The ID CaseBook

The ID CaseBook provides instructional design students with 25 realistic, open-ended case studies that encourage adept problem-solving across a variety of client types and through all stages of the process. After an introduction to the technique of case-based reasoning, the book offers four sections dedicated to K–12, informal learning, post-secondary, and industry clients, respectively, each comprising varied, detailed cases created by instructional design experts. All cases, alongside their accompanying discussion questions, encourage students to analyze the available information, develop action plans, and consider alternative possibilities in resolving problems. This revised and updated sixth edition attends to the profound impacts that public health crises; urgent access, equity, and inclusion needs among diverse learners; and a rapidly expanded reliance on digital learning formats have had on the design of learning today.

Peggy A. Ertmer is Professor Emerita of Learning Design and Technology in the College of Education at Purdue University, USA.

Krista D. Glazewski is Executive Director of the Friday Institute and Associate Dean for Translational Research in the College of Education at North Carolina State University, USA.

Adrie A. Koehler is Associate Professor of Learning Design and Technology in the College of Education at Purdue University, USA.

Jill E. Stefaniak is Associate Professor in the Learning, Design, and Technology program in the Department of Workforce Education and Instructional Technology at the University of Georgia, USA.

The ID CaseBook

Case Studies in Instructional Design

Sixth Edition

Edited by
Peggy A. Ertmer, Krista D. Glazewski,
Adrie A. Koehler, and Jill E. Stefaniak

NEW YORK AND LONDON

Designed cover image: Front cover artworks by Cathy Thorson (top-left), Sheila Monzon (top-right), Peggy A. Ertmer (bottom-left), and Elizabeth Seabert (bottom-right). Back cover artwork by Colleen Nelson.

Sixth edition published 2024
by Routledge
605 Third Avenue, New York, NY 10158

and by Routledge
4 Park Square, Milton Park, Abingdon, Oxon, OX14 4RN

Routledge is an imprint of the Taylor & Francis Group, an informa business

First edition published by Merrill/Prentice Hall 1999.
Fifth edition published by Routledge 2019

ISBN: 978-1-032-40723-4 (hbk)
ISBN: 978-1-032-37930-2 (pbk)
ISBN: 978-1-003-35446-8 (ebk)

DOI: 10.4324/9781003354468

Typeset in Minion & Gill Sans
by Apex CoVantage, LLC

Jim Quinn, through his vision, inspiration, and tireless efforts in the first five editions of this text, has created a lasting legacy. We owe him (and Elvis Presley) a deep debt of gratitude.

Contents

Editor Biographies

Peggy A. Ertmer is Professor Emerita of Learning Design and Technology at Purdue University. She continues to be passionate about the use of case- and problem-based learning at all levels. Her most recent efforts comprise identifying and implementing effective facilitation strategies to support instructors' and students' case analysis efforts. Dr. Ertmer is extremely grateful that *The ID CaseBook*, now in its sixth edition, continues to provide a rich resource for both instructors and students of instruction design.

Krista D. Glazewski is Executive Director of the Friday Institute and Associate Dean for Translational Research in the College of Education at North Carolina State University, where she offers leadership in K-12 educational innovation across North Carolina and beyond. Her work investigates how and under what conditions teachers might adopt and adapt new practices, with a focus on complex problem-solving and collaborative inquiry supported by foundational and emergent technologies. Her work has resulted in numerous contributions, over 70 publications and $10 million in external funding, primarily from the National Science Foundation, US Department of Education, and the Department of Defense. She is a former middle school teacher originally from New Mexico.

Adrie A. Koehler is Associate Professor of Learning Design and Technology at Purdue University. Her professional interests include the consideration of instructional strategies in teaching and learning processes. Specifically, she has explored these topics through investigating ways emerging technologies can be used for instructional purposes, how instructors develop a presence in online settings and the impact of this presence, and methods to best facilitate case-based instruction. She has facilitated case learning experiences with high school, undergraduate, and graduate students, as well as with adults as a training tool.

Jill E. Stefaniak is Associate Professor in the Learning, Design, and Technology program in the Department of Workforce Education and Instructional Technology at the University of Georgia, USA. Her research interests focus on the professional development of instructional designers, decision-making processes, and contextual factors influencing design in situated environments.

Contributor Biographies

Lewis R. J. Archer is currently a doctoral student and pilot for a fractional airline. Prior to this, he has held various positions in both aviation and higher education including regional airline pilot, flight instructor, aviation professor, and assistant chair. Lewis earned a bachelor of science in aeronautics and a master of science in aviation and is currently pursuing a doctor of education with an emphasis in instructional design from the University of North Dakota. He holds an FAA Airline Transport Pilot certificate with Dash 8 series and Challenger 300 series type ratings and an FAA Flight Instructor certificate.

Ismahan Arslan-Ari is Associate Professor of Learning Design and Technologies at the University of South Carolina. She is also the director for the South Carolina Center for Assistive Technology and Educational Research. Her research mainly focuses on multimedia learning, online learning, and technology integration in special education.

Erin D. Besser is an educational technology enthusiast. She is Associate Professor in Educational Technology at Cal State Fullerton. She has taught courses related to instructional design, educational technology, educational learning theory, technology integration, and technology skill development. As a former K–6 educator, she holds a valid California Multiple Subject teaching credential with three supplementary authorizations, is an ISTE-certified educator, has received several Google Educator certifications, and has received awards for her innovation in teaching. Her research interests include the intersection of collaborative instruction and technology, digital badging as a mechanism for learning, using digital tools to leverage teaching and learning, and technology within teacher education.

Elizabeth Boling is Professor of Instructional Systems Technology, Indiana University, Bloomington, and was previously Department Chair, Associate Dean for Graduate Studies, and Executive Associate Dean in the School of Education. She holds a BFA and MFA in printmaking. She has worked as illustrator, interface designer, and production manager in the field including at Apple, Inc., before joining Indiana University. She is the editor-in-chief of *International Journal of Designs for Learning* and was the co-editor of the *Handbook of Research in Educational Communications and Technology,* fifth edition. Her research interests include visual design for information and instruction, as well as design theory, pedagogy, and practice.

Stephanie Bowles is a doctoral student in the Learning, Design, and Technology program at Penn State and is currently affiliated with the Augmented and Mobile Learning Research group. Her research deals with understanding informal learning settings and creating immersive technologies for learning. She is currently a LinDiv fellow, dealing with bridging the gap between human-computer interaction and linguistic diversity. She has worked for over seven years as an expert educator and program coordinator in higher education and academies in the United States and abroad, received military training, and holds certifications in iOS development and data analytics.

Lillyanna Faimon is a doctoral student in the Learning, Design, and Technology program at Penn State University. She received a BS in cognitive science from Indiana University and a MS in learning, design, and technology from Penn State University. She is an educational researcher, facilitator, and instructor and is currently working with the Augmented and Mobile Learning research group and the Playful Learning research group. Her research interests focus on the intersection of STEM and the arts, STEAM and maker education in supporting learning, interest development, and engagement in informal and out-of-school learning environments.

Xun Ge is Professor of Learning Sciences and Technologies at the University of North Texas. She teaches graduate courses related to instructional design and learning technologies for various educational and training settings, including problem-based, project-based, inquiry-based, game-based, makerspace, and immersive virtual reality learning. Her primary research includes designing scaffolding tools and strategies to support student critical thinking, self-regulation, ill-structured problem-solving, and decision-making. She has found *The ID CaseBook* a great resource of real-world cases to develop instructional design students' expertise in problem representation and generating adaptive solutions to various complex and multifaceted instructional design problems.

Noah Glaser is Assistant Professor at the University of Missouri's School of Information Science and Learning Technologies, where he is also the director of the Information Experience Lab. Noah primarily conducts design research to create learning interventions that use innovative technologies such as virtual reality, video games, mobile devices, and artificial intelligence. He is particularly known for his work on developing innovative, immersive learning systems for neurodiverse learners and has conducted research using EEG and eye trackers to better understand how people learn and interact with technology.

Sangeetha Gopalakrishnan, PhD, is Assistant Dean of Online and Learning Innovation at the College of Education at the University of Illinois at Urbana-Champaign. In her role, she provides strategic leadership in conceptualizing and implementing traditional and non-traditional online programs to meet the needs of diverse audiences and oversees all aspects of online program administration at the college. Her research interests include best practices and leadership strategies for implementing successful online programs at universities, technology integration in teaching, and instructional design. She also has extensive experience teaching online in the field of learning design and technology.

Michael M. Grant is Associate Professor at the University of South Carolina and a past president of the Association for Educational Communications and Technology. He is an education scientist, teacher, keynote and workshop presenter, author, and consultant to K–12 schools and in higher education. His research considers the design and development of technology-enhanced learning environments with a focus on inquiry methods, such as project-based and problem-based learning, where learners make their knowledge visible. Dr. Grant earned his PhD in instructional technology from the University of Georgia and a bachelor's and a master's degree in industrial education from Clemson University.

Colin M. Gray is Associate Professor in the Luddy School of Informatics, Computing, and Engineering at Indiana University Bloomington, where they are the director of the Human-Computer Interaction Design (HCI/d) program. They hold appointments as Guest Professor at Beijing Normal University and Visiting Researcher at Newcastle University. Their research focuses on the ways in which the pedagogy and practice of designers informs the development of design ability, particularly in relation to ethics, design knowledge, and learning experience.

Kharon Grimmet is Clinical Associate Professor of Special Education at Purdue University in West Lafayette, Indiana. Prior to receiving her doctoral degree in special education from Indiana University-Bloomington, she taught first grade and fourth grade and was a life skills special education teacher—all at the elementary level. Dr. Grimmet prepares future special educators as she coordinates Purdue's Online MSEd in Special Education and Licensure Program. Her research interests include special education teacher preparation, mentor and induction programs, and post-secondary educational opportunities for individuals with disability.

Miranda Hawks is Assistant Professor in the WellStar School of Nursing Department at Kennesaw State University. She holds certifications in e-learning design and online teaching and learning from the University of Georgia (2022) and completed the Governor's Teaching Fellows Institute of Higher Education program in 2019. Dedicated to student success, Miranda focuses her research on physical activity and nutrition beliefs of early adolescents in the US Southeast using ethnography. She collaborated in Vietnam on evidence-based nursing practice through the Vietnam Practice Improvement Project in 2017, which led to an ongoing partnership for nursing curriculum revision. Her research intersects global population health, curriculum evolution, anthropology, and cultural humility.

Carole Hruskocy has more than 30 years of experience in curriculum, teaching, and instructional design. Her expertise includes curriculum, course design, assessment, learning design evaluation, and professional development. She has also served as a Quality Matters reviewer. Dr. Hruskocy has managed national and international curriculum projects. As Director of Learning Design, she leads a global instructional design team and collaborates with institutional clients. Dr. Hruskocy holds a BS in education, MA in curriculum with an emphasis in instructional design, and a PhD in curriculum, instruction, and assessment from Purdue University. She is also a national board-certified health and wellness coach.

Kun Huang is Associate Professor of Learning, Design, and Technology at the University of Kentucky. Her research aims to uncover learners' behavioral, cognitive, and motivational patterns across a variety of settings such as problem-based learning, game- and simulation-based learning, STEM education, and online learning. She has published research works in journals such as *Educational Technology Research & Development*, *British Journal of Educational Technology*, and *Educational Technology & Society*.

Woei Hung is Professor and Graduate Director of the Instructional Design and Technology program in the College of Education and Human Development at the University of North Dakota. His research areas include problem-based learning (PBL), complex problem-solving, systems thinking and modeling, concept mapping and formation, and microlearning. He has published numerous journal articles and book chapters in the areas of PBL problem and curriculum design. He is currently a co-editor of *Interdisciplinary Journal of Problem-based Learning*. He is also an executive board member of the PAN PBL Association of Problem-Based Learning and Active Learning Methodologies.

Alan Jones is Clinical Assistant Professor for the WellStar School of Nursing at Kennesaw State University. He is a medical-surgical board-certified registered nurse (RN-BC) through the American Nurses Credentialing Center and is a certified nurse educator (CNE) through the National League for Nursing. He received his PhD in nursing from Emory University, his master's degree in nursing education from University of West Georgia, and his bachelor's degree in nursing from Georgia State University. He specializes in nursing education with an emphasis on distance learning modalities and received a post-master's certificate in online teaching and learning from University of Georgia.

Jiyoon Jung is Assistant Professor of Instructional Technology at Valdosta State University. She used to be an English teacher and a program officer for English learning contents in South Korea before earning her PhD from Indiana University. She developed her interest in using cases to provide authentic learning experiences to those preparing to be future professionals in their fields in her doctoral years. She still uses—and creates—cases to illustrate real-world complexity and uncertainty, promote critical thinking, and facilitate meaningful discussions among students.

Charles Keith is a doctoral student in the Learning, Design, and Technology program at Penn State University. He received his MEd in curriculum and instruction from the University of Nevada, Las Vegas, and has worked as an instructor in both formal and informal settings for over five years across K–12 and university settings. He is currently a graduate researcher within the Augmented and Mobile Learning Research group and a fellow in the NSF Research Traineeship program called Linguistic Diversity Across the Lifespan (LinDiv). His research interests include STEM-based mobile learning and the use of technology in informal learning environments.

Adrie A. Koehler is Associate Professor of Learning Design and Technology at Purdue University. Her professional interests include the consideration of instructional strategies in teaching and learning processes. Specifically, she has explored these topics through investigating ways emerging technologies can be used for instructional purposes, how instructors develop a presence in online settings and the impact of this presence, and methods to best facilitate case-based instruction. She has facilitated case learning experiences with high school, undergraduate, and graduate students, as well as with adults as a training tool.

Susan Land serves as Head of the Department of Learning and Performance Systems within the College of Education at Penn State (University Park). She is also Professor in the

Learning, Design, and Technology program. Land's research investigates frameworks for the design of open-ended, technology-enhanced learning environments. Land is a Co-PI on a grant funded by the National Science Foundation titled "Transforming Outdoor Places into Learning Spaces," which examines the design of mobile, augmented reality (AR) technologies to support science learning in outdoor community spaces. The project engages visitors to "see the unseen" science around them. Her research is part of the Augmented and Mobile Learning Research Group (sites.psu.edu/augmentedlearning).

Jason K. McDonald is Professor in the Department of Instructional Psychology and Technology, at Brigham Young University. He has also worked in the instructional media industry as an instructional designer, manager of e-learning, account manager, and organizational executive. Dr. McDonald's research focuses around advancing instructional design practice and education. He teaches classes in instructional design, project management, storytelling for educational purposes, learning theory, and design theory.

Stephanie L. Moore is Assistant Professor in Organization, Information, and Learning Sciences at the University of New Mexico. She is also a fellow with the Barbara Bush Foundation for Family Literacy working on learning technologies for adult literacy. She previously worked as a director of instructional design and senior instructional designer on online learning initiatives. She teaches on ethics as design, reframing ethics as a design activity whereby designers tackle complex problems and dimensions of instruction using design activities. She and Heather co-authored the recent book *Ethics and Educational Technology: Reflection, Interrogation, and Design as a Framework for Practice.*

Valerie Morgan is a learning design consultant. She continues to enjoy learning design and diverse, complex design challenges the field presents. Val is thrilled to be a part of the sixth edition of *The ID CaseBook.*

Christie Nelson completed Purdue's Educational Technology Program in 2001. She was an Instructional Designer for global consulting organizations as well as boutique e-learning firms in her early career. After moving to Australia, she led the Instructional Design Team at The Learning Group in Sydney. Christie now balances her time between instructional and graphic design work and parenting.

Gamze Ozogul is Associate Professor in the Instructional Systems Technology (IST) Department at Indiana University. She received her PhD degree in educational technology from Arizona State University (ASU) in 2006, and completed a post-doc in electrical engineering at ASU. She was an associate director of research and evaluation at ASU prior to joining Indiana University. Ozogul's expertise focuses on instructional design, development, and evaluation of online, computer-based, and face-to-face learning environments. Her research specifically focuses on instructional design and implementation of feedback and various instructional strategies on outcomes, learning and engagement.

Susan Pedersen is Associate Professor in the Learning Sciences program in the Department of Educational Psychology at Texas A&M University. Her research interests lie in the design of games and virtual environments for STEM education. Recent projects include Planet K, a game for undergraduate electrical engineering students, and the VELscience project, in which she led a team in the design of virtual environments for learning (VELs) capable of engaging learners in student-directed inquiry, both funded by the National Science Foundation. Her research examines the design of game components for their support of player engagement and learning as well as the impact of classroom implementation practices during game-based learning. She was the lead designer of *Rigglefish,* winner of three national and international awards, including the Adobe Innovation in Interactive Media in Education Award in 2011, and a finalist in the Interservice/Industry Training, Simulation, and Education conference (I/ITSEC) Serious Games Showcase and Challenge and *Hurricane Hal,* which was runner-up for the AECT Immersive Learning Award in 2012.

Jennifer C. Richardson is Professor of Learning, Design, and Technology at Purdue University. Jennifer has been teaching and conducting research in distance education for the past 25 years and feels that these two processes advance one another. She focuses on evidence-based practices in online learning environments and preparing instructional designers. Specifically, she researches strategies and design for teaching online, social presence, gauging learning in online environments, and the community of inquiry (CoI) framework. She was named the Mildred B. and Charles A. Wedemeyer Award for Outstanding Scholar in Distance Education and is also an OLC Fellow.

Amy Rogers received her master's degree in instructional psychology and technology from Brigham Young University. She has worked as an instructional designer in a variety of settings, including higher education and public services. Currently she works as an instructional designer for a tech company in Lehi, Utah. When she's not working, Amy enjoys riding scooters around the block and jumping on the trampoline with her three kids.

Freddi Rokaw earned her MSEd from the online Learning Design and Technology program at Purdue University in 2013. She is an instructional designer who has worked with Fortune 500 companies, such as Disney, Apple, PayPal, and Google/YouTube. Freddi has experience working with the George Lucas Educational Foundation, a startup in Silicon Valley, and a financial services company supporting the entertainment industry and creating a certification program at an architectural software company in Pasadena, California. She loves volunteering for non-profit organizations that serve children and music.

Enilda Romero-Hall is an award-winning scholar and Associate Professor and Coordinator of the Learning, Design, and Technology PhD program at the University of Tennessee Knoxville. She also serves as the program chair for the AERA SIG Instructional Technology and Advising Editor to the Feminist Pedagogy for Online Teaching digital guide. In her research, she explores the design and development of interactive multimedia, faculty and learners' digital literacy, and networked learning in online social communities. Her other research areas include innovative research methodologies; culture, technology, and education; and feminist pedagogies.

Matthew Schmidt, PhD, is Associate Professor at the University of Georgia (UGA) in the Learning, Design, and Technology Department. His primary research interest includes design and development of innovative educational courseware and computer software with a particular focus on individuals with disabilities, their families, and their providers. His secondary research interests include learning in extended reality (inclusive of virtual reality, augmented reality, and mixed reality) and learning experience design.

David L. Solomon is Learning Architect for IC Axon in Montreal, Quebec. He is deeply humbled that instructional design students and instructors have been using his case in *The ID Casebook* for more than 15 years! David enjoys using case-based learning in his corporate training practice to establish relevance and facilitate transfer of training on the job.

Bill Solomonson is Associate Professor and Chair in the Department of Organizational Leadership at Oakland University in Rochester, Michigan. His research interests include the client-consultant relationship, organizational performance improvement, and equity in education. He is a former member of the board of directors for ISPI as well as a former member of the Steering Committee for the Alliance for Excellence in Online Education (A4EOE). He has consulted with Ford Motor Company, General Motors, Audi, Volkswagen, Chrysler, Delphi, Henry Ford Health Systems, Siemens, US Army, Wayne State University, Beaumont Hospitals, Kellogg's, Fiat, Raytheon, and others.

Jill E. Stefaniak is Associate Professor in the Learning, Design, and Technology program in the Department of Workforce Education and Instructional Technology at the University of Georgia, USA. Her research interests focus on the professional development of instructional designers, decision-making processes, and contextual factors influencing design in situated environments.

Heather K. Tillberg-Webb is Associate Vice President of Academic Technology at Southern New Hampshire University in Manchester, NH. She previously served as Associate Provost of Systems, Planning, and Administration at Lesley University in Cambridge, MA. She stays engaged with teaching in the master's of education in the Health Professions program at Johns Hopkins University and the Learning Technologies and Design program at the University of Missouri Columbia. Her research interests focus on technology philosophy and its intersection with educational technology practice and ethical instructional design. She earned her PhD in Instructional Technology from the University of Virginia in 2007.

Monica W. Tracey is a Professor of Learning Design and Technology in the College of Education at Wayne State University. Tracey embraces teaching and research on the designer, including developing designer professional identity, empathic design, and the designer's use of a moment of use context for design action. She has over 60 publications concentrating on design including a recent book *Cultivating Professional Identity in Design: Empathy, Creativity, Collaboration, and Seven More Cross-Disciplinary Skills.*

Daniela Rezende Vilarinho-Pereira received her doctoral degree in Human Development Processes and Health from the University of Brasilia, Brazil. During her doctoral studies, she was a visiting scholar at the Giftedness, Creativity, and Talent Development Program at the University of Connecticut. She is currently pursuing her second doctoral degree in Learning Design and Technology at Purdue University. Her research interests include creativity and innovation, talent development, and digital technology integration in education.

Shahron Williams van Rooij is Associate Professor Emerita, Learning Design and Technology program of George Mason University's College of Education and Human Development. She also has more than 20 years of industry experience. She continues to conduct research and to consult on projects in Organizational Studies, Human Resource Development, Learning

Leadership, and Workplace Learning. Her book *The Business Side of Learning Design and Technologies* was published by Routledge. Her most recent projects are Reflective Practices in Non-Academic Workplace Settings and a casebook on leadership and learning.

Brent G. Wilson is Professor Emeritus within the School of Education and Human Development at the University of Colorado Denver, where he taught for many years in the Learning Design and Technology program. Brent's core interests center on instructional design foundations—our evolving identity as a field and how we approach problems of practice. His teaching and writing focused on big questions facing learning designers such as: What is good instruction? And what can we do to help everyone benefit from learning supports and programs? Brent is a big believer in knowledge embedded in practice—such as the present volume!

Michael L. Wray is Professor of Hospitality Management at the School of Hospitality, Rita and Navin Dimond Department of Hotel Management, Metropolitan State University of Denver, and retired Army Lieutenant Colonel specializing in food service and logistics. His professional credentials include a Sommelier Diploma, Certified Culinary Instructor, Certified Wine Specialist, and Master Certified Food Service Executive. At Metro State, Dr. Wray has been the lead visionary for several public/private partnerships resulting in capital developments for the hotel and learning center, www.springhillsuitesdenver.com; the on-campus brewery, www.tivolibrewingco.com; and a regional food insecurity charity, www.foodforthoughtdenver.org.

Heather Toomey Zimmerman, Professor of Education at Penn State University, is a learning scientist who studies how multiple learning experiences contribute to the development of knowledge, practices, and identity toward (or away) from science. Her interests include designing for informal institutions, technology to support learning across settings, environmental education, STEM learning in rural communities, learning in makerspaces, and family learning. She has published in *Journal of Research in Science Teaching, Science Education, International Journal of Science Education, Research in Science Education, Journal of Museum Education, Environmental Education Research, International Journal of Computer-Supported Collaborative Learning*, and *Museums & Social Issues.*

Foreword

Preparing the next generation of instructional designers is a challenging endeavor for both novice and experienced instructional design (ID) educators across the globe. The increasingly complex competencies demanded by these nascent professionals continue to evolve as our field matures. As soon as we think we have identified the numerous competencies for instructional design professionals, the learning situation and workplace change, and call upon ID professionals to use different competencies than used before. Instructional designers must be agile and reflective professionals, capable of working across different organizational ecosystems (e.g., military, higher education, business) to meet the needs of a diverse array of learners with different backgrounds while also meeting the increasingly challenging organizational priorities of their employers.

Instructional design requires a multifaceted set of competencies ranging from conceptual knowledge of how humans learn to procedural knowledge of how to create robust learning experiences and environments for learners. Instructional designers must be strong communicators with the ability to work independently and collaboratively across environments with multiple, time-sensitive, complex projects and stakeholders with different interests, skills, and agendas. Instructional design professionals in the 21st century not only enhance the knowledge and skills of their target learners but also provide an in-demand service to organizations attempting to maximize the potential of their human talent. Organizations across the planet need ID professionals to help carry out their strategic plans and operationalize their tactics into tangible outcomes. Taking all of this into consideration, the task of preparing our next generation of instructional designers requires educational resources and processes capable of exposing emerging instructional designers to the mixed array of real-world problems they will encounter in their workplaces.

The ID CaseBook, now in its sixth edition, is perhaps one of the most valued and respected resources available to ID educators and aspiring instructional designers in our community. Inspired by problem-based learning and the case study teaching method, *The ID CaseBook* offers a rich set of case studies presenting ill-structured ID problems from the perspective of a designer working in a specific professional context (e.g., higher education, business). The case studies provide asymmetric information about the ID problems presented, leaving the readers to make decisions and predictions based on the information available. The readers of these case studies are immersed in real-world ID situations with different types of stakeholders (e.g., subject matter experts) coming to life on the pages. These ill-structured problems can be addressed using many different interventions and solutions found in the ID arsenal. The cases all require readers to make important design decisions that will ultimately influence the outcome of the case. These design decisions are the basis for fruitful classroom discussions that extend students' thinking into new experiences.

Perhaps the most useful aspect of *The ID CaseBook* is the multiple ways in which the case studies themselves can be used across educational programs. The case studies can be integrated into face-to-face, blended, or online ID courses to augment and enhance the authenticity of the course learning experiences, resulting in students better prepared to transfer newly-learned competencies to real-world ID settings. The case studies can be intensively examined as an independent learning activity requiring problem-solving and creative thinking, and critically examined in class discussions and debates in which the instructor scaffolds the conversation. Students can present their competing ideas and solutions and discuss the likely outcomes of different approaches to the problems. I have even seen these case studies used as part of comprehensive or qualifying examinations in academic programs. I have been using *The ID CaseBook* since I started teaching instructional design more than a decade ago, and I continue to go back to this exceptional resource for inspiration on how to best teach instructional design ideas to my students.

The ID CaseBook inherently shifts the nature of the pedagogy in the classroom away from the "sage on stage" model of learning to the "guide on the side" model. This student-centered approach to teaching and learning ID provides educators with options, flexibility, and the ability to tailor learning experiences to the needs of their students. Educators seeking to create immersive, authentic, engaging, and challenging learning experiences around instructional design will find *The ID CaseBook* a natural choice for their students. *The ID CaseBook* continues to be a reliable and useful educational resource for everyone in the ID community.

Albert D. Ritzhaupt, PhD
Professor of Educational Technology, University of Florida
Editor-in-Chief, *Journal of Research on Technology in Education* (JRTE)
President, International Board of Standards for Training, Performance, and Instruction (IBSTPI)

Preface

Education within the professions isn't always as effective as we would like. Within a number of professions, including instructional design (ID), educators and employers often report that graduates are unable to apply what they've learned during their education to the solution of problems in professional practice. The consistent theme in these reports is the "inert knowledge problem" (Bransford, 1993, p. 174, paraphrasing Whitehead), which refers to graduates who have acquired domain knowledge but who are not adept at applying their knowledge to the solution of common problems in the discipline (Stefaniak & Hwang, 2021; Stepich & Ertmer, 2010).

Instructional design educators have long recognized this problem and have developed various approaches to integrate the development of practical skills with the acquisition of conceptual knowledge. Nearly 30 years ago, Rowland et al. (1995) created a "design studio" (p. 231) in which students worked collaboratively to solve ID problems that gradually increased in complexity. The tradition of studio education has been documented with other ID programs, such as the University of Georgia (Clinton & Rieber, 2010) and Indiana University (Boling & Smith, 2014). Jonassen and Hernandez-Serrano (2002) provided students with stories that had been elicited from experienced instructional designers as a way to help them gain "conditionalized" knowledge (Bransford et al., 2000, p. 43).

In each of the above approaches, students were asked to apply their emerging instructional design knowledge and skills in the context of "real-world" situations. This allowed students to apply their conceptual knowledge and develop their technical skills while working on realistic, complex problems. We argue that in such complex contexts, students are sourcing what others have documented as "precedent knowledge" (Boling & Gray, 2018; Gray et al., 2016). Precedent is a critical component of design activity built on awareness and experience, which Boling and Gray discussed as multi-sourced and possessing a narrative quality. That is, individuals generally provide a narrative account for the source(s) of their design work, which they leverage to apply to a current context or situation.

In the tradition of studio education and narrative storytelling, the case teaching approach used in this book enables ID educators to convey the complexity and ill-structured nature of ID. By tackling the problems presented in the cases, students gain the skillfulness needed to operate creatively and effectively in the often unclear, uncertain, and open-ended contexts in which ID is performed. In addition to practicing specific ID skills, case-based teaching and learning requires students to recognize and explore, in depth, a range of problems occurring within any given situation. In addition, working through a large number of cases enables students to experience multiple, varied problem situations to a much greater extent than would be possible through a single internship or practicum experience. This experience, coupled with ongoing reflection on their learning, hastens students' abilities to apply their emerging knowledge as they examine ID issues within a broad range of settings.

WHAT IS A CASE STUDY?

Wasserman described a case study as a "darn good story" (1994, p. 44). According to Barnes et al. (1994), a case study presents students with a "partial, historical, clinical study of a situation which has confronted a practicing administrator or managerial group" (p. 44) and asks them to provide solutions to the problems presented in the situation through analysis, reflection, and discussion. In this text, we use an approach to case studies that is based on the business school model—that is, case studies are problem-centered descriptions of design situations, developed from the actual experiences of instructional designers.

The cases in this book are designed to be dilemma oriented: each case ends before the solution is clear. Students are expected to evaluate the available evidence, to make reasonable assumptions as necessary, to judge alternative interpretations and actions, and, in doing so, to experience the uncertainty that commonly accompanies design decisions. In particular, we hope that by analyzing the cases presented in this book, students will learn how to identify ID problems and subproblems; to recognize the importance of context in tackling such problems; and to develop, justify, and test differing plans for resolving ID problems.

ORGANIZATION OF *THE ID CASEBOOK*

We like to say that cases do not teach themselves and, as such, would like to highlight the considerable resources within *The ID CaseBook* that support learning from cases. In "The Case-Learning Process: Strategies and Reflections," we provide students with suggestions and strategies for how to approach learning from case studies. Although students are typically excited about using cases in their ID courses, commonly they are also apprehensive, as they generally have little familiarity with this approach. We have found that providing detailed suggestions, up front, on how to approach case-based learning can considerably lessen students' initial concerns.

The 25 case studies in the text are divided into 3 sections based on audience and context: "K-12 and Informal Learning," "Post-Secondary," and "Industry." The case matrix included at the end of this preface allows both students and instructors to see, at a glance, the variety of situations that the cases address.

NEW TO THIS EDITION

- The sixth edition of *The ID CaseBook* consists of 25 instructional design case studies, including 11 new cases as well as 14 of your favorite cases from the previous editions.
- Together, the new and "returning" cases provide students with wonderful opportunities to examine a variety of demanding situations involving a wide range of contents, contexts, and audiences.
- New cases offer opportunities to explore the use of ID in informal learning contexts; provide more emphasis on ethical considerations in ID practice, as well as more nuanced

treatment of diversity, equity, and inclusion. New cases also reflect how ID processes were used to address the unique challenges presented by the pandemic.
- The sixth edition offers an increased focus on designing instruction for complex content, including examples of practice within crisis conditions, military contexts, and expanded professional contexts.

As in the previous five editions, each case consists of a case narrative and two sets of discussion questions designed to invoke ID practice. The *case narrative* includes relevant background information for the case, such as the problem context, key players, available resources, and existing constraints. In addition, each case includes relevant data or artifacts presented in a variety of forms and formats.

The two sets of discussion questions at the end of each case to are intended to stimulate students' thinking and to provide a focus for class discussion. The first set of questions—*Preliminary Analysis Questions*—asks students to identify and discuss specific issues from the case, to consider the issues from multiple perspectives, to develop a plan of action to resolve problems, and/or to specify possible consequences resulting from their recommended plans. The second set of questions—*Implications for ID Practice*—requires students to think more broadly about the issues presented in the case from the point of view of ID theory and practice.

INSTRUCTOR MANUAL

We believe the *Instructor Manual* (IM) offers essential support to instructors who have adopted *The ID CaseBook*. Specifically, the *Instructor Manual* includes:

- *Case Matrix:* The summary matrix allows instructors to see, at a glance, the particular content, audience, and contexts addressed by each case.
- *Teaching Suggestions for Using Case Studies:* This comprises a comprehensive set of suggestions for: structuring a case-based course; preparing for, facilitating, and debriefing case discussions; and assessing students' performances/progress in the analysis process.

In addition, for each case, the *Instructor Manual* contains:

- *Case Overview:* A description of the case, encapsulating the key ideas and insights that students should garner from the case study.
- *Case Objectives:* The supporting concepts/principles learners need to use in analyzing the case issues; the knowledge, skills, and/or attitudes students should gain from their case analyses and discussions.
- *Debriefing Guidelines:* Substantive suggestions from the case authors regarding how to think about the case, including additional teaching suggestions specific to the case. In addition, some authors have provided additional background that might further assist instructors in facilitating case analysis and discussion.

It is our hope that the combined features of *The ID CaseBook* and the *Instructor Manual* provide both students and instructors with a challenging and rewarding learning experience. If you or your students have suggestions for future editions, we'd love to hear from you! Our e-mail addresses are pertmer@purdue.edu, kdglazew@ncsu.edu, akoehler@purdue.edu, and jill.stefaniak@uga.edu.

ACKNOWLEDGMENTS

Throughout the development of this 6th edition, we have benefited from the support, advice, and encouragement of many individuals, including the contributing authors, a supportive editor, insightful students, supportive colleagues, patient family members, and thoughtful reviewers. Without the contributions of all of these people, this book would not have been possible.

First, we thank all the authors who contributed to this volume. We have enjoyed working with all of them, for they have made our work interesting and enjoyable. We firmly believe that each author has added something unique to the text and sincerely appreciate the time they gave to develop and revise their cases. For your information, we have provided a brief biography of each author in the "Contributors' Biographies" section. In addition, we wish to thank the four artists who shared their talent with us for the cover of this text: Sheila Monzon, Elizabeth Seabert, Cathy Thorson, and Colleen Nelson.

Our current and past students continue to be influential in shaping many of the details of the text, particularly in making suggestions for how to think about the case-learning process. We are also grateful to our colleagues who were willing to pilot the cases in their courses and to provide valuable formative feedback that improved numerous aspects of the cases. And although Jim Quinn is no longer an editor on this text, his fingerprints are all over this book. His leadership and oversight have played a crucial role in the success of the past five editions. We owe him a huge thank you for helping to make this text what it is today.

In addition, we thank our editor Daniel Schwartz for steadfastly supporting our endeavors over the years and playing a pivotal role in the creation of what we anticipate being a valuable sixth edition. We were also assisted in the design and development process by the insights and suggestions from several reviewers, including . . .

The Instructor Manual can be accessed at: www.routledge.com/9781032379302

Peggy A. Ertmer
Purdue University

Krista D. Glazewski
North Carolina State University

Adrie A. Koehler
Purdue University

Jill E. Stefaniak
University of Georgia

REFERENCES

Barnes, L. B., Christensen, C. R., & Hansen, A. J. (1994). *Teaching and the case method: Text, cases, and readings*. Harvard Business School Press.

Bransford, J. D. (1993). Who ya gonna call? Thoughts about teaching problem solving. In P. Hallingen, K. Leithwood, & J. Murphy (Eds.), *Cognitive perspectives on educational leadership* (pp. 171–191). Teachers College Press.

Bransford, J. D., Brown, A. L., & Cocking, R. R. (Eds.) (2000). *How people learn: Brain, mind, experience, and school*. National Academies Press.

Boling E., Gray C. M. (2018) Use of precedent as a narrative practice in design learning. In B. Hokanson, G. Clinton, & K. Kaminski (Eds.), *Educational Technology and Narrative* (pp. 259–270). Springer. https://doi.org/10.1007/978-3-319-69914-1_21

Boling, E., & Smith, K. M. (2014). Critical issues in studio pedagogy: Beyond the mystique and down to business. In B. Hokanson, & A. Gibbons (Eds.), *Design in Educational Technology: Issues and Innovations* (pp. 37–56). Springer International Publishing: https://doi.org/10.1007/978-3-319-00927-8_3

Clinton, G., & Rieber, L. P. (2010). The studio experience at the University of Georgia: An example of constructionist learning for adults. *Educational Technology Research and Development, 58*(6), 755–780. http://doi.org/10.1007/sl 1423-010-9165-2

Gray, C. M., Seifert, C. M., Yilmaz, S., Daly, S. R., & Gonzalez, R. (2016). What is the content of "design thinking"? Design heuristics as conceptual repertoire. *International Journal of Engineering Education, 32*(3), 1349–1355.

Jonassen, D. H., & Hernandez-Serrano, J. (2002). Case-based reasoning and instructional design: Using stories to support problem solving. *Educational Technology Research and Development, 50*(2), 65–77. https://doi.org/10.1007/BF02504994

Rowland, G., Parra, M. L., & Basnet, K. (1995). Educating instructional designers: Different methods for different outcomes. In B. B. Seels (Ed.), *Instructional design fundamentals: A reconsideration* (pp. 223–236). Educational Technology Publications.

Stefaniak, J. E., & Hwang, H. (2021). A systematic review of how expertise is cultivated in instructional design coursework. *Educational Technology Research and Development*, 69, 3331–3366, https://doi.org/10.1007/s11423-021-10064-x

Stepich, D. A., & Ertmer, P. A. (2010). "Teaching" instructional design expertise: Strategies to support students' problem-finding skills. *Technology, Instruction, Cognition, and Learning, 7*, 147–170.

Wasserman, S.1994. *Introduction to case method teaching: A guide to the galaxy*. Teachers College Press.

Case Matrix for the Sixth Edition

Title	Subtitle	Content	Audience/Context
K–12 and INFORMAL LEARNING			
1. Michael Bishop	Implementing Gaming Technologies in Traditional K–12 Contexts	Middle school science (genetics)	K–12 teachers
2. Tameka Jackson	Blue Ridge Academy Online	Customizing online education	K–12 teachers
3. Marisol Valencia, Fiona Huang, and the Team	Designing and Conducting Evaluation Post-Pandemic	Conducting an evaluation of a project to promote parental involvement in instruction	K–12 teachers
4. Lynn Dixon	Designing a Learning Platform to Celebrate World Wetlands Day	Wetlands	Visitors to an aquarium
5. Autumn Leifson	Developing a Mobile App That Supports Family Engagement Outdoors Through Informal Learning	Pollination	Visitors to a local arboretum
6. Maria Martinez	Developing a Virtual Reality Training Program for Autistic Adults to Use Public Transportation	Developing virtual reality training to support the use of public transportation	Autistic adults
POST-SECONDARY			
7. Lucas Baily and Ellie Miller	Addressing Low Pass Rates Among Student Pilots	Reliability of instructor-administered assessments	Students training to become certified pilots
8. Suzie Beckett and Adam McSweeny	Developing a Role-Playing Simulation	Understanding aging and deepening empathy toward elderly persons	Undergraduate students
9. Amelia Kelly, Sara Brody, and Andrea Huffman	Designing a Military Think-Tank Workshop	Information related to all aspects of military life	Military families
10. Anthony Cerise	The Care, Feeding, and Growing Pains of a Multidisciplinary Undergraduate Program	Team-based course design in higher education	Faculty, students, and administrators in higher education

(continued)

(Continued)

Title	*Subtitle*	*Content*	*Audience/Context*
11. Andy Parker and Casie Hammond	Designing Online Labs for Undergraduate Engineering Education	Mechanical and electrical engineering	Remote undergraduate engineering students
12. Lindsey Jenkins	Piloting Case-Based Learning in a Blended Learning Nursing Curriculum	Undergraduate nursing courses	Nursing school faculty
13. Victoria March	Tackling Complex Content and Managing SMEs	Oncology—liquid cancers	Experts in radiation biology and physics
14. Megan Martin	Redesigning a Course to Promote Equity and Increase Student Success	Kitchen operations	Culinary arts program
15. Jenna Powell	Designing a Competency-Based Licensure Program	Technology integration for preservice teachers	Faculty teaching in pre service teaching programs
16. Tess Primeau	Redesigning Curriculum for International Learning Contexts and Global Partnerships	Undergraduate professional education	Underserved global populations
17. Parvathy Ramanathan and Mohana Ganesan	Redesigning a Workshop to Increase the Impact of Social Workers' Efforts in a Developing Country	Preparing social workers for professional practice	Social work students in India
18. Jane Rogers and Kayla Wilson	Navigating Between Instructor and Student Needs	Video production	Online undergraduate students
INDUSTRY			
19. Desmond Brower	Handling Challenges When Subcontracting as an External Needs Assessor	Data collection strategies	Sales personnel
20. Maggie Lochs	Aligning Process at Global Training Innovations	Data collection strategies and navigating difficult conversations	Learning and development professionals
21. Raul Ramirez	Designing Educational Materials for a Neurodiverse Patient Population	Strategies for working with diverse patient populations	Healthcare professionals
22. Fiona Roberts	Joyne-ing a Learning Team as a Startup Company	Technical skills; communication and interpersonal skills	Field specialists at startup company
23. Cassie Standage	Developing a Workplace Violence Prevention Training	Workplace violence prevention	Firefighters
24. Jack Waterkamp	Managing Scope Change in an Instructional Design Project	Software development training	System administrators, software trainers
25. Scott Hunter	Developing Online Assessment in an International Setting	Sales consultant certification	Automobile industry

Introduction: The Case-Learning Process—Strategies and Reflections

Peggy A. Ertmer, Krista D. Glazewski, Adrie A. Koehler, and Jill E. Stefaniak

> Stories are always drawn from life, from both the general qualities we distill from experience and the particular qualities we discern in careful observation, but they get their power from going beyond this basis in fact . . . From the standpoint of a reader or listener, stories are revealing journeys that we can take multiple times, discovering new things in each telling.
>
> (Parrish, 2006, p. 73)

Storytelling has been part of the human experience since people learned to communicate with symbols and words and continues to be a regular part of our lives today. We tell stories to gain attention, elicit emotion, illustrate our position, humanize a situation, explain the complexity of something, make distinctions, build commonalties, and create meaning (Bruner, 1986, 1990; Jonassen & Hernandez-Serrano, 2002; Kolodner, 1992). But perhaps a more meaningful idea to consider is what you, as the learner, have to gain from the stories of others, and more specifically, what you have to gain from the experiences and stories of other instructional designers. As Parrish (2006) noted, stories offer a medium for making sense of experiences, providing a means for bridging analysis and synthesis. Historian, novelist, and journalist Jeanette Winterson (2021) has taken these ideas further in arguing that humans comprise not just nature or nurture, but also narrative:

> Humans are narrative. The stories we hear. The stories we tell. The stories we must learn to tell differently. Humans have been telling stories since time began—on cave walls, in song, in dance, in language. We make ourselves up as we go along. Who we are is not a law–we're not like gravity. We are an ongoing story.
>
> (p. 179)

We argue that stories provision us to act, understand, and problem solve toward a future that we are creating for ourselves. As such, acting, understanding, and problem solving from within the stories of others has the potential to yield many different forms of knowledge

(Jonassen & Hernandez-Serrano, 2002). By analyzing the design stories of others, you have opportunities to understand the diverse types of knowledge you are drawing on, recognize areas for growth, and reflect on your developing identity as an instructional designer (Stefaniak & Hwang, 2021).

Swan et al. (2020) categorized three types of expert knowledge: procedural (e.g., instructional design [ID] methods and procedures), conditional (e.g., making adjustments based on project developments), and conceptual (e.g., facts and theories). ID represents an ill-defined skill that is largely dependent on the context in which it is practiced and occurs within a series of iterative decision-making cycles as designers consider both existing constraints and available resources (Jonassen, 2008; Stefaniak & Hwang, 2021). In other words, there is no single set of principles and procedures that can be applied in the same way in every situation. Although there is no formula for good design (Brown & Green, 2018; Cates, 2001), there is evidence to suggest that the more we know about ID, and the more we practice solving ID problems, the more "expert" we become (Bransford et al., 2000; Ertmer & Stepich, 2005; Gibbons, 2014; Stefaniak & Hwang, 2021; Swan et al., 2020). As Swan et al. (2020) pointed out, "if instructional designers can better understand the development of expertise—specifically the structural components of expertise and their interactions—they can design experiences more intentionally to better prepare students" (p. 2552).

We hope that the cases in this text provide you with the kind of opportunities you need to initiate the development of your instructional design expertise and evolving identity. The case studies are purposefully complex and, by design, do not lend themselves to simple, "right" answers. The goal of the case method is not to help you find answers to every possible design issue but rather to increase your understanding of the types of complex problems professional designers encounter in their everyday practice and to prompt personal awareness of the design decisions you are making. We expect that by analyzing and reflecting on a variety of complex design situations you will be better prepared to solve similar problems in your own ID practice. This assumption is based on the practices of case-based reasoning.

CASE-BASED REASONING

Imagine a designer who is asked to develop and facilitate a workshop for a group of experts. The designer is charged with prompting these experts to brainstorm potential solutions to address the difficulties military families face as they navigate major (e.g., deployment, changing duty stations) and day-to-day (e.g., youth sports, filing taxes, childcare) events—events that are complicated by information overload created by countless websites with potential resources. While the designer has previously developed and facilitated learning experiences across a variety of contexts, she has no experience with military personnel, their families, or those supporting them. Her client informs her about the challenges facing these individuals and pushes for a specific type of technological solution. However, her training and experience lead her to question these directives, as it seems premature to determine specific options at this point in the process. Instead, what seems most critical is for her to gain an understanding of the variety of experiences that exist among the military families she is tasked with helping.

As she considers her limited experience with military contexts, she reflects on the experiences of her friend—a single mother whose ex-husband was in the military. She remembers her friend sharing her frustrations with trying to find an in-network healthcare provider for her son, who had military insurance. Complicating their situation was the fact that they both lived far from a military community. Her client had not mentioned specific family dynamics, but thinking of her friend prompted her to realize that across military families, there were bound to be countless dynamics that complicated the process of finding needed resources. At the same time, she considers her experiences facilitating workshops for adults. These events have primarily involved working with teaching professionals and graduate students aspiring to become educators. However, when she first transitioned from being a high school teacher to working with adult learners, she realized that designing for adult learners differed in significant ways from designing for teenagers. For instance, adult learners typically were more self-directed and could draw on more life experiences as a part of the learning process. Thus, although neither situation was exactly the same as the current one, both of her prior experiences represented case examples that she could use in approaching this project. This type of reasoning, from direct and indirect past experiences, is known as case-based reasoning (CBR) (Tawfik & Kolodner, 2016).

Formally defined, case-based reasoning involves "using old experiences to understand and solve new problems" (Kolodner, 1992, p. 3). Individuals leverage prior knowledge and understanding that informs the current situation, provided that their knowledge is readily usable. For these reasons, Kolodner et al. (2004) argued that it is not enough to have extensive experience; this experience must be reflected on and interpreted for meaning, relevance, and lessons learned. Only then can the individual use it as a relevant case to reason from in future applications. In other words, each meaningfully interpreted experience becomes a case in their memories, and it is helpful to think of this collection of cases as a metaphorical case library. From our earlier example, you know that the ID professional applied reasoning from two separate cases in her case library—her prior experience designing workshops for adult learners and her related interactions with a military family.

ATTENTION, STUDENTS: STRATEGIES FOR LEARNING FROM CASES

Although case methods have been used in business, law, and medicine for more than 100 years, it is likely that this will be one of your first experiences with the case approach. This may give rise to a wide range of feelings—excitement, nervousness, curiosity, intimidation, frustration, or any combination. In addition, you will probably have a lot of questions: *How do I analyze a case? How long should a case analysis be? How will I know if I've done it right? Where will I find the information and resources I need to solve the case problems? Do you have examples of completed case analyses?*

Based on our experiences, students are typically excited about using case studies in instruction. However, they often feel a little apprehensive as well, possibly because of their unfamiliarity with this approach. We have written this section, addressed to you specifically, because we have found that initial concerns can be lessened by describing, up front, the types of tasks you will be expected to complete, as well as some of the adjustments you may need to make in your current learning "mindsets." As one of our former students noted:

> In my opinion, if students were told up front that this style of learning (case-based instruction) feels slow and cumbersome at first, and that they should read and re-read the information in the case a couple of times, do what they need to visualize and better understand the scenarios—it might be easier to adjust to. I think case-based learning is a valuable and interactive method that just takes a different mindset than most students are used to.

We think this student makes two excellent suggestions: tell students what this approach *feels* like and tell them *how* to do it (i.e., analyze a case). Although we don't really believe that we can tell you exactly how it feels to learn from cases or how you must go about analyzing a case, we offer a few thoughts and suggestions related to these two elements of the case-learning experience. We begin with suggestions on how to adopt a reflective mindset and then provide strategies and procedures for analyzing a case.

DEVELOPING A REFLECTIVE MINDSET

One of the primary goals of professional education is helping novices "think like" members of the profession (Shulman, 1992) and facilitating "professional identities that align with the complexities and expectations they will encounter in the real world of design practice" (Tracey et al., 2014, p. 316). This entails being able to look back on practice as a way to understand experience (Schön, 1983), engaging in an internal process of reflection and inquiry as a way to improve future practice (Tracey et al., 2014), and drawing lessons learned from design experiences (Tawfik & Kolodner, 2016). According to Hartog (2002), this type of skillful inquiry takes "time, commitment, and practice" (p. 237).

Reflective practice helps instructional designers take stock of the countless adjustments they make as new information becomes available or clients ask for changes during ongoing projects. McDonald (2022) argued that ID students should be given opportunities to practice three different types of reflective practice: reflection-in-action, reflection-on-action, and reflection-for-action. Reflection-in-action occurs when individuals intentionally pause to reflect on their actions while they are still in the middle of completing tasks (Schön, 1983). Reflection-on-action occurs after a project has been complete. As such, instructional designers may take time to think about what went well, what they had to adjust, or what challenges they experienced during the project. Killion and Todnem (1991) suggested a third type of reflection that builds upon Schon's work called reflection-for-action. During reflection-for-action, instructional designers might contemplate how they can apply what was learned from one project to a future project.

Mature, reflective thinkers are able to view situations from multiple perspectives, search for alternative explanations of events, and use evidence to support or evaluate a decision or position (Kitchener & King, 1990). Furthermore, they are "active and reflective agents of innovation whose storehouse of design precedents feeds professional judgment and action in the design space" (Tracey et al., 2014, p. 316). These qualities form an essential part of the mindset that we believe facilitates learning from case studies. We provide additional guidelines here, gleaned from our own experiences and those of our students, as well as from the results of a research study conducted by one of the authors (Ertmer et al., 1996).

- There is no one right answer. If you enter the case-learning experience with this idea firmly planted, you are less likely to be frustrated by the ambiguity inherent in the case-study approach. Additionally, you should keep in mind that not all proposed solutions hold the same value. There are many approaches to the issues in each case. The solutions you propose will depend as much on the perspective you take as on the issues you identify. Some solutions will please more stakeholders, address more barriers, and work more readily within specific constraints compared to other solutions. Accept the fact that you will not know how to solve each case. Furthermore, if you have no clue where to begin, give yourself permission not to know. Then begin the analysis process by paying attention to how others analyze the case based on their personal experiences.

- After you have analyzed the case, you may want to know how the designers in the cases "solved" the problems. However, this is not as helpful as you might think. Being frustrated by a lack of answers can actually be very motivating. If you're left hanging after reading a case, chances are you'll continue to ponder the issues for a long time to come.
- There is more than one way to look at things. One of the advantages to participating in case discussions is that you get the chance to hear how others analyzed the case and to consider multiple points of view, thus gaining a more complete examination and understanding of the issues involved. Not only will listening to others' ideas allow you to see the issues from different points of view; it will also force you to consider exactly where you stand. By paying close attention to what others have to say, you can evaluate how their views fit with your own. As a result, you will learn more about who you are, where you are coming from, and what you stand for. Your views of others, as well as of yourself, may be broadened. Research has demonstrated that students who value case discussions as an important part of the learning process and invest effort into participating into these discussions exhibit more complete problem-solving processes compared to peers who were less invested in the discussions (Koehler et al., 2022).
- Keep an open mind; suspend judgment until all ideas are considered. This suggestion builds on the previous one. Come to the case discussion with an attitude of "Let's see what develops." Begin by regarding your initial solutions as tentative. Listen respectfully to your peers; ask questions to clarify and gather additional information, not to pass judgment on ideas different from yours. As one of our students recommended, "Be flexible and open-minded. Remember that problems can be attacked from many different angles." Use the case discussion to gather additional data. In the end, your final recommendation should be informed by the collective wisdom of the whole class yet still reflect your own best judgment.
- Be leery of assumptions and generalizations; avoid seeing things in extremes. If data are ambiguous or there is little evidence to support why case players behaved as they did, be cautious of the assumptions you make. Be especially careful to state your assumptions tentatively, suggesting uncertainty. Furthermore, be careful about making assumptions that allow you to propose easy solutions. Before going down any single solution path, ask yourself if the assumptions you are making are realistic, based on the facts of the case.

  Along these same lines, be careful not to generalize your observations beyond the data provided. Avoid using labels or slogans that lump people together. If you're inclined to see things in black and white, or all or nothing, stand back and look at the words you use in your analysis. In general, you should avoid words such as *always, never, everybody,* or *nobody*. Stick close to the facts when describing the issues, drawing conclusions, and making recommendations.
- Expect to get better; focus on the analysis process. At the beginning of a case-based course, you may feel overwhelmed with the challenge of trying to solve case problems. It is important to recognize, first, that this is not uncommon. Many students initially feel overwhelmed and apprehensive. Second, as with most skills, recognizing that design skills and knowledge improve with practice is equally important. Furthermore, most students actually start to enjoy the challenge involved in analyzing problematic situations. If you maintain the mindset that you learn as much from the analysis process as you do from identifying a potential solution, then your case-learning experience will be less frustrating. The analytic process is at the heart of the case method. Pay attention to the progress you make in analyzing the cases. Did you consider all the issues? Did you look at issues from the varying perspectives of the key players? Have you based suggestions

on available data? In short, become comfortable with the complexity and uncertainty involved with the ID process, embrace failure in the safe space case learning affords, and focus on developing design thinking strategies versus perfect solutions (Stefaniak, 2021). If your skills are improving in these areas, you're gaining in precisely the ways promoted by the case approach. And remember that learning is a lifelong process. You'll never know all there is to know about designing. Yet each experience with design situations should move you closer to thinking and acting like a professional designer.

- Take time to reflect. According to Campoy (2005), "Good problem solvers review their efforts and the results to incorporate what they have learned for future reference" (p. 197). However, reflection is commonly overlooked during problem-centered learning (Tawfik & Kolodner, 2016). Reflection is a recurring theme in our discussion of how to approach a case study. Quite simply, that's because we believe that reflection enhances everything that happens in the case method. According to Shulman (1996), "We do not learn from experience; we learn by thinking about our experience" (p. 208). Reflection, as a form of metacognition, is a prerequisite for deep learning and is key to developing your case library for future retrieval in case-based reasoning (Kolodner et al., 2004). Furthermore, reflection "enables designers to examine their thinking, their behaviors, design situations, and concerns from team members and stakeholders" (Hong & Choi, 2011, p. 688).

  It is true that a case analysis takes more time to complete than traditional course assignments. Yet there is little to be gained by trying to rush the process. Acting or responding impulsively decreases the chances that you will gather all the relevant information, examine all the potential courses of action, and consider the many possible ensuing consequences. Take time to think. Ask questions of yourself, your peers, and your instructor. Hills and Gibson (cited in Grimmett & Erickson, 1988) describe how reflective practitioners might go about their work. The development of this type of reflective mindset can begin with your work on these cases:

  > As you go about your work responding to phenomena, identifying problems, diagnosing problems, making normative judgments, developing strategies, etc. think about your responses to situations and about what it is in the situation, and in yourself, that leads you to respond that way; think about the norms and values on which your judgments are based; think about the manner in which you frame problems, and think about "your conception of your role." "Surface" and criticize your implicit understandings. Construct and test your own theories.
  >
  > (p. 151)

- Expect to engage in productive struggle. The development of ID expertise is a gradual process that takes time; you can expect to demonstrate both expert-like thinking and novice-like thinking across cases you analyze (Koehler et al., 2018). After reflecting on their experiences learning complex content, one group of students came to the realization that "struggle, the emotional and intellectual work associated with complex learning, was an important part of the sensemaking process" (Fiock et al., 2022, p. 44). The struggle itself was motivating to them and prompted awareness of where they needed to keep working. The key is to maintain a positive mindset and to understand the struggle—both its causes and the factors that contribute to that struggle, including the emotions you experience—then, you can identify how best to move forward.

- Enjoy yourself. As indicated earlier, the case method may at first feel like a strange and difficult way to learn. Yet, even when students indicate that learning from case studies can be frustrating and "unnerving," they also admit that it is exciting and valuable. Being actively involved, working with stimulating case material, having a chance to express your ideas and hear those of others—these are all enjoyable aspects of case learning. We think one of our students summed it up wonderfully: "I like how cases challenge you and frustrate you. My advice is to relax. Let the ideas flow. Don't say, 'This isn't possible.' And, most of all, be confident that what you are doing now will pay off in the future."

STRATEGIES FOR ANALYZING A CASE

There are a variety of ways to effectively analyze a case study. We offer the following as one possibility:

1. Understand the context in which the case is being analyzed and discussed. If your instructor is using this text to supplement another, then the cases will probably be used to provide real-world examples of the content or design steps you've discussed. This context can help focus your attention on relevant issues, questions, and concerns related to your readings and other coursework. Also, each case includes a set of focusing questions at the end. You may want to read these questions first, as a way to "prime the pump." Reading case questions before you read the case may help you read more meaningfully and more effectively.
2. Read the case. Your first reading should probably be fairly quick, just to get a general sense of what the case is about—the key players, main issues, context, and so on.
3. Read the case again. Your second (and subsequent) reading(s) should be much slower: taking notes, considering multiple perspectives, thinking about alternative solutions and consequences. The benefits you reap from your case analysis will relate to how much time you spend—not necessarily reading it, but reflecting on what you have read.
4. Analyze the case. This is probably the "fuzziest" and thus most overwhelming step of the whole case-analysis process. Assuming that you have already identified the facts of the case, relevant information, key players, context, and resources and constraints, we recommend that you address the following questions/points during your analysis:
   a. Who are the key stakeholders in this case? How would each stakeholder describe the primary issue in the case?
   b. Given the stakeholders' various perspectives, what do you see as the primary design issue(s) in the case?
   c. List any assumptions you make about information that is missing from the case. As much as possible, support your assumptions with evidence from the case. Why are your assumptions reasonable?
   d. Generate a list of potential solutions related to each issue.
   e. Specify possible consequences (pros and cons) of each solution.
   f. After weighing the advantages and limitations to each solution, make a recommendation for action.
   g. Describe how your recommendations address the issues listed in points a and b. Reflect on the extent to which you think that the suggested solution will solve the primary issue(s).

5. Actively participate in class discussion. The case class is a learning community—together you, your instructor, and your peers are working to gain a more complete understanding of the case situation and possible solutions. Your active participation and listening are important. You must listen carefully to what others are saying so that your questions and contributions can move the discussion along. Coming to class prepared is critical to your ability to participate in, and benefit from, the case-learning experience. The overall value of the discussion will depend on you and your peers' abilities to regulate the collaborative experience (Hakkinen et al., 2017). Don't rely on your instructor to determine the purpose of your discussion. Find ways to make it meaningful for you personally and work to remove any barriers you are experiencing (Koehler et al., 2022).
6. Reflect on the case-learning experience. Boud (2001) advocated the use of reflection at three different points during a learning experience: at the *start*, in a preparatory phase when you start to explore what is required of you, as you become aware of the demands of the situation and the resources you bring to bear; *during* the experience, as a way of dealing with the vast array of inputs and coping with the feelings generated; and *after* the experience, as you attempt to make sense of it and index it for future application.
7. Take advantage of technology affordances to support problem solving and reflection. For instance, if you are participating in asynchronous discussions, the online forum preserves the ideas being shared, offering you opportunities to consider ideas in a flexible manner or to revisit posts to fuel reflection (Koehler et al., 2020). As another example, social media offer opportunities to connect with experts and content, to see how experts and peers interact with meaningful content and to create an identity as an instructional design professional (Koehler & Vilarinho-Pereira, 2023). These tools can support your efforts to understand case problems more fully (e.g., using YouTube to familiarize yourself with an unfamiliar learning context; connecting with an expert in the field) and devise effective solutions (e.g., sharing ideas and gaining feedback from connections, accessing archived materials for precedents). Optimize connections within your class and beyond.
8. Identify the emotions you experience throughout the case learning process. As noted previously, you will likely experience several different emotions while analyzing cases. Effectively monitoring your learning experiences requires metacognitive awareness of yourself and the task at hand (Pintrich, 2004). Labeling and reflecting on your emotions promote regulation and greater well-being by allowing you to make sense of your experiences and manage your actions (Brown, 2021).

The case method provides opportunities for facilitating a reflective approach to learning. Starting with the first step in the analysis process, as you consider the context in which you are studying a case, you are immersed in a reflective process. As you implement your analysis approach, you complete a variety of activities that are inherent in a reflective design approach; that is, you "test the waters" through a process in which you consider previous experiences, connect with your feelings, and draw upon your existing repertoire of images, metaphors, and theories (Smith, 2001).

Finally, at the end of a case analysis, reflection helps you make sense of your experiences, deepen your understanding of the case, and solidify the case example for future retrieval. By reflecting on both the products and the processes of your learning experiences, you gain insights essential to improving future performance. Reflection can link past and future actions by providing you with information about the strategies you used (learning process) and the outcomes you achieved (learning products). It allows you to take stock of what has happened and to prepare yourself for future action. As noted by one of our former students:

> I have enjoyed the opportunity to reflect upon my performance (on my case analyses) because I think that it encourages me to take stock of where I have been, where I am, and where I need to go on the road to expertise. Self-reflection may, at times, be painful, but the gains stimulate growth and improvement necessary to become the best instructional designer possible.

BECOMING AN ID PROFESSIONAL: REFLECTING ON YOUR CASE EXPERIENCES

It should be evident by now that one of our primary purposes for using case studies as an instructional approach is to facilitate your growing ability to think like an ID professional. As in all professions, learning to "think like a designer" does not happen overnight. Furthermore, as noted earlier, reflection has been established as a valuable part of this process, as experience alone doesn't assure learning (Weil & Frame, 1992). As Exter and Ashby (2022) pointed out, design problems have many potential solutions and instructional designers should evaluate "problems, ideas, constraints, and potential outcomes" through "reflective thinking to stay cognizant of their actions and decisions, and how these impact the design process itself" (p. 255).

As you analyze the cases in this book, and particularly as you come to the end of using the book, we ask you to consider how you learned from the case studies, and then more broadly, as a beginning ID professional, how you might use cases in your own design work.

First of all, consider what it was like trying to learn from case studies. Use the following questions to stimulate your thinking about the case-learning experience:

- How interesting, valuable, and relevant was the case approach?
- How challenging and/or frustrating was it? What features contributed to the challenge level? Should these features be altered, and if so, how?
- How would you describe your attitude toward using case studies as a learning tool?
- What strategies did you use to analyze each case? Did you use a systematic approach, or was it more hit-and-miss?
- Did your approach change over the course of the semester, and if so, how?
- What did you do when you hit a "snag"? (Did you give up? Did you consult other resources? Did you talk to other students?)
- What advice would you give to other ID students who are just beginning a course/text like this?

Second, we ask you to put on a different hat, so to speak, and look at the use of case studies from the point of view of a designer rather than a student of design. Use the following questions to stimulate your thinking regarding the usefulness of the case method as a teaching strategy:

- What particular design situations might be amenable to the case approach?
- Are there situations where the case method would not be appropriate?
- Are there any specific types of learners who would or would not benefit from the case approach?
- What different purposes might cases serve (e.g., building interest and motivation, contextualizing learning, enhancing problem diagnosis and problem-solving skills) in the education of instructional designers?

- How might cases be used with novice learners, advanced beginners, and so on?
- How might cases be used in professional development courses for practicing instructional design professionals?

We hope that reflecting on questions such as these will help you feel comfortable using the case approach when you begin designing and teaching your own courses and workshops. We believe that cases offer a powerful means for facilitating the development of ID expertise. At the end of this course/text, as you look back on your own experiences using *The ID CaseBook*, we certainly hope that this is true for you, and wish you well in confidently employing the case method in your future instructional design practice.

REFERENCES

Boud, D. (2001). Using journal writing to enhance reflective practice. In L. M. English & M. A. Gillen (Eds.), *Promoting journal writing in adult education: New directions in adult and continuing education* (Vol. 90, pp. 9–18). Jossey-Bass. https://doi.org/10.1002/ace.16

Bransford, J. D., Brown, A. L., & Cocking, R. R. (Eds.). (2000). How experts differ from novices. In *How People Learn: Brain, mind, experience, and school* (pp. 31–50). National Academies Press.

Brown, A. H., & Green, T. D. (2018). Beyond teaching instructional design models: Exploring the design process to advance professional development and expertise. *Journal of Computing in Higher Education, 30*, 176–186. https://doi.org/10.1007/s12528-017-9164-y

Brown, B. (2021). *Atlas of the heart: Mapping meaningful connection and the language of human experience*. Random House.

Bruner, J. (1986). *Actual minds, possible worlds*. Harvard University Press.

Bruner, J. (1990). *Acts of meaning*. Harvard University Press.

Campoy, R. (2005). *Case study analysis in the classroom: Becoming a reflective teacher*. Sage. https://doi.org/10.4135/9781452229775

Cates, W. M. (2001). Introduction to the special issue. *Educational Technology, 41*(1), 5–6.

Ertmer, P. A., Newby, T. J., & MacDougall, M. (1996). Students' approaches to learning from case-based instruction: The role of reflective self-regulation. *American Educational Research Journal, 33*(3), 719–752. https://doi.org/10.3102/00028312033003719

Ertmer, P. A., & Stepich, D. A. (2005). Instructional design expertise: How will we know it when we see it? *Educational Technology, 45*(6), 38–43. https://www.jstor.org/stable/44429251

Exter, M., & Ashby, I. (2022). Lifelong learning of instructional design and educational technology professionals: A heutagogical approach. *TechTrends, 66*(2), 254–264. https://doi.org/10.1007/s11528-021-00657-x

Fiock, H., Meech, S., Yang, M., Long, Y., Farmer, T., Hilliard, N., Koehler, A. A., & Cheng, Z. (2022). Instructional design learners make sense of theory: A collaborative autoethnography. *Educational Technology Research and Development, 70*(1), 31–57. https://doi.org/10.1007/s11423-021-10075-8

Gibbons, A. S. (2014). Eight views of instructional design and what they should mean to instructional designers. In B. Hokanson & A. S. Gibbons (Eds.), *Design in educational technology* (pp. 15–36). Springer. https://doi.org/10.1007/978-3-319-00927-8_2

Grimmett, P. P., & Erickson, G. L. (1988). *Reflection in teacher education*. Teachers College Press.

Hakkinen, P., Jarvela, S., Makitalo-Siegl, K., Ahonen, A., Naykki, P., & Valtonen, T. (2017). Preparing teacher-students for twenty-first-century learning practices (PREP 21): A framework for enhancing collaborative problem-solving and strategic learning skills. *Teachers and Teaching, 23*(1), 25–41. https://doi.org/10.1080/13540602.2016.1203772

Hartog, M. (2002). Becoming a reflective practitioner: A continuing professional development strategy through humanistic action research. *Business Ethics: A European Review, 11*, 233–243. https://doi.org/10.1111/1467-8608.00281

Hong, Y. C., & Choi, I. (2011). Three dimensions of reflective thinking in solving design problems: A conceptual model. *Educational Technology Research and Development, 59*, 687–710. https://doi.org/10.1007/s11423-011-9202-9

Jonassen, D. H. (2008). Instructional design as design problem solving: An iterative process. *Educational Technology, 48*(3), 21–26. https://www.jstor.org/stable/44429574

Jonassen, D. H., & Hernandez-Serrano, J. (2002). Case-based reasoning and instructional design: Using stories to support problem solving. *Educational Technology Research and Development, 50*(2), 65–77. https://doi.org/10.1007/BF02504994

Killion, J. P., & Todnem, G. R. (1991). A process for personal theory building. *Educational Leadership, 48*(6), 14–16.

Kitchener, K. S., & King, P. M. (1990). The reflective judgment model: Ten years of research. In M. L. Commons, C. Arman, L. Kohlberg, F. A. Richards, T. A. Grotzer, & J. Sinnott (Eds.), *Adult development: Models and methods in the study of adolescent and adult thought* (Vol. 2, pp. 63–78). Praeger.

Koehler, A. A., Cheng, Z., Fiock, H., Janakiraman, S., & Wang, H. (2020). Asynchronous online discussions during case-based learning: A problem-solving process. *Online Learning, 24*(4), 64–92. https://doi.org/10.24059/olj.v24i4.233

Koehler, A. A., Cheng, Z., Fiock, H., Wang, H., Janakiraman, S., & Chartier, K. (2022). Examining students' use of online case-based discussions to support problem solving: Considering individual and collaborative experiences. *Computers & Education, 179*. https://doi.org/10.1016/j.compedu.2021.104407

Koehler, A. A., Ertmer, P. A., & Newby, T. J. (2018). Developing pre-service teachers' instructional design skills through case-based instruction: Examining the impact of discussion format. *Journal of Teacher Education, 70*(4), 319–334. https://doi.org/10.1177/0022487118755701

Koehler, A. A., & Vilarinho-Pereira, D. R. (2023). Using social media affordances to support ill-structured problem-solving skills: Considering possibilities and challenges. *Educational Technology Research & Development, 71*(2), 199–235. https://doi.org/10.1007/s11423-021-10060-1

Kolodner, J. L. (1992). An introduction to case-based reasoning. *Artificial Intelligence Review, 6*, 3–34. https://doi.org/10.1007/BF00155578

Kolodner, J. L., Owensby, J. N., & Guzdial, M. (2004). Case-based learning aids. In D. H. Jonassen (Ed.), *Handbook of research for educational communications and technology* (2nd ed., pp. 829–861). Erlbaum.

McDonald, J. K. (2022). Preparing instructional design students for reflective practice. In J. E. Stefaniak & R. M. Reese (Eds.), *The instructional design trainer's guide: Authentic practices and considerations for mentoring ID and ed tech professionals* (pp. 29–37). Routledge.

Parrish, P. (2006). Design as storytelling. *TechTrends, 50*(4), 72–82. https://doi.org/10.1007/s11528-006-0072-7

Pintrich, P. R. (2004). A conceptual framework for assessing motivation and self-regulated learning in college students. *Educational Psychology Review, 16*(4), 385–407. https://doi.org/10.1007/s10648-004-0006-x

Schön, D. A. (1983). *The reflective practitioner: How professionals think in action*. Basic Books.

Shulman, L. (1992). Toward a pedagogy of cases. In J. H. Shulman (Ed.), *Case methods in teacher education* (pp. 1–30). Teachers College Press.

Shulman, L. S. (1996). Just in case: Reflections on learning from experience. In J. A. Colbert, P. Desberg, & K. Trimble (Eds.), *The case for education: Contemporary approaches for using case methods* (pp. 197–217). Allyn & Bacon.

Smith, M. K. (2001). Donald Schön: Learning, reflection and change. *The Encyclopedia of Informal Education*. Retrieved January 28, 2013, from http://www.infed.org/thinkers/et-schon.htm

Stefaniak, J. (2021). Leveraging failure-based learning to support decision-making and creative risk in instructional design pedagogy. *TechTrends, 65*, 646–652. https://doi.org/10.1007/s11528-021-00608-6

Stefaniak, J. E., & Hwang, H. (2021). A systematic review of how expertise is cultivated in instructional design coursework. *Educational Technology Research & Development, 69*, 3331–3366. https://doi.org/10.1007/s11423-021-10064-x

Swan, R. H., Plummer, K. J., & West, R. E. (2020). Toward functional expertise through formal education: Identifying an opportunity for higher education. *Educational Technology Research & Development, 68*, 2551–2568. https://doi.org/10.1007/s11423-020-09778-1

Tawfik, A. A., & Kolodner, J. L. (2016). Systematizing scaffolding for problem-based learning: A view from case-based reasoning. *Interdisciplinary Journal of Problem-Based Learning, 10*(1). https://doi.org/10.7771/1541-5015.1608

Tracey, M. W., Hutchinson, A., & Grzebyk, T. Q. (2014). Instructional designers as reflective practitioners: Developing professional identity through reflection. *Educational Technology Research & Development, 62*, 315–334. https://doi.org/10.1007/s11423-014-9334-9

Weil, S., & Frame, P. (1992). Capability through business and management education. In J. Stephenson & S. Weil (Eds.), *Quality in learning: A capability approach in higher education* (pp. 45–76). Kogan Page.

Winterson, J. (2021). *12 Bytes: How we got here. Where we might go next*. Grove Atlantic Press.

Part I

K–12 and Informal Learning

1

Michael Bishop

Implementing Gaming Technologies in Traditional K–12 Contexts

Susan Pedersen

Michael Bishop was at Oakdale Middle School early last May when the results of the recent state-wide proficiency tests were released. He'd been meeting with middle school teachers involved in pilot testing the educational games his team had developed for middle school science classes. As he left the training session he found Nancy Levin, the district-level science curriculum specialist, in the hallway, talking with Paul Russell, the Oakdale principal. Michael, a researcher at the university and the director of the project developing the science games, had been working with Nancy for two years now, and they had an easy relationship. So, he approached her smiling, not yet realizing how serious the conversation would be.

The results were disappointing. The state proficiency exam had been revised two years earlier to include new open-ended question types, including short essays and tasks that asked students to show their work (such as plotting a point on a graph), all of which were scored by humans and could receive partial credit. In the previous year, the district average on the new eighth-grade proficiency tests trailed the state average by 8%. However, district administrators had argued that because it was the first year for the new test format, the results were not necessarily indicative of a problem. For the most part, parents were understanding, and there had been little pushback, but everyone knew that this argument wouldn't hold water a second year.

That summer, the district curriculum specialists developed strategies designed to boost scores across reading, math, and science. Committees of teachers had convened over the summer to assess alignment of the curriculum to state standards and write open-ended test items to be used along with the existing bank of multiple-choice items for practice throughout the school year. In the fall, teachers participated in training sessions on preparing students for these new types of items. And schools developed pull-out and after school programs for students who fell just short of proficiency in any of these subjects. Confidence in these approaches ran high in the district office, and school officials had waited eagerly for the confirmation of their effectiveness that the proficiency test results would provide. But the results showed exactly the opposite. The district average for eighth grade had fallen by 8% while the state average had risen by 2%. This left the district trailing the state average by a whopping 18%. The results of tests at the fifth-grade level were slightly better, but they still trailed state

DOI: 10.4324/9781003354468-2

averages by 11%. Michael knew that in this state, such a drop typically had consequences for district personnel, and he wondered if some of this would fall on Nancy's shoulders.

So, Michael was not entirely surprised six weeks later, after school was out for the summer, to get an email from Nancy announcing that she had decided to take an early retirement, and that her replacement would be Tara Jones. She did not mention Michael's project. Michael was surprised at the formality of the email, so he tried calling Nancy, both then and two days later. She returned neither call. Michael then contacted Tara to set up a time to meet to discuss the science game project.

Tara called Michael two days later. "I've had a chance to sit down with our superintendent to discuss your project, and I'm afraid that we've decided to withdraw," Tara told Michael. "We've decided to move to a personalized learning approach and plan to work with a vendor to completely revamp our science curriculum for grades 4 to 8. I'm afraid we simply can't spare the class time to participate in your research study. We have nothing against games, and we know that yours are designed to be educational, but each of your games takes over a week to play, and that's just too much time. The cohort you're working with will be eighth-grade students next year, and since that's the grade in which kids take the science proficiency test, we've really got to work on preparing them. Now, I understand the problem we're causing for your project and that it will probably be an issue with your funding agency, but I'm sorry, the decision has been made."

FINDING A NEW PILOT SITE

Michael was frustrated. Now in the middle of the project, he needed to recruit another school district to pilot-test the games. So after taking a few days to consider his pitch, Michael called three different district offices and followed up with emails; one never responded, and the other two formally declined to participate without even meeting with Michael. Michael decided to take a different approach and asked a colleague who had some contacts with district-level science coordinators to make some introductions. This led to conversations with administrators from five districts.

Michael felt as if he had to pitch the games to a skeptical audience, something he didn't like doing. He also knew that these administrators had full schedules, so he needed to give them enough detail to grab their interest but not overwhelm them, address issues head-on, and make sure they could see the potential these games had for both learning and motivation. He sent an attachment to each of the administrators before their conversation (see Figure 1.1) summarizing the game approach.

He began these conversations by explaining, "Each game addresses specific grade-level science concept standards, and does it in a way that makes it more likely that kids will understand and remember them. But more importantly, these games address inquiry standards. Kids ponder complex problems, ask questions, look for existing information, design investigations to gather data to answer their questions, support their decisions with evidence, and communicate their reasoning to classmates. Because the games are designed to be played in class, students come to mirror a scientific community, talking a lot with each other about how to do things, and debating what evidence is needed to make a claim. Typically, different students end up becoming 'experts' on different components of the game." Michael then walked the administrators through the game model, answering questions as they arose. He made sure to emphasize how motivated students were during the game: "Even kids who normally seem unmotivated in science class stay on task and are enthusiastic."

Rigglefish

Game Description: *Rigglefish* is a game designed to address middle school standards related to genetics and scientific inquiry. In *Rigglefish,* learners take on the role of Dr. Waters, a geneticist tasked by the government with developing a source for Omega X, a fatty acid that can be used as a protectant against a deadly bioweapon. That source is the rigglefish, a recently discovered species of fish rich in Omega X. Rigglefish can be red, orange, or yellow, but only the yellow ones produce high concentrations of Omega X. Rigglefish also possess some traits that make them difficult to breed in captivity, including a sensitivity to low pressure environments, sharp spikes, and their distinctive wiggle. Players must breed a mating pair of rigglefish that can be farmed to provide a source for the needed protectant.

Game Component	*Example: Rigglefish*
A Complex Task: Each game presents a complex, ill-structured task which requires students to engage in student-directed inquiry	Students must breed a mating pair of fish that are purebred for four key traits. To accomplish this task, students determine, through observation and testing, the phenotypes and genotypes of fish they collect, then breed these fish to obtain the target fish.
Opening Scenario: Video introduction to problem; provides a compelling backstory, but does not tell learners what to do	Student is cast in the role of Dr. Waters, a geneticist who receives an urgent request from the government to develop a source for Omega X, a protectant against a deadly new bioweapon. Task must be completed before enemy agents discover the lab where players are working.
A Virtual Environment: A confined space that contains all the tools and resources learners need; players spend very little time on navigation	Students work in a top-secret underwater lab with four rooms: bathysphere, sample room, pressure room, and breeding room.
Virtual Scientific Instruments: Virtual models of real-world scientific instruments, simplified to emphasize key characteristics relevant to student learning; students must interpret the data the instruments return	Sample Instruments: Bathysphere: Used to collect rigglefish for testing and breeding Sample tanks: Used to observe rigglefish and determine phenotypes and genotypes of each Gel electrophoresis and PCR (Polymerase chain reaction): Determine a fish's genotype for wiggle trait Breeding tanks: Breed rigglefish and select offspring for further testing and breeding
Information Resources: All information needed to handle the task is provided within the game so that learners do not need to search online; information is divided among resources, which discourages reading without a purpose	Sample Resources: Genetics guide: Information on topics such as dominant, recessive, co-dominant, and incompletely dominant alleles Punnett square: Interactive square that players can use to determine possible offspring; connects genotypes with phenotypes
Expert Modeling Videos: An expert thinks aloud about how he or she would handle different tasks within the game, making scientific thinking overt; videos available on demand	Menu allows students to ask questions such as: • What should I do first? • How can I tell the genotypes and phenotypes of different fish? • How do I breed a fish without a wiggle?
Tool Demonstration Videos: These show how each tool within the program functions	Videos on how to use the following: • Bathysphere • Sample tanks • Pressure tank • Gel electrophoresis • PCR • Punnett square • Breeding tanks

FIGURE 1.1 Game description sent to district personnel describing the game model, with examples from one of the games, *Rigglefish*.

Michael then discussed the potential impact on standardized test results, citing results from the National Assessment of Educational Progress (NAEP) that demonstrated how games and other technology-based approaches, which engage students in higher-order thinking, were correlated with higher outcomes on standardized tests than traditional approaches. He then provided a few examples of both objective and subjective test items that students should be able to complete after playing one of the games, *Rigglefish*, and argued that games like this could prepare students for both the traditional multiple choice questions as well as these new types of items.

Bailey Richards, the science curriculum specialist in the Weyman Independent School District (ISD), seemed genuinely interested in games as a means to engage students in scientific inquiry and agreed to meet with Michael and let him present the games to her. But, like Tara Jones, she balked at the amount of time required. "We hit a lot of topics in those middle grades and yes, we want depth, but we have to go deep quickly. So, we want inquiry, but we really have to guide them through it so they don't spend a lot of time just trying to figure out what to do. Your games look great, but these kids aren't used to having to figure so much out for themselves. I think you would find a lot of kids wasting time not knowing what to do. Maybe advanced learners would be able to handle something like this, but I don't think this would be an efficient use of time for the average learner."

Amelia Perez, the assistant director of STEM education in a large urban district, expressed a similar concern about the amount of class time the games required. "We already have a very full curriculum and teachers struggle to get their kids through everything while also trying to meet each child's needs. I would suggest that you have kids play the game as homework, then come into class and discuss it for part of class the next day. If the game is really engaging you might get them to do it. But I don't think that would work for all kids. A third of our kids come from economically disadvantaged backgrounds. During the pandemic our district provided mobile hotspots for kids without high-speed internet access at home but that resource is no longer available."

Laura Kenner and Daniel Brown, the science coordinators in two neighboring districts that had received ratings in the satisfactory range on the proficiency tests in the previous two years, raised other issues as well. Many of their teachers had left the profession during the pandemic, and their districts had struggled to replace them. But teachers' growing concerns over safety, pay and benefits, and even state politics meant that these districts continued to suffer from high levels of turnover. Daniel told Michael, "You talk about teachers 'scaffolding' and 'debriefing' during these games, but half of our science faculty are in their first or second year of teaching. Those are advanced teaching skills, and I don't think every teacher is really prepared to implement those games the way you intend." Laura expressed similar concerns and added, "It's great that you have funds to provide stipends for teachers, especially since pay raises have not kept up with inflation and teachers could use some extra money, but we're seeing so much burnout among our faculty. You want teachers to commit to two weekends and several after-school meetings; it's a lot."

Jim Harrington, the assistant superintendent for curriculum in Mason ISD, a large district where the middle school ratings on the proficiency tests fell into the excellent to exemplary categories, met with Michael for over an hour and seemed to really enjoy playing one of the games Michael's team had developed, even though he hit a couple of bugs. He was less concerned than the others about the length of the games themselves but raised another issue about the time required. "I know some of these approaches have great potential, and I think that's certainly true for your games. And, I also know you have to pilot-test them somewhere, but I feel like we really need to protect our kids from spending too much time on that sort of thing. We've had university folks come into our schools before, and they want to have kids complete a lot of surveys and tests and try out new materials and approaches. But not all of them are ready for prime time. Even in your game, there were some bugs; those could bring a class to a screeching halt and end up wasting time. And you want them to complete pretests and surveys and interviews. We just can't spend that sort of time on research."

Interestingly, none of the school personnel Michael spoke with argued that games were inappropriate in science education. In fact, many of them seemed enthusiastic about the use of games in education. In the end, Bailey offered to let Michael implement the games in pre-AP classes in two middle schools. Laura asked if he would like to work with the after-school science clubs at two of the schools in her district, and Daniel suggested he consider summer programs. They liked the games; they just didn't want them in their regular science classes.

A major purpose of the games Michael's team was developing, and the purpose for which they had received funding, was to hone an innovative model to use technology to increase the engagement of all students in scientific inquiry in their science classes. This was consistent with the Next Generation Science Standards, which emphasized critical thinking and inquiry-based problem solving anchored in programs that reflected how science was practiced in the real world. Restricting use of the games to gifted students, after-school programs, and science summer camps seemed like an admission that these goals weren't appropriate for regular kids in regular classes. Michael wondered if there were ways to make them more appealing to school districts. Nancy had given him some good advice, such as trying to keep the games to a maximum of eight days and including tool demonstration videos, and he had adjusted the original model for the games accordingly. However, this had been insufficient to make the games appealing to anyone who wasn't already an advocate of this type of approach. In considering what the options might be, Michael sought advice from people in diverse fields.

GETTING ADVICE

Michael recruited a small group of people with expertise in different areas to participate in an advisory session. Craig Dawson, the director of science education for the state education agency, had 20 years of teaching experience in middle and high school science classes and was a strong advocate of inquiry-based learning. Michael had attended a couple of talks he had given but did not know him well. Bob Blanchard was a game designer who had spent nine years in California working on some triple-A game titles, then moved two years ago to lead game design in a midsize company located in the same town as the university. Michael had met him the previous year when he was conducting interviews with gaming professionals as part of a research project led by a colleague at another university. Antonia Fisher was a professor of science education at Michael's university. She had projects of her own and had pleaded lack of time when Michael had invited her to be a co–principal investigator on his project. However, Michael had known her for years and valued her opinion, so he was glad she'd agreed to participate in the advisory session. Despite their busy schedules, they were able to meet for a four-hour block in early August.

Michael began the meeting with introductions followed by a presentation of the game model, similar to the one he had given district administrators. He then showed them the opening scenario of *Rigglefish* and let them play for about 40 minutes (see Figure 1.2). This

FIGURE 1.2 Players use the bathysphere in *Rigglefish* to collect fish they can study and breed.

was enough time for everyone to capture fish and try out the different tools, including the breeding tank (see Figure 1.3). They all chatted as they played, commenting mostly on features they liked and asking questions about how to accomplish specific tasks. It was obvious they enjoyed the game and wanted to figure out how to breed the target fish.

Michael began transitioning the group from playing *Rigglefish* to discussing the project. "What I'd like from you is your advice on moving forward with the design of these games." He then explained about the withdrawal of one district from the pilot test and the responses from other districts. "We'd like to see these games implemented in middle school science classes, not only with pre-AP or gifted students, but with regular education students as well. Is that reasonable? And we need enough buy-in from the teachers that they will participate in training on how to implement the games so that they support but not direct learners. Do we need to design these games differently in order to make them attractive to teachers and districts? Or should we give up on that and design for a different audience?"

Craig Dawson shifted in his seat. "That's a tough one, Michael. Teachers and administrators are concerned about those tests, but really what we're all concerned about is making the best use of instructional time. Games are highly engaging, but do students learn as fast or as deeply as they do through other approaches? Unless you can build a case that these games engage students in real science and that this causes them to learn better and faster, you're going to continue to have the sort of pushback you've gotten so far. Now I know that standardized tests have a bad reputation among academics and we're certainly trying to move to tests that better reflect what happens in classrooms and in the real world, but they're still the best tool we have for identifying schools that are failing and students who need help. So you've got to be able to show that your games lead to learning that shows up on those tests."

Antonia Fisher responded, "I think that's a somewhat unrealistic expectation, Craig. Performance on those tests depends on a lot of factors. I would say that if you can show that you

FIGURE 1.3 The breeding tank in *Rigglefish* allows players to cross fish to breed offspring with desired traits.

are successful in getting kids to engage in scientific practice within the games, that's enough to justify their use. The science education community has been trying for decades to incorporate better opportunities for kids to engage in authentic scientific practices and from what I noticed playing your game, I think it's pretty clear that players 'do science' in it. In particular, what resonated with me was that I could see kids collaborating and debating the best ways to tackle various parts of this problem, just like the three of us did as we played. That type of critical thinking just doesn't happen often enough in our science classes."

"I agree that the game encourages higher-level thinking," Craig replied. "I think that's great. All I'm saying is that if you want buy-in from schools, you're going to have to show an impact on performance. I'd recommend creating a bank of test items that teachers can use either as warm-up activities or homework, or perhaps even embed them in your games. Kids reach certain checkpoints and they answer a few questions to test their understanding. That would allow both the teachers and the students to see how much they understand."

Bob Blanchard objected, "Games are great at gathering data about players. There's no need to incorporate multiple-choice questions because you can tell through gameplay what a player does and doesn't understand. Now it's difficult to pull that data out of games and make it really usable for teachers, but it can give a much better picture of what players understand."

Michael cut in, "In fact, we're working on that right now. We've got a game-based assessment component built into two of the games, and we're looking at that data to refine the assessment and then validate it."

Bob continued, "That's great. That's a huge potential of games, and if you can figure out how to look at not just content knowledge but inquiry skills, that would be amazing. But as far as incorporating multiple-choice or short-answer questions in the game: that would break up gameplay, distract the player, and kill motivation. You might be able to do some of that in a homework exercise, but I suspect that as soon as those worksheets come out, the type of critical thinking you're trying to get at here will disappear."

Antonia replied, "I think that's a real danger. You know, Michael, schools need alternatives. If the only types of learning materials out there are ones that prep students for tests, where are the models of alternative approaches? Where are the materials those innovative teachers can use? You have a vision here, and it's a pretty good one, so I say stick with it. These games won't be for everyone, but if you can find a few partners who believe in this work and show impact on the types of things that really matter, then you've done something important."

"What do you mean by 'really matter'?" Craig asked.

Antonia was growing passionate. "By the time a student finishes high school, he or she should have adopted the habits of mind that good scientists have. For example, they should bring the type of healthy skepticism that scientists have to making decisions in all areas of their lives. By that I mean that they should expect—no, *demand*—evidence for claims that others make. And they should think critically about whether that evidence is unbiased and valid. I think games like this can support that type of thinking. I think kids are likely to challenge each other about what claims they make and that they are going to want to defend what they are doing. In other words, they're going to ask each other for evidence and offer it themselves when challenged. That's incredible. That's what we should want out of our educational system. Achieving a goal like that—that should be the measure of success."

Craig smiled. "That's all fine and good, but you have to consider the realities of the classrooms where you want your games played. In addition, you have to think about the teachers and students who play them."

Antonia nodded and said, "What I question about these games is whether you really support teachers in using them well. It takes time to learn to use an approach as different as this effectively, and like you heard from those district administrators, you have to consider the realities of what it's like to be a teacher right now."

Bob added, "I worked on an educational game, and we did some testing in schools. As soon as the teacher was the one managing the implementation, we had problems. That's not a slam at the teachers; this was pre-pandemic, and I don't know about burnout. They were quite professional and even enthusiastic, but they started telling the kids to do things that we'd never anticipated. In particular, they would show them specific strategies and tell them to play that way, even though there were multiple effective strategies. It undermined the whole gameplay experience in that the kids were not really figuring things out for themselves. You really have to provide good teacher training if you want them to support, rather than direct, the inquiry experience."

"But teachers are going to need to hold students accountable for learning while they are playing," Craig said. "Otherwise, what are you going to do about kids who get off-task?"

Michael responded, "Actually, we don't see a lot of off-task behavior."

"Perhaps you haven't seen it because you're there leading the class and the approach is novel," said Craig. "But when you've got a class of kids with diverse needs and a teacher who isn't experienced or entirely comfortable with the approach, you're going to have some kids get confused and off track. The teacher has got to have some control to bring them back on task. There have got to be checkpoints and at least a few definite assignments with due dates. Otherwise there's a danger of a lot of time being wasted."

"Michael," said Antonia, "if you are really looking for a pure implementation of your games, then you might seriously consider summer camps and homeschool markets. That would allow you to implement your vision of the games while at the same time learn about effective implementation strategies. Once you know how to optimize the player experience, you might be able to try that out in a school setting. There have been a variety of innovations that have caught on outside of classrooms, and once they were really polished, started being adopted by schools."

Michael tried to get the group to identify areas of consensus about how he should move forward with the project, but he didn't get very far. Beyond agreeing that the games had merit, their opinions diverged too much to coalesce into an action plan he could walk away with. The lofty principles Antonia espoused resonated with Michael's own beliefs about the goals of science education, but he also recognized that sticking with his vision might mean that the games were doomed to irrelevance. Even if he could find a few teachers or schools willing to pilot-test them, they would probably never achieve broad dissemination in middle schools under their current design. Michael left the meeting realizing he had a lot of thinking to do.

Preliminary Analysis Questions

1. Identify the different barriers Michael encountered when he tried to convince school district personnel to implement the games in middle school classes. What questions do you think educational game designers must consider when designing a game for K–12 contexts?
2. What arguments could Michael make to convince school administrators and teachers about the potential benefits of educational games?
3. Why does Michael feel so strongly about *not* putting the game in an after-school program? Discuss the pros and cons of Michael's decision.

Implications for ID Practice

1. What characteristics of middle school learners must designers consider when planning educational games? Provide specific examples.
2. Identify the different contexts in which an educational game might be played and how those contexts affect design decisions.
3. How can teachers assess student learning through educational games?
4. How are the factors affecting the adoption of a game in this case similar to or differ from efforts to introduce other innovations (e.g., problem-based learning, mobile devices) in schools?

2

Tameka Jackson

Blue Ridge Academy Online

Michael M. Grant and Ismahan Arslan-Ari

DR. JACKSON OBSERVES AN ISSUE

Scanning a table of grades on her aging laptop's screen, Dr. Tameka Jackson thought to herself: *There's something here that just doesn't feel right*. Dr. Jackson was Lower School Head (grades K–8) for Blue Ridge Academy, and the end-of-course grades for both history and math in grades 7 and 8 seemed off. The spread of the online course grades was lower for this school year than the previous year (see Tables 2.1–2.2). Comparing just the onsite and online distribution of math and history grades in the current year, it was clear the percentage of *A*s was lower. This obviously resulted in a higher proportion of *B*s, *C*s, *D*s, and even *F*s. Focusing on just the math scores, though, less than a quarter of the online students scored *A*s, with more than half of the onsite students scoring *A*s. "That seems significant to me," Tameka thought. In history, there was less of a difference: Most onsite students scored *A*s (about 60%), while the online students were pretty evenly split between *A*s and *B*s—and there were no *D*s or *F*s online, but those grades were pretty rare for Blue Ridge students anyway. Tameka pursed her lips, knitted her brow, and reflected on how Blue Ridge Academy progressed to this point.

Blue Ridge Academy was a charter school system with brick-and-mortar locations in Memphis (TN), Nashville (TN), Little Rock (AR), and Houston (TX). There was a total of nine schools (i.e., K–8 and high schools) across the four cities, and each site possessed its own personality. Memphis, Nashville, and Houston were all situated in urban settings. The Little Rock site, however, was located on the outskirts of the city which tended to be more rural. Memphis and Nashville—based on the locations in their respective cities—served predominantly African American students who lived in tightly packed one- and two-story apartment complexes. Houston (given its proximity to the southern US border and the changing demographics of Texas) primarily served a Latinx population, who lived with their families in extended-stay motels, apartments, rental houses, and single-family homes. Little Rock's students were almost evenly split between white students and minority ethnicities, including African American, Latinx, and Hmong students. Students at the Little Rock site were from blue-collar and single-parent families who lived in apartments, small houses, or manufactured homes. Throughout the charter school system, white students tended to come from

DOI: 10.4324/9781003354468-3

TABLE 2.1
Percentages of Students' Math Grades

		Site				*Grade Level*		*Overall*		
Academic Year	*Student Grades*	*Nashville (TN)*	*Memphis (TN)*	*Little Rock (AR)*	*Houston (TX)*	*7th*	*8th*	*Total*	*Onsite*	*Online*
Year 1	A	54.5	47.1	65.6	46.4	47.6	58.3	53.7	53.7	—
	B	18.2	43.5	25.8	26.2	33.3	25.0	28.6	28.6	—
	C	18.2	9.4	8.6	17.9	14.3	12.5	13.3	13.3	—
	D	9.1	—	—	9.5	4.8	4.2	4.4	4.4	—
	F	—	—	—	—	—	—	—	—	—
Year 2	A	36.4	28.2	49.5	36.9	33.3	41.7	38.1	53.5	24.4
	B	36.4	44.7	24.7	35.7	42.9	29.2	35.1	27.7	41.7
	C	9.1	27.1	17.2	17.9	14.3	20.8	18.0	13.8	21.7
	D	18.2	—	—	9.5	9.5	4.2	6.5	5.0	7.8
	F	—	—	8.6	—	—	4.2	2.4	—	4.4

TABLE 2.2
Percentages of Students' History Grades

		Site				*Grade Level*		*Overall*		
Academic Year	*Student Grades*	*Nashville (TN)*	*Memphis (TN)*	*Little Rock (AR)*	*Houston (TX)*	*7th*	*8th*	*Total*	*Onsite*	*Online*
Year 1	A	63.6	64.7	66.7	44.0	61.9	58.3	59.9	59.9	—
	B	27.3	17.6	24.7	46.4	28.6	29.2	28.9	28.9	—
	C	9.1	17.6	8.6	9.5	9.5	12.5	11.2	11.2	—
	D	—	—	—	—	—	—	—	—	—
	F	—	—	—	—	—	—	—	—	—
Year 2	A	54.5	45.9	50.5	61.9	57.1	50.0	53.1	61.6	45.6
	B	27.3	45.9	40.9	19.0	28.6	37.5	33.6	23.9	42.2
	C	18.2	8.2	8.6	9.5	9.5	4.2	6.5	9.4	12.2
	D	—	—	—	—	4.8	4.2	4.4	—	—
	F	—	—	—	9.5	—	4.2	2.4	5.0	—

wealthier, middle-class—albeit lower-middle-class—families, but all students received free breakfast and lunch.

Blue Ridge Academy used a curriculum referred to as classical education, which focused heavily on the liberal arts. Each student was provided a Chromebook for in-class and at-home learning. Blue Ridge Academy staff coordinated with state and municipal social services programs, local internet service providers, and cellphone data service providers to supply low-cost and free internet access (such as mobile hotspots) to all their students.

In the early phases of the pandemic when schools were shuttered, the Blue Ridge Academy schools followed their local and state laws, which were inconsistent across the charter school system. Teachers and staff adjusted to at-home synchronous courses, using Google Classroom and Google Apps for Education since the charter school system already used gmail. And they were ahead of the curve compared to other school districts because Blue Ridge already provided internet access and Chromebooks to their students.

For the previous school year, Blue Ridge Academy selected Canvas as its learning management system, which integrated Zoom video conferencing and Google Apps for Education. Recognizing that classes were going to be offered at a distance, the CEO of Blue Ridge Academy, Darren Thompson, alerted parents. The fallout was significant. Some parents unenrolled their students to be homeschooled or taught in pods with several other families and an experienced teacher. It was obvious that wealthier families were the ones leaving the charter schools for alternatives. The loss of state-appropriated funds for each student withdrawal hit Blue Ridge Academy's budget hard.

However, feedback from parents and students during the remote teaching and at-home learning indicated that there was a desire for high-quality online schooling to continue. For several reasons, including student health, learning preferences, student anxiety, caring for siblings, and supporting family income, virtual schooling worked for a sizable number of students at Blue Ridge Academy schools.

For the current school year, Blue Ridge Academy opted to begin Blue Ridge Academy Online, a virtual school for grades 7–12. Courses included students from across the charter school system. To avoid loading additional responsibilities onto their teachers, Blue Ridge Academy opted to purchase online courses (charged by the student or seat) aligned with their classical curriculum from Xplains Learning, a San Francisco–based education and learning technology company that offered online courses to schools and districts throughout the United States. The courses were asynchronous with course content published into a proprietary learning management system and supplemented by multimedia and screen recordings. While the course content and learning management system were provided by Xplains, the courses were taught by Blue Ridge Academy teachers from any one of the four sites. Blue Ridge Academy Online teachers were available to video conference with students during the school day, and they were available in the afternoons by text messaging and email.

DR. JACKSON CONTEMPLATES TAKING ACTION

A text message *doo-da-doo!* alert jolted Dr. Jackson back from her memory. With a sideways glance at her phone to see who the message was from, she decided she could ignore it.

But this was only the first year of the online academy, Dr. Jackson thought, and she knew she was comparing the online grades to the onsite grades—which wasn't a completely fair comparison. Dr. Jackson leaned back deeply into her comfy office chair. *Am I seeing something that isn't there? Let's see if the teachers can tell me anything that might explain the differences.* She dashed off an email to the two seventh-grade teachers and two eighth-grade teachers to see if they could supply any more details.

A few days later Dr. Jackson was still puzzled. She ran her fingers through her wavy hair, weary from thinking about what she should do. The replies from the teachers had been little help. The summary on her laptop screen listed some instructional issues but nothing substantial to tackle (see Figure 2.1).

Their feedback speaks to the students experiencing challenges, she thought. *But it's not anything concrete to go on.* From the teachers' responses, Dr. Jackson picked up on students' need for additional time for completing assignments and additional requests for meetings with

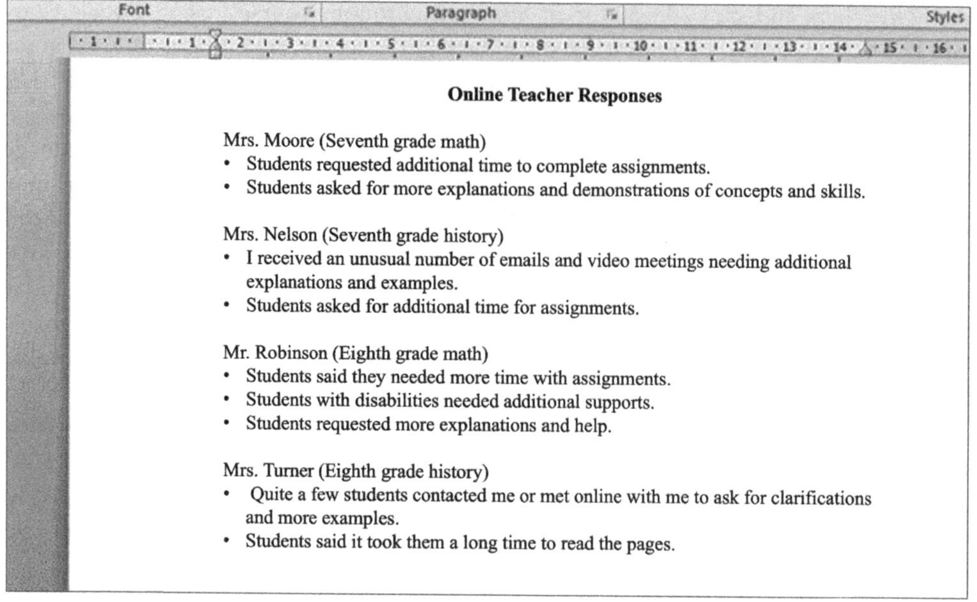

FIGURE 2.1 List of teacher feedback and challenges with online courses.

teachers. She could tell that students needed supplemental scaffolding with explanations and examples to support the online instructional content. *How much of this is just teachers and students adjusting to learning online full-time?* Dr. Jackson wondered.

Dr. Jackson's fingers scrolled across the laptop's track pad and selected another document. Parent and student comments from the online courses' evaluations had been collected in a laundry list. Dr. Jackson scanned through the various broad remarks on her screen:

> Sakara didn't have any problems . . . Hwah-jung thought the writing was difficult . . . My internet was really slow watching the videos . . . It took me longer to read the pages . . . The narration and transcript weren't really helpful for Ja'nelle, so we asked for help from Mrs. Moore to explain the math concepts . . . Some of the writing was hard to read . . . Mr. Robinson was a great teacher. He explained what I didn't understand.

Internet bandwidth problems. Possible student accessibility issues. Probable reading level challenges. And more requests for help from the teachers. *These comments weren't really going to help confirm specific issues either*, she thought.

Dr. Jackson ran her fingers through her dark hair again, expelling a sigh and glaring at the unhelpful computer screen. She still did not know enough about the problems to make any recommendations to remedy them. She was unsure based on the anecdotal evidence from the teachers, parents, and students whether there *were* issues with the courses or if this was an adjustment period to online schooling for the teachers and the students. *There's not enough here*, she thought as she shook her head, closed her eyes, and sighed again. *None of the data are specific enough for us to make changes. There's no one thing I can point to that would make a difference*. In short, she felt it was difficult to make any decisions based on a data point of one.

So, with little evidence to move on, Blue Ridge Academy continued to use the four seventh and eighth grade courses from Xplains Learning for the following school year. To provide at least some kind of follow-up, Dr. Jackson asked the seventh and eighth grade teachers to pay particular attention to any issues to see if there were areas where Blue Ridge could improve the experience for students.

THE FOLLOWING YEAR: DR. JACKSON DETECTS A PATTERN

Now with another school year behind her, Dr. Jackson anticipated summer's slower pace and spending more time with her family. Her slender fingers scrolled down the end-of-year report on the laptop's bright screen. She was always increasing the brightness settings on her laptop and her phone. *Who could read on a dimmed screen? I really need to change that setting.* She paused intermittently, scanning the grades. She stopped hard about half-way down the report, scrutinizing the online grades. *Something's definitely not right*, she thought. The grades for the online seventh and eighth grade students were still an issue. The distribution of the online students' grades was lower again than that for the onsite students' grades (see Tables 2.3–2.4).

Scrutinizing the overall math scores for the onsite students, the proportions of students earning the different letter grades were reasonably consistent: More than half of students were scoring *A*s with about 30% scoring *B*s. Overall history scores depicted onsite students performing well with 80% or more scoring *A*s and *B*s. Online students, though, seemed to struggle more in both math and history. In math, about 75% of the students' grades were spread across *A*s through *C*s. And while not as low, in history, the scores trended lower. *Our students are not performing as well online. Something must be done,* she thought. *This is the second year.*

TABLE 2.3
Percentages of Students by Letter Grades Earned in Math (A–F)

		Site				*Grade Level*		*Overall*		
Academic Year	*Student Grades*	*Nashville (TN)*	*Memphis (TN)*	*Little Rock (AR)*	*Houston (TX)*	*7th*	*8th*	*Total*	*Onsite*	*Online*
Year 1	A	54.5	47.1	65.6	46.4	47.6	58.3	53.7	53.7	—
	B	18.2	43.5	25.8	26.2	33.3	25.0	28.6	28.6	—
	C	18.2	9.4	8.6	17.9	14.3	12.5	13.3	13.3	—
	D	9.1	—	—	9.5	4.8	4.2	4.4	4.4	—
	F	—	—	—	—	—	—	—	—	—
Year 2	A	36.4	28.2	49.5	36.9	33.3	41.7	38.1	53.5	24.4
	B	36.4	44.7	24.7	35.7	42.9	29.2	35.1	27.7	41.7
	C	9.1	27.1	17.2	17.9	14.3	20.8	18.0	13.8	21.7
	D	18.2	—	—	9.5	9.5	4.2	6.5	5.0	7.8
	F	—	—	8.6	—	—	4.2	2.4	—	4.4
Year 3	A	27.3	36.5	41.9	17.9	28.6	33.3	31.3	57.9	7.8
	B	36.4	18.8	32.3	54.8	38.1	33.3	35.4	28.3	41.7
	C	18.2	17.6	8.6	17.9	19.0	12.5	15.3	4.4	25.0
	D	—	27.1	8.6	9.5	9.5	16.7	13.6	9.4	17.2
	F	9.1		8.6	—	4.8	4.2	4.4	—	8.3

TABLE 2.4
Percentages of Students by Letter Grades Earned in History (A–F)

		Site				*Grade Level*		*Overall*		
Academic Year	*Student Grades*	*Nashville (TN)*	*Memphis (TN)*	*Little Rock (AR)*	*Houston (TX)*	*7th*	*8th*	*Total*	*Onsite*	*Online*
Year 1	A	63.6	64.7	66.7	44.0	61.9	58.3	59.9	59.9	—
	B	27.3	17.6	24.7	46.4	28.6	29.2	28.9	28.9	—
	C	9.1	17.6	8.6	9.5	9.5	12.5	11.2	11.2	—
	D	—	—	—	—	—	—	—	—	—
	F	—	—	—	—	—	—	—	—	—
Year 2	A	54.5	45.9	50.5	61.9	57.1	50.0	53.1	61.6	45.6
	B	27.3	45.9	40.9	19.0	28.6	37.5	33.6	23.9	42.2
	C	18.2	8.2	8.6	9.5	9.5	4.2	6.5	9.4	12.2
	D	—	—	—	—	4.8	4.2	4.4	—	—
	F	—	—	—	9.5	—	4.2	2.4	5.0	—
Year 3	A	45.5	28.3	41.9	61.9	47.6	41.7	44.2	71.1	20.6
	B	27.3	45.9	49.5	9.5	28.6	37.5	33.6	14.5	50.6
	C	27.3	25.9	8.6	9.5	23.8	8.3	15.0	4.4	24.4
	D	—	—	—	—	—	8.3	4.7	5.0	4.4
	F	—	—	—	9.5	—	4.2	2.4	5.0	—

We've got to do something to help the students. This can't continue. Two years' worth of data made Dr. Jackson more confident actions were needed.

With a quick text message, she asked Blue Ridge Academy's CEO, Darren Thompson, to drop by her office when he had time. Later that afternoon, Thompson's stout frame filled her doorway. A band of white hair circled his balding head and contrasted with his florid face. "What can I help with, Tameka?" he rumbled as she looked up. She motioned for him to take a seat in a club chair across from her.

Dr. Jackson filled him in on the issue with the online courses. Thompson and Dr. Jackson discussed the situation and the feedback. They were unsure whether Xplains Learning would even be willing to make changes to any of their courses, specifically based on Blue Ridge Academy's request and without charges for customization; Xplains' courses were "packaged as-is" with customizations requiring significant charges based on extensiveness.

"I'll follow up with Xplains and get back to you," Thompson said as he walked out of the office. "Anything else I need to know?"

Dr. Jackson shook her head no. "Not at this point. Let me know what you hear."

After an email exchange with Xplains' CEO, Thompson assured Dr. Jackson that some (hopefully small) changes to the courses were possible. Xplains had been amenable to revisions since Blue Ridge Academy teachers were the ones teaching the courses and the changes would only affect Blue Ridge Academy students. The sentiment from Xplains Learning was that Blue Ridge Academy was a great client, and Xplains Learning was glad to make some modifications to improve students' learning. Blue Ridge Academy, however, would need to provide data, feedback, and recommendations to Xplains' instructional design team to help make any adjustments for the next school year. And that needed to happen as quickly as possible to be ready for the next school year's start date.

DR. JACKSON PLANS AN INVESTIGATION

With Xplains Learning open to course revisions, Dr. Jackson felt more at ease. *Okay. We can do this*, she thought. *I need to get the Accreditation and Curriculum Department on board and start an in-depth evaluation.* She already had the course's assessment data, so she began crafting an email to request a survey for the online students and their parents. To provide the best feedback and recommendations to the Xplains Learning team, she wanted to target different components of the online courses in the survey, including the different videos and multimedia that were embedded, the examples, the assessments, and the readings or lectures. She also wanted to specifically address some of the issues that had been raised by the teachers last year and mentioned in the parents' comments, like accessibility of the contents and teacher support. In addition, she thought it would be a good idea to conduct interviews with some of the students and the four teachers. Again, Dr. Jackson felt it was important to explore the effectiveness and appeal of the online courses' contents and any specific issues that may have been experienced, such as accessibility and technology barriers.

Would assessment data, parent and student survey data, and student and teacher interview data be enough? she wondered. She thought so. *It was quite a bit of data, and it should point to where changes could help.*

She finished up the email and sent it on. She then went back to a previous message Thompson had sent. She clicked through several email folders to locate it, scanning the dates and subject lines. *Ah. There it is*, she thought, skimming through the message's text. When she had the evaluation data in hand, she would work with Xplains Learning's lead instructional designer, Kiara Adams, and her team to recommend the areas for improvement to the courses.

I hope Kiara and her team are open to real changes that will help improve the courses for our students, she worriedly thought. *And not just what was easiest to change. Or worse*, she thought, *be resistant to changes altogether*. She didn't have any indication that it would be the case, and Xplains' CEO had stated they were open to changes. *Let's just hope that's the case.*

Dr. Jackson opened a new message in her email:

> Dear Ms. Adams, I want to introduce myself and provide you with an update with where we're at with collecting data to revise our courses.

She described the data she had requested and that she hoped to follow up in the next 10 to 14 days with the data. She asked if they could go ahead and set up a video conference meeting for the review. With some apprehension, she settled on a closing for the message:

> I look forward to working with you and your team.

It was best to establish a friendly relationship with them, she thought. And she *was* looking forward to working with them to improve the courses. The students' learning was at stake.

Less than ten minutes later, a *dung-dung* announced a new email message, and Dr. Jackson quickly read a short reply from Kiara. *Wow. She's fast*, Dr. Jackson thought, smiling to herself.

Several folks were copied on the message. Dr. Jackson assumed they were the others on the instructional design team since all their emails ended with "id.xplains.com." The brief message said they were looking forward to working with Dr. Jackson too, and Kiara had suggested a date about two and a half weeks out with a suggestion for the morning. With a quick check of her online calendar, Dr. Jackson thought, *That should work,* and she replied to confirm the meeting.

DR. THOMPSON, KIARA, AND THE TEAM PUZZLE OVER THE DATA

A few days after they had confirmed the meeting to review the evaluation data, Dr. Jackson received an unexpected email from Kiara at Xplains Learning. Kiara was asking if Dr. Jackson would like to have analytics from the learning management system downloaded for their review at the meeting? Kiara offered to pull the average number of logins, average times on pages and curriculum units, and average grade scores by units.

Huh. I hadn't even considered collecting the system's data, Dr. Jackson pondered. *But I'm not sure what it could tell us either.* Dr. Jackson replied, communicating her unfamiliarity (and skepticism) with the system data and its usefulness. After a couple of quick email exchanges, Dr. Jackson and Kiara settled on waiting to request the learning management system analytics until they had discussed the other data.

Three days prior to the scheduled video conference with Kiara and the instructional design team, Dr. Jackson forwarded the evaluation data that had been collected and analyzed. While she hadn't had a chance to fully review it herself yet, she wanted to get the findings into the instructional design team's hands as soon as she had received it (see Tables 2.5–2.6.).

TABLE 2.5
Findings from Survey for Math Classes

	Site				
	Nashville (TN)	*Memphis (TN)*	*Little Rock (AR)*	*Houston (TX)*	*Overall*
Subscales	*M (SD)*	*M (SD)*	*M (SD)*	*M (SD)*	*M (SD)*
Ease of course	4.28 (0.80)	4.31 (0.70)	4.14 (0.38)	4.31 (0.70)	4.26 (0.65)
Helpfulness of examples	3.67 (0.66)	3.50 (0.46)	3.43 (0.53)	3.75 (0.38)	3.59 (0.52)
Helpfulness of the multimedia content (videos, images, animations, audio, etc.)	3.83 (0.43)	2.75 (0.46)	3.71 (0.64)	3.56 (0.50)	3.47 (0.65)
Clarity of the text	3.06 (0.46)	2.94 (0.42)	3.64 (0.38)	3.31 (0.65)	3.22 (0.56)
Quality of the instructional content	4.28 (0.91)	4.00 (0.59)	2.50 (0.71)	4.31 (0.70)	4.11 (0.83)
Ease of navigation within the course	2.61 (0.49)	3.69 (0.59)	2.50 (0.71)	3.94 (0.73)	3.19 (0.88)
Quality of the assessment activities (assignments, quizzes, tests, etc.)	3.04 (0.26)	3.04 (0.38)	2.91 (0.32)	3.83 (0.80)	3.04 (0.83)
Helpfulness of the course resources	3.83 (1.12)	4.00 (0.66)	3.64 (0.75)	3.88 (0.64)	3.84 (0.80)
Appropriateness of the learning activities (readings, discussions, lectures, etc.)	3.28 (1.33)	3.94 (0.82)	3.57 (0.61)	3.88 (0.52)	3.66 (0.92)
Satisfaction with the teacher support and interaction	4.28 (1.03)	4.19 (0.75)	3.79 (0.57)	4.44 (0.50)	4.19 (0.76)
Feedback quality	4.50 (0.87)	4.00 (0.76)	3.93 (0.98)	4.44 (0.49)	4.23 (0.79)
Accessibility of the course	2.44 (0.33)	2.63 (0.33)	3.04 (0.30)	3.88 (0.50)	2.97 (0.67)

Note: Survey scale—from 1 (strongly disagree) to 5 (strongly agree).

TABLE 2.6
Findings from Survey for History Classes

	Site				
	Nashville (TN)	*Memphis (TN)*	*Little Rock (AR)*	*Houston (TX)*	*Overall*
Subscales	*M (SD)*	*M (SD)*	*M (SD)*	*M (SD)*	*M (SD)*
Ease of course	4.13 (0.52)	3.81 (0.84)	3.93 (0.19)	2.75 (0.60)	3.65 (0.79)
Helpfulness of examples	3.89 (0.86)	3.94 (0.50)	4.07 (0.19)	3.00 (1.00)	3.72 (0.82)
Helpfulness of the multimedia content (videos, images, animations, audio, etc.)	4.22 (0.71)	2.88 (0.35)	4.29 (0.39)	2.81 (0.53)	3.55 (0.87)
Clarity of the text	4.28 (0.97)	4.06 (0.50)	2.50 (0.58)	2.56 (0.42)	3.41 (1.05)
Quality of the instructional content	4.28 (0.56)	4.06 (0.56)	4.00 (0.58)	4.13 (0.36)	4.13 (0.51)
Ease of navigation within the course	2.78 (0.62)	3.63 (0.44)	2.50 (0.65)	3.94 (0.73)	3.22 (0.83)
Quality of the assessment activities (assignments, quizzes, tests, etc.)	3.00 (0.43)	3.81 (0.59)	2.93 (0.61)	4.13 (0.88)	3.47 (0.81)
Helpfulness of the course resources	4.11 (0.65)	4.00 (0.66)	3.64 (0.75)	3.93 (0.63)	3.94 (0.66)
Appropriateness of the learning activities (readings, discussions, lectures, etc.)	3.33 (1.30)	3.94 (0.82)	3.57 (0.61)	2.94 (0.32)	3.43 (0.90)
Satisfaction with the teacher support and interaction	4.28 (1.03)	4.19 (0.75)	4.36 (0.38)	4.50 (0.54)	4.48 (0.48)
Feedback quality	4.50 (0.87)	4.19 (0.46)	4.29 (0.49)	4.43 (0.50)	4.43 (0.49)
Accessibility of the course	2.56 (0.53)	2.44 (0.62)	2.57 (0.61)	3.56 (0.50)	2.78 (0.71)

Note: Survey scale—from 1 (strongly disagree) to 5 (strongly agree).

The survey results had been analyzed with averages overall, by site, and by courses. Excerpts from the interviews with the four teachers and students from different sites were also presented (see Figures 2.2–2.3).

On the morning of the video conference, Dr. Jackson scrolled through her social media feeds on her phone as she waited for everyone to arrive.

"I think we're just waiting for one more team member to arrive, Dr. Jackson," Kiara spoke into her webcam. *Ding-doo!* sounded the video conferencing system, announcing a new arrival. "Ah, there's Jamil now. That's everyone."

"Oh great!" Dr. Jackson replied. "I want to thank you all for attending this morning, and I really appreciate your willingness to help our students with any revisions we may recommend."

"We're glad to, Dr. Jackson," Kiara responded. "We found your data really interesting."

"I did, too," Dr. Jackson said as her brow furrowed. She leaned in closer to the laptop's camera. "It seemed that the overall scores were somewhat misleading in that different sites were experiencing different challenges."

"We noticed that too," Kiara answered. "It was like the students did not experience the same courses."

"Exactly," Dr. Jackson began. "After I reviewed the data, I felt like I needed to do some further research about what students in general had experienced during the pandemic and specifically what online students may still be experiencing. I then wanted to look at our

Student Interviews

Nashville site

- "Yeah, like, some of the math problems did make sense to me. They were, like, talking all about stuff, like, that I didn't know about.... Nah, it wasn't the math. It was more, like, the stuff it was talking about, like the word problems and stuff." (African American, seventh grader)
- "Yeah, I, like, tried to use my phone, you know, to like read and discussion posts and take quizzes and stuff. But not, like, everything worked. Like, I couldn't get to the discussion posts and stuff so I had to wait and do that on my Chromebook." (African American, eighth grader)
- "The math programs tend to be the most difficult considering the nature of my learning disability.... I find that I am more relaxed in an online class since I don't have an audience looking at me in class." (White, eighth grader)
- "MAKING SURE READINGS ARE ACCESSIBLE for screen reader users!" (White, eighth grader)

Memphis site

- "You know, the transcript for the videos in math class was completely useless. Gosh, I was so frustrated. They weren't synched with the video, so it was terrible trying to match up what Mrs. Moore was showing us on the screen." (African American, eighth grader, auditory impairment)
- "I just wished we'd had more choices in the assignments for social studies. We just kept writing papers over and over." (African American, seventh grader)
- "I most liked that I could work at my own pace.... The least favorite part is overcoming the obstacles, like learning how to use different programs I had never used before." (White, eighth grader)
- "Canvas was confusing sometimes to determine when assignments were due." (African American, eighth grader)
- "I work much better with in-person classes and tangible objects (homework, exams), but I had to do the online academy because of my health and COVID, so having everything on a screen made it incredibly hard to concentrate and memorize things." (White, seventh grader)
- "I know I have to learn this social studies stuff for stuff, but what's it matter to, like, a Black kid living in Memphis? How am I going to use this? Is it just so I can get into college and stuff?" (African American, seventh grader)

Little Rock site

- "It was kind of hard to understand some of the examples in the word problems and the homework sheets. So I just, like, asked Mrs. Moore about them." (White, seventh grader)
- "I had to like, look up a bunch of the words in the units to see what they mean, and I had to like, start and stop the videos a lot to look up the words ... and it just took, like, forever." (Latina, seventh grader)
- "Like, a lot of the stuff just wouldn't work on my phone. I wish it had, you know. I have it with me all the time, so I tried to like check on class stuff. But some of it just wouldn't show up." (African American, eighth grader)
- "Oh my gosh, the word problems! They were so hard to understand, some of them. I wasn't sure what they were talking about. There was this one, like I remember, it was talking about buying stuff at a bodega on the corner. I, like, didn't have any ideas what it was talking about, so I just skipped it and asked Mr. Robinson about it, and he was like, it's like a convenience store, but don't worry about it and do the math." (African American, eighth grader)
- "I would have like to, you know, done something other than the worksheets in social studies. We've got all of this technology, like Chromebooks and stuff, and we just did worksheets and papers." (Hmong student, eighth grader)

FIGURE 2.2 Excerpts from student interviews.

Student Interviews continued

Houston site

- "I wished I could have had the text read to me. It would have been easier than reading all the English words.... I'm better at understanding English than reading all the words. We speak Spanish at home, so I'm always translating back and forth in my head.... I tried to get my phone to read the text to me a lot, but it just wouldn't work." (Latina, eighth grader)
- "It was hard to understand some the examples in the math videos." (Latino, seventh grader)
- "There was like this one word problem in the last math unit video that so did not make any sense to me. It was like, talking about sitting on a stoop talking to your grandma and like, some recipe for dim sum. I didn't have any idea what it was talking about, so I just kind of ignored it and tried to do the math.... Yeah, there were examples like that in the videos that didn't really make a whole lot of like, sense to me." (Latina, eighth grader)
- "You know, I really would have liked more assignments, where we like made stuff, like presentations and stuff.... I also kept asking Mrs. Turner, like, what was happening like in Texas and Mexico while the European explorers were conquering everybody." (Latino, eighth grader)
- "I don't know if this is what you're looking for or not, but it kind of felt like the social studies class wasn't made for me, like a kid living in Texas and stuff. I didn't always get what I was supposed to get out of it, like what did it mean for me." (Latina, eighth grader)

FIGURE 2.2 Continued

Teacher Interviews

Math Courses

- "The students with disabilities, like auditory and visual disabilities, really needed a lot of extra support. The course materials and videos really weren't sufficient for them to be successful, and I felt really bad that I wasn't able to help them better.... I wish I had been able to edit some of the materials to provide better examples or more examples or even an explanation that I thought would have helped. But, I couldn't edit the course." (Mrs. Moore, seventh grade)
- "I think it would have been so much better to have been able to edit at least parts of the course. It was so frustrating, and it really added more work on my part to have to send out a course announcement email with a link to a video or with a lot of explanation about a concept or skill that students seemed to be having problems with. I wish I'd have been able to just go into the course materials and make some edits, add some stuff directly into the course. I think it would have been easier and better for the kids." (Mr. Robinson, eighth grade)
- "Definitely some of the examples used in the math units didn't make sense for the kids. I got a lot of questions about examples or questions that had nothing to do with the math. Instead, the kids were asking about things like, What's a stoop? What's dim sum? What's a bodega? (Those were from some of our last units.) These were all parts of questions that set the context for the math problems, but my students didn't know what they were. They weren't applicable to my students. You have to live in places where those things are common for them to relevant to you." (Mr. Robinson, eighth grade)
- "I felt really bad for the students with disabilities. The course materials and videos really didn't support them in the best ways. I tried to send them additional videos or I tried downloading the videos and tried to caption them better, but it could have been a lot better for them. I asked our learning support specialist if she had any suggestions, and she really didn't since we couldn't edit the courses. So, I spent a lot of time teaching one-on-one with students who needed it." (Mr. Robinson, eighth grade)

History Courses

- "I kept asking Dr. Jackson if there was a way we could edit parts of the courses. She said because the way the courses were set up, we couldn't. It was really frustrating to not be able to. I felt like I had to add or create some scaffolds or supports and send those to the students, but I felt like it would have been better if they had just been part of the course for the students to access.... I also wanted to provide some alternatives to the assignments that were required as part of the courses. I felt like doing the worksheets and papers was monotonous, and it really didn't allow the students to personalize or differentiate the assignment. I would have liked to be able to allow the students to choose a different format, like a presentation or a video, or integrate some of their own cultures into their assignments. But the way the assignments were set up, that just wasn't possible." (Mrs. Turner, eighth grade)
- "My students based in Houston emailed and contacted me a lot about examples or explanations. They were really wanting to know about the historical issues that had impacted immigrants and other peoples from Mexico and Latin American." (Mrs. Nelson, seventh grade)

FIGURE 2.3 Excerpts from seventh and eighth grade teacher interviews.

Teacher Interviews continued

- "I found that the Latino/Latina students were really inquisitive about their heritages. They wanted to know more about how the historical issues we were discussing had impacted their ancestors. You know, a lot of our history content centers on white European experiences and it tends to be Western-centric or US-centric. So, it's really reasonable for students with Mexican or Latin American heritages to question and want to know more about what was happening elsewhere.... Where I didn't think I succeeded very well was with our few Hmong students. I think maybe if I'd have been able to adjust some assignments maybe I could have may the course more accessible and relevant to them." (Mrs. Turner, eighth grade)
- "I know students struggled with the reading. My students who are English language learners and their primary language at home isn't English really struggled with the texts. I had a couple of students tell me they tried to play the text on their phones so it would read it to them, but it didn't work. I searched out a website where they could copy and paste the text so it would read it to them, but it was really cumbersome. It wasn't easy to do, and I had to request the site be unblocked by our school filter." (Mrs. Nelson, seventh grade)

FIGURE 2.3 Continued

individual sites to see what may be impacting our students, how they were experiencing the courses, and how the courses could be affected.

"One piece of research from multiple news articles and national surveys that I found significant—I knew it intuitively based on the demographics of our students at each site—was that African American and Latinx students were more likely to remain learning online when schools reopened. And these students were more likely to have to care for siblings and have fewer parental supports. Also, other students who may be medically vulnerable and need accommodations for learning are more likely to be choosing online courses, and these account for many of our students at our different sites. So, while our online courses have worked well for some students, other students are not being served well, especially our racial minorities and students with disabilities, which is a significant issue we must address."

"I completely agree, Dr. Jackson," Kiara added, "and we also noticed some common issues and some site-specific issues. To speak directly to your point, it was evident in both the survey data and the interviews that students at the Memphis and Nashville sites experienced accessibility issues with our course content. Even for the students for whom English was a second language, we need to do a better job so that our content is accessible across different devices and for speech-to-text. This isn't an issue we've seen in other schools who may have students using our Classical Curriculum courses . . . but I don't think we've had such a diverse range of students using our courses before. So, that's definitely a problem we have to make sure to take care of."

"Yes, yes," Dr. Jackson responded excitedly. "I also wanted to highlight what I considered to be a more subtle issue. In the student interviews and the teacher interviews, I thought it was powerful to note that some of the instructional content wasn't relevant to our students. Because of where they live or their cultural backgrounds, they were unfamiliar with content or contexts used as the basis for practice items or assessments. For example, one of our Houston students mentioned a video for her math class that contextualized the problem with sitting on a stoop and making a recipe for dim sum. For this student in Houston, this type of context with details didn't make sense. Even in an urban city like Houston, they don't have apartments with stoops, and I got the sense that this student had never heard of dim sum. So, we must figure out a way to allow the teachers to contextualize the instructional content so that it's culturally appropriate for the local site and student backgrounds. I feel passionately that this issue is one that is critical for our students' success."

The instructional design team members' heads bobbed up and down in agreement. Without missing a beat, Kiara jumped in: "We saw that too, and as someone who's in charge of developing the content for courses like this, I can see that we need to do a better job at integrating a variety of cultural backgrounds in our curriculum or allowing the content to be modified. It was also evident to me that the teachers were frustrated and hampered by their lack of access to edit the content or modify the assignments, especially to address relevance. Those are not typical permissions we provide to teachers, but it is possible to adjust those settings."

Dr. Jackson breathed a sigh of relief and leaned back deeply into her chair, the leather making a crinkling sound. "So where should we start, Kiara? Should we identify overall issues then go site by site and talk about what can be changed?"

"Sounds good," Kiara replied. "Can we also plan to identify which issues are priorities along with how extensive the change is and how difficult it will be to implement?"

Preliminary Analysis Questions

1. After reviewing three years' worth of grades, Dr. Jackson noted a difference in the distribution of online students' grades. To identify the causes of this change, what questions do you think Dr. Jackson should ask the instructional design team based on the data provided?
2. Although Dr. Jackson remarked on the distribution differences between the onsite and online math and history grades, the difference was less in history grades. Examining the survey and the interview data, what differences did you identify between the math and history courses for each site? What issues did the students experience in math and history courses? What are your thoughts about what might attribute to the greater decrease in math scores?
3. What differences have you observed in the students' math and history scores by grades? What could be the reason for the difference between the grade levels?
4. What suggestions do you have for Dr. Jackson or the instructional design team for collecting the additional data to determine the issues at each site?
5. Now that you have identified the issues associated with the online courses and possible causes for these issues, assume the role of Dr. Jackson and the instructional design team. What recommendations should be ranked as the highest priority given the potential for customization charges for Nashville by Xplains Learning? What would be required to accommodate the three other sites (i.e., Houston, Memphis, and Little Rock)? What would you like to advocate for in terms of priorities for the Nashville site?
6. The courses offered by the online program of Blue Ridge Academy are not self-paced and the courses were facilitated by Blue Ridge Academy teachers from any one of the four sites. What could be the roles of those facilitators to address the challenges and adaptations at each site?

Implications for ID Practice

1. How would you describe the importance of learner analysis in designing an online course in culturally diverse settings? What are some of the specific student characteristics an instructional designer should consider? What type of data sources could be used to collect data in learner analysis?
2. What questions can you ask about data you receive to ensure inferences and explanations can account for the decrease in the online students' grades locally?
3. What are some of the key considerations you should examine when converting a face-to-face course to an online course to meet the needs of all students, including students with disabilities and English language learners? Discuss the challenges of developing an online course for diverse students, including individuals with disabilities and English language learners.

3

Marisol Valencia, Fiona Huang, and the Team

Designing and Conducting Evaluation Post-Pandemic

Gamze Ozogul

SEPTEMBER 26: THE EMAIL

Dr. Marisol Valencia, co-owner of Instructional Design and Evaluation Solutions (IDES), was going through her emails in her home office while drinking her morning coffee. This had become a ritual for starting her days since they had closed the office building and approved remote work for all company employees during the pandemic. As she scrolled through the unread messages, an email from the State Department of Education grabbed her interest. After the pandemic, the State Department of Education and IDES had been in various consulting meetings to discuss topics and collaborate on projects. These topics were related to learning loss, emergency remote teaching, equity, and access issues related to technology in rural parts of the state. Marisol took another sip of her coffee and clicked on the email thinking this might be a request for another collaboration meeting, possibly to discuss parent involvement and student success in K–12 online schools and emergency remote teaching, which they did not get to discuss last time. The subject line of the email read "Interested in this project?" As Marisol clicked on the email, the following message opened in her browser (see Figure 3.1).

Marisol skimmed through the email fast at first and then read it one more time slowly, considering the availability of the IDES team and identifying their other commitments. Even though they had a few pressing timelines, she thought the IDES team could use a project to help them move forward from the pandemic. She took another sip of her coffee and forwarded the email to her associate, Fiona Huang, adding, "What do you think?"

Marisol and Fiona founded IDES together after working for several years as instructional designers and evaluation experts in the Center for Research and Evaluation for Teaching Excellence at an institution of higher education. After gaining confidence and experience in that setting, they decided to be their own bosses, and so they had founded IDES seven years ago. They took special pride in being women owners and hiring other women and minorities. They were doing okay before the pandemic, securing projects, and were able to build a strong team. But during the pandemic, they had to release five of their employees and were forced

DOI: 10.4324/9781003354468-4

Subject: Interested in this project?
To: Marisol Valencia <MValencia@ides.com>
From: Devin T Ford <DevinTFord@departmentofeducation.gov>
Date: September 26, 8:11 a.m.

Hello Dr. Valencia,

It has been a few months since our last Zoom discussion and since you provided us with the landscape report for the state online learning in K-12 schools. We gathered the building principals and presented your report.

The reason I am reaching out to you today is, well, we had funded another project before COVID and that has been going on for the last 4 years but with the pandemic, we didn't get to do an evaluation and collect data on it. Below are a few details. I am wondering if you and your team would be interested in doing a late-stage program evaluation, just to capture what school sites were doing before the pandemic and how they shifted during the pandemic in regards to the project goals, use of the funds, and implementation.

Duration: 4 years started before the pandemic and will be concluding at the end of this school year

Number of school sites: 10 (across demographically and geographically diverse locations in our state, most of the schools are rural)

Funds: $75,000 per school site, per year, for implementing the project

Project goal: The goal of the project is to improve teachers' use of authentic instruction and to increase parent involvement in the selected 10 school sites. One of our consultants at the time provided evidence that authentic instruction and involving parents improved student engagement and learning outcomes. Our consultant suggested we use a four-step process that they developed.

Project kickoff: A one-hour information session was held at the State Department of Education building by inviting one self-selected teacher leader from each school site. These teacher leaders were asked to lead the efforts to implement the school improvement project at their school sites.

During the kickoff, the 4-step process was shared with the teacher leaders, and they were asked to communicate these to the other teachers and administrators at their sites, and to use this process as a road map for improving their schools.

1- Develop a set of learning goals shared by the school community.
2- Develop a shared vision based on these goals.
3- Determine where each school is now concerning the vision.
4- Develop and implement a plan to close the gap between the vision and where each school currently stands.

Additionally, the teacher leaders were asked to embed the two key features—authentic instruction and parent involvement—into their schools' instructional practices, as suggested by the consultant.

What do you think? Interested? We don't have tons of funds, but we have $75,000 to allocate to your team for conducting the retroactive evaluation and informing me about what each school did to meet project goals and how the funds were spent. Looking forward to your response, and happy to have a brief Zoom meeting if you and the team are interested.

Thank you, Devin (They, them)

FIGURE 3.1 Email from Devin to Marisol.

to function as the "lean version" of their team. Now post-pandemic as project requests had been picking up, they were able to rehire two of their core team members, full time, to work on various instructional design and evaluation projects.

Marisol kept reading her other emails, and before long, Fiona's reply appeared at the top of her inbox. Fiona wrote, "Let's find a time to talk to Devin. This sounds like a late-stage evaluation. Collecting data from the pandemic years will be a challenge, well . . . if the schools even kept up with the project considering all the remote emergency teaching plans they had to come up with overnight. Let's get a date and time on the calendar to meet Devin."

SEPTEMBER 29: THE ZOOM MEETING

The Zoom meeting between Marisol, Devin, and Fiona was scheduled for late afternoon. At the scheduled time, three faces appeared in the Zoom room. Marisol greeted everyone with a warm hello and a big smile. She was at her home office and her cat Tuesday was on her lap. Devin was at their office building and greeted them all by saying hello to Marisol, Fiona, and Marisol's office buddy. Fiona was participating from her home office, and said, "Great to see you, Devin. Your email sounded intriguing, tell us more."

Devin, with a smile, said, "Well . . . I am in a bit of a time crunch. I reached out because I have a project that needs to be evaluated before it comes to an end in the next few months. The project is called the 'Achieving Schools Project.' It started three years ago, before the pandemic . . . so this year, by the end of this school year, we will be concluding the project as funding was allocated for a total of four years. With the pandemic occurring, our State Department of Education offices have had too many issues to deal with, as you can imagine, so we did not get to collect any implementation or outcome data on this project at all. So, it's looking like a late-stage evaluation, just to capture what happened at each participating school site, despite the pandemic."

"Ha! Sounds like this meeting should have taken place three and a half years ago, but I understand, none of us envisioned schools going to emergency response teaching overnight," responded Fiona.

After a short pause, Devin lowered their voice. "You are right! Well, when we started the project, we did not envision all the support we needed to provide for schools across the state for technology, teacher professional development, parent communication materials, or to transport students to Wi-Fi locations so that they could access their schoolwork. Now, hopefully, we are past the pandemic emergency remote teaching phase, and the State Department of Education and our consultant want to know what happened at the school sites as a result of this project, how they adapted to the pandemic, and what we can do better next time for similar projects, both during "normal" times and during future crises."

Marisol straightened her posture in her chair and put Tuesday on the floor slowly. She said, "So, are you saying we would have about eight months to design, develop, and implement an evaluation that captures what happened during the past four years of the project, of which two years were during the pandemic?"

Devin responded with a cringe, "That's about right. But the good thing is that you would have two additional months to write up your report."

"Hmmm, thankfully. Well, it seems like a very tight timeline. We will need a few days to discuss this amongst ourselves before we can get back to you with a decision. Tell me a bit about the context and scope," asked Marisol as she scrolled through the upcoming months on her calendar.

"Understandable. Okay. We hired a consultant to look into our lower-achieving school sites just before the pandemic. He—well, Dr. Nadal—conducted document reviews and a few site visits to those low-achieving schools. After his visits and data collection, he suggested that we can improve the local schools by asking them to use a four-step process he had developed, and while doing that to focus on the themes of authentic learning and parent involvement. He said these two foci are game changers as he had read about them in the *21st Century*

Schools and Trends magazine. In that magazine, there were articles about both of these trends making a difference in student progress and learning outcomes. For authentic learning, he shared that if students are continuously presented with instructional activities that engage them in situated problems in real-life contexts, they are more likely to be interested and willing to learn. For parent involvement, the articles highlighted that students whose parents are involved with schoolwork and school life are more likely to succeed and—"

Without allowing Devin to finish their sentence, Marisol jumped in, "Wow, hold on, so he based the entire project process on articles from one magazine and developed a four-step process to apply this in low-achieving school sites in the state?"

Devin nodded and said, "Yeah, and he was able to bring in the seed funding to match our funding sources—so we said why not give it a go and see if it works and makes a difference in the selected ten schools."

Fiona unmuted her microphone and said, "I am not familiar with the four-step process he proposed, but it will be very interesting to see what these schools did with these two initiatives, especially in the pandemic context. I have been reading the pandemic landscape reports written about the rural schools and their efforts during the pandemic to deliver emergency remote teaching. These two things, depending on how the schools operationalized them, are two variables that may have helped with their student success and engagement during emergency remote online learning."

Devin responded, "Certainly, will be interesting to see how schools pivoted and adjusted."

Marisol nodded and said, "Okay, so tell us more about the project and how you introduced it to the school sites, before knowing that we would be hit with this pandemic?"

Devin straightened their posture and started explaining. "Our consultant had outlined a four-step process for each school site to follow, which included these two key features: parent involvement and authentic instruction. Every school was asked to implement the same four-step process, although they had flexibility in terms of implementation. We emailed 18 elementary school principals and asked if they wanted to be a part of this project. The principals of ten elementary schools, in demographically and geographically diverse sites spread across our state, agreed to participate. Since the beginning of the project, these schools have been receiving $75,000 each year for implementing the project. Unfortunately, after the pandemic started, we have not required any progress reports, nor have the schools made any specific requests for support from us, nor any other, um—"

Again, without allowing Devin to finish their sentence, Fiona jumped in, "Wow, hold on, so we have no reports up to this point? Well, it certainly makes sense with the pandemic. All schools needed to deal with that as a priority. For us, as the potential evaluators, I am more concerned about the tight timeline and the scope of the evaluation project. Since there has been no previous data collection or reporting on the project, and school sites have continued to receive the yearly funds without having to report on their progress, this certainly will add complexity to the evaluation. Also, I imagine the direction of their project plans and implementation might have changed during the pandemic."

Devin replied with a confident tone, "Based on our previous work together, I know that if anyone could help us with this evaluation, it would be you and your team, Marisol and Fiona. If you would like to take a few days to think it over, that is fine. Perhaps we can meet on Friday. I could invite our consultant to attend too if you like, so you can ask any questions you might have."

Following the Zoom meeting, the next day, Fiona and Marisol scheduled a meeting with their two staff on Zoom. Fortunately, all teams were very experienced in instructional design and evaluation. Marisol had earned a bachelor's degree in Spanish and had a PhD in instructional design and technology from a highly respected program. Fiona had earned a bachelor's degree in computer science and had also completed a master's degree in instructional design and technology. Two staff members, Bahar and Sophie, were both experienced in instructional design and evaluation, and both had a bachelor's degree in education. Bahar had a master's degree in measurement sciences and evaluation, and Sophie had earned an MS degree in educational technology.

SEPTEMBER 30: IDES TEAM MEETING

All four members of the IDES team signed into the Zoom meeting promptly at 10:00 a.m. as scheduled. All team members were sitting in their home offices, sipping either their teas or coffees, when the meeting started. Marisol greeted them with a smile and said, "Good morning, team, looks like we have been offered a new project that has a tight timeline but sounds interesting. And it will keep us busy for the next eight months. I don't know too much about the project yet, but I received an email from Devin, the director of Special Projects and Students' Success Office at the State Department of Education. We met with Devin briefly yesterday. We will have one more meeting with Devin and the consultant who came up with this school's project idea and project directions. Okay, let me find the email. This is what I have so far. Okay, hang on for a second, let me share my screen." She shared her screen (see Figure 3.1).

After taking a few minutes to review the email, the team began to prepare initial questions for the consultant. It didn't take the team long to realize that there were many aspects to consider before accepting the project and before possibly beginning their evaluation in two weeks. All four started to ask questions one after another: "Was there any further contact with schools other than this one-hour kickoff meeting?" "How were the terms related to authentic learning and parental involvement defined for the teacher leaders during the information session?" "How was the money used . . . ?" "So, could schools pick what they wanted to work on—as long as they used the four-step process and included the two key features?" and so on.

Suddenly Fiona said, "Okay, okay, so many aspects to clarify. I'm thinking that at least this is a good sign we are interested in the project. Bahar, why don't you start a document to keep a list of our questions so we can be sure to ask them in the meeting with the consultant?" Bahar created a live document and started typing as the team brainstormed more questions. At the end of the IDES team meeting, they had a list of questions to ask (see Table 3.1).

TABLE 3.1
Sample Questions from the Team's List

- What definition was provided for authentic instruction?
- Were examples given to the teacher leaders?
- How was parent involvement defined?
- How did the donor come up with these four steps?
- What do they mean by the comment that "achievement will improve"? What is the definition of achievement in the context of this project?
- Why does the donor think these two key features are important?
- Were the lead teachers given any specific instructions on how to implement the project?
- How much flexibility were schools allowed to make adjustments based on their contexts?
- How would you like us to approach this evaluation, knowing that during the second year there was a pandemic and schools engaged mainly in emergency remote teaching ?

OCTOBER 2: MEETING WITH THE CONSULTANT

The team was eager to meet with Devin and the consultant, Dr. Nadal. When the IDES team appeared one by one on the Zoom screen, Devin and Dr. Nadal were already in the Zoom room. After initial greetings and introductions, Devin explained to Dr. Nadal that the IDES team was about to be hired to evaluate the Achieving Schools Project.

With her characteristic eagerness to get going, Marisol started the conversation, saying, "Dr. Nadal—"

Dr. Nadal jumped in and said, "Please call me Alex."

Marisol smiled and continued, "Alex, I was wondering if you could give us a little background on this project. Maybe you could start by telling us why you selected parent involvement and authentic instruction as the two key features of this school improvement effort for student success?"

"Well, as a developmental psychologist who has a doctorate in educational psychology, I think a lot about kids' experiences in schools, and what we can do to keep them engaged, when schools are teaching various subjects in a stand-alone and abstract fashion. It was this way 40 years ago when I went to school, and it is the same now. When I think about my childhood, I think that some of the key things that were missing were opportunities for my parents to be involved in my education, and as a student, I didn't think my teachers provided very interesting instruction. Lectures, lectures, and more lectures. To this day, I can't remember anything from a single lecture."

"But what I do remember vividly," continued Alex, "is how my fourth-grade science teacher taught us about the stages of a butterfly's life by having butterflies in our classroom. I didn't have much instruction like that. When I got my education and understood more about what makes learning experiences permanent, what makes instruction interesting are these types of experiences, situated in authentic contexts. So, I wanted to offer through my expertise these features in a more systematic manner. That's why I came up with the idea of the four-step process, with the two features for each school to follow. And now with technology, there are so many opportunities. I wanted to give schools enough freedom, as they know their own needs and contexts best, to decide what they wanted to work on, but to use the four-step process, and use these key features that have research-based evidence to improve student success and engagement."

The team was listening intently. Sophie unmuted her microphone and asked, "So how did you explain the four steps and two key features to the teachers in these schools?"

After a moment of pause, Alex turned to Devin and said, "Correct me if I'm wrong, Devin, but didn't you have a one-hour information session with the teacher leaders, at the beginning of the project, before we released the funds in the first year?"

Devin nodded, and then added, "That's correct. It wasn't a very formal meeting; I would not call it training. I would call it an information session. We gathered the ten teacher leaders together, and we informed them about the project's four steps and the two key features. We introduced the teacher leaders from different schools to each other, answered any questions they had, provided lunch, and then they left to begin working on ideas for the implementation of their projects at their school sites."

"And since then, did all school sites receive the funds to implement the project?" asked Bahar.

"That's correct, Bahar," responded Devin.

As Marisol listened to the answer, she jumped in, "Devin, what examples do you have of implementations in the schools as a result of this project, well . . . if you have any?"

"I'm not too familiar with what the schools did with the project funds or how they implemented the project," responded Devin. They continued, "I heard from one teacher that they started a school garden, and in another school, they added more clocks on the walls to help students learn to tell the time when asked, and I know one school purchased VR headsets and software for historical site visits, but there are many other implementations that I'm not aware of. However, I think you will find variability in each school's implementation and scope, due to the lack of uniform guidelines given to the schools and how they shifted and responded to emergency remote teaching during the pandemic."

"I am assuming it was the pandemic that got in the way of follow-up and yearly formative evaluations, right? And now that the project is coming to an end, you want to do a summative evaluation, since we missed the opportunity for formative evaluation, to capture what happened at each school site. Right?" asked Fiona.

Devin responded, "Well, I guess initially we were just so eager to get the project started at the beginning of the new school year, that we didn't have much time to think about evaluation in addition to suddenly being hit with the pandemic. But now that the project is ending, both Alex and the State Department of Education would like to know how the project was implemented at each school site, and what shifts happened during the pandemic. What did each school do about the key features and the steps?"

"Okay, we will do our best to capture this information. I'm wondering, did you provide specific definitions to the teachers for 'parent involvement' and 'authentic learning' in the information meeting?" Sophie asked.

Bahar jumped in, "It seems like these terms could have multiple definitions or interpretations."

"We went with Alex's vision on that," said Devin and turned to Alex.

"Well, parent involvement was obvious, right? Involve parents in school activities. Simple." If they had been in the same meeting room, Fiona and Marisol would have exchanged glances, but they both remained silent. Alex continued, "Authentic instruction was described as providing students with learning experiences within an authentic context. Most teachers should already know what it stands for."

"Yes, this is exactly how I described it to the teacher leaders," said Devin and continued, "and I also used Alex's butterfly example to illustrate the ideas."

OCTOBER 4: IDES PLANNING MEETING

Following the meeting with Devin and Alex, the evaluation team decided to accept this challenging evaluation project and met to develop an evaluation plan and draft data collection instruments. "We need to know how funds were spent at each site. I have serious concerns that these school sites received the yearly funds without ever being asked to report back, and with the pandemic happening, they might have spent it on whatever they needed. We will need to triangulate self-report data so we can distinguish between what teachers say they did and what they did; how they spent the actual project funds, and how they organized the project in each school," Marisol stated.

Fiona added, "I am also concerned that it will be difficult to determine what happened as a result of this project versus what would have happened as a result of each school's normal efforts to meet state and federal requirements, and to function during the pandemic. Sophie and Bahar, what do you think?"

Sophie unmuted her microphone and responded, "It will certainly be a challenging project due to the tight timeline and the use of post hoc data. Participants have to rely on their memories of what happened. In addition, there are a lot of other challenges related to the unclear definitions and directions given to teachers in the ten demographically diverse, geographically dispersed schools, and a possible shift in project focus at each school site in the second year. We just need to find out what happened at each school site related to project goals and budget and report that."

Fiona agreed and reiterated to the team that the client had not made any specific evaluation demands, other than wanting to know what happened at each site in relation to the four steps and project key features, how schools shifted their project focus, and what could be done better next time. She added, "Let's think about what data we need to collect, how to collect it, and who to get it from."

During the rest of the meeting, the team came up with a task schedule for the next eight months (see Appendix 3-A) and made decisions about instruments for collecting data. First, they decided to conduct a single site visit for two days at each school site and, if schools were not open to accepting visitors for on-site visits, to conduct virtual site visits. Additionally, they decided to develop a survey to gather general information from both teachers and parents and then to conduct a limited number of in-depth phone or Zoom interviews with the lead teachers, other teachers, and parents after analyzing data from the initial surveys and going over the findings. They also developed a checklist to use during their site visits (or during virtual site visits) for systematically recording observations related to the key features and four-step process. The IDES team decided to ask each lead teacher and principal for artifacts (e.g., budget for how they spent the project funds, event flyers, relevant student work) related to the project during the previous three and a half years. They decided to ask questions geared to project efforts for year 1 (pre-pandemic), years 2 and 3 (pandemic years), and post-pandemic to capture data and details concerning the implementation of the project for these specific implementation times.

"Okay, let's meet again first thing next week to work on the instruments. Before that, let's all think about what we would like to ask of whom and how we can triangulate our data. Please draft some interview questions and bring them to our next meeting," said Marisol as she pushed back her chair and stood up.

OCTOBER 10: DRAFTING DATA COLLECTION INSTRUMENTS

Sophie began, "Let's make some decisions about teacher interviews. First, let's ask them how they applied this four-step process, and how they implemented the two key features in the first year."

Marisol responded, "Well, if we ask them how they applied these components, aren't we assuming that they implemented them? Would we be prompting them to find, or maybe even create, examples to tell us? Maybe they didn't even hear about these project steps and key features! How can we know if they were aware of these things? Maybe, instead, we should ask if they were aware of these terms, if these terms were introduced or communicated by the lead teacher, and if so, how?"

Bahar jumped in, saying, "Well, again we would be asking in such a way that the teachers may try to respond in a politically correct way. I mean, wouldn't they just say that they were aware of these terms to protect their lead teachers? Maybe we should start by asking if they heard about this 'Achieving Schools Project' and what they know about it. We can see if they refer to any of the project features in their responses and what they can recall regarding these features."

Fiona nodded in agreement and stated, "Let's ask broad questions initially, and later we can follow up with more specific questions to capture how they applied these features and how they shifted during the pandemic" (see Appendix 3-B).

Later in the same team meeting, the team began to tackle the parent involvement component. Marisol said, "We need to figure out what schools did to involve parents. From our meeting with Devin and Alex, I don't think they were given a very clear definition of this term in their initial meeting. Also, think about it, three and a half years have passed since that meeting. For example, based on our meeting with the donor, what do you think they meant by parent involvement? Maybe they meant parents were involved in the school, like through the PTA?"

Fiona responded, "Maybe, but based on what Alex said, parent involvement could also have meant that the parents helped their kids with their schoolwork—which would be natural during emergency remote learning. But is it related to project efforts or just naturally happening? For example, parents might be helping with their kids' homework at home or doing school projects together with their children at school in the first year. During the pandemic, parent involvement might have increased naturally as kids did more schooling at home—but what we need to find out is: was there a project effort to involve parents specifically as a part of this project during emergency remote teaching?"

Bahar intervened, "Well, we actually may have a general idea what parent involvement or authentic instruction is, or we can look up definitions from literature, but since we need to design an evaluation specific to this project, we need to find out how these terms were operationalized in each school."

After a pause Marisol added, "Alex defined parent involvement as including parents in school activities. So that's what we will take as the operationalized definition. Let's write down a question to ask the lead teachers how they defined parent involvement, and we can look for alignment among lead teachers. We can also ask the same question of other teachers to determine what they did to meet this criterion of parent involvement. Additionally, we can ask parents how they were involved with their kids, what school events they were involved in the past three and a half years, and their overall perceptions of being involved in the children's school. Lastly, we can ask them to recall involvement during first year and then during the pandemic specifically to capture the shift."

"And we also need to find out how they allocated project funds to support those activities," Sophie added, "and whether this was a result of the project, as opposed to a regular occurrence due to the school or district culture, or pandemic efforts. We should look for actual data that support what lead teachers, teachers, and parents are saying, and look for direct connections to project efforts. For example, if they said that they held a parents' night for something, let's see if we can find a budget item or a flyer related to that, or if they say that during the pandemic they created LMS training materials to involve parents and held virtual training, did they use project funds?"

"Yes, let's do that. Seems like we're close. Sophie, can you finish drafting the teacher survey, and Bahar, can you finish drafting the parent survey? Let's move forward," said Marisol.

JANUARY 30: TEAM'S SITE VISIT REPORTS

Fiona began, "What a busy few months it has been. Well, we have visited, either virtually or in person, all the school sites. It was good that we were able to physically visit four sites and also do six virtual site visits. And we went all the way to the border for one of them. I can't believe that it didn't occur to us to plan for this, but I think the biggest curve ball was that we didn't anticipate that we would need to translate our interviews and surveys into Spanish, find translators to conduct and record the interviews, and have the transcripts of the interviews translated back into English."

Sophie jumped in, "Yeah, also good that we considered virtual site visits. Some schools are still not open to any visitors, as they are still recovering from the pandemic."

Marisol nodded in agreement. "Yeah, this translation stuff put us behind on the timeline and added an extra line to our budget. Anyway, we need to analyze all the data, synthesize findings, and prepare a concise report for Devin."

Bahar stated, "As I completed my first in-person two-site visits, what I observed was that each school did *something* to meet the project requirements, but the implementations were unique to their contexts and needs. Because this project was developed and delivered with vaguely defined implementation details, we will be reporting on a variety of different applications that happened at the school sites."

"All schools needed to shift and adjust during the pandemic—well, that's what I can tell informally from my virtual and in-person visits," added Sophie.

Fiona reached for her laptop and pulled up her observation records from her first two school sites visits, one in-person and one virtual, and shared them on the screen (see Appendix 3-C).

"Wow, you've got it organized, Fiona," said Marisol with a smile. She was impressed with her go-getter attitude.

"Yes, but I'm only reporting on observations and data from the first two sites I visited. Well, *visited* meaning I had one in-person visit, and one virtual," responded Fiona. "Look at how different they are. For example, in school A they looked for ways to involve parents, whereas in school B they tracked the 'physical visibility' of parents at the school site. I think this is probably due to the lack of clear definitions when they started. During the pandemic, things shifted, but these two sites stayed kind of close to the core of project directions. I think that is because the efforts they put forward were able to be a resource or support to students during emergency remote teaching."

Marisol added, "Also, at school B, they sent someone to an authentic instruction workshop to build expertise in year 1, whereas in school A, they simply implemented what they believed qualified as authentic. And during the pandemic, they tried to use these principles of authentic instruction for delivery of online instruction in both schools."

Sophie said, "I also have ten responses from the parent surveys that were received from three schools. Two other schools reported that the parent surveys kept coming back empty, or the online versions were not being completed. Apparently in some sites, parents were asking for a translation. But I brought some initial survey responses and my notes." (see Appendix 3-D)

As they looked at Sophie's summary table, Marisol said, "Well, obviously we can see a problem at school C in terms of parent involvement and communication with parents, as the parents who responded to the survey reported not hearing about the project, said that they were hesitant to visit the school, and shared they didn't get much support or communication from the school during pandemic. It may be the school culture, but it seems that there is a communication issue, at least from these parents' points of view—"

Marisol jumped in and said, "Let's wait for more responses and see what others say."

Bahar added, "Based on the virtual and in-person site visits and parent survey responses, it looks like we will see a lot of implementation variability across sites. The trick will be to identify what happened as a result of the $75,000 project funds versus what the school was already doing regularly, before the project, and how they used the funds."

Marisol said, "Also, look at school A. They developed a system to track student achievement data even during the pandemic. They kept using the data to inform their decisions on afterschool programs or supplemental instruction." She paused for a moment and then continued, "Yes, we have our work cut out for us to determine how much the changes in student achievement, if any, can be attributed to the project funded by the State Department of Education."

Fiona sighed, "So, where do we go from here? Let's see what the rest of the data shows. It's going to be difficult to capture the results of the Achieving Schools Project retrospectively."

Preliminary Analysis Questions

1. Critique the team's plan for an evaluation of a project that was nearing the end of a four-year funding period. For each component of your critique (e.g., getting familiarized with project, interacting with clients, data collection plan, initial reporting components), describe if, and how, the team could have developed an improved approach.
2. During the October 10 planning meeting, the evaluation team attempted to account for potential bias during data collection.
   a. Critique the questions on the parent survey (Appendix 6-D). For each question, decide whether or not you think it needs improvement. Provide your reasoning.
   b. For each question that needs improvement, create an improved question, and explain your rationale.
3. What issues do you foresee happening while doing on-site and virtual site visits to collect data? What type of adjustments are needed to collect data for different types of site visits?
4. How can the team use the information that Fiona presented? Develop a revised evaluation plan that the IDES could use to assess the outcomes of the Achieving Schools Project.

Implications for ID Practice

1. How can instructional designers integrate flexibility into their evaluation processes for projects that will be implemented in multiple contexts (or capturing change based on unpredicted factors like a pandemic?) What factors should be considered during evaluation planning and implementation?
2. How can evaluators make sense of data that come from different sources but point to contradictory findings?
3. Describe the role of interim feedback in monitoring the evaluation process.
4. Describe complications that can result when project teams do not invest in evaluation during the project planning process.

Appendix 3.A

Task Scheduler

Action	*Person(s) Responsible*	*Deadline/Timescale*
Meet with the State Department of Education to discuss project objectives and expectations	IDES, Dr. Nadal, Devin	September
Submit evaluation plan proposal for approval	IDES Team	October 15
Collect existing data and documents from the information session and background from the State Department of Education	IDES Team	October 15
Initiate and introduce the team to school teacher leaders, and ask for existing data to be shared with the team	IDES Team	October 20
Design and develop evaluation instruments and submit them to the State Department of Education	IDES Team	October 20
Receive feedback from the State Department of Education on evaluation instruments	IDES Team	October 25
Complete 1st round of on-site and virtual visits with participating schools; send out surveys	IDES Team	October 27-Jan 25
Conduct phone/Zoom interviews	IDES Team	Jan25-March 24
Analyze preliminary data	IDES Team	March 27-April 7
Meet with the State Department of Education to provide an update on preliminary findings	Devin	April 12
Conclude survey data collection	IDES Team	May 19
Analyze complete evaluation findings and complete draft report	IDES Team	June 30
Submit a draft report to the State Department of Education	IDES Team	July 3
Provide feedback to the evaluation team on the summary report	Devin	July 17
Present the final report to the State Department of Education and the donor	IDES Team	August 11

Appendix 3.B

Example Interview Questions, Issues, and Iterations

Evaluation Questions	*Interview Question Drafts*	*Issue*
Teachers *How can we capture what they know about the 4-steps and key features without curing participants?*	Iteration 1: How did you apply the 4-step process in year 1?	*This assumes they applied the process.*
	Iteration 2: Were you introduced to the 4-step process by the lead teacher?	*Teachers may respond "yes" to protect the lead teacher. Also, may encounter self-presentation bias.*
	Iteration 3: Have you heard about the Achieving Schools Project?	*Again, they may say yes. So, a follow-up is needed to see what they know about it.*
	Final Question:	
Parents *How can we capture what parents know in a way that will let us see if it can be attributed to the project?*	Iteration 1: Are you aware of the "Achieving Schools Project"?	*Parents may say "yes" to protect the teachers. The name of the project is so generic parents may confuse it with other initiatives.*
	Iteration 2: Tell us if you have been more involved with your kids in the last 3.5 years.	*Parents may say yes as it is the acceptable answer expected by society. Also with the pandemic, they might have to be more involved. So, first year and pandemic, maybe separate questions.*
	Final Question:	
	Potential Follow-up questions:	
	Other questions related to parents:	

Appendix 3.C

Sample Individual School Summaries

	School Site A (In Person Visit)	*School Site B (Virtual Visit)*
Goals set by schools (by following the 4-step process)	—Improve translation services for communication with parents. —Increase parent and community involvement by opening a computer lab to parents twice a week. —Help students succeed	—Implement special attitude programs for students and teachers (STAR: Stop, think, act, right) —Make parents more visible in school events, bring them to school —Revise curriculum to meet current academic needs
Activities (to meet project goals)	—Hired contract translator on site, available Mon-Wed-Fri, to provide translation for visiting parents, and most home communications. —Started new parent involvement activities: reading, writing, and computer skills nights or weekend camps (along with onsite childcare) —Began to track achievement data by assigning a team leader for several subjects (Math, Science, Language Arts, Social Studies) —Started sending student progress reports more frequently.	—Developed a planning document for improving attitude and school culture —Organized movie nights for students and parents —Organized subject-specific planning groups (Math, Science, English only) to review the current curriculum, teaching methods, and district goals. —Sent one science teacher to a science center workshop on authentic learning, and had that teacher present to other science teachers
Outcomes	—Defined a new vision statement and set measurable goals Monitored progress monthly —Improved communication and involvement of parents, especially Spanish-speaking parents. —Used outcome data to monitor student progress —More parents volunteered in school activities	—Positive cultural change has occurred among teachers and students —Early-out Wednesdays were given to teachers to spend on curriculum improvement —School initiated two school-wide learning projects, within school post office service, and school garden —Sent surveys to parents to gather information about their availability and interests to attend further events. Kept track of the numbers of parents attending in-school events and observed an increase as variety increased.

	School Site A (In Person Visit)	*School Site B (Virtual Visit)*
The primary use of funds (triangulated with budget/artifacts and reported by multiple stakeholders)	—Hired a translator 3 days per week during the school year. —Hired hourly lab assistant for after-hours and parent help, tutors for science and math nights —Held a project-sponsored retreat for teachers to review and revise the vision of the school	—Supported attendance for authentic learning workshop at Science Center (travel, registration, per diem). —Hired a coordinator for the culture change program —Sponsored 2 per semester movie nights —Provided funding for the school garden project —Printed surveys, and provided funding for school events that involve parents (astronomy night, cooking night, baseball night, cultural dance night)
Major challenges	—Half of the parents are monolingual Spanish speakers; roughly another 10% are neither Spanish nor English speakers (refugee populations from Zimbabwe and Mozambique) The initial focus for the project on authentic learning wasn't perceived clearly by the foundation, felt like it resulted in conflicts with the district. In the second year, they switched the focus more to the four steps and parents. —Teachers needed training for using technology —Parents were hesitant to attend school activities —Teachers needed professional development on tracking student progress, data-based decision-making, and creating alert systems for student progress	—Parents lack time and willingness to visit the school —Teachers resisted trying authentic learning in their classes (due to limited time and budget for meeting state standards) —Fifty-seven percent of students are of Mexican origin, having just arrived from Mexico in the last 1–5 years —Forty-four percent turnover among teachers in the last two years. Many trained teachers departed during the pandemic.
Evaluator comments	—Parents interviewed indicated they were enthusiastic about school efforts to involve them, but they are still hesitant. Parents reported school staff has been welcoming to them. The attendance numbers are stable for events, with a slight increase since it began. Comprehensive student progress information is made available by teachers and sent home frequently (in English and Spanish). Teachers didn't do authentic learning activities, as there was a big push for standardized testing. There is an opportunity to increase parent involvement with the addition of translation services for the Zimbabwe and Mozambique refugee populations.	—Due to the hesitancy of the teachers to embed authentic learning in each of their classes, the school initiated two authentic learning projects and sent a science teacher to a workshop on authentic learning. Students, parents, and teachers are very enthusiastic about this project. The lead teacher has concerns regarding sustaining the garden without the project funds. The same goes for parent involvement activities. Schools may need to look for further funding to sustain these. STAR program became the culture of the school, and created a positive influence on interactions amongst students and teachers. Teacher turnover is a major issue. The school needs to look at the reasons behind this as well as plan to train new teachers so they can quickly pick up where others left off.

Appendix 3.D

Parent Responses to Selected Survey Questions

Responses to selected questions from the survey	*School Site A*	*School Site B*	*School Site C*	*Comments*
	2 parents	*4 parents*	*4 parents*	
Have you heard about the Achieving Schools Project?	Yes (1) No (1)	Yes (3) No (1)	No (4)	Compare with teacher leader and teacher efforts for the project and what they say they did with parents, and how they informed them about the goals of the project.
How did you hear about the project?	From volunteering in school	From principal (3)	Haven't heard (4)	SITE 3: Communicating project to parents
Have you been involved in the project?	Yes, from PTA	Yes (2) From parent workshops No (1)		
How many children do you have at school?	1 (1) 2–3 (1) 4–5	1 (2) 2–3 (2) 4–5	1 (2) 2–3 (2) 4–5	
How do you get information about your child's progress at school?	Teacher conference (2)	Report card (3) Teacher conference (1)	Report card (3) Call school (1)	
How often do you visit the school before the pandemic?	Once a week (2)	Everyday (2) Once a month (2)	Once a month (3) Once a semester (1)	
What meetings did you attend at the school last year?	PTA meetings (1) Teacher conferences (2)	Curriculum night (4) Parent-student movie nights (3)	Holiday Coffee (1) Site Council (1) Teacher conference (4)	

Responses to selected questions from the survey	*School Site A*	*School Site B*	*School Site C*	*Comments*
	2 parents	*4 parents*	*4 parents*	
How comfortable do you feel visiting the school?	Very comfortable Comfortable Neutral (1) Not comfortable Very uncomfortable (1)	Very comfortable (1) Comfortable (3) Neutral Not comfortable Very uncomfortable	Very comfortable Comfortable Neutral Not comfortable (4) Very uncomfortable	Sites 1& 3: Hesitant parents seem to show up here . . .
How would you rate the school's efforts to involve you in school-related activities?	Excellent Good (2) Neutral Not good Poor	Excellent Good (4) Neutral Not good Poor	Excellent Good Neutral (1) Not good (2) Poor (1)	SITE 3: Parents don't seem to know about school efforts to involve them. GET MORE SURVEYS.
What special events or activities did your school organize within the first year? What special events or activities did your school do during the pandemic to involve you with your kids during the pandemic?	Having a translator in the math tutor room (1) Sending announcements to cell phones (1)	STAR program (2) Astronomy night (1) Professional development for parents to use LMS (1) Texting due dates for student assignments	Xmas cookie sale Support troops event (2) Holiday Coffee Baseball game Snail mail communication on how to do things on LMS (2) Texts on missing assignments (1)	SITE 2: Aligned with school observations, and reported events No communication from the school Felt lost

4

Lynn Dixon

Designing a Learning Platform to Celebrate World Wetlands Day

Christie Nelson

Lynn Dixon is an instructional designer at a small e-learning company in Sydney, Australia, called Telopea Learning. Telopea Learning creates technology-based learning solutions for a variety of clients including banks, insurance companies, government departments, and the retail industry. It's a fast-paced working environment with tight deadlines. However, the company also encourages a fresh, lively atmosphere, with music playing, frequent company fun days, and sporting events. Lynn often wonders how she's meant to keep her clients happy while having all that fun!

Lynn has been working at Telopea Learning for almost a year. She took this job after she moved to Australia from the United States, where she grew up. Although Lynn had very similar work experiences in the United States, she has discovered some interesting differences between American and Australian workplace cultures. The Australians seem much more casual about things, whereas her American colleagues tended to be very "by the book." Lynn has a master's degree in educational technology with a focus on instructional design (ID). She was surprised to learn that many of her colleagues at Telopea Learning did not have ID degrees; instead, many were hired in from other disciplines and had acquired their learning on the job. As a result of her formal education and experience, Lynn was quickly regarded as one of their best designers and asked to take the lead on many projects.

A NEW PROJECT FOR LYNN

It's now 9:00 A.M. on Monday, and Lynn has already been at her desk for a couple of hours. Coming in early allows her to get her to-do list organized and to make sure she's ready for the week ahead, before others arrive and need to talk with her, ask questions, troubleshoot issues, and so on. People are starting to arrive now, and the familiar hum of phones ringing, keyboards clicking, and conversation fills the large open-plan workspace. Lynn glances up and sees her colleague, Janette Parks, giving her a wave from across the room. Lynn recognizes the look on Janette's face—*she's going to ask me to do something.* Janette is the head of the sales team at Telopea Learning. It's an important role—Janette is the person who secures project work for the company with new and existing clients. Lynn finds herself wishing she could be more involved in these conversations, because there often seems to be a disconnect

DOI: 10.4324/9781003354468-5

between what is sold to the client and what the company is capable of achieving within the time and budget allowed. It's a problem that Lynn often finds herself having to resolve. Janette is walking over to Lynn's desk now.

"We've got a really exciting new project kicking off this week, and I'm told you're going to be the lead on it," Janette begins excitedly. Lynn gets a nervous feeling in the pit of her stomach; she's already quite busy and wonders how she'll fit another project into her schedule. "It's working with the Marine Park on a learning platform for the Aquarium in Cairns (see Figure 4.1 for a map of Australia) to celebrate World Wetlands Day. This project is amazing, Lynn—we get to help them choose the best technology solution to deliver some super cool content!" Lynn's interest picks up. Lately, she's been working on some really mundane projects, and the idea of doing something for a public institution is appealing. "We need to fly up there for a day trip on Wednesday to get things started. Can you run the kickoff meeting?"

Janette tells Lynn more of the project details. The Aquarium has been closed to visitors for a couple of years because it needed some significant renovations. As a part of these renovations, they are building a new wetlands exhibit to enhance the already impressive collection of fish tanks and aquatic exhibits. The new exhibit will include visual displays, 25,000 liters of water, 800 fish, and a 3-meter-high waterfall, all designed to show the connection between the wetlands and the Great Barrier Reef. The team responsible for the exhibit is led by Laura Barton, who works in the government department responsible for the Aquarium. Laura wants to provide a technology-based option for visitors to explore and learn more about the wetlands, in conjunction with the physical exhibit. Telopea Learning has been initially contracted to provide a strategy and design for the solution. Laura is working with another provider on hardware and installation for other parts of the Aquarium, and if needed, Telopea Learning could partner with them on delivering this project.

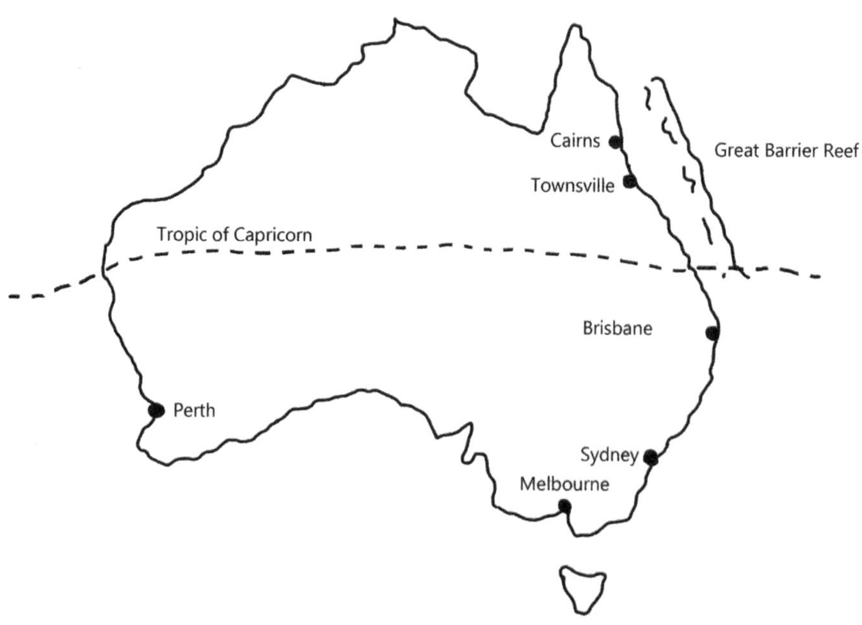

FIGURE 4.1 Map of Australia.

For the first time in a while, Lynn is thrilled to be taking on a new project. This is the type of work she imagined herself doing when she was in graduate school. She is excited about getting involved with the client during the early planning stages in order to identify the best solution. Often in her role, by the time she meets with a client, the solution has already been chosen: a website, an app, an online course, and so on. In those cases, Lynn is unable to weigh in about what would be best from an instructional design perspective. And unfortunately, sometimes her clients haven't chosen the best option! From what Janette tells her, the team at the Aquarium is open to a variety of delivery options, and they are genuinely interested in getting expert advice from Telopea Learning.

Lynn spends the next day getting her other projects in order and doing some initial reading about museum- and aquarium-based learning. Many institutions are using apps to support their exhibits, as well as highly visual wall projections. Lynn also checks out the Aquarium's website. She concludes that visitors to the Aquarium are diverse in nearly all categories—age, educational background, primary language, reading ability, and so on. Most of Lynn's projects have had very specific, well-defined audiences, so there are a lot of new factors to consider. On Tuesday night, she sets her phone alarm for 5:00 A.M. in order to make it to the airport on time for their early morning flight to Cairns.

A VISIT TO THE CLIENT SITE

Lynn steps off the plane into the warm and humid Queensland sun on Wednesday morning. It's a refreshing feeling after leaving Sydney on a chilly winter morning. The difference in climate she experiences is similar to the difference when traveling from New York to Florida or the Bahamas. Lynn is a bit chagrined that she finds Sydney winters cold after enduring harsh Chicago winters for the previous five years, but she does sometimes. Now she can feel the warm, humid air opening her sinuses and rousing her out of her sleepy haze. She and Janette catch an Uber and head over to the Aquarium. They get out of the car and walk up the front steps. The Aquarium is still closed to visitors; however, many of the renovations are complete and looking impressive! Lynn suppresses her childlike enthusiasm before donning her professional façade. Just inside the front gates, Lynn sees a couple of friendly looking people waiting for them by a large fish tank. Laura introduces herself and Ben Williams, the education manager at the Aquarium, and suggests they take a quick tour before getting started. Lynn welcomes the chance to walk around and stretch her legs.

A world of bustling marine life and colorful coral envelops them as they make their way through a maze of tunnels that go around, above, and through enormous tanks of water. They step into the construction area for the new wetlands exhibit. Ben shows Lynn and Janette the waterfall and fish tank. Lynn is impressed and excited that she will be working to support such an amazing educational environment.

They leave the exhibit area and sit down in a meeting room. Lynn hands out the meeting agenda and some sample project documents (project plan, phases, etc.) to Laura and Ben. They begin by discussing their roles and responsibilities. Laura is the project sponsor—she works for the government and is busy with several other projects—so, she wants to be involved only in the initial decisions, major reviews, and signoffs, not in the day-to-day decisions once the team starts designing and implementing the technology solution. That responsibility falls to Ben, who will coordinate directly with Lynn and also serve as the subject matter expert (SME). Ben will be available to answer Lynn's questions and will also complete all preliminary reviews and provide feedback for the project deliverables. He will manage the project timeline on the client side and report progress back to Laura. He's also the resident wetlands expert. Ben readily admits that he could talk about the wetlands for hours, if permitted. He hands Lynn some brochures, books, and posters, as she wonders how she'll carry them all onto the plane back to Sydney! He also promises to send her even more information electronically.

Ben then provides an overview of the general requirements for the technology tool. First of all, he emphasizes that the tool needs to be well-utilized. A government grant has provided the scope for a significant investment into this tool, as long as the Aquarium can provide evidence of its use and impact. The theme of the new exhibit is Connections—between the Great Barrier Reef, the wetlands, and the catchment areas. The various displays in the exhibit will demonstrate the relationships and interconnectedness among these three environments. Ben and Laura are hoping the tool can really emphasize and reinforce these relationships. They also want it to provide information about the different types of wetlands. In addition to being used at the Aquarium, the team would like the tool available at several regional information centers, if possible. Laura suggests that the tool should somehow acknowledge each of these regional areas by name and description, because each has provided significant funding and support for the project. Another important theme should be the role wetlands play in Aboriginal culture and heritage. Laura isn't sure how this could be depicted, but Ben thinks there might be some Aboriginal stories included in the materials he provided. Lynn agrees to keep this in mind as she is looking through the materials.

The group stops for a minute and then begins brainstorming ideas for the solution. Ben enthusiastically describes his idea for an animation showing a bird flying high in the sky, zooming around looking down on the catchment, then quickly flying down into a more detailed billabong setting. Lynn's eyes widen as she throws Janette a sideways glance. Janette has a way of encouraging clients to think big, even if their budgets and timeframes are small. For this project, it will be important to indicate to the Aquarium team what different levels of investment will get them. At this point Janette chimes in and reviews the project statement of work, which specifies different levels of "interactivity" and the corresponding cost. Zooming animated bird life would require a higher level of investment. Lynn is reminded of her frustration with these metrics. What really defines interactivity versus technical complexity? How can she reliably judge the interactivity of the ideas they were discussing? This is one feature she's always wanted to improve about the way her company sells and quotes on projects.

Ben reminds them of another requirement. They want to be able to measure how much time any user spends on particular content areas and then generate a report that indicates the most popular and longest viewed topics. This will allow them to identify areas for improvement and changes for future versions. Janette nods to indicate that this can be included in the project scope and mentions to Lynn that Telopea Learning's technical developers shouldn't have an issue with making this happen. Janette then reminds Ben and Laura that audio narration can be included in the solution; however, the hiring of professional voice talent to do recordings would be an additional cost. As an option, the team could use voices from individuals who work at Telopea Learning.

At this stage, Lynn steers the conversation back to how a typical project should run and provides some more detail about next steps. Lynn will return to Telopea Learning's office in Sydney and review all the content that Ben has provided. She'll decide what information is most relevant to include in the solution and summarize this information in a high-level instructional design document. This document is important as it will form an agreement between Telopea Learning and the Aquarium about what learning objectives they will achieve with the solution. She will also produce a summary of technical delivery options with examples of how the content areas could work in each. This should help the team decide which option makes the most sense for the Aquarium. Laura and Ben are looking forward to seeing this and remind Lynn to call them if any questions come up as she is working. Everyone is happy as the meeting concludes. As they are walking out, Laura quickly mentions to Lynn that she could easily get access to a pilot group of users if needed. There is a senior citizens group that regularly tours the Aquarium and often does small volunteer projects for them. Lynn and Janette say their thanks and goodbyes and grab an Uber back to the airport. Lynn's stomach begins growling. *Why isn't there ever time to eat on these day trips?*

LYNN REFLECTS ON INITIAL CLIENT MEETING: WHAT NOW?

Before takeoff, Janette quickly catches up on her messages. Lynn exhales, relaxes into the headrest, and closes her eyes for just a moment. This is always an enjoyable part of a day trip—the work is done, and now she's on her way home. As she begins contemplating how she's going to tackle this project, she is interrupted by a slight nudge and question from Janette.

"So, Lynn, what is your next step with this?"

"Well, it's going to take some time for me to review all this content. I think Ben gave me three times more than I'll end up using. Once I get some ideas about major themes, I'll start working on the high-level design document. I'll also need to do some research about the technology options. I'm looking forward to this—I'm really interested in how museums are using apps and other technological advancements to enhance the visitor experience."

"Great. So, when do you think you might be able to get something back to them? Can you also do a project plan by the end of this week? We'll need to let them know when their first review is coming so they can notify their stakeholders."

"Sure, Janette. I have to tell you it seems like Ben has some pretty high expectations about the 'bells and whistles' that might appear in the solution. Do you think he understands the impact of these on cost?"

"Oh, we looked at a lot of demos together during the Zoom meeting we had before they decided to work with us. Don't worry, Lynn—if you run into any issues just bring me back into the loop. Remember, they could have some flexibility to spend big here." The flight attendant then announces that the plane has reached its cruising altitude and that electronic devices are now safe to be used, reminding passengers to ensure that their phones are switched to airplane mode. Janette returns to her messages from the day.

Lynn rests her head again and stretches out her legs. Although the wetlands content is certainly more exciting than insurance product training (her other big project at the moment), she has some concerns. The lack of definition around the delivery medium is overwhelming, especially given the diversity of the learning audience. Lynn makes a mental note to do more research on this. How do you design something that works for so many different types of people? She wonders if Telopea's graphic designer could give her some ideas. Also, how is she going to fit this work into her already fully scheduled week? She contemplates an ideal world where this is her only project and she has unlimited time at her disposal to make it really amazing. Unfortunately, this is not Lynn's reality. Lynn hopes she'll be able to keep everyone as happy as they were at the conclusion of today's meeting. She begins to drift off to sleep as the flight to Sydney continues.

DESIGN DOCUMENT REVIEW

Two weeks have passed, and Lynn is about to participate in an online meeting with Ben and Laura to discuss their review of her design document (see Figure 4.2). She hasn't yet started the summary of technology options. She thought it was more important to nail down the content learning objectives and level of interactivity before diving into different ways to best deliver the solution.

Lynn finds a conference room and joins the online meeting. Ben and Laura haven't arrived yet. While waiting, she looks over their comments. They seem to be generally happy with the design, but it sounds like they just want more—of everything. Lynn wishes Janette could have been involved in the call, but she was asked to attend an "important meeting" at the last minute. Salespeople—they always seemed to have important meetings. Although Lynn wishes she could do everything the client wants, she knows she'll also have to make sure they have the budget to make it all happen.

Beep. Ben and Laura have just joined the meeting.

"Hello, there," Lynn says.

"G'day!" Ben seems to be in a cheerful mood, which relaxes Lynn a little.

"Thank you for sending your review comments," Lynn begins. "We'll go through them together so you can be sure I understand all of your points. I'm sorry that Janette couldn't be here, but I'll get her to follow up on any issues pertaining to the project later today if needed, okay?"

Laura responds, "No worries. We really liked the design, Lynn. It's a great start. Isn't it exciting to imagine what this thing is going to look like? We've never been involved in this sort of project before, and so far, we're really enjoying it." She continues to discuss what they liked about the design, including the use of the "Regional Showcase." She mentions that there are now several more regional wetlands they need to include here. She also liked the section about "Types of Wetlands."

Ben then joins in to discuss some of their concerns.

"Lynn, I am not sure where we're going to see anything about the Aboriginal relationship with the wetlands," he begins. "Can we include some of their storytelling? It would be great if we could get someone to read an Aboriginal Dreamtime story. Hmmm, you probably don't have anyone of Aboriginal descent working at Telopea Learning, do you? I think people might be confused by your American accent!"

"No, we don't," Lynn replies. "But we can look into hiring an actor if you think this is critical—I'll just have Janette provide you with a cost estimate."

"I reckon I can find someone here. We could probably fly them down to you for a recording session, too, or look into getting a recording done here."

"Okay, that sounds promising. I was actually wondering if you had considered involving the local university in the project. They might have access to more content resources, or people of Aboriginal descent to help us out," says Lynn.

"That's a great idea, Lynn," Ben responds. "I'll look into it."

Ben continues to discuss some other issues. "I know we haven't yet started discussing how this will all be delivered; however, for those sections with high levels of interactivity, I was hoping to see a game or fancy animation. Could we do something cool for the 'Threats to Wetlands' section? I'd like the users to really understand the impacts that urban development is having on the wetlands, such as pollution, as well as the effects the wildlife population is

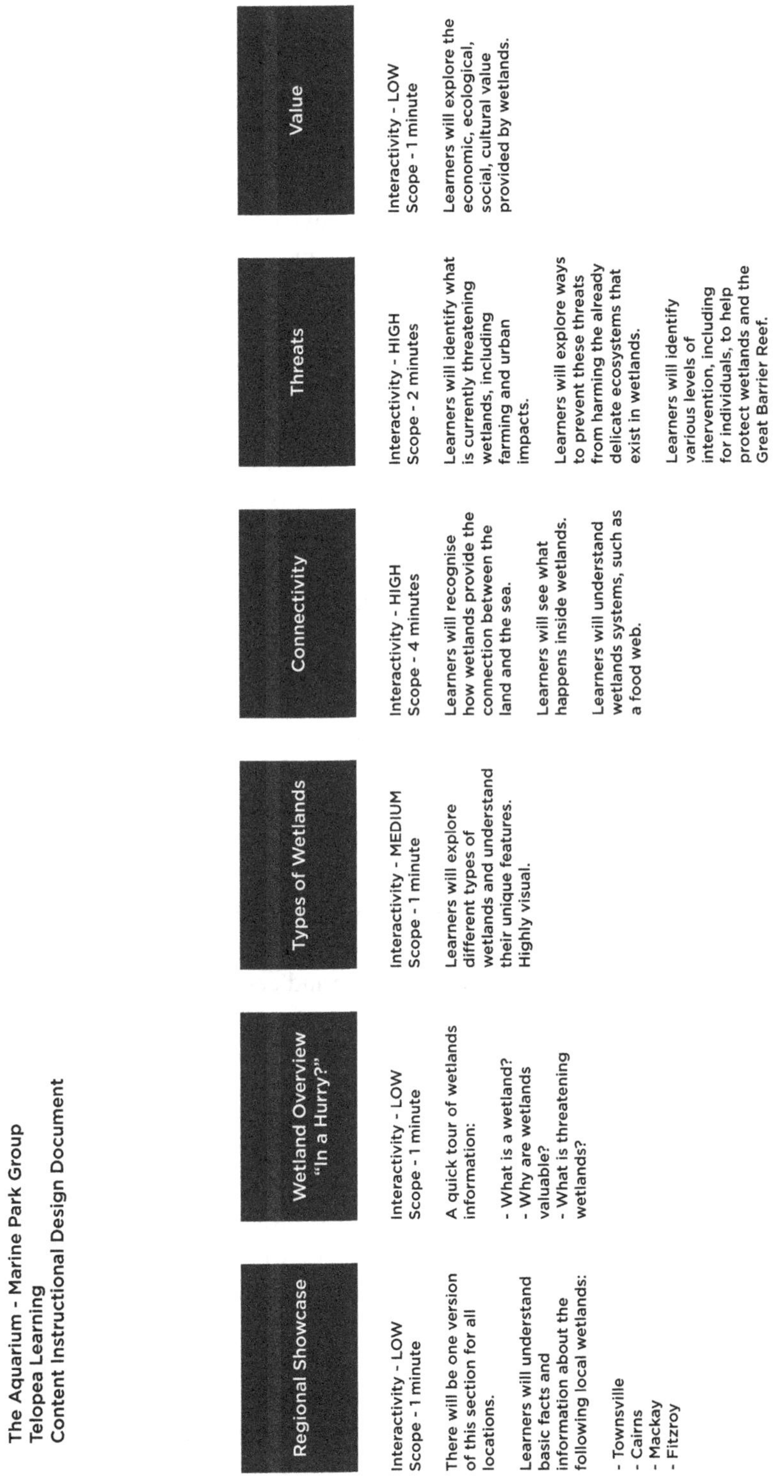

The Aquarium - Marine Park Group
Telopea Learning
Content Instructional Design Document

Regional Showcase	Wetland Overview "In a Hurry?"	Types of Wetlands	Connectivity	Threats	Value
Interactivity - LOW Scope - 1 minute	Interactivity - LOW Scope - 1 minute	Interactivity - MEDIUM Scope - 1 minute	Interactivity - HIGH Scope - 4 minutes	Interactivity - HIGH Scope - 2 minutes	Interactivity - LOW Scope - 1 minute
There will be one version of this section for all locations. Learners will understand basic facts and information about the following local wetlands: - Townsville - Cairns - Mackay - Fitzroy	A quick tour of wetlands information: - What is a wetland? - Why are wetlands valuable? - What is threatening wetlands?	Learners will explore different types of wetlands and understand their unique features. Highly visual.	Learners will recognise how wetlands provide the connection between the land and the sea. Learners will see what happens inside wetlands. Learners will understand wetlands systems, such as a food web.	Learners will identify what is currently threatening wetlands, including farming and urban impacts. Learners will explore ways to prevent these threats from harming the already delicate ecosystems that exist in wetlands. Learners will identify various levels of intervention, including for individuals, to help protect wetlands and the Great Barrier Reef.	Learners will explore the economic, ecological, social, cultural value provided by wetlands.

FIGURE 4.2 Lynn's design document.

feeling. I also couldn't tell how we could use a fancy bird's eye animation of the catchment area. You remember the one I told you about during our meeting?"

Lynn hesitates for a moment, unsure how to respond. She begins by addressing the game request. "I think we could definitely come up with some ideas for a game. Costs can increase quickly as games become more complicated; however, I imagine we could do a type of discovery activity where learners investigate the impact of different types of development, such as cane farming. This could be fun!

"About the animation, I'm going to have a chat with Janette about how much we can do. We are only able to use the graphics that you have provided for us; however, we can manipulate them to some extent. We could probably come up with a nice high-level view of the catchment with some help from you."

"Well, I'd be super-keen to come down for a working session with you and the graphic designers if you like—that shouldn't be an issue!" Ben is always so enthusiastic, it's hard for Lynn to say no.

Laura jumps in with one final point. "Lynn, I'd like to understand more about how you're going to cater to the variety of visitors the Aquarium receives every day. As you've seen, we've got everyone from school-aged children to senior citizens attending the exhibits. There are some significant world authorities on wetlands who will be interested in viewing it. We also get a lot of international visitors who may only speak a little English. How are you going to ensure that the solution will be relevant to everyone?"

Lynn was expecting this question, as it has been something she also wondered herself. "Well, Laura, I think we'll have to get a bit further in the design process before this becomes apparent. I do think that some of the content areas will be more relevant to particular audiences than others. However, the combination of all sections should provide a bit of something for everyone."

"Okay, that makes sense," Laura replied. "I look forward to the next step, then!"

Lynn breathes an internal sigh of relief that Laura was satisfied with her answer. This is definitely something she's going to have to think through further. And with that, along with the typical discussions about what would be coming next, they conclude the meeting.

Lynn returns to her desk and reviews her growing to-do list. Various issues of concern are swimming around in her head. In addition to the audience issue that Laura raised, many other questions remain unanswered. She really needs to get working on the delivery solution analysis. She puts her notes aside for a moment and decides to run downstairs for a chicken Caesar wrap and some hot chips.

Preliminary Analysis Questions

1. Lynn needs to design a solution that works for a variety of learners. How would you design the Wetlands learning experiences so that they provide something for everyone?
2. What technology solution would you recommend to support the Wetlands exhibit and why? Consider the learning environment, audience characteristics, average time someone will spend, etc.
3. Lynn's initial design document is basic. Assume you are using the technology solution recommended in Question 2, choose one section and provide more detailed instructional design strategies that you would use to deliver the content, using sketches and diagrams.

4. Ben is an enthusiastic subject matter expert with a lot of grand ideas. How can Lynn keep him happy while still managing the project within an agreed budget?
5. Lynn perceives a disconnect within Telopea Learning between the sales and design teams in regard to what can be achieved within a particular budget for a project. How would you work to improve this situation within Telopea Learning?

Implications for ID Practice

1. What are some visual and instructional design strategies that would be unique to aquarium- or museum-based learning? What are some instructional design challenges when designing for this scenario?
2. Instructional designers often don't have time to perform any type of detailed analysis before beginning a design document. In what ways can designers incorporate an initial analysis "on the fly"?
3. Interactive resources are becoming more and more learner-driven, meaning that learners choose what they view; they control the sequence of information and the amount of time they spend. How can instructional designers design such resources knowing that their learners may not approach them in a systematic way?

5

Autumn Leifson

Developing a Mobile App That Supports Family Engagement Outdoors Through Informal Learning

Charles Keith, Lillyanna Faimon, Stephanie Bowles, Susan Land, and Heather Toomey Zimmerman

Autumn turned around in her office chair, thinking about her most recent design project. *With all these new opportunities to learn about the natural world at our Arboretum, I wonder what STEM curriculum we could draw from to make our mobile learning app more versatile for a wide range of families. One family did mention something about interactive elements, such as drawing or drag-and-drop activities in the app . . . Hmm, I guess it's time to do more research.*

Autumn Leifson, an instructional designer for the Educational Outreach Office at Garden University, was struggling to think of new ideas for designing effective place-based science learning opportunities for families visiting the Arboretum. As part of her new job, she had been tasked with leading the design of a new mobile informal learning app to be used on families' phones or tablets as they visited Garden University's Arboretum. As explained to Autumn by her new supervisor, Dr. Flores, the app, called *Arboretum Adventurers*, was to be completed in partnership with Garden University's Arboretum to allow visiting families to learn about the science in their communities.

Arboretum Adventurers was, undoubtedly, Autumn's biggest project since she had been hired. The project, to be completed within a two-year timeline, was being developed with families of younger children (ages 5–12) in mind, focusing on using mobile technologies to support STEM learning in the garden while also supporting families' unique interests and choices about what they wanted to learn during their visit. Garden University's Arboretum aimed to design the *Arboretum Adventurers* app to help visitors engage in self-directed, place-based science learning about local plants and pollinators. Stakeholders at Garden University's Arboretum wanted quick progress on the app, ensuring that the pilot version would be completed within one year. Designs for the app would change as Autumn observed participants' uses and analyzed their feedback.

The initial design of *Arboretum Adventurers* focused on several learning objectives and design conjectures (see Figure 5.1) that Autumn had created to guide the initial design of the pilot version of the app. Autumn used these objectives to create design conjectures to guide learning experiences for families based on interest-driven learning, where families' interests

DOI: 10.4324/9781003354468-6

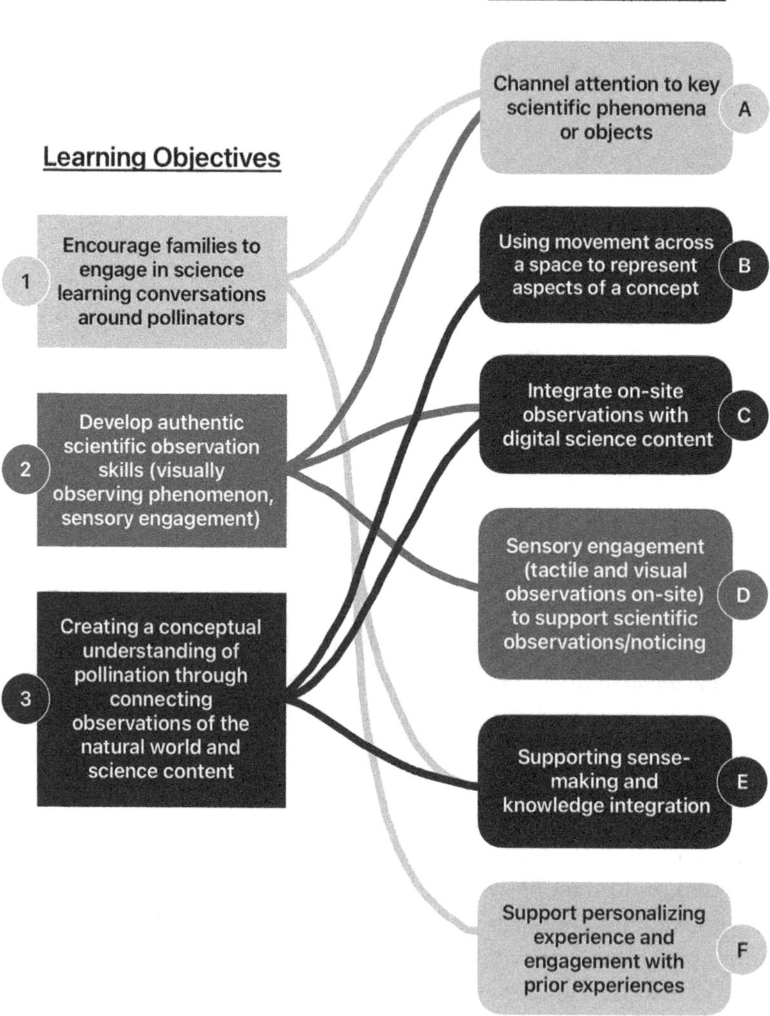

FIGURE 5.1 Arboretum Adventurers learning objectives and design conjectures.

drive what they want to learn, as well as place-based learning, which leverages the garden space itself as a resource for science learning (see Figure 5.2).

MOBILE LEARNING APP USABILITY TESTING AND USER FEEDBACK

The next steps in Autumn's work on *Arboretum Adventurers* involved usability testing and formative evaluations of the app through observing the hands-on experiences of participating families. Waking up early on a beautiful Saturday morning at the end of the summer semester, Autumn quickly prepared for the day. She grabbed her keys and headed for her office where she packed all of the materials she would need for pilot testing the app. Knowing that visitor feedback and experiences would be key in influencing future app design updates, Autumn brought tablet computers with the app pre-loaded onto them, body-mounted cameras to record visitors' perspectives while they used the app, and a clipboard with prepared

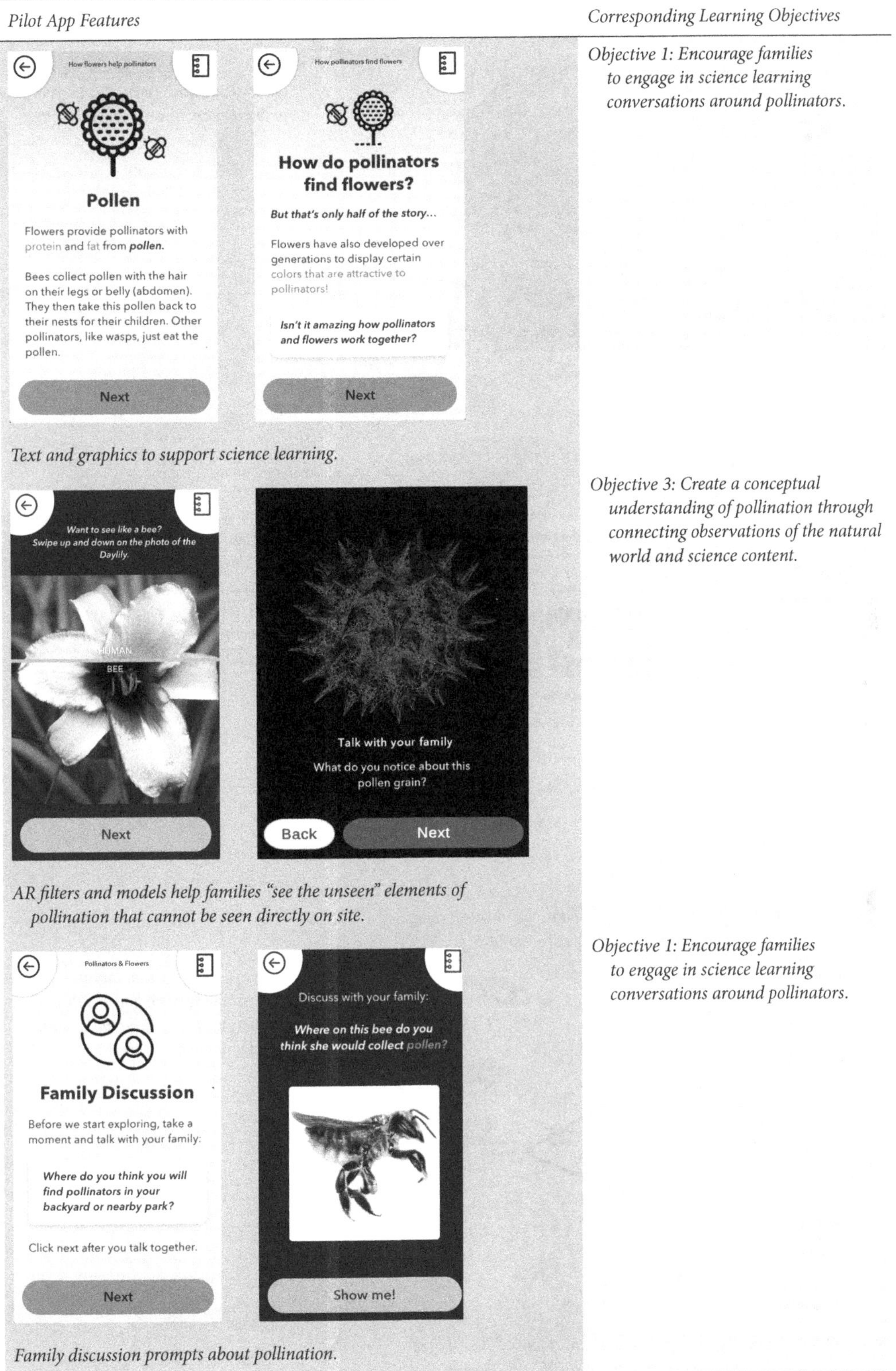

FIGURE 5.2 Arboretum Adventurers app features and learning objectives.

Pilot App Features	*Corresponding Learning Objectives*
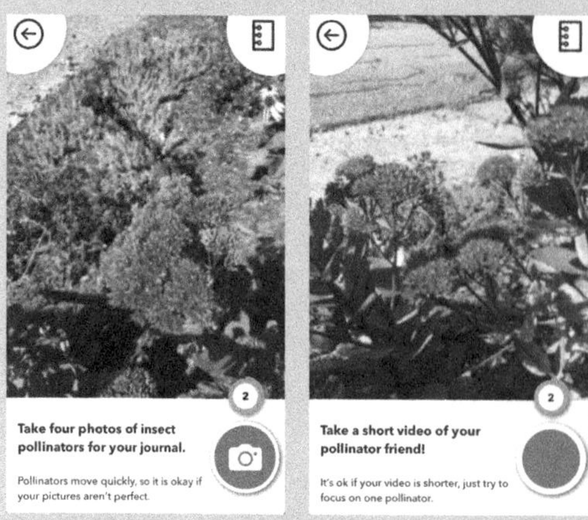 *Photos and videos taken by families to support their interest-driven observations of pollinators.*	*Objective 2: Develop authentic scientific observation skills (visually observing phenomenon, sensory engagement).*
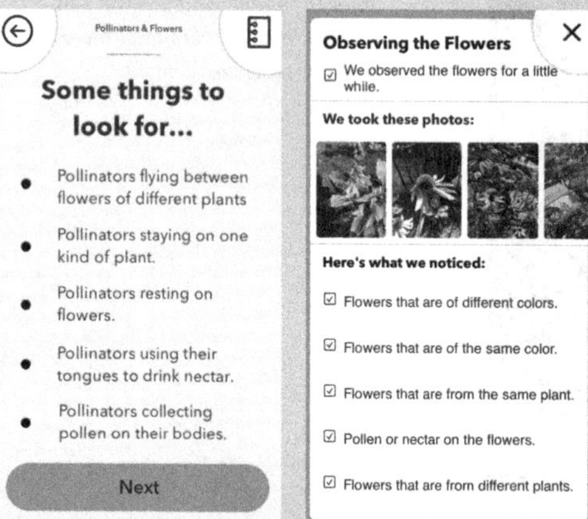 *Supporting families to observe and notice pollinators through reflecting on their photos with observation checklists or prompts.*	*Objective 2: Develop authentic scientific observation skills (visually observing phenomenon, sensory engagement).* *Objective 3: Create a conceptual understanding of pollination through connecting observations of the natural world and science content.*
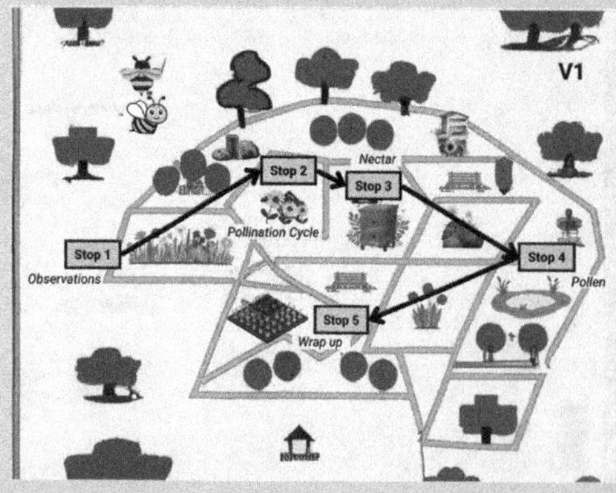 *Wayfinding map through the garden to support family place-based learning about pollinators as they observe different elements that impact pollination.*	*Objective 3: Create a conceptual understanding of pollination through connecting observations of the natural world and science content.*

FIGURE 5.2 Continued

formative evaluation questions for families to answer after they were done using the app at the Arboretum. Screen recordings of each tablet would be collected while families tested *Arboretum Adventurers* to provide additional insight into how they utilized the tablet and on-screen elements during their testing. All of these materials would provide Autumn with ample tools to evaluate the success of *Arboretum Adventurers* in providing families with informal learning experiences while engaging with the garden's outdoor spaces.

With the help of Dr. Flores, Autumn set up the necessary materials in the heart of the Arboretum, along with a sign that read "Learn about pollinators in the Pollinator Garden today! Come test our newest mobile learning app!"

Autumn looked down at her clipboard, reviewing the questions and wondering how the participants would engage with the app. As part of the project, Autumn planned to ask the participants questions to better understand how families felt about the app, their likes and dislikes of its current usability and design, and any information about what they had learned while using the app to understand if the intended learning objectives were being met.

Within the first 15 minutes of setting up, two families had arrived. Dr. Flores turned to Autumn and said, "I'm curious to hear what families like about the app! Hopefully, they can learn a lot today."

One family approached Autumn while the other spoke with Dr. Flores. "Good morning! We saw your sign and were interested in testing your app. Can our family participate?" the mother asked. This first family comprised two parents, a mother, and a father, as well as their two children, a daughter aged eight and a son aged six. "That would be great, let me get you all a tablet and video recorder," Autumn replied. After asking the family questions regarding their prior experiences with mobile learning apps from her clipboard, the family set out to test *Arboretum Adventurers* for themselves.

Half an hour later, the family returned having completed the app activities. Autumn reviewed her formative evaluation questions (see Figure 5.3) and prepared to discuss what the families had learned from their activities and how they had interacted with the app.

"And our last question today is, 'What was something that your family learned or thought was cool during your experience with the app?'" asked Autumn.

The daughter, aged 6, quickly responded, "I really liked watching the butterflies! We saw so many on one flower. I think they liked . . ." The daughter struggled to look for the word she was thinking of.

The father jumped in, pointing to the spot where they had seen the butterflies, and said, "Yeah, they really liked the nectar on the milkweed!" He turned to Autumn and added, "We really did have a lot of fun today observing all the pollinators. Following the prompts was a bit of a challenge, especially the science content. My wife and I tried to connect the more

Learning Questions	User Experience Questions
What part of your learning experience today helped guide your conversations about pollination?	What location or content interested your family or kept you the most engaged during the experience?
Could you describe the process of pollination to me? (Directed at kids)	Which elements of the app helped you and your family observe pollinators today?
What was something that your family learned or thought was cool during your experience with the app?	If you could change anything about the app, what might that be?

FIGURE 5.3 Autumn's formative evaluation questions.

'sciencey' words with what we were observing, but even we didn't know all the terms. My daughter is such a fan of us reading to her, but she struggled today with some of the more 'sciencey' talk. If the app could have adjusted for her reading level or even provided some audio elements that could have read her the content, I feel like that would have helped her. We had such a great time today, there wasn't a single stop where we weren't all talking and making observations. The photo-taking activities were probably our favorite parts of the app!"

Autumn was concerned to hear that the app hadn't worked perfectly for the family and thought back to the original goals of the stakeholders, including the Educational Outreach Office. If the app was to work for a diverse audience, it would have to take into account reading level and other factors that she hadn't considered earlier. Rewording some of the prompts and science content would probably be necessary when considering new changes to the app. While the stakeholders felt that having sound in the app would distract from the experience of other visitors, Autumn was sure there was some other way to adjust the content to work for a variety of learners.

"I'm so sorry that happened!" Autumn replied. "Thank you for the feedback. We can certainly look into adjusting the reading level. If we were unable to add all of these features, like the audio elements, what other activities do you think might help identify the pollinators and their actions?"

The mother turned to Autumn and replied, "That's a good question . . . Our kids are so interested in drawing. They liked taking pictures, but they wanted to draw all the flowers and pollinators that they saw today. That might have been fun for them. Again, I think we were all a bit confused with some of the scientific words . . . I wish we could have used labels for the plants and pollinators at some point."

Autumn jotted their suggestions down. Her initial reaction to hearing the recommendation regarding labels made her think of a drag-and-drop activity, which she thought might help prompt connections between participants' photos and the science content. After finishing her notes, Autumn replied, "Thank you so much for your feedback and all of your help today!"

Soon after this first family had left, the second family, comprising three early middle school-aged boys and their parents, finished their experience with *Arboretum Adventurers*. Autumn listened closely as Dr. Flores asked the same formative evaluation questions.

"So, what location or content interested your family or kept you the most engaged during the experience?" asked Dr. Flores.

"We loved the pond!" screamed the boys.

The mother laughed and quickly followed up, "Yes, we did love the pond. We loved it so much that we weren't able to complete all of the app activities today. We hope that's alright."

"Absolutely! What kinds of observations were you able to make during your visit to the pond today?" asked Dr. Flores.

After their brief conversation, Autumn realized how differently this family had utilized the app as a learning tool in comparison to the first family. While the first family had struggled with some of the science content and prompts, it seemed that the second family only had good feedback to provide on those elements of the app. However, they had been so focused on their observations of finding pollinators at the pond that they actually observed much of the other wildlife there as well, such as the pond's growing turtle population. Autumn realized that these additional factors may have taken attention away from some of the key learning activities and concepts that they wished families to engage in within the app.

EDUCATIONAL OUTREACH OFFICE INTERNAL EVALUATION

Following the first pilot testing for *Arboretum Adventurers*, Autumn reviewed the screen recordings of the tablets, body camera footage of families using the app, responses to formative evaluation questions, and general feedback provided by families after using the app. Her notes highlighted different aspects of the app that families enjoyed or had problems with. From her analysis of the data, she found that several families commented on the difficulty of the science terminology in relation to completing the prompts. Additionally, she noted how many families enjoyed the photo-taking activities, but the location in which these activities took place greatly impacted how engaged many of the families were during their time at the Arboretum. Locations, such as the pond, proved to be quite distracting and took away from activities in which families were intended to observe pollinators. However, this might also be a positive outcome, as the app worked alongside families' interests in what they wanted to explore. For some families, the abundance of wildlife in the area drove interest in other observations. Autumn created a table to note these findings in comparison to the intended learning objectives and app design elements to identify more patterns and findings on the pilot testing and feedback provided (see Figure 5.4).

Learning Objectives	*Design Elements to Support Learning*	*Notes*
1. Encourage families to engage in science learning conversations around pollinators	AR features, family discussion prompts	- The science language (pollination, nectar, pollen) could be too advanced for younger children, and sometimes for older children and parents, but parents could scaffold discussions around them if they had content knowledge. - Family discussion prompts helped to guide family talk around the science content and connections to prior knowledge or experiences.
2. Develop authentic scientific observation skills (visually observing phenomenon, sensory engagement)	Photos and videos of observed phenomenon, observation checklists and prompts	- Families mentioned how much children enjoyed taking pictures of the different things they observed (*interest-driven learning*). - Majority of families actively engaged and discussed the behavior of pollinators when prompted (*place-based learning*). - Families used gesture and conversation to communicate about their observations to each other and in videos.
3. Creating a conceptual understanding of pollination through connecting observations of the natural world and science content	Wayfinding map, AR features, family discussion prompts, observation checklists and prompts	- Science content was discussed in family discussion prompts but not often in connection to the photo-taking activity or other augmented elements of the app—videos and checklists seemed to scaffold this more. - Families seemed less engaged with the science content than with interactive aspects of the app, such as photo-taking tasks. - Families had issues with app-directed, place-based learning at locations with lots of stimuli (i.e., pond); however, some families enjoyed the balance of app-directed activities with their own interests; others were easily distracted by other features or animals (turtles, fish, playing in the water) and commented on difficulty focusing on observing pollinators or connecting content.

FIGURE 5.4 Autumn's notes of Arboretum Adventurers' pilot testing.

The next step in the development cycle included presenting this information to the Educational Outreach team to help decide which elements of the app were most important to update. Future app testing was scheduled at the end of the spring semester when the pollinators would once again be abundant at the Arboretum. The team, including Autumn's supervisor, Dr. Flores, met early on a Friday morning in November. Each reviewed the notes that Autumn had emailed them earlier in the week as she presented her thoughts.

"Well, thinking about how we can make STEM learning more engaging in outdoor environments, I think that we need to consider how families identify pollinators while using the app. Many families did try to identify pollinators on the flowers, but the children were often focused on completing the pollinator photo-taking activities. From my observations, it seemed that the children became so excited with all the wildlife at particular locations that they focused photo-taking on several animals that caught their attention, even those that weren't pollinators. While we can say that the families had meaningful interest-driven, place-based observations, this challenged how often the families were able to make connections back to the directed science content and document their observations of pollinators. Also, after finishing the photo-taking tasks, it seemed that the children often lost interest in our follow-up information screens that explained pollination and the transferring of pollen."

After jotting some notes down, Dr. Flores looked up and responded, "Great observations, Autumn. So, it seems that the first thing we need to do is try to identify ways in which we can help families understand these terms and make connections to their observations. It seems we may also consider where we position the science content in the app, whether that's before or after our photo-taking activities. Autumn, you also mentioned that some families wanted to draw or physically interact with the tablet when they tested the pilot. That might be something to consider as well. Do you think that might be an important component of supporting STEM learning at the Arboretum?"

Autumn looked back through her notes on the data analysis, trying to identify just how many families had made comments about wanting these types of activities. "I think it might be important to add because it allows families to capture their observations and note what is important to them! A drag-and-drop style activity may help families make connections with their photo-taking engagement and conceptual understanding. I'll do some reading to see what I can find about the role of matching activities and reflection when learning. I think we should also consider where the app is routing families through the Arboretum. I remember that several families had commented that they spent the majority of their time at the pond because of all of the turtles and fish they could observe. I'm not sure if we have time now, but considering changes to the wayfinding map and route that families take while completing the activities might help minimize distractions during the families' learning experiences. That sounds like a plan, though I'll contact the app development team and see what they think. I think I might reach out to our pollination scientists at the university as well; they might have an idea of how to better approach the pollination observation and explanation for participants."

Before the meeting concluded, other staff provided comments on design changes for the app. They reemphasized that Autumn's concerns regarding the app providing fun and engaging STEM learning opportunities were crucial to the Arboretum's needs and wished her the best during the app redesign process.

MOBILE LEARNING APP DEVELOPMENT TEAM UPDATES

Autumn's discussions with her colleagues and the pollination scientists led to new ideas for how to improve *Arboretum Adventurers* for the second version. The pollination scientists, comprising entomology and botany professors on campus, encouraged Autumn to consider how families might engage with understanding the process of pollination. The previous version of the app relied on the photo-taking process to help families observe pollinators while introducing important content, such as pollen and nectar on the following screens. However, the pollination scientists recommended that participants may need a variety of opportunities to interact with the complex concepts within the app. Autumn thought back to the suggestions for different interactive elements that could be included, such as a drag-and-drop labeling activity, where participants could link the key concepts to the photos taken or the drawings that users made. This would work best for families with prior experiences with pollinators, as the pollination scientists agreed that drawing or labeling important concepts on the photos taken could help families make connections to prior knowledge. Autumn wondered if families that did not have prior experiences with pollinators would also benefit from this activity. She also thought to ask the experts about other possible locations at the Arboretum that may attract pollinators, as she remembered how the wildlife at the pond stop was redirecting families away from the app's pollination observations. Autumn made notes on the previous app design with her tablet, marking textual changes for possible revision, in addition to a small sketch of the wayfinding map redesign to share with the development team (see Figure 5.5).

When advocating for these app changes, Autumn emphasized that photo taking and the locations at which app activities took place helped create opportunities for place-based and

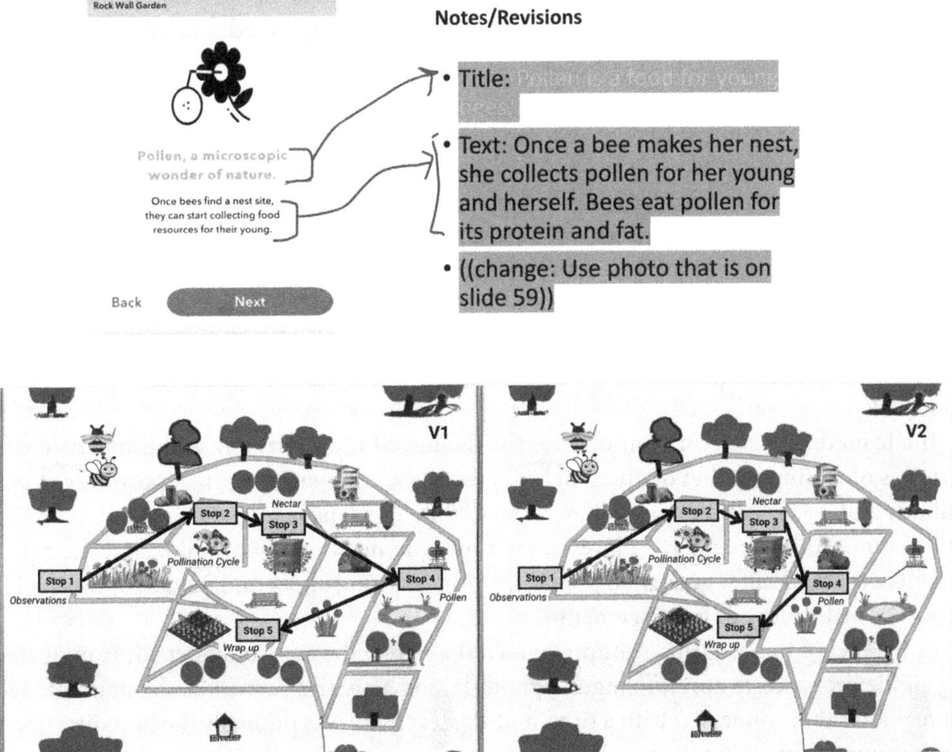

FIGURE 5.5 Notes and suggested revisions for Arboretum Adventurers text (top), stop location and wayfinding map suggested revisions (bottom).

interest-driven learning. Including activities such as these would help meet the foundational goals for both Garden University's Arboretum and the Educational Outreach Office in facilitating interactive learning in outdoor environments. Additionally, these activities would address the learning objectives expected of the stakeholders, as families would engage in scientific observation and create conceptual understanding in connection with their observations at the Garden University Arboretum.

After having spent several months collaborating with her instructional design team and the pollination experts, Autumn was able to schedule a meeting with the app development team during the first week of February. This team had developed the pilot version of *Arboretum Adventurers* and was eager to hear about Autumn's updates. While a prominent part of the team, the developers' work, on projects *other* than Autumn's, was also heavy, often involving multiple assignments from various departments across campus. Luckily, Hillary and Dave, two senior developers within the graphic design and programming team, were able to attend the meeting and see Autumn's presentation.

After Autumn shared some of the initial findings and successes of the pilot app, she began asking questions related to the redesign. Turning to Hillary and Dave, Autumn asked, "Do our recommendations require a lot of new programming and changes on your part? Do you think this can be done easily? We were hoping to have the app ready by early April to meet our deadlines."

Hillary looked up from the revision list Autumn had provided. "Well, you've presented a lot of great ideas. Although I think your timeline may limit what we can do, adding text changes should be easy, but incorporating some of these other revisions into the app by the deadline may be challenging. What do you think, Dave?"

"I agree. Let's discuss the possibility of some of the additional options that you listed here. You were also considering changing the route in which the app guides families through the Arboretum. That might require some serious shuffling of the app's current assets and activities," said Dave.

Autumn took a moment to consider their comments and reflect on a realistic timeline in which these changes could be completed. "Well, along with text changes, I think adding a feature that allows users to take multiple photos and select one for a drag-and-drop activity may be most important. That way users will have an opportunity to view their photos and select one that they wish to engage with further. That could help address some of the key issues the pollination scientists brought up. We can consider changes to the recommended route later."

"I think that would work. Adding in a feature to take multiple photos would certainly be possible within the timeline, as well as possibly adding a drag-and-drop type of interaction," said Dave.

The team deliberated on their options for the rest of the afternoon. Autumn's main concern was providing families of different backgrounds and experiences an opportunity to both connect and learn with the pollination topics while they engaged with Garden University's Arboretum. Both she and Dr. Flores agreed that the needs of each visitor and their prior experiences could differ greatly, so providing more learning opportunities and options might help with mobile learning engagement.

At the end of the meeting, Autumn agreed that while the app could benefit from including all the proposed features, fixing the photo-taking activities to include the option to take more photos that connected with a drag-and-drop activity was probably the best direction to move forward with, given the timeline. A drag-and-drop labeling activity would be a valuable addition in providing the experience that the Arboretum wanted, while making changes to the wayfinding map and rerouting families through their Arboretum activities may have to be completed in the next iteration. "I appreciate your help in getting this all done!" Autumn said as she left the meeting. Autumn shared her notes of possible revisions for the next step of the redesign with the development and research teams. She noted what changes would and would not be possible based on the developers' current resources and timeline. This also helped her consider possible what-if scenarios if road bumps occurred and every change could not be implemented quickly (see Figure 5.6).

PRESENTING THE FINDINGS AND NEW REVISIONS TO STAKEHOLDERS

A month later, the app development team gave Autumn an update on their programming efforts. While they were able to make quick changes to the text and the location of some of the information pages, the development of the drag-and-drop activity was slightly delayed. Although they believed they could finish it before the projected app testing date in April, this was not guaranteed. Updates were also made that allowed users to select a photo to interact with after completing each photo-taking activity, as well as a back button if users needed to revert to previous information pages. However, as expected, changes to the wayfinding map that could guide families on a different path through the Arboretum required more time to complete and would possibly be included in the next development update.

Autumn was pleased to hear of the updates but was nervous about the drag-and-drop component being finished in time. Incorporating a new interactive element into the app meant that families could connect pollination concepts with their observations of pollinators through their photo-capture activities. Additionally, this would incorporate the recommendations by the pollination experts and meet the goals of the Arboretum in providing elements of self-directed science learning for visitors in connection with place-based learning.

With these new updates ready to test, Autumn spent the next weekend at the Arboretum to ensure elements of the new app worked properly. After checking every element and trying

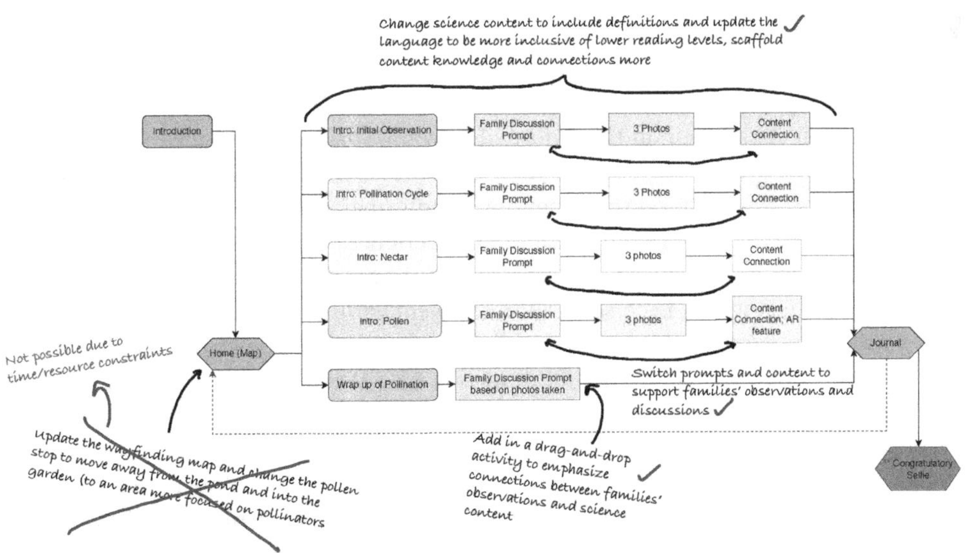

FIGURE 5.6 App development outline and possible updates before discussion with team and consultants and after.

her best to "break the app" during a beta testing phase, Autumn was happy to have completed the *Arboretum Adventurers* activities on several tablets with no issues. She just hoped that the developers could finish the drag-and-drop activity by mid-April, with enough time to beta test it before the next usability tests.

Autumn knew that it would be important to update the Arboretum stakeholders on these updates to the app as well as the timeline for testing the new app onsite. Daisy, the director of the Garden University Arboretum, was Autumn's main point of contact. While Autumn had provided Daisy with updates throughout the year, Daisy was interested in updates to the app that would fulfill Garden University Arboretum's needs to provide outdoor science learning opportunities for visitors. Autumn drafted an email and was able to schedule a meeting with Daisy onsite at the Arboretum at the end of March.

"We're in the process of updating *Arboretum Adventurers* based on family feedback and user interactions from the pilot testing last summer. Many of the families had fun with the app but did have trouble utilizing all aspects of it," said Autumn.

Daisy was happy to hear that the redesign was going smoothly. "That's great! What elements were the most challenging? Were families able to engage with the Arboretum as we discussed? The new flower gardens should allow visitors to see more pollinators this year!"

"They were. Families were very excited to observe the pollinators, flowers, and other aspects of the garden. The Arboretum has a lot that interests families, and the app has helped direct their attention. However, some of the families also had difficulty understanding some of the pollination content, especially connecting it to their real-world observations in the Arboretum. After working with our pollination experts, we consolidated what we wanted families to learn from the app. The development team is working on adding a drag-and-drop activity that works in conjunction with the photo-taking activities, which should help clarify how the science content can be observed at the Arboretum. That activity should, hopefully, be ready in time for our next app testing date," said Autumn.

Daisy nodded, "That's great news, I am looking forward to hearing how the testing goes and the next evolution of the app."

"Thanks, Daisy! I'm looking forward to sharing our findings with you and any future updates to the app," Autumn said.

After the meeting with Daisy, Autumn hoped that all of the app features would work, including the drag-and-drop activities, and wondered if these additions would help families engage with their mobile app in this informal learning space. She reflected, "Well, the app isn't finished yet, but the next round of testing is sure to bring to light how different users and families interact with the app." Designing for informal, outdoor learning environments had brought different challenges than had her experiences with classroom learning. If the changes weren't done on time, Autumn might have to consider new ways to address some of the redesign suggestions. Each suggestion was kept within Autumn's revision document, which was sure to come in handy. Hopefully, the drag-and-drop activity could be added soon, but if not, there were sure to be other ways to help families connect their observations to the content. Autumn wondered, "If we can't add edits to the app, I wonder if we could provide families with picture cards that displayed the science terms and an example image of the term that might connect back to the app content?" There was more design work to be done, and Autumn would continue to reevaluate her notes, observe more families for possible design changes, and work alongside the developers to implement feasible changes within the timeline of the project.

Preliminary Analysis Questions

1. Each year the Arboretum attracts a diverse audience ranging in reading levels, accessibility needs, interests, family dynamics, and prior understanding. What steps could Autumn and her team take to address the needs of this variety of learners?
2. Autumn worked through the first round of formative evaluation feedback from families and provided the stakeholders with her findings. What important details does she bring to the meeting? What information could she provide in future meetings to help the team make decisions for improving the app?
3. Based on the families' experiences with the mobile learning app (*Arboretum Adventurers*), what other strategies could be used to help families engage in place-based learning and make observations of pollinators outdoors in ways that both promote science learning and provide a fun activity for families to do together?
4. Considering the stage of the app after Autumn speaks with the development team, what are some possible next steps for Autumn to formatively evaluate families' uses of the redesigned app? How could this help guide future app redesigns?

Implications for ID Practice

1. How can instructional designers address the diverse needs of a target audience during the design of a mobile app ? Consider the two families presented in this case as you describe the characteristics of an effective process to meet diverse needs.
2. Informal learning may present challenges that differ from formal learning experiences. How might an instructional designer identify these differences and create an effective design for appropriate audiences?
3. It is often impossible to include all of the suggestions and recommendations made to improve the design of a technological solution (e.g., a mobile app). How can instructional designers use the formative evaluation process to assess the effectiveness of newly implemented changes?

6

Maria Martinez

Developing a Virtual Reality Training Program for Autistic Adults to Use Public Transportation

Matthew Schmidt and Noah Glaser

The *Innovative Impact* adult day program for autistic adults buzzed with activity as program associates prepared for their day of vocational training and learning to use public transportation. Among them was Karl Stevens, director of the program and a passionate advocate for providing effective and equitable training for autistic adults. As he made his way through the busy halls, Karl couldn't help but notice the unease and anxiety etched on the faces of some of the program associates. He knew all too well the struggles that came with using public transportation and the barriers it posed for autistic people.

Karl knew that the program associates needed structured, formal training to prepare them for the challenges of using public transportation. He recognized that without proper guidance, navigating the complex world of shuttle systems, shuttle stops, maps, and schedules could be overwhelming and daunting for autistic users. Sensory overload is a significant hurdle. The bustling crowds, loud noises, and unfamiliar environments often trigger anxiety and sometimes sensory meltdowns, making it difficult for autistic individuals to cope with the overwhelming stimuli. Another obstacle was the unpredictable nature of public transportation. Delays, schedule changes, and unexpected disruptions could interrupt routines and create potential distress for autistic individuals, who often rely heavily on predictability and structure to be successful. To be sure, autistic individuals can find adapting to these unexpected circumstances challenging. Further, a range of social aspects, associated with using public transportation, can present additional difficulties. Interacting with drivers, knowing where to sit, and navigating other systems require effective social communication skills and the ability to process information quickly. However, since the program lacked funding and resources to provide formal, structured training, the associates had to rely on ad hoc, on-the-fly instruction with little formal structure. This led to uneven and sometimes ineffective results, and many program associates struggled to navigate the public transportation system provided by the university.

Karl had recently been introduced to Maria Martinez, a seasoned researcher with a PhD in instructional design. Karl had been impressed with her tech-savvy expertise and passion for helping autistic learners. They had discussed the problem of providing more formalized

DOI: 10.4324/9781003354468-7

FIGURE 6.1 Text message conversation between Karl and Maria.

training for using public transportation in the *Innovative Impact* program. The following is a screenshot of their ensuing text message conversation (see Figure 6.1).

Later, Karl received a phone call from Maria. "I completely understand, Karl," said Maria. "It's a complex problem, but I think I have an idea. What if we use virtual reality simulations?"

"Virtual reality?" Karl raised an eyebrow skeptically. "I'm not sure that's feasible for *Innovative Impact*."

"It's more feasible than you might think," Maria replied. "VR can be really effective for potentially dangerous training situations. With VR, we could create a simulation that mimics using public transportation in the real world but without the risks and barriers that your program associates face. It could provide a structured, safe, and repeatable training environment."

Intrigued, Karl responded, "Okay, I'm listening. How would we even begin with something like that?"

Maria smiled, "Let's start by doing some ride-alongs with your program associates. Then we can think about how we can translate those procedures into a VR simulation."

"Wow, sounds pretty cool!" Karl exclaimed. "When do we start?"

"I'm meeting with my team later today," responded Maria, "I'll give you a shout when we know more."

AT A LATER DESIGN MEETING

"Okay, team, we've got a big challenge ahead of us," Maria shared. "As you know, we're looking at designing a virtual reality training program for autistic adults to learn how to use public transportation. The goal is to increase their independence and access to vocational training."

The room buzzed with excitement with this news. While Maria fielded questions and explained the situation, Jonah, the lead designer, asked, "Aren't there potential risks associated with using VR, especially for vulnerable learners? I have read about cybersickness being an issue."

"I agree," said Keith, the lead developer. "My kid has a VR headset at home. I tried it once and it made me feel sick. Like, a lot! We need to find a way to create a learning experience that doesn't make our associates feel sick."

"Exactly," said Maria. "We have a responsibility to mitigate any potential adverse effects while also delivering a training program that meets the needs of autistic adults. Let's put our heads together and come up with a design that achieves both goals."

The team nodded in agreement, ready to tackle the challenge ahead.

CONSIDERING INDIVIDUAL DIFFERENCES

Excited by the possibility of providing an effective, efficient, and safe learning experience for autistic adult learners, the design team got to work scoping the problem.

"Hey, Maria," said Keith, "I was wondering if we could talk a bit more about the audience. I don't want us to overgeneralize and assume everyone on the spectrum is the same."

Maria responded, "That's a great point, Keith. We need to acknowledge the diverse needs of our audience so we can create a truly inclusive training program."

"I agree," Jonah interjected. "So, what exactly do we need to consider?"

"Sure," replied Maria reassuringly. "One of the first things we need to recognize is that autism is a spectrum condition, which means that autistic people can have a wide range of abilities and needs. For example, some autistic people may have challenges with social interaction, while others may have remarkably strong visual and memory abilities." Maria shared a presentation on autistic strengths and challenges with the team (see Figure 6.2).

"That was super helpful," Jonah replied. "So, how do we make sure our training program is accessible to people with so many different needs but also amplifies autistic strengths?"

"Since you brought up the issue of potential adverse effects," Maria replied, "we also need to be mindful of the potential for sensory overload. VR experiences can be quite immersive and visceral, so we need to be careful not to overwhelm our users. Perhaps we can provide options for users to adjust the intensity of the experience?"

"Yeah, we could do that!" exclaimed Jonah. "We could make it so they can adjust the brightness or sound levels . . ." Trailing off, Jonah continued, "It sounds like we have a lot to consider."

"We do," agreed Maria. "By creating a training program that is truly inclusive and accessible, we can help promote independence and success for our users." She paused, "I'd also like to talk to you all about gender considerations in our design."

"What do you mean?" asked Keith.

"Well, autism presents differently in males and females," Maria explained, "and social experiences can be quite different based on gender. We need to be mindful of that and make sure we are designing interventions that are inclusive and appropriate for all."

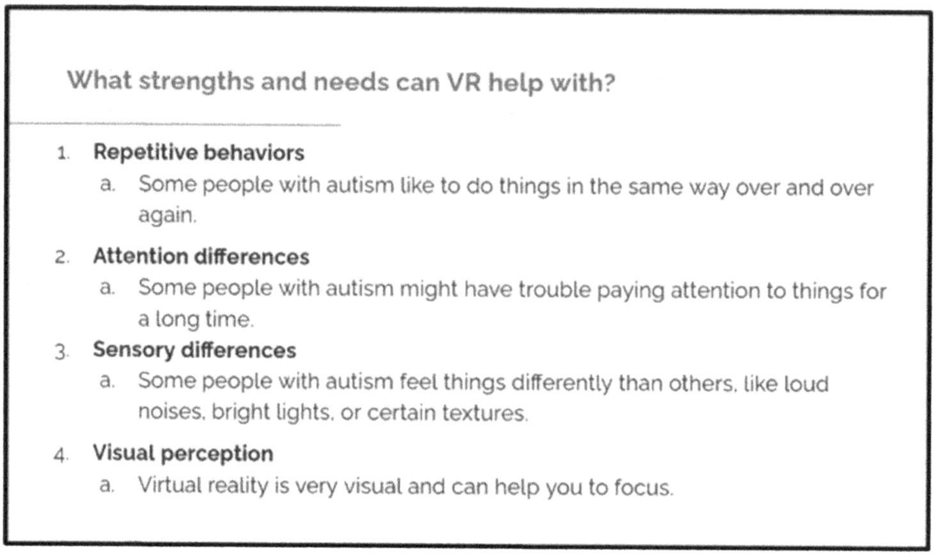

What strengths and needs can VR help with?

1. **Repetitive behaviors**
   a. Some people with autism like to do things in the same way over and over again.
2. **Attention differences**
   a. Some people with autism might have trouble paying attention to things for a long time.
3. **Sensory differences**
   a. Some people with autism feel things differently than others, like loud noises, bright lights, or certain textures.
4. **Visual perception**
   a. Virtual reality is very visual and can help you to focus.

FIGURE 6.2 Slide from Maria's presentation aligning autistic strengths and needs with VR.

"Ah, I see what you mean," Keith nodded. "Yes, that's definitely something we should consider. Do you have any suggestions on how we can approach this?"

"We are fortunate to have a diverse team that includes people with different backgrounds and experiences," Maria replied. "That will be a big help. But we also need to do some research specifically focused on gender and autism and incorporate our findings into our design process."

"That's a great idea," Jonah responded. "It sounds like one of our goals will be to create an experience that is truly helpful and effective for everyone in our target audience."

"Exactly," Maria responded, "and we also need to be mindful of the language we use and the imagery we include in our interventions. We don't want to perpetuate harmful stereotypes or assumptions about gender and autism."

"Thank you for explaining that, Maria," Keith replied. "It's an important aspect of our work that we need to make sure we are addressing. But I have another question. You keep referring to the *Innovative Impact* associates as 'autistic adults,' but my girlfriend says that the correct term is 'adults with autism spectrum disorder.' Are we using the wrong term?"

"That's a good question, Keith," Maria responded. "We need to ensure that our language reflects and respects inclusivity. When I refer to someone on the spectrum as an autistic person, that's what is known as 'identity-first' language. When your girlfriend refers to them as a person with autism spectrum disorder, that's what is known as 'person-first' language."

"Yeah," Keith replied, "that's what my girlfriend was saying. She said person-first is meant to acknowledge the individual as a unique person first, and then recognize their autism as, like, a part of their identity. So why don't we do this?"

"There is some debate about this," explained Maria, "but the research suggests that autistic people tend to prefer identity-first language. My inclination is to defer to how autistic people prefer to be referred to, but there is no universal 'right answer' to this question. Ultimately, the point is to make sure that we are treating everyone with respect and dignity."

"That's cool and all," Keith replied, "but at the end of the day, I just need to know what language to include in our simulation."

"I understand," Maria said. "To your point, we really just need to show that we respect individual preferences. As a team, we need to remain open and responsive to the preferences expressed by the individuals we are designing for.

"Keith, it seems straightforward to me," Jonah said. "It's more about being flexible and adaptable in our language to accommodate diverse perspectives among the autistic community. It's less about the words themselves and more about respect."

"That's solid," says Keith. "I can get behind respecting our users, for sure."

"Excellent!" Maria exclaimed. "Our goal is to create an inclusive environment that values and respects the voices of autistic adults. By using identity-first language as a default and being open to person-first language when preferred, we can demonstrate our commitment to inclusivity."

TROUBLES ARISE IN THE DESIGN PROCESS

Three months later, the design team huddled around a table in the conference room, surrounded by whiteboards, half-empty C4 energy drinks, and Post-it notes.

Keith scratched his head in frustration. "How are we supposed to create a VR training environment for autistic users when there's no guidance on how to do so?"

Maria nodded in agreement. "That's the million-dollar question, Keith. We haven't been very successful at finding any guidance in the academic literature."

Keith responded, "Well, we can't just wing it and hope for the best. The *Innovative Impact* director, Karl, keeps telling me that we need to involve autistic users in the design process and make sure we're getting their input and feedback every step of the way." He continued, "And we need to keep in mind the limited budgets and tight timelines we're working with. We have months, not years, to develop this thing. We need to find a way to make this work within our constraints."

The team sat in silence for a moment, contemplating the challenge before them.

"Well . . . based on the results of our procedural task analysis," Maria considered, tapping her pen against her notebook, "we have a really solid outline of every step of the process for using the university shuttle, and so far, it's provided a workable roadmap for the VR simulation. But, Jonah, I understand you're concerned about some roadblocks, right?"

"To put it mildly," Jonah replied, "we know that for autistic users, we need to make scenarios in our virtual environment very similar to the real world, right? So, we want to create a sim that allows users to practice in a way that is as close to the real world as possible."

"Yes, that's right," responded Maria. "We want to be able to address the tendency toward concrete thinking of many autistic people."

"I get that, and that's what we're trying to do with the bus model. So, after users have completed the previous training steps, we need to make the bus model arrive on a set schedule, just like a real bus would do. But here's the catch—the virtual world toolkit we have been using for this, *FidelityForge*, is still in alpha. Its documentation and standards are barely usable. We can't reliably animate objects. I've been trying to get the bus model to arrive based on a schedule, but it keeps breaking. Honestly, it's kind of a mess."

Looking up from his phone with a concerned expression on his face, Keith casted his phone screen to the large projector, "Um, it might be worse than that. Check this out." As Keith scrolled through a screen announcing that *FidelityForge* had decided to cease development and discontinue the software, the team looked on in disbelief.

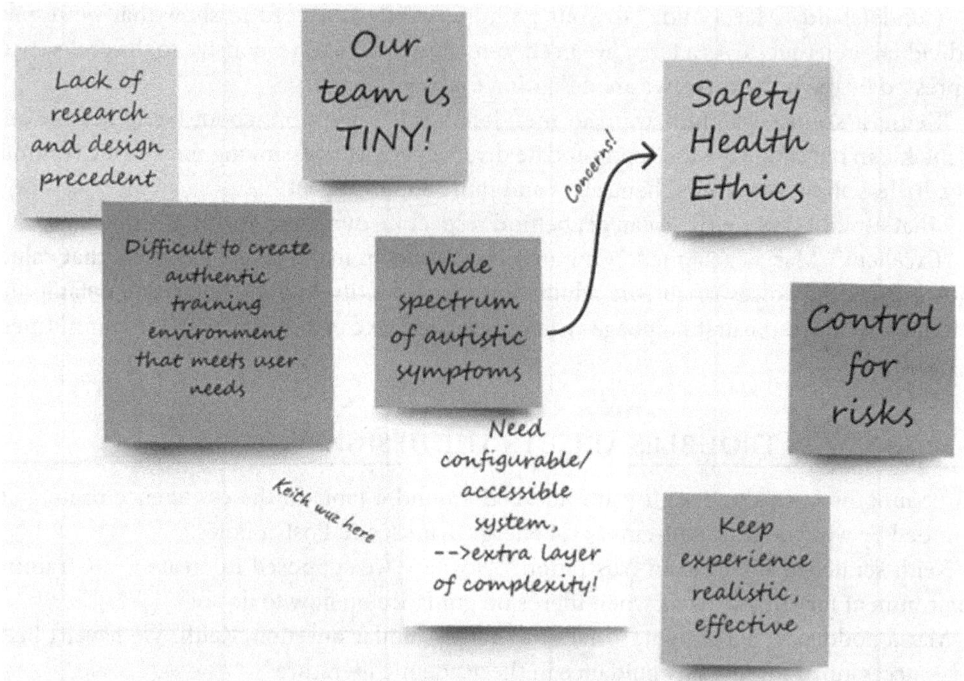

FIGURE 6.3 Whiteboard with sticky notes capturing project challenges.

Jonah, visibly affected by this development, exclaimed, "I can't believe this! We were finally starting to make some progress with *FidelityForge*. Now we're gonna have to start from scratch, and we're already behind schedule." A despondent mood settled on the design team.

"Not to be a bad news bear, but there's more," Keith piped up after a few minutes of discomfort. "Remember how I mentioned Karl's concerns about how we might not be doing enough to make the simulation accessible and inclusive for autistic learners? I kind of underplayed that. He's pretty unhappy that we haven't been including *Innovative Impact* program associates in our design process. Like, really unhappy."

Jonah chimed in, "This might be a serious missed opportunity. If we haven't included autistic people in our design process then how can we say we are a learner-centered design shop? We haven't even spoken to our learners once."

"Yikes on bikes!" Maria responded. "These are super valid points. To be fair, I'm not sure we could have avoided any of these challenges. We've stretched ourselves to the limit and we've been moving as fast as we can. But that doesn't mean we don't have to deal with these challenges. Let's take a moment and try to lay out all of these issues."

Heading to the whiteboard, Maria started sketching out her ideas, intermittently asking for input from the team. As the myriad of challenges come together, the design team started to wonder if they had bitten off more than they could chew. Maria stepped back from the whiteboard and read the Post-it notes to the team (see Figure 6.3).

ANOTHER MEETING WITH THE INNOVATIVE IMPACT DIRECTOR, KARL STEVENS

Karl Stevens listened attentively as the design team laid out their concerns and challenges. After a moment of thoughtful silence, he leaned forward and spoke up.

"You know, these issues you've brought up are indeed complex and not easily solvable. But perhaps we can view them as opportunities rather than roadblocks," Karl suggested, his voice filled with a mix of curiosity and determination. "While I may not have expertise in all these areas, one thing that I feel strongly about is involving autistic users from the *Innovative Impact* program directly in the design process, and it's my job to advocate that you do so."

Maria nodded. "That's a valid point, and we agree it is a crucial step forward, Karl. Although we have done some usability studies with the associates, we haven't meaningfully included them in our design process so far. We want to change this. Users' firsthand insights and experiences will be invaluable in shaping the training environment. We need to hear their voices and involve them throughout. Perhaps this is an opportunity for a reboot."

Jonah leaned back in his chair; his expression was contemplative. "It's true that we can't rely solely on VR best practices or what researchers say about what autistic users need. How many of those researchers are autistic? And so much of the research is vague and even contradictory!"

"The literature is not the most helpful," Maria responded. "And, you're right, Johan. From what I can tell, none of the researchers were autistic."

"Yeah, no," Jonah said, "we have to engage with our users directly. You know, co-create the solution together. We need to ensure that the training isn't just accessible. It's got to genuinely address the perspectives and challenges that our users experience."

Keith chimed in, a glimmer of hope in his eyes, "Solid! But we are going to have to step out of our comfort zones. You know, like reaching out to autism communities or centers or whatever they're called. Advocacy groups, too. Maybe we can do interviews or focus groups, so we can learn how to adapt our approach based on their feedback. Probably won't be easy, but I'm stoked!"

Maria responded, "I don't want to be negative, but if we're going to go this route, we need to start thinking about how we can balance involving autistic users with our limited resources and tight timelines. Our funding and timeline are already stretched thin. We need to bear this in mind as we consider how to do justice to user needs and ensure a quality outcome."

Karl leaned forward. "That's fair. We need to find that balance. I will reach out to a small group of autistic users from *Innovative Impact*. I have three or four people in mind already. I could even set up a regular meeting every week to gather feedback. It's possible to incorporate it into their daily schedules, as well. I understand it's not a perfect representation, but I would support this as a step in the right direction."

Keith nodded. "Yeah, that's super solid! Maybe as we make progress, we could, like, involve even more autistic users. That would let us expand the platform, and maybe do virtual focus groups . . . We could use collaborative tools to do remote studies . . . So many opportunities for activities!"

"Whoa, slow down there, Keith," Maria laughed. "We need to make sure we don't compromise our timeline. There are only so many of us." Looking at her teammates with a sense of cautious optimism in her eyes, she continued, "That said, maybe involving autistic users could help us address many of the challenges we face."

As the team left the conference room, a renewed sense of purpose filled the air.

KEITH CATCHES A LUCKY BREAK!

Maria opened her email to the following message (see Figure 6.4).

Exciting News and a Little Dilemma

Retention: Inbox (3 years) Expires: Sun 6/21/2026 11:40 AM

Johnson, Keith

To: Martinez, Maria <maria.martinez@university.edu>

Thu 6/22/2023 11:40 AM

Hi Maria,
I wanted to share something cool with you. Remember that side project I've been working on with the engineering folks? Well, we've come up with a software using 360 video for virtual campus tours. And guess what? I think we can use it to tackle the FidelityForge predicament! At least part of it.

Since FidelityForge is going away, I had this idea to offer our 360 video software to the team for free. It adds a whole new layer to our training by using video modeling techniques. It's like next-level stuff, and I can't help but get excited about the possibilities.

Picture this: combining our VR simulation with immersive video-based training. It could be a game-changer for teaching public transportation skills to the Innovative Impact associates. I mean, how awesome would that be?

Also, about involving the autistic community more in our design process - if we go with this 360 video tool, I think it's more important than ever. The user insights and experiences are super important to create a top-notch training sim, so we gotta listen and learn from them, IMO

Can you help with scheduling a team meeting? I've got a few ideas up my sleeve, but I want everyone's input on this. Looking forward to chatting about this. Shoot me an email or give me a call when you're free. Can't wait to hear your thoughts!

Thanks,

Keith Johnson

"Don't believe everything you read on the Internet just because there's a picture with a quote next to it." - Abraham Lincoln (2021).

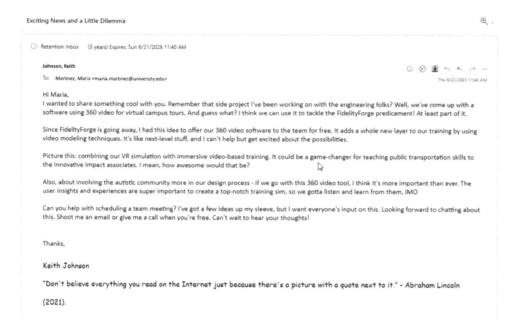

FIGURE 6.4 Email from Keith Johnson to Maria Martinez about the possibility of using a new tool in the project.

ADDRESSING THE LINGERING ISSUES

Keith, Jonah, and Maria gathered in the lab, ready to tackle the pressing decision ahead of them. The team had explored two primary options to address the problem of *FidelityForge* no longer being available. First, they had considered finding a common, off-the-shelf VR solution. Second, they had considered using a VR development environment such as *Unity* or *Unreal Engine*. However, none seemed satisfactory. They knew they needed a fresh approach.

Keith spoke up first, voicing his concerns. "I've been looking into off-the-shelf VR solutions; they are all kind of garbage. If we are going to create an awesome environment for autistic users, that's going to require customization. None of these pre-packaged tools provide that."

Jonah nodded in agreement, adding, "I've also been researching VR development environments like *Unity* and *Unreal Engine*. They offer more control, but they come with their own set of challenges. We would need to invest time and effort to master the tools, and we can't afford to overlook the long-term support and compatibility aspects. That said, I'm nearly done with the getting started tutorials."

Maria chimed in, her brow furrowed with thought, "It's a tough decision. Off-the-shelf solutions might save us time, but they could compromise the quality and customization we need. Plus, they might just go away! On the other hand, diving into VR development environments will require significant resources and learning curves."

Keith looked at his teammates, his eyes reflecting a newfound determination. "I think we need to approach this differently. We can't settle for a one-size-fits-all solution. What if we take an agile development approach? I've been reading about this CHUDS framework that emphasizes collaboration, iteration, and flexibility. It could be just what we need."

Maria asked, "What is the CHUDS framework?"

Home - Design - The CHUDS Design Framework

CHUDS Framework

- **Contextual:** The first pillar of the CHUDS framework emphasizes the importance of understanding the context in which a design solution will exist. Every design has unique challenges, be it cultural, environmental, or technological. By comprehending the context thoroughly, designers can tailor their solutions to align with the specific requirements and constraints of the situation.
- **Human-centered:** At the heart of the CHUDS framework lies the user. Design solutions must prioritize the needs, behaviors, and preferences of the target audience. Conducting user research, gathering insights, and empathizing with users allows designers to create experiences that genuinely resonate. By placing users at the forefront, designers can craft solutions that make a meaningful impact in their lives.
- **Usable:** Usability is a critical aspect of any design solution. It focuses on making interfaces, products, and experiences intuitive and easy to use. A usable design ensures that users can accomplish their goals efficiently, without unnecessary confusion or frustration. By employing user-centric design principles and conducting usability testing, designers can continually refine and improve the usability of their solutions.
- **Delightful:** Design has the power to evoke emotions and create lasting impressions. The delightful aspect of the CHUDS framework emphasizes the importance of crafting experiences that go beyond functionality. By incorporating aesthetics, visual appeal, and elements of surprise and joy, designers can create solutions that leave a memorable and positive impact on users.
- **Sustainable:** In today's world, sustainability is a pressing concern. Designers have a responsibility to consider the long-term impact of their creations on the environment, society, and economy. The sustainable principle of CHUDS encourages designers to incorporate eco-friendly materials, energy-efficient components, and promote responsible consumption. By prioritizing sustainability, designers can contribute to a more balanced and resilient future.

FIGURE 6.5 Webpage with overview of the CHUDS framework.

"Oh, you don't know?" Keith responded. "It's an agile software development approach that stands for 'contextual, human-centered, usable, delightful, and sustainable.' It's specifically for immersive learning. Some guy named Noah Glaser invented it. I saw him present it at the *VR Learning Nerd* conference. Seemed like a pretty productive approach. Here's a link to his website."

Maria entered the URL and casted her phone screen to the projector (see Figure 6.5).

Jonah nodded slowly. "I have heard of this CHUDS you speak of, and I agree. CHUDS could help us adapt to the challenges we're facing. We can prioritize the critical features and functionalities while cutting down on unnecessary bells and whistles. Hmm. CHUDS is one way we might be able to stay focused and deliver something that matters and is sustainable."

Maria added, "I really like CHUDS! Agile is a solid idea, too. But we still need to make informed decisions moving forward, and the key decision right now is whether we use an off-the-shelf software tool or create our own VR experience."

EPILOGUE

With their collective agreement, the trio embarked on a hands-on examination of the available software options. They wanted to experience the process firsthand and assess any potential issues or limitations. Keith, Jonah, and Maria dove into the realm of *Unity*, testing the importing of their existing digital assets.

As they explored, they stumbled upon a treasure trove of *Unity* plugins. These tools aligned with their needs for rapid prototyping and offered features like easy avatar development, bus animations, multiplayer networking, and non-playable character control. Excitement filled the room as they realized the potential these plugins held.

Their exploration proved invaluable, providing them with insights and a foundation for their ultimate decision. The team now had a clearer vision of how they might navigate the challenges ahead, armed with an agile mindset and on their way to selecting the right tools for the job.

Preliminary Analysis Questions

1. In what ways did the lack of existing research or design precedent for autistic adults impact the design team's decision-making process? How did they address this challenge?
2. The design team faced a range of challenges around using an emerging technology with a vulnerable population, including health, safety, ethics, etc. How did they mitigate these challenges? What additional steps could they have taken to ensure the safety and well-being of their users?
3. The design team recognized the need to create a configurable and accessible system to accommodate the wide spectrum of how autistic symptoms present. What design strategies did they use? How effective were these strategies in meeting the needs of their target audience? What other strategies might have been employed to ensure the success of their VR intervention?

Implications for ID Practice

1. How can an instructional designer ensure ethical considerations are taken into account when designing for individual differences, such as disabilities or cultural backgrounds?
2. What ethical considerations should an instructional designer consider when designing interventions for autistic people?
3. What steps can instructional designers take to ensure their interventions do not perpetuate harmful stereotypes or biases toward certain individuals or groups, such as those based on gender, race, disability, etc.?
4. How can an instructional designer approach designing interventions that consider the unique needs and preferences of individual learners, while also ensuring the interventions are effective, efficient, and appealing?
5. How can instructional designers navigate the challenges of choosing between off-the-shelf solutions and custom solutions when utilizing emerging technologies?

Part II

Post-Secondary

7

Lucas Bailey and Ellie Miller

Addressing Low Pass Rates Among Student Pilots

Woei Hung and Lewis R. J. Archer

The chair of the Aviation Department at Western Plains University, Lucas Bailey, was in his early 30s and had established a solid record as a young professional. Although he was in his first year as department chair, he was previously employed as a commercial airline pilot for a few years, joining the department ten years previously as a flight instructor.

MONDAY, 8:10 A.M.

As he sat in his office, Lucas looked out the window contemplating the weather. "Finally, the sun is out! The students and instructors should be able to get a lot of flying done today!" he thought before turning on his computer to start his day. Upon opening his email client, an email with a red "!" and the subject line "Concern with First-Attempt Pass Rates" caught his attention. "Oh no," he thought to himself, "this doesn't look good. How bad is it?" He took a deep breath and clicked on the email (see Figure 7.1).

After reading Joel's email, Lucas pondered how to tackle this problem. He mumbled, "Well, I kind of knew this was coming, but I didn't expect it this soon." He logged into the assessment system and started to pull out the private pilot end-of-course test data to see if he could find any clues that might suggest what the problem was. While he was completely immersed in the data, Dillon Jefferson popped his head into Lucas's office. "Hey, did you hear that Mark is leaving for SuperJet?"

Shifting from his work, Lucas sighed, "What? No! Not another one. We have lost so many flight instructors over the past two years—just as air travel has finally recovered from COVID. Industry pay is just too good for us to compete with."

Dillon continued the conversation as he walked into Lucas's office and took a seat across his desk, "Yeah, I heard that they also give their new hires accelerated career advancement opportunities and sign-on bonuses. Who wouldn't want that? Even pilots, who I would be hesitant to hire, have all landed jobs. These airlines are really pushing their hiring standards to the lowest legal levels, which is pretty scary."

Lucas looked frustrated and sighed. "Yeah, I know, but market dictates standards, right? I heard that some airlines are even exploring options to maneuver around the legal

DOI: 10.4324/9781003354468-9

From: O'Brien, Joel
Sent: Friday, March 17 4:55 P.M.
To: Bailey, Lucas
Subject: Concern with First-Attempt Pass Rates

Reply | Reply All | Forward | ...

Good morning, Lucas-

Today, I checked the first-attempt pass rates for our private pilot end-of-course tests. I see that the pass rate for the oral portion of the assessment is 91.3%, whereas the flight portion is only 80.7%.

You may not know this, since this is your first year as department chair, but it is imperative that students score at or above 90% to ensure our ability to retain examining authority. Without it, our students would need to pay additional money to conduct an external checkride with a designated examiner to earn their Private Pilot certificate, as opposed to them doing their end-of-course test with one of our own check instructors. We both know that the FAA does not have the resources to conduct the amount of checkrides that would be required for our students, which means our students would be subject to significant training delays if we lost examining authority.

Could you please analyze the situation and come to me with some suggestions on how we can improve our pass rate?

Joel O'Brien
Dean, School of Aerospace Sciences
Western Plains University

FIGURE 7.1 Email from Joel O'Brien to Lucas Bailey.

experience minimums, and plus, the demand for pilots means a lot more students for us as well . . . It's a good career opportunity and quick return-on-investment. Having too many students is a good problem to have, but not having enough instructors to meet the demand is *not*."

Dillon replied, laughing, "It's easy for the industry to dump the problem on us, right?"

Lucas's frustration was turning to anger. "Now that we are having a hard time maintaining a sufficient number of flight instructors, we actually have had to lower our own hiring standards *and* accommodate rapid advancement opportunities in order to retain them."

Dillon shifted his eyes, nodding toward the hallway, and said, "Is that why I am seeing a lot of young faces walking around the building nowadays?"

Lucas nodded in agreement. "Yeah, these young flight instructors who were hired during this recent hiring boom now account for approximately 90% of our entire flight instructor workforce in the department, and yes, you are right—they are, on average, 21 years old. The youngest instructors are only 19 years old."

Dillon was surprised by what he heard. "Huh, then how many flight hours do they have I wonder?"

"Well, most have between 300–500 hours, which is significantly lower than the 800–1,000 hours the senior flight instructors in the department have. Besides the number of flight hours, their overall proficiency and professionalism seem subpar. Some of them required additional training during the onboarding process. Others have posted some questionable things on social media recently. I had to talk to one instructor last week who was texting on his phone during a flight lesson," Lucas stated bitterly.

"Gee, no wonder I've heard some complaints from the students too," Dillon said with realization.

Lucas responded swiftly, "Oh? Like what?"

Dillon didn't think that it was his position to tattle on other instructors. "Well, I don't like to gossip, but you can ask some of the students. Got to run. I am late for a meeting!"

After Dillon left, Lucas slowly refocused his attention on the end-of-course test data that he had been working on. "Hmmm, that's interesting," he pondered. "I wonder if there is a connection between students' low passing rates and the different flight instructors. But, where should I begin? Oh, yeah, Ellie! She'd be the perfect person for me to consult with. Okay, let me see if I can reach her."

ELLIE'S OFFICE

Ellie Miller, in her 50s, was a senior instructional consultant at the Center for Teaching Excellence (CTE) and a part-time instructor for the Instructional Design and Technology program at the university. She had more than 25 years of instructional design consulting experience with instructors at the university as well as private companies. Having just finished a virtual meeting with a biology professor wanting to redesign her undergraduate class using team-based learning, Ellie was preparing to take a 5-minute break and grab her third cup of coffee of the day, when the phone in her office rang.

"Hello, this is Ellie Miller at the Center for Teaching Excellence. How may I help you?" Ellie spoke into the receiver.

A voice answered. "Hey, Ellie, this is Lucas, your old friend over in Aviation!"

"Hi, Lucas, great to hear from you. How have you been?" Ellie responded.

"Well, things are going well. I am the department chair now. It's been busy, but I am learning a lot, which is great. How about you?" Lucas replied jovially.

"It's been great. The university finally recognized the importance of helping instructors improve their teaching skills and use best practices to design their instruction. So, we are in the process of expanding our office to provide better services to the campus."

"Wow! That sounds exciting! This is good timing for my phone call actually! So, I have a favor to ask," Lucas continued tentatively. "You know how our aviation students have to take a final test to get their pilot certificates, right? Well, the passing rate has been dropping, and the dean is concerned. Do you think you can help us figure out what the problem might be and strategize how we might boost the passing rate?"

Ellie paused. "Hmmm, this doesn't sound good. I don't think we can solve this problem over the phone. Why don't we set up a time to discuss this in more detail?"

Excited, Lucas said, "Sure, that would be great! How about next Tuesday at 2:30 p.m. in my office?"

"That's fine," Ellie replied. "In the meantime, could you send me all the final assessment scores and the assessment protocol so I'll have a better idea what you are referring to?"

"Will do!" Lucas hung up the phone, breathing a sigh of relief (see Table 7.1).

TABLE 7.1
Examiner Data and Profiles (Past 5 Years).

Student Name	*Knowledge Test (First)*	*Knowledge Test (Second)*	*Block 1 Stage Check*	*Examiner*	*Block 2 Stage Check*	*Examiner*	*End-of-Course Test*	*Examiner*
Amanda Castaneda	82%		Satisfactory	Jeremiah Jones	Satisfactory	Dillon Jefferson	Satisfactory	Jeremiah Jones
Annie Santiago	99%		Satisfactory	Robert Pierre	Satisfactory	Phyllis Francisco	Satisfactory	Amelia Carpenter
Corinne Grant	78%		Satisfactory	Jeremiah Jones	Satisfactory	Juliette Andrews	Unsatisfactory	Harrison McDonald
Jenny Potter	82%		Satisfactory	Robert Pierre	Satisfactory	Nicholas Archibald	Satisfactory	Will Anderson
Stacy Downs	96%		Satisfactory	Robert Pierre	Satisfactory	Dillon Jefferson	Satisfactory	Will Anderson
Marina Hutchinson	89%		Satisfactory	Robert Pierre	Satisfactory	Juliette Andrews	Satisfactory	Ashley Williams
Jayne Mckinney	90%		Satisfactory	Juliette Andrews	Satisfactory	Ashley Williams	Satisfactory	Robert Pierre
Sadie Mcdonald	74%		Satisfactory	Juliette Andrews	Satisfactory	Robert Pierre	Unsatisfactory	Amelia Carpenter
Goldie York	92%		Satisfactory	Jeremiah Jones	Satisfactory	Will Anderson	Satisfactory	Ashley Williams
Kaye Cordova	S4%		Satisfactory	Dillon Jefferson	Unsatisfactory	Phyllis Francisco	Satisfactory	Jeremiah Jones
Veronica Guerrero	83%		Satisfactory	Phyllis Francisco	Unsatisfactory	Alexander Barker	Satisfactory	Dillon Jefferson
Flossie Lara	82%		Satisfactory	Robert Pierre	Satisfactory	Amelia Carpenter	Satisfactory	Alexander Barker
Claire Norman	85%		Satisfactory	Robert Pierre	Unsatisfactory	Raymond Johnson	Unsatisfactory	Alexander Barker
Estella Barton	96%		Satisfactory	Dillon Jefferson	Unsatisfactory	Amelia Carpenter	Satisfactory	Nicholas Archibald
Crystal Olsen	83%		Satisfactory	Phyllis Francisco	Satisfactory	Nicholas Archibald	Unsatisfactory	Amelia Carpenter
Mallory Avila	88%		Satisfactory	Ashley Williams	Unsatisfactory	Amelia Carpenter	Satisfactory	Dillon Jefferson
Mattie Sosa	63%	92%	Satisfactory	Amelia Carpenter	Satisfactory	Robert Pierre	Unsatisfactory	Raymond Johnson
Adela Knapp	81%		Satisfactory	Ashley Williams	Unsatisfactory	Harrison McDonald	Satisfactory	Will Anderson
Norma Wagner	87%		Satisfactory	Jeremiah Jones	Unsatisfactory	Juliette Andrews	Satisfactory	Nichole Archibald
Sheree West	76%		Satisfactory	Amelia Carpenter	Satisfactory	Ashley Williams	Satisfactory	Juliette Andrews
Natalie Maldonado	60%	89%	Satisfactory	Robert Pierre	Unsatisfactory	Harrison McDonald	Unsatisfactory	Will Anderson
Kimberly Pena	95%		Satisfactory	Alexander Barker	Unsatisfactory	Raymond Johnson	Satisfactory	Dillon Jefferson
Tonia Meza	86%		Satisfactory	Alexander Barker	Unsatisfactory	Raymond Johnson	Satisfactory	Dillon Jefferson

Nikki Pace	87%		Satisfactory	Jeremiah Jones	Unsatisfactory	Harrison McDonald	Satisfactory	Phyllis Francisco
Trisha Proctor	64%		Satisfactory	Amelia Carpenter	Satisfactory	Dillon Jefferson	Unsatisfactory	Harrison McDonald
Concepcion Ritter	62%	94%	Unsatisfactory	Raymond Johnson	Unsatisfactory	Harrison McDonald	Satisfactory	Nicholas Archibald
Charmaine Diaz	70%		Satisfactory	Robert Pierre	Satisfactory	Robert Pierre	Unsatisfactory	Amelia Carpenter
Rosalyn Nichols	92%		Satisfactory	Juliette Andrews	Satisfactory	Will Anderson	Satisfactory	Phyllis Francisco
Aileen Cross	83%		Satisfactory	Jeremiah Jones	Unsatisfactory	Amelia Carpenter	Satisfactory	Alexander Barker
Susanne Kim	93%		Satisfactory	Jeremiah Jones	Satisfactory	Alexander Barker	Unsatisfactory	Harrison McDonald

Note: Minimum passing score for Knowledge test is 70%. The student can have as many retakes as they wish to get to that threshold.
Block 3 (end of course) in combination with a passing score on the knowledge test determines issuance of the certificate.

TUESDAY, 2:30 P.M.

In his office, Lucas was waiting for Ellie to arrive for their meeting. Ellie appeared at the door of Lucas's office right on time. Lucas raised his head and saw Ellie. "Hey, Ellie, c'mon in! Thanks for helping me out with this. I really appreciate it!"

As she pulled a chair out and sat down across the desk from Lucas, Ellie replied, "No problem, I am glad to help. So, let's get to it. First of all, could you fill me in with a little background as to how this final assessment works?"

Lucas gave Ellie a quick overview of the assessment protocol. To be certified as pilots, the students are required to pass a series of formal assessments by the end of each training course. For example, in the Private Pilot course, the students must pass a knowledge test, two-stage (progress) checks, and an end-of-course test. These are based on standards defined by the Federal Aviation Administration (FAA). A pilot applicant must successfully complete the knowledge test and end-of-course test to be certified. The knowledge test is a traditional multiple-choice written examination, while the stage checks and end-of-course test include both an oral exam and flight examination, utilizing human raters who are called examiners.

Ellie pondered Lucas's brief explanation of the final assessment, then slowly replied, "I've looked at the assessment protocol that you sent, but it's kind of vague. So, I am still not quite sure I fully understand it. Can you explain how the examiners conduct the stage checks and end-of-course test?"

Lucas quickly responded, "These assessments are conducted in a one-on-one environment. The examiner serves as the rater of a pilot applicant's performance on both the oral and flight examination. The examiner will score them as either satisfactory or unsatisfactory but is required to utilize a set of established standards to guide this decision, called the FAA airman certification standards, or ACS for short."

Ellie followed up on Lucas's response and asked, "OK, so, your students will be taking these assessments with someone from the FAA? Do the examiners work for the FAA?"

Lucas replied, "No. Actually, our aviation program is certified by the FAA as a 14 CFR Part 141 institution, which means we are authorized to provide structured flight training, administer the formal assessments, and recommend issuance of pilot certificates and ratings without requiring students to complete an FAA-administered assessment. However, to keep this privilege, the program has to maintain a 90% overall first-attempt passing rate on our end-of-course test. So, if this rate falls under this threshold, we could lose the privilege of examining authority, which will not only cause significant training delays for our students, but also damage the school's reputation, and even worse, lead to the loss of students."

Hearing Lucas's further explanation about Part 141, Ellie understood the concerns of the department: "I see. No wonder this concerns the dean. So, who are the examiners administering the end-of-course tests in your program?"

Lucas felt slightly frustrated and couldn't hide it from his tone. "Previously, we used our most experienced flight instructors as our examiners. The problem is, we have lost so many of our experienced instructors to the airlines recently, that now we must rely more on our younger, less experienced instructors."

Ellie followed up on Lucas's response immediately. "What kind of training do they receive to be an examiner?"

Lucas pursed his lips. "The FAA requires that examiners be trained but doesn't require anything specific. There are no FAA regulatory requirements to maintain a minimum level of reliability, nor is there any minimum regulatory structure or content that must be provided in an examiner training program. The training on how to use the assessment checklists is simply a matter of the examiners who have done it before telling the new examiners how to use the checklists based on their own experiences."

Ellie leaned forward a bit when she asked, "Did you say checklist? Is that what the examiners use to assess the students? Do the examiners also use rubrics or any other types of instruments?"

"Well, the FAA does not have standardized assessment instruments, so we created checklists based on the FAA airman certification standards. But no, we don't have rubrics" (see Figure 7.2).

At this point, Ellie thought she might have a lead that could prove productive, "Huh, I see. Okay, have the ratings been pretty consistent across the examiners?"

Grade	Tasks
0 U M S X	FAA Aviation English Language Standard (AELS)
0 U M S X	Preflight Assessment
0 U M S X	Flight Deck Management
0 U M S X	Engine Starting
0 U M S X	Taxiing
0 U M S X	Before Takeoff Check
0 U M S X	Communications, Light Signals, and Runway Lighting Systems
0 U M S X	Traffic Patterns
0 U M S X	Normal Takeoff & Climb
0 U M S X	Soft-Field Take-Off & Climb
0 U M S X	Short-Field Take-Off and Maximum Performance Climb
0 U M S X	Steep Turns
0 U M S X	Ground Reference Maneuver
0 U M S X	Pilotage & Dead Reckoning
0 U M S X	Navigation Systems & Radar Services
0 U M S X	Diversion
0 U M S X	Lost Procedure
0 U M S X	Maneuvering During Slow Flight
0 U M S X	Power-Off Stall
0 U M S X	Power-On Stall
0 U M S X	Basic Instrument Flight Maneuvers
0 U M S X	Recovery from Unusual Flight Attitudes
0 U M S X	Emergency Descent
0 U M S X	Emergency Approach and Landing - Off Airport
0 U M S X	Systems & Equipment Malfunctions
0 U M S X	Emergency Equipment & Survival Gear
0 U M S X	Slip to Landing
0 U M S X	Go-Around/Rejected Landing
0 U M S X	Normal Approach & Landing
0 U M S X	Soft-Field Approach & Landing
0 U M S X	Short-Field Approach & Landing
0 U M S X	After Landing, Parking, and Securing

Grade Legend:

0 Not attempted
U Unsatisfactory
M Marginal
S Satisfactory

FIGURE 7.2 Email from Lucas Bailey to Ellie Miller.

"Well, actually, there have been some complaints from the students that the stage checks and end-of-course tests are too subjective."

Ellie quickly jumped on this clue and asked, "Can I see the profiles of these examiners and their ratings of students' end-of-course assessments in the past five years?"

Lucas replied, "Sure!" Lucas pulled up the files of the examiners and turned the screen toward Ellie. "Here they are" (see Table 7.2 and Table 7.3).

Ellie carefully examined the profiles and data on Lucas's screen, then turned on her own laptop and opened the student scores file that Lucas had sent. She compared the data between Lucas's screen and her laptop for a while, then turned to Lucas.

"Hmmm . . . interesting . . . The examiner's data and profiles kind of confirm my suspicion that the examiners might have played a role in this issue. When I was first examining the student scores, I kind of noticed that the satisfactory and unsatisfactory scores seemed poorly correlated to students' knowledge test scores but better associated with certain examiners. Look, if we divide the students' ratings into 'satisfactory' and 'unsatisfactory' groups, you can see that different examiners tend to be associated with certain groups. Not all the examiners show this tendency, but the numbers are noticeable. And now the examiners' data and profiles confirm my suspicion."

TABLE 7.2
Flight Instructor Demographics.

Evaluator	*Age*	*Flight Experience (Hours)*	*Employment (Years)*	*Pass Rate*
Amelia Carpenter	24	425	2.6	73.30%
Will Anderson	21	478	1.2	88.90%
Ashley Williams	21	421	1.2	92.10%
Robert Pierre	21	408	1.2	100.00%
Jeremiah Jones	22	368	0.6	98.80%
Dillon Jefferson	29	544	7.7	100.00%
Raymond Johnson	19	362	0.6	48.50%
Phyllis Francisco	22	518	2.6	82.50%
Harrison McDonald	23	486	0.6	64.50%
Alexander Barker	19	312	0.6	86.80%
Nicholas Archibald	21	435	1.2	95.80%
Juliette Andrews	20	358	0.6	88.00%

TABLE 7.3
Flight Instructor Demographics.

Academic Year	*Avg. Age*	*Avg. Experience (Hours)*	*Avg. Employment (Years)*
1	28	643.2	2.1
2	29	675.1	2.3
3	26	582.3	2.0
4	23	465.8	1.9
5	21	426.3	1.7

"As a matter of fact, I am not surprised by your observation," Lucas agreed. "After hearing some gossip from a colleague, I talked to a few students. And yeah, it has started to become a known fact circulating among the students that if you get a 'hawk,' good luck!"

With a look of confusion, Ellie asked, "What's a hawk?"

Lucas smiled and said, "Well, students have labeled some examiners 'hawks' and others 'doves,' meaning, if you get a hawk as your examiner, you are likely to get an unsatisfactory score, and if you get a dove, lucky you! So, in very general terms, hawks tend to fail students, and doves tend to pass students. I would say, from what I could see, the tests *are* pretty subjective. I even heard that a few students who failed their end-of-course tests were considering transferring to another pilot school or giving up getting their pilot licenses all together because they thought the test was so subjective and unfair."

Ellie again felt that she was getting closer to finding something that might offer clues to the problem, "How many examiners are evaluating a single student on their end-of-course test?"

Lucas replied, "Just one."

Ellie responded cautiously, "Mmm, I see. Now, it does look like the hawk and dove examiners are playing a role here. The personality factor could affect the reliability of their ratings and therefore skew the overall passing rate, especially if there is no formal training on how to objectively evaluate students' performances to produce reliable ratings. *But* we need to be careful before jumping to conclusions too fast. I want to gather more information and be sure other possibilities are also examined. Is it possible for me to talk to some of the different examiners?"

Lucas nodded. "Sure, I can arrange that!"

MEETING WITH THE INSTRUCTORS

In the conference room in the Aviation Department, Ellie, Lucas, and Dillon were already chatting while waiting for another instructor, Harrison, to join the meeting. Dillon was a 29-year-old senior instructor, and Harrison was a 23-year-old junior instructor. Two minutes after the time the meeting was supposed to start, Harrison rushed into the conference room.

"Sorry, I'm late. There's construction everywhere on campus. The roads are blocked, and I couldn't find a parking space close by!"

Lucas was not happy about Harrison's tardiness but did not show his displeasure. "We are glad that you are here now. Okay, thanks, everyone, for coming. Since this is your first time meeting Ellie, why don't you guys introduce yourselves?"

Dillon looked at Harrison and noted he didn't seem up to speaking first. So, he introduced himself. "Sure! I am Dillon Jefferson, I've been a flight instructor in the aviation department for over eight years, and I am currently a lead instructor."

Then, Harrison introduced himself. "Harrison McDonald, I am also a flight instructor, just joined the aviation department two years ago."

"Okay, great. I've invited Ellie, who is an instructional design consultant from CTE, to help us with the end-of-course test pass rate issue."

Ellie smiled at everyone in the room and introduced herself, "Hi, I'm Ellie Miller. Thanks for having me. Perhaps we can start with both of you describing the criteria you use for awarding a satisfactory score on the end-of-course test?"

Harrison jumped right in and confidently said, "I may be a rookie, but I think human lives and aircraft safety top everything else. So, I think it is important to hold the students to the highest standards. Every step in every flight procedure needs to be executed with 100%

precision. The FAA standards are clear; the assessment checklists are clear. I don't see why the students are complaining if they can't perform at the level they are supposed to. I think they just feel entitled."

After hearing what Harrison said, Dillon replied slowly, "Well, I 100% agree with you on holding students to the highest standards, Harrison, no doubt. However, while the standards and assessment checklists may seem straightforward, in reality, when you are in the air, things are a lot different and more unpredictable than how they are on the ground. So, some flexibility and critical thinking may be necessary. Besides, the standards are guidelines, not rigid prescriptions of the steps of the procedures. As long as the students perform the steps well enough, that is just fine. They don't have to perform every step in the manual to a T."

Harrison replied irritably, "Well, I respectfully disagree. We don't need Santa Claus here to baby these students, and we shouldn't. What we really need is to be a safeguard to protect people's lives and properties by filtering out unqualified pilots. We should score their performances by following the FAA's standards. What we need is precision, not flexibility."

Dillon sighed. "That's why students avoid you, Harrison. Several students have told me they thought you were unreasonable, only focused on minute, insignificant details and that you can't see the big picture. Yes, the standards are clear, but they depend on how you interpret them."

To make Dillon's point more legitimate, Lucas added, "Well, we do need to consider how students perceive this. I've received a few complaints from some students, and they were considering transferring to other flight schools because they felt they were being treated unfairly."

Not concealing his anger, Harrison responded, "We are not here to please students. If we let unqualified students pass, then when they start flying for the industry, what kind of reputation would our flight school have? If we produce 'enough' low-quality pilots and release them to the industry, do you think word wouldn't eventually get back to the FAA? I am not the only one who is proud of enforcing standards!"

Noting Harrison's rage, Dillon kept his cool and replied, "What you say is absolutely right, but if we don't reach the 90% passing rate, we may all be out of a job."

Lucas added, "Harrison, Dillon is talking about our Part 141 examining authority. But what you said is also true—that we can't ruin our reputation in the industry. Losing students, losing our privileges, or ruining our reputation—none of these is what the dean or I want to see."

To steer both instructors away from personal emotions and get back to the issue at hand, Ellie asked, "What about the students' performances during the program before they take the end-of-course assessment? Is there a correlation between the students' GPA and their performances on the end-of-course test?"

Lucas replied, "Not that I could tell, based on the data we have. Also, you may notice in the dataset that I sent you that the majority of the students who got unsatisfactory scores also passed the knowledge test, which is all multiple-choice questions, with no human raters involved."

After hearing all the accounts from the two instructors and Lucas, Ellie offered a hypothesis about the passing rates issue. "Well, the end-of-course tests are conducted in a one-on-one environment, with an examiner serving as the rater of a pilot applicant's performance on both the oral and flight examination. Subjectivity and rater reliability are the main concerns here. So, the final assessment checklist itself and how examiners interpret the FAA standards and score students' performances might be something we need to take a closer look at."

Lucas was pleased to learn that there was a potential solution to the problem and queried hopefully, "So, do you recommend we re-evaluate and redesign the assessment instrument and administering protocol?"

Ellie immediately replied, “Yes, that would be the first step at this point, given what we know so far. Of course, we should survey how everybody has been conducting their assessments and perhaps collect other information so that we can be sure that redesigning the assessment instrument is the right solution . . . see if anything else needs to be in place.”

Dillon agreed enthusiastically, “Yeah, I think that’s a good idea.”

Unsurprisingly, Harrison was not happy with what he heard. “Well, you guys do whatever you like. I have no objection, but I just don’t think there is a problem here.”

Lucas concluded the meeting and thanked everyone for coming. “Well, okay, I’ll take this to the dean and see what he says.”

After the meeting, Lucas drafted a memo reporting the findings and recommendations and sent it to the dean (see Figure 7.3). Three days later, Lucas was working on the annual evaluations of the instructors in his office, when the phone rang.

MEMO

DATE: April 15

TO: Joel O’Brien, Dean of School of Aerospace Sciences

FROM: Lucas Baily, Chair of Aviation Department

SUBJECT: Preliminary Report on *pilot students’ first attempt passing rates*

To address the issue of pilot students’ low passing rates on the end-of-course test, a redesign of the assessment instrument used by the examiners to evaluate pilot students’ end-of-course test is recommended. This recommendation is based on a series of data collections and analyses, including the students’ test scores, examiners’ profiles, and other data over the past five years, interviews of a number of aviation instructors and pilot students, as well as the consultation with Ellie Miller, who is a senior instructional designer from the Center for Teaching Excellence on campus.

The results of the investigation suggested that the scoring of the students’ performances has not been consistent among examiners, which may have skewed the students’ final outcomes. While other possibilities cannot be completely ruled out, examiners’ inconsistent scoring seems to be the most likely cause of the issue, with the data that we have so far. Ms. Miller suggested that the department start by reexamining the evaluation tools and administering protocols that all examiners are currently using and eventually develop a standardized evaluation instrument.

FIGURE 7.3 Memo from Lucas Bailey to Joel O’Brien.

"Good morning, Lucas. How are you?" greeted Joel warmly.

Sitting down, Lucas replied, "Good, how about yourself?"

"Oh, same old, same old . . . Hey, listen, I got your report on the students' first attempt passing rates investigation. Thanks so much. You did a great job."

"Thank you. So . . . what do you think?" Lucas asked in anticipation.

"I think that is a great recommendation. But do you think having a new evaluation instrument will solve the problem entirely?" suggested Joel carefully.

Feeling unsure, Lucas answered, "Well, I don't know. I will need to talk to Ellie and see what she says."

"You know what, why don't you talk to her and see if we can have her as a designated consultant for this project." Joel added determinedly, "We can't afford to fail at this."

"Okay," Lucas replied, satisfied. "I will email her" (see Figure 7.4).

From: Bailey, Lucas
Sent: Thursday, April 6, 8:05 A.M.
To: Miller, Ellie
Subject: Explore solutions to the low passing rate issue

Reply | Reply All | Forward | ...

Hi Ellie-

I've given our preliminary report to Joel, and he would like to assign you to serve as the designated consultant for this project and help us solve the inconsistent ratings issue and explore solutions to the problem. Of course, we will discuss this with CTE regarding how to allocate your time to this project. Do you think you can give us your plan for this project and a list of other data or resources you will need to get started sometime soon?

Thanks!

Lucas Bailey
Aviation Department Chair
School of Aerospace Sciences
Western Plains University

FIGURE 7.4 Email from Lucas Bailey to Ellie Miller.

Preliminary Analysis Questions

1. Ellie was cautious about focusing too heavily on the instructors' "hawk" and "dove" personalities and perspectives. What other factors might have contributed to the low passing rate among the students? How could Ellie confirm these factors?
2. Critique Ellie's suggestion for redesigning the final formal assessment. What additional data would offer insight for understanding the problem situation?
3. What steps can Ellie take to ensure the reliability of the redesigned assessment instruments and administering protocol?
4. How does a high-stakes context, such as aviation training, influence potential solutions?

Implications for ID Practice

1. What kinds of data can designers use to inform decisions regarding assessment redesign efforts?
2. How can instructional designers assure that assessment protocols are highly reliable in unpredictable, dynamic test environments?
3. What are key considerations when designing and implementing assessment instruments that will be used in high-stakes environments?

8

Suzie Beckett and Adam McSweeny

Developing a Role-Playing Simulation

Enilda Romero-Hall

THE PROJECT

At the end of the spring semester, Drs. Lorena Colombo and Adam McSweeny, both assistant professors at the Bianchi Institute of Technology, received notification from the Institute's internal grant coordinator that they had been awarded $25,000 for a project titled *Myths and Misconceptions About the Aging Process*. The project involved the design and development of a web-based role-playing simulation, intended to increase undergraduate students' understanding of the aging process and deepen their empathy toward elderly individuals.

BACKGROUND

Lorena was a third-year assistant professor with expertise in the developmental processes associated with aging. She taught senior-level courses in developmental psychology and was knowledgeable of students' perceptions of the elderly and the important role that perspective taking played in promoting empathy toward others. In this newly funded project, Lorena served as the project co-manager and subject matter expert (SME). The outcome of the project would be used in Lorena's Aging & the Elderly course, taught in the psychology department. Although Lorena was described as a nice, easy-going person by her colleagues and students, she was often doubtful of her decisions and worried significantly about other's approval and their impressions of her scholarly work.

Adam was a faculty member in instructional technology. He taught courses in instructional design (ID), development of multimedia instruction, and distance learning. He had earned a bachelor's degree in business administration and both master's and doctoral degrees in instructional design and technology. He had also obtained a specialization in modeling and simulation. Colleagues described Adam as a professional, hardworking, and creative individual, as well as a caring team player and a good listener. Like Lorena, he was a third-year assistant professor in a tenure-track position. Adam was known for saying, "Fake it 'til you make it," particularly when faced with anything stressful or challenging.

Earlier in the year, Lorena had reached out to Adam after learning of his expertise in simulation development. "As I reviewed your portfolio, Adam, one area of research that caught my

DOI: 10.4324/9781003354468-10

attention was your recent experience in the design of a pain management simulation using role-playing activities and animated characters."

Adam smiled as he responded, "That was one of my favorite projects during my post-doc. It was a great collaboration with the faculty in the nursing department at my previous institution."

Lorena was interested in changing the way she taught her courses. She wanted to include more innovative activities in her classes. "I thought that a similar application could be used to engage my students and foster their understanding about the aging process. I would really like to add a role-playing activity in my class. It would be great to have my students interact with authentic characters in a simulated environment to stimulate empathy and increase their knowledge of the aging process."

Adam wanted to know more. "What are the current learning activities?"

Lorena mentioned that typically students read about the aging process in a book and then interact with elderly individuals as part of the service-learning portion of the course. Lorena proposed a potential collaboration between them to design and develop a simulation. Without hesitation, Adam agreed that a role-playing web simulation with aging characters seemed to be a good fit for the instructional needs of the students in Lorena's class.

Lorena and Adam began their work by conducting a literature review focused on both the psychology and instructional design literature. They looked specifically at tools and strategies designed to increase awareness of the aging process and dispel misconceptions about geriatric individuals. After conducting the literature review, Lorena and Adam realized that what they were planning to do was both novel and innovative compared to other tools and interventions. Existing tools required expensive equipment, significant user training, and were not easily accessible by all learners at the same time. For example, some other institutions used bodysuits that helped students understand the physical limitations of elderly individuals. Unlike the other tools available, the web-based simulation that Lorena and Adam planned to design and develop could be deployed using an Internet connection and a web browser. Multiple students could access the web simulation at the same time, from multiple locations (as long as there was Internet connectivity).

SUMMER MONTHS (JUNE AND JULY)

That June, after hearing that they had received funding, Lorena and Adam met several times to start planning the simulation. During their first meeting, Lorena mentioned, "I am so excited that our simulation project was funded!"

Adam was also thrilled, "This will be a great learning tool to assist the undergraduate students enrolled in your Aging & the Elderly service-earning course."

Lorena knew that this would be a tool that other faculty in her department would appreciate using in their courses. She also thought it could lead others to consider adding educational technology elements in their psychology courses, and told him, "I shared the news with the chair of the psychology department and she was ecstatic! Since this course is offered regularly each fall and spring semester, the web simulation could be used extensively by psychology majors."

Adam had already brainstormed on his own and had a vision for what the simulation would entail. "Great! I have been thinking about the simulation and envision that it could include three scenarios. Each scenario could feature an aging individual who is experiencing

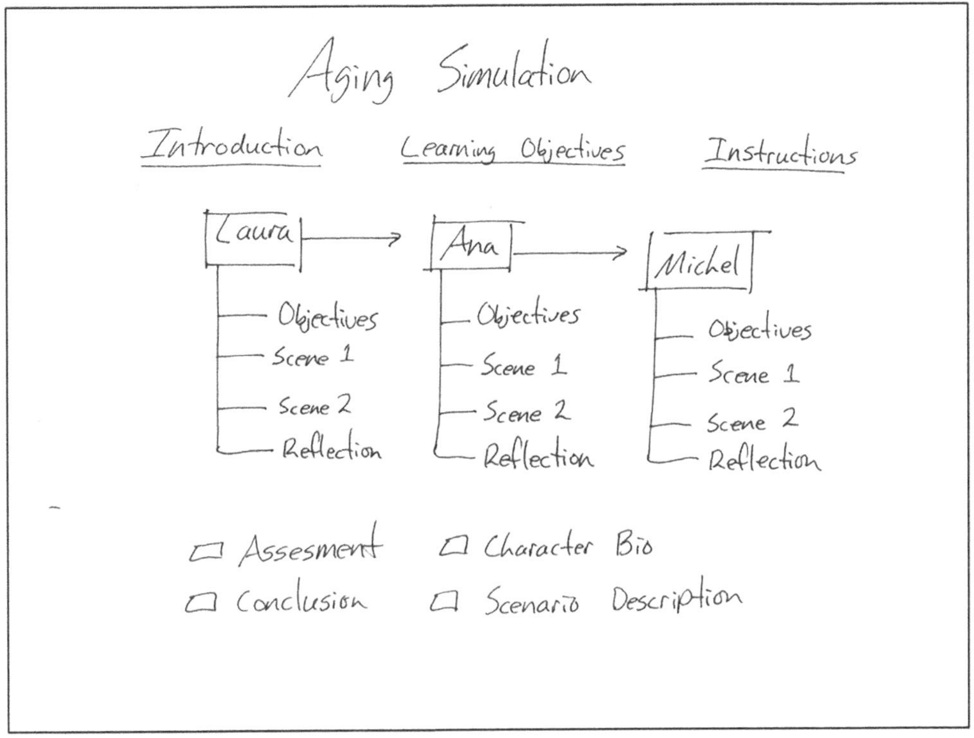

FIGURE 8.1 Design sketches of the role-playing simulation.

a range of emotions, social situations, and illnesses commonly experienced by the elderly" (see Figure 8.1).

Lorena was also ready to share her thoughts on the content. "Yes, ideally we could design each scenario to confront myths and misconceptions associated with aging, which would allow students to better understand age-related changes. We should also keep in mind that one of the main goals is to stimulate empathy and concern for the elderly."

Adam agreed, "Absolutely! To ensure students can relate to the content of the simulation we can ask the learners to select a virtual character—an aging individual—and then roleplay a specific scenario with that character. Each scenario could include biographies of the characters involved, instructions on how to navigate the role-playing activities, a description of the setting, reflection activities, generative strategies, and an assessment."

Adam was brimming with big ideas and had yet to provide specific details on how the simulation would be developed, especially given the limited budget and software availability. Lorena's vision and expectations for the simulation were high. However, details on the role-playing components or the development phase were rarely articulated during their conversations. This was due, in part, to the fact that Adam felt it would be best to have these conversations primarily with the instructional design project assistant, who they had not yet hired.

The project timeline Lorena and Adam had proposed in the grant document comprised a one-year design and development period (see Figure 8.2). The institution required outcomes to be shared in a grant report by the end of the academic year. The resources for this project

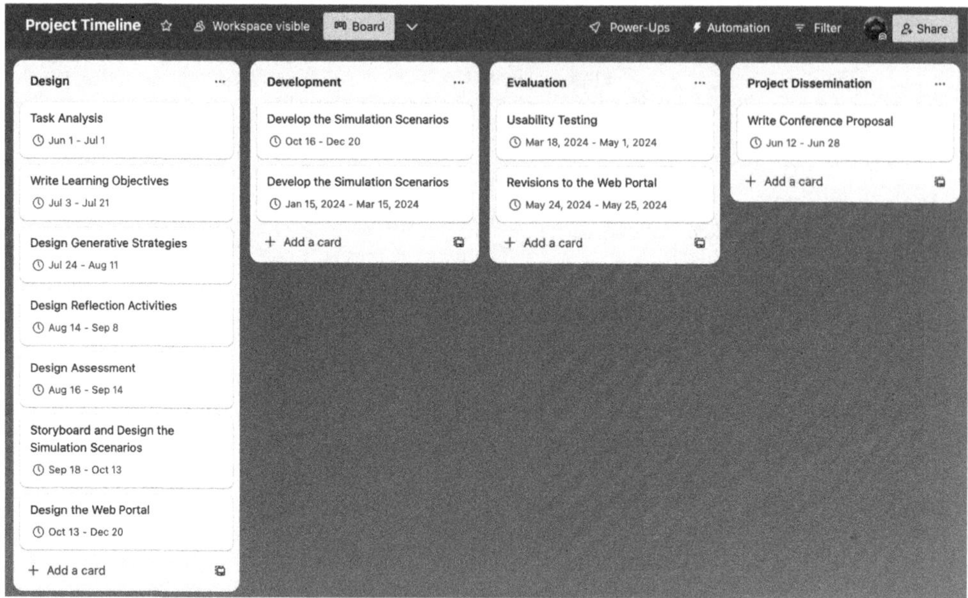

FIGURE 8.2 Project timeline of the design and development process.

included personnel (project co-managers, project assistants, student assistant), hardware and software, and office space. Most of the resources were covered through the grant funds provided by Bianchi (see Figure 8.3).

Since Lorena's role included serving as the SME on the content of the simulation, she began searching for research that addressed specific physical, sensory, social, and emotional experiences known to affect geriatric individuals, as well as misconceptions associated with these experiences, to help guide the topics that would be addressed in the scenarios. Adam focused on the content presentation within the animations. During one of their meetings in June, Adam suggested translating the text into conversational exchanges between virtual characters in the simulation and reflection activities. "Lorena, how about, instead of having text on the screen describing various activities of elderly individuals, we present two characters who talk informally about social gatherings they had attended with family and friends?"

Adam had previously reviewed the literature on the pros and cons of audio versus text content presentations. He knew that research results on the topic were mixed; however, for the purpose of this project, it seemed more engaging to use animated characters with voices. Lorena agreed with the suggestion, "I like that type of content presentation! We could do the same for sensory issues. Instead of presenting text-based information on traditional sensory issues that occur with aging, the characters could show signs of sensory deterioration."

To help Lorena visualize this type of interaction, Adam provided an example. Lorena was enthusiastic. "Great idea! So, for example, we could have the virtual geriatric character ask another virtual character to repeat a comment because he/she could not hear it clearly. This could all be followed by a direct question and a reflection about the scenario."

Adam also mentioned to Lorena that it would be important to represent a diverse set of people in the web-based simulation. More specifically, they decided that their characters would include a Caucasian female, a Hispanic female, and an African American male. Adam and Lorena believed that this representation of diversity would help learners identify more closely with the characters given the diverse student population at Bianchi.

Summary Budget Worksheet

Applicant Name: **Lorena Colombo / Adam McSweeny** **Department:** **Psychology / Education**

List **all** funding requested for this project from **all** Grants/Awards.

Shaded Boxes indicate that restrictions apply; refer to the guidelines for allowable expenses.

Budget Item	Budget Request for One or Multiple Grants		
	Development	**Research**	**Experiential**
Personnel/Salaries			
Faculty salary/stipend	$ 12,000.00	N/A	N/A
Student salary/stipend	$ 6,000.00	$.	$.
Technology/Software:			
Laptop Computer	$ 3,000.00	$.	$.
Web Hosting Platform	$ 500.00	$.	$.
Unity Pro	$ 2,040.00	$.	$.
Travel:			
Airfare or other	$.	$.	$.
Local travel (car rental, mileage, etc.)	$.	$.	$.
Lodging (i.e., hotel)	$.	$.	$.
Per diem	$.	$.	$.
Fees, Equipment, Supplies and Outside Services:	list below		
Microphone	$ 150.00	$.	$.
Headphones	$ 200.00	$.	$.
Usability Testing Participants [stipend]	$ 500.00	$.	$.
Voiceover Participants [stipend]	$ 250.00	$.	$.
Office Supplies	$ 200.00	$.	$.
	$.	$.	$.
	$.	$.	$.
	$.	$.	$.
	$.	$.	$.
	$.	$.	$.
	$.	$.	$.
	$.	$.	$.
	$.	$.	$.
TOTAL	**$ 24,840.00**	**$.**	**$.**

FIGURE 8.3 Project budget submitted with the grant proposal.

THE HIRING PROCESS (AUGUST)

Once the design documents (see sample in Figure 8.4) had been drafted, Lorena and Adam moved on to the task of hiring a project assistant. Adam believed that the ideal candidate would be someone with media and programming skills, who could help develop the simulation. Rather than posting the job opening on the university website, Lorena recommended that Adam consider hiring one of his current students. Lorena was unsure of the skills the student would need in order to work as a project assistant, but she trusted that Adam would hire a student who would be an asset to the team.

Suzie was a graduate student in the instructional design and technology master's program and was completing her last year of coursework. She was soft-spoken and very business savvy.

Scenario Flow with Learning Content
Scene One

Introduction:
Older adults often experience challenges to their well-being. For this activity, you should imagine that you are experiencing what happens to Laura. Put yourself in Laura's shoes and think about how she feels. Laura is 87 years old. She has just had lunch with some friends and stops by the pharmacy on her way home.

Dialogue:
- Pharmacist: Hello, how are you doing today?
- Laura: I'm feeling great! I just had lunch with some friends. It was a fun time!
- Pharmacist: That sounds nice. How may I help you today?
- Laura: Could you please fill these prescriptions for me?
- Pharmacist: Sure, I can fill these right now.

Assessment:
Participant is asked to match Laura's emotion with the correct emotion.
A correct answer of "happy" must be given to proceed with the simulation.

Knowledge Blurb:
Participant is asked to proceed to the Knowledge Blurb

When participating in physical activities of daily living, older adults are overall happier when they have the option to make choices in their activities, they can understand the activities, and they can relate to the activity. Positive feelings owing to physical activities in daily living depend on the extent that psychological needs are satisfied. Older adults favor engaging in physical activities where they can relate to others (Kanning and Hansen, 2016).

Reference
Kanning, M., & Hansen, S. (2016). Need satisfaction moderates the association between physical activity and affective states in adults aged 50+: an activity-triggered ambulatory assessment. Annals of Behavioral Medicine, 51, 18-29. doi: 10.1007/s12160-016-9824-6

Reflection:
Please consider the experiences of most elderly individuals. Imagine you experience Mary's situation. Take a moment to think about how this would make you feel.

FIGURE 8.4 Scenario flow with content.

She had a fun and expressive personality. Others enjoyed working with her and described her as a team player. Before enrolling in the program at Bianchi, Suzie had earned a master's of business administration (MBA) from a large public university and a bachelor of science in industrial engineering. In addition to her studies, she had been working as an ID intern for a local company for 20 hours per week.

Adam hoped that Suzie could work an additional ten hours a week on this project and immediately scheduled a meeting to discuss the project with her. The meeting was scheduled for mid-August, just a few weeks before the fall semester began. At the start of the meeting, Adam described the aims and goals of the project, "Suzie, I'm so glad you could meet with me today."

Suzie mentioned how honored she was that Adam had thought of her for this project. Adam proceeded to discuss the project, "I think it will be of interest to you. I am working with my colleague, Dr. Lorena Colombo, on the design and development of a web-based simulation that will include role-playing aspects in which the learner engages with animated characters. The goal of the web-based simulation is to dispel myths and misconceptions about the aging process."

Suzie listened attentively, clearly interested. "It sounds fascinating! Tell me more."

Adam started to provide details on the role Suzie would have in the project. "You would be tasked with the creation of the animated characters and provide audio feedback."

Suzie thought this project would be of great benefit to her. "This sounds like a great project in which I could use my development skills, but I do have a few questions. What is the timeline of the project?"

Adam was hopeful that the timeline would work well for Suzie, but he knew that taking on an additional project could be stressful for her. "Great question. We are aiming to complete the project by April next year. The bulk of the development work, which includes creating the animated characters, will occur from August to December this year."

Suzie thought that the amount of time for development was probably adequate. However, Suzie also wanted to know how many hours she would be expected to work on the project.

Adam responded, "We were thinking that the project assistant would work for ten hours per week during the development portion of the project."

Suzie hesitated for a few minutes, as she thought about her final semester as a student and her existing internship. "I am just a little bit concerned about how these hours would fit into my already full schedule." Still, she was thrilled to have this opportunity. "You know, I do think I can manage my schedule. You can count on me! I am eager to join the team and collaborate with you and Dr. Colombo."

Adam reassured Suzie that he would be available for support, and that it would be valuable for her. He also reminded her she had already successfully made it through the heavy project courses in her program. "Furthermore," he added, "if you'd like, we can set it up for practicum credit, so it fits in your program of study. I will be supervising and guiding you anyway, and it would be good to formalize that. Plus, this is a position that you could list on your resume as an authentic ID experience. Also, you will have the opportunity to learn some new software."

Suzie immediately thought back to her instructional media course, which she had completed early in her ID master program. "I am a little nervous about my ability to develop the animations, but I am ready to take on the challenge." She made a mental note to review the applications she had learned in the multimedia class.

Adam thought it would be a good idea to go over the planning materials. "Since you are here, would it be okay if we go over the design documents? I have them opened on my computer screen."

Suzie agreed it would help her gain an understanding of the plan. "Yes, that would be great! I am eager to learn more about the project. I want to know what you and Dr. Colombo have in mind for the simulation."

Adam began by sharing what he and Lorena had worked on during the previous summer months—the drafts of the goals and objectives of the simulation. He commented on several elements that would be part of the simulation. "We are planning to have three characters as part of the simulation, and each character will have a unique scenario. The goal is to have an introduction with objectives, two scenes per scenario, and a reflection at the end of each scenario."

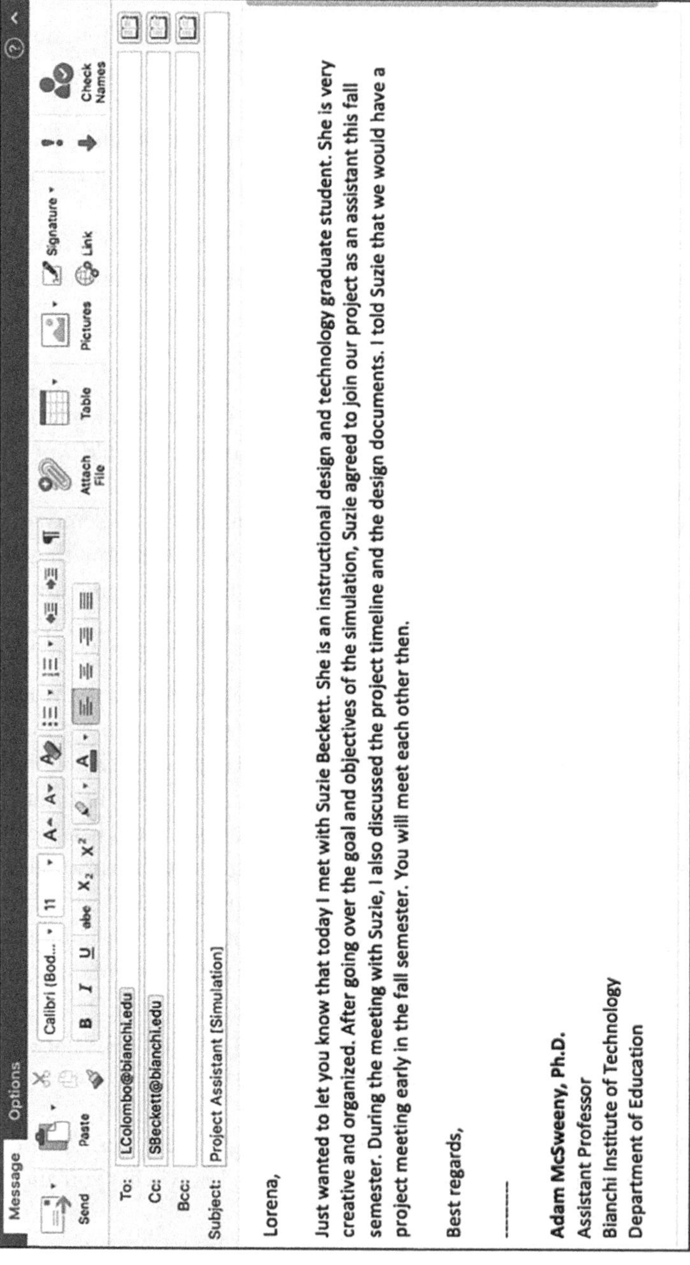

To: LColombo@bianchi.edu

Cc: SBeckett@bianchi.edu

Bcc:

Subject: Project Assistant [Simulation]

Lorena,

Just wanted to let you know that today I met with Suzie Beckett. She is an instructional design and technology graduate student. She is very creative and organized. After going over the goal and objectives of the simulation, Suzie agreed to join our project as an assistant this fall semester. During the meeting with Suzie, I also discussed the project timeline and the design documents. I told Suzie that we would have a project meeting early in the fall semester. You will meet each other then.

Best regards,

Adam McSweeny, Ph.D.
Assistant Professor
Bianchi Institute of Technology
Department of Education

FIGURE 8.5 Email to Lorena from Adam after the initial meeting with Suzie.

Suzie was glad to hear that the simulation would provide objectives and a reflection component at the end. She wanted to know more about the scenes. She asked, "What would be included in the different 'scenes?'"

She listened intently, trying to understand every detail of the design, while Adam elaborated. "For each scene, we have drafted an outline. The outline includes the introduction message that will be spoken by an animated character, who will play the role of the narrator throughout the simulation. It also includes the script dialogue between the characters in the scene, the activity that the learner will perform after viewing the animation, and a short knowledge blurb about the aging process."

At the end of the meeting, Suzie was starting to see and imagine the flow of each scenario. She was already planning to take some time to read over the design documents and gain a better sense of the overall goal of the simulation. Adam mentioned that he would email her the documents and that Suzie should feel free to email him if she had any questions.

After the meeting, Adam emailed Suzie the design documents he had drafted in collaboration with Lorena, stating the objectives of the project. Adam also reiterated in the email that Suzie would be tasked with the development of the scenery, recording of the animated voices, development and animation of the virtual characters, and rendering of the animations. Suzie would also receive credit for the required ID practicum for the master's program. A follow-up email was sent to Lorena to ensure she was kept in the loop (see Figure 8.5).

After hiring Suzie as the project assistant, Lorena thought it would also be beneficial to hire at least one psychology student to help ensure relevant content within the role-playing activities. She contacted a few psychology students who had expressed interest in earning independent study credit for the semester. In exchange for their efforts on the project, Lorena would provide a grade at the end of the semester. Almost immediately, one of her students, Johanna Duncan, responded that she would be delighted to be part of the project in exchange for independent study credit. Dr. Colombo promptly welcomed her onto the team and emailed other members to let them know Johanna would be helping with the project.

THE FIRST TEAM MEETING (SEPTEMBER)

The first week of September, Adam emailed an invitation to the team to a project kickoff meeting in his office. The objective was to go over the goals of the project, identify regular meeting dates/times, and get started with project tasks based on the timeline stated in the grant proposal. After everyone completed an online poll, they decided on a location, date, and time for the following week.

During the meeting, everyone was very excited to finally meet each other. Adam started the meeting by welcoming the team. "I'm so glad we can finally see each other face-to-face! Thank you for answering the online poll to set our meeting times. It looks like gathering every two weeks works for all of us. After this meeting, I will send an email with our scheduled dates from September until December."

Following this, all the team members introduced themselves and expressed their excitement for the project. Suzie began, "Dr. Colombo it is a pleasure to meet you!"

Lorena responded, "Great to meet you as well, Suzie! I heard great comments from Adam about your instructional design skills."

Johanna also introduced herself. "Very nice to meet you, Dr. McSweeny. Based on my meeting with Dr. Colombo, the project sounds extremely interesting." Lorena made sure to share, with Adam and Suzie, that Johanna was one of their best senior psychology students.

Since Johanna was put on the spot, she felt it was appropriate to clarify how little she knew about the ID field. "Dr. Colombo, thank you for your kind words. But I have to be honest, I am not very familiar with instructional design. So, what is the process?"

Adam realized that this was a great way to start the conversation about the ID process and how it applied to the project. "Well, to give you a bit of background, the ID process focuses on the creation of engaging learning experiences. Some of these experiences are face-to-face and others are online. For this project, we will be creating an online multimedia experience. Dr. Colombo and I started the process back in July with the analysis phase. During that phase, we determined the objectives of the simulation."

Lorena interjected to mention how they had also conducted an analysis to determine which content to include in the simulation based on existing research. She asked Adam to provide more information about the scenarios: "Perhaps, we should also discuss the scenario descriptions and storyboards."

Adam began by sharing more background about the already completed tasks. "Yes, good point! Before Dr. Colombo and I determined the objectives of the simulation and completed the task analysis, we made a few key decisions. We decided that it would be good to have three animated characters and each character would have his or her own scenario. With that in mind, at the end of July, we storyboarded and documented the design process for each scenario."

Suzie chimed in, "When I reviewed the design documents you sent me, Dr. McSweeny, I noticed that each character's scenario is based on different age-related issues, as well as myths and misconceptions about the aging process."

Lorena quickly responded by adding, "Well, since we want to address a range of topics in the simulation, it was important to create variations on issues using the different animated characters. Also, the animated characters deal with a range of social situations and illnesses commonly experienced by the elderly."

Johanna was happy to know that her team members knew so much about the ID process and could provide guidance. "Dr. Colombo and McSweeny, you have done so much already! What are the next steps?"

Since Adam had given Suzie the design documents a few weeks ago and that was the next main step in the process, he asked her to share her ideas for developing the animations that would be part of the web simulation. "This is where Suzie comes into play. She will be working on the development of the simulation. Suzie, can you tell us what you have in mind for the development process?"

Suzie was prepared for this. "First, I want to create an audio recording of the scripted conversations. The public library has a great audio-recording booth with professional equipment. I can book it for next week."

Privately, Lorena thought the plan to move forward with audio recordings was too rushed since the scripts hadn't been finalized, but she trusted the designers' judgment.

Adam supported this first step. "I like that idea. Let me add 'audio recording' to our action items."

"Since we are talking about the scripts and audio recordings of the scripts, I want to make sure I mentioned this to both of you. When I was reviewing the materials and documents that you sent me, I noticed that the scripts were not representative of diverse aging individuals as you had planned and written in the design document," stated Suzie.

Lorena wanted to get more feedback on the scripts, so without hesitation she asked, "Can you be more specific?"

Suzie, an African American woman, explained, "The expressions, vocabulary, and exchanges used to create the script are representative of White Americans. It is unlikely that an African American or Latinx elderly person would talk or express themselves as represented in the script."

Suzie continued sharing her plan: "I highly recommend revisions to the script so that they represent the cultural, racial, and ethnic group you aim for in the design documents. After I get copies of the revised and reviewed scripts, I want to select the individuals who will be doing the voice recordings. I have a couple of friends whose voices would work perfectly for these characters, but if you have any other volunteers, please let me know."

Adam suggested that maybe Johanna could be the voice for one of the characters. Johanna was ecstatic. "I have never done something like this before, but it sounds like fun!"

Suzie added, "I will also start working with the software to develop the characters. I want to make sure the characters I develop accurately represent your vision. But most importantly, we have to make sure the dialogue is completely finalized. Once the audio is recorded and I start connecting it with the animated characters, it will be difficult to make changes."

As Suzie shared her ideas about the different tasks, Lorena seemed concerned about not being able to make changes to the audio or animations. She wondered how often changes *could* be made throughout the development process. However, Adam reassured her the scripts would be finalized and approved by both of them before recording the audio. Yet, Lorena felt it still was imperative to ask, "But what if I want to change the dialogue between the characters after I see the animations?"

Suzie wanted to make sure that Lorena understood what it would entail to make changes after the recordings from the script were made, so she guided Lorena through the process. "Well, it would be best to keep changes to a minimum once we combine the audio and the animated characters. The software we are using syncs the pre-recorded and edited audio tracks with the animated characters. The output is an animated character with sync mouth movements to the audio track. So, changes to the script would require three things: (1) re-editing the audio track, (2) re-syncing the audio with the animated characters, and (3) re-rendering the scenes."

After listening to Suzie describe the process for re-rendering the scenes and how it would be problematic to make edits, Lorena expressed her concerns. "I just want to make sure that the output is something that truly represents the vision I have, as you mentioned before."

Suzie felt that it was important to set clear expectations from the beginning. "Well, I have to be honest. There are limitations with the development software. I hope I am not being rude as I say this, but the simulation is not going to look like a Pixar movie."

Adam interrupted, "Yes, but also it is not going to look like a student project. We are going to work hard to make the animations look as professional as possible regardless of the limitations of the software."

Lorena seemed very confused by both statements, but she felt again that it was important for her to trust the expertise of Adam and Suzie. She had also made notes about the feedback on the scripts. Lorena, a White American woman, was planning to work closely with Johanna, who identified as Afro-Latinx, to improve diversity representation in the scripts. Clearly, there was a cultural and diversity dimension to the scripts that she had overlooked and needed to rectify.

The last statements that Suzie shared with the team related to the other elements that would be part of each scene: "I want to be sure to mention that there are several other aspects of the scenes that I need to consider. For example, I need to work on secondary characters, scenery, the narrator, and the different angles of the animations."

Johanna followed up by offering her support: "If there is any way I can be of help, please just let me know."

TEAM DYNAMICS AND TENSION

After the first meeting, Suzie created a plan with specific deadlines for the development of the scenery, recording of the animated voices, development and animation of the virtual characters, and rendering of the animations. Suzie estimated that her portion of the development would be completed in about four months. This would allow Adam enough time to work on the web portal beginning in January of the following year. Suzie shared her plans via email with the rest of the project team.

The initial interactions between the members of the design team were very collaborative and open. All team members attended the scheduled meetings regularly. The project co-managers were very accepting of each other's ideas for the scenarios and seemed to have similar expectations for what the final product should entail. However, as the design and development processes continued, the team started to experience some tension, which appeared to result from their disagreement on the logistical decisions and conceptual framework that would guide the design of the simulation.

Given his background with instructional simulations, Adam felt very comfortable outlining the key elements needed for an effective multimedia learning experience for an instructional role-playing simulation. These key elements included:

- a list of instructional objectives
- proper simulation instructions
- the availability of help resources
- prompts to aid the learner
- adequate and timely feedback

Lorena seemed concerned that these elements would take away from the natural interaction students would have with the role-playing activities. She seemed far more interested in including perspective-taking theory and empathy-inducing activities in the simulation. For example, Lorena wanted the simulated scenario to prompt students to assume the role of an elderly person, experience one negative and one positive age-related issue, make decisions based on outcomes associated with the issue, reflect on the experiences, and learn about the concepts of the aging process. She wanted to have a less prompted process and to engage students in a reflection of their biases, preconceptions, and stereotypes of aging individuals and the aging process.

To deal with this tension, Lorena and Adam each storyboarded their own versions of the web portal containing the simulation elements. One storyboard included Lorena's perspective: an introduction to the simulation, access to the simulation scenarios, and the references. The other included Adam's recommendations, with some different elements: an introduction to the simulation, simulation instructional objectives, simulation manipulation instructions, access to the simulation scenarios with inclusion of help resources and feedback, and the references. The project co-managers agreed to delay their decision on whether to include objectives, instructions, prompts, help resources, and feedback later in the project timeline but before the end of the development process.

Adding to the existing tension, the project was to be executed with software that was completely new to Suzie since Adam had already selected the software that would be used prior to hiring her. However, after receiving the design documents, Suzie began to familiarize herself with the software—watching tutorials on YouTube and Atomic Learning. Some of her co-workers at the local ID firm where she worked as an intern used the software to develop animations. She started asking them questions as she developed the different elements of the scenarios.

Lorena seemed to have very high expectations regarding what the animations should look like. Specifically, she wanted the animated characters to look as realistic as possible. Furthermore, she wanted the characters that represented elderly individuals to show significant physical signs of aging. Lorena also wanted to incorporate feedback mechanisms that could potentially lead to perspective taking for the learners. However, this feature was difficult to achieve due to limitations with the software. When Lorena realized that Suzie had very little experience with the software, she was afraid that her expectations would not be met.

Lorena was very resolved that the team develop a product that she would feel proud presenting to her colleagues in the psychology department and that her students would use. However, Lorena's unfamiliarity with the development process, specifically related to creating animations (including voice recording, editing of audio recording, character development, and scenario development), made for a scattered review, feedback, and editing process. Suzie had already specified the dates by which she would have a certain number of animations ready for review (with incorporated audio and movement). Once Suzie made the animations available for review, Lorena would take a significant amount of time to provide feedback. It was clear to Adam and Suzie that Lorena was struggling to juggle her duties on the project with other work obligations such as teaching and other research projects.

The Wednesday after Thanksgiving, Suzie and Lorena scheduled a meeting to review the third scenario together. Two weeks before the meeting, Suzie sent an email to the team, providing access to the scenes from the third and final scenario. Adam had already provided feedback via email, but Lorena had requested to meet in person with Suzie. That afternoon, Suzie walked into Lorena's office on campus. Lorena greeted her and asked if Suzie had a good Thanksgiving. "I hope you had a nice and relaxing time with your family."

Suzie responded, "Yes, it was great to have a long weekend and take a mental break. It has been a very hectic few months for me."

Lorena replied, "I completely understand and can totally relate. Well, I wanted to go over the scenes from scenario three with you. To be honest, I have not looked over them. Perhaps, I can open the scenario on my computer, and you can walk me through it." Suzie took a deep breath; she was really hoping Lorena had at least looked at the scenario.

Suzie started by reading over the design documents she was provided for this specific scenario. Afterward Suzie described the character. "This animated character is named 'Michel.' He is an 82-year-old African American male. I used the development software to change his posture and hair color. The default hair color in the software is black. I wanted our character to have white hair."

Lorena interrupted, "That is all great, but I am really interested in the features of the different scenes that lead to perspective taking and empathy."

Suzie wanted Lorena to get a full picture of the scenario and the development process, so she felt somewhat frustrated by Lorena's request. However, Suzie thought this was the perfect opportunity to work toward a shared understanding of the design of the simulation.

Suzie then started by sharing the development of the second scene within the third scenario. This scene featured tone of voice and facial emotions to convey sadness (in the animated character).

Lorena thought it was effectively executed but was not very impressed after watching the animations. "I know you and Adam mentioned that this would not be the same quality as a Pixar animation, and I guess that is fine as long as the animations truly capture the feelings and perspective we want the students to experience. It may have not come across that way before, but these elements are more important to me than the realism of the characters."

Suzie smiled and mentioned that she considered herself well-versed in the development of meaningful learning experiences. "There is extensive literature, including peer-reviewed articles, that highlight the key design elements of animated pedagogical characters in multimedia learning environments. We used these design elements as part of the development process in the company where I work as an intern to create authentic learning experiences. I did not mention it before to you, although I mentioned to Dr. McSweeny that I would keep this research in mind as I worked on the development of the scenarios." Lorena was interested in learning and reading more about the articles Suzie mentioned, so she quickly asked if Suzie could share them with her.

Preliminary Analysis Questions

1. What design and development priorities did the team discuss for creating a simulation to meet the project goals?
2. Describe the team's various perspectives on the relationship between authenticity and student learning.
3. Evaluate the design process being used in this project. To what extent did the team build a shared understanding of the process?
4. Evaluate Adam's approach to addressing diversity in the simulation. What else should the team consider when building the scenarios?
5. How can the design team ensure a high-quality simulation while balancing a fixed budget, time constraints, and software limitations?

Implications for ID Practice

1. How do issues related to team dynamics (e.g., expectations and communication) affect the practice of instructional design? Suggest strategies to facilitate a mutually beneficial relationship among team members from different disciplines.
2. How much authenticity is needed to achieve the cognitive and affective goals of a simulation scenario?
3. How do instructional designers prioritize input from multiple stakeholders (e.g., SMEs, clients, users) and manage diverse expectations to ensure positive team dynamics?
4. How can instructional designers address modifications during the design process? What challenges will instructional designers face if unable to plan for adaptability of the design?

9

Amelia Kelly, Sara Brody, and Andrea Huffman

Designing a Military Think-Tank Workshop

Adrie A. Koehler, Erin D. Besser, and Jennifer C. Richardson

EARLY JANUARY

"You have a strong outline for your literature review," Dr. Amelia Kelly reassured Sara Brody, a first-year PhD student. Amelia, an associate professor in Learning Technologies, had worked at Central Midwest State University (CMSU) for eight years. "Before you go, do you have any other questions?"

Sara peered down at her notes before hesitantly responding, "No . . . I think you've addressed all of my concerns."

"Well, let me know if you run into any problems," Amelia added. "So, let's set up a time to meet again two weeks from now. Do you think you can have your articles reviewed by then?"

Removing her phone from her pocket to access the calendar, Sara replied, "That seems reasonable. So, two weeks from now . . . Thursday, same time?" Nodding, Amelia confirmed, "Great! I'm adding it to my calendar now." With that, Sara shut her computer, gathered her notes, and slid everything into her backpack. "I really appreciate your help, Dr. Kelly." Smiling, Amelia encouraged her, "You're doing great work, Sara. Keep it up!"

As Sara left her office, Amelia reflected on the number of graduate students she had mentored at CMSU. Currently, she was advising ten doctoral students and working with several other graduate students on various projects. Over the years, she certainly had dealt with a variety of different personalities and work styles. Smiling to herself, she thought Sara seemed to be on the path to success even if she had some self-doubts at this point. With Sara, as with her other students, Amelia would mentor her through her first year of coursework in the Learning Technologies program, and then support the development of relevant skills such as conducting research studies, working with clients, and gaining design and teaching experience.

Glancing at the clock, Amelia realized she still had 15 minutes until her faculty meeting started, just enough time to scan the emails that had accumulated in her inbox. Scrolling through the list, she came across an e-newsletter for the Armed Forces Family Support

DOI: 10.4324/9781003354468-11

Armed Forces Family Support Center January

NEWSLETTER

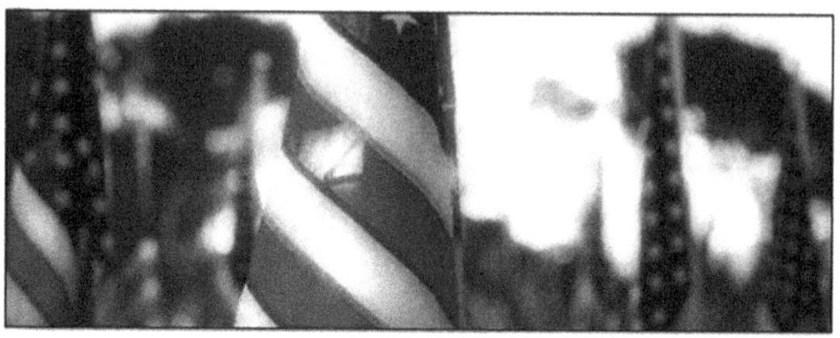

AFFSC's mission is to research topics impacting military personnel and their families who are making the transition from civilian to military life

AFFSC Spouse Symposium

The AFFSC will host an e-symposium for military spouses on Saturday, March 10. The event will offer resources for military spouses transitioning from civilian life to the military lifestyle. Interested individuals should e-mail Jessica Adamson (jadamson@@affsc.org).

Research Participants Needed

The AFFSC is interested in the perspectives of military members who have been enlisted or commissioned for less than a year. Please visit our website for details.

AFFSC Goals

With funding from the Department of Defense, the Armed Forces Family Support Center was created to address the following goals:

- Conduct research focused on improving policy, practice, and networks supporting military families
- Develop products and support services for military
- Create opportunities for civilian groups to partner with programs supporting military families

FIGURE 9.1 Armed Forces Family Support Center e-newsletter.

Center (AFFSC), a nonprofit organization with which she was completing some Department of Defense grant work (see Figure 9.1). Seeing the e-newsletter reminded Amelia that they had $5,000 left in the grant account, which would need to be spent on work related to the project by June 30. So that she wouldn't forget to do it later, she immediately emailed Karen Livingston, the director of AFFSC, to see what remaining work needed to be completed in order to tie up the project. Amelia then headed down the hall toward the conference room to meet with her colleagues.

PROJECT INITIATION

As Amelia was returning to her office after the meeting, the faint ping of her phone indicated a new email. She was surprised to see that Karen had already responded to her email (see Figure 9.2). After reading Karen's response, Amelia realized that this would be a great project on which to involve some graduate students, giving them the opportunity to take the lead on an authentic experience. In addition, she could use her mentoring skills while primarily serving in a supporting role. Most of the program's graduate students had some experience working with K–12 educators, higher education faculty, and even a few business and industry clients. However, in this project, the client and the target audience represented a less familiar demographic: the military.

Because Amelia saw this as a project in which she'd be minimally involved, she immediately realized that she would need to select graduate students who were self-starters and good

From: Livingston, Karen <livingston@affsc.org>

Sent: January 18 at 12:02 PM

To: Kelly, Amelia <akelly@cmstate.edu>

Subject: RE: DoD Grant

Yes, I have a project in mind for you. What I have in mind is for you to organize an online 'think tank' day or meeting to address the problem of how best to help military families to make sense of the complete morass of information they have to deal with regarding support programs. I can say more when we meet if this idea is of interest to you, but I'm envisioning something in late March to mid-April, 20 or so folks, a full-day work session, with AFFSC covering the expenses for actually doing the day.

Sound interesting?
Karen—
Karen Livingston
Director: Armed Forces Family Support Center

From: Kelly, Amelia <akelly@cmstate.edu>

Sent: January 18 at 10:21 AM

To: Livingston, Karen <livingston@affsc.org>

Subject: DoD Grant

Karen,

We still have $5,000 of grant funds available in the DoD account. Is there some additional work that is needed that I could help with?

Amelia

Amelia Kelly, Ph.D.
College of Education
Central Midwest State University

FIGURE 9.2 E-mail correspondence initiating project work.

problem solvers and who had strong communication skills to work directly with the client. Amelia asked herself, "Who should I consider among the current graduate students? Are there any students who might have an interest in this particular demographic? Would any students already be familiar with the target audience? Who was advanced enough to actually meet these criteria? And who could be counted on to do good work?"

KICKOFF MEETING AND INITIAL PLANNING

At ten minutes before 10:00 a.m. on February 16, Amelia, Sara, and Andrea Huffman headed to meet Karen at an on-campus coffee shop. The three women made small talk as they walked, agreeing that a meeting over coffee seemed like the perfect setting for the brisk, gray day. Both Sara and Andrea welcomed the opportunity to informally engage with their mentor, as she often shared fun stories from grad school, interesting experiences as a new assistant professor, or various current projects. These interactions with Amelia offered glimpses into Amelia's professional progression and prompted them to reflect on their own aspirations and identities—something they struggled with and frequently discussed. Upon entering the cozy coffee shop, they were comforted by the warm air, saw Karen seated at a table next to the window, and quickly placed their drink orders. With a smile and wave, Amelia led the pair to meet Karen. "Good morning, Karen! How are you? I would like to introduce you to Sara Brody and Andrea Huffman, the talented grad students I told you about," Amelia said warmly. Both Sara and Andrea had previously worked in K–12—Sara as an elementary teacher and Andrea as a high school business teacher. Andrea had just finished her first year in the Learning Technologies PhD program. Karen stood to greet the team, extending a handshake to Sara and Andrea while adding, "I'm doing well, thank you." As everyone settled into their seats, Sara and Andrea removed tablets and pens from their bags to take notes during the meeting.

"Karen, I've shared your basic idea for a 'think-tank' day with Sara and Andrea, but maybe you could tell us a little more about what you have in mind," Amelia suggested.

"Sure," Karen started, "the Department of Defense invests significant resources in trying to minimize potential negative effects of military service on service members and their families. Many supportive policies and programs are made available around the world, along with additional resources provided by private philanthropies and employers, non-governmental organizations, and state and local governments."

Pausing to take a sip of her coffee, Karen continued speaking directly to Amelia, "Obviously, many of these resources are available online, providing military families with the potential for increased support. However, these online resources can change rapidly, resulting in a confusing and ever-changing landscape of possibilities that is difficult for families to sort through, particularly if they are already struggling with challenges, such as deployment, changing duty stations, finding medical care, and so on. For instance, this could involve locating information related to a major life event like preparing for a duty station in Okinawa and determining what is needed with vaccinations, moving, finding housing, and living internationally. Or finding resources for day-to-day things like finding an answer to a tax question, participating in youth sports on base, or finding the correct phone number for an office on base. Accessing on-base resources is not always feasible for families with spouses who work, as the hours are limited and typically overlap with standard business hours–really underscoring the need for easy access to helpful resources. Although various websites, which are not government or military sponsored, offer support programs and information, there are useful resources those websites cannot list because they don't have the authority or the inside information needed to share specific details on these resources. Also, the websites may lack features that families might find helpful."

"I wonder what she means by that?" Andrea thought to herself, as she forced herself to focus on Karen's continuing description of project details that were becoming increasingly unclear to her.

"In addition, not all websites are trustworthy or provide accurate information. The goal of this 'think-tank' meeting is to convene experts to wrestle with the thorny problem of how best to connect military families with online resources available to them, given the constraints that exist when trying to accomplish that goal. In other words, facilitate a productive conversation . . . an experience, where experts can brainstorm solutions to these challenges. Additionally, I think an online venue would serve as the most convenient option to bring diverse perspectives together to consider the challenges facing military families."

Andrea thought that she had understood the basics of the problem—a combination of military family members' difficulties in using the resources as well as poorly designed online resources, but she couldn't help but feel a little overwhelmed by the description Karen had just provided and uncertainty about what a think-tank day actually involved, not to mention, an online think-tank experience.

Sara looked up from the notes she had been taking and asked, "I understand you want a group of individuals to address these problems that are facing military families. So, what do you envision for the think-tank event?"

Karen considered the question before answering, "I really see a range of possible outcomes, but that is where I'm counting on your expertise." Still looking at Amelia, she continued, "First, as I mentioned, this will give experts an opportunity to really think about this problem. Also, I'm thinking this same group might be up for writing a white paper on the topic. I'm hoping that this could lead to funding for a technology solution to the problems facing these families."

Andrea jumped into the conversation, "You mentioned experts—who do you think would be best qualified to participate in the workshop?"

Without hesitation, Karen replied, "I am relying on you to do the heavy lifting in terms of figuring out who to invite, helping me determine the substantive approaches, structuring the day, and so on. But, I'll use my contacts to assist you with recruitment. Also, my assistant, Jessica Adamson, is available to help you."

"So, logistically," Amelia started, "you're still thinking about a one-day event six to eight weeks from now?"

"Yes, that's right," Karen responded. "My team will handle setting up the online platform and sending the link to attendees." Turning to Sara and Andrea for the first time, Karen said, "To understand the complexity of the problems, I suggest that you also conduct interviews with several individuals who have experienced these types of problems firsthand."

"Do you have any contacts who might be willing to be interviewed?" Andrea asked.

"Sure. At our organization, there are a couple of ladies whose spouses previously were in the military. Also, we have a gentleman who is an Army veteran. I can give you their contact information. I'll send you some other contacts as well," Karen answered.

Just as Karen was finishing her response, her cell phone began beeping. "I really must be off to my next engagement. I look forward to seeing what you come up with for the think-tank event. With several weeks, you should have plenty of time to create something that provides an in-depth look at this problem and meet the goal of envisioning a solution that helps connecting military families with online resources." Karen zipped her coat and exited the coffee shop.

"I need to head to a department meeting," said Amelia. "But, before I go, what are your initial reactions to the project?"

"I'm still wrapping my head around what Karen told us. It all seems really vague," Sara started.

Andrea wasn't sure what to say exactly. She didn't want to appear incompetent, but at this point, she couldn't even think about how to respond. She said, "I think I need some time to consider what Karen shared with us."

"Well, let's set up some time to discuss next steps," Amelia decided. The group planned to meet in Amelia's office in exactly one week.

Amelia headed to her meeting across campus, thinking to herself, "This is a really broad project, but luckily it seems that Karen has some leads. This should be okay." Meanwhile, Sara and Andrea headed back to their shared office in the College of Education. As they walked, they discussed the meeting.

Andrea started, "Was it just me, or did you feel that Karen pretty much ignored us when relaying project details?"

"Yes! I hope that's not a bad sign for having a good client relationship!" Sara agreed. "And yet she says that she expects us to do the 'heavy lifting' for this project. And, what exactly is a think-tank event anyway?"

Shaking her head, Andrea admitted, "I'm not really sure, but I hope we can figure that out soon—I don't want to let Amelia down. She's been so supportive in giving us opportunities like this to develop our design skills. Sometimes I worry I'll never get the hang of projects like this. I feel like such an imposter. What do you think of conducting several interviews?"

Sara frowned, "With only about two months—at the most—before the think-tank workshop, conducting, reviewing, and analyzing interviews could be a pretty time intensive commitment."

Andrea nodded and wondered aloud, "I'm sure hoping that some of Karen's contacts will be willing to participate." The pair decided that their next step would be to take some time before their meeting with Amelia to investigate both the problem under consideration and the suggested format.

UNDERSTANDING THE PROBLEM

To prepare for their next meeting with Amelia, Sara and Andrea devised a tentative plan to explore the problem that the workshop was intended to resolve and to review the demographics of military personnel and their families. After discussing the initial meeting details, they believed that understanding both of these components was crucial for recruiting representative participants for the think-tank day, as Karen really didn't answer their question regarding who she envisioned participating in the workshop. Both women agreed to meet up prior to their meeting with Amelia to consider Karen's requests.

The sun streamed through the small office window, despite the snow on the ground and the chill in the air. Sara sat at her computer and opened up a browser window. Andrea sat nearby with her tablet gently resting on her lap.

"Before we start investigating the problem, let's look at some military personnel statistics," suggested Andrea.

Soon the pair had compiled a list of statistics from various military websites (see Figure 9.3).

"Wow!" Sara exclaimed. "The military personnel are extremely diverse. No wonder focusing the target audience is challenging."

After the women had studied the data, Sara suggested, "Let's try to put ourselves in the shoes of these service members and try searching for information on a specific topic."

Notes and Statistics Regarding Military Personnel

- Active-duty branches: Air Force, Army, Coast Guard, Marine Corps, Navy, Space Force
- Reserve branches: Air National Guard and Air Force Reserve, Army National Guard, Army Reserve, Marine Corps Reserve, Navy Reserve, Coast Guard Reserve
- Total active-duty service members by branch:
    - Air Force: 328,888
    - Army: 482,416
    - Coast Guard: 40,487
    - Marine Corps: 179,378
    - Navy: 343,223
- The total number of military personnel is greater than 3.5 million (with the largest groups being active duty [37.8%], ready reserve [30.9%], DoD civilian personnel [24.9%]).
- Active duty comprises 82.3% enlisted personnel and 17.7% officers with 17.3% female members and 82.7% male members.
- The average age of active-duty personnel (28.4):
    - 25 years old or younger: 44.4%
    - 26–30 years old: 21.5%
    - 31–35 years old: 15%
    - 36–40 years old: 11%
    - 41 years old or older: 8%
- Military personnel race demographics:
    - American Indian or Alaska Native: 1.0%
    - Asian: 4.9%
    - Black or African American: 16.9%
    - Multi-racial: 2.6%
    - Native Hawaiian or other Pacific Islander: 1.1%
    - Other/unknown: 3.2%
    - White: 70.5%

    (*Note:* 17.7% of the total military force identifies as Hispanic or Latino)
- Military family demographics active-duty and reserves
    - Family members (spouses, children, adult dependents): 2,129,656
    - Single with no children: 46.8%
    - Married to a civilian, with children: 29.4%; married dual-military: 2.1%
    - Married to a civilian, no children: 12.9%; married dual-military, no children: 3.2%
    - Single with children: 5.6%

FIGURE 9.3 Military demographic notes.

"Great idea! Why don't we start with healthcare?" suggested Andrea. The office grew quiet as Sara and Andrea began their research. A cloud outside partly covered the sun causing the small office to become slightly darker. After both women had a chance to review several sites, Andrea broke the silence. "I can definitely see how people would become frustrated simply trying to find resources and then figuring out if the information is even accurate. For instance, pull up ArmedForcesDirectSupport.com (see Figure 9.4). This is a pretty typical website based on what I've found. Look at how much information is available. Even if someone had experience with military life, I still think navigating this website would be pretty challenging, and that's assuming that you already had an idea about the specific information you were seeking.

"I'm thinking about what Karen mentioned about planning for a duty station in Okinawa and getting required vaccines. Trying to find requirements took a little sifting. In one discussion forum, I read about a family with a baby that was not eligible to receive all of the required vaccines until she was at least six months old, which resulted in the family being separated from the military member and moving at a later date. Preparing for an international move would be pretty different if the military member was single compared to if the military member was married with children . . . And this is thinking about things from a healthcare perspective—there would be several other considerations like locating housing, moving belongings, getting appropriate documentation for all family members, and so on."

"I agree, the sheer lack of organization is overwhelming," Sara added, as a fine dusting of snowflakes outside their window caught her eye.

"I think we can work with this as a starting point for the workshop. Let's ask Amelia to help us with next steps in our upcoming meeting," Andrea offered.

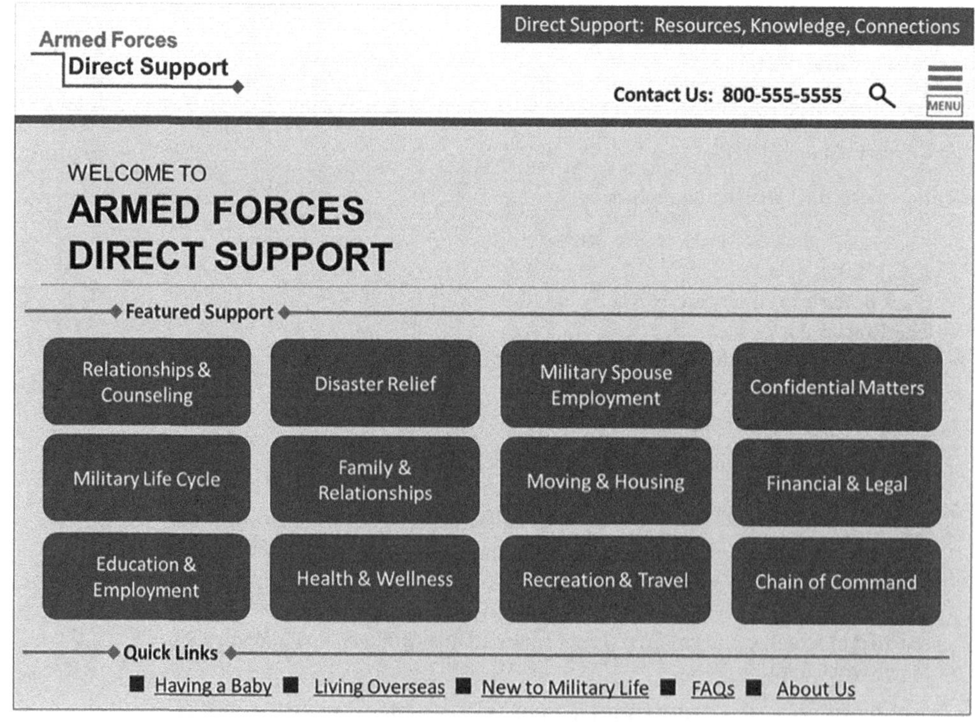

FIGURE 9.4 Armed forces direct support website.

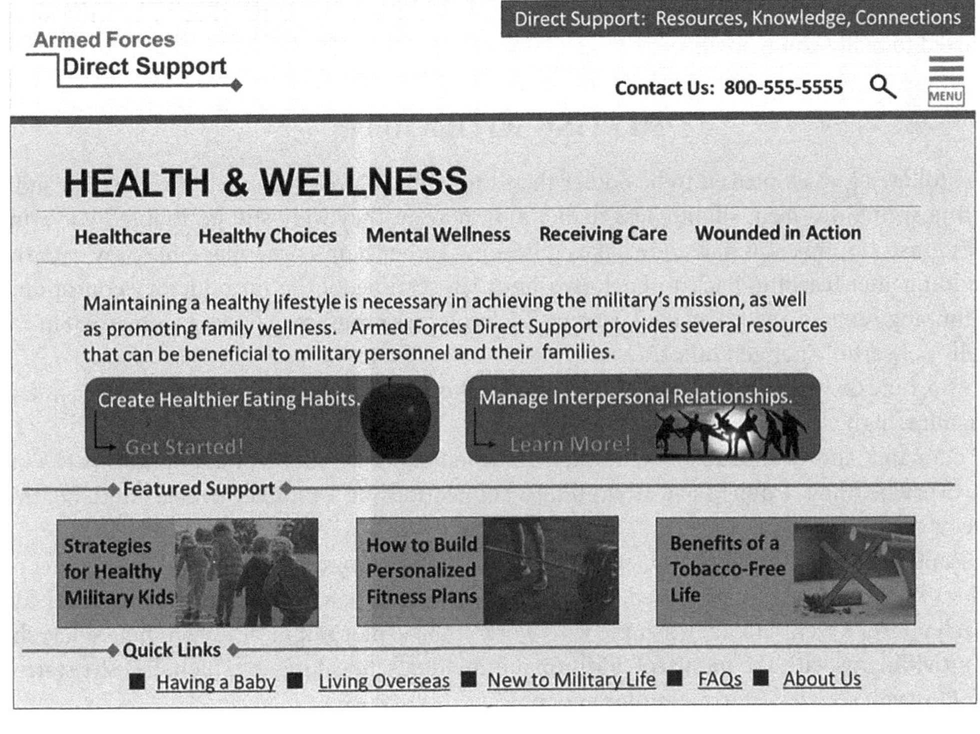

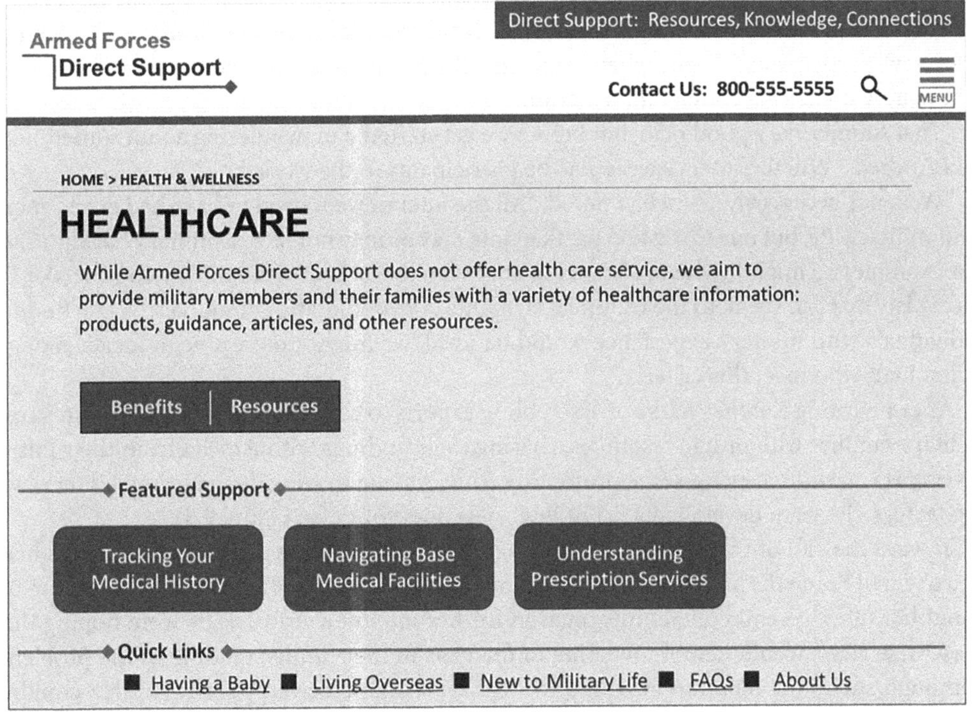

FIGURE 9.4 Continued

The two women closed their office and headed home to their families before the snow started to really come down.

MEETING WITH AMELIA

The following week proved to be cooler than the week before. Even with the calendar indicating spring was near, slightly less than a month away, they were still undoubtedly in winter's grasp. Andrea still had snowflakes glistening in her hair as she made her way into the building after teaching back-to-back two-hour lab sections of the introductory educational technology course offered by the Learning Technologies program. All three women sat in Dr. Kelly's cheerfully painted office.

"So, how do we feel about this project and working with our client, Karen?" Amelia asked, encouragingly.

Sara and Andrea looked at each other, and then Sara offered, "To be honest, this is a little overwhelming. I don't have any military connections or a military background. So, this seems so daunting."

Amelia smiled. "I understand—it is a very different demographic. Luckily, I have someone who has agreed to be interviewed, and I think I might have a few additional contacts I can reach out to. Karen said a few people who work at the center might be able to help. Plus, she is providing us with the names of additional individuals. Speaking of which, has she started sending you contact information for anyone?"

Looking at Sara, Andrea responded, "I haven't received anything. Sara, have you?"

Sara shook her head.

Amelia suggested, "How about we start with the types of questions you'd like to ask the interview participants? Then, when you send Karen the questions for approval, you can follow-up with getting contact information."

"That sounds like a good plan, but before we get started, I'm wondering about something," said Andrea. "Will the interviewees also be participants in the workshop?"

"Well, not necessarily," Amelia offered. "All the interviewees need to have had experiences with military life, but our workshop participants may or may not have a military background. For example, we might invite professors or staff who've worked with military contracts or IT specialists that can speak to the technical elements of disseminating resources. While finding individuals with military experience would be ideal, we might not be able to locate enough individuals who meet this criteria."

After revisiting Karen's charge of assembling experts to consider a solution for connecting military families with online resources, sharing their findings with Amelia from their initial investigation, and receiving some prompting from Amelia to consider additional interviewing factors, the team developed a list of interview questions (see Figure 9.5).

Toward the end of the meeting, Andrea agreed to clean up the questions with Sara's help and to email Karen the first draft of the questions in order to get feedback and also to follow-up about her offer to send contact information for her interview leads. They were hoping that these interviews would help fill in some of the gaps in their understanding of the problem. Although she didn't mention anything for fear of being perceived poorly, Andrea couldn't shake an uneasy feeling she had about completing the interviews. With a short timeline and a tight budget, no solid leads, and the time commitment required for conducting and analyzing interviews, she wondered how they would manage to complete this task. While working with a different professor on an unrelated project, Andrea had voiced concerns about the

- *Are you or your spouse in the military?*
- *What is your family structure?*
- *How long have you or your spouse been enlisted or commissioned?*
- *Where do you normally receive most information related to needs associated with military life (e.g., relocation)?*
- *When you need information on needs associated with military life (e.g., healthcare), where do you go?*
- *What types of problems/frustrations have you experienced with locating information on needs associated with military life (e.g., housing)? Can you describe a specific situation/story to help me understand?*
- *What types of technology do you use?*
- *How do you use this technology to support any concerns or needs you have related to military life?*
- *Have you experienced challenges with using technological tools or resources when trying to locate information related to military life? If so, can you describe one?*

FIGURE 9.5 Draft questions for military family interviews.

required time commitment, only to be told, "Don't be lazy—this is what it's like when you're getting a PhD."

Sensing Andrea's uncertainty, Amelia asked, "Is everything okay, Andrea?"

Andrea managed a smile, forced the thought from her head, and shared another real concern she had. "Yes! I guess I'm just nervous about completing the interviews because I don't have much experience doing them."

Sara agreed that she was also anxious about the interview process.

"Try not to be nervous," Amelia reassured them. "These are initial questions, but you'll want to think of additional follow-up questions that will be helpful to ask. Creating follow-up questions will help you prepare for the conversations and lead to more developed responses from the interviewees. Plus, you'll think of other things to ask when you're in the moment."

Andrea's uneasiness only increased when several more days passed without receiving a response from Karen. After a quick check with Sara, they decided to ask Amelia for help, which led to a series of emails (see Figure 9.6).

After receiving Karen's email, Andrea received a text from Sara seeking her thoughts on Karen's response (see Figure 9.7). As the women texted back and forth, Andrea couldn't help feeling thankful for the easy relationship she and Sara shared. The friendship offered support for making sense of their developing professional identities.

PLANNING FOR AFFSC THINK TANK

A week later, Sara and Andrea felt more confident about their progress on the project. Sara settled into her campus office, removed her coat, logged onto her computer, and put in her wireless earbuds. Once she had logged into her computer, she clicked the chat button on her video conferencing application. "Hey, Andrea!" Sara greeted her friend as her screen came into view. Andrea was sitting at the kitchen table as her two red-headed boys could be heard playing in the background. "I'm glad we were able to find a time to chat with everything going on," Sara said.

"I have been thinking about the format of the workshop, and I think that we could use a hook to help engage the think-tank experts," suggested Andrea.

"Well, is there some way we can showcase the experiences of one of the interviewees?" asked Sara. "I like that idea—what about a short movie to introduce the problem?" suggested Andrea as a little face appeared behind her for a brief moment.

From: Huffman, Andrea <ahuffman@cmstate.edu>
Sent: February 24 at 8:11 AM
To: Livingston, Karen <livingston@affsc.org>
CC: Kelly, Amelia <akelly@cmstate.edu>; Brody, Sara <sbrody@cmstate.edu>
Subject: AFFSC Workshop- Interview Questions and Contacts

Hello Karen,

Sara and I plan to interview individuals for the AFFSC project. From these interviews, we hope to gain a clear idea of the problem from the point of view of individuals experiencing it.

We plan to ask the questions in the attached document. How do these sound? What suggestions do you have?

Also, you had mentioned in our meeting that you could connect us with individuals to interview. Do you have that information for us?

We look forward to your feedback!
Thanks,
Andrea

Andrea Huffman, Doctoral Student
College of Education
Central Midwest State University

From: Huffman, Andrea <ahuffman@cmstate.edu>
Sent: March 1 at 8:33 AM
To: Kelly, Amelia <akelly@cmstate.edu>
CC: Brody, Sara <sbrody@cmstate.edu>
Subject: AFFSC Workshop - Interview Questions and Contacts

Hey Amelia,

So, Sara and I have received no response from Karen on our questions for the interviews. Should we just proceed with the contacts that you connected us with? We don't want to wait too long and not be ready for the big day. Also, do we have a date for the event?

Thanks!
Andrea

Andrea Huffman, Doctoral Student
College of Education

From: Kelly, Amelia <akelly@cmstate.edu>
Sent: March 1 at 10:07 AM
To: Huffman, Andrea <ahuffman@cmstate.edu>
CC: Brody, Sara <sbrody@cmstate.edu>
Subject: AFFSC Workshop - Interview Questions and Contacts

Let me try one more time.

Sent from my iPhone

From: Kelly, Amelia <akelly@cmstate.edu>
Sent: March 1 at 10:17 AM
To: Livingston, Karen <livingston@affsc.org>
CC: Brody, Sara <sbrody@cmstate.edu>; Huffman, Andrea <ahuffman@cmstate.edu>
Subject: AFFSC Workshop - Interview Questions and Contacts

Hi Karen,

Can you let Andrea & Sara know when you might be able to get them some feedback so they can go ahead and get some interviews set up. We just want to make sure they have included info that is in agreement with what you were thinking. Also, some information on potential interviewees.

Thanks,
Amelia

Amelia Kelly, Ph.D.
College of Education
Central Midwest State University

From: Livingston, Karen <livingston@affsc.org>
Sent: March 2 at 3:40 PM
To: Huffman, Andrea <ahuffman@cmstate.edu>
Subject: RE: AFFSC Workshop - Interview Questions and Contacts

Fine. Follow these up with probes as you learn about the issues, and you'll learn more ideas to ask about. I'll look forward to seeing the agenda. I thought I had previously hooked you up with Terri Andrews, who is a military spouse. Dave Rankin in our office is a military veteran who might also have a good perspective - Terri can do introductions for that. Tina Zendejas also could help.

Karen

Karen Livingston
Director: Armed Forces Family Support Center

FIGURE 9.6 E-mail exchange.

"That makes sense," Sara continued. "What if we approached this in a problem-centered way? For example, we could start with a movie showcasing a typical problem facing military members or their spouses and how they tried to solve it using Internet resources. Then, the rest of the morning can be dedicated to prompting the participants to think through different aspects of the problem and potential solutions. We can use breakout rooms for this part, and then, in the afternoon, we can engage them in several scenarios that focus on solutions."

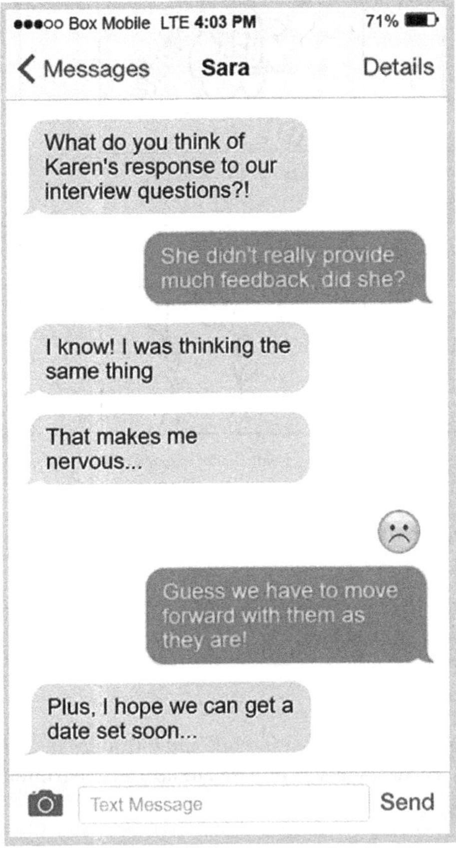

FIGURE 9.7 Text conversation between Sara and Andrea.

"That sounds great!" Andrea offered. "Since Karen wants the think-tank participants to really wrestle with the problem, we could ask participants to think through real-life scenarios from the different stakeholder group perspectives, like a military spouse with children, a young new military member, a single parent, et cetera. How would you like to divide the work?"

"Why don't I create a high-level storyboard for the introductory movie, and you create a detailed outline of the agenda for the workshop?" Sara suggested.

"That works," Andrea agreed. "Let's plan to send these drafts to Amelia in a few days to see what she thinks."

As planned, after creating the initial drafts, Sara sent Amelia the storyboard and agenda outline (see Figures 9.8 and 9.9).

MEETING WITH KAREN

After receiving timely feedback from Amelia on their draft workshop materials, Andrea and Sara immediately forwarded their ideas to Karen. At the same time, they found themselves in the familiar state of becoming apprehensive about their timeline, as a week passed before receiving a response from Karen. When she did finally reply, she agreed to a meeting to discuss the workshop.

Opening scene representing all branches

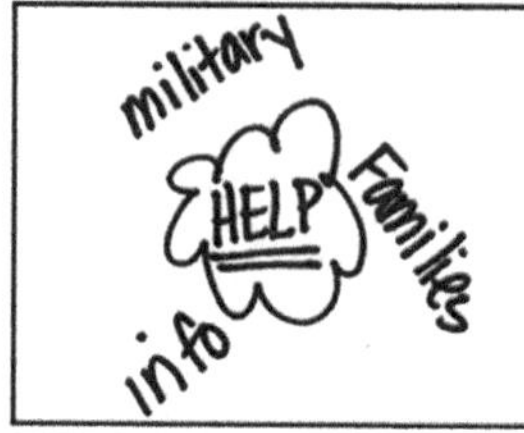

Introduction of the problem

Example of the problem from a military family's perspective

Sample search for information illustrating problem

Interviews with military members

Next steps toward a solution

FIGURE 9.8 Draft introductory movie storyboard.

Proposed AFFSC Think-Tank Day Agenda

<u>Kick Off the Meeting</u>

- **8:00–8:15, Greetings:** Karen will welcome everyone and introduce the project.
- **8:15–8:45, Introductions:** Participants will be asked to take a couple minutes to introduce themselves.

<u>PART I: Exploring the Problem</u>
(Goal: Participants fully understand the problem.)

- **8:45–9:00, Overview of the Day:** Andrea and Sara will provide an overview of the day (including objectives) and answer any initial questions.
- **9:00–9:20, Introduction to the Problem:** Movie focusing on interviews with service members and spouses relating their experiences searching for and locating information related to common challenges (e.g., relocation, financial planning). Additional information from interview findings will be presented to participants.

Work in Small Breakout Groups

- **9:20–9:40, Military Family Structure Activity:** Participants will identify potential needs of various military service member family structures and resources that can potentially meet these needs:
  - Single, recently enlisted
  - Married, no kids, recently enlisted
  - Married, 3 kids, senior military member
  - Single parent, 2 kids
- **9:40–10:10, Mini-Case Activity:** Participants will work in breakout groups (pairs/threes) and be assigned a mini case. As they are working, they will answer these questions, from the perspective of an assigned stakeholder:
  - What information is the stakeholder seeking?
  - What are the most important attributes of the relevant stakeholder?
  - What resources can the relevant stakeholder potentially access?
  - What problems and challenges do the stakeholder encounter?

(Note: *Participants will each be given a Google Doc link and asked to complete a table that can be easily shared with the rest of the group.*)

FIGURE 9.9 Draft agenda for the think-tank event.

- ▶ **10:10–10:35, Debrief:** Facilitators will pull up each group's work:
  - Ask participants to share their answers to the questions.
  - Ask participants to identify common themes across reported answers.

(Note: *These themes will be recorded using a Google Doc for all to see.*)

- ▶ **10:35–11:05, Exploring Online Resources:** Participants will receive an "official letter" from the US military encouraging them to explore specific online sources (e.g., armed forces direct support, social media sites). Facilitators will ask participants to consider the letter and the following questions from the point of view of the stakeholders discussed in their case:
  - What resources did you access (as recommended in the letter and others not from the letter)?
  - What resource(s) proved the most beneficial?
  - What are strengths and weaknesses for the resources you reviewed?
  - Think about the most important attributes of the stakeholders in your case and the resources that you've reviewed. Identify the most relevant issues with the resources from the perspective of your assigned stakeholder.

(Note: *Participants will each be given a Google Doc link, and asked to complete a table that can be easily shared with the rest of the group.*)

- ▶ **11:05–11:50, Report Findings:** Facilitators will pull up participants' findings via the Google Doc. Participants will be asked to share what resources they viewed and their thoughts on that resource. For example, the facilitator will ask the first group, "What is one resource that you accessed? What are your thoughts about this resource's strengths and weaknesses?" Then, the facilitator will ask other groups if they have accessed that resource and have anything else they would like to add. This method will be repeated for several online resources.
- ▶ **11:50–11:55:** Karen will wrap up the morning session.
- ▶ **11:55–12:45, Lunch Break:** Participants will each be given a preloaded gift card to order lunch and have it delivered to their location.

PART II: Exploring Potential Solutions
(Goal: Participants identify specific ways that the identified problems can be addressed while weighing pros and cons.)

- ▶ **12:45–2:45: Work in Small Groups**
  1. Facilitators will display results from the first activity.
  2. Participants will work in breakout groups and discuss potential solutions for each identified problem:
     - Identify a range of solutions to address the identified problems. After evaluating several solutions, decide on your best 2–3.
     - What implications do military realities have for each proposed solution? What are the benefits and limitations of each proposed solution?
  3. Participants will be given the following prompt:

Recently, the AFFSC posted a call for grant proposals to promote the exploration of using Internet technologies in the dissemination of supportive information to military families. You have decided to submit a proposal. Specifically, in the proposal, the AFFSC would like to hear how you would design a specific solution that meets the diverse needs of military members and their spouses. Be sure to consider how this solution addresses aspects of current resources.

4. Participants will work in small groups to design a solution that addresses the diverse needs of military stakeholders. Participants will develop short presentations (approximately 10 minutes) using PowerPoint or another tool.

- ▶ **2:45–3:00, Break**
- ▶ **3:00–4:00, Proposed Solutions**
  - Proposed solutions will be revisited/discussed—how can we use the strongest features from each potential solution to address the problem?
  - How is scalability being considered?
  - Karen's concluding thoughts

FIGURE 9.9 Continued

Sara and Andrea walked from the College of Education building to the nearby coffee shop to meet Karen. Although the day was crisp, there were signs of spring all around them. Both women felt confident and even excited about presenting Karen with their plans for the workshop. They made their way into the coffee shop several minutes early, finding a quiet corner in the cafe. Andrea took out her tablet and Sara organized her notes. Karen appeared before them, "Hello, girls." As pleasantries were exchanged, Karen took a seat and placed her smartphone purposefully on the table in front of her and looked directly at the women.

With that, Andrea began. "In thinking about how we envision the workshop, we wanted to include a creative element that not only hooks and engages the think-tank participants, but that begins to explore the scope of the problem."

"Yes, we have conducted three interviews—including ones with Tina Zendejas and Terri Andrews. We also interviewed Meredith Kowalski, someone that Amelia connected us with. We plan to incorporate these into a short video." Sara paused.

Andrea found herself thinking, "We would have had a fourth interview if one of the contacts that Karen had provided hadn't declined for 'professional reasons.' "

Her thoughts were interrupted as Karen interjected, "Three interviews? Three is not nearly enough to fully understand the problem military families face in seeking out information. I suggest you do more interviews and also post a message at some of the social media sites where young military spouses tend to congregate and see if you can find any additional folks who would be willing to talk with you. I am disappointed that this wasn't considered before now."

Although Sara felt a bit defeated, she continued, "After considering the goal for the workshop, we decided that it would be useful if we used a problem-centered approach to engage the think-tank participants in considering the issues."

Before Sara could continue, the women were interrupted by a tall man with graying hair and a large smile gracing his face. "Karen!" he exclaimed.

"Mark! It's so good to see you," Karen replied.

Andrea and Sara exchanged glances and looked at their notes as the two shared a few words.

"I would love to catch up with you and Margaret soon. As you can see, I am in a meeting with these two undergrad students, but contact my assistant, and we'll have lunch."

As the man walked away, Karen turned swiftly and looked directly at Andrea and Sara. "Frankly, I am disappointed. I was hoping you would have the audience consider a way technology could solve this problem. Specifically, I was thinking that you could use the structure of websites like Kayak, Yelp, or even TripAdvisor as a way for military people to narrow the scope of the information available, as well as determine its credibility. I suggest you incorporate those types of sites as a way for the participants to attempt to solve the issues. Do you think you can do that?"

"Of course, Sara and I can take a deeper look at these types of technologies and find a way to incorporate something like them into our plans," offered Andrea with a smile trying to ease the tension.

"And you mentioned additional interviews," added Sara. "How many do you think would be ideal?"

"I suggest you review the plan with Dr. Edmund Tanaka to be sure that it makes good sense to him. Personally, I can't decide whether it is a little too structured for such a sophisticated group of data folks, or if it is just what is needed to help them get 'inside the heads' of the typically young, inexperienced folks who are in the position of needing these services. Jessica has Dr. Tanaka's contact info. He will be able to provide additional feedback on what you have here. If you have any other questions, ask Jessica or Dr. Tanaka for help. I have another meeting I need to get to."

With that, Karen grabbed her smartphone and headed out of the coffee shop. As she walked away, Andrea thought, "She never answered our question, and who is Dr. Tanaka?"

"Wow . . ." Andrea sighed. "I really didn't see our meeting going that way."

"Me neither," Sara responded. "I'm not sure how we are going to complete more interviews, create activities for the technological aspect that Karen wants, *and* receive feedback from Dr. Tanaka in the time we have left before the workshop. With the workshop date set for April 16, that leaves us just a little over three weeks. By the way, do you know who Dr. Tanaka is?"

Andrea shook her head.

Sara continued, "Plus, we didn't even have a chance to discuss recruitment of the workshop participants. Karen never really shared who should be invited to the workshop, but today she mentioned 'data folks.' How many participants have agreed to come?"

Andrea accessed a file on her tablet, "According to my notes, we have two information technologists, a communication professor, two veterans, and a couple of military spouses . . . Oh, and a former homeland security specialist. So . . . what does that make? Eight?"

"I don't know how we'll be able get everything done in such a short timeframe with our heavy teaching commitments. We'll both have 50 student projects to grade at the end of the week." Andrea frowned.

"Plus, you have your prelims, and we have that paper to finish in our *Issues and Methods in Research Design* course," Sara added.

"With all these extra hours, have you stopped to calculate how much our hourly pay would be?" Andrea asked. "I'm not sure, but it can't be good, and it just keeps getting worse. This project seemed like such a good way to earn some money to help pay for that conference we both wanted to attend," Sara sighed.

NOW WHAT

A couple of days following their meeting with Karen, Sara and Andrea sat in Amelia's office recapping the details and expressing their uncertainty about how to move forward with the workshop. With only three weeks until the event, they felt at a loss regarding how to address Karen's new requests. As Amelia listened to Sara and Andrea, she couldn't help but wonder how such a seemingly simple request for a one-day online workshop had become so problematic.

Preliminary Analysis Questions

1. Critique Sara and Andrea's approach to the design of the think-tank workshop, including their use of a problem-centered approach, their development of interview questions, and their use of a video to highlight stakeholders' perspectives.
2. In this case, Amelia wanted to provide an authentic experience for Sara and Andrea. Evaluate the mentoring strategies that she used in this case. How did Amelia's mentoring approach influence the progress and outcomes of the project?

3. From the beginning of the project, Sara and Andrea's relationship with Karen was strained. What factors contributed to this strain? What could have been done, if anything, at the outset of the project to build a better relationship?
4. At the end of the case, Karen presents some new challenges for Sara and Andrea. Moving forward, what actions might Sara and Andrea take to complete the project?
5. One challenge facing Sara and Andrea is that they are still developing their professional identities. Consider the different roles that the women embrace during the case (e.g., graduate student, instructional designer, mentee). How do their developing identities impact various aspects of the project, and what steps can they take to effectively navigate their various roles?

Implications for ID Practice

1. What design options are open to an ID professional when access to important information is either vague or limited?
2. How should ID consultants work with clients who fail to share ownership of an ID project but who expect the consultant to do the "heavy lifting?"
3. At times, in the advanced stages of design, clients make additional project requests, which weren't established upfront. How can ID consultants handle these types of situations while being mindful of managing client expectations, scope creep, and constraints?
4. Describe the strategies a mentor needs to use when team members have varying levels of knowledge and experience. How do these strategies specifically impact the design process?
5. Describe elements of effective mentoring for new ID professionals entering the ID workforce. Provide recommendations for what it takes to be a good mentor and a good mentee.

10

Anthony Cerise

The Care, Feeding, and Growing Pains of a Multidisciplinary Undergraduate Program

Elizabeth Boling and Colin M. Gray

THE INTEGRATED DESIGN PROGRAM (IDP)

Hustling across campus at Mid-State University, Anthony Cerise, an associate professor in the College of Education, juggles his backpack, his morning coffee in a paper cup, and the agenda he just printed for a meeting to which he hopes he will not be late. His scarf is flapping across his face thanks to a stiff fall breeze, blinding him off and on, but in a stroke of luck he spots the campus bus in time to flag it down, only spilling a little coffee as he does so. He sprints up the bus steps and flops down on a worn vinyl seat just behind the driver, who sees him on this route between the education and engineering buildings often enough not to require his campus ID when he boards. Good thing, too; he doesn't have a hand free to fish his wallet out of his pocket. It was also fortunate that he caught the bus, he thinks; it's important to arrive on time today without having to sprint. This meeting is being held to discuss issues with the IDP (or, as the dean always states in full, the Integrated Design Program). Showing up disheveled, let alone late, would not put him on the right foot. Sure, the program is a big success—that's the problem, in fact; it has grown so large and so quickly that he and his colleagues desperately need to confer on where it is coming apart at the seams. But Anthony is keenly aware of the tensions which have existed in the program since the beginning, not to mention those between the program and the administration right now. As the leader of the faculty team which designs and implements the program, he works to keep an even keel and to exude confidence on behalf of them all. He'd like to maintain that presence. More than that, he doesn't want to give Roger Went, head of the administrative steering committee, any reason to carry back to the other deans an impression that their current growing pains are any worse than they really are. Despite the ballooning enrollments in IDP, or perhaps because of them, Anthony knows there are those on campus who wouldn't mind seeing this program shut down. It is drawing enrollments away from other majors, including those currently contributing to the multidisciplinary effort as partners. Others, he suspects, are eyeing the program as a candidate for moving online with outsourcing for recruitment and program management, the idea being that if it is growing as a campus program, it will surely be a moneymaker online. If he and his fellow colleagues cannot handle their current

DOI: 10.4324/9781003354468-12

growing pains, he worries that the institutional support they need will be withdrawn or that the program might be effectively taken out of their hands.

HOW IT STARTED

As the bus rumbles across campus, Anthony takes a drink of his coffee and considers how far the program has come since the early days. He smiles wryly, thinking about one of the first meetings he and his program colleagues had around the design of the program. Although they were all excited about the multidisciplinary work they were embarking on, they had stalled immediately over their individual understandings of a studio-based program.

Coming from a background in Human-Computer Interface Design, Marta de la Torre was used to large courses in which the hands-on component of learning centered around project teams who found places to work together all over campus, including in libraries and in the student center. "A lot of them work in each other's dorm rooms," she had laughed, describing her HCI studio class, "and they all use their laptops to share their documents and prototypes online. I call it the paperless studio!"

Jack Sanders had been appalled as Marta spoke. He was naturally a quiet guy, but he had interrupted her almost rudely—"How could you possibly provide adequate guidance to 40 or 50 students at a time?" he asked incredulously. "Especially when you're not right there in the moment to see them working and to discuss with them what they're doing? I mean, that's just how studio teaching works!" His first few years of teaching in Communications Design had been very traditional, with small groups of students working independently in dedicated spaces open to them 24/7 where they spread their work-in-progress over every free surface, and where they ate and sometimes even slept as their project deadlines approached.

"Marta, is it even ethical to have students doing design work outside of a studio space?" Jack asked earnestly.

"Are you saying I have not been teaching ethically?" she shot back.

Anthony had needed to think on his feet during that meeting! Quickly he had suggested that they turn their attention to listing the core activities each one of them believed that studio students should carry out, *then* discuss when and where these activities would take place, recognizing that this new program might have to look different than those of their collective experiences. For himself, he added, he had some experience blending face-to-face consultations with instructors and online work with project teams in prior studios, some of them with large enrollments. They might be able to work out a plan, he suggested, and over several days they managed to do so and even to reach some productive compromises in understanding. The current plan (see Figure 10.1), although space intensive, was working well, he reflected. Two classrooms, which were recently upgraded with reconfigurable tables and chairs, were booked two hours a day for three days each week. These were used for class meeting hours, which were organized flexibly for critique, demonstration, guest speakers, and other formats. Therefore, those classrooms were left open for other classes a substantial amount of the time, while a third, smaller classroom was designated to the studio program, full time, as a workspace. Because these were close together, they formed a sort of center for the program, with the workroom as the hub. They'd had to work through Jack's concern that some students never used the workroom, and they found themselves routinely requesting more hours in the class meeting rooms, but Anthony felt the plan had been successful for the most part.

The same had been true for their co-teaching model. Originally, they had decided that co-teaching would allow them to bring their separate areas of expertise together naturally

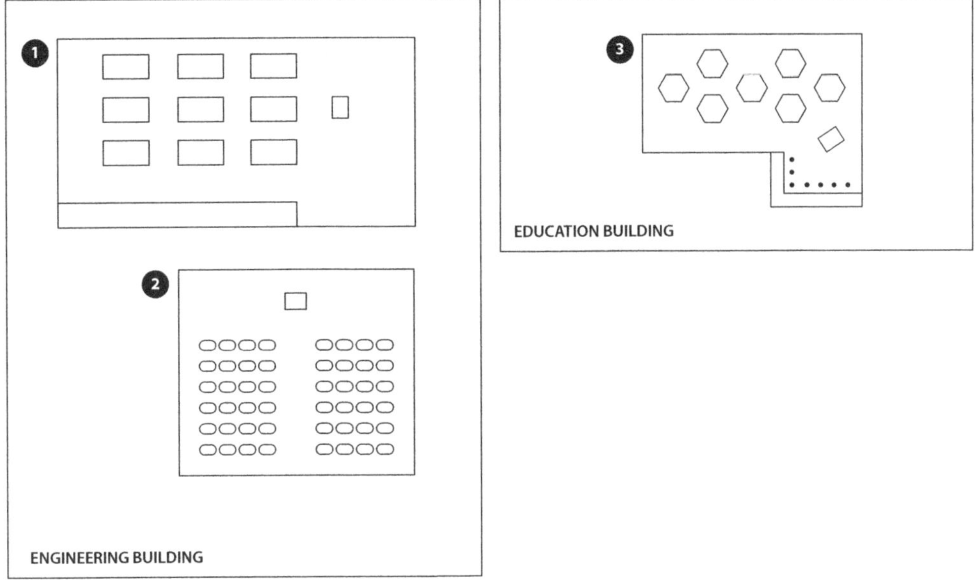

FIGURE 10.1 Floor plan sketches of three rooms used in program.

and help them align disparate elements of the program which were drawn from different disciplines to form a coherent, and rich, curriculum. With classroom experiences in common and tangible student work to discuss, working out conceptual issues proved to be manageable, if not easy. Anthony recalled an especially lively discussion one midterm when Jack suggested awarding minimum points to half the project teams because their project boards were "painfully ugly, almost unreadable," while Marta was excited about the manifestly high level of attention those same teams had paid to incorporating user perspectives into their draft designs, and he himself was wrestling with the extreme variation in quality between the teams' written reports. Recognizing, and reconciling, how they placed value on these aspects of project work led to significant cross-domain discussions about the outcomes of teaching and how the workplaces they envisioned for their students after graduation differed across fields of practice. This had proven to be important work in shaping the program, especially now that the question of assessment was becoming ever more central in the focus of both the faculty and the administration.

Anthony couldn't quite recall whether the push for explicit documentation of program quality assessments had come from the administration first, or whether he and his colleagues had already begun discussing competency versus mastery-based assessment when the word came down about program quality. Whichever it had been, Anthony did remember his surprise when Jack had remarked in a program meeting, "We're preparing these folks for work as designers out in the world; wouldn't a competency approach to assessment make the most sense for us?" While he thought of Jack as a more traditional educator than Marta, she was the one who pointed out that committing to a competency system would require dismantling their current program and starting all over again. She wasn't ready to go that far but volunteered to work with Anthony on identifying some shared strands of competencies across the core courses in the program. They had settled on several aspects of studio—collaborative project work, engagement in the studio culture through critique participation and peer

FIGURE 10.2 Student mock-up of a "Studio Pioneers" t-shirt.

mentoring, and regular opportunities for feedback on projects prior to turn-in—as a percentage of the overall grade for all core courses in the program.

He had appreciated how open Marta was about these changes, especially after Andrea Xin joined the program. At that memory he winced a little, and not just because his coffee was now growing cold. He reminded himself that they had needed to add a member of faculty because the program had been growing, and that Andrea arrived with a promising set of credentials. The problem had been, he thought, that her experiences in engineering design had been with relatively large-scale courses, often 50 or 60 students in what they called "design labs," and that these experiences had seemingly imprinted her with a rigid view of how design should be taught. He also admitted to himself that he, Marta, and Jack had already built up a shared vision of the program among themselves. They were trying to share that vision with Andrea and to be open to her influence on the program. But now she was pushing relentlessly for what she termed "the only fiscally rational model," which relied on growing classes to the maximum size possible and using a kind of sink or swim approach to teaching which kept the effort required of instructors manageable.

This was an ongoing tension because, at least from Anthony's perspective, it was difficult to contemplate stepping away from the hard work they had done getting this program to a viable place. At the start, when there was no appropriate textbook, no real culture of studio in place to model for new students how the courses were supposed to function, and no alumni group or social structure within the program to support students, the faculty had poured much time and effort into co-design, working side by side with their first groups of students, the "pioneers" (see Figure 10.2). They had co-developed norms for studio participation and expectations, nurtured that first group to a point of development where they could serve as mentors to incoming junior students, and created a self-sustaining structure for the program in which intangible but critical elements of a studio approach were now in place.

These felt too precious to lose now, but Anthony reflected that serious pressures might work against keeping them intact, with Andrea only a part of that dynamic. Her emphasis on larger programs as a fiscal concern was not just an individual position; he knew that this viewpoint was more and more common in program planning conversations around campus, and recognized their team would have to grapple with it sooner or later.

HOW IT'S GOING

Anthony recognized that there were growing tensions within the program, although he did not agree with Andrea about what they were. For one thing, what she saw as an inappropriate burden of work on faculty, he saw as a strength of the program even though he understood that if they did have to scale the program up even further, possibly even outsourcing some of its administration, its current hands-on structure would make that difficult. At the same time, they had built a solid base of cohort relationships and connections among students that kept all students invested. Further, the program was growing increasingly focused on LX (Learning Experience) Design, with the students more engaged inside the studio program and less involved with the external computing, communication, and teacher education areas from which they had been drawn. As a result, it was less robust as a cross-disciplinary program than it had once been.

There were other tensions as well, he reflected, including several which had unfortunately been precipitated—or exacerbated—by the COVID-19 pandemic of 2020. He mentally ticked off some of the other tensions. The mentorship model had been shown to be somewhat thin in the area of addressing overall student wellbeing, as sudden and prolonged isolation underscored situations in which the personal struggles of students were affecting their ability to engage with learning in the studio. More practically, students, whose aging or underpowered laptops had been serving them well enough, found that they could not keep up with the multiple demands placed on them by videoconferencing, using cloud services for multiple channels of document sharing and project coordination, and shifting to digital tools for group work that previously had been accomplished using physical materials like sticky notes and index cards. Speaking of materials, during the sudden move online in March 2020, all of them had scrambled to develop new materials that supported revised activities and documented key parts of learning experiences which had been tacit before. These were shared between the instructors for their own use and use with their students, but it had become clear that no agreement existed regarding who owned which materials and therefore who should be updating them or how to resolve differences when the materials were used differently than the creator had intended. He was concerned that if anyone new came onboard, this issue would just become more complicated.

Beginning before the pandemic and continuing today, Anthony recognized another concern which was increasingly bothering him. While, at first, they had a problem because all the students were beginners and they had no senior students who could mentor their peers effectively, the period when a mentoring system functioned well for them had been, in his view, relatively short. Almost from the start, more male native speakers of English had emerged in leadership roles than did women, students of color, and non-native speakers of English. Students who were quick to speak up and whose voices carried, including online, took on key positions in project teams and were looked to by the junior students in preference to others. Efforts of instructors to identify and nudge students who needed more confidence to step into leadership roles had not been fruitful. In fact, isolation of non-native speakers had become the norm, as had their relegation to lesser roles, or even placeholder type roles, on their project teams. He knew that some teams reported the pressure of deadlines as an unintentional factor in sidelining minority students, but more than one student had confided in him their belief that issues of culture and race had actively excluded them from leadership, from central roles in team efforts, and even from feeling they did not belong in studio or could not "own" it in the way their peers could. This element of the program was going to need serious attention, and very soon, so that they had a plan before enrollment grew so large that some kind of scaffolding process for equitable leadership could no longer be put into place and function effectively.

Glancing out the window of the bus, Anthony notes that he has been utterly caught up in his thoughts. They have ranged over many aspects of the program, seeming to take quite a bit of time, but it has only been a ten-minute ride, and here they are. He isn't sure he is ready for this meeting. Setting the program up, pulling people together and working with them to make it a success, seeing it through the move online and then back on campus had been difficult, rewarding work. Right now, though, it seems as if everything up until today may have been the least part of the effort. This meeting isn't going to be easy. He exits the bus, tossing his coffee cup into a nearby trash bin, and strides toward the engineering building.

THE MEETING

Arriving in a conference room adjacent to the office of the engineering dean, Anthony greets Roger Fuller, engineering professor and chair of the Steering Committee for the IDP. See Figure 10.3 for the organizational chart of the IDP steering committee and relationships to the engineering committee and deans.

"Good to see you, Anthony!" Roger booms. "Ready to get down to work?"

"Sure thing!" Anthony can feel himself gearing up to match Roger's energy and pace. Roger has been a strong advocate of the program, and Anthony respects him. He has found, however, that Roger can get moving so fast that he can miss the finer points of an argument. It helps when Anthony ramps up his own style a bit so that he stays in Roger's view and can catch his attention at the right moments. "You got the agenda I sent out?" he asks Roger. He knows the meeting may not go according to his agenda, but at least his issues are on the table and more likely to be covered than if he just waits for a chance to bring them up.

"You bet!" Roger replies, pushing copies into the middle of the table.

"Oh, thanks." As Anthony takes out his notebook and pen, his colleagues arrive, shedding their coats and greeting him as they enter the room. Jack's dean, Ram Khatun, has accompanied him to the meeting, and Anthony is glad to see him. He is level-headed, always willing to offer ideas that might move a project forward or solve problems. He nods to acknowledge Ram and the others, but before he can speak, Roger is off and running.

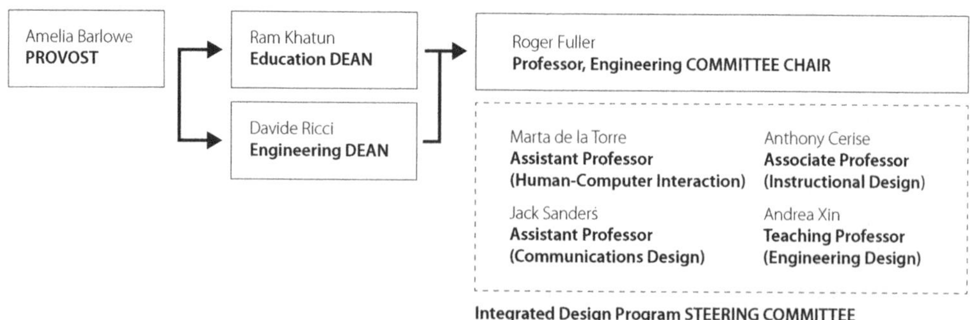

FIGURE 10.3 Organizational chart describing the Integrated Design Program steering committee and relationships to the engineering committee and education and engineering deans.

"So," he begins, not referring to the agenda, "let's start by getting this out of the way—one of your colleagues has gone over my head to the provost regarding the program design and the insupportable workload it puts onto faculty—her words, not mine."

Anthony winces. He might have known. He immediately flashes back to a conversation he had with Andrea and Jack on Slack (see Figure 10.4). As much as they had worked to calibrate expectations with Andrea and adjust elements of the program around the expectations she had brought from her discipline, he knew that she considered the demands of studio teaching to be excessive—and that she blamed her colleagues for this instead of viewing it as a different, and valid, pedagogy. Anthony is not as worried about the interpersonal issue here as he is about how Andrea's complaint could open up more questions about budgets and class sizes. He's imagining an administrator with a calculator, thinking, "This program has fewer students per class than other programs, but teaching is taking too much faculty time? Not a winning equation."

Sure enough, Roger forges ahead with exactly this idea. "I'm sure you're working out any personal differences among yourselves," he says, "but the provost is asking me about the scale of the program in reference to workload, and I share her concerns." He looks around the table. "There's not an open faculty line to throw at this problem right now, and don't forget that we're a research institution, people. You know I'm IDP's top champion—but are we striving for high levels of innovation in teaching at the expense of faculty research time? Is that realistic?"

Drawing a breath to reply, Anthony finds that Jack is already speaking. "Roger, I don't see this as a question of excessive workload; it's—it's just more than required to run students through canned projects as quickly as possible." Anthony winces again even as he gives Jack a mental pat on the back. The studio format had not been part of Jack's experience at first either, but he certainly had embraced it and was now defending it—albeit at the risk of offending Roger with this obvious reference to some large "production line" engineering courses.

Anthony adds, "I agree with Jack. This has been an academic culture issue, primarily. We are working on it and on calibrating how each of us handles our course sections so that students are getting equivalent experiences in each one."

"I'm glad to hear that," Roger says, "because I do have some less than happy news today. With reference to the first agenda item, Budget Issues, we do have budget cuts on the way,

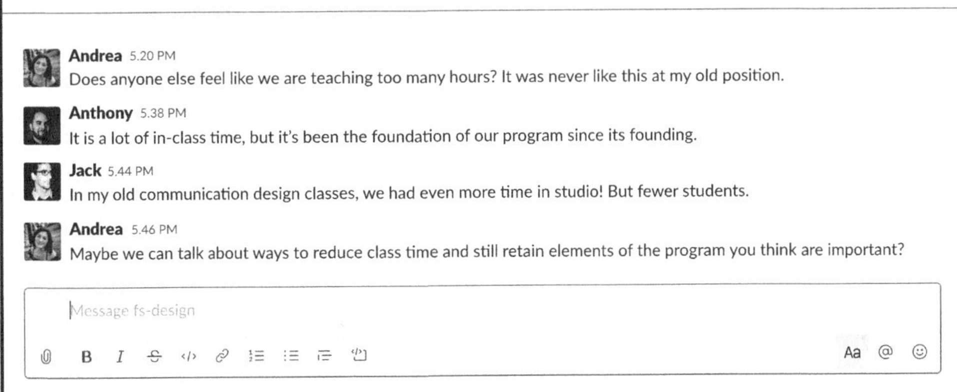

FIGURE 10.4 Message exchange on Slack among the program faculty indicating differences in expectations regarding studio teaching.

unit-wide, am I right, Ram?" The engineering dean nods. "Right," Roger repeats. "So, we need to discuss two aspects of IDP that I anticipate will be targets for the provost. As we've discussed before, team teaching in studio courses is a luxury we can't afford anymore. With your rising enrollments we are going to need every faculty member to teach a broader range of courses, and we won't be hiring new lines until existing faculty are at full load without doubling up for team teaching." He glances around, pausing. "I suspect the other issue is not going to be a surprise either. Even though the IDP numbers are growing, and we anticipate that trend continuing, we're going to have to examine how we are allocating space to the program."

He's right, Anthony thinks. Neither of these points is a surprise. Theirs is not the only program competing for space, and despite the growth in their enrollments, he knows that a faculty line, even at the assistant level, is a hard sell—and that their student numbers will not warrant a new hire for some time to come.

"We've been discussing these issues, of course, Roger," Anthony begins. "In fact, Marta has led us in considering how to redistribute the teaching assignments across studio and topics courses. Marta, could you talk a bit about our tentative plan?"

"Sure," Marta says, sitting forward. "We're close to a plan that will phase out team teaching over a couple years as our newest and largest cohort moves through the program. Each of us will follow them into a topics course and then keep teaching that course until there is just one person assigned to studio. Our peer mentor program is going to fill in the gap, we think. We're overhauling that too—we want more diversity in our mentors, so it's a good time to rethink what we're doing with them in the studio. All we have to do is hold new enrollments steady for a couple years while we get the new plan going. We think it will be a win-win, though, for the program."

"That's right," Anthony agrees. "The bonus is that we can hold our use of classroom space to the current level and save on adjunct salaries as we cover the topics courses. We're looking forward to stabilizing the program at this point while we address some of our growing pains." He stops and looks to Roger, then to Ram. *Uh-oh*, he thinks. *This was our big good news, and it is not going over well.* Roger is fiddling with a pencil, not meeting his glance, and the ordinarily upbeat Ram has a little frown line developing between his eyebrows. Anthony braces for what will come next.

"Actually," Roger says, clacking his pencil down on the desktop, "the provost's thinking was heading in a different direction." He picks up a stack of brochures and begins to hand them around the table. Anthony notes quickly that one is from an "academic services" company and the other is from an "online programs partner." His heart sinks. "Two directions, actually," Roger goes on. "And I have to say, one or both look promising. For starters, they build on growth instead of holding us stagnant."

Anthony, Marta, and Jack peruse the brochures quickly. Anthony has a fair amount of information about these kinds of academic corporations; a colleague across campus is involved with a graduate program using a well-known service that oversees everything about their program except syllabus review.

Not aware he is frowning, he looks up to see Roger holding out a flat palm to him and saying, "Before you say anything! We'll need time to think through the issues, of course. And even though he's asking about it, the provost has not given an ultimatum."

"I hope not," Jack blurts out, waving the brochures in the air. "How would something like this even work? I mean, yeah, we have a lot more happening online now, but not the whole program! That was a stopgap, not a long-term plan. In fact, it left us with some problems that we're still cleaning up—some of our students were really shoved to the edges of participation in team projects while they were working online. And we're still rewriting the studio syllabus every semester trying to get this cross-disciplinary studio refined. Another thing—where would the instructors come from if we let a corporate partner hire them? I mean, where would they find someone who can teach online studio? Or are you saying that has to go too?"

Seeing that Jack is getting agitated, and noting the mutinous look on Marta's face signaling that she might be about to join him, Anthony breaks in quickly. "I hear you, Roger. The provost has heard about these options and is just asking how they might work and *if* they might work at all, right?"

"One hundred percent," Roger responds, nodding vigorously. "Looking for input from you guys, that's all. Now, having said that, and knowing the program as I do from the perspective of the steering committee, I will point out a couple of positives. An outsourcing service plan alone can relieve you of all administrative and advising duties. It would probably double enrollments at minimum, and this would allow for more faculty hiring right away, even free up time for further development of the program. And if we opted for the partnership—well!" Roger seems excited now. "These contracts typically return funds directly to programs. A good agreement with the campus could leave each of you with time *and* funds for innovation, in this program and in other areas."

Jack is still struggling; he's scanning the information in the brochure for corporate partners to offer online programs. "They're talking about a 'faculty liaison' here. What does that mean? A member of the faculty?" He looks around the table as Marta quickly takes a second look at the materials.

"I suggest looking at their online sites," suggests Ram. "I expect many questions will be answered there."

"Right, right!" booms Roger, standing and pushing the meeting agenda to the center of the table. "Great idea!" He pauses and looks Anthony square in the eye. "I've promised the provost a short report from you in a week's time."

Anthony returns his gaze. He's not a little unhappy; for all his aggressive manner, Roger has been a strong advocate of the IDP up until today, and it is not good news to see that he is obviously taking his direction from the provost now. He may not have had a choice, but it is still something of a blow. "What should it cover?" he asks.

"Oh. Well, probably best to outline what it would take to follow one or the other of these possible plans. And if you don't think either one is a possibility, I recommend that you explain why—and also explain plans for continuing to scale up the program, preferably quickly." For a minute, he sounds supportive again, although his message is not positive. "Honestly, guys, I appreciate where the program is now. It's been a fantastic success in so many ways. But the idea of holding it down to current enrollment is just not going to fly."

Shrugging on his coat in the now silent room, Roger exits with Ram following, leaving Anthony and his colleagues in silence. After a minute, they gather up the brochures they've been given and rise to leave. "Walk across campus with me?" Anthony asks the others. "We can talk about this on the way."

THE FUTURE

The three colleagues head out of the building, and Anthony can tell that Jack is still agitated, while Marta is unusually quiet. It is clear to him that they are going to have to scrap the plan they had worked out previously for pausing the growth of the program unless they can work out a strong rationale and demonstrate how the program would grow later. He doesn't want to cut off discussion immediately though. He wants to hear what the others have to say, so he waits for the inevitable—an outburst from Jack.

"Well, they could have told us before we spent all that time working on a plan!" Jack blurts out. Then he laughs suddenly. "But look at it this way—Andrea would love to outsource the program! Sooo much less work!" He sobers again. "I don't like the sound of it, though," he grumbles.

Marta speaks up, neither joking nor grumbling, although she is clearly worried. "Did you see in the brochures about 'faculty liaison' and 'faculty coordinator'?" What does that really mean—and who would do it?"

"It means someone turns into an administrator without getting paid for it," says Jack.

"Oh, that's not good," Marta observes. "Someone junior will get stuck with it." Anthony can tell that, as a junior member of the faculty, she's picturing herself in the role.

"Maybe let's start with the possible benefits," he suggests.

"Such as?"

Anthony glances at Jack. "I'm not sure," he says, taking advantage of the group pausing at a crosswalk to think quickly. He's also a little off balance after the meeting and admits to himself that ideas are not flooding into his head. "Well, uh . . . ," he begins. "Well, hmm. In a way, Jack might be right. If we went online with an academic service company, we might all work less in the studio, but that might give us more time to develop the program . . . work on issues like unequal opportunities for leadership and mentoring among our students. It's a big problem that we have just started to address."

Jack snorts a little. "I don't see it going that way, though," he argues. "An outsourcing company will want a stable program they can recruit for and advise for. And a service company taking the program online will want the same. How do they scale up to hundreds of students like they promise here," he waves a brochure, "if we are going to tinker with the program—innovate—all the time? And another thing," he races on. "I bet once we hand over our courses to them, that's the last time we really get to revise them, let alone the overall program."

"And what about the student-to-student mentoring part of the program if it goes online?" Marta puts in. "And the real time back-channel feedback during critiques? Will we be able to bring in practitioners for design sprints?" Anthony knows these are elements of the current program that Marta has worked hard on and that she's invested in as distinctive, positive contributors to the effectiveness of the IDP. "I mean, maybe we could work out how to get those things online—but would a service company be able to reproduce them? They hire adjuncts to handle the big classes, I think. Where would they find adjuncts to do those things?"

"Good question," Anthony responds. "But we have that problem right now too. Bringing new people onto the faculty of this program, at least as it is designed right now, is always going to be a bit of a culture shock, and we've already seen what a problem that can be."

The others nod. Jack checks his phone for the time. "Hey, I have to head to my car," he says. "My day to pick up the kids. I'll be in tomorrow and check with you all about getting together to discuss more."

Marta and Anthony say a quick goodbye to Jack and continue on together. "This seems so complicated," Marta starts after a minute.

"I agree." Anthony nods. "But it does seem as though we have maybe four possible paths forward. Maybe we can map those out and then tackle the complicated details."

"Yeah. Okay. Well, one is outsourcing the recruitment and management for the program. Or take it online to a full-service company that also teaches the courses."

"Or dig in and defend our original plan. Or—and I'm not sure about this one—maybe take it online ourselves, without the support of a service company," Anthony finishes, as they arrive at the door of the building housing the IDP studio. He frowns. "Only one of those actually results in IDP as we recognize it now." They enter the building, and Anthony promises to send an email for the purpose of organizing a meeting to tackle the provost's assignment. "It needs to be soon," he emphasizes as they part in the hall, heading for their separate offices.

A minute later, flopped down in his office chair with his coat still on, Anthony wills his mind to settle for a minute. When thoughts continue to swirl, he decides to call into play the tools that he teaches his own students. He shrugs off his coat and scarf and grabs a whiteboard marker. Quickly erasing the notes on the large board next to his desk, he lists the four options he had laid out minutes ago across the top, then begins to list stakeholders down the side of the board—students, faculty, administrators. "Which of these options will serve each stakeholder best?" he muses. Suddenly a fifth option occurs to him, a phased plan like their original one, but in this plan the program grows quickly now, and they work out issues with it in a series of agile design sprints before stabilizing it to go online. Glancing at his short list of stakeholders, he realizes it needs to be more complicated—senior students, junior students, and marginalized students, for example, and campus-level administrators in addition to unit-level ones, or adjunct versus permanent faculty. Pretty soon he is scribbling notes in each cell of this improvised matrix and using two additional colors of marker to add notes about the resources, available and still needed, to realize benefits for certain stakeholders under each possible plan. Adding a third color for disadvantages each option might bring to a stakeholder group, Anthony pauses. "I need everyone's perspective on this," he thinks, and, energized by the prospect of laying out their situation in detail so they can examine all facets of it together, he takes a picture of his white board and dashes off an email to Jack, Marta, and Andrea to get their perspectives. "This won't solve everything," he acknowledges, "but I hope we can figure out some possible risks and benefits right now, so that we know what information gathering we need to do and what options are really on or off the table for us. I'm not sure exactly how yet," Anthony explains to the group, "but we are going to be moving forward!"

Preliminary Analysis Questions

1. What is the position of the IDP faculty in relation to other stakeholders of the program? How has it changed over time?
2. Is Anthony's framing of their current design problem accurate? Could the problem be framed differently?
3. What assumptions are the IDP faculty making about these issues and what more do they need to know?
4. What are the core issues that the faculty team will need to consider before they write their report and concretize their recommendations? Which issue(s) might they prioritize and why?
5. What might be gained or lost from each path they could take? Who might gain or lose, and how might this be different for those in variable positions of power?
6. How might the IDP faculty address this situation outside the parameters that they are using now?

Implications for ID Practice

1. How should IDs balance the benefits of novel pedagogical approaches with the limitations of those approaches based on modality (onsite versus online)? Based on administrative implications like enrollments and facilities?
2. What can IDs do to build alignment among diverse types of co-designers with different beliefs or conceptual models of learning?
3. What can IDs do within complex situations to build and maintain equitable environments for students who are marginalized in one or more dimensions?

11

Andy Parker and Casie Hammond

Designing Online Labs for Undergraduate Engineering Education

Stephanie L. Moore and Heather K. Tillberg-Webb

Dean Elise Taylor appeared suddenly in the doorway of Andy's office.

"The state wants us to take on a new STEM education initiative, and I need to chat with you about it. Walk with me to my office?"

Andy Parker was the associate dean for undergraduate education in the College of Engineering at Blake University. Although he met frequently with the dean on many initiatives, it was rare that she popped in unannounced and asked for his immediate attention.

As they walked, Dean Taylor started to explain, "State officials are really focused on small community revitalization around the state, and they're directing some federal money toward STEM education in particular. One of their main priorities is building pathways for students to get their associate's degrees at their local community colleges and then access a four-year undergraduate degree in a STEM discipline. But they don't want those students to have to relocate. They want them to be able to stay in their local communities, go to school there, and maybe get internships or jobs there. The hope is that these students will eventually go on to grow their own STEM-related businesses and create jobs in those cities and towns. It's part of the state's attempt to address economic downturns due to loss of other industries in those areas. And they want *us* to offer that four-year pathway."

Dean Taylor's tone in the last sentence conveyed a sense of annoyance. Blake's engineering school was one of the top-rated schools in the country, and they got there by focusing on traditional engineering research. Dean Taylor had defined her career doing that kind of research, and she viewed educational initiatives as diversions from the university's research agenda. She felt it was her responsibility to maintain and even grow the school's standing and research funding.

"They selected us because of our reputation, and they think an engineering degree, in particular, is the way to go. I think they're expecting us to build one of those online programs . . . ," she said, then trailed off for a bit. "I don't know, Andy. I just don't think those are any good. I don't see how that fits with our culture. Faculty are not going to want to do that."

As they reached Dean Taylor's office, they sat down to discuss further. Dean Taylor continued, "We are really getting pressure from the state and from the university's Board of Governors and the Provost's office on this. And, they're already putting out press releases and

DOI: 10.4324/9781003354468-13

making this a big deal. I don't think we can say no. So, we need to figure out a solution. Here's their recent press release" (see Figure 11.1).

Dean Taylor pushed a copy of the press release toward Andy. Andy had a PhD in engineering and thought he might apply his engineering design training to this initiative. He was a thoughtful innovator, always aiming to identify new opportunities but also spending time conducting careful research and gathering information. "Why don't we create a task force with some of our business partners, faculty, and contacts in the community colleges? Let's start a process to learn more about the parameters of this."

The dean agreed, and Andy reached out to their various contacts in industry and at community colleges across the state. He also began gathering information about the specific engineering areas the community colleges offered. Andy quickly found that mechanical engineering (ME) was the most commonly offered major, followed by electrical engineering (EE). The options really tapered off after those two. He also began to explore implications related to accreditation and discovered that ABET, the body that accredited engineering programs, didn't offer any guidance on online programs. What he did find were some statements indicating that ABET wasn't sure *how* to accredit online programs, so they weren't accrediting them just yet. That raised red flags for Andy—if Blake offered one of their accredited programs online, could the on-campus program lose its accreditation?

During a meeting with the task force, Andy raised some of these questions to the group. "In doing some research into what the community colleges offer, I found that most students will be coming to us with some background in either mechanical or electrical engineering. But, I also looked for guidance from our accreditors regarding online learning. However, instead of finding any clear guidance, ABET's guidelines gave me pause. I don't know if we could lose accreditation for a program by moving it online, but we need to be careful."

One member of the task force was Sandra Chavez, an associate professor in mechanical engineering. Andy had invited her to the meeting assuming the ME department would be a critical connection, and he wanted to facilitate a more collaborative relationship with them.

FOR IMMEDIATE RELEASE

New STEM Degree Opportunities for Students in Rural Communities

Blake University to launch an online engineering program that students can complete from home.

As part of the state's initiative to revitalize industries in areas hard hit by recent economic downturns, funding will be provided to Blake University to launch an online program that will allow students to complete a bachelor's in engineering from wherever they live in the state. This will create new educational opportunities for residents in many areas that have limited access to higher education. It will also support communities in growing their own talent in industries that generate jobs and boost their local economies.

Governor Kate Bryant said, "We are excited about such an innovative program that will make a real difference for the people of this state. With our flagship university leading the initiative, I am sure this will be a great opportunity that will make this state even more attractive for business."

The initiative will involve collaboration between the community college system and Blake University. University leaders anticipate the program will begin to offer courses in the fall of next year.

FIGURE 11.1 Press release by Governor Bryant's office announcing the new STEM remote learning initiative.

Sandra was doing traditional engineering research but had discussed some of her work on engineering education in a faculty meeting. As just one example, she had recently used some grant money to purchase a recording booth and had it installed in her office for making multimedia content for students. Sandra was an MIT graduate with a penchant for tinkering and exploring. Andy believed that she could be a strong contributor to planning and designing courses for this initiative.

"Well, we do have that non-accredited degree option, the engineering sciences degree, that we created so we could get more creative with our curriculum," Sandra noted. "What if we used that as a shell to design something for this project?"

"That's a great idea, Sandra. We have a lot of flexibility with that program, and there's no accreditation to lose. It could even be interesting to see if maybe we could work *with* ABET to articulate guidelines and standards for an online undergraduate engineering degree."

Sandra added, "We could certainly integrate a component of mechanical engineering that is already part of that curriculum, instead of our accredited one."

"Yeah, I like this direction," Andy said. "What about students who are at community colleges where they have an electrical engineering focus?"

Sandra offered, "Right now, there's a lot of work at the nexus of mechanical and electrical. Think robotics as an example. The term most folks use for that is 'mechatronics.' What if we assembled a mechatronics curriculum for this degree from our existing mechanical and electrical courses?"

At this point, one of the business partners jumped in. Alysse Cardaño was the Director of Operations for an aerospace company headquartered in one of the larger metro areas a few hours up the road from the university. Their company had worked on several research and development initiatives with the university, so they had a well-established partnership.

"I have to say, I really like this idea," Alysse noted. "We are experiencing a higher need for employees who have that very mix of skills and knowledge. We're increasingly using automation in our facilities, and employees need a mix of knowledge on both the mechanical and electrical aspects. But people with that mix are rare. Most people have one or the other skill set. I think this mechatronics pathway could also give these students a competitive advantage in the job market. If you do go that route, I think we might also be interested in creating some internship opportunities for the students."

Andy had also invited the community colleges to nominate some of their students to the task force. Felicia Givens and Gregg Anders were both sitting quietly during the discussions, so Andy asked them directly for their thoughts and input.

"Felicia and Gregg, it's great to have you both join us. Since we're doing this for you, are there some things you think we're missing or not addressing?"

Felicia sat forward, "Well, thank you for inviting us. I think first I want to say, I'm excited about these options. I never thought I would be able to attend Blake because it's so far away and moving just isn't an option. I really like the mechatronics idea. I can see how that would be useful and lead to the kinds of jobs I think students are hoping they can get. I think my questions relate to better understanding what the classes are going to look like. Will they be online or will we have to drive to campus for some parts of the program? Will we be a separate program or can we come for events at Blake? And, I still don't have a good sense of cost. Plus, I don't know where to go for information on Blake's website. I'm finding the financial aid aspects difficult to understand and get support for."

"I have a lot of the same questions and am running into the same issues so far," Gregg added. "I'm also excited about being in classes with other students at Blake and hopefully being able to connect with some other students or student groups. Do you know how we're going to access the library or how we'll be able to form study groups and things like that? And what kind of access will we have to the professors?"

"These are great questions!" Andy replied. "I'm making notes. Right now, I don't have very clear answers, but we need to make sure we're building a support system for you, not just classes. I need to work with different areas of the university to make sure we're building access to the entire university, not just class sessions."

Felicia added, "I guess, to be honest, I worry about feeling like an outsider. I mean, my impression is that a lot of students at Blake come from wealthier families. They may not have to work like many of us do. I don't know how well we can relate to each other."

"Well, to return the honesty, I would like to get some of our current students out of their bubbles," Andy replied. "I also think that they need to learn how to work collaboratively as part of remote or distributed teams. In industry and government, a lot of the work is with others who are at company sites around the world or with other researchers at labs around the country."

Alysse chimed in, "That's a great point, Andy. You're right. Our employees don't just work with folks in a nearby office. They must be able to connect with people at other locations and figure out how to work on distributed teams. I like that term. If students could develop those teamwork and collaboration skills in this program, that would be great."

As the task force talked further, a clear plan was taking shape, and the team was identifying important student needs. Andy reported back to Dean Taylor, apprising her of the idea to use the engineering sciences curriculum as a sort of lab space for developing the program, as well as the feedback from their business partners supporting the mechatronics direction. In the interim, Dean Taylor had also been talking with other deans about online learning. Some had expressed significant reservations and struck cautionary tones, but some others—including some at other programs that were ranked more highly—had said they were planning to build their own online initiatives and were very keen on the possibilities. Dean Taylor was still very ambivalent.

"Okay. I think this is a good plan, but I still have my doubts about whether the program will be any good if it's offered online. I worry whether that will hurt our reputation and whether the students in this program will actually learn anything. But, let's start putting this together and, as you suggested, just experiment with it."

Over the next few days, Andy started reaching out to as many colleagues as possible in the mechanical and electrical engineering programs to initiate conversations about online or remote classes. He wanted to better understand the curricular details and also wanted to foster some buy-in and support. However, while he was starting to envision some creative learning opportunities, his colleagues varied greatly in their acceptance of, or resistance to, online learning. During one meeting with a group of colleagues, one tenured professor in mechanical engineering, Matt Brown, flatly protested: "Those students who go to community colleges and take online classes just aren't the same caliber as *our* students. Online just isn't as good as a classroom setting where I can see their eyes and really get a sense of what they understand. Maybe this is something that they can do in the humanities or education, but it's just not possible for engineering. This is really going to degrade the quality of learning for our own students."

Nobody contested this statement during the meeting, and several nodded in agreement. Afterward, however, a few faculty members followed up directly with Andy. They had concerns about online learning, too, but they also saw some interesting possibilities. Two in particular—Rajeesh Patel and Petra May, both in mechanical engineering—were championing the idea of virtual labs. Rajeesh was a senior, tenured, full professor who was interested in investing more in engineering education after spending the last 25 years on more traditional engineering research. He also had been involved in some international collaborations that gave him more of a window into efforts being undertaken in other countries.

"I've been keen to develop a virtual or remote lab for one of our mechanical labs," Rajeesh started. "Some of our counterparts in Europe are doing R&D on virtual and remote labs, and agencies like NASA are starting to express serious interest in the ability to conduct remote lab experiments in places we cannot send human beings, like Mars or deep-water research. This could be a really interesting area for us to expand our research into, get some external funding, and oh-by-the-way develop some labs for this initiative."

Rajeesh shared some examples of virtual labs being developed overseas (see Figure 11.2). "Here are some examples I pulled up on the web for you to take a look at. Some of these are news items, but some of these are research papers colleagues are publishing on remote and online labs. I think these are great examples both of what's being developed and researched and how this has practical application in a variety of settings that our engineering graduates might work in."

Petra chimed in, "I've been looking more into simulations as well. NSF requires us to incorporate educational research into many of our proposals now, so I've been reading more about educational simulations. It has me thinking about some possibilities around what we might be able to do in undergraduate engineering education more generally."

Petra was an associate professor. She expressed to Andy in confidence that she wasn't really focused on promotion to full professor yet because she was much more interested in

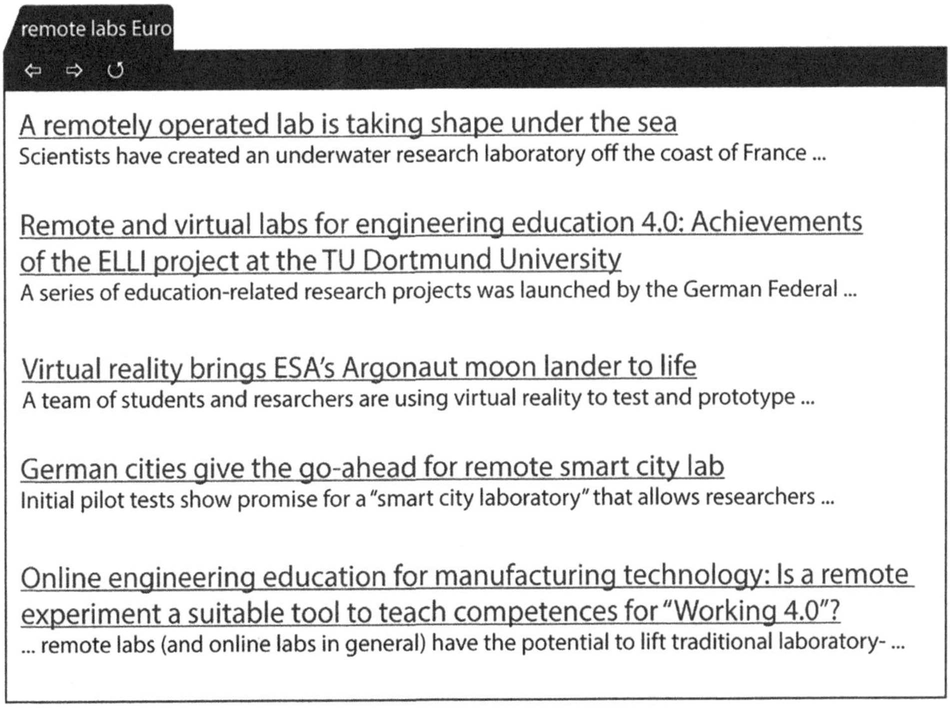

remote labs Euro

A remotely operated lab is taking shape under the sea
Scientists have created an underwater research laboratory off the coast of France ...

Remote and virtual labs for engineering education 4.0: Achievements of the ELLI project at the TU Dortmund University
A series of education-related research projects was launched by the German Federal ...

Virtual reality brings ESA's Argonaut moon lander to life
A team of students and resarchers are using virtual reality to test and prototype ...

German cities give the go-ahead for remote smart city lab
Initial pilot tests show promise for a "smart city laboratory" that allows researchers ...

Online engineering education for manufacturing technology: Is a remote experiment a suitable tool to teach competences for "Working 4.0"?
... remote labs (and online labs in general) have the potential to lift traditional laboratory- ...

FIGURE 11.2 News and research articles on remote labs in Europe.

engineering education research and development, something that Dean Taylor had explicitly stated was a low priority.

While clearly there was still more work to do with many other colleagues on developing their courses for online offerings, Andy was relieved to have some potential collaborators—especially around the labs. "The labs are going to be the trickiest part," he thought. "We're going to need some good old-fashioned creative problem solving in this space. Maybe, just maybe, we could also identify ways to innovate and develop new lines of research."

As part of his research into online and distance learning solutions, Andy was learning more about this field called "instructional design." The more he read about it, the more he liked its design orientation. "This resonates well with engineering design," he thought. "I think we should try to bring in someone who can think like a designer, but who can help us design something effective that's grounded in research on learning." After consulting with the dean, Andy decided to conduct a job search to find a director of online design to lead this effort. That search yielded a finalist—Casie Hammond—who had led the design of other online learning efforts before. Andy specifically liked that she had been a lead instructional designer in building graduate online learning programs and that she had worked with faculty across a range of different disciplines already. He also really liked that she had a PhD and often described how research informed effective online learning efforts. He believed this would help make the case to other faculty that this online learning initiative could be done well.

"One thing that really intrigues me about this opportunity is its potential for new frontiers in online learning," Casie conveyed during the interview process. "Although I've designed a lot of online learning courses and programs, I haven't seen much yet around virtual or remote labs. I imagine this initiative would likely need to crack open that design nut. It could be a great chance to develop truly new and innovative solutions, and we could wrap research around it as well."

This resonated with Andy's own expanding vision and the ideas being expressed by Rajeesh and Petra as well.

While the classes would be relatively straight-forward, it was becoming clear in conversations with the faculty who taught the engineering labs that the required lab activities each posed different sets of design requirements and considerations. There was no one-size-fits-all solution to the labs. To make this new program work, there would need to be some agreement on the standardization of the lab experiences. Also, many of the students they would be serving lived hours away from the campus. The staffing requirements for in-person labs were intense—there were several full-time staff members employed to help manage the expensive equipment and lab facilities. If labs were offered virtually, the same level of oversight required for the physical materials would not be needed. Andy was certain Casie could help puzzle through the best design of these virtual labs to make optimal connections between the learning goals, resource constraints, and instructional requirements. In addition, some of Casie's prior work included instructional design in a center whose primary mission was serving learners with various physical and learning disabilities.

"I hadn't really thought about accessibility issues before; can you tell me more about how you addressed accessibility in online learning?" Andy inquired during the interview.

"Sure," Casie started. "Back when I first started working in design, this was a relatively unexplored area. Today, there are a lot of checklists for accessible websites, but at the time we had to figure everything out on the fly. We did add things like alt tags and closed captioning, but we also dug deeper to really think about web page and web site architecture. For example, we switched all the pages to HTML with CSS because the CSS can be edited or swapped out by users so they could redesign the site using different colors, font sizes, and so that worked better for their particular needs. We also worked with end users to test site usability and navigation and discovered that the interface was imposing significant cognitive load, so we reworked our interfaces both in terms of layout as well as using embedded messages that screen readers would pick up on to send blind users the same messages and cues that sighted users were getting."

Andy really liked how Casie evidenced a research and design spirit in devising solutions and testing them, not just picking flashy technology or waiting for others to generate ideas. And, her work with accessibility suggested she would more naturally fold diversity considerations into their design processes. Andy was convinced that Casie possessed the design mindset he was looking for.

As Casie started her role, Andy approached her about attending a conference on virtual and remote field research at Langley Air Force Base and asked her to find what she could on current research and resources. Casie figured the conference would be a great way to develop more comfort with the engineering context, so she signed up. As part of its preparatory materials, the conference organizers had sent out some advance readings on the use of virtual and remote technologies for government and defense work and research. One of those readings was a white paper by researchers at different research sites including NASA's Ames Research Center and Johnson Space Center. She also compiled some resources on virtual labs she thought they might want to reference along with a list of tools others were using to build virtual labs (see Figure 11.3).

Casie was really intrigued by the real-world applications of remote labs and the caché of agencies like NASA generating some innovations. She thought this might provide ideas and help persuade some more reticent faculty. She also started curating examples of virtual labs at other universities that she could share with Andy including one at California State Polytechnic University and some other resources from universities around the world.

Once Casie was back at Blake, she met with a number of lab instructors and sat in on their in-person lab sessions. In nearly every case, the instructor teaching the lab class insisted that students must have hands-on experiences with the equipment.

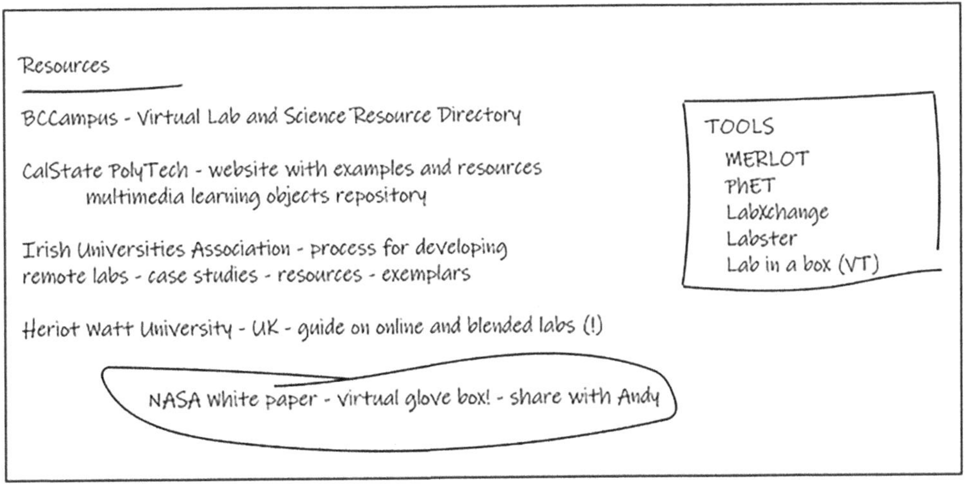

FIGURE 11.3 Casie's notes on resources and tools for virtual labs.

"They need to be able to turn the knobs, hear the hum of the engine as it starts whirring," Matt said as Casie observed his mechanical engineering lab. "You just can't get the full experience online."

Casie paused to think. "How can I build credibility with Matt and also pique his interest in possibilities for virtual engineering labs?" She recalled some examples from the Langley conference materials and presentations and thought maybe some real-world cases might persuade him.

She replied, "I've just read a white paper out of Langley about NASA's experimentation with remote labs and 'virtual gloveboxes' for research on remote planets. I think the Navy is experimenting with some of this as well, so they can complete research missions that are in spaces they don't want to send people. What if we thought about preparing students for those sorts of environments? What if they'll have to use equipment where they can't hear or feel it and will have to rely on other feedback and information?"

Matt paused. "Well . . . they wouldn't be using this exact piece of equipment for that, but I take your point."

Casie quickly tried to pick up on this opportunity. "I think it could be fascinating to unpack the decision-making aspects of their use of this equipment, maybe even consider how we might use virtual or remote options to throw curveballs to students that they could possibly experience in the wild."

Matt countered, "Yeah, I see where you're going . . . but students love these labs. They come to Blake for engineering in part so they can physically access equipment they can't access elsewhere. I just don't see our on-campus students being willing to give that up."

After the meeting, Casie reflected on how difficult it may be to get some key instructors to buy-in to virtual labs and online learning. Matt brought up a good point about the on-campus students' expectations, but it would be resource intensive to have two versions of the same lab. Plus, Andy had communicated a vision of on-campus and off-campus students learning together to build stronger connections and community. Casie brought this interaction back to Andy, looking for additional feedback on how to strategize to get buy-in from the faculty for the use of virtual labs. Andy suggested they start with more eager partners, so he set up a meeting with Casie, Rajeesh, and Petra to discuss their ideas for labs. This meeting proved to be more positive but also introduced several complex possibilities.

"One thing I think a remote lab could really facilitate is international collaboration on research," Rajeesh explained. "Already in Europe, teams are located in multiple countries working together—some remotely, some on-site—to run tests and experiments." He shared the same examples with Casie that he had shared earlier with Andy.

Casie didn't want to lose sight of the learning needs for students as well. If they could capitalize on multiple potential uses for both learning and research, then perhaps there was a sweet spot here. "That's fascinating. Could you share more so I can read up on it? And, we could even share this with students to make these labs more relevant for them. So, in terms of preparing students to work on this kind of equipment, what kinds of situations would you want them to experience as part of their labs?"

This moved Rajeesh and Petra into discussing what the on-campus labs currently looked like. In addition, they discussed the technical details of how the labs were currently set up.

"What I really think we should do is rethink the labs," Petra responded. "Right now, these environments are so controlled because we can't have students tinkering and accidentally blowing things up. This equipment is expensive and can be very dangerous. In fact, we can't do it like other labs where we can just send them kits. It's way too dangerous for students to do some of these things on their own unsupervised, and there's no way they could afford that anyway."

"When you say 'rethink the labs,' what do you have in mind?" Casie queried.

"Well, what if, for example, we *could* let the students experience catastrophic failures that stem from their decisions or oversights? Couldn't they do that safely in a virtual lab or simulation?" Petra wondered aloud. "I also have been thinking about how this might allow us to provide more access to labs. Right now, labs are in buildings that are locked for about half of the hours in a day. What if . . . what if we could 'unlock' them so students could spend more time running tests, doing labs, and generally just tinkering like engineers do?"

"That is a really interesting idea, Petra! I was just reading about the idea of 'productive play' and how some engineers and computer scientists would hack into labs at Michigan or other places so they could spend many additional hours just tinkering. That tinkering could be really productive learning!" Casie waxed on about time-on-task and schema development, and Petra was really intrigued by the learning sciences aspects.

Petra paused. "But, I do have a question for you, Casie. If we design it simply as a simulation, does it become too much of a game to the students? Are there some downsides to learning?" She paused again, and Casie could see the wheels turning as Petra started imagining options. "What if we tied the simulation to an actual physical lab so students had some sense that something real might happen if they do enter in the wrong parameters or hit the wrong button? Would that up the stakes enough?"

Casie replied, "That's a good question, Petra. I think we need to carefully consider affective aspects of the design as well—like stress. I'll also do some digging to see if I can find anything that speaks to this. And some of our decisions will really depend on what it is we want the students to take away. We should write some clear statements on what we want them to get from the labs so we can design to those ends. But then I also wonder about unanticipated learning—both negative and positive. What if you could enable students to go beyond? Maybe not every student will do that, but if we give them an environment where they can truly explore, we may just nurture some real future superstars."

Petra and Rajeesh were starting to get excited, and Petra noted how much she liked thinking about this as a design problem. The team seemed to be clicking, but they were also generating a lot of different ideas, many of which were technically complex and expensive. Casie began to worry a bit that some were too complex for her to even understand, so she would need to really trust her colleagues on their ideas.

Back in their offices, Andy and Cassie reflected on their meeting with Rajeesh and Petra. Andy raised the question of lab fees for engineering students. It was very typical for colleges of engineering to charge additional lab fees, and Andy was trying to think through how to fund what sounded like some very expensive development.

Whereas most of the traditional students at the university were full-time students whose parents had college degrees, many of the students who would be admitted from the community colleges were first-generation college students. These learners also typically worked in part-time jobs or in internships while they were studying, in contrast to their on-campus peers who generally could focus all their attention on their studies and would attend the same classes and labs with them. During some on-campus meetings and observations, Casie had caught some derogatory comments about those who had opted to study at community colleges. There seemed to be the general feeling that if students were "smart enough" they would have just enrolled in Blake in the first place. Casie started to worry whether the remote students would be viewed as less capable in the online classes and labs. "In thinking about the new students we'll be reaching, I worry about affordability. It could be that we remove barriers by using online and remote solutions only to introduce additional access barriers because of costs, especially if we have to raise fees. I'm not suggesting we don't charge fees, but I think we should consider the financial realities for this new group of students," Casie offered.

"Yes, that's a good point. Maybe we can get one of the companies to give us a small development grant? Let's think on this some more and then brainstorm some other possible solutions," Andy replied.

"I think we also need to consider what we can do to make sure the students from the community colleges feel like they belong and are equally 'our students,'" Casie added. "If we have separate sections, for example, it could perpetuate some negative beliefs I've been hearing and make the remote students feel like they never truly were a part of the university. Maybe there are some things we can do in the classes as well as things around the classes, like some events or some type of community building," she brainstormed.

"Those are excellent points, Casie, and I've heard those comments, too," Andy said. "Let's think about some solutions that could help the students transferring from community colleges feel like they belong to Blake and Blake belongs to them."

"Talking about physical access also makes me think about your accessibility work," Andy said to Casie, "Do you have some thoughts on anything we should be doing there?"

In all the excitement over the technical possibilities, Casie had temporarily forgotten about accessibility. It wasn't a topic that came up during her initial discussions with the engineering faculty or in other conversations on campus, especially compared to projects she had worked on before. She was a bit embarrassed she didn't bring it up herself. Her mind raced as she started thinking through various accessibility implications.

"There are a lot of potential accessibility issues here. Some of them I'm not even sure we have clear solutions for yet. Since virtual environments and simulations are newer, we'll probably have to generate solutions from scratch. I don't think we can simply add alt tags and video transcription. I mean, some of that will still apply, but we should test the virtual labs in particular with some students who have visual or other impairments to see what barriers they experience," Casie brainstormed out loud.

Andy suggested that Casie identify others on campus who were working on accessibility issues. Casie looked forward to following up on that idea. It was a comfortable space she was eager to get back into. She located one person, Jun Lau, in a central administration role who mentioned accessibility in her online profile, and she set up a meeting with Jun. As they discussed accessibility, Casie described some of her past work and shared that she was eager to incorporate it into her work here.

"Oh, we don't tend to have a lot of students with disabilities here, so it isn't something we pay much attention to," Jun replied.

Casie was stunned. This was an educational institution, and the federal laws were pretty clear. Furthermore, often many more students have disabilities than openly declare them. Statistically, the university very likely had more students with accessibility needs than Jun realized. But Casie also did not want her approach to frame the issue as a legal concern only. For one thing, that could be perceived as antagonistic, and she did not feel she was in a position to take this on in addition to the pushback to online learning. Additionally, Casie preferred to frame the issue more as a teaching and learning concern rather than compliance. That would put the focus more on solutions that actually support learners.

Casie struggled with how to respond to this aspect of the design. She was feeling a sense of responsibility to try to generate *something*, and especially now that Andy had raised the question, she felt she could not in good conscience simply ignore it. Folding this into the lab designs would be challenging, especially since there were no additional resources, and it would require a significant amount of time from her.

As Casie sat in her office reviewing her notes and reflecting on her many conversations—with all the possibilities, constraints, pushback, and eager ideas—she wondered: *Can we really rethink the paradigm for labs? Could we do that in a way that benefits* all *learners, on-campus and online? How can I foster more buy-in and support for online learning? And how am I going to address accessibility if I don't have many resources for that? How can I ensure that our distance students get an equally great learning experience?*

Preliminary Analysis Questions

1. How can Casie design the online engineering labs so that both program and student needs are met? What are some design options that might enhance learning opportunities for all students, both face-to-face and remote?
2. What are the unique needs of first-generation learners in an online engineering program? What are some possible systemic supports and designs, as well as course-level strategies, that might address these learners' needs?
3. List the constraints Casie encounters when designing an accessible online engineering program. As an example, consider some of the ways in which her preferred accessibility solutions might be constrained by systemic factors, such as infrastructure and capacity (or lack thereof). Discuss strategic ways Casie could work within these constraints.

Implications for ID Practice

1. What tools can designers use to uncover cultural (traditions, values, ways of working, etc.) and organizational (policies, resources/infrastructure, communication loops, incentives and disincentives, etc.) aspects of a design problem? How might those tools help manage tensions in the design process?
2. Generate some examples of times when design needs—including ethical considerations—conflict with each other. For example, transparency and confidentiality are common assumed goods, but both cannot be optimized simultaneously. How can designers navigate these tensions in their work?
3. Reflect on what it means to frame ethical considerations as design specifications rather than as evaluative judgments. What are the implications for design practice?

12

Lindsey Jenkins

Piloting Case-Based Learning in a Blended-Learning Nursing Curriculum

Xun Ge and Kun Huang

The authors thank Maribeth Moran, professor at the University of Oklahoma College of Nursing, for allowing us to adapt her nursing case for use in this text.

As Lindsey Jenkins steps into her office, she realizes that she has worked for exactly one month at the Brooks Health Science Center School of Nursing (SON) as a faculty-rank instructional designer. Lindsey holds a PhD in instructional design and technology. Before joining SON, Lindsey had three years of experience as an instructional designer at another nursing institution and six years of college teaching experience.

Sitting in front of her computer, she looks at her Outlook calendar, and her eyes focus on a meeting event scheduled for 2:00 p.m. This is the first time she is going to host a meeting with two nursing professors about a course redesign pilot project. She feels a little bit anxious while anticipating and preparing for the meeting. With a deep breath, she tries to focus on the things she is going to discuss at the meeting. She is deep in thought as she reflects on what she has seen, heard, and experienced during her first month's work, which flickers across her mind like scenes from a movie.

INITIAL MEETING WITH DR. BARBARA MILLER, ASSOCIATE DEAN

On her second day of work, Lindsey met with Dr. Barbara Miller, the associate dean of academic affairs at SON. As Lindsey came into Barbara's office, Barbara stood up and greeted her. "Welcome aboard, Dr. Jenkins! We are very glad that you have joined SON." After some chatting, their conversation moved to the projects Lindsey would be working on.

"Let me give you some background information about SON," said Barbara. "There are five schools in the Brooks Health Science Center, and SON is the largest. We have more than 1,000 students, including undergraduate, master's, and doctoral students. Each degree level has different tracks."

"The school is indeed quite large," Lindsey said. "I read from the school website that there are more than 100 faculty members."

DOI: 10.4324/9781003354468-14

"Yes," Barbara said, "and 70% of them are full-time faculty. They are the ones you will be working with the most."

Barbara continued, "The main purpose in creating your position was the need for curriculum redesign at the school. Our school's percentile rank has traditionally been around 70 in NCLEX, you know, the National Council Licensure Examination."

"Yes," Lindsey said, "I'm familiar with NCLEX from my previous work."

"Okay, great," said Barbara, who then explained to Lindsey that in the past three years SON's performance in NCLEX had dropped, especially in the content area of physiological adaptation. "Physiological adaptation has been a weak area in our school's NCLEX performance. In the past three years, student performance has steadily decreased" (see Figure 12.1).

"The drop in performance on NCLEX was not too surprising," said Barbara, "because over the past couple of years our schoolwide student survey also indicated a decrease in students' satisfaction with the quality of their education."

Barbara continued, "One of the main curricular challenges facing us right now is shifting our focus to critical thinking. In recent years, NCLEX has been placing an increasing emphasis on assessing students' critical thinking skills. Also, we have accreditations going on at both SON and the Health Science Center as a whole—each calling for a curriculum to promote students' critical thinking skills. The dean and I, as well as the school curriculum committee, saw the synergy between improving students' performance on the board exam and meeting accreditation standards. We thought that by redesigning the school's core curriculum to focus on enhancing students' critical thinking, we could address both needs at the same time. That's why we hired you. Your training and expertise in education will help us with the curriculum redesign."

"Are you considering piloting the redesign in a few courses before it is implemented more widely?" asked Lindsey.

Barbara replied, "Yes, in fact it was decided that two courses would be the pilot courses—Acute and Chronic Nursing I and II—since physiological adaptation topics are heavily

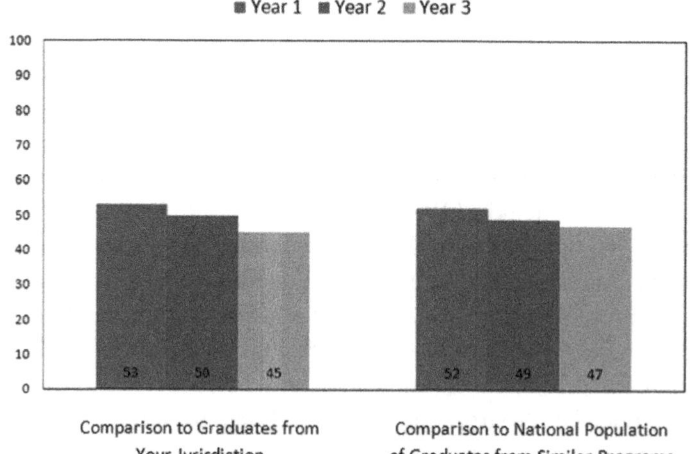

FIGURE 12.1 SON's NCLEX test reports over the past three years.

addressed in the two courses. Based on what we learn from the pilot, we can roll the redesign to the rest of the undergraduate core courses."

"That sounds like a good plan," said Lindsey. "Let me make sure that I understand the tasks clearly. The school is currently looking to redesign two courses with a focus on promoting students' critical thinking. After piloting these courses, we will turn our attention to the ultimate goal, which is to redesign the entire undergraduate core curriculum."

"That is correct," said Barbara. "About the two courses: Acute and Chronic I is offered to juniors in the spring semester. Professor Gina Smith teaches the course. Acute and Chronic II is a senior course taught in the fall by Professor David Cunningham. Gina has already tried using case studies in Acute and Chronic I to promote critical thinking among students. As I recall, you're familiar with case-based learning?"

"Yes, I am," said Lindsey. "I worked with nursing faculty to write cases in my previous job, and we also developed the cases into several interactive learning objects for online modules."

"Great," Barbara said. "I have attended a couple of case-based learning workshops at some nursing conferences. I think real-world nursing case scenarios can really help our students develop critical thinking skills. Students should be able to assess a patient's condition, identify and prioritize health care needs, develop a care plan, and evaluate its effectiveness. Actually, two months ago, we invited an expert in case-based learning to give a professional development workshop to our faculty."

"So, it sounds like case-based learning is an agreed-upon approach for curriculum redesign," commented Lindsey.

"Yes—the curriculum committee likes the approach, and the dean supports it, too." Barbara continued, "So, for the curriculum redesign initiative, you will be the lead person to coordinate the effort. You will work closely with David and Gina on the pilot project. Oh, you will also work with Jason Haung, our instructional technology specialist. He will be able to contribute to this project from the technology perspective."

"I understand. So, what does the timeline look like?" Lindsey asked.

Barbara said, "We are looking at a one-year pilot period. Right now, we are in the middle of the spring semester. Between now and fall, you can do some planning and build a model for implementing case-based learning. Then, in the following spring and fall, the model will be piloted in the two courses. The pilot will be evaluated, and we hope that the results will provide us with some insights for implementation at a larger scale."

"One thing is very important," Barbara added. "We are looking for evidence of improvement, which is what the accreditation bodies will look at, too. So, the evaluation of the pilot courses is going to need some good planning. We hope that the findings will help support our argument for adopting case-based learning across the entire core curriculum."

Lindsey came out of the meeting feeling both anxious and excited to start. She was excited that she had an opportunity to apply her knowledge and experience in this pilot project. At the same time, Lindsey felt a little concerned that she had been handed a project with predetermined approaches that was already under way.

GATHERING MORE INFORMATION

To learn more about the colleagues she would be collaborating with in the first year, Lindsey spent some time on the school website looking up information about the two professors. The school's online faculty profiles showed that Gina was an assistant professor in SON. She held a master's of science degree in nursing and a PhD degree in higher education. She joined

SON two years ago and had been teaching Acute and Chronic Nursing I ever since. Before joining SON, she had more than 10 years of teaching experience in another school of nursing. David held a master's of science degree in nursing and had been with SON for nearly 20 years. He had received several teaching awards throughout his tenure at SON.

In the following weeks, Lindsey was able to meet the two professors, both of whom agreed to give Lindsey access to their course websites. With Jason's help, Lindsey accessed the two courses through the school's course management system. She found that both were large classes, with more than 120 students in each course. The course syllabi indicated that both courses were taught primarily online, but with some face-to-face sessions. The students met with the instructor only during the first class and the five exam sessions. For the rest of the semester, the students studied the course materials independently online.

The resources for both courses were well organized in content modules. Learning materials were mostly readings, PowerPoint slides, and narrated PowerPoints recorded by the two professors. Most modules had a quiz at the end. There was a discussion forum in both courses, which was available for students to ask any course-related questions. Lindsey saw several students' posts asking questions about assignment requirements and deadlines.

Curious about how Gina had used cases in her course, Lindsey looked for sample cases and found one in a narrated PowerPoint. In several slides, Gina introduced a case scenario followed by a set of questions (see Figure 12.2).

After looking at the case, Lindsey thought that the questions at the end of the case were not directly linked to the patient scenario, and virtually no critical thinking would be required to answer the questions. This reminded Lindsey of her experiences with the nursing faculty in her previous job—the first drafts of cases that the faculty handed to her were very similar to what Lindsey saw here.

In the subsequent slides, Gina thoroughly explained the symptoms, treatment, and prevention of the disease presented in the case, and how nurses should take care of patients with the disease. She also stressed some common misconceptions in caring for the disease. In fact, Lindsey found that the most engaging part of Gina's narrated PowerPoint was her sharing of past experiences and the lessons she had learned as a nurse in caring for patients with the disease. Lindsey thought that it would be great to integrate Gina's experiences into the case scenario. For example, the patient could be presented with multiple symptoms, and students could be asked to assess the urgency of the symptoms, decide what to take care of first, and explain the rationale for their decisions.

Thinking that she would gain more insights into the current teaching of the courses, Lindsey asked Barbara for a copy of students' evaluations of the two courses from the past year (see Figure 12.3 for quantitative ratings). Lindsey also reviewed the students' comments in the course evaluations (see Figure 12.4 for representative examples of students' comments). The evaluations appeared to show some consistent patterns across the two courses in terms of their strengths and weaknesses.

After doing some more research, Lindsey decided that she was ready to set up a meeting to start the course redesign pilot project. In her email to David, Gina, and Jason, Lindsey indicated that the goal of the meeting was for them to review the current status of the two pilot courses and identify the needs or areas to be addressed by the project.

Case Study
• T.C. is a 7-year-old girl who was brought to the clinic where you work by her grandmother. Her grandmother states that she has "lost her appetite," complains of headache and abdominal pain, and that her urine "looks just like coke." On exam, you find that she is lethargic and appears unwell. Her vital signs are 136/98 98–116–28, with occasional crackles on chest auscultation. Her urinalysis reveals the following data:
Case Study
• Color: reddish-brown
• Appearance: cloudy
• Odor: normal
• Sp. gravity: 1.035
• Protein: 3+
• Glucose: negative
• RBCs: too many to count
• WBCs: 10 per low power field
• Casts: 15
Questions
1 What other information do you need to obtain from the child and her grandmother?
2 T.C. is diagnosed with poststreptococcal glomerulonephritis. Discuss the pathophysiology of this disease process, including the etiology.
3 What are the symptoms of glomerulonephritis?
4 What are some common methods (treatment options and drugs) for treating poststreptococcal glomerulonephritis?
5 Discuss three ways nurses can help prevent the occurrence of glomerulonephritis.
6 Compare and contrast dietary restrictions of glomerulonephritis with those of nephrotic syndrome.
7 How would you care for a patient with poststreptococcal glomerulonephritis?

FIGURE 12.2 Gina's PowerPoint slides illustrating a case study with patient information and questions.

THE MEETING

Lindsey arrives at the meeting room early. She has brought along two articles on best practices in writing and teaching with cases in medical education to share with the two professors at the meeting. On entering the meeting room, she checks the display system to make sure that it works properly.

Course Evaluation Report: N3134 Acute & Chronic Nursing I		
Teacher Performance	**Average**	**School Average**
1. Knowledge of the subject matter	3.8	3.6
2. Communication and explanation of subject matter	3.4	3.2
3. Organization of course materials	3.8	3.2
4. Encouragement of class interaction	2.0	2.5
5. Stimulation of student interest in the subject matter	2.1	2.9
6. Responsiveness to student inquiries	2.5	3.0
7. Respect for students	3.4	3.4
8. Overall rating of the instructor	3.3	3.2
Course Evaluation Report: N4134 Acute & Chronic Nursing II		
Teacher Performance	**Average**	**School Average**
1. Knowledge of the subject matter	4.0	3.6
2. Communication and explanation of subject matter	3.3	3.2
3. Organization of course materials	3.3	3.2
4. Encouragement of class interaction	2.3	2.5
5. Stimulation of student interest in the subject matter	2.5	2.9
6. Responsiveness to student inquiries	2.5	3.0
7. Respect for students	3.6	3.4
8. Overall rating of the instructor	3.2	3.2
Key: 1 = Poor 2 = Fair 3 = Good 4 = Excellent		

FIGURE 12.3 Quantitative summary of course evaluations of the two courses.

Gina arrives shortly. After greeting each other and some brief chatting, Lindsey asks, "So, how is it going with the Acute and Chronic I class?"

"It's going quite well. We just had the first exam. Students seem to have done well," Gina replies.

Lindsey remarks, "That is great! I visited your course website and saw some cases in your narrated PowerPoints. I really liked the sharing of your own experiences as a nurse. And I learned a few things myself!"

"I'm glad that you liked it, Lindsey. Yes, I have tried to incorporate at least one case in each narrated PowerPoint. I want the students to be able to relate the information for each disease

Course Evaluation Report
Question
• What were the specific weak points of the course?
Comment
• I feel I needed more support. While the recorded lectures were easy to understand, and the tests were okay, I got stuck when practicing NCLEX questions. I feel this course did not prepare me for the board exam.
• We received a lot of information about acute and chronic diseases, but were not taught adequately how to apply the information in real situations.
• There was not much opportunity to actually talk to the professor to get my questions answered. Usually when I had a question when watching PowerPoint, I had to figure it out myself.
• The quizzes and exams often focused on trivia. It would be very helpful if they made more of an effort to reflect the boards.
• The online offering of this course made it hard for us students to interact with each other. But I learn best by studying together with other students. I had to form a study group with two other students to meet regularly. We learned quite a lot from each other.

FIGURE 12.4 Qualitative comments in the course evaluations of the two courses.

type to some actual patients instead of simply memorizing all the symptoms, pathophysiology, drugs, and treatment. I think this process is very important to promote students' critical thinking."

"You mentioned critical thinking," says Lindsey. "How is the content of the Acute and Chronic I connected to critical thinking, which I presume is one of the learning goals for the class? Educate me here, Gina."

"Of course!" Gina responds. "We certainly want students to develop a good understanding of acute and chronic conditions and their diagnoses and treatments, but that knowledge is not enough. The reality of caring for patients with acute and chronic conditions can be quite complex that requires us nurses to assess the situation, prioritize care, and make timely decisions. This learning goal can be hard to accomplish for our students."

"In addition to the cases in your PowerPoints, do you assign students other cases to work on?" asks Lindsey.

"Not at this time. That will be my next step. It takes time to write cases, and it's a steep learning curve for me, which is why I am very glad that you have joined us, Lindsey. With your help, I feel more confident in revising my course."

At this time, David steps into the room. Lindsey welcomes him, saying that she and Gina were just talking about the cases in Acute and Chronic I. Then the three of them sit down at a table.

"Why don't we get started while waiting for Jason?" Lindsey says. "First, thank you for coming to this meeting. I thought that this would be a good time for us to sit down together and discuss the course redesign pilot project. I know that you attended the case-based learning workshop a while ago, and Gina has been using cases in her courses. As you know, I am new here. My charge is to work with you on the two pilot courses and to evaluate the outcomes of these courses in terms of improving students' critical thinking skills. I have been learning ever since I came on board. Your course websites helped me a lot, but I still have some gaps to fill. Perhaps you can help orient me so that I can better understand the two courses. From there, we may be able to brainstorm some ideas for the project."

"That sounds like a good plan," says Gina. "I'd be happy to share with you any information about my Acute and Chronic course. I certainly appreciate your help in finding a good way to do case studies."

"Talking about the workshop," says David, looking at Lindsey, "I personally don't think it was very helpful. The speaker was not from the nursing or even medical field. The examples she gave at the workshop were not related to nursing. For business and social sciences, it is easier to do case studies because there are no right or wrong answers. But for nursing, it is different." He turns to Gina. "Gina, the cases might work better for your Acute and Chronic I. But for Acute and Chronic II, I have a lot to cover in each module. I still don't know which part I can give up for case studies, not to mention the time needed to develop those cases."

Lindsey responds, "I understand. Nursing is indeed different from some other disciplines. However, the model and the underlying principles for learning apply, regardless of discipline. Actually, I brought these two articles on using cases in medical education." She hands the two copies to David and Gina and continues, "The articles offer some great guidelines for writing cases and teaching with cases. One of the authors actually did a study, and the findings were very positive about case teaching. David, I can work with you and Gina on developing cases, but of course I will need to rely on your content expertise."

Turning to Gina, Lindsey asks, "Gina, for the cases you present in your narrated presentations, do students have a chance to work on them before getting your answers from the PowerPoint?"

"Yes," replies Gina, "I want to make sure that they have really worked on the cases before watching my PowerPoint. So, for each module, I first assign readings and cases to students for them to work on. They have to submit their case responses by a deadline before I post my narrated PowerPoint with answers. I wish I could read all of their responses, but it is simply impossible for me to read or grade 126 of them. So, I give them participation points for submitting the case responses, because otherwise many students would not really work on the cases."

Recalling students' comments that they had little opportunity to interact with each other, Lindsey asks, "Have you thought about letting students discuss the cases or do some other online collaborative work?"

"Yes, I did try it before. I asked my students to post their answers to a discussion forum and encouraged them to discuss the case on the forum. But they didn't really discuss with each other. Instead, they only posted their answers, and that was it. So, I dropped the discussion forum later on."

"Have you thought about using some tools like a wiki to have groups of students work on the cases together?" asks Lindsey.

"A wiki?" David chuckles. "Like Wikipedia? I really don't like Wikipedia because it has very little credibility with me."

"Well, actually, both have similar characteristics, but think of it this way—both can be collaboratively edited by those with permissions. A course or content wiki allows a group of people to write and edit one single document at the same time."

Gina looks doubtful. "I actually tried wikis in the nursing research class the first semester I was here. I put students in groups to work on a research paper and encouraged them to use a free wiki website to work on the paper together. But it didn't work very well. Most of the students ended up posting comments instead of really collaboratively writing and editing the paper. They tended to post comments like 'Great job!' or 'Here are some useful resources'—things of that nature. There is another issue related to the use of a wiki. Jason told me that since the wiki website was a free service, it did not have a service contract with SON. If the system goes down or if there's any technical issue, there will be no support available. So, I kind of gave up using wikis at that point."

Jason, who has arrived a little late at the meeting, has been listening and keeping silent. As his name is mentioned, he smiles and nods at Gina and then adds, "I have tried my best to provide technical support to the SON faculty, but sometimes I feel overwhelmed by the volume of questions and requests coming from the faculty. When I joined SON six years ago, the volume of support was not this high. But now, 70% of SON courses are either blended or completely online. It is hard to stay on top of everything. With the course management system alone, I've got enough questions and requests for help. If each faculty member uses different free software, it is just not possible for me to answer all the questions, including questions as trivial as 'How do I create a page in wiki?' I wish I could provide all the IT support requested, but honestly it is just impossible."

Gina says, "I don't blame you, Jason. We've got to find a way to deal with these issues if we are going to encourage faculty to use technology in their teaching . . . Now back to wikis. Even though I stopped using a wiki after my first attempt, I would love to give it a second try now that Lindsey might be able to help me use it as a tool for students to work on cases. Lindsey, if you can help me find out how to use wikis to facilitate students' discussion of cases, and especially how to assess students' contributions to a wiki, that would be wonderful."

"Absolutely," says Lindsey. "I'd be glad to. Let's arrange a time for another meeting."

"That will work. Thanks, Lindsey," says Gina.

David says, "Although I haven't tried case studies, I do value discussions and group work. I think it's a great way for our students to learn. In fact, before my courses went online, I used to do a lot of discussions in my class, and the students really liked it. However, based on my experience, I just think it'd be hard for students to discuss online, especially for a case. Each student may have a different answer, and the discussion may go nowhere when they aren't in one room talking face-to-face. I'm not a big fan of technology, and our current course management system has already given me enough headaches when we switched to it from another system two years ago. But if you can find ways to give students the same opportunities to discuss and collaborate using the course management system or some other system, I'm willing to give it a try."

The meeting ends at 3:00 p.m. because David has to leave for another meeting. Based on the information she's been given, Lindsey now has a bigger picture of the pilot project. When she returns to her office, she plans to summarize her observations, list all the areas of needs to be addressed, and formulate an action plan for the next steps to be sent to the two professors and Jason.

Preliminary Analysis Questions

1. What ID issues have you observed in this case? How would those issues affect the implementation of case-based learning?
2. Develop a plan of action for Lindsey to assist faculty members in developing, implementing, and evaluating case instruction that is aligned with the principles of a case-based approach and serves to achieve the desired learning outcomes.
3. How would you explain the educational benefits of the case-based learning approach and the use of collaborative tools, given David's current understanding?
4. How would you work with the faculty to ensure that case-based learning helps to meet the learning goals of the two courses? What additional approaches would you explore to support the learning goals (e.g., knowledge about acute and chronic care, critical thinking skills, communication skills)? How can the two courses best work together to achieve these goals?
5. What can Lindsey recommend to the dean regarding the technology constraints and challenges that Jason highlighted in the meeting?
6. What considerations should Lindsey be weighing for the pilot evaluation in Gina and David's courses?

Implications for ID Practice

1. How would you encourage students to use technology effectively for collaboration to solve the problems presented by the cases? Provide some specific examples.
2. What are the challenges of promoting new approaches to teaching and learning in an existing curriculum, especially in an online learning environment?
3. What are the core elements that need to be included in the evaluation of the case-based learning approach to assess students' critical thinking?

13

Victoria March

Tackling Complex Content and Managing SMEs

Valerie Morgan and Monica W. Tracey

Victoria March, an independent learning designer, was sitting at her desk, working on a project when she received the call. She knew it was coming. Dr. Claire Philips, a professor of learning design at Wexford University, contacted her a few months prior to discuss a relatively large grant for which the university had applied. She also wanted to discuss Victoria's role in the grant, should she accept the offer. On the call several months prior, Claire had explained that the grant was a three-year, 1.2-million-dollar award focusing on the treatment of "liquid" cancers. "This grant is groundbreaking in two ways," she said. "First, this is the first multidisciplinary grant in the history of Wexford University. Second, this grant will provide a setting for oncology specialists from all over the United States to participate in a five-day course analyzing state-of-the-art cancer treatments."

"This," Claire exclaimed to Victoria, "rarely happens! We have a wonderful opportunity to make a difference." She had asked Victoria if she were interested in coming on board as the lead designer, should they procure the grant. "Are you in?" she had asked. "Yes, of course," Victoria responded. Victoria had always believed in the benefits of engaging in diverse design projects and knew that she did her best work under demanding, rigorous conditions. The Wexford project was unlike any she'd worked on before, so she thought it would be the perfect challenge. Victoria had worked with Claire several times in the past, and Claire's projects had never failed to challenge or stretch her as a designer.

Victoria was appreciative that Claire considered her a good fit for what seemed to be a highly worthwhile project, even though she had yet to fully comprehend its potential impact. Victoria reflected on all of this as she listened to Claire today. Claire told Victoria that they were awarded the grant and asked Victoria if she were still able to join the IDBRC (Integrating Disciplines for Blood Related Cancers) project as lead designer and if so, could she attend the kickoff team meeting to talk about specific details of the grant. "I am one of two principal investigators (PIs). You'll be able to meet the other PI from the School of Medicine, and the two co-investigators, one from the School of Medicine and the other from the School of Education and Human Services. You will also meet the other learning designers. We hope by the end of this meeting," Claire continued, "to have a better understanding of the focus of the project, the content we need to work with, and what the team will be doing for the next three years."

DOI: 10.4324/9781003354468-15

Victoria agreed to attend the kickoff meeting and shortly afterward, she and the other designers received a brief email along with an informal agenda. They were asked to be prepared to introduce themselves, brainstorm design processes, receive assignments, and create a meeting schedule.

SETTING

Wexford University (WU) is a nationally recognized research institution in the northwest US, offering over 400 academic programs through 15 schools and colleges to 33,000 students. Wexford University students come from over 60 countries around the globe.

WU's School of Medicine has over 1,100 medical students. Strong emphasis is placed on integrating basic and clinical sciences through research. WU is a research intensive (R1) institution with more than $75 million in research funding. Historically, Wexford's faculty had not pursued funding for interdisciplinary grants; however, a mandate from the president of the university required faculty to apply for funding to work on interdisciplinary projects. This collaboration between the School of Education and Human Services and the School of Medicine was the first of its kind at Wexford University.

YEAR 1: KICKOFF MEETING, SEPTEMBER 19

Claire Philips opened the meeting by introducing herself and passed out a packet to everyone that contained several documents. Claire said, "Let's first have a look at the organizational chart and IDBRC team member sheet, in your packet, so we can get to know each other (see Figure 13.1 and Table 13.1).

"Let me start our introductions. I am a professor of learning design here at Wexford University and one of the principal investigators on this project along with Wayne Jameson, who you will meet shortly. I, along with Wayne and the co-investigators, contributed to the writing of this grant. My role on this team is to assume responsibility for conducting this project and leading the team of learning designers. Unfortunately, one of us could not be here today.

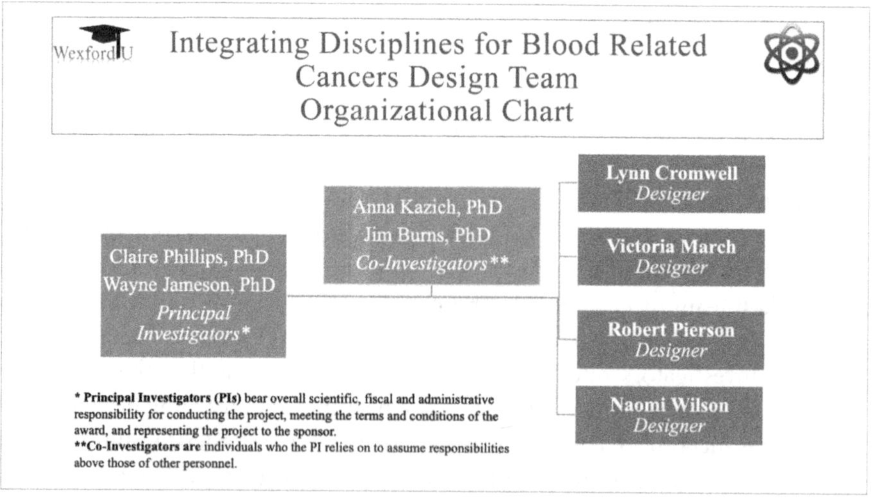

FIGURE 13.1 IDBRC organizational chart.

TABLE 13.1
IDBRC Team Members

Role	*Name/Affiliation*	*Background/IDRBC Responsibilities*
Principal Investigator *(Bears overall scientific, fiscal, and administrative responsibility for conducting the project, meeting the terms and conditions of the award, and representing the project to the sponsor)*	**Claire Phillips, PhD** Professor of Learning Design at Wexford University	Collaborated with Wayne Jameson to write the grant. Leads the team of learning designers and is the primary point of contact for SMEs, Wayne Jameson and Jim Burns.
Principal Investigator *(Bears overall scientific, fiscal, and administrative responsibility for conducting the project, meeting the terms and conditions of the award, and representing the project to the sponsor)*	**Wayne Jameson, PhD** Professor of Oncology, Wexford University School of Medicine	Collaborated with Claire Phillips to create the fundamental outline for the course. Radiobiology SME to all learning designers.
Co-Investigator *(Assumes responsibilities above those of other personnel)*	**Anna Kazich, PhD** Assistant Professor of Education Evaluation and Research at Wexford University	One of the original authors of the grant. Leads all the assessment activities of the grant.
Co-Investigator *(Assumes responsibilities above those of other personnel)*	**Jim Burns, PhD** Professor of Oncology, Wexford University School of Medicine	Assisted Wayne Jameson with the conception of the fundamental outline for the course. Pathology SME to all learning designers.
Learning Designer	**Victoria March, MS** Independent learning design consultant	Ten years of diverse design experience. Former undergraduate student and graduate assistant of Claire Phillips. Designs learning activities for the course. Maintains communication with keynote speakers.
Learning Designer	**Lynn Cromwell** Curriculum developer at Craft Community College	Current graduate student in the Wexford University Learning Design Program. Designs learning activities for the course. Maintains communication with keynote speakers.
Learning Designer	**Robert Pierson, MS** Librarian at Wexford University	Worked with Dr. Phillips on master's degree project. Assists in the design of activities for the course. Maintains communication with keynote speakers.
Research Data Collection Learning Designer	**Naomi Wilson** Graduate research assistant for Claire Phillips	Background in business. Responsible for research data collection and analysis generated from the grant. Designs learning activities for the course. Maintains communication with keynote speakers.

Jim Burns, a co-investigator on the grant, is unavailable today. So, let me introduce you to my fellow principal investigator, Wayne Jameson."

"Hello, everyone. As Claire mentioned, my name is Wayne Jameson, and I am a professor of oncology here at the Wexford University School of Medicine. I assisted Claire in creating the outline for this course. Going forward, I will serve as the radiobiology subject matter expert, or SME, to the learning designers on our team. Claire just mentioned that Jim Burns will not be with us today. Jim Burns will be the SME for pathology. His current responsibilities in the medical school have been such that, as Claire just mentioned, he is not able to be here today, so, again, my apologies."

Next, Anna Kazich explained that she also contributed to the grant writing, that her interest is in research, that she has a degree in learning design, and that she would lead the assessment activities associated with the grant. As team members continued to introduce themselves, Victoria couldn't help but feel disappointed that Jim was not present. She had hoped to meet both the SMEs and hoped that Jim's absence would not become a problem down the road. In any case, she was next to speak and described how her most challenging project to date was working overseas leading a design team. "I know that the overseas job helped me become a better designer because of its sheer rigor and multiple constraints." She went on to say how that experience, along with other client projects, ultimately prepared her to contribute to this project, which she anticipated would be rigorous as well.

Lynn Cromwell, a curriculum developer for a local community college said that she was a new master's student and was eager to contribute what she knew about curriculum design. "I've had several years' experience as a curriculum designer at Craft Community College. I think it could really help us on this project." Robert Pierson described his position as a librarian at Wexford for about a year and stated that his passion is research. He thought that for him, exploring this complex medical content would be really interesting and relatively easy. He added, "I have really good connections with the library staff here and can easily do research within the library system."

Naomi Wilson described her main responsibility as collection and analysis of the research data generated by the grant and said that she would serve as a learning designer on the team as well.

Once the introductions were complete, Wayne asked everyone to take out the Program Overview document from their packets, so they would all understand the fundamental vision of the course (see Figure 13.2).

"This document summarizes the goal of the grant," he explained. "The first paragraph speaks to the status of cancer in America, and the second paragraph provides more detail about the course itself." Wayne said that he would turn it over to Claire for more specific course details but asked if there were any questions. No questions were asked but based on the looks on the faces of the designers, it was clear that they needed to understand more about the program to fully envision what this course might look like. Subsequently, Claire provided more detailed information about the team, the course timeline and goals, and the participants. She projected several slides and began with a few team basics (see Figure 13.3).

"I'd like us all to remember a few basics. I will be guiding the designers through this process. Keep in mind that this collaboration is a new experience for all of us. Now, let's look at what we know about the course so far" (see Figure 13.4).

Claire cautioned the group that none of the details of the project had been fleshed out yet. Then, she provided more detailed information about the program participants. Claire continued, "The next two slides are a good estimate of who our audience is and how we expect them to participate." As Claire reviewed the slides, the designers began to see the composition and the expectations of the cohort (see Figures 13.5 and 13.6).

IDBRC

Program Overview: Integrating Disciplines for Blood Related Cancers (IDBRC)

Cancer impacts most people one way or another in the United States. Future growth in the number of older adults and minorities is leading inevitably to a corresponding increase in overall cancer incidences. There is an increasing demand, worldwide, for therapies in cancer treatment. To address this problem, a 3-year grant was awarded to support the design and evaluation of a course for oncology specialists.

This 1.2 million dollar grant awarded to the School of Medicine and the School of Education and Human Services at Wexford University supports the development of an innovative and advanced 5-day collaborative multidisciplinary course integrating radiobiology, pathology, and radiation therapy and is targeted at all specialists within oncology, dedicated to the treatment of liquid or blood-related cancers. We hypothesize that by providing this course on integrating radiobiology, pathology, and radiation therapy we will produce more effective researchers, clinicians, and educators who have the desire to plan research and pursue careers in academic oncology and who will have the ability to work effectively across fields. This will ultimately improve blood-cancer patient care and cure rates.

Course Outline

Participants will:

- Attend lectures from internationally recognized experts in their fields followed by question and answer sessions.
- Engage in structured, collaborative, problem-based activities.
- Plan constructive research that tests potential developing technology and treatment practices.

FIGURE 13.2 Program overview.

The IDBRC Team

- Claire leads the team of learning designers.
- The SMEs have never worked with learning designers and vice versa.
- This is a new experience for all team members.

FIGURE 13.3 Team basics.

IDBRC

Integrating Disciplines for Blood Related Cancers

- What we know so far...
  - Course: June 4 through June 8
  - Five-day classroom-based course
  - Keynote speakers on Days 1 through 4
  - Day 5: wrap-up

FIGURE 13.4 What we know about the course so far.

Participants

- PhD or MD/PhD in Radiation Biology or Physics
  - Medical Physicist – 56% of cohort
  - Radiation Oncologist – 10% of cohort
  - Radiobiologist – 34% of cohort
  - All may be currently working as educators
  - Experienced in their respective fields

FIGURE 13.5 Audience for the project.

Participants must be willing to:

- Collaborate in teams
- Solve problems
- Work together on multidisciplinary goals
- Provide support for different treatment approaches

FIGURE 13.6 Expectations of cohort.

IDBRC – Audience Personas

The following is an audience assessment for the upcoming IDBRC course. Participants are MD, MD/PhD, or PhD in Radiation Biology or Physics.

1. Participants are on the cutting edge in their areas of expertise. Physicians MUST continue to develop and learn throughout their careers. They are ALL motivated learners.
2. Participants are used to complex problems. By the very nature of their areas of expertise, they are used to and welcome dealing with complex problems.
3. Participants are very busy people and do not like to waste time. Give them the information that they need to know as background information, so they can get to the complex problem! Provide pre-reading if necessary and present the content so that the specialists in different areas of expertise can understand each other. Remember that the learning will take place as they solve the complex problems, so the lectures are the foundation and must provide the foundational materials.

To provide you with a clearer picture of the audience members, review the personas of two professionals you might expect to see in the course:

Persona 1
Medical Physicist – 56% of cohort

- Faculty level
- Recognizes their desired career trajectory
- Wants to be in research (academic) arena
- Hungry for information – yet has enough experience to solve problems

Persona 2
Radiobiologist – 34% of cohort

- Senior level
- New to radiation

FIGURE 13.7 Audience personas.

Claire then asked the team to take out the IDBRC—Audience Personas document that further described the participants they should expect to see in the course (see Figure 13.7).

"It is important to have a clear picture of who our audience is when we work together to create this course. To be the best designers, we must meet the learners where they are, and to do that, we must know who they are and where they are in their respective careers," she explained. "You can see how this document provides us with a good assessment of, not only the percentages of different disciplines that will be represented, but also examples of where participants might be in their careers." Claire directed the team to take a few moments to review the document and asked for questions before moving on. Though there were no questions, the designers were glad to see the audience persona document as it provided a helpful visual representation of the cohort.

Claire then said, "Now let's turn our attention back to Wayne so he can give us a little more detail about the course."

Wayne began by describing the role of the keynote speakers. "Each day, two keynote speakers who are experts in their fields, and who draw quite a following, will be scheduled to present cutting-edge lectures on a theme we have predetermined, based on the keynotes' expertise. One keynote speaker will present about the biology aspects of their theme, and the other keynote will lecture about the physics aspects of their theme. If you have a look at this slide, you'll see how each day has been assigned a theme" (see Figure 13.8).

Victoria couldn't help but note two potential issues. First, the SMEs had never worked with learning designers before. In her experience, this meant that the design team would need to continuously educate the SMEs throughout the project about what learning design is and the designers' roles in the project. And second, as Wayne and Claire had indicated earlier, even though Jim was identified as a significant SME on the project, he was not in attendance for this important first meeting.

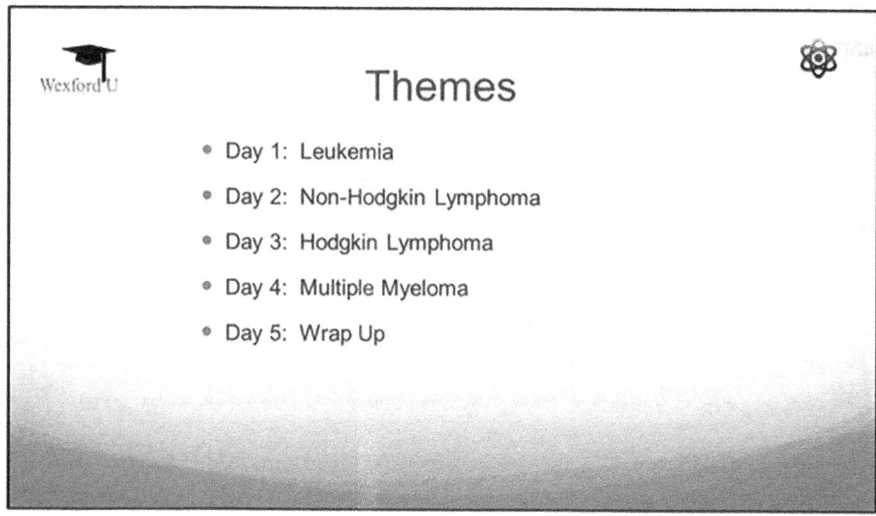

FIGURE 13.8 Themes for each day.

TABLE 13.2
Initial Plan

Kickoff Meeting Brainstorming Session		
Goal	*Instructional Activity to Meet Goal*	*Designer*
1. Collaborate	Speed storming	Anna
2. Solve problems	Clinical trial	Robert
3. Work on a multidisciplinary patient case	Clinic simulation	Victoria
4. Argue different treatment approaches	Treatment option debates	Naomi

After Wayne and Claire finished their presentations, Claire addressed the design timeline. "The design timeline is tight, to say the least. The project launches June 4. We'll need one month to produce materials with our desktop publisher and time to develop and pilot instructional materials. Let's plan to meet every two weeks to keep the project moving forward." Claire continued, "Now, we need to do some brainstorming. We know what our goals are for the participants for the five days. Let's brainstorm ideas for instructional activities that will achieve these goals, and then, let's assign designers to specific activities. Claire posted large pieces of Post-it easel paper on the wall, and after 60 minutes, the team had agreed to an initial plan (see Table 13.2).

Once the activities were identified, Wayne distributed a list of the keynote speakers with their contact information. Wayne noted that some of the keynote speakers were local and some were from out of town, and he suggested that they schedule meetings with those who were local as soon as possible. In the case of the out-of-town keynote speakers, he recommended that they be contacted via phone or video chat. Wayne asked that in these meetings, the designers discuss the project, gain content information from the keynote speakers, and answer any questions they might have. The designers then selected speakers they would visit and decided to work in pairs to visit the local keynote speakers (see Table 13.3).

TABLE 13.3
Learning Designer Assignments

Learning Designer Assignments			
Day	*Theme*	*Keynote Speakers*	*Designers*
Day 1	Leukemia	James Solomon—R Samuel Jones—P	Victoria*/Robert
Day 2	Non-Hodgkin lymphoma	Joseph Franks—R Stephen McCann—P	Robert*/Victoria
Day 3	Hodgkin lymphoma	Mark Willson—R Damien DeJong—P	Naomi*/Lynn
Day 4	Multiple myeloma	Allen Samosia—R Albert Shimko—P	Lynn*/Naomi

R = Radiobiologist
P = Medical physicist
*** = Lead designer***

As the meeting wrapped up, Claire reminded everyone that there would be another design meeting in two weeks. The designers walked away from the meeting with assigned keynote speakers and content areas, and activities to pin down and develop.

MEETING WITH KEYNOTE SPEAKERS—ONE WEEK LATER

Both keynote speakers for day 1 were local, so Victoria and Robert set up a meeting with Drs. Solomon and Jones. Prior to the meeting, Victoria and Robert discussed their goals for the meeting: (1) to provide Drs. Solomon and Jones with an overview of the IDBRC project and (2) to discuss the content of their keynote lectures to help them with the design of their instructional activities.

Victoria was excited, but somewhat apprehensive, about the meeting. She envisioned that following the meeting, she and Robert would better understand how the design team could integrate the keynote lectures with the activities they would design. However, sitting with Drs. Solomon and Jones, Victoria realized that Wayne and Jim had not discussed many details of the program with the keynote speakers. After Robert and Victoria provided an overview of the program, Drs. Solomon and Jones asked what was required of them. "What kind of keynote lecture do you want, overview or cutting edge?"

"Cutting edge," Victoria replied. Before Victoria could continue, Dr. Solomon interjected, "Good. Well, I've been teaching medical students for some time now, and I've tried other teaching methods. That push-pull with students can sometimes be a challenge, but I have found that traditional didactic lecture works well for student learning. I'd have to be convinced to deviate from a method that has worked best in the past." Victoria reiterated that the goal of the course was collaboration among oncology specialists, and so, was not supposed to look like a typical course. "This is envisioned as a highly collaborative course among professionals who do not typically interact."

Dr. Jones asked about Robert's and Victoria's role in this project. Robert explained that they were learning designers for the course. The keynote speakers looked perplexed, "Learning designers?" they asked simultaneously. Victoria knew then that she needed to provide more detail about learning designers and their roles in the course design. "We are from the

School of Education and Human Services and have been hired to design the IDBRC course. As learning designers, we work with professionals who are subject matter experts, or SMEs, who know the content that needs to be taught. We are responsible for developing course goals and learning outcomes, and then creating appropriate learning activities for the target audience."

Dr. Solomon asked for examples of activities that might be designed. Victoria explained that the design team was still in the early stages of design, so the activities were not fleshed out yet. There was awkward silence as the keynote speakers tried to process this information. Victoria and Robert fumbled through the rest of the meeting trying to generally explain what the five-day course would entail. Victoria was keenly aware that her lack of understanding of the content scope and complexity of this project was apparent to the keynote speakers. Robert and Victoria walked out of the meeting concerned that they had not been able to convey to the keynote speakers what they were expected to do. Did the keynote speakers have a better understanding of the course and their parts in it, or were they just more confused? How could they reassure them that she and Robert have the project under control?

As Robert and Victoria walked to the parking garage, Victoria took the opportunity to pick Robert's brain about the clinic simulation activity she had to design. She believed that the clinic simulation would require expertise in web development, and she didn't have a contact for one. Robert excitedly told her that he had worked on a different project with a web developer, Jack Lee, who was wonderful and thought that he could help them. He offered to reach out to him to see if he could attend the next design meeting and think about how the clinic simulation might work. Victoria contacted Claire to inform her that Robert had found a web developer whom he thought might be appropriate for the project and would like to invite him to the next meeting. Claire agreed and explained that if they hired him, he could be paid out of the design budget in the grant.

DESIGNING AND SMES

Robert phoned Victoria to tell her that he had contacted Jack who was eager to work on the project and that he was available to attend the next design meeting. He wanted to bring ideas to the meeting and asked if he and Victoria could speak beforehand. Victoria agreed that a quick videoconference would help her explain what she's looking for and what Jack needed to do to create the prototype for the clinic simulation. Victoria had already produced a storyboard concept of the simulation and wanted to convey to Jack what specifications were needed to create an initial model for the next meeting.

At the start of the videoconference, Victoria outlined the simulation content and specifications with Jack. However, as they talked, Victoria realized that she could only go so far with the discussion without greater knowledge of the content. She assured Jack that she would get back to him with as much content as she could in the next few days, in time for him to create a prototype. When she finished her call with Jack, she immediately emailed Wayne and Jim asking for help understanding the content well enough to produce an initial, functional simulation for the next design meeting, if possible. She thought it might be best to set up a conference call with both at the same time. Wayne responded to the email quickly and informed her that Jim would be out of the country at a conference for the next several days, but that he was available to speak via phone, so they could at least begin to discuss the radiobiology content. The pathology content would have to wait until Jim returned.

Victoria called Wayne immediately. After sharing pleasantries, they got right down to discussing the course. Victoria said, "As you know, the theme for the first day is leukemia, so we need to find a time for us to work together on the content."

"Yes, indeed," he responded, sounding like he understood his role in the design for the first time. She further explained that she had a web developer attending the next design meeting who would be assisting with the development of the clinic simulation. Victoria and Wayne set an appointment for the next day to discuss the radiobiology content and to outline the basic framework of the simulation. Victoria wanted Jack to have the simulation framework and some of the content for the design meeting. After the meeting, Victoria contacted Jack to inform him of the outcomes of the meeting, so he could begin to develop the model.

DESIGN MEETING: OCTOBER 1

The designers, along with Jack, assembled in Claire's office. Robert introduced Jack to the rest of the team explaining how he had used Jack's expertise on a previous project and that Jack would be working with Victoria on the clinic simulation. Claire then asked the designers to identify any constraints they were currently facing. A common theme emerged: the inability to get in touch with keynote speakers and SMEs. Claire told the designers that she would contact Wayne to address this issue.

Claire moved the group past the constraints to focus on the clinic simulation. At this point, Victoria asked Jack to explain how he created the prototype (see Figure 13.9).

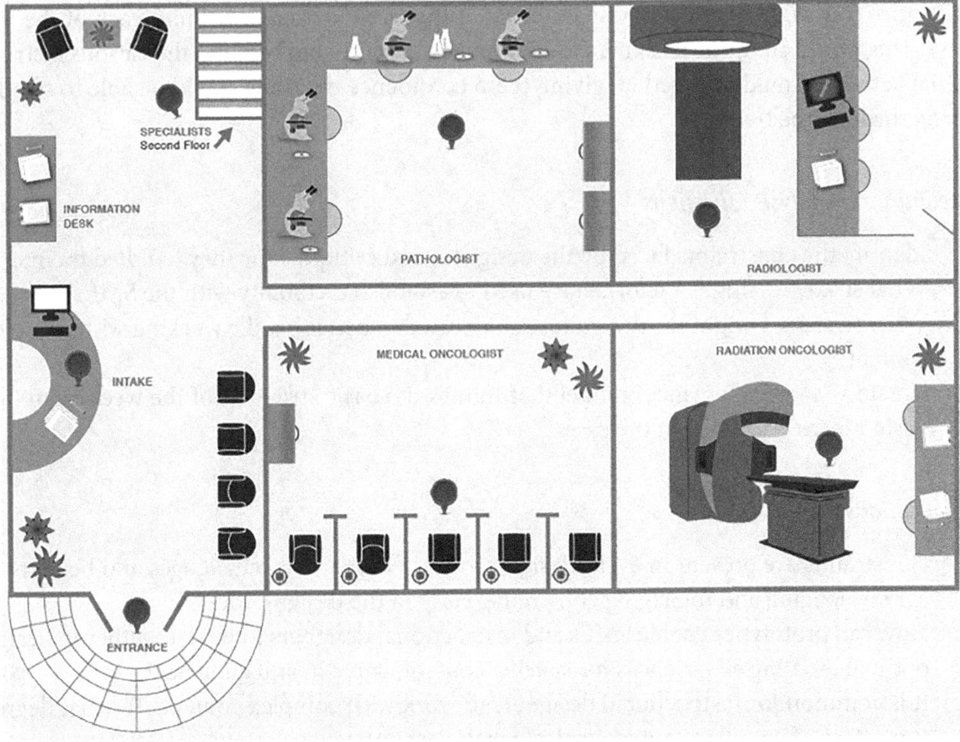

FIGURE 13.9 IDBRC prototype.

"Well, inside the clinic, you can click on different rooms and access whatever information you choose. You can profile a patient," he said. The designers thought they were getting somewhere. As a team, they could see the structure and how a user could access different pieces of information, but they couldn't see or verbalize how to create the activity. They were still stymied by their incomplete understanding of the content and the difficulty accessing and working with the SMEs. Victoria said, "I was able to meet with Wayne to get some of the radiobiology content, but I think that if we can get both of the SMEs in the same room, and nail down the content, we would be able to design the simulation and use it as a daily, collaborative icebreaker for all four of the themes." Given the inaccessibility of one of the SMEs, she was unsure of this happening, but she still recommended that idea to the group. The group agreed that the simulation had great potential to be a daily icebreaker.

As the meeting progressed, Claire recognized that the team was becoming overwhelmed by concerns about the content and were failing to "see" the design. She took the lead. "We can design this without understanding the content, don't you see?"

Lynn quickly drew her hands up to her eyes like she was trying to focus a pair of binoculars. "No! No, I can't see it! Help me see it!"

Everyone burst out laughing, a comedic break much needed at that point. Claire understood what the team was feeling, but at the same time she knew that she had assembled a talented group of designers, and she was trying to get everyone past this perceived constraint. "We must focus our design on the learners. What learning experiences do we want the learners to have? If we just focus on the content, we will lose the learners!"

To start moving the process forward, the team decided that if they created a document, which they called IDBRC Course At-A-Glance, this would help them see the framework of the entire course. It would be a visual format of the week broken down into each of the five days. This would allow the designers to see how the keynote speakers and the various instructional activities could fit together, giving them confidence that they would be able to see the forest through the trees.

Preliminary Analysis Questions

1. Identify the constraints faced by the designers and critique how they handled them.
2. What strategies might Victoria have used to establish credibility with the SMEs?
3. What strategies might the design team have used to better handle working with complex content?
4. Create a "week at a glance" model that frames the basic structure of the week using the design ideas presented in the case.

Implications for ID Practice

1. Constraints are present in every design project. What are the challenges and benefits to acknowledging and managing constraints early in the design process?
2. How can prototypes enable SMEs and instructional designers to work together to design optimal learning experiences for specific content, context, and audience?
3. It is common for instructional designers to work with complex content. To what degree is mastery of complex content critical when designing instruction?

14

Megan Martin

Redesigning a Course to Promote Equity and Increase Student Success[1]

Michael L. Wray and Brent G. Wilson

CHARGE FROM THE DEAN

It's a rainy day as Megan Martin arrives to meet with Carlton Edwards, the dean of consumer sciences at San Antonio Technical University (SATU). Stepping into the dean's suite, she laughs as she shakes the rain off her raincoat. "I always enjoy the rain, being from Texas!" SATU is an open-enrollment institution in downtown San Antonio, and its academic programs change rapidly as it continually adapts to workforce needs. Eight months ago, Megan accepted a faculty development position at SATU, where faculty have come to appreciate the instructional design support she provides. At any given time, Megan consults on 12–15 projects with both faculty and administration. Curriculum development and assessment is a part of the job, but her primary role is to support faculty in shifting their instructional practice to ensure inclusive programs for students wishing to transition from school to work—and helping to promote universal design of learning (UDL). Megan's graduate training had used UDL as a framework for reaching diverse audiences—giving students options for different media, activities, and means of engagement.

Gesturing toward the nearest chair, Dean Edwards welcomes Megan into the office. "Thank you for meeting with me. Your evaluation of our programs is one of my highest priorities right now, and I know your findings will make a significant difference to us. The School of Consumer Sciences was recently reorganized due to the fast growth and departure of Management Information Science (MIS) and Business Analytics, which became their own school. Consumer Sciences now has an array of vocational and professional studies programs: Fashion Merchandising, Hospitality, Nutrition, and Culinary Arts.

"As you may know," Dean Edwards continues, "MIS has a high number of both enrolled students and larger classes, which had served to balance our smaller programs, particularly those with less students per class. So now, every program must stand on its own two feet. We are starting our evaluation with Culinary Arts. The program is small but highly regarded. I asked you here to review the appropriateness of our teaching approaches and the quality of our students' learning experiences. I am hoping you can produce some great ideas for improvement."

DOI: 10.4324/9781003354468-16

Megan is looking forward to jumping in but just a little anxious about the prospects. She has heard accolades about the program coordinator, Claudetta Moreno, a charismatic instructor who is active in the culinary community and often featured in local media as an expert in Latin American cuisine. Megan asks, "I understand that Claudetta teaches and coordinates the program. How successful are the graduates?"

Dean Edwards responds, "Well, the program is cohort-based, accepting only 15 students each year; however, only eight graduate each spring. But those who succeed in navigating the program are very sought after with a near 100% job placement rate.

Megan was silently doing the math on graduation rate, somewhere just over 50%—an exceedingly small percentage, and Megan's shock was obvious. "Why do you think that almost half of the students fail to graduate?"

Dean Edwards pauses and responds, "The word is out on Claudetta—she is a challenging instructor with exacting standards for classroom performance and the required industry experience. She maintains strict standards both in the classroom and in their applied work settings, any student can tell you that!"

"Students have both classroom and work requirements?" Megan is curious—how do instructors manage that dual oversight? Learning in authentic settings is great, but is every student ready for workplace pressures?

Dean Edwards responds, "Yes, students are on the job from the get-go—or maybe it is the second term they start working, I am not sure. Claudetta can fill you in on the details. She teaches the Kitchen Operations course, which is one of the first classes students take in their first year. The second-year students are the management team. If the first-year students do not achieve a grade of B or higher, they are removed from the cohort and are replaced by students on the program wait list and must reapply to enter another cohort." Megan mentally pictures a reality TV show where poor performers are kicked off the island—or out of the kitchen. Dean Edwards continues, "The Operations course is a feeder into the program, offered each term because of the high number of students who don't make it through."

Megan continues to take notes. "Sounds like a high stakes teaching approach," she observes and inquires further, "Are you concerned about the low rate of student success in this first course? What do you think is going on?"

Too many questions, Megan tells herself, slow down! To Megan, encouraging multiple means of student expression is so important—and learners can engage better if the classroom is inclusive and inviting to all learners.

After a pause and a sigh, Dean Edwards responds, "I've had a few students in my office in tears, feeling overwhelmed by the course."

Megan asks, "Does failure deter recruitment?"

"No, students flock to her. She has quite the following as the expert of Modern Latin Cuisine. She came to us from a culinary school in Oaxaca, where she also owned a restaurant."

"She taught and ran a restaurant?" Megan asks with eyebrows raised.

"Not just any restaurant, but a Michelin-starred resort fine dining restaurant. Her Mod-Mex Cuisine cookbook captured a James Beard Award—or something like that." Dean Edwards adds, "Let me just say though: with enrollments more of an issue now, I don't want to lose any students unnecessarily."

Dean Edwards continues, "Our problem is complicated. We want quality graduates and the cachet that comes with this elite program—but we need to retain more students and grow the program—even scale it up somehow." Laughing, he concludes, "I'd like you to figure out how we can be more inclusive, improve retention, and maintain a quality program—all at the same time!"

"Piece o' cake!" Megan replies, recognizing the pun as she says it. Complicated indeed! "Thanks for your time, Dean Edwards. I think I would like to visit with Claudetta."

Dean Edwards replies, "I will give you much more than that! How about a personal tour and lunch in our student-run restaurant, Toro?"

Megan smiles. "Toro?"

"Yes," Dean Edwards replies enthusiastically. "It is in the top five on *Yelp* for San Antonio restaurants. It is so good," he adds, "specializing in steak of course, hence *Toro*, but it's also the presentation, the sauces, and those desserts!"

"I think that would be wonderful; please lead on, Matador," Megan chuckles. "We're off," Dean Edwards responds, shaking hands, and briskly walking with her from the office to the student restaurant.

TOUR AND LUNCH

Megan is ready to take it all in: the student chefs, the famed Claudetta, and the restaurant—or is it a reality show set? Dean Edwards shows her the student culinary labs where students prepare the meal before service. She is impressed to see everyone in crisp uniforms, each busy and involved in food production. "What are the differences among the kitchens?" she asks.

Dean Edwards explains that there are three kitchens. "In the skills lab, students work on knife and basic cooking skills." He adds, "In the skills kitchen students practice the recipes on the menu in Toro; there is also a bake shop where they hone their baking skills. Most of the desserts are fully prepped prior to service, just requiring plating." Next, Megan is shown the production kitchen that serves the restaurant or as Dean Edwards commented, "where the magic happens." "Take a look," he adds, "you can tell the first-year students as they are in a solid white cap and checkered pants, while second-year students have a black cap with solid black pants."

It is easy to see who is in charge as they walk to the production kitchen. As the two move toward the sound of voices, clanging pots and pans, and knives chopping, there is no mistaking Claudetta. She is regal in her tall white hat and immaculately pressed white coat with her name embroidered in cursive. The pens and thermometer in the arm pocket appear consciously chosen, as is the bright colored apron, reflecting the colors of Mexico, matching the flag on her collar and corresponding piping. Standing with an air of authority, she peers toward the spot where finished food will soon emerge. She smiles constantly, nodding frequently while calling out timing "Service up!" as a nervously excited first-year student named Jason responds, "Yes, Chef!"

The pace is fast, especially for first-year students scurrying around their work areas, receiving some support from second-year students but most instruction from Claudetta: "Fire, one pollo en molé poblano, one duck blandas!"

Immediately Jason clears the sweat from his brow with a dish towel and responds sharply, "One molé poblano, one duck, yes, Chef!"

A student assistant, name-tagged Jenna, takes over and commands sharply, "Order up! Two Toro grill, a molé roja sub blandas with greens, other with molé vérde."

Jason's response is not as fast this time, as he says timidly, "One Toro roja, yes, Chef."

After a pause, Claudetta, sensing a need to clarify, sharply notes, "You got it?"

"No, Chef," he responds timidly, "is that greens on both?"

"No," Claudetta responds as she walks to the side of the station, speaking clearly, "Jenna needs two orders: First is a Toro grill with the red molé—but no tortillas, they want grilled greens. The other steak is subbing the roja with the green molé, but with standard tortillas, got it?

"Yes, Chef," he replies.

"Yes what?" Claudetta says, turning to include Jenna.

A slow but accurate response from Jason ensues, "One Toro roja, sub greens, one Toro vérde side blandas, yes, Chef!" He finishes assuredly.

"Good, good." Claudetta continues, "Jenna, take over expediting, I'm on tables."

Returning to the production line, Jenna quickly ends her chopping of cilantro with a quick scrape into a container, wiping the knife with a wet towel from a red bucket marked SANITIZER, and bounds spiritedly to the front of the serving line. Poised and proud in her role as expediter, Claudetta moves briskly to the dining room, straightening her chef coat and removing the kitchen towel from her apron without breaking stride.

Dean Edwards and Megan take a seat in a small dining room adjacent to the production kitchen. Megan is greeted by a server, Aiesha, who promptly smiles and says, "I know you, Dean Edwards," then turning to Megan, she asks, "Your first time here?"

"Yes, I'm looking forward to it—smells amazing!" Megan smiles back.

"Well, welcome to Toro!" Aiesha responds. "So, I'll tell you what we are about. We have seven kinds of molé, and blandas, special tortillas that are light and fluffy.

"I love molé," Megan responds.

Aiesha confirms, "Oh yes, Chef Moreno uses a traditional preparation from where she grew up in Mexico. My favorite is the Coloradito. It's spicy, but not too spicy, because it has chocolate in it as well."

"That sounds great to me, the chocolate seals the deal," says Megan, laughing.

Aiesha excuses herself as she pours water from a brightly colored clay pitcher, saying, "You can look over the menu to choose your sides, and I'll be back."

The menu is a crisp parchment with an abstract logo of a bull and the word 'Toro' on the front cover. Megan quickly becomes immersed in reading about the seven types of molé. Aiesha did not mention the Amarillo with Indian curry spice—a shock to Megan as are some of the other varieties from Oaxaca.

With appetite in full gear, Megan turns to the back cover of the menu where there is a picture of Claudetta with her biography. Claudetta hails from the eastern part of Oaxaca, bordering the state of Chiapas. She lived in a multi-generational family of Oto-Manguean-speaking Zapotec peoples, indigenous to modern-day Mexico, and worked in the family restaurant. She learned traditional recipes from her grandmother, Yatzil, and Aunt Tia Ariché. Claudetta learned English in secondary school before being accepted to the Culinary Institute of America. Following school, Claudetta had stints in NYC and Chicago, returning to the coastal resort town of Huatulco as an executive chef, where she earned a Michelin star.

Megan orders the pollo with coloradito molé, with both grilled greens and squash blossoms stuffed with cheese. Dean Edwards does not need to review the menu, stating firmly, "The usual for me, Aiesha. Turkey with molé vérde but bring an extra side of blandas so Megan can have some." He turns to Megan, insisting, "You have to try them, it's a must."

Before long, the food arrives. "The pollo coloradito for the lady, and for Dean Edwards, we have the turkey vérde and extra blandas." Megan gasps as she takes in the sight and aroma of the plate. The chicken is on skewers, blackened by the grill, and placed over the grilled greens. A light dressing of oil and herbs is drizzled over both with an inviting ramekin of molé for dipping. The feature, however, is clearly the squash blossom—thinly sliced summer squash curled in the shape of a flower, resting on a bed of tomatillo salsa and a side of flash fried squash blossom with gooey quesillo cheese oozing from one side. Not even glancing at Dean Edwards's plate, Megan is excited with anticipation as she focuses squarely on her own plate. Megan sighs. "It smells wonderful!" Dean Edwards nods agreement and passes a side plate of steaming blandas Megan's way, smiling as they both begin their meal.

When their plates are empty, Aiesha arrives and offers dessert, which Megan declines, but Dean Edwards certainly does not. When it arrives Megan regrets saying no. The dessert is pan de yema, a traditional sweet bread, topped with sesame. Claudetta's version is a bit different than the usual, with a French ganache filling, and lavender honey drizzle accompanied with a side of cinnamon and cayenne hot chocolate. Megan settles for piñon coffee as she quietly recovers from her food coma.

While enjoying her coffee, Megan ponders how best to advise Claudetta. The chef's approach seems very much about strict conduct of the kitchen and her own specific approach toward cuisine—not exactly a student-centered environment. She is intrigued: how *does* one fit UDL principles into an authentic environment where people fill specified roles with low tolerance for error?

Megan recalls her graduate training: UDL is about providing multiple means of representation, engagement, and expression—yet the Toro kitchen is like a highly polished machine. Granted, UDL does fit the school's focus on student success at a broader level. Student-advisement tools are in place in all departments, using predictive analytics based on demographic, LMS, and other student data. Megan keeps thinking about the students weeded out of Claudetta's system, who are not ready to handle the Kitchen Operations course. The work/school experience seems a success for some—but at considerable cost. *Do we have to accept that half the students with an interest in culinary arts will not finish?*

After the meal Megan is anxious to talk to Claudetta directly about her course and the amazing meal. She thanks Dean Edwards for his time and firmly shakes his hand, contemplating how she may approach Claudetta.

MEETING THE CHEF

Megan knocks on Claudetta's door and wonders, what is she like, really? As the door opens, Megan is greeted warmly as Claudetta says, "Dean Edwards told me you would stop by—so how are you? How was lunch?"

Megan is immediately relieved as Claudetta's demeanor is less intimidating over a desk than across a cooking station. Stepping into the office, the two begin a conversation to break the ice. "Thanks for a great lunch!"

"It is a true pleasure, "Claudetta responds. "I'm glad you had the chance to see the students working. It is important that they get real-world skills. We focus on their ability to add value, day one in the workplace. Nothing like a dining room and kitchen—the best schooling there is."

Glancing at her watch, Claudetta continues, "When Dean Edwards told me you were coming, I immediately began to look forward to how you could help us improve our program. I am excited about our work together. How can I help you get started?"

Megan reflects for a moment and responds, "Perhaps we could start by telling me about past successes. Tell me about your history with the university and what you consider the strengths of the program."

Claudetta begins a recap of her story on the menu cover. She is a past president of the local American Culinary Federation chapter, which helps, as she knows most of the restaurant operators where she can place students for their work experience requirement.

"Since I arrived," Claudetta explains, "I have instituted a student dining room that produces meals three days a week, like you saw today. Before that, we had no outlet for the student work; most of the food production was in the classroom only. Students like to see the public enjoy the meals they produce!"

Megan agrees. "I certainly enjoyed it!"

Claudetta continues, "When I arrived, we had problems with students' professional standards, lack of a consistent skill set among students, and poor feedback from employers. I've worked hard to reverse these problems."

"What do you mean, professional standards?" asks Megan.

"It's about skills and performing to standard in the kitchen," Claudetta explains. "Our students need to perform in a professional kitchen, deliver quality food, and have strong basic knife skills, food sanitation competencies, cooking techniques, and the ability to perform in a fast-paced kitchen with long hours and hard work."

"How do they show that they have achieved these standards?" Megan asks.

Claudetta hands Megan her student inspection sheet for the day (see Figure 15.1). "Prior to a production day, students have a skills lab day where they are given their assignments and I tell them what standards they need to meet. But it's more than that," Claudetta adds. "I follow the tell-show-do approach to learning."

"How does this look in the culinary arts?" Megan asks.

"I tell them what has to be done, then I show them how to do it—we call that a *culinary demo*," Claudetta responds. "I assign them tasks on an inspection sheet [see Figure 14.1] and organize them by groups [see Figure 14.2]."

Inspected by Student Group Leader (Year 2) and Graded by Chef Instructor

Ware Washer/Triple Sink Area

___ Triple sinks drained and cleaned: no food in drains, sides of sinks clean, no standing water on draining areas
___ Ware washer emptied: no standing water on either side
___ Ware washer food screen emptied
___ Ware washer chemicals need replacing? Please let chef know if empty or getting close

Demo Area

___ Demo area cleaned on top and underneath

Prep/Hand Sinks

___ Hand sinks clean: no food or stains, handles and spigot clean
___ Vegetable sink clean: no food in drains, walls of sinks clean, garbage disposal clean, no standing water on either draining side
___ Prep sink in work station area clean: no food in drains, walls of sink clean
___ Prep sink beside cage clean: no food in drains, walls of sink clean

Large Dry Goods Cage

___ Floor of area swept, debris free, no food on floor
___ Shelves neat and organized
___ Open products closed properly
___ Outdated items discarded

Spice Area

___ Shelving clean
___ Spice containers neat, clean and organized

FIGURE 14.1 Student inspection sheet.

Walk-In Refrigerator
___ Floor swept/mopped
___ Proper placement of products: cooked/veg on top of shelves, raw products on bottom
___ All open/prepared items labeled
___ Out of date items discarded
Walk-In Freezer
___ Floor debris free
___ Products organized/labeled
___ All open/prepared items labeled
___ Out of date items discarded
Large Equipment
___ Stove tops/ovens cleaned: no food, sides of ovens cleaned, inside free of food, guard shelving underneath clean, shelves on top clean and grease free
___ Large mixer clean: underneath and surrounding area
___ All carts cleaned: shelving, handles and legs
Equipment Cage/Shelves/Small Equipment
___ Pots, pans and miscellaneous equipment neat and orderly and placed upside down
___ Shelving clean
___ Equipment on top neat and orderly and placed upside down
___ Plastic containers, measuring cups, etc. neat
___ Bus tubs holding equipment clean
___ Sheet pans clean and grease free and placed upside down
___ Scales clean and put away
___ Cutting boards in proper place
Floors
___ Swept and debris free
___ Deck brushed and squeegeed
___ No standing water
___ Drains free of debris and clean
HACCP Log
___ Filled out completely and turned in to Chef
Refrigeration Log
___ Noted, dated and initialed
___ Made Chef aware if temperature is in danger zone
Security
___ Cages/Cabinets locked
___ Walk in locked

Comments:

Student Signature: **Instructor Signature:** **Group:** **Grade:**

FIGURE 14.1 Continued

"Look here," she says, pointing to the group assignments and inspection sheets. "Each week they rotate groups, so they get a different experience, but only second-year students take a leadership role. The first-year students must perform to standard in the skills lab before production when we have customers for lunch. The second-year students are the group leaders and get graded on how well they inspect the work of their groups. I check how well they inspected their group's work, and if it's not right, they do it again until they get it."

Claudetta crosses her arms as she breathes deeply and adds, "This is what works. Experienced students prep the demo. I show them the food. They must perform to standard and

	Wks 1–3	Wks 4–6	Wks 7–9	Wks 10–12	Wks 13–15
Sous Chef Group (Year 2) Fill triple sinks Fill pails/disburse HACCP log Fridge temps Expedite Final kitchen check	1	2	3	4	5
Demo Group (Year 2) Demo mise en place Clean demo area Scour hand sinks/walls Scour prep sink/walls Clean SS tables	2	3	4	5	1
Floor Group (Year 1) Sweep floors Deck brush floors Squeegee floors Mop walk in	3	4	5	1	2
Organizer Group (Year 1) Clean shelving Organize equipment/shelves Organize dry storage Organize walk in/freezer Clean/organize reach ins Empty garbage/clean cans	4	5	1	2	3
Dishwashing Group (Year 1) Finish *general* dishes at end of class Drain sinks/ware washer Scour triple sinks/walls Scour ware washer, ware washer area/walls Put away remaining dishes	5	1	2	3	4

All groups/students must:

1. **Wash/sanitize own dishes**
2. **Put away dishes in an organized manner**
3. **Clean any large equipment used by group (oven, stovetop, etc.)**
4. **Clean any small equipment used by group (mixers, etc.)**
5. **Ensure dining area is clean and neat (no cups, soda cans, trash, etc. left in dining room). Straighten tables and chairs. Wipe off tables.**
6. **Assist any other group or members when own work is done**

No one leaves until everyone is done!

FIGURE 14.2 Kitchen clean-up schedule by group number.

maintain a clean, efficient workspace. This is how first-year students practice their skills and second-year students learn to supervise and are graded on how well the group performs."

Megan studies the list of work tasks, organized by group and job duty, but noticeably without a clearly communicated standard or an inclusive approach, consistent with UDL. Some students would surely prefer to see a picture of an organized workstation and instructions on how to perform these tasks. And what if a student is visually or hearing impaired? Some students read slower and need more time than others to absorb the material. Could they receive instructions in different formats? In advance?

Megan also wonders how much time students have for *reflection* as they proceed through the apprentice-based program. Megan looks up from her reading. "Hmm. It seems very thorough and focused on quality as you said." Careful not to sound too critical, Megan asks, "Do students follow a recipe too? I am amazed how exacting and perfect each plate looked—and tasted—at lunch."

Claudetta smiles and responds, "Oh sure, they have my book, and their culinary standards manual for reference. But the recipes are for the skills lab. Production day is about tasks and inspections."

Megan decides to probe further. "Do you use our Canvas online system to post materials? Some of our faculty use videos with subtitles for those with hearing disability, and in large format font if necessary. As you know, some students learn differently, each in their own way."

Claudetta responds quickly, "Well I do not use Canvas; it is not used in the real world. This class is about a professional kitchen—fast-paced, with limited time to stop and read a book or look up a recipe online. They need to perform to standard in real time and complete their checklists or they will not survive in the workplace."

Megan senses the need to slow down the interrogation. "Well, given that the food is as good as it is, any of those students can likely cook as well as most of the chefs in town."

Claudetta smiles and responds, "Perhaps so, but there are some good chefs in town! But you're right: Our students work for some of the best restaurants in town. Prior to us starting our own student dining room, they tended to arrive at work very green, and we'd get complaints that they didn't take to task quickly or understand the pace or operation of a kitchen at all."

Claudetta sighs. "I view my role as preparing them for success in the industry. Kitchens are a community. The chef is the center of that community. To become a chef, you must learn all the kitchen aspects. I'm never far removed, but students need to practice *leading* a kitchen, checking, and tasting food before it goes to the table. So, mostly they are gaining skills that are the norm in a kitchen, but they also get to be in charge at times."

Claudetta continues, assuredly stating, "If they can't perform, they can't be a chef, so they need to learn that here and early in their schooling. I'd rather they fail here in their first year than later on the job. I created Toro to mimic the real world. I want them to get the standards down here before they go out into the industry. Local chefs know our students can talk the talk and walk the walk."

Claudetta adds proudly, "Our students get jobs—good jobs—for a reason: they deliver on day one."

Megan responds, "Sounds like it works for about half of your students, but many students fail. Do you have a sense why so many of the students entering the Kitchen Operations course are removed from the cohort because of a low grade, and why only about half of the students who enter each semester complete the program?"

"Yes, this is a huge concern for me," responds Claudetta. "I'm hoping to look into this more with your help. I don't think we're doing everything we can, and I'm sure we could do more. I'm hoping that you and I can come up with interesting ideas to put into practice."

Megan stands to leave. "You've given me a lot to think about. Let me get back to you soon with some notes and observations, then we will figure out a way to move forward toward increasing retention and student enrollment, while maintaining the prominent level of quality graduates you are known for producing."

"That sounds wonderful," answers Claudetta, as she stands to see Megan out. "If I can be of further help, please feel free to reach out." Shaking hands, Megan leaves the office with a full mind and tummy. "Maybe I should have had that dessert!" she muses, returning to her car, umbrella in hand. The rain is gone, and the sun is shining again.

On the drive home, Megan continues to turn ideas around in her mind. She is both impressed and unsettled by her visit with Claudetta and the dean. Is it possible for a high-pressure classroom to be inclusive for all learners, or must it be either "get it" or "get out?"

"This project will certainly be a challenge," Megan says to herself as she continues her drive home, "but I think I can make it work."

Preliminary Analysis Questions

1. This case deals with a conflict of competing values within the culinary arts program. How would you frame the conflicting values evident in the conversation between Megan, Claudetta, and the dean? Megan's focus on equity seems bedrock for instructional designers. What other values are coming into play in this case—and how are they conflicting?
2. UDL introduced in the case is about multiple methods for increased accessibility. No other models or theories are really mentioned. What other ID principles might apply? How important are authentic opportunities for practice and real-life connections? How do different ID principles get combined or integrated into a single case of practice?
3. Megan has only begun her review of the culinary arts program. What further data should be gathered to provide suggestions for improving the program?
4. Imagine you are an experienced ID consulting with Megan. Provide suggestions for completing her study in a way that respects the "wisdom of practice" already inherent in a successful program—while helping the program work for a broader range of students.

Implications for ID Practice

1. Some programs are highly competitive and demanding, in both admission and performance outcomes required of graduates. How do we apply equity values to such programs? What does accessibility really mean for a program that is highly selective by design?
2. How should we judge quality in an instructional program? What values, standards, or ideals should we look to when planning and growing an instructional program?
3. Rigorous apprenticeship programs can give enormous discretion to supervisors, increasing the risk of coercion or exploitation of student workers. What kinds of data could be used to detect problems?
4. Professionals like Megan develop their expertise by close attention to both theory and practice. What kinds of conflicts have you experienced between textbook approaches and everyday concerns of practice? How can we combine the best practices of a wise colleague on the job and an insightful professor from school?

NOTE

1 This case is a major reworking of the earlier case of Beth Owens by the same authors. Megan Martin retains the culinary context but shifts the theoretical framing from behaviorism versus constructivism to equity, inclusion, and student success.

15

Jenna Powell

Designing a Competency-Based Licensure Program

Adrie A. Koehler, Daniela Rezende Vilarinho-Pereira, and Kharon Grimmet

YEAR 1: POTENTIAL DIRECTIONS

"Hey, Jenna! Do you have a minute?" Jenna Powell turned to see Vanessa Middleton smiling and walking toward her. Jenna and Vanessa, both professors in the College of Education at Mid State University, were serving on a team charged with revamping their teacher education programs. Jenna was an assistant professor in the Educational Technology (EdTech) program, while Vanessa was a clinical associate professor and the coordinator of Mid State's Special Education online master's program.

"Sure!" Jenna stopped, completely facing Vanessa and replied, "What's up?"

"So, I know that you've been promoting the importance of preparing all the preservice teachers to work across blended and online environments, and I've been thinking a lot about blended and online methods—I think there is potential to transform our special education program."

The women agreed to meet soon to discuss opportunities for preparing special educators to effectively teach across face-to-face, blended, and online learning environments.

Once Jenna returned to her office, she took a moment to reflect and check her notes on the Innovating Teacher Education Project (ITEP). The previous spring, she had been selected as the EdTech representative for the initiative and attended a week of all-day meetings during the summer. While attending these meetings, Jenna learned that in the revamped program, preservice teachers would complete more field hours, attend seminars focused on tying theory to practice, and select a pathway related to either special education, English language learners (ELL), or gifted education (see Figure 15.1). When she inquired about adding a pathway for educational technology, program leaders explained that the special education, ELL, and gifted education pathways would result in preservice teachers (PSTs) earning an additional license. Because the College of Education had not been approved for an educational technology-related license, there was no real interest in adding a specific pathway for educational technology. When Jenna heard this, she was disappointed as she believed it would have been a way to improve how preservice teachers

DOI: 10.4324/9781003354468-17

Year 1	Year 2
■ Introduction to Teaching ■ Policy and Law ■ Multicultural Education ■ Educator Service in Communities ■ Field Placement and Seminar	■ Motivation in Learning ■ Introduction to English Language Learning ■ Teaching Gifted Children ■ Inclusive Classrooms ■ Learning Differentiation ■ Field Placement and Seminar
Year 3	**Year 4**
■ Educational Technology Foundations ■ Methods ■ Field Placement and Seminar ■ Pathway Selective 1 (ELL, SPED, or Gifted) ■ Pathway Selective 2 (ELL, SPED, or Gifted)	■ Evaluation and Assessment ■ Classroom Management ■ Pathway Selective 3 (ELL, SPED, or Gifted) ■ Student Teaching

FIGURE 15.1 Core education courses.

were being prepared to integrate technology. Currently, PSTs enrolled in undergraduate programs were required to complete only one educational technology course, with most taking it during their freshman or sophomore year. Moreover, as more requirements were being added to the revamped programs, the educational technology course had been cut from three credit hours to one credit hour.

These events had prompted Jenna to investigate new opportunities for preparing PSTs to effectively use educational technology. First, she found that the State Department of Education offered a license in blended and online teaching (see Figure 15.2 for an overview of license standards).

Jenna felt excited when she looked more closely at the standards. Although the license was titled "blended and online" teaching, it seemed to broadly relate to using technology across all environments to meet learners' diverse needs, support the design and implementation of learning experiences, and develop professional and communication skills. E-learning days were increasingly being used by school districts to cover snow days and teacher professional development, learning management systems were a common tool in most K–12 classrooms, and the number of online K–12 schools was continuing to grow. Given this, Jenna believed that current teachers needed to be prepared to use technology across learning environments and licensing PSTs in blended and online teaching could be worthwhile. Jenna couldn't help feeling excited as she imagined designing a program where PSTs received *more* educational technology training and were qualified to teach across diverse environments. She was eager to share her ideas with her colleagues.

GROWING CHALLENGES

However, soon, Jenna's enthusiasm was tested. As she began to share her idea at meetings, not everyone agreed that it was a meaningful path to pursue. At one ITEP meeting, attended by representatives from the different teacher education programs, Lisa Brighton, the chair of the ITEP, shared Jenna's idea of licensing PSTs in blended and online teaching.

One professor immediately responded, "Why would we do that? Why would it be worthwhile to license preservice teachers in blended and online teaching? Most have no plans for teaching in an online school."

State Department of Education
Blended and Online Teaching Standards

Standard 1: Learning Environments- pedagogical considerations across face-to-face, blended, and online learning

Standard 2: Learner Motivation and Engagement- designing for learner engagement and motivation in blended and online environments

Standard 3: Digital Design- understanding and using design principles and technologies across learning environments

Standard 4: Assessment and Evaluation- using best practices and tools for assessing and evaluating online teaching and learning

Standard 5: Diversity, Inclusion, and Equity- identifying student diversity and designing for it in online and blended environments

Standard 6: Digital Citizenship- understanding legal and ethical considerations in blended and online learning, promoting effective digital practices, and modeling appropriate behavior in online environments

Standard 7: Professionalism- using effective communication and professional habits in blended and online environments

FIGURE 15.2 State blended and online teaching standards.

She also had hoped that a blended and online teaching license might create the opportunity for an additional pathway for preservice teachers. However, Lisa shared that creating an educational technology pathway similar to the other three pathways was not a viable option at this point in the initiative. Although frustrated from the unexpected negative reactions from some colleagues and not getting the green light to create a blended and online teaching pathway, college and team leadership was supportive, and Jenna continued to develop a vision for a new and improved educational technology experience for PSTs.

She wondered, "How can I gain faculty buy-in for the licensure? If there isn't a blended and online teaching pathway, how will I get preservice teachers interested in pursuing this license?"

At the end of the semester, Jenna submitted documentation to the Program Convener Council (PCC), a group of approximately 30 College of Education program leaders from the various teacher education programs and college administrators, to gain conceptual approval for offering a new licensure pathway. After minimal discussion, everyone voted unanimously to approve the new program. The next step would be to get final approval from the PCC and the State Department of Education, which required Jenna to develop a detailed overview of the licensure program structure, implementation plan, and needed resources.

Blended and Online Teaching License & Online SPED MS Program

- Certification Requirements
  - Apple Teacher
  - Google Certified Educator Level 1
  - How do we include certifications into the program?
- Nature of SPED
  - What are special considerations unique to SPED? How do we prepare teachers to work with diverse needs in blended and online settings?
  - Who are key stakeholders that special educators work with (e.g., parents, case managers, paraprofessionals)? How do educators effectively work with these individuals in blended or online environments?
  - What do accommodations look like in online settings?
- Preparing SPED teachers for blended and online teaching and learning
  - Managing online discussions
  - Engaging students in online settings
  - Evaluating student work
  - Communicating with stakeholders, using a variety of technologies
  - Using various educational technologies (e.g., LMS, video conferencing, screencasting)
- Format of program
  - What existing assignments are focused on designing learning experiences and supporting diverse needs? How can a blended and online component be incorporated with these?
  - What will a blended and online clinical experience look like? Can this be incorporated with existing structures or are additional partnerships needed?

FIGURE 15.3 Meeting notes.

In the meantime, Jenna and Vanessa continued meeting and discussing how they could prepare special educators to successfully work in blended and online teaching environments. From these discussions, Jenna maintained a running list of topics that would need careful consideration (see Figure 15.3).

YEAR 2: MOVING FORWARD

As the COVID-19 pandemic set in and educators at K–12 schools and universities were forced to make drastic changes to how they were developing and delivering learning experiences, interest in, and buy-in to, Jenna's plan for licensing PSTs in blended and online teaching steadily grew. In fact, college leadership had decided that all PSTs should be licensed in blended and online teaching. Although she was grateful for the support and the opportunity to increase the level of educational technology preparation that PSTs were receiving, she was uncertain how she could prepare all PSTs across diverse programs. There were over ten different undergraduate teacher education program areas in the College of Education, all with different courses of study; an online special education master's program, with most of the participants already teaching; and an early childhood education program, housed in a different college within the university. Jenna also wondered how she would address another major constraint.

In one meeting, Lisa shared with Jenna, "Often, licensure pathways require learners to take a specific series of courses, but there is no room in any program of study to require PSTs to take additional courses to meet requirements for this license."

To help her brainstorm, Jenna scheduled time with Shane Crosby, another professor in the EdTech program. Shane had helped Jenna with every step of the process and managed the current foundational educational technology course. As she waited for Shane to join the Zoom call, she reviewed an EdTech online master's student's portfolio. A few years earlier, the EdTech online master's program had shifted to a competency-based approach, in which students were required to demonstrate specific skills by the end of their programs. Jenna had begun to wonder if possibly a competency-based approach might be useful in addressing some of the constraints she was experiencing related to the development of the blended and online licensure.

She jumped when Shane joined the call and enthusiastically greeted her. "Hey there! How are you doing?"

Laughing, Jenna replied, "You scared me! I guess I was deep in thought, reviewing this portfolio."

Shane smiled. "One of the master's student's portfolios?" Seeing Jenna nod, Shane continued, "I've already finished reviewing mine for this term."

Jenna grimaced. "It must be nice. I still have four left to review by tonight." Jenna paused and went on, "Reviewing the portfolios does have me wondering about something. Do you think there might be a way to use a competency-based approach to create the blended and online teaching licensure pathway? Using the same badging system somehow?"

Shane leaned back in his chair and asked, "So, what would that look like? Thinking of our EdTech online master's students, they all take the same courses and even have courses dedicated to submitting evidence, reflecting on their experiences, and earning their competency badges."

Jenna nodded. "Yeah, that's definitely part of the challenge. While there are many different undergraduate teacher education programs with differing requirements, there are core courses that all PSTs are required to take. However, the early childhood education program is housed in a different college. So, it doesn't share all the same core courses, but there is some overlap with the College of Education programs. Then, of course, the online special education master's program has a completely different set of courses. But that's kind of the beauty of competencies—that would allow us to identify common skills without necessarily creating identical learning experiences across programs to develop those skills. So, in other words, all teacher education students would receive the same prompts for each competency, but they would have room to demonstrate their understanding in individual ways."

Shane nodded slowly. "So, if we created blended and online teaching competencies these could be used across programs, and there could be many different ways to demonstrate skills in these areas. Plus, that could help us overcome the limits of having only a one-credit hour course to prepare preservice teachers for all their educational technology use. I've always thought our current educational technology foundation course was somewhat limited because students take it so early in their programs, and it is just a single course that likely seems separate from their other education courses. However, we would have to get faculty buy-in to design learning experiences that align with the competencies throughout each program. We would be relying on content to be covered in other courses." Jenna agreed, "Yes. Faculty buy-in would be a major consideration in a setup like this—we have to be really mindful of not creating something else for instructors to add to their courses, as everyone is already so maxed out; we have to make it as easy as possible for this to work. Since our EdTech foundations course has been reduced to one credit hour, and we do not want to lose our teaching assistant lines, I thought maybe we could potentially shift their roles a bit to support the design, development, implementation, and evaluation of the competencies. If we are going to get things set up and effectively help so many different faculty members with technology integration, our workload will really increase."

Shane smiled. "Okay. If we go this route, we just need to figure out how to create learning experiences that align with competencies across the ten plus undergraduate CoE programs, the early childhood program, and the online special education program, all without common courses or without adding any new courses where learners might earn the actual badges, *and* expect an intensified workload."

Jenna smiled back and winked. "Yep! When you put it that way, it all sounds so easy."

They laughed and agreed to think more about how a competency-based approach might work.

Following the brainstorming session, Jenna felt several different emotions at once. First, she felt thankful that she worked with such supportive colleagues in EdTech. While Shane had raised valid concerns, he didn't dismiss her idea of using competencies, and Jenna knew that he would continue to help her find ways to navigate these challenges. She also felt overwhelmed. When she agreed to be the EdTech representative to the ITEP, she wasn't quite sure what to expect. As an assistant professor working toward tenure, she really didn't need an additional program to oversee, but she felt passionate about improving teacher education. Previously, she had been a high school social studies teacher. Transitioning into the teaching profession after graduating from her undergraduate program had been tough, and these challenges had led her to pursuing graduate school to find ways to support other PSTs through this transition. Finally, somehow, she also felt excited to be working on a project that prompted a reconsideration of how PSTs are traditionally prepared and an opportunity to infuse more educational technology into courses across an entire curriculum.

After giving herself time to reflect on and embrace her emotions, Jenna refocused and thought more about developing competencies for a licensure program like this. Of course, they could use the state standards to help form these, but something had been bothering her. She worried that if they designed a competency-based blended and online teaching license, some broader aspects of technology integration might be missed. This prompted her to consider the International Society for Technology in Education (ISTE) standards and compare these to the blended and online teaching standards. Using these two sets of standards, Jenna tentatively outlined competencies that might be used to guide a licensure program. She then shared these with her EdTech colleagues, including a former instructional coach at a local middle school. After a few rounds of revisions, she believed she had a solid set of competencies (see Appendix 15A). Then, she began working on the application to gain state approval for a new license (see Appendix 15B).

YEAR 3: WORKING WITH THE ONLINE SPECIAL EDUCATION MASTER'S PROGRAM

After Jenna received final approval from the PCC and from the State Department of Education, she considered options for implementing the new licensure pathway and had another brainstorming session with Shane. The two agreed that while there were many potential ways to go about this process, they believed that working with Vanessa to implement the competencies in the special education online master's program was a viable option. First, Vanessa had always been an enthusiastic supporter of the blended and online teaching initiative.

Second, unlike the many undergraduate programs with differences in courses and requirements, all students in the special education program took the same courses and had the same requirements, resulting in a less complex setup than the College of Education undergraduate programs. Third, the online special education program employed two full-time faculty members, which would reduce the complexity of meeting with several different faculty members. Finally, from their previous meetings, Jenna knew that Vanessa's team was renovating the entire online special education master's program. Jenna believed this would be great timing to find ways to integrate the competencies. If Jenna could work with Vanessa to develop a strong program for the online special education program, she hoped that she could adapt elements that were created for other programs.

To discuss plans for implementing the competencies into the online special education program, Jenna agreed to start attending Vanessa's weekly team meetings. Vanessa's team consisted of Elise Pell, a clinical instructor and former special educator; Nancy Catchings, a part-time administrative support professional; and Yusuf Altan, a postdoctoral researcher. Additionally, Juliana Barbosa, an EdTech doctoral student and Jenna's advisee, joined the meetings to support implementation efforts.

Prior to the first meeting, Jenna and Juliana created notes to help them prepare (Figure 15.2). Briefly skimming these notes, Jenna joined the Teams call to find everyone else joining too. "Good morning!" Vanessa greeted everyone enthusiastically, flashed a big smile, and continued, "So, you'll notice we have some extra people at our meeting today. I think you all know Jenna, and I would like to introduce you to Juliana Barbosa, a doctoral student in the EdTech program. Jenna and Juliana will be joining our weekly meetings to help with our program renovation—specifically offering support in how we can integrate the blended and online teaching competencies and help make sure we are graduating the best special educators in the nation!"

Both Jenna and Juliana smiled and waved at everyone. "Before we get started with any specific plans, I think discussing the program's background will be helpful," Vanessa shared. "When I started working at Mid State University in 2014, I was responsible for developing the online master's program. Since there was a lot of pressure to get the program up and running, we often felt like we were . . . what's the phrase? Building the plane while we were flying it!" Vanessa laughed as she continued, "Most of our students are already in classrooms teaching, many on emergency licenses. We offer two different programs: "mild only" licensure and "mild and intense" licensure. Students can typically complete their programs in seven semesters, which does include summers. Students take two courses a semester, each seven weeks long. Across these courses, we have three sets of standards we must address: Council for Exceptional Children Preparation Standards, Council for the Accreditation of Educator Preparation Standards, and Council for the Accreditation of Educator Preparation Advanced Standards. Student cohorts start at three times a year: fall, spring, and summer. We typically have around 10–20 students starting each semester and around 100 students in the program at any one time."

Vanessa paused. "Do you have any questions so far?"

Jenna laughed and exclaimed, "Three sets of standards? No big deal! Who is responsible for designing the new courses in your program?"

Vanessa laughed. "You're looking at it! We are a small, but mighty team. We do have limited term lecturers that teach in our program and who may be able to help, but Elise, Yusuf, and I are responsible for the redesign."

Jenna followed up, "When do you plan to start the new program?"

Vanessa smiled sheepishly. "Well, we are hoping to start rolling out the new courses this summer because we really need to get moving for accreditation purposes. Since we don't really have the time or resources to build all of the courses before this summer, we will have to be building courses for the semester ahead."

Juliana chimed in, "I have a question. Are courses offered through Brightspace?"

"Good question," Vanessa responded. "We've used a different LMS, but we are working on transitioning all courses to Brightspace. We aren't too familiar with Brightspace, but we're hoping you can help us with that too!"

"Great! Thanks!" Juliana replied. "Can I ask another question?" Vanessa nodded, and Juliana continued, "Do you have a common structure that you plan to use for the courses?"

"Well, I want us to rethink how we've done everything in the past and come up with a more supportive environment. I've been thinking a lot about this, and I'm hoping we can use a similar structure for each course to promote consistency as students transition from one course to the next. While our courses have traditionally been seven weeks long, I am thinking we can change to eight-week courses. Then, possibly, you guys can use the additional week for blended and online competencies."

Jenna pondered this proposal. "I really like having dedicated space for covering the blended and online teaching competencies and helping learners consider technology integration in special education. My only concern is that the technology piece will feel separated from the special education content. Shane and I have had many conversations about this, and we don't want technology integration to become a situation where we are a guest speaker in someone's class once a semester."

Vanessa nodded. "Yes, I understand what you mean, and I am not suggesting that is the only place we address the technology piece. I agree we need to also be sure that it's infused throughout the courses we are offering."

"Okay! Good!" Jenna replied. "We will need to provide opportunities for the students to develop skills related to the competencies—not that this needs to take place only through coursework, since most of them are already teaching. One more thing, as Juliana and I do not have expertise in special education, I know we will need your help with creating authentic learning experiences and thinking through the unique considerations that come with designing for the special needs of students."

"Absolutely!" Vanessa responded. The meeting wrapped up with Jenna and Juliana agreeing to come up with some initial ideas for meeting the competencies and covering technology integration.

Following the meeting, Jenna and Juliana discussed next steps, and over the next few weeks, the team came up with a tentative plan for covering the competencies and technology integration. During the summer, the EdTech program hired a new faculty member, Tom Sharpton, who took over responsibility for building the badging system that would be used to manage the competency process.

YEAR 4: MONITORING COMPETENCIES IN THE ONLINE SPECIAL EDUCATION MASTER'S PROGRAM

Jenna looked at her calendar to prepare for her week ahead. She wondered how it could be possible that it was already July and another fall semester would soon be starting. Although things were moving along with integrating the competencies into the special education master's program, projects like this were messy. Jenna reflected on the overall program and how they might best monitor and improve things moving forward.

Preliminary Analysis Questions

- What constraints is Jenna facing as she creates a blended and online teaching licensing program? Given these constraints, what design challenges did she face while using the competency-based approach?
- Critique Jenna's design and implementation of the competency-based license with the online special education master's program, noting areas of potential future challenges and opportunities. What key design and management aspects should she be mindful of to boost success in the online master's program and inform the design and implementation of the licensing program for the undergraduate programs?
- What type of support will Jenna and Juliana need from Vanessa and her team to create authentic learning experiences and adapt the technology integration and the blended and online competencies to meet the needs of the students in the special education online master's program?
- Jenna is faced with balancing standardization and customization. On one hand, Jenna will have to create a standardized experience that offers consistency across all teacher education programs. On the other hand, she has the opportunity to create customized experiences for each teacher education program. How can she manage these dimensions strategically? Where are there potential opportunities and challenges?

Implications for ID Practice

- Discuss the pros and cons of using a competency-based approach to prepare preservice teachers to effectively use technology across face-to-face, blended, and online learning environments. Consider the perspectives of the instructional designer, the instructor, and the students.
- Discuss the possible challenges instructional designers can face when not all people involved in a project buy into their proposal. What are some strategies that can help them overcome this problem?
- What potential issues may arise if you work with a client who is agreeable and open to new ideas?
- Discuss the risks and benefits associated with creating online learning experiences for special needs populations.

Appendix 15.A

Overview of Competencies

Competency 1: Educational Technology Foundations
Part 1: *Educational Technology and Learning Environments*—Preservice teachers will consider the continuum of learning environments (e.g., face-to-face, blended, fully online) and identify online and blended management tasks.
Part 2: *Educational Technology Terminology and Tools*—Preservice teachers will consider hardware and software used across face-to-face, blended, and online environments to design and manage learning.
Competency 2: Educational Technology and Learner Needs
Part 1: *Educational Technology and Learner Diversity*—Preservice teachers will consider student diversity and how to design for diverse needs using educational technologies across face-to-face, blended, and online environments.
Part 2: *Educational Technology, Community, and Presence*—Preservice teachers will consider safe, supportive, and inclusive learning environments and how to develop these environments across modalities (face-to-face, blended, and online).
Competency 3: Educational Technology Design Principles
Part 1: *Educational Technology and Theories and Principles of Instructional Design*—Preservice teachers will consider major design principles, theories, and concepts related to effective design across face-to-face, blended, and online experiences.
Part 2: *Educational Technology and Instructional Strategies*—Preservice teachers will consider design and adaptation strategies in face-to-face, blended, and online learning environments to meet student needs and how technological tools can be used to create meaningful experiences.
Competency 4: Educational Technology, Leadership, and Professionalism
Part 1: *Educational Technology and Professionalism*—Preservice teachers will consider state and federal standards in the establishment of learner procedures and expectations for blended and online learning and the development of professional work environments (including strategies for staying abreast of emerging technologies and trends)
Part 2: *Educational Technology, Leadership, and Communication*—Preservice teachers will consider strategies for engaging stakeholders, using culturally appropriate communication, and preparing learners to be digital citizens.
Competency 5: Educational Technology and Facilitation
Part 1: *Educational Technology and Learning Management*—Preservice teachers will consider using educational technologies for communication, feedback, monitoring, resources sharing, etc. for diverse student needs in blended and online courses.
Part 2: *Educational Technology and Assessment*—Preservice teachers will consider formative and summative assessment strategies for blended and online environments and using educational technologies to support authentic assessment

Appendix 15.B

Excerpt from State Application

State Department of Education
Application Form

Address
Mid State University—College of Education
100 N Campus Blvd

Method of Delivery (onsite, online, hybrid)
Onsite, Online, Hybrid

Program contact name(s) and email address/addresses

Jenna Powell	Shane Crosby
jpowell@midstate.edu	scrosby@midstate.edu

Required Information/Documentation
Provide a brief overview and rationale for the program, including each of the following:

- **Purpose or goal of the program:**
  Upon completion of this program, participants will be eligible for a license in blended and online teaching. Through this process, Mid State teacher education graduates will be prepared to design, develop, implement, and evaluate effective teaching and learning experiences across diverse educational environments (e.g., face-to-face, blended, online) and to effectively use technology as part of this process.
- **License earned upon completion:**
  Blended and online teaching license add-on
  - **Degree major awarded upon completion:**
    Candidates for this license include teacher education candidates from a variety of programs. This license is an add-on to their primary degree and academic major.
  - **Reason(s) program should be approved:**
    + *Expertise of Educational Technology Faculty:* The Educational Technology faculty members at Mid State University are highly experienced with the design and development of online programs and the use of educational technology and have received numerous awards for their efforts.

- ***CAEP Technology Requirements:*** In the new 2020 standards, CAEP requires that "providers ensure that candidates model and apply approved technology standards (e.g., ISTE, state standards) as they design, implement, and assess learning experiences to engage students and improve learning."
- ***Online Learning Trend:*** Over the last several years, the number of students learning online has continued to increase. This trend suggests that online and blended learning has become a mainstay in contemporary teaching and learning.
- ***Online K–12 Options:*** While higher education has seen dramatic increases in online course offerings, the number of online K–12 programs also continues to increase.
- ***E-Learning Days:*** In recent years, the State Department of Education has established the use of "e-learning days" in schools.
- ***Blended Learning:*** Even in traditional brick and mortar K–12 schools, technology is increasingly used in ways that combine both online and face-to-face elements (e.g., the increasing use of learning management systems).
- ***Ongoing Pandemic***: The ongoing global pandemic has greatly disrupted educational processes and made clear the importance of preparing preservice teachers to handle unexpected disruptions.

Sequence of experiences required for candidates to complete the program:
Traditionally, in teacher preparation programs, preservice teachers are required to complete stand-alone educational technology courses; however, infused technology approaches show promise for providing a full consideration of discipline-specific educational technology use. Additionally, infused technology is consistent with CAEP requirements. Using the blended and online teaching standards, paired with ISTE standards, we have developed specific competencies that teacher education graduates will be expected to master upon completing their programs. Through this approach, there will be no additional courses or field experiences required beyond those in students' current plans of study. Rather, these experiences will be modified to emphasize different learning environments (e.g., face-to-face, blended, online) and appropriate instruction across these settings.

Candidates will be expected to demonstrate five competencies, with each of these competencies requiring two parts:

1. Educational Technology Foundations
   a. Educational Technology and Learning Environments
   b. Educational Technology Terminology and Tools
2. Educational Technology and Learners
   a. Educational Technology and Learner Diversity
   b. Educational Technology, Community, and Presence
3. Educational Technology Design Principles
   a. Educational Technology and Theories and Principles of Instructional Design
   b. Educational Technology and Instructional Strategies
4. Educational Technology, Leadership, and Professionalism
   a. Educational Technology and Lifelong Learning
   b. Educational Technology, Leadership, and Communication
5. Educational Technology and Facilitation
   a. Educational Technology and Learning Management
   b. Educational Technology and Assessment

16

Tess Primeau

Redesigning Curriculum for International Learning Contexts and Global Partnerships

Carole Hruskocy

A few months back, Tess Primeau, a professor of curriculum and instructional design at Mountain University, had been encouraged by her colleague, Kaley Wilson, to apply for a curriculum lead role for revision and development of a set of education courses designed for a global audience. Tess recalled how Kaley had rushed into her office that day.

Kaley had exclaimed, "Tess, you *have* to apply for this curriculum lead role! I would apply but since I'm not an instructional designer, I don't have a chance. This is the same project that's recently been highlighted on the university website. Essentially, our program provides the online courses and grants the degree."

Tess, smiling at Kaley's enthusiasm, said, "Slow down! I know a little bit about the project, but clearly, you know much more. What can you tell me?"

Kaley sat down in Tess's overstuffed office chair and shared what she knew about the project, "The courses to be revised and developed are part of a diploma offered by International Learning Opportunities for All or ILO_All. ILO_All is a non-profit organization focused on offering free, tertiary education to individuals who might not have access to higher education opportunities. ILO_All partners with various universities in the United States, including ours. The student population for the courses might be located in refugee camps around the globe, such as in Kenya and Malawi, and in areas of high economic need, in countries such as Afghanistan, Jordan, Chad, India, or Myanmar, as well as in the United States. Tess, with your background and professional interests, this project was meant for you!"

Tess had previously worked as an instructional designer in both a corporate and higher education capacity. Currently, she was managing a master's degree program in curriculum and instructional design (ID) at Mountain University for which she had developed curriculum and online courses. Tess agreed that the project seemed to be a good fit for her background and goals, which included expanding and applying her ID skills to international development work. Tess had always had a passion for diverse cultures and enjoyed immersing herself in international settings so that she could experience new cultures firsthand. In fact, Tess had recently returned from Liberia where she had begun work on the development of a K–12 school. Tess saw this new job prospect as a win-win situation that might offer

DOI: 10.4324/9781003354468-18

Subject: ILO_All SME Position
From: Anthony Jones <ajones@ILO_All.org>
To: Dr. Tess Primeau <tprimeau@mountain.edu>
Date: August 28 7:26 A.M.

Dr. Primeau,

Thank you for your recent application for the role of Curriculum Lead and Subject Matter Expert (SME) to the International Learning Opportunities for All (ILO_All) initiative. The selection committee met, and I am delighted to offer you the position of Curriculum Lead and SME for our concentration—Education.

This concentration is one of three concentrations and is part of the 30 courses being developed for ILO_All's revised Diploma in Liberal Studies program. All courses will be 8 weeks long and will be delivered online to students at ILO_All's learning sites around the world. An exciting challenge is to develop courses that are multicultural and sufficiently flexible to be delivered globally with minimal adaptation.

To enable us to recruit faculty to teach these courses, our aim is to have the courses ready by the end of March with the intention that the first of them will be available to students next August.

The first step in this process will be to convene a meeting to introduce you to ILO_All with key inputs from ILO_All colleagues, site-based staff, and former students. More specifically, we will outline the work of ILO_All's Curriculum Oversight and Steering Committee (COSC) and the curriculum framework it has developed for the ILO_All programs. During the meeting you will engage with the pedagogical framework that supports course design and begin work on the education concentration. This three-day meeting will be held in October, in Washington, DC.

Looking forward to meeting you soon!

Sincerely,
Anthony

FIGURE 16.1 Email message from CAO Anthony Jones to Dr. Primeau.

opportunities for international travel, expanding her network, advancing her curricular and ID skills, and using her skills to create impactful work for the greater good. She truly believed this job was a perfect fit for her—both professionally and personally.

As the fall semester had just begun, Tess was wondering when she might hear back from ILO_All about her application for the curriculum lead role. Tess opened her email to start her day and was excited to see an email from the chief academic officer (CAO), Anthony Jones of ILO_All, stating that she had been accepted for the role (see Figure 16.1)!

Tess rushed into Kaley's office to share the good news. "Kaley, I got the ILO_All job!"

Kaley jumped up from her desk to give Tess a hug and exclaimed, "You will be perfect for this job! I'm so excited for you and know how much this job means to you."

Kaley and Tess began to discuss the project details. "Who do you think the other SMEs will be for the education concentration?" Kaley wondered. "And what does 'sufficiently flexible' mean?"

"I'm not sure," responded Tess. "And, I wonder how all of this work could be done by March?" As Tess walked back to her office these questions, and more, were on her mind, but she knew that the three-day meeting would provide the opportunity to have her questions answered.

On a crisp October day, Tess arrived in Washington, DC. The first meeting day was overwhelming as a wealth of information was shared about the project background, goals, and curriculum revision plan. But, Tess began to find answers to some of her questions.

NON-PROFIT ORGANIZATION AND PROJECT BACKGROUND

The mission of the ILO_All organization is centered on values such as care for others and community, leadership, service learning, reflection, and action. A focus of the organization's educational work is consideration of students' cultures and experiences within the required learning activities. For example, education students in a Kenyan refugee camp might be asked to reflect on their personal educational experiences to select a teacher who had a positive impact on them, describing the skills and/or dispositions this teacher illustrated, which they might want to emulate as teachers. Or, students might be asked to reflect on the United Nation's Sustainable Development Goals, as well as the academic challenges they themselves have encountered to develop a plan for becoming change agents in their communities. ILO_All referred to its educational philosophy as creating "open doors and windows" that would allow students to infuse their own local cultures and experiences into their learning.

The organization itself spanned the globe and had been operating for four years. The chief executive officer (CEO), Jane Fields, was located in the northwestern United States. The chief academic officer (CAO), Anthony Jones, was located in Europe. The chief information officer (CIO), Maria Rhodes, was located in the eastern United States. Maria oversaw the curriculum and managed course development including work done by instructional designers and media and web developers. Mountain University (MU) provided the online courses for ILO_All and granted the diploma. MU also employed a project director who was responsible for qualifying instructors, approving and monitoring course assignments, providing instructor support, and conducting course evaluations. A second university, Eastern Atlantic, provided IT support including the learning management system (LMS) and email services. While the program was delivered online, ILO_All established learning centers in several countries (e.g., Kenya, Malawi, Chad, Afghanistan) to provide students access to necessary technology. Learning centers employed a site coordinator who supported the students, managed the technology, and at times, facilitated student discussions (which created a blended course format). However, not all locations had a learning center. Online tutors, typically volunteer university faculty, were also an available resource.

THE FOUNDATIONAL CURRICULUM AND THE THREE CONCENTRATIONS

Tess was fascinated by the international connections of the organization and was curious to know more about the curriculum. She also wondered how the challenges associated with having multiple stakeholders in multiple locations might impact the revision project. She recalled that students completed a 45-credit, three-year program that culminated in a diploma in liberal studies, but she wanted more details on how the online courses were decided upon and developed. She was happy to see that the rest of the morning would be spent on curriculum.

Maria began with an overview of the program. She explained that in the first two years, students completed ten foundational courses that covered topics such as writing, communication, ethics, art, religion, math, science, sociology, and politics. Then, in the third year of the program, students selected from one of three academic concentrations: education, business, or social work. Just as Tess was about to ask about program goals and objectives, Maria began to share the skills and dispositions that framed the initial dialogue on the program that had occurred five to six years prior to the project inception. She shared the expectation that all courses address the skills and dispositions. Maria also shared a list of the ten diploma courses. Tess captured the information in her notes (see Figure 16.2).

As Tess reflected on the skills and dispositions, she was struck by the preponderance of what appeared to be a "Western-centric" or "Global North" perspective. She heard a few whispers among the other faculty and SMEs, "This list seems so culturally bound."

Tess was happy to know that she wasn't the only one with concerns about an overly Americanized curriculum. So, Tess asked Maria, "What additional background can you share on how the curriculum was determined?" and "How do we know these skills and dispositions translate across cultures and settings?"

Maria smiled and nodded, as though she expected these questions, and replied, "The topics for the ten foundational courses were determined by the organization's curriculum committee, which comprised deans and other university representatives from the United States and Europe. Learning objectives and competencies were conceptualized through the lens of intellectual, emotional, and social skills. Additionally, experience, reflection, and action—core tenets of the organization—helped frame curricular decisions."

A faculty participant asked Maria to expand on this information.

Maria added, "For example, 'experience' was addressed in foundational courses such as science, math, communications, writing, and ethics; courses in the arts, political thought, sociology, and religion were connected with 'reflection.' 'Action' was emphasized in specialized courses in the three concentrations. Therefore, the resulting objectives for the diploma encompassed a wide range of skills and dispositions such as critical thinking, disciplinary knowledge, communication, and ethical reasoning."

Tess scanned the room to determine the faculty's responses—based on their facial expressions, it appeared that they were clear on the answers Maria provided. Tess, herself, didn't feel

Skills and Dispositions Tied to Objectives and Competencies	**Foundational Courses in the First Two Years of the Diploma**
Analytical skills	*Academic Writing*
Critical thinking	*Interpersonal Communication*
Communication skills	*Dynamic Algebra*
Disciplinary knowledge	*Introduction to Physical Science*
Knowledge application	*Ethics and the Human Person*
Ethical reasoning	*Interdisciplinary Arts*
Life-long learner	*Religions of the World*
Diversity/culture appreciation	*Introduction to Political Thought*
Self-awareness	*Introduction to Sociology*
Community engagement	*Elective (student selected)*

FIGURE 16.2 ILO—all program completion skills, dispositions, and list of diploma courses.

quite so certain about the curriculum framework and was still unsure of the match between skills, dispositions, and cultures. She was beginning to wonder about the project's feasibility and found Maria's abstract descriptions challenging.

Tess made a mental note to learn more about the multi-cultural, multi-lingual, multi-ethnic audience and contexts and to revisit her second question with Maria at a later time. She refocused on her goal of ensuring the education curriculum illustrated a true international perspective. For now, and with this additional information on the "big picture" behind the curriculum, she was ready to focus on the curriculum revision task.

THE CURRICULUM REVISION TASK—DESIGNING THE EDUCATION CONCENTRATION

After a morning of learning about the organization's history, goals, and progress-to-date, Tess's mind was reeling with more questions about her role and the revision task than before she arrived. Gratefully, just before lunch she was introduced to the ILO_All instructional designer on the redesign project, Kate Young, who seemed to have a wealth of knowledge about the program, having previously visited a few learning sites and taught courses for the program. Tess found Kate to be easy-going and immediately felt they would work well together. Kate and Tess were scheduled to spend the second half of the day reviewing project documents and processes.

Over lunch, Tess asked Kate for more details on her fellow course writers and the project deadline, "Kate, I don't see other education SMEs here. Who will I be working with on the design of the education courses? What would their backgrounds be? How much freedom do we have in designing the courses? How do we ensure that the courses are designed for an international audience? And how feasible is the ten-month deadline?"

Kate smiled acknowledging all of the unanswered questions at this point in the project. She added, "ILO_All will put out a call for course writers once the DC meeting concludes.

Tess asked, "And what is the timeline for completion?"

Kate shared, "The education courses won't be due until the last stage of our development cycle, which will probably be in another year and a half, so we have plenty of time."

Tess breathed a sigh of relief.

Tess was also curious to know more about the reasons behind the curriculum revision. She wondered again about the various stakeholders and their roles in curricular decisions. But first she wanted to know more about the revision project. So she asked Kate, "Can you tell me more about why the program is being revised?"

Kate's response gave Tess the first ah-ha moment of the day. Kate shared, "Feedback from students, instructors, and learning site coordinators indicated that the courses needed to be revised to better fit a global audience. The initial set of courses had been written for American students from Mountain University. Therefore, American themes and references were common. For example, the education courses regularly referenced United States educational standards."

Tess asked, "Can you give me an example of something from the curriculum?"

Kate recalled, "Well, there was one course discussion question in which students were asked to visit their local Starbucks to observe communication behaviors."

Kate and Tess chuckled as Kate shared this example, yet, at the same time, Tess was surprised at how such curricular gaps could exist in the first place. She had a feeling that designing for this international audience who lived "at the margins" and in various locations could present design challenges not yet imagined.

As the plane lifted off from Dulles airport, Tess reflected on the project and all that she had learned during the three-day meeting. She began outlining all of her tasks ahead and created a priority list of to-do items. She reflected on some earlier concerns about the multi-cultural, multi-lingual, multi-ethnic audience and contexts and the need to include a true international perspective in the education courses. She was tired but, at the same time, excited about the work ahead and returned home ready to jump into the project.

RECRUITING COURSE WRITERS

The first task on Tess's list was identifying five courses that would comprise the education concentration. Tess recalled a conversation in DC with the CIO. Maria had shared that the first course would be a foundations course and that she had already selected a course writer.

Tess was a bit surprised by this decision since discussion about the curriculum had not yet taken place, and so she had asked Maria, "What can you tell me about the course writer?"

Maria replied, "I asked Vivian Davis to write the first course. Vivian has previously taught courses in the program, including the existing foundations course."

Tess felt better knowing the Vivian was selected based on her experience with the program and thought Vivian could bring a helpful perspective to the project.

Maria also provided suggestions for other course topics but ended with, "I'm eager to learn what course topics you might suggest."

To inform her course suggestions, Tess felt it was important to gain input from professionals in the field. She consulted with education colleagues, sought information through social media, and interviewed learning coordinators at two of the organization's refugee camp sites. Tess reflected on the information gathered, reviewed the current education courses, and drafted five course topics. In addition to educational foundations, the topics included educational psychology, learning environments, cultures, exceptionalities, and practical teaching. Tess emailed the topics to Anthony and Maria and scheduled a video call. She knew they would be touching base with Jane, the CEO, on the topics. A week later they connected on a call and discussed the proposed topics and whether the topics covered the basics of what a teacher should know and do. Tess was smiling as the call came to a close—the topics were approved!

Now that the course topics were identified she was eager to move the project forward. A second item on Tess's to-do list was selecting the remaining course writers. Anthony and Maria were posting a "call" on the organization's website for course writers experienced in education fields that matched the proposed course topics. The call emphasized international teaching experience. The first call resulted in nine applicants, but after Jane, Anthony, and Maria reviewed the applications they agreed that the "right" people had not applied. The applicants had educational backgrounds but did not have international experience. Tess received an email from Maria with an update on the application process and shared the team's frustration with the first set of applicants. Maria asked Tess to reach out to her contacts and colleagues to assist with a second call for course writers.

Eager to help out, Tess reached out to a number of education organizations, blogs, and social media groups with invitations to apply as course writers. A second call was posted on the organization's website. Unfortunately, the second set of applicants also lacked international experience. Frustrations were high since precious time was being spent on recruitment. Vivian had been identified as one writer, and in DC, Tess had agreed to write a course.

So three SMEs had not yet been identified. Since the application calls had not been successful, Jane, Anthony, Maria, and Tess reached out to personal contacts in an effort to recruit a team of educators. This recruitment strategy resulted in hiring the remaining course writers. All writers were experienced higher education faculty with practical teaching experience. Despite efforts to recruit international faculty, only one writer, Niley Chen, fit this category. Niley was born in Fiji and had international teaching experience; she was currently working at a South Pacific University as an instructional designer. A second writer, Frank Taylor, was retired faculty from Northwest Coastal University in the US and had visited ILO_All's refugee camp learning sites in Kenya and Malawi to consult with learning site coordinators. The third writer, Bridgette Clark, was an educational psychology professor employed at Flatlands University, a midwestern United States institution. She did not have international teaching experience but had worked with Tess on a previous design project. Due to the challenges in locating course writers and time constraints, Bridgette was hired.

CURRICULUM PLANNING MEETING

With course writers selected, Tess began planning the agenda for a three-day curriculum meeting. Several weeks before the meeting, Tess sent an email to the course writers detailing the information she had gathered from the DC meeting and her initial attempts to complete an analysis of the audience and context (see Figure 16.3). To help with organizing the project work, Tess also shared a link to a shared site where the course writers could upload their documents. She also saved a copy of the information in the email on the shared site.

Nine months after the DC meeting, on a hot July weekend, a meeting was convened at Mountain University to conceptualize and design the five-course education concentration. All education course writers, along with Kate and Anthony, attended the meeting. Maria was unable to attend but briefly joined the meeting virtually through video conference to open the meeting, welcome the team, and provide a brief synopsis of the task at hand. As curriculum lead, Tess led the rest of the meeting starting with the agenda and outcomes for the team: (1) complete a curriculum scope for the education concentration, (2) establish concentration outcomes, and (3) conceptualize course topics/content for the individual education courses.

Anthony, in a business-like manner, offered a brief history of the project and lessons learned from the pilot years including the identified need to have courses designed for a multi-cultural, international audience. He also shared that while the courses were online, they might not always be completed in a true online fashion but rather in a blended approach. Anthony explained, "Some of the students complete their coursework at a learning site or center. Not all students have access to technology outside of a learning site." Anthony also clarified that the education students would have already completed two years of the program, or 10 courses, prior to beginning the education concentration.

Being new to the project, Bridgette and Niley asked for more information about the audience for whom they would be designing courses.

Anthony nodded and replied, "No two sites are the same."

Tess smiled and nodded as she reflected on her own attempt to further understand the audience and context. Tess reminded the writers of the audience and context information she had shared in the pre-meeting email and accessed the information on the project shared site, displaying the information using the projector and screen. She allowed time for the writers to review the information and asked if there were any questions.

Subject: **Overview of ILO_All Audience and Context**
From: Dr. Tess Primeau <tprimeau@mountain.edu>
To: Niley Chen <nchen@sopacific.edu>, Bridgette Clark <bclark@flatlands.edu>, Vivian Davis <vdavis@ILO_All.org>, Frank Taylor <ftaylor@nwcoastal.edu>
CC: Kate Young <kyoung@ILO_All.org>
Date: June 12 9:48 A.M.

Hello Education Course Writers!

I am excited to be working with you all on this important project. I've been gathering background information on ILO_All and potential students to help inform our ID work. Below you'll find a summary of information I gained through the context and audience analyses.

ILO_All enrollment history
Over the initial four years of the project:

- 2,747 have enrolled in the diploma program
- 1,089 women; 1,546 men
  - Note: At least 30% of the students must be women (goal of ILO_All)
- 20% have withdrawn (some students are relocated)

Acceptance into the program:

- Eligibility—dependent on the site (ideally have evidence of secondary education)
- English test
- Written essay, 2 pages (assessed according to a rubric by volunteer faculty)
- On site interview (with scoring rubric)
- Age—no restrictions (secondary level education; perhaps from 18–60 years old)

Audience analysis
General:
Students will vary in age; cultures will span the globe. Students will likely have prior education experience, possibly at a secondary level; English will not be their first language; some may have access to personal technology, some will not; many will have suffered deep, personal loss; and, all are motivated to advance their current situations.

Specific to the field of education, access to public or private schools to observe or practice teaching skills will not always be feasible.

Site specific:
Site A—refugee camp of 28–30K; has institutionalized its management of refugees; camp has been there a long time; collect people at the border and take them to camp; as a result, very many nationalities

Site B—around 200,000 refugees; multi-ethnic, religion, language

Site C—majority are Syrian; 20% Iraqi with a mix of other nationalities including Palestinian and other African nations

Site D—not a site but partnered with a school; mostly high school students; has begun offering teacher training; students have low opinions of the local higher education sites; tend not to be refugees; residents of the local community; marginalized because of the availability and quality of higher education

Site E—tend not to be refugees; have no access to higher education; may be academically less prepared due to the years of disorder/strife in the country.

Context analysis

Students might complete the course work alone, if they have access to personal technology. Students (especially refugees) might complete the work in a common space (called learning center or learning site). Group work is common in the learning sites.

FIGURE 16.3 Email message from Tess to education concentration course writers.

Urban sites: Learning centers may be located in a city. These students tend to work at home. If working at home the ability to work may be difficult, lots of family around; lighting may not be available; students stay at center as long as possible to get work done; almost a "flipped experience" from the typical online learning experience (work done off site/at home).

Implication for Assignments: Consider limiting paper assignment length to 3–4 pages rather than a lengthier paper.

I hope this information offers a perspective on the diverse audience and context for which we'll be developing courses. We'll talk further about the audience and context at our meeting.

I look forward to working with you all on this project, and I'll see you in a few weeks!

Tess

FIGURE 16.3 Continued

Bridgette, who Tess knew to be focused and task-oriented, asked, "Can you share how the analysis was completed? I found the information you shared helpful, but a bit of background will be even more helpful."

Tess offered background on where and how the audience and context information was gathered, explaining her challenges, "I ran into some bumps in the road trying to gather some solid information on our audience and context. What we know is that the audience and learning sites are dispersed across the globe. I tried to gather information from students by sending out a survey. But I learned that responding to a survey is problematic because of students' limited access to technology outside of the learning site."

Niley, who seemed open and agreeable, chimed in, "I imagine both technology access and reliability are challenges. So how did you gather information from students?"

Tess added, "The site coordinators told me that interpreting students' language might also be an issue, so they suggested that I email surveys directly to them and they would share the survey with current and former students. I suggested we might set up synchronous calls so that I could talk in real time to the students, but the limited access to technology was a constraint and also impacted their work. For example, site coordinators will download all articles, videos, or materials that are part of a particular lesson the evening before the class session. With all materials downloaded before class, the coordinators are able to work around bandwidth issues and focus on the lesson."

Niley nodded and asked, "So, how did that work out?"

Tess smiled and replied, "Well, I found that their concerns about survey responses were right. Two students responded, and the input they gave wasn't helpful. There was a definite issue with written communication. So, as the coordinators predicted, the information I received did not provide additional perspective on the audience."

Anthony added, "Tess's efforts are commendable. The challenges she encountered were not surprising and illustrate a few of the many challenges we encounter with this program. But we overcome such challenges every day."

Tess was pleased by Anthony's support adding, "I didn't stop at the students. I sought additional sources of information and was able to interview two learning site coordinators. I also spoke with folks who had visited some learning sites. As a matter of fact, Kate and one of our fellow writers, Frank, have both visited learning sites."

Tess then invited Kate and Frank to expand on the audience and context.

Kate replied, "No two audiences are the same—across learning sites and even *within* learning sites. For example, in the Kenyan refugee camp there are multiple cultures found within the camp. You might have students from 'opposing tribes' or ethnic groups with differing religious or political beliefs."

Frank added, "Initially these situations are sensitive, but a significant benefit observed from this project is that the line between cultures becomes blurred as students begin to engage with each other."

Kate shared that the answer to the context question was just as challenging to answer: "Each context differs as some students complete the work alone in their homes and others complete the work at a learning center, such as the center in the Kenya refugee camp."

Frank agreed with Kate's analysis of the context, adding, "The program is projected to expand to additional settings, so future contexts and audiences are unknown."

Aware that Vivian had not yet participated in the conversation and remembering that Vivian had taught a few courses in the program, Tess invited her to share her thoughts on the students.

Vivian shared, "There is no easy way to describe the audience. But the students are highly motivated to learn and embrace education as a life-changing experience."

Tess thought her response to be short, considering her experience with the program. Tess felt unsure about Vivian's interest in the project having not been involved in hiring her. She made a mental note to connect with Vivian during the first meeting break.

Closing the conversation, Anthony light-heartedly summarized, "Essentially there is no specific audience demographic or defined learning context."

Bridgette and Niley's expressions seemed to say, "Okay, this is a unique design challenge."

Tess recognized those expressions from her own experience trying to gather information on the audience and continued to ponder how she would lead a curriculum project for an audience that was multi-cultural, multi-lingual, and multi-ethnic and with a vague, or unknown, context.

The focus of the meeting then shifted to curriculum. To get the curriculum discussion underway, Tess presented draft outcomes for the education concentration (see Table 16.1). She was eager to gain consensus on the outcomes to help guide further dialogue. The team offered input on the outcomes, which Tess then revised; revisions were minor.

With the outcomes decided, Tess began to facilitate a brainstorming session with guiding questions developed after the DC meeting.

Tess began, "What does an effective teacher know? What does an accomplished teacher do in the performance of their duties? What evidence can education students offer relative to what they know or do?"

With a roomful of educators, rich discussion ensued. Some discussion focused on which educational theorists were important to cover and whether they should be called theories or models. Niley shared, "Knowing how diverse our audience and the context might be, I feel strongly that theorists outside of the United States (US) are important to include."

Knowing Vivian had experience teaching in the program, Tess specifically asked her, "What insight can you share about the importance of covering international theorists in the education courses?"

Vivian replied matter-of-factly, "My experience has been that students really *want* to know about Western ways of teaching. They are eager to learn how to teach differently than the traditional lecture format by which they were taught. At the same time, students have

TABLE 16.1
Draft Outcomes for the Education Concentration

International Learning Opportunities for All (ILO_All)
Education Concentration Outcomes 1. Examine frameworks for teaching including Danielson's (2009) four domains of 1) planning and preparation; 2) the classroom environment; 3) instruction; and 4) professional responsibilities. 2. Explore cultural diversity through social, ethical, philosophical, and historical perspectives with implications for student needs. 3. Apply theories of learning and development to select appropriate learning strategies, develop effective lesson plans, promote motivation, and create effective learning environments. 4. Illustrate professionalism through dialogue on philosophical beliefs on teaching and learning, ethics, community relationships, research-based learning strategies, and construction of a resource portfolio. *Danielson, C. (2009). Implementing the framework for teaching in enhancing professional practice. ASCD.*

shared how their cultural contexts might impact their abilities to actually implement Western strategies."

Bridgette interjected, "Students may not always know what they need to learn. Effective teaching is effective teaching, no matter the culture or setting."

Vivian tilted her head and said, "I respectfully disagree. For example, some of the classrooms where these students might eventually teach can have 100 students or more. So, integrating a constructivist approach is nearly impossible, and classroom management strategies clearly differ from global north classrooms."

Niley, knowing first-hand about cultural diversity and teaching, agreed with Vivian's point and suggested, "Perhaps we can develop a list of contextual challenges these students might encounter."

Frank concurred and shared his perspective from having visited some learning sites: "Other students might run into constraints due to government mandates. For example, in Malawi, government schools follow a particular prescribed curriculum and teaching approach. However, private schools have more freedom, and these teachers are eager to implement more contemporary instructional strategies."

Vivian added, "So I think presenting what might be called 'Western theorists' is a workable strategy as long as we provide students with an opportunity to research other theorists and apply the theories to their own contexts."

Bridgette proposed, "Let's be sure to capture the importance of including diverse theorists as we move forward with our planning."

Tess was optimistic about Vivian's contributions and thought this conversation served as an important reminder of the complexity of the design project relative to the audience and context.

A second main discussion covered whether, or how, to address standards, such as national and state standards for a multi-cultural audience.

Vivian shared, "We might introduce the concept of education standards, but it's not necessary to cover specific Western education standards since the students may or may not have to comply with standards for their individual countries."

Discussion continued about what fundamentals beginning teachers should learn.

Circling back to previous discussion on educational theories and models, Bridgette commented, "Of course, I'm biased toward educational psychology, but I do feel that such a course is essential. I'm thinking we can introduce theory and models in the ed psych course and then include further study on theories and models in the remaining courses."

Frank agreed and strongly supported the need to address classroom management: "If I might offer a reminder, my observations at the sites point to how complex the teaching contexts might be for these students. Classroom size can range from small classrooms to classrooms of 100 or more!"

Kate concurred and shared what she felt was a gap in the previous ILO_All education curriculum, "In the past, students in the program were not expected or required to conduct actual practice lessons."

Just as Tess was about to share her surprise, Bridgette replied, "Whoa! How can we endorse a curriculum that doesn't provide students with opportunities to practice teaching? I think we would all agree that this kind of practice is essential."

Niley added, "I'm also surprised to learn this about the previous curriculum, and I wholeheartedly agree with Bridgette that opportunity to practice teaching is essential for these students. But I'd like to know how feasible such practice is given the variety of learning contexts."

Kate added her perspective from working with a few of the refugee camps, "Not all learning sites could provide for this practical teaching opportunity, at least not as we typically envision a practice teaching experience. For example, students in a refugee camp would not be able to practice their teaching outside of the refugee camp, but they *could* practice teaching a lesson to their peers or perhaps refugee children."

Tess felt the tension in the room ease as the course writers nodded.

Bridgette replied, "That's really important information. I think we can all live with that option."

The other course writers nodded in agreement and determined that such practical teaching experience was important to embed in the curriculum, even if the practice audience was a group of peers.

Discussion continued about the essential elements of an education curriculum with consensus focused on the importance of covering outcomes, assessment, instructional strategies, lesson planning, and professionalism. Tess felt good about the way the meeting was moving forward and captured the group's input in a table, grouping their ideas into categories (see Appendix 16-A). The writing team also applied backward design to conceptualize the final, capstone course experience and to understand what scaffolds would be necessary, across all courses in the concentration, to enable students to successfully complete the capstone.

With a solid outline of themes and topics, Tess shared the five courses she, Maria, and Anthony had agreed upon after the DC meeting: Educational Foundations, Educational Psychology, Learning Environments, Instruction across Cultures and Exceptionalities, and Practical Application of Teaching/Capstone. Discussion shifted toward the five courses. The team compared the table of themes and topics against the courses and found a close match.

To avoid making assumptions about whether the five courses would best prepare students, Tess asked, "So what are your thoughts on these courses?"

Kate, Niley, Bridgette, and Vivian nodded in approval.

Frank commented, "I think these courses would provide the foundation the students need and would improve upon the current curriculum. I feel good about where we are heading."

Tess was pleased with this feedback, especially since Frank had visited several of the learning sites.

As a next step, the team shared thoughts on what each course might cover and, with only minor edits made to the titles and course sequence, ultimately agreed on the courses. Course assignments were then discussed among the team, with team members sharing which course best matched their experiences and expertise. Tess explained that Vivian had been selected to write the first course, Foundations. Even though faculty were selected for a specific expertise and experience, Tess was pleasantly surprised with how quickly and easily faculty came to consensus on which course each of them would write.

Tess's excitement was growing as she was starting to "see" the project become reality. Using the agreed upon themes the team had just discussed, she created a second table (see Table 16.2), and the team began mapping the competencies and learning progressions to define where a topic would be introduced (I), developed (D), and mastered (M). The group discussed whether "mastery" could actually be achieved in a four-course concentration. Kate offered a reminder on the ILO_All program: "Remember, the diploma is a step below an

TABLE 16.2
Education Concentration Competencies and Learning Progressions

Competencies	*Educational Foundations*	*Educational Psychology*	*Learning Environments*	*Cultures and Exceptionalities*	*Practical Application of Teaching/ Capstone*
Learner standards	I	D		D	D
Theories or models of learning	I	I D	D	I D	D—revisit models and theorists
Education theories	I	I D	D	D	D
Learning/instructional strategies	I	I D	D	D	D
Lesson planning (plan/ design)	I—concept of lesson planning + examples; scaffold across concentration courses	I—cover learning outcomes/ objectives	I—cover lesson plan template elements; write a lesson plan	D—cover differentiation; UDL in lesson planning	D—revisit lesson plan from previous courses; create new lesson plan and apply to teaching of a lesson
Assessment/evaluation/ data	I	D	D	D	D
Learning environments/ communities of learners	I	D	D	D	D
Objectives/outcomes	I	I	D	D	D
Content knowledge			I	D	D
Ethics	I	D	D	D	D
Fundamentals of knowledge (pre-assessment; culture, diversity)	I	D		D	D
Professionalism/ disposition	I—teaching philosophy		D	D	D—revisit philosophy from 1st course
Management/motivation	I	D	D	D	D
Technology		I	I	I D	D

associate's degree." With this important reminder, the group agreed that "mastery" could not be expected.

As the team was working through the Foundations course, Vivian shared, "That course has already been developed. I wrote that course several months ago, and it's done."

Kate, the instructional designer, added, "Yes, I've been working with Vivian. Maria gave permission for Vivian to work on the course months ago, and it's pretty much done and in production."

Tess could hear the room go silent. She took a moment to collect her thoughts and then cautiously suggested, "Vivian, your perspective is so important to this project. Now that we have a curriculum map, perhaps you might review and, if necessary, revise components of your course."

Vivian shook her head and replied, "My course is done. I agreed to attend this meeting, but I won't be attending any other meetings this weekend. Maria and Kate have said this was okay since my course is already done."

Tess's initial concerns about leading a curriculum project for an ill-defined audience now just got bigger. Sensing the growing tension in the room, Tess quickly turned the matter at hand into an opportunity and said, "Vivian, with your experience teaching in the program and now developing a course, can you help us understand how we might account for a varied audience and context in our course designs and how we might ensure a multi-cultural perspective? What strategies did you use to address these issues?"

Preliminary Analysis Questions

1. Tess and the writing team were tasked with designing curriculum for a multi-cultural, multi-lingual, and multi-ethnic audience who lived in varied, or unknown, contexts. What specific strategies might she integrate into the curriculum planning phase and the curriculum design to account for the ill-defined audience and context?
2. One challenge in this case was recruiting course writers/faculty with international experience. What factors impacted the selection of course writers and to what extent did these decisions impact the resulting design? Suggest additional recruitment strategies that Tess and her colleagues might have implemented.
3. Tess and the course writing team were surprised to learn that the first course was already developed and in production. How can Tess ensure that the agreed upon themes are integrated into the first course? What should her next steps be in the curriculum development process?
4. Instructional designers are often brought onto a project after high-level decision-making has occurred. What decisions were made before Tess joined the project? How did these decisions impact the project? How would you address these challenges?

Implications for ID Practice

1. How do you design for a varied audience and varied contexts? What strategies can you use to meet the changing needs of an ill-defined audience?
2. Completing a front-end, audience analysis is an essential step in the ID process. When an analysis is either not possible or does not provide sufficient information what design decisions are impacted? How might the project proceed?

3. Working with multiple team members and across multiple locations is common in ID projects. What skills did Tess evidence and what was missing? Outline a professional development plan to "fill in the gaps" for the skills you will need for working with multiple team members and multiple locations.
4. Cultural awareness is an important skill in the designer tool kit. How can instructional designers surface their own deeply held cultural beliefs and understandings? How can they design in a way that is culturally relevant to the target audience?

Appendix 16.A

Education Concentration Common Themes and Topics Across Courses

	Vivian's course: Educational Foundations	*Bridgette's course: Educational Psychology*	*Frank's course: Learning Environments*	*Niley's course: Cultures and Exceptionalities*	*Tess's course: Practical Application of Teaching/Capstone*
Professionalism/ standards	Introduce Danielson, Domains 1–4	Danielson, if appropriate	Reference Danielson, especially Domain 2	Reference Danielson, whichever domains are appropriate	Synthesize concentration concepts through review of Danielson
Personal philosophy	Draft	Revisit/revise specific to educational theories Integrate theories into philosophy	Revisit/revise specific to learning environments Connect teaching philosophy with classroom management expectations and processes	Revisit/revise specific to cultures and exceptionalities Connect teaching philosophy with diverse learners	Revisit/revise for final assignment; integrate concepts throughout the concentration
Lesson plan template	Introduction to lesson planning with exposure to examples; introduce the lesson plan template with reference to the capstone lesson plan; introduce unit plans *Could this course offer opportunity to do more with the lesson plan?	Introduction to learning outcomes/ objectives and practice writing outcomes; the start of a first lesson plan draft; plan will be completed across the next two courses; plan revisited in capstone for feedback/ revisions	Introduction to the other elements of the lesson plan with practice by completing a draft of the elements (with the exception of differentiation and UDL—this will be address in Niley's course)	Completion of differentiation/UDL section of the lesson plan template (use their lesson plan from Frank's course to build this final section) Possibly adapt a lesson that includes an assessment to meet the needs of diverse learners	Critique existing lesson plans; create a new lesson plan with application of the lesson plan through micro-teaching; create presentation

	Vivian's course: Educational Foundations	*Bridgette's course: Educational Psychology*	*Frank's course: Learning Environments*	*Niley's course: Cultures and Exceptionalities*	*Tess's course: Practical Application of Teaching/Capstone*
Theories of learning	Content includes: Gardner—multiple intelligences Constructivism Experiential learning: TED Talk video, "How to Learn from Mistakes" by Diana Laufenberg Learning theories discussion. First view TED Talk video, "Teaching with the World Peace Game" by John Hunter UNESCO resource—How Children Learn: (Something to consider across courses; a nice supplement to theories of learning)	Traditional theories 1. Behaviorism—Skinner 2. Cognitivism—Wundt 3. Social learning theory—Piaget, Bandura Contemporary theories 1. Constructivism—Bruner, Vygotsky 2. Experiential learning—Kolb 3. Situated learning—Lave 4. Connectivism—Siemens, Downes Perhaps revisit Hunter TED talk from Vivian's course to explore what theories are evidenced	Implications of the theories for the classroom Wenger—Communities of practice Gardner, multiple intelligences Constructivism Perhaps revisit TED talk to explore what theories are evidenced relative to type of learning environment Hunter espoused: Hunter TED Talk video	Analyze the theories against various cultures and exceptionalities Gardner, multiple intelligences Freire—liberation pedagogy Vygotsky—contextual learning	Personalize the theories for your setting; reflect on concentration readings and videos: How will you organize the learning space? What theories will you use? As a learner how do you learn best? What theories support your style?
Diversity/cultures	Content includes: UNESCO "Universal Declaration on Cultural Diversity" pages 10–17 UNESCO resource: Emotions and Learning Gender Religion Inclusion	Cultural/ethnic diversity Gender	Perhaps revisit from Foundations course: UNESCO resource, Emotions and Learning Gender Religion Disabilities Inclusive environments	Perhaps revisit from Foundations course: UNESCO resource, "Universal Declaration on Cultural Diversity" pages 10–17 Perhaps revisit from Foundations course UNESCO resource: Emotions and Learning Gender Religion Disabilities Inclusion	Cultural/ethnic diversity Gender Religion Disabilities Inclusion
Portfolio—selected key assessments/ artifacts	Select 1–2 key assessments from the course for students to include in their portfolio (key assessments evidence a majority of the course outcomes)	Select 1–2 key assessments from the course for students to include in their portfolio (key assessments evidence a majority of the course outcomes)	Select 1–2 key assessments from the course for students to include in their portfolio (key assessments evidence a majority of the course outcomes)	Select 1–2 key assessments from the course for students to include in their portfolio (key assessments evidence a majority of the course outcomes)	Build final portfolio; complete reflection question(s)
Additional readings based on location and audience					

17

Parvathy Ramanathan and Mohana Ganesan

Redesigning a Workshop to Increase the Impact of Social Workers' Efforts in a Developing Country

Sangeetha Gopalakrishnan

Mohana Ganesan stared at the spinning disk on her phone screen that said "reconnecting." She had lost track of the number of disruptions that had occurred during this video call with Parvathy Ramanathan. It made a long conversation seem even longer. Parvathy, or Paru to people who knew her, lived in New Delhi, India's capital. Located in the north of the country, the union territory of Delhi had a population of over 18 million. With its historical monuments bearing testament to India's checkered past, Delhi presented the juxtaposition of calm and chaos, ancient and modern, poverty and affluence, and backwardness and progress. Many residents of Delhi came from various parts of the country and spoke different Indian languages as their mother tongue. These residents represented India's cultural and linguistic multiplicity, while the temples, mosques, and churches that dotted the cityscape portrayed its religious diversity. The diversities and contradictions seen in Delhi were characteristic of India.

Mohana knew all too well that the quality of calls to India from the US—especially internet-based calls—was unpredictable and easily affected by both the chronic power shortages across India and the weather. The long hot summers and the heavy monsoon rains caused frequent power outages and disrupted telecommunication. Indians often joked that all it took for a bad connection was a crow sitting on the phone line. Paru had been telling Mohana about her recent workshop at Kadal University, a state-run regional university. Kadal was located in Rameshwaram, a small town on the Pamban Island at the southern tip of the Indian peninsula. Mohana recalled visiting the ancient Rameshwaram temple on the seashore, famed for its beautiful long corridors.

When the call reconnected, Paru reported cheerfully, "It's raining here. Maybe that's why the connectivity is bad today."

Mohana rolled her eyes and grinned. "At least this time we aren't interrupted by monkeys!" she quipped. During a previous conversation, Paru had put the call on hold because she thought monkeys had entered her home! Paru had explained that unruly monkeys living

DOI: 10.4324/9781003354468-19

in the trees in her Delhi neighborhood terrorized residents by entering their homes, eating their food, breaking cell phones, and turning everything topsy-turvy. Marauding monkeys had been a neighborhood menace even during her student days in Delhi, Mohana remembered. Even though India was changing rapidly in many ways, many things in India never seemed to change.

Paru was wearing a beautiful peacock-blue handwoven silk saree with golden threads, which she had gracefully pleated. Mohana had always admired the way Paru elegantly draped sarees. "As I was saying," Paru continued, "I'm looking at expanding my workshop for the social work students at Kadal University and wanted to explore the option of using an online format. So that is why I wanted to talk to you."

Mohana worked in faculty development at Lakeshore University, an urban research institution in Chicago. She had earned a PhD in instructional technology from the same university and now taught in both face-to-face and online formats. Mohana was born and raised in Madras, or Chennai, as it is now known. It was India's fourth largest city and situated on its southeastern coast on the Bay of Bengal. Several years ago the city's name had been officially changed back to Chennai, its original name before the British colonized the country. India was asserting its hard-won independence in various ways. Even so, the colonial influences on India ran deep, had become integrated into the fabric of India, and, like the widely spoken English language, were hard to extricate. Mohana still referred to her hometown as Madras, because that was the name she had used for most of her life, including up until the time she left India. She had heard someone say, "Chennai is a city, Madras is an emotion," and that somehow seemed to explain how she related to her hometown.

Mohana had come to the US, almost two decades ago, for graduate studies. Although she chose to remain in the US, she made annual trips back to India and stayed in contact with family and friends there. She and Paru had been roommates at North India University (NIU) in Delhi. Paru was also originally from Madras, and the two had immediately bonded over their homesickness. They had missed the spicy *sambar* and *rasam*, curried lentil and tamarind sauces, and rice dishes of Madras, its juicy mangos, fragrant jasmine flowers, graceful coconut trees, and the pleasant ocean breeze on a hot day. They also had shared an aversion to the bitter Delhi winters, a season that had been completely unfamiliar to them. People from Madras, they had said laughingly, knew only two seasons, summer and monsoon. Eventually, they learned some Hindi, the primary local language, started wearing *salwar kameezes* with colorful *duppattas*, the North Indian traditional outfits, ate *dhal* and *rotis*, lentils and wheat flatbreads, and became quite like the *Delhiites*. Mohana visited with Paru during her trips home, but they didn't talk much about their work. However, knowing about Mohana's expertise with online learning, Paru had asked to consult with her about expanding her workshop for social work students.

As Mohana glanced at her computer she was again reminded why these conversations with Paru were difficult—not only because of the call quality but also because of the 12-hour time difference between them. It was hard to match energy levels when one was pumped up for the day and the other ready for bed. But Paru had always been a night owl, and she was passionate when she talked about her work. Unfazed by the late hour and interruptions, Paru continued to speak energetically.

Mohana had just made herself a cup of steaming hot "filter coffee," as it was known in South India, to distinguish it from what many considered an inferior alternative, instant coffee. It was made by brewing finely ground dark-roast coffee in a traditional brass or stainless steel filter and adding frothing milk. Filter coffee was a favorite for many South Indians, including Mohana. Many years ago, she had purchased a small stainless steel coffee filter from Madras so that she could have filter coffee in the US, an important morning ritual for her. As Mohana sipped on her beverage, she reflected on Paru's educational background and career path. Paru had a master's degree in library and information sciences and had worked as a librarian for several years for the cultural and educational arm of an international organization in Delhi. She also remembered that Paru had set up an automated library system for a technology research company. And now, Paru was conducting workshops for students in the Master of Social Work program at Kadal University.

Setting aside her coffee and picking up her note pad, Mohana said, "Paru, tell me again how you became involved with Kadal University. How did you make this jump from being a librarian to teaching social work students?"

Paru smiled broadly and said, "Yeah, my background and qualifications are unusual for someone engaged in what I am currently doing. I came to the development sector through the information and knowledge route." Mohana looked quizzically at her. Paru explained, "I transitioned into working with international agencies and non-governmental organizations (NGOs) that were doing community development in India by helping them with their library systems. As part of their development efforts, these agencies engaged in community outreach through educational programs. I began helping them disseminate information to their beneficiaries. And then I gradually became involved in training. I know it is an atypical career path."

"Maybe. But it makes sense," said Mohana, smiling.

"Good," said Paru and continued, "You asked about my involvement with Kadal University. It really began about six years ago. At that time I was conducting ten-day workshops on NGO management all over India. The workshops focused on showing NGO workers how to enhance organizational effectiveness through better program delivery. These workshops were offered under the auspices of my current employer, Dilli Chakra, with funding from international development agencies."

"Interesting. So, what type of organization is Dilli Chakra?"

Paru explained that Dilli Chakra was a large non-profit organization headquartered in Delhi. Together with international aid agencies and other non-profit organizations, Dilli Chakra worked with NGOs in India to increase their impact. It did so primarily through knowledge dissemination and educational programs rather than by engaging in any fieldwork itself. As a developing country with a population of over one billion, India had acute shortages that the government could not completely address. Mohana knew, by virtue of having grown up in India, that it fell to NGOs to meet some of these needs. But she was unfamiliar with the nature of social work programs undertaken by the NGOs.

Mohana said, "Can you contextualize NGO work in India for me a bit? Are these NGOs Indian or internationally run? Can you give me a sense of what kind of social work projects NGOs engage in?"

Paru replied, "Well, NGOs in India are both internationally and nationally run, but more the latter. There are dire needs in every aspect of Indian life—from poverty alleviation and primary education and vocational training, to empowerment of women, importance of vaccination, female infanticide, child labor, human trafficking, caring for the disabled and elderly, animal welfare, tiger conservation, elephant poaching, and environment and climate change. You name it and NGOs probably work in that area."

"How do the NGOs get established and funded?"

"Anyone can set up an NGO—you have to complete the paperwork and register it with the Indian government. The NGOs can be large—those funded by major international aid agencies tend to be large and have a big geographical reach, or they can be small and local. Funding could be through international agencies, Indian corporations, grants from the Indian government, and individual donations. Nowadays, crowd sourcing is also an option but the smaller NGOs are often unaware of that avenue for funding."

Mohana remarked, "I imagine that the NGOs are generally strapped for resources."

"Yes, very much so. NGO work in India is constrained by a severe lack of resources, which is compounded by poor planning, implementation, and evaluation of interventions, all of which interfere with effective delivery of services. A big question in India is how do you enhance the effectiveness of an NGO? One of the huge challenges in India is that NGOs implement projects with the best intentions, but do little to ascertain the impact of their work."

"I see. What kind of background and training do NGO workers have?"

"Oh, most individuals who work in NGOs, at least those whom I have come across, don't have formal education in social work or any training in community development. Rather, the NGOs I've seen are often established by those who have a passion for helping others and a big heart! These are the folks who see a problem and want to fix it. Often they have meager financial means themselves. They simply want to make a difference in the communities they serve. But invariably they don't bring a structured approach to their work—they learn by doing. And, sadly, passion and a big heart don't always bring about the changes they want."

"So, are the NGO workers who have a formal education more effective in their work?" asked Mohana.

"Not necessarily. Unfortunately, even those NGO workers are often unable to apply the theoretical knowledge learned in their programs. This is one of India's paradoxes. I don't know how it is in the US, but here in India it is not the norm for people engaging in social work to inform themselves about best practices when planning interventions. More often than not, they just jump in with whatever idea they have. Even those who are aware of the notion of following best practices have no real understanding of how to do this in the situations they face."

Mohana nodded, "Applying theoretical knowledge gained in the classroom to everyday practice can be a challenge for many of my students here in the US as well."

Paru continued, "Dilli Chakra and other international development agencies in India believed that better NGO training was needed, specifically that which moved the training of social workers from the theoretical into the practical realm. The ten-day workshops on NGO management were intended to address these deficiencies. Since NGOs are resource-strapped, participants were offered financial assistance by international development agencies to attend the workshops. These workshops were publicized within the community of social workers and NGOs by word of mouth rather than by formal marketing and they were well received by the participants."

"How many workshops did you offer and how many participants did you have?"

Paru closed her eyes and thought for a moment. "Let's see, I think we must have offered about 30 workshops on NGO management, and we probably had about 40 participants in each."

Mohana observed, "So, around 1,200 participants then. That is impressive. It certainly seems like there is a hunger among NGO workers to know more about NGO management."

"Indeed! Rather than large NGOs that were relatively well-established, the ten-day workshops were targeted at small and mid-sized NGOs."

"How many workers would a small, mid-sized, or large NGO typically have?"

"It is hard to say. I don't know if there is a standard by which NGOs in India, or even worldwide, are categorized by size. In my experience, the smaller NGOs could have as few as 5 workers, the mid-sized, 10–15, and the larger NGOs could have, say, 30 workers or more. I have also come across NGOs with less than 5 workers as well as large, internationally funded NGOs with 50–100 workers. We targeted NGOs having a staff of about 5 to 8 people who worked at the local level, and we selected NGOs that had some credibility in the region they served but were not growing or being very impactful. Often, workers at these NGOs lacked formal education in NGO management. But even if they had some formal training, it was predominantly theoretical, and so they felt extremely ill-prepared when they began fieldwork."

"You mentioned NGOs that are not growing or impactful—what does that mean?"

"Let me illustrate that by using the example of an NGO working on, say, human trafficking. It is a serious problem in India affecting children, teenage girls and boys, and women. There are several facets to this problem that an interested NGO, working in a specific village or geographical service area, needs to know. These include the reasons for trafficking and the ways in which it occurs, how to increase families' awareness of trafficking, how to set up vigilante groups, how to build an awareness campaign in a community or village, the type of messaging that has to go into wall posters, and how to achieve and measure the impact of their work, among many other things. If, for example, an NGO focusing on child trafficking does not grow beyond the 20–25 children it began working with initially, then it is not sufficiently impactful. When it comes to community development, NGOs should also have an exit strategy, meaning that, after three to five years of their involvement, members of the community should be able to take over and sustain the work initiated by the NGOs. Simultaneously, the social workers in the NGO should begin considering their next initiative, because an NGO's effectiveness is tied to creating communities that become self-reliant."

"I see. That makes sense. In what ways do the NGO workers feel unprepared?"

Paru answered, "So, when it comes to establishing and managing an NGO, there are several basic skills that many NGO workers lack, such as how to plan a project and determine its timeline, how to link with technical expertise, how to expand the geographical reach of the NGO, how to get the target audience to become involved and inculcate a spirit of inquiry, and how to raise money. The NGO workers often don't know basic work processes, such as the importance of record keeping, data gathering, creating links between information, or deploying technology for all of this. Also, they don't know how to put together proper documentation to ask for funding. They suffer from a lack of experience in grant writing, poor research skills, and language barriers. In addition, many of them are only fluent in the regional Indian language and don't speak English."

Mohana interjected, "I suppose since a lot of information is available only in English, their lack of English language skills limits their access to that information."

"Very much so! All of these act as barriers to applying for funding and ascertaining the impact of their work."

Mohana furrowed her brow and tapped her pen on her notepad. She said, "I also know that carrying out development programs in India is highly complex because of its great diversity. An American colleague asked me how many languages are spoken in India, and I had to look it up. According to one source, there are over 20 languages—with about half of them having distinctly different scripts—and over 700 dialects. And then I checked another source and the numbers were somewhat different. There is no agreement even on that!"

"Right!" said Paru, grinning. "India is diverse in every way imaginable. Remember our initial reactions to the *kadhi* we used to get at the NIU cafeteria back then?"

Mohana smiled at the memory. Kadhi was a spicy sauce made out of yogurt, and they had tasted it for the first time at NIU. It had been so different from the *mor kuzhambu* of South India, which was also made with yogurt, but had coconut in it, presumably because there are coconut trees in the south. And even in the North, the kadhi was made a bit differently in each state. Across India, there is so much variation in food and culture. In the Indian context where different states, regions, villages, communities, tribes, and ethnic groups have multiple linguistic, cultural, political, and religious influences, it's enormously challenging to address social problems. There is no one size that fits all of India.

MOVING SOCIAL WORK TRAINING FROM THE THEORETICAL TO THE PRACTICAL

Mohana observed, "So, all that began six years ago, right? How did those ten-day workshops lead to your current involvement with Kadal University?"

Paru beamed and said, "As with so many things in India, it was word of mouth! Having heard about these NGO management workshops, a handful of Indian universities approached me to conduct similar workshops for students in their Master of Social Work programs, and one of those was Kadal University. A student who had just graduated from Kadal's social work program and was volunteering in an NGO happened to attend my workshop and was so impressed that he recommended it to the department chair at Kadal!"

Mohana smiled back and said, "As an educator, I know that this kind of validation from students about the relevance of what they learned is terrific!"

Paru nodded in the characteristic Indian way, which most Westerners found intriguing and said, "Most of the department chairs and faculty who approached me were convinced that their social work curricula were failing to teach students to design results-based interventions."

Although Mohana was from India, some of the terminology that Paru used was new to her or had an entirely different connotation in the American context. Feeling the need for clarification, Mohana asked, "What do you mean by results-based interventions? Can you give me an example?"

Paru thought for a moment and said, "The NGO must be able to specify the results they want to achieve—measurable short-term, mid-term, and long-term results. The NGO also needs to articulate how they would achieve those results. Let me go back to the example of an NGO wanting to work on the issue of human trafficking. For this issue, they need to decide on the specific population they want to focus on, such as, say, young women in the 25-to-28-year-old age group. They should ascertain the geographical area they will cover and decide which aspects of trafficking they will address. This could include prosecution, rescue, rehabilitation of rescued, policy development to prevent trafficking, setting up vigilante groups in the villages, or identifying potential centers or 'red-light areas' where young women are trafficked. If the NGO decides to focus on, say, the rehabilitation of these young women then they need to list specific ideas for rehabilitation, who they will rehabilitate, and how.

"For example, rescued young women from the villages who are illiterate can be taught specific vocational skills so they can become financially independent. Further, they can be counseled on how to look after themselves, how to live with dignity even within modest means, and how to deal with the possibility of not being accepted by their families. The NGO needs to be able to measure the effectiveness of their interventions, and of course, finding ways to do this is not easy. Even if they can quantify some interventions easily, such as how many rescued women they trained on, say, jewelry making, how can they measure if the rescued women's quality of life improved over a period of time? Also, cost-effectiveness needs to be a consideration. I could go into more details of the complexities, but does this help you understand what I mean when I say the NGOs need to be engaged in results-based interventions?"

Mohana nodded and said, "Yes, I definitely have a better understanding now."

Paru raised her eyebrows and said emphatically, "The problem with the social work curriculum at many Indian universities is that it is so theoretical, leaving students ill-equipped to apply what they learned in the classroom when they engage in fieldwork. Faculty at many universities, especially government-run institutions, are neither required nor motivated to update their curricula."

Mohana mused that Paru's description of faculty motivation may sound exaggerated to an American audience. Having lived in the US for many years, she knew that there were differences in how Indians and Americans dealt with and reported facts. Indians often tended to overgeneralize whereas in the American culture, people were careful not to. On the other hand, perhaps, as a compensatory mechanism, most Indians rarely took comments like these too literally, but rather tended to interpret anything they heard with a grain of salt. Even though Paru's statement sounded like an exaggeration, being from India, Mohana knew that it was probably not that far from the truth.

Paru shook her head in frustration. "Not only that, but the approval process for any sort of curriculum change is inscrutable, hugely time-consuming, and political, so faculty just don't want to deal with it. Rather than revise their curricula, some departments decided to add on my workshop, because that did not require them to go through major approval processes. The social work department at Kadal University decided to replace a theoretical paper on NGO management in their Master of Social Work program with my workshop."

A CLOSER LOOK AT THE WORKSHOP STRUCTURE

"Being sought after by those universities to do NGO management workshops for them must have been very exciting!" Mohana remarked approvingly.

"Of course!" said Paru, grinning widely. "And remember that I don't have a doctorate, which typically one has to have to teach at most Indian universities. But it took some figuring out. To begin with, I was unable to spend ten days at a stretch away from my office delivering workshops at universities. So, I changed the ten-day session structure to two five-day modules and modified it to specifically target university students. I wanted my workshop to provide students with a more hands-on approach to creating new NGOs, as well as sustaining existing ones. For these students to be able to make any difference in people's lives in the communities they serve, they need to be able to think more creatively about the problems the communities face, identify how they are interlinked, and come up with innovative ways to solve them."

"So, can you give me a sense of what you want students to be able to do when you talk about problem solving?"

"Well, let's say students suggest raising awareness among villagers to address the issue of trafficking of young women. Students need to figure out how they will do this. What are effective ways to run a messaging campaign? If they suggest distributing flyers and putting up wall posters, what will the message be? How will they create and distribute them? How will they reach the villagers who are illiterate? And they need to be fully aware that lack of awareness is only one facet of the human trafficking problem, and by raising awareness, they are only addressing a single facet of a complex problem."

"I see. Speaking of complex problems, you also mentioned climate change earlier. I'm intrigued. How does climate change figure into social work in India?"

"In a big way!" said Paru. "Did you hear about the mass farmer suicides in India? There are studies that attribute the increase in farmer suicide to climate change."

Mohana remembered reading reports about the thousands of farmers who committed suicide in India in recent years. The numbers had reached staggering figures. The reasons had largely to do with crop failure, which then led to farmers sinking deeper into debt, which led to their inability to sustain their families and themselves. Utter hopelessness drove massive numbers of farmers to take their lives. Although the government was trying to help address the plight of farmers, it was inadequate.

Paru explained, "Climate change patterns are affecting people in the farming communities. Farmers are heavily dependent on rivers, lakes, and bore wells for irrigation. Illiterate farmers don't know why we are experiencing changing and extreme weather patterns—for instance, excessive and/or untimely rains, large-scale flooding of farmlands, or unexplained, prolonged drought which completely depletes ground water. The agricultural landscape in India is changing and crops don't behave like they used to. Because the income of the farming community is solely dependent on agriculture, when crops fail, their entire livelihood is lost. NGOs bring in agricultural experts who help the community explore different options, such as growing alternate crops, studying soil patterns, seeking alternate livelihoods, or migrating to a different geographical location."

"So, NGOs are needed to help study the situation and community."

"Exactly. So, the role of social workers in addressing the effects of climate change is becoming increasingly critical."

"I can see how the need for information dissemination and education is significant. If we could go back to the workshop structure, what do the students do in the workshop?"

"Over the duration of the two five-day modules, students have to identify a real problem in the community; propose a plan, on paper, for establishing a new NGO or organizing an existing NGO to address this problem; and present strategies for effectively managing that NGO. Students work in teams of five to seven. Typically, there are about 35–40 students in the workshop and so there are about five to eight teams. Each team works on one community problem they have identified. So, by the end of both modules, or ten days, the entire class will have drafted about five to eight proposals for various projects. Let me send you a document showing you the topics I cover" (see Table 17.1.).

"That seems like a good approach to achieving your objectives!" Mohana observed.

Paru shook her head and frowned. "But, you know, students hardly open their mouths in the classroom. They aren't used to developing individual projects or taking ownership of their learning. Typically, students don't present or participate actively in the classroom, nor are they encouraged to do so. Students are told what to say and think—they tend to be quite passive. They aren't expected or taught how to identify or solve problems." Mohana knew that most Indian classrooms were lecture-based and emphasized rote learning; students were

TABLE 17.1
NGO Workshop: Content and Structure

	Topic	*Subtopics*
	Module 1	
Day 1	Goal setting	Short-, medium-, and long-term planning; results-based planning
Day 2	Problem analysis and identification	Problem identification tools; eliciting community participation and stakeholder involvement
Day 3	Project management	Drafting and presenting project proposals; applying for funding
Day 4	Deploying technology	Leveraging technology tools for project management
Day 5	Record-keeping and reporting	Data management tools and processes
	Module 2	
Day 6	Managing finances	Fiscal responsibility and management
Day 7	Human resource management	Empowering and nurturing workers
Day 8	Networking and sharing	Seeking and sharing best practices
Day 9	Understanding changing weather	Climate change and its impact
Day 10	Entrepreneurship	Creating entrepreneurs

assessed mostly on how well they memorized and regurgitated information rather than how well they applied knowledge. So certainly, the social work program at Kadal University was no exception.

Mohana wanted to know more about Paru's workshop design. She flipped the page on her note pad and asked, "What reading material do you assign students?"

"None."

Mohana raised her eyebrows in surprise. Paru said with some seriousness, "I really don't want to assign them anything theoretical. They get plenty of that in their regular coursework. Rather, I typically use PowerPoint presentations, and in class, I discourage note taking." Mohana frowned because this seemed to contradict what she believed to be the role of note taking in learning. Paru exclaimed, "I don't want them just copying the PowerPoint slides. Otherwise, they are likely to just memorize what's on the slides without even trying to process what is on them. You know how it is in India, surely!"

"I do," said Mohana, nodding. She knew that Paru's statements would sound stereotypical in the American context, but they actually were true of the vast majority of learners in India. Nevertheless, she was still somewhat uncertain about Paru's ban on note taking.

Sensing Mohana's skepticism, Paru said emphatically, "I can tell you it works! They are forced to pay attention. Anyways, I structure my presentations to incorporate discussions for about 2.5 hours each morning, and then teamwork is done for about 2 hours in the afternoon."

"So, that is 2 hours for each of 10 days, about 20 hours then. By American standards it seems unrealistic for students to produce what they are expected to in that timeframe. Is there some preparatory work done by the students before the workshop begins?"

Paru shrugged and responded, "No, there is no preparatory work. In the US, people tend to be more specific about such time and effort calculations. It is not that literal here in

India—the learning environment is rather different. On some days, I may just shorten the morning discussion session and give them more time for teamwork. And after the afternoon session, students often stay back and continue to work in their teams for a few more hours, well into the evening. They view it as homework and are quite motivated and don't mind putting in some more hours. That is quite amazing."

Mohana was used to her students in the US coordinating their schedules and setting up times outside the class for working on group projects. She asked, "Why is this surprising?"

"Well, students at Kadal come from small towns and villages, and so home life, cultural events, and religious festivals always take precedence. If there is a family event on Saturday, they may just skip classes and leave early on Friday. Or, if there is a wedding in the family, they may miss an entire week of class." Mohana knew that what was considered extended family in the US was considered family in the Indian context. So, Indians attended many weddings, which usually lasted multiple days. Paru continued, "Students don't always stay in class even for the time they are supposed to. There is no strong impetus to study and do coursework. It is quite unusual for students to spend time doing group work. Even the department faculty are surprised to see the students working together late into the evening of their own free will."

"Interesting! During the workshop, how do you keep students engaged in the learning?"

"I encourage students to participate. They need to respond to my discussion prompts. I ask them to share their experiences. It is all very conversational."

"I see. So, how do you know students are learning, Paru?"

"Each day, I can tell by how students apply the morning discussions during the afternoon group work. But learning happens, holistically, over the entire duration of the ten-day workshop, at various stages. The learning process entails four distinct stages: first, students develop a real-world problem focus; next, teams of five or six students draft a blueprint for setting up an NGO; then, teams present and defend their blueprints and other teams ask questions; and finally, I also provide input."

Mohana asked, "So do you teach in English or Tamil?" Tamil is the language spoken in Tamilnadu, the Indian state where Kadal is located. Being originally from Madras, the capital of Tamilnadu, both Mohana and Paru spoke Tamil fluently.

Paru replied, "Well, students' English fluency is limited, especially in spoken skills. I do my presentations and facilitate classroom discussions in both English and Tamil. During team work, some students may present in Tamil only. Although English is the official language of instruction at Kadal University, faculty often switch to Tamil to communicate with students. Many faculty also come from the small towns near the university, and they too are more comfortable with Tamil."

Mohana shifted in her chair and adjusted her web camera. "Let me switch to another topic, Paru. What about students' technology skills and their access to technology resources?"

"Since students come from the rural areas around Kadal, their experiences with technology are limited. But they are used to going online and engaging with social media, primarily on smart phones, which most own. The department has about seven or eight computers. But in the classroom, the students use their smartphones to look up information. They use the lab computers to work on the slides for their presentations."

Mohana thought about the explosive increase in the use of mobile phones in recent years in India. In a country with a high illiteracy rate and where many houses did not have electricity and running water, this proliferation of mobile phones, across education and income levels, was remarkable. She vividly remembered her surprise in seeing a familiar, yet unusual, sight during one of her visits to India. She had been on a road trip with family, traveling past rural areas, when they had stopped for some tender coconut water at a roadside stand. She saw a farmer riding a typical bullock cart through the lush green paddy fields. He was wearing the traditional *veshti*, a rectangular cloth worn around the waist and sometimes tucked between the legs, and was shirtless, in the 100°F degree weather. But he was also speaking on a mobile phone. The striking contrasts in this image intrigued her. Many among India's vast illiterate population had become mobile phone-savvy, and even those in India's struggling lower middle class could now afford smartphones, albeit the less expensive ones.

Mohana reflected, "It sounds like you are deviating from the norm in terms of how you teach. What is the response?"

"Well, the faculty of the social work department at Kadal have completely bought into my practical workshop on NGO management in lieu of the theoretical paper that students used to complete. The paper was not application-oriented but my workshop is. It is actually more intensive and more work than the paper. Faculty tell students, 'You are lucky to have this addition to the master's program!' You know, in the Indian context such full-hearted support of a change initiative is unusual. I think faculty acceptance of this switch in the curriculum has contributed to students viewing it favorably as well. Faculty are surprised that students are actually talking in my workshop. They want to sit in on my sessions and see what it is that I do differently to get the students to talk!"

Mohana asked Paru whether a workshop evaluation is conducted at the end of the two five-day sessions. Paru replied, "Well, faculty feel that the students are exiting with useful skills. Villagers and the heads of the NGOs, where students work, report that the students who have completed my workshop are making a difference. Students who have graduated and found employment reported that their job prospects improved because they took this workshop."

"That is terrific! It sounds like the workshop evaluation is more anecdotal then?"

Paru tilted her head to one side as she considered Mohana's question and said, "Yes, I suppose. In India when something is good, or bad, word gets around pretty quickly. Reputation is everything. But I do want to do a more formal evaluation of how students fare in the field. Students do complete a survey at the end of each day, but I rarely glean anything useful from it because they tell me everything is fine."

Mohana was not surprised as she knew that culturally these students would probably shy away from providing feedback that may be perceived as critical of the instructor.

PROPOSED WORKSHOP EXPANSION

"So that is where things are now after six years, right?" Mohana asked.

"Yes!" said Paru nodding. "The master's program is a two-year program. Currently, the two five-day modules are incorporated into the first and second half of the second year of the master's program. The modules are six months apart and only for five days each. I really want to extend learning beyond these sessions. Up until now, students engaging in fieldwork haven't had a formal way of discussing what they are experiencing when they apply their workshop learning during their fieldwork. I want to provide for a learning-application-feedback loop, and this is what I want to enable with the expanded workshop."

Mohana asked, "So currently do the students do anything between the two modules?

"Between the two modules, students work on assignments, which comprise developing more examples of problem analysis and project development. And, then, when they go to the NGOs for fieldwork, they are expected to assess the NGOs using the analysis and development approaches learned in the first module. Before the second module, they send me their work, and I schedule a video conferencing session with each of them at least once. It is not all that formal."

"And how often do students engage in fieldwork during the program?"

"Students engage in fieldwork two days a week and work on a variety of social issues. However, unfortunately, this type of involvement by the students is bringing about little actual, sustained change. Social work students need to be able to work with local leaders in the communities they are engaged in. Sadly, students aren't in a position to impact the work of the NGO, but neither are many NGOs positioned to leverage the contributions of the students."

Paru noted, "Ideally, I would like students to apply what they are learning in the workshop in their fieldwork, note what worked and didn't work, come back to the classroom to debrief, hone their skills some more, and then go back to do more fieldwork. A second goal for the expanded workshop is to get students to leverage what is already known about what works in the field rather than reinvent the wheel. They really need to hear from other social workers in the field, share their experiences with them, and learn from them. I would love to invite experts from different fields to talk to students on a variety of topics."

Mohana interjected, "Are there any written accounts from NGOs and social workers about successful interventions in the field and lessons learned that you could share with students?"

Paru replied, "There is little documentation about what NGOs are doing. NGOs are isolated. For example, you may have four NGOs in the same village working on the human trafficking issue and even on the same facet of the problem. Although they are feeling good that they are doing *something* they are not as effective as they could be if they worked together. For instance, if one NGO focused on rescuing trafficked women, and the other NGO worked on their rehabilitation, together they would have more impact on the problem in that village. In general, there needs to be better ways for NGOs to share their experiences and pool their scarce resources. So another challenge is the duplication of work across NGOs."

Paru also emphasized the importance of partnerships between universities and civic organizations in affecting change in their geographical service areas. She drew attention to a new law in India stipulating corporate social responsibility. It required large corporations to invest 2% of their profits into social projects. Paru said, "Corporations and academic researchers need to join forces in driving social change. There need to be ways to measure how social work students are affecting change. If there are such data, corporations may be willing to fund academic programs. So, a third goal of the expanded workshop is to explore ways to gather such data."

Mohana asked, "So how do you envision the workshop being expanded?"

Paru wanted to expand the workshop from two to four modules, which would span the entire two years of the master's program to address some of these shortcomings and needs. The expanded workshop would include two modules in the two halves of the first year (see Table 17.2).

THE CHALLENGE: DOING EVEN MORE WITH LESS

"But the thing is," Paru explained, straightening her saree and furrowing her brow, "I really can't be onsite for the additional two modules. I am practically doing this pro bono and can't take time off work."

"What do you mean you are doing this for free?" Mohana asked incredulously. Mohana had always guessed that Paru was not making big bucks given the nature of her work, but

TABLE 17.2
Proposed Workshop Expansion

Current Structure of Workshop		
1st Year	1st 6 months No workshop	2nd 6 months No Workshop
2nd Year *Note: Paru goes to the university for the first 5-day workshop. At the workshop, students identify a need for an NGO in a geographical location, propose an intervention, and specify how results will be measured. Students learn how to document the intervention, understand funding and so on as per the topics for the 10-day session outlined in Table 1.*	1st 6 months Module 1 • Goal setting • Problem analysis and identification • Project management • Deploying technology • Record-keeping and reporting	2nd 6 months Module 2 • Managing finances • Human resource management • Networking and sharing • Understanding changing weather • Entrepreneurship
Proposed Expanded Workshop		
1st Year	1st 6 months Current module 1	2nd 6 months Current module 2
2nd Year *Note: The two 5-day sessions in the 2nd year primarily are application-oriented and entail applying the learning. The objective is for students to relate their learning to an actual real-life situation in an existing NGO. (By the time students start with this module they do have the theoretical knowledge of how to set up an NGO.)*	1st 6 months Module 3	2nd 6 months Module 4

pro bono? "So, what do you gain from making this change? Doesn't this actually add to your time commitment?"

Paru shrugged. "After the initial years, the international development agencies' funding cycle expired. Kadal was unable to compensate me much for my workshops. But I decided to continue to offer the workshops practically for free because I believe it can, and is, making a difference in the education of the social work students who, in turn, are better equipped to make an impact on the communities they work in."

Mohana smiled admiringly at Paru's commitment. Paru had always been generous with her time and efforts when it came to helping others and had a big heart.

"So, I am wondering if, and how, online learning can be deployed?" Paru asked expectantly.

When Mohana finally got off the phone at the conclusion of the long video call with Paru, she was still feeling somewhat annoyed by the call quality. Is India making *any* progress, Mohana wondered, ruefully. But then, she reminded herself, the call quality had been pretty good during their previous few phone conversations. A few years ago, video calls to India using mobile technologies were a mere fantasy, so India was rapidly progressing, at least in certain sectors. As she finished writing up her notes, Mohana rubbed her eyes and looked through the large open windows of her suburban Chicago home. She was an avid gardener and maintained a beautiful yard. Had rabbits chewed on her plants, again? Darn. At least here in the American Midwest, she did not have to watch out for monkeys entering her home.

CAN "AMERICAN" LEARNING DESIGN AND TECHNOLOGY HELP?

Mohana got into her car and set out on her daily commute to her university located in downtown Chicago. It was a beautiful late summer morning, but the air felt less humid and the sunlight seemed to have turned softer and more golden, a harbinger of fall. As she drove toward downtown, she reflected on her conversation with Paru. Her music app came on and the shuffle play setting pulled up one of her favorite Bollywood songs, bringing back memories of her student days in Delhi. She remembered the scorching Delhi summers. The dorms at their university had no air conditioning. She and Paru would try to cool the verandah outside their room by throwing buckets of water on the cement floors. The floors would sizzle and almost instantly dry because they were so hot! The traffic on the interstate leading to Chicago was thick and moved slowly, but it was nowhere as horrendous as the congestion, noise, pollution, and utter chaos of Indian roads.

Her mind switched back to her workday. In her annual budget she had asked her university for funds to update two of the four multimedia instructional and collaborative spaces she oversaw. But she had received approval for updating only one room. Although she was disappointed, she was glad for the support that she got. Today, she needed to discuss the installation of large touch-screens in the newly redesigned student collaborative learning spaces and plan the faculty training sessions on their new learning management system (LMS) with the instructional designer. Her work environment in the US had resource limitations, but they were nowhere as acute as Paru's.

Paru had been skeptical about how online components might be integrated into her workshop. "I really don't know how much of what you do in the US would work here," she had said. Kadal University could not afford an LMS such as the ones used in the US. The department, at best, had a handful of computers and would need university funding to establish a computer lab. Internet connectivity and power outages were challenges at Kadal as they were in most parts of India. So, the university would need to improve its wired and wireless networks.

Paru had reiterated that establishing adequate communications infrastructure, expanding the curriculum, developing content for online components, and inviting experts were all ideas that had costs attached. Also, any changes she proposed to the workshop modules would need to be sustainable and would require resources that neither Paru nor the university had. She had mentioned, more as an afterthought, that the department chair seemed willing to make a case to the university about strengthening the communications infrastructure and was even considering applying for some grant funding. "But that is really a long shot," Paru had said.

Mohana wondered how could she apply the instructional design she taught and practiced in the US in the Indian context and adjust her "Western" approach to the complexities of Paru's situation?

Preliminary Analysis Questions

1. Identify the relevant cultural and contextual factors in this case. Analyze how these factors affect the learning design issues.
2. Given Mohana's cultural and educational background, does she have an *insider* or an *outsider* perspective in this case? What are the advantages and disadvantages to having each perspective as an instructional designer?

3. How might Mohana adapt instructional design practices to address the constraints in the Indian context?
4. Create a plan that Mohana can use to address Paru's needs with regard to the expanded workshop using an online format. Consider the limitations of deploying a standard LMS in Paru's situation and explore non-conventional technology options to deliver instruction including but not restricted to mobile devices such as telephones, and social media and communication software such as Facebook and WhatsApp, specifically in the Indian socioeconomic context.

Implications for ID Practice

1. There are a number of practical implications for a US-educated instructional designer working in a developing country. Consider the following:
   a. Different populations may have different beliefs about what constitutes learning, how best to bring it about, and how to assess it. How might a US-educated instructional designer engage with these beliefs, especially if they are antithetical to their own beliefs?
   b. Resources are commonly an acute paucity in the developing world. How can an instructional designer practice "good" instructional design even with extreme resource limitations? What are some strategies that could be helpful?
   c. When designing instruction for the developing world, what factors should inform an instructional designer's choices for technologies for learning?
   d. How can instructional designers deal with the implementation and evaluation issues that occur in the developing world?
   e. Different populations may have different work ethics and communication practices. How can instructional designers work with these populations?
2. Assume you are invited to be an instructional design consultant for a client in a developing country:
   a. What does designing solutions *for* versus *together with* the client mean to you?
   b. How can an instructional design consultant counteract the tendency to want to "fix" what they might perceive as not being "normal," especially in terms of different ideas about learning?
   c. How would you translate your ideas into action?
3. Instructional design consultants need to possess cultural, linguistic, geographical, and socio-political competence. How might designers gain these competencies during their graduate programs?

18

Jane Rogers and Kayla Wilson

Navigating Between Instructor and Student Needs

Jiyoon Jung

Dr. Jane Rogers, a former high school English teacher, had become an assistant professor of educational studies at Merryville University, a regional comprehensive university located in southern Georgia. The university offered fully online master's programs designed for working professionals seeking to change or advance their careers.

A NEW COURSE ASSIGNMENT

Two weeks prior to the start of Jane's first semester at Merryville, she had a meeting scheduled with her department head, Dr. Jerold Hobson, to discuss the courses assigned to her. As Jane entered Dr. Hobson's office, he warmly greeted her, saying, "Welcome to Merryville University, Jane. Please have a seat. I hope you're settling in well."

Taking a seat, Jane replied, "Thank you, Dr. Hobson. The move went smoothly, and we're all adjusting well."

Dr. Hobson continued the conversation, saying, "I'm glad to hear that! As I mentioned in my earlier email, you'll be teaching a master's course called 'Instructional Videos.' While I used to teach this course at a different university, it's a new addition here. I can provide you with my previous syllabus, but you'll need to handle the course development. Are you familiar with D2L, Design to Learn?"

Dr. Hobson continued as Jane shook her head. "Well, D2L is the learning management system that we use. It's very similar to other major learning management systems such as Canvas."

Jane responded, "Okay. I have used Canvas before."

"Good," said Dr. Hobson, "it's pretty straightforward. However, if you need help, you can visit the eLearning Center on campus. They provide professional learning sessions about D2L. I think you will enjoy teaching this course because it fits your expertise in information literacy and video-based content development."

Jane responded, "Great! I am super excited to teach this course. It seems to offer a great opportunity to discuss media literacy in an authentic manner. I love it when I can easily contextualize learning to resemble real-world settings. I think it really enhances student

DOI: 10.4324/9781003354468-20

learning. What are the student demographics for this course? What's the typical student like? Do you know?"

Dr. Hobson answered, "This course focuses primarily on learning one specific video editing tool, Adobe Premiere Pro. Since most students in the course are K–12 teachers, few have ever used it. However, currently there are at least two professional video content developers enrolled in your course who may have more experience. But don't worry. They should know this course is for beginners." Dr. Hobson and Jane continued their conversation a little more, and Jane left his office with a lot to think about as she planned her next move.

Jane was concerned about the potential diversity in students' experience levels, but she had to rush development as the semester was about to start. She adopted the two textbooks Dr. Hobson recommended and planned to develop content based on the sequence of the book chapters. In order to save development time, she was also advised by Dr. Hobson to use the Premiere Pro tutorials on YouTube as opposed to trying to create her own.

DESIGNING THE NEW COURSE

As Jane considered potential class activities and learning artifacts, she tried to follow the principles of authentic learning design proposed by Herrington et al. (2014), which had stuck with her from her doctoral years. The authors suggested focusing on authentic contexts, authentic tasks, modeling, multiple roles/perspectives, collaborative construction of knowledge, reflection, articulation, coaching/scaffolding, and authentic assessment to promote deep learning.

Jane thought, "I could provide learners with an authentic task of creating instructional videos that they could use in their own settings . . ." As she was brainstorming, she created

Week	Module/Topic	Reading	Graded Activity and Assignments								
			Discussion (5%)	Script (5%)	Storyboarding (10%)	Interview video (15%)	Demonstration video (15%)	Audio (5%)	Graphics (5%)	Instructional Video (30%)	Quiz (10%)
	Unit 1: Getting started										
W01	Orientation	Syllabus Dockery (1, ACA Objectives)	Introduction								
W02	Process, concepts, project set up	Dockery (1, 6) Jago (1, 2)	Reverse storyboarding	X							
W03	Theories and principles	Jago (3, 4)	Video analysis		X						
	Unit 2: Practice your skills										
W04	Video editing techniques	Jago (5~9)	Reflective learning journal								
W05	Interview & Action scene	Dockery (2, 3)				X					
W06	Audio	Jago (10, 11)						x			
W07	Graphics & Exporting	Jago (15, 16)							x		
W08	Green screen & slide show	Dockery (4, 5)					x				
Midterm											
	Unit 3: Be a producer										
W09	Development	Review	Reflective learning journal							o	
W10	No Class – Spring Break										
W11	Preproduction	Review	Peer critique – Script							o	
W12	Production	Review	Peer critique – Storyboard								
W13	Production / Postproduction	Review									x
W14	Postproduction	Review								o	
W15	Student presentation	N/A	Peer critique - Video								x
W16	Wrap up	N/A	Course reflection Post-survey							x	

FIGURE 18.1 Semester 1 course schedule.

a rough course schedule, consisting of three key components she thought were important to cover: introduction to the basics of instructional videos, learning video editing skills, and an authentic project. These later became "units" in the final course schedule (see Figure 18.1).

In particular, the first unit, Getting Started, covered basic concepts and the process of video production, technology setup, and multimedia learning design principles. The second unit, Practice Your Skills, focused on learning how to use Premiere Pro through the creation of two short videos (Interview and Demonstration), and the final unit, Be a Producer, focused on completing a longer instructional video with less instructor guidance.

While developing the course schedule, Jane also brainstormed ideas highlighting the main instructional design strategies that aligned with the nine authentic learning design principles (see Figure 18.2). The strategies were constantly refined as she revised the schedule to meet the practical constraints (e.g., content coverage, development time, reasonable sequence).

Once the plan was set, Jane started creating materials to assist with the weekly activities and assignments. As instructional supports, Jane provided steps, resources, and tools for the learning activities (e.g., textbook readings, scripting, storyboarding, video production and editing, discussions, reflective journaling). These were organized by week in the university's learning management system, D2L.

AUTHENTIC LEARNING DESIGN PRINCIPLES...

- ☐ Authentic Context
  - ✓ Access to the tool (Premiere Pro)
  - ✓ Lists of existing resources and tutorials
- ☐ Authentic Task: "Create a 5-7 minutes long instructional video one could use in their own setting"
- ☐ Modeling → selected instructional videos from YouTube
- ☐ Multiple Roles/Perspectives → Class discussions on "good" instructional videos
- ☐ Collaborative Construction of Knowledge → Peer review
- ☐ Reflection → after each module...
- ☐ Articulation → Class presentation of student videos → Video gallery?
- ☐ Coaching/Scaffolding → Practice Tasks & on-going instructor feedback → Focus on trying. No harsh grading!
- ☐ Authentic Assessment → Rubric
  - ✓ Content & Format: Length, Professionalism
  - ✓ Theory Application: Coherency, Contiguity
  - ✓ Production: Video/Audio Quality, Dynamic/Engaging Scenes
  - ✓ Post-Production: Instructional Cues, Effects/Transitions
  - ✓ Supplementary Materials

FIGURE 18.2 Jane's notes on main instructional strategies.

AFTER THE FIRST IMPLEMENTATION

The first implementation of the newly designed course went by fast for Jane. Because the course had not been fully developed prior to implementation, she constantly had to push herself to develop new content as she published a new module each week.

After the first semester, Jane reviewed her students' reactions from the course evaluation forms. Some students commented that it was a "great class" that effectively taught complex concepts, but more students thought the class was too challenging. One student commented, "Dr. Rogers taught the course as if all students were familiar with video editing. It was a very confusing course, and the assignments were not well explained." Several students expressed wanting "video tutorials." Students also talked about grading being too slow and too harsh.

Frustrated, Jane decided to get some external help. She asked other faculty members for suggestions, and they recommended contacting the eLearning Center on campus.

FIRST CONSULTATION WITH THE INSTRUCTIONAL DESIGNER

After consulting with colleagues, Jane made an appointment at the eLearning Center near the beginning of the summer term. The center had a team of instructional designers and technologists who supported faculty, staff, and students' online, hybrid, and educational technology needs.

Two highly capable instructional designers worked in the eLearning Center. However, like other units at the university, the center was suffering from budget cuts while managing a heavy workload. To worsen the problem, one of the center's instructional designers was placed on a multi-year project involving major instructional design work. This left the other instructional designer, Kayla Wilson, to support all faculty needs related to online instruction at the university.

Kayla had worked as an instructional designer at Merryville for three years. Previously, she worked as a media specialist at a local middle school, but after completing a master's degree in instructional design (ID) at Merryville, she fell in love with ID work. She enjoyed working for the university where there was a relatively long history of online learning. One day in May, Jane sent a help request to Kayla.

Using the archived course, Kayla completed a formal evaluation of Jane's course using a rubric created by the eLearning Center. In reviewing the evaluation, Jane noted that Kayla pointed out several areas for improvement: students' weekly workload, information presentation in the syllabus and the course schedule, as well as strategies for providing visual support to accommodate diverse learning needs (see Figure 18.3).

Upon receipt of the evaluation, Jane asked Kayla for a virtual consultation. After a short friendly conversation, Jane got to the point: "Thank you, Kayla, for all of the suggestions. There are certainly areas I can work on based on your feedback. I am not sure how much content I should cut. I want my course to help students create an instructional video-given a request-just like they would be expected to do in the real world. I did not think what I asked in this course was too much."

Kayla responded, "I see your point, Dr. Rogers. However, you should acknowledge that your students are not traditional students. They mostly work full time and have family members to take care of. With these students, it's sometimes better to focus on a limited number of key activities, provide clearer guidance, and do more formative than summative assessments. And of course, as you know, this is a mostly asynchronous online class."

Overview

To evaluate the course, the overall structure and content of the course were reviewed, along with how they contributed to student comprehension and learning success.

This is a rigorous course that engages students through discussion forums, quizzes, and several multimedia production activities and projects, so there are learner-content and learner-learner interactions.

There are two required textbooks, as well as a number of tutorials and supporting resources for students to review. This extra time must be taken into consideration when calculating the workload hours for each week. Estimates can be listed in the course schedule for students (see recommendation below).

The alignment of module objectives to course content is thorough. However, the way this information is presented in the syllabus is confusing. Consider simplifying the layout by modifying the course schedule into a detailed "course map" with module names, topics, open/close dates, learning objectives, types of assessments (i.e., quiz, discussion, etc.), and specific learning activities (see recommendation below). Also, it's important to provide a clear explanation of **why** students need to know the material and **when** they will apply the knowledge.

Additionally, the course should follow Universal Design for Learning (UDL) principles whenever possible, so there are fewer barriers to student learning and outcomes are more achievable. According to Amanda Morin (n.d.), Writer and Senior Expert at Understood, some students prefer learning new information visually. Others learn better by listening to information, by finding patterns, or by working with other people. Most students learn best through combinations of these areas of strengths.

The following evaluation and recommendations show research-based reasoning for restructuring the course based on instructional design best practices, UDL principles, and the Course Design Rubric utilized at Merryville.

FIGURE 18.3 Overview of Kayla's evaluation of Dr. Rogers' course.

After pausing a moment to reflect, Jane commented, "I think I can reduce the number of videos students are asked to create, which will eliminate the need to use two textbooks. But when it comes to providing clearer guidance, I am not sure how clear it needs to be. Sometimes, I think all they want is the answer. They asked me for samples, but I don't want to limit their creativity by giving them specific examples. I do share the basic steps they should follow for assignments through support-like hints, but it sounds like they expect step-by-step guidance. I want to help my students, but giving detailed guidance goes completely against my beliefs about authentic tasks. I actually want them to struggle a bit."

Kayla responded, "Dr. Rogers, I understand what you are saying. But what if your ideas of 'struggling a bit' are, in fact, too much for your students to handle? Sharing student samples helps ease student concerns about course grades because it allows them to visualize your expectations."

Jane admitted reluctantly, "I see your point. However, realistically speaking, I currently have no time or energy to create a sample for my students. I also am not sure what level of work I should show my students to reference. I don't want my students to think that the work is impossible for them to accomplish, but I also do not want to show a sample that is mediocre—I want the samples to be good."

Kayla nodded, and Jane continued, "Since this course is new, I don't have any past student work to show my current students. My tasks are intentionally open-ended to allow

1. Manage student workload
    - Reduce the number of unguided video production projects
    - Expand weeks spent on Premiere Pro practice with guidance
    - Reduce student time spent on steps that are not crucial (e.g., script writing, storyboarding).
2. Organize content around topics (not weeks)
   → students get a better sense of what they are learning
3. Provide tutorials or student samples when possible.
4. Use multiple modes of supporting learning: video tutorials, job-aids, and synchronous sessions.
5. Simplify the weekly assessment rubric & clearer expectations.

FIGURE 18.4 Jane's list of course revisions.

students to work on their choices of real-world topics. I am already stretching myself to provide quality feedback each week, tailored to everyone who is doing something slightly different, not to mention the two other courses I have had to develop and teach at the same time. I am using rubrics, but it's sometimes just too much to understand why and how my students make mistakes in their uniquely designed assignments to provide meaningful feedback."

After the conclusion of the first consultation, Jane and Kayla agreed to meet in a week, once they both had a chance to consider remaining questions regarding how to streamline the instruction and effectively design and facilitate an online problem-centered course. A week later, Jane met with Kayla and created a list of revisions for the course (see Figure 18.4). Based on the list, Jane worked with Kayla for a couple of days to streamline the course content and develop additional learning resources.

FIRST COURSE REVISION FOR THE SECOND IMPLEMENTATION

The three-unit structure of the course was kept for the second implementation in the following spring semester. However, Jane made multiple changes. First, she replaced the two short video production tasks (e.g., interview and demonstration videos) and other multimedia component development tasks (e.g., audios, graphics) with a series of weekly practice tasks focused on learning major skills (e.g., applying effects and transitions) in hopes to better prepare students.

In fact, Jane made many design changes to reduce the overall student workload. For example, she decided to use one textbook (instead of two) and integrated the pre-production tasks, such as script writing and storyboarding, as informal components of the final video production project. She also kept only one quiz (instead of two), one peer review activity

Week	Module/Topic	Reading	Activity	Project	Pts.
1	0. Getting started	Ch1, Ch2	Kick-off meeting (2%) Quiz: Syllabus quiz Discussion: Meet-and-Greet Practice: Set up a Premiere Pro project (3%)		5
2	1. Tools and practice	Ch16	Learn: Video production tools and practice Practice: Export and share (3%) Discussion: Which type of instructional video should I make? (4%)	Submit: Script	7
3	2. Theories and principles	TBD	Learn: Theories and principles for video-based learning Discussion: How should I chunk my learning content? (4%)		4
4	3. Creating and editing videos	Ch3-Ch6	Practice: Record a quality video (3%) Practice: Organize a sequence (3%)	Submit: Storyboard	6
5		Ch7-Ch9, Ch12	Practice: Enhance video quality (3%) Practice: Apply effects and transitions (3%)		6
6	4. Creating and editing audios	Ch10-Ch11	Practice: Record a quality audio (3%) Practice: Enhance audio quality (3%)	Edit the storyboard	6
7	5. Using Graphics	Ch15	Practice: Apply simple graphic motion (3%) Discussion: Create an Animation	Start preparing assets	3
8			Practice: Apply the multimedia learning principles (3%) Discussion: What strategies should I use to maximize the impact of the video on learning (4%)		7
Midterm					
9	6. Other Techniques & Review	CH13-Ch14	Practice: Color correction/grading, compositing techniques Quiz: Review (4%)	Submit: Project Plan (10%)	14
10	No Class –Spring Break				
11	7. Instructional Video Production		Workshop: Opening and body sequence (Schedule a check-in meeting with the instructor for personalized assistance on the project. A slot will be offered each week. A student needs to attend one of them.) (Check-in meeting, 2%)	Submit: Screenshot of assets Start editing on PP	2
12					
13					
14					
15			Discussion: Publish and share	Multimedia assets and sequences properly packaged	0
16	Wrap up		Workshop: Complete the Project Report Student Opinion of Instruction	Submit: Project Report (40%)	40

FIGURE 18.5 Revised course schedule.

(as opposed to three), and one semester-end reflection (instead of requiring the three reflective learning journals at the end of each unit).

Furthermore, Jane revised the discussion activities to better support students to successfully complete the final instructional design project. She used driving questions to orient students to think about the instructional video they would create in the latter part of the semester. The three questions were as follows: *Which type of instructional video should I make? How should I chunk my learning content? What strategies should I use to maximize the impact of the video on learning?*

To further help students easily understand the design intent and navigate the new course, Jane added synchronous meetings to be held at the beginning of the semester (i.e., kickoff meeting) and during the final project period (i.e., individual check-in meetings)

During development, Jane attempted to present the revised course design information in a more student-friendly manner. She revised the course schedule as a roadmap to foreground the weekly learning activities, the project, and the points to be earned each week (see Figure 18.5). The modules were also labeled by topic at the first level, as opposed to by week. Modules that spanned multiple weeks included sub-modules labeled by week.

A key change was reflected in the support material provided for the skill-building practice tasks. In total, she had 11 practice tasks, and 10 of these were worth 3% of the course grade each. Previously, such practice tasks, were guided minimally with instruction, requirements (specification of the expected outcomes), and tips. The tips were mostly text-based and included hyperlinks to external resources. Recognizing how students were generally in need of more targeted support, Jane created a presentation for each practice task this time and provided more detailed and multimedia-based guidelines (see Figure 18.6).

Table of Contents › Week 04-05 › Interview video

Interview video

Instructions

Shoot and edit a two minute video in which you interview one or more subjects about a given topic. The final product will be an informational video aiding viewers in learning more about the given topic.

Requirements

- Length: about 2 minutes
- Format: interview (outdoor/indoor with some background noise during recording) + B-roll
- Topic: Your choice
- Edit with Adobe Premiere Pro CC
  - Reduce noise and reduce rumble using the Essential Sound panel
  - Change the volume using the audio keyframes
  - Add a background music where appropriate
  - Perform basic color correction (white balance, tone, saturation) using the Lumetri Color panel
  - Add a jump cut
  - Add a B-roll clip
  - Change a clip speed/duration at least once

Tip: Plan your interview questions or action scenes prior to shooting.

Submission

- Submit a zip file of your project file and the media assets used.
- Submit the edited interview video

Table of Contents › Creating and Editing Videos (W4-W5) › Submit Your Practice Task Outcomes

W4a: Submit Your Practice Task Outcomes

Instructions

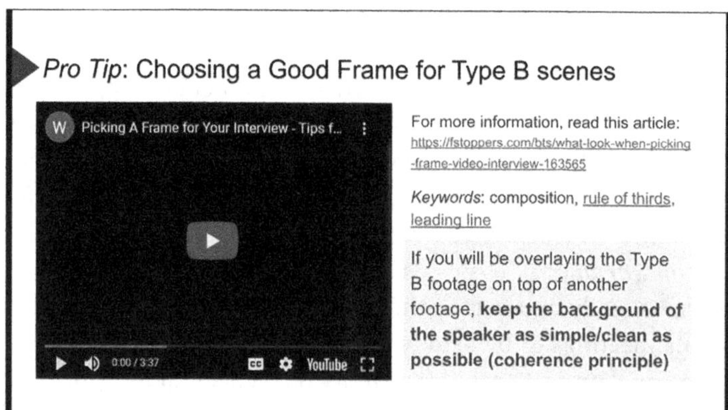

Record Type A, B, and C scenes that are about 10 seconds long each and demonstrate the following:

- The Type A scene (voice-over presentation) have at least two instances of narration-text/image syncing.
- The Type B scene (lecture/interview) have good lighting and background (composition).
- The Type C scene (demonstration) have shots from two different angles OR include a POV shot and a full shot OR .

Save each recording with a file name indicating the scene type and the content. For example, if you recorded a voice-over presentation on the concept of photography, you will name the clip as "A_photography."

Submit the three types of scenes recorded as file attachments. For this assignment, audio/narration needs to be included but its quality does not need to be of a concern.

FIGURE 18.6 Minimally guided (top) vs. guided (bottom) practice tasks.

THE SECOND IMPLEMENTATION

Similar to Jane's first semester, the second spring semester went by quickly, and the class had already moved into its last instructional module after spring break. Jane was offering synchronous project check-in sessions with individual students. So far, students appeared to be less stressed about completing the weekly practice tasks to learn basic Premiere Pro techniques. There were still some emails asking for additional help, but it was manageable for Jane. However, one student's comment during the check-in session caught her off guard.

The student, Becky, said, "I know you are doing your best, but I feel like I am failing this course. I am never going to be a professional videographer but what you expect me to do every week is just beyond overwhelming, and I constantly find myself trying to keep up to get a passing grade."

Jane was a little confused because the student did not stand out in the gradebook as someone needing extra help. She asked the student empathetically, "Becky, I am sorry that you are feeling that way. Can you share why you are feeling so overwhelmed with the class?"

Becky responded with some hesitation, "I have a minor case of dyslexia so trying to read your instructions while performing the steps with Premiere Pro has been very challenging. I chose this class because I thought it would be a fun video making class without much need for reading instructions. Your guidelines are certainly helpful, but they are too much to read. I tried to use the screen reader, but it did not work well with the visuals and embedded materials."

Jane responded with surprise and a bit of embarrassment, "Oh my! I had not thought about those. I am sorry you had to go through it. Let me figure out if there is anything I can do to minimize your burden."

SECOND CONSULTATION WITH KAYLA AND COURSE REVISION

After the session with Becky, Jane reached out to Kayla to get more help. Once Jane explained her situation, Kayla shared a checklist that summarized how to meet the Americans with Disabilities Act (ADA) requirements in online courses (see Figure 18.7).

Kayla commented, "Strategies for following some of these guidelines are as easy as turning on the closed-captioning feature when recording or uploading the tutorial videos. I think the biggest area of concern in your course is that you have embedded slides and videos or images without text descriptions, which makes reading hard for screen readers. I can help you meet these guidelines later in the summer. For now, I think it's best to format your instruction and guideline documents properly and avoid using embedded elements. I can also show you how you can add descriptions to an image."

At the suggestion of more updates, Jane felt frustrated that she would be required to spend additional time and effort on continued development. But she agreed to attend to the ADA guidelines when publishing new materials for the remaining weeks of the semester to support her students. Jane decided to use easily downloadable Word documents with necessary images and hyperlinks to be ADA compliant, instead of creating slide presentations with embedded images and videos to ensure accessibility while minimizing her development workload.

When the semester was over, Jane was glad that she was finally able to ask Kayla for more help. Kayla was assigned to another big project for the summer, but she agreed to help Jane as this was something she had previously agreed to do. Together, they reviewed and created

Type	Guideline	Yes	No	N/A
Link	• Use text descriptions for the links, instead of "click here."			
Text	• Use sans serif fonts for easy readability. • Use dark font colors on light backgrounds (preferably use black text on a white background). • Avoid extremely bright colors as a background color. • Use one font throughout the site. • Avoid overuse of ALL CAPS, **bold** or *italics*. • Avoid underlining words, as the screen reader can mistake it for a navigation link.			
Image	• Use images for a clear purpose. • Use image files that are optimized for efficient loading. • Limit the use of animated images to only those that contribute to the learning experience supporting the course content. • Avoid animated or blinking images, text or cursors. These can cause seizures for some people. • All images have alt texts/long descriptions attached to them.			
Audio/Video	• Use audio/video files with clear quality. • Use audio/video files with an adequate length to meet the goals of the activity. o Without being too large to restrict users' ability to download the file on computers with lower bandwidths. o Without adding unnecessary information. • Provide a written transcript or closed captioning for all audio/video files. • Use audio/video files that requires a player that is compatible with multiple operating systems and requires only a standard and free plug-in.			

FIGURE 18.7 Checklist for ADA compliance in online courses.

the guidelines for the remaining practice tasks to better comply with the ADA compliance checklist, resulting in another busy summer.

SECOND COURSE REVISION FOR THE THIRD IMPLEMENTATION

In addition to developing accessible Practice Task Guidelines, Jane revised the course content by cleaning up the module structure. In particular, she provided Module Instructions for each module (see Figure 18.8), documents that listed learning objectives and described an overview of the weekly activities. Jane also prepared a Practice Task document (specifying the task with required edits and examples) and a Practice Task Guideline document (detailing learning resources, task specification, and assessment criteria) for each practice task in Module 3.

Jane further reduced the number of practice tasks from 11 to 7 by removing some of the video editing techniques that were not frequently used by previous students. Jane also informed students that they could perform practice tasks to create video sequences and resources for use in their final instructional video projects, so they could save time with the project.

LAST CONSULTATION: HOW FAR DO I NEED TO GO?

After the third implementation, Jane again reviewed student feedback. While the overall course evaluation score improved, the students still wanted more guidance on how to perform certain tasks and "an actual sample video of the expectations of the practice tasks."

M3. Practice Tasks (W4-W9)

Learning Objectives

- Effectively utilize video editing tools (e.g. Adobe Premiere) for instruction.
- Effectively utilize audio editing tools (e.g. Adobe Audition) for instruction.
- Render video products in formats for online delivery.
- Prepare for industry-recognized post-production skill certification exam (eg, Adobe Certified Associate exam).

Module Overview

Prior to this module, you should have access to Premiere Pro, Audition, Media Encoder and have read Chapters 1-4 of the textbook. These chapters explain basic but technical concepts, including program interface (p. 22) and set up, you should know before you start editing with Premiere Pro. You should also have learned the basics of instructional video design, including multimedia learning principles.

We will focus on practicing your video editing skills in this module, which is designed to span across ***six*** weeks. Each week, you should read the **Weekly Activity** instruction sheet that summarizes weekly assigned **Readings** with instructor highlights and **Practice Tasks**, consisting of key Premiere Pro editing tasks sequenced to follow a common post-production process. Sometimes, you have an additional assignment designed to prepare you for the larger video projects (**Video Project Prep**).

Week	Textbook Reading	Practice Task	Video Project Prep
4	Ch5. Editing Video—The Essentials Ch6. Working with Clips and Markers	Recording Set Up and Cut Edits	Draft "Project Overview" and "Project Timeline" of the report for instructor feedback.
5	Ch7. Adding Transitions Ch8. Editing Video—Advanced Techniques Ch13. Applying Color Correction and Grading	Precision Edit, Color Grading/Correction, Transition, and Nesting	Work on the project on your own as planned. Make sure important recording schedules are set. Optionally, you can submit a script or storyboard for instructor feedback.
6	Ch7. Adding Transitions Ch10. Editing and Mixing Audio Ch11. Improving Audio	Improving Audio and Mixing	
7	Ch9. Putting Clips in Motion Ch12. Adding Video Effects	Motion Effects with Ease In/Out, Tracked Masking, and Inserts	
8	Ch14. Exploring Compositing Techniques	Compositing, Graphic Layering	
9	Ch15. Creating New Graphics Ch16. Exporting Frames, Clips, and Sequences	Highlighting, Title and Logo, Animation, Exporting and Sharing	

FIGURE 18.8 Module instruction (top), practice task (middle), and practice task guidelines (bottom).

W4 Practice Task: Recording Set Up and Cut Edits

Create a less-than-a-minute-long interview video with A-roll and B-roll shots for general audience to view on a computer screen (landscape mode).

Required Edits

a) Includes clips with names indicating A-roll and B-roll.
b) Include a jump cut within your B-roll shots.
c) Include a J or L cut to cover a portion of the A-roll audio with B-roll video

Example

Watch from 0:07 to 0:53 of this video by XXX.

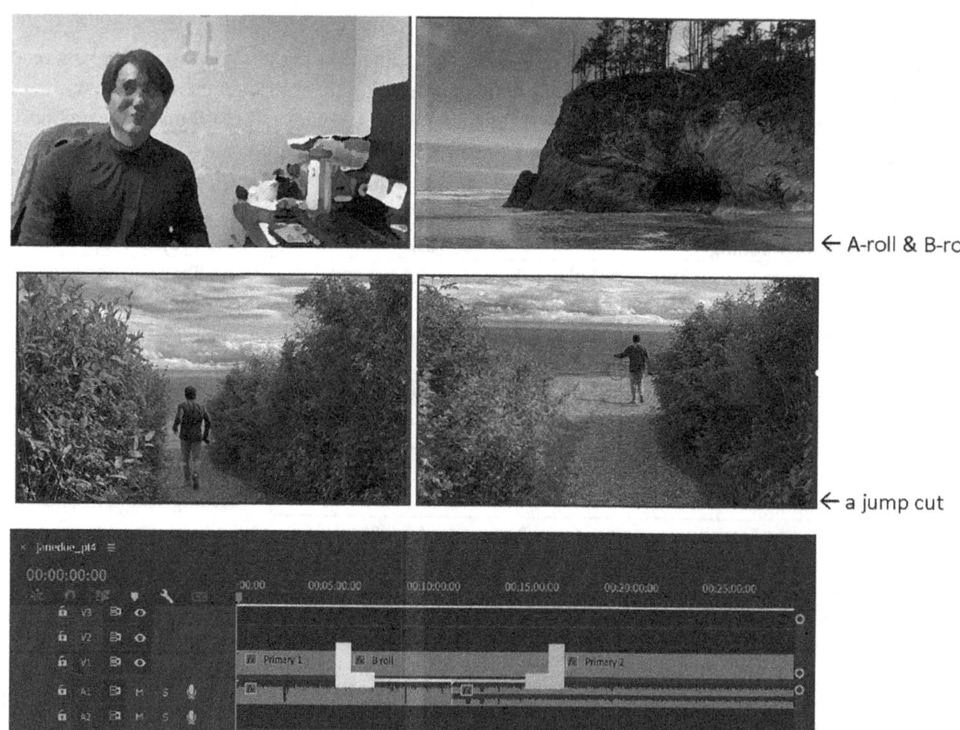

← A-roll & B-roll

← a jump cut

← J or L cuts should be evident through the screenshot of your timeline panel where the cut edits are performed.

FIGURE 18.8 Continued

W4 Practice Task Guidelines: Recording Set Up and Cut Edits

RECORDING SET UP >>

If you are doing a cooking video, your A-roll will be yourself describing what recipe will be introduced, why you chose the recipe, and what kind of audience this video is targeting. Your B-roll will then be a scene of the kitchen with yourself moving in it to prepare for a shoot (e.g., the video clip on this page).

If you are doing an interview video, your A-roll will be the interviewee talking about something while the B-roll is a scene describing the things that are talked about.

Shooting footage can be challenging for one person. If you have a family member or a friend who can help you as the person behind the video camera or the person who would be performing action for your video, you are more than welcome to *have an assistant*.

For a steady shot, place the camera on a flat and stable surface or get a camera tripod/stand/holder. Make sure there is no obstacle between the camera and the main character.

You can use your phone camera, as long as it produces good quality videos. However, keep in mind that you *record in a landscape mode*, as opposed to a portrait mode.

Because you don't know if the footage is good enough, it would be wise to *take multiple shoots* for the planned scenes.

1. **Write a script** for your A-roll (about half a page) based on the information in the "Key Messages" column of this spreadsheet. You should assume that the scripted messages will be narrated by an interviewee later. For the Practice Task, you will read the script.
   Schedule the actual interview during Week 4 ~ Week 9 (before the Spring Break).
2. Ideally you would create a storyboard to visually plan for shooting. You are not required to do the storyboard this time, but here is a template (word, pdf) for your reference.
3. Prepare the equipment. Video camera, mic, stand, lighting, etc. Make sure that you test your audio before you record the scenes. Although it is not required, having good lighting enhances your video dramatically. If you are interested, watch this video about 3-point lighting set-up for more information. Set up with the following considerations:
   a. **Location**: Pick a location that is thematically appropriate, interesting, and has good lighting. Remove any unnecessary clutter. Which room to choose? Location Scouting 101 – Tips for Shooting Professional Video Interviews
   b. **Frame**: Now that you have decided the location, what background will you be shooting against? What angle should you have for your camera? Test out different frames to pick the one that best works for your video. Which frame to choose? Picking a Frame for Your Interview – Tips for Shooting Professional Video Interviews. Check out this video on Rules of Framing and Composition for information on: The Rule of Thirds, Symmetry, Leading Lines, Leading Room or Head Room, Depth, Size Equals Power, how these rules should be used.

FIGURE 18.8 Continued

Another student wanted "live class sessions" or tutorials demonstrating the features of the software. A couple of students however wanted more projects, "more smaller projects/videos would be helpful." Another student commented, "If we could work on the final project throughout the semester instead of the last few weeks . . ."

Jane sat in her office and wondered, "Even if I had time to provide all they wanted me to provide, the course would no longer be what I want it to be. This was supposed to prepare students to be job-ready, but I doubt that a person with this much video editing skills would be competitive in professional positions."

Jane looked at her third version of the course, which appeared drastically simplified and highly structured from her perspective. She questioned how many accommodations were enough. She thought that some of the students were taking advantage of the tasks that were overly simple. Those who seemed familiar with the tool had posted their work really early in the semester, or they showed up for the mid-point check-in meetings with little work done and were still able to complete the project with fair quality. Reflecting on all this, Jane sat down and wrote an email to Kayla in frustration (see Figure 18.9).

From: Rogers, Jane <jrogers@merryville.edu>

Sent: May 10 at 11:36 A.M.

To: Kayla Wilson <kwilson@merryville.edu>

Subject: Thank You

Kayla,

Thanks for meeting with me again.

When I first designed the course, I did not want to provide step-by-step guidelines or worked samples as I believed these constrained students' thoughts and learning. I also thought that graduate students would be more self-directed and prefer flexibility in their coursework. I wanted my students to be able to problem solve on their own, eventually without assistance, through this course. This is what I thought should have happened.

The course already looks like spoon-feeding to me, and my students want even more. I am not sure what to do. How far do I need to go to meet the students' needs?

After all of these revisions, my students are still wanting more guidance. First, I thought that these students could easily find the resources—including the video tutorials—that they needed online, like through YouTube, given how popular these topics are these days. I actually had a couple of students who had their own YouTube channels. For these students, I feared that the course would be too easy and boring. But I guess I was wrong. And frankly, it has been really hard trying to develop all the supporting materials as I was teaching. Knowing that it is never going to be enough really frustrates me.

Any advice?

Jane

Jane Rogers, PhD
Assistant Professor

FIGURE 18.9 Jane's last email to Kayla.

Preliminary Analysis Questions

1. Consider the concerns Jane experienced at the beginning, throughout, and at the end of the case. How did these concerns stay the same and how did they change?
2. What are some of the unique challenges Jane faced when designing an online, graduate-level course that promotes self-directed learning and open-ended problem solving?
3. How can Jane support the development of her students' problem-solving skills without frustrating her students or over-structuring the authentic tasks?

Implications for ID Practice

1. How much support is "just right" when designing an authentic learning environment that asks students to complete more open-ended and real-world problem-based assignments?
2. How should an instructional designer (or faculty designing online courses) address accessibility concerns in online course design? Whose responsibility is it to ensure that the course is ADA compliant?
3. What are different ways in which diverse learner needs (motivational, intellectual, developmental, physical, linguistic, emotional, or cultural) could conflict with providing authentic learning experiences? How should designers balance these needs?

REFERENCES

Herrington, J., Reeves, T. C., & Oliver, R. (2014). Authentic learning environments. In J. M. Spector, M. D., Merrill, J. Elen, & M. J. Bishop (Eds.), *Handbook of research on educational communications and technology* (4th ed., pp. 401–412). Springer.

Morin, A. (n.d.). Learning options for your child's thinking style. Understood.org. https://www.understood.org/articles/learning-options-for-your-childs-thinking-style

Part III

Industry

19

Desmond Brower

Handling Challenges When Subcontracting as an External Needs Assessor

William L. Solomonson

FRIDAY, AUGUST 3

Desmond Brower, an independent performance consultant working in the areas of manufacturing and retail, was looking through his inbox, when the email, "Subject: Needs Assessment Opportunity" caught his eye (see Figure 19.1). So far this had been a good year for Desmond and he had been getting about as much work as he could handle, which offered him the luxury of being able to be somewhat selective in his choice of clients and projects. At the same time, Desmond knew that landing new projects was always a business imperative, and a needs assessment project did not present itself every day. He opened the email and read it with interest.

Tim Mcrue was a project manager with Xultant Learning, a company that Desmond had consulted with in the past. He and Tim had met once or twice, but they had not yet worked together. Desmond looked up Tim's online profile to read a little more about him. According to LinkedIn, Tim was an instructional designer with about ten years of experience. He'd worked at Xultant Learning for about two years. His education was similar to Desmond's—an undergraduate degree, and a master's degree in instructional design. Desmond had continued to complete a Ph.D. but he knew that it was more common for practitioners to earn a master's degree.

Desmond re-read the email from Tim. He liked this orderly approach to updating and standardizing the curriculum. He smiled, knowing that he had a reputation for being a bit of a data nerd, but he also knew that front-end analysis could mean the difference between a worthwhile evidence-based project and a potential waste of time and money.

In his 25 years in the business, Desmond also knew that these kinds of projects were all too infrequent, as most companies struggled to justify the time and effort required to be data-driven. Desmond thought back through the projects he had already completed this year. They were what he considered to be "typical" corporate training projects related to sales products, enterprise software updates, safety, and policy updates. Realistically, he knew he already had nearly as much work as he could handle, and taking on this project would preclude him from accepting any other projects until it was completed. However, Desmond believed this was a

DOI: 10.4324/9781003354468-22

Subject: Needs Assessment Opportunity
To: Desmond Brower <desmondbrower@dbrower.com>
From: Tim Mcrue <t.mcrue@xultantlearning.com>
Date: August 3, 8:35 a.m.

Hi Desmond,

We've landed a new project that focuses on a needs assessment for Lenker Foods, Inc., based in Atlanta. They're planning to update and standardize their onboarding across three sales roles. They're also planning to review their overall curriculum. I'm wondering if you would be interested in the needs assessment phase of the project. This would involve gathering data and then creating learning impact maps and learning paths.

Please let me know if you're interested.

Best,
Tim

FIGURE 19.1 Project inquiry email to Desmond Brower from Tim Mcrue.

Subject: Re: Needs Assessment Opportunity
To: Tim Mcrue <t.mcrue@xultantlearning.com>
From: Desmond Brower <desmondbrower@dbrower.com>
Date: August 3, 10:15 a.m.

Hi Tim,

Yes, I'm interested. It sounds like a challenging and meaningful project to the client. Let's set up a time when we can discuss more details. For example, when is the project kickoff, what are the expected timeline and deliverable due dates, and is there a statement of work that you could share with me?

Best,
Desmond

FIGURE 19.2 Email response from Desmond Brower.

project that strongly matched his interests. Even with all the consulting work he already had, this seemed like a good project to take on (see Figure 19.2).

Later that day, Tim sent Desmond a copy of the final proposal that Xultant Learning had delivered to Lenker Foods, which outlined the scope, timeline, and deliverables of the project, as well as an example of each. From his previous work with the company, Desmond knew that forwarding the proposal to subcontracting consultants was standard protocol for Xultant Learning. This allowed him to review, in-depth, the entire project proposal.

Desmond knew that if he took on the project he would work directly with the client and would be responsible for creating the deliverables to the client's satisfaction. He reflected on the many times he'd worked on other projects when information was only verbally disseminated through a team leader or project manager, and how it had often led to unnecessary misunderstandings, rework, and client and vendor frustration.

Proposal: Lenker Foods Sales Onboarding

[Page 2] . . .Xultant Learning will conduct a needs assessment, as the first step in creating a learning path for three key sales roles within the Lenker Foods organization. The three roles are sales managers, customer service representatives (CSR), and merchandising specialists.

[Page 4] . . .Interviews will be conducted by Xultant Learning with leaders and individual performers in each of these three roles. Deliverables will be three (3) learning impact maps, three (3) learning paths, and up to twenty (20) specification sheets.

[Page 5] . . .All final deliverables will be received by Lenker Foods no later than the end of business on January 15.

FIGURE 19.3 Key excerpts from the Xultant proposal.

Desmond also knew from his previous experiences working for Xultant Learning that his sub-contractor role would be as invisible to the end client as possible. In other words, in the eyes of Lenker Foods, Desmond would simply be an employee of Xultant Learning. Additionally, he knew that most of the major decisions of the project had likely been determined during the proposal phase, before he engaged with the project. Unfortunately, this meant that pre-arranged processes or deliverables might act as constraints on his ability to determine "new" solutions based on the needs assessment's results, or his insights.

Desmond read the proposal with several things in mind (see Figure 19.3). What specifically was Xultant Learning contracted to do for Lenker Foods? Who were the clients within Lenker Foods? What exactly would he be doing? And what was the time frame?

Desmond could see that the needs assessment was a part of a larger project. Lenker Foods was committed to an onboarding effort for its sales force, one that included rethinking its training curriculum and developing new role-specific courses. According to the documents that Tim sent, the people in the three sales roles interact directly with Lenker Foods' customers, as well as the buyers and managers of stores, and so have an important role in terms of sales and support. The first client deliverables would be learning impact maps. Desmond knew that these were key documents that would ultimately determine the direction of the project as well as ensure that role-specific learning needs would align with organizational goals. Additionally, since these were the first deliverables the client would see, they would be especially important in building trust in the client relationship.

A learning impact map would be created for each of the three sales roles. It is typically built as a one-page document that specifies the critical tasks, the required knowledge and skills to accomplish those tasks, the individual results that demonstrate accomplishing the tasks, and the organizational goals that are impacted by the critical tasks (see Table 19.1).

The learning impact maps, once approved by the client, were necessary prerequisites to the design of the learning paths, which show the courses or learning events that support the development of the knowledge and skills necessary to accomplish each role's critical tasks (see Table 19.2). Desmond loved this systematic approach to performance. Focusing first on what people need to do to achieve organizational goals, followed by designing learning interventions directly aligned to meeting those needs, is a roadmap for effective and efficient instructional design. Each deliverable of the project met a targeted design step that logically

TABLE 19.1
Learning Impact Map: Lenker Foods' Customer Service Representatives

Critical Tasks	*Required Knowledge/ Skills*	*Individual Results*	*Organizational Goals*
Answer phone calls/email inquiries to support customer needs	• Critical thinking skills • Product/process knowledge	90% or higher ratings on customer interaction surveys	Be the customer's #1 food product supplier
Communicate issues to sales managers promptly	• Prioritization skills • Communication skills	Issues are communicated to sales managers within 1 hour of receiving input from the customer	Be the customer's #1 food product supplier
Upsell customers on top-selling products	• Product/process knowledge • Communication skills	5% increase on orders taken from upsells	Increase "Right Rice" sales from $1 billion to $2 billion within three years

TABLE 19.2
Learning Path: Lenker Foods' Customer Service Representatives

0–30 Days	*31–90 Days*	*91 Days–1 Year*	*1–2 Years*
• Lenker 101 • Our brands and products • CSR processes	• Customer interactions • Up-selling 101 • The annual marketing calendar • Supporting your regional teams	• Writing a return authorization • Problem-solving workshop • Critical thinking workshop • Developing the business relationship	• Advanced Excel for CSRs • Advanced Access for CSRs

drove the next deliverable. The design of each deliverable was critical as it would govern all design decisions made downstream from it. So, identifying the required knowledge and skills in the learning impact maps was vital as they would directly determine the necessary content in the learning paths.

As part of developing the learning path, Desmond would also conduct a review of the existing sales curriculum of Lenker Foods to determine what learning events already existed and what would need to be added.

The 20 specification sheets mentioned in the proposal would specify prerequisites, learning objectives, delivery methods, and deliverables for each learning event's overall goals (see Table 19.3). These would provide instructional designers in the next phase of the project with design content templates to make the design and development processes as effective and efficient as possible.

Desmond needed to know what he would be paid to determine if the remuneration was acceptable for his time and effort and asked Tim to send him a contract. The contract specified a flat fee for working on the project that was within Desmond's typical payment range. This meant that he would maintain his targeted hourly rate. Desmond decided this was an exciting project and signed the contract. He was ready to begin work!

TABLE 19.3
Specification Sheet: Lenker Foods' Customer Service Representatives—"Supporting Your Regional Teams" Course

Specification Sheet	
Activity name	Supporting your regional teams
Learners	Lenker CSRs
Duration	30 minutes
Pre-requisites	The marketing calendar (e-learning)
Overall goal	In this 30-minute e-learning course, Lenker CSRs will learn about the five most common ways they will actively provide support to regional sales managers and merchandising specialists.
Learning objectives	After this course, Lenker CSRs will be able to: • List the five most common ways they will support the regional sales teams • Describe the roles of sales manager and merchandising specialist • Identify key events on the annual marketing calendar • Identify the timing at which key communications are sent out to the regional sales network
Delivery method	E-learning
Deliverables	Interactive 30-minute seat-time course with multiple modules; job aids of the annual marketing calendar; 15-question test pool
Comments	The successful completion of this course certifies a CSR as ready to complete the critical tasks on the job. This course should be completed within 90 days of hire.

KICKOFF MEETING, AUGUST 15

"Welcome back to Xultant Learning!" Tim said as Desmond walked into the conference room for the internal kickoff meeting. "And thanks for coming, Desmond. I just wanted us to sit down together before meeting with the client."

"Great," said Desmond. "It's nice to meet you in person, Tim." After exchanging some pleasantries, Desmond continued, "From my previous work with Xultant, I know that we want my role to be as seamless as possible for the client. Part of my consulting philosophy is that it's my job to best serve the end client's needs, in this case, Lenker Foods," he added. "That builds the relationship, and I find everything falls in line from there."

"Okay," said Tim with a slight laugh. "But just remember you work for Xultant Learning." Desmond nodded and smiled to communicate he understood this, but didn't laugh. Even with serving the Lenker Foods' client "invisibly," Desmond was aware that he also served Xultant Learning, and specifically Tim, as its main point of contact.

Tim continued, "So, the good news is that I worked on the proposal, so I'm pretty familiar with it. The project will start this month, and the three learning impact maps are due to our Lenker Foods client by the first of October. So, that gives us about six weeks. The three learning paths are then due at the beginning of December, and the specification sheets are due by the middle of January."

"That sounds good and reasonable," said Desmond.

Tim added, "Our process is that each deliverable gets reviewed internally—on this project that would be me doing the review—then it's reviewed by the client, feedback is collected, and revisions are made by you with a final deliverable that is then submitted to the client."

TABLE 19.4
Project Team and Roles

Team Member Name	*Company*	*Role*
Desmond Brower	Xultant Learning	Needs Assessor
Tim Mcrue	Xultant Learning	Project Manager
Lisa Conlin	Lenker Foods	SME, Project Manager
Sameesh Asoka	Lenker Foods	SME
Marcus Zacharius	Lenker Foods	Project Owner

Two days later, Tim and Desmond sat down again in the conference room, this time for the external kickoff meeting. The conference call line beeped as the two Lenker Foods' learning managers called in. Tim answered and started the meeting.

"Welcome, everyone! I'm Tim Mcrue, and I'll be the project manager for Xultant Learning on this project. The purpose of this meeting is to introduce our team members so we can get to know each other, and then we'll review the project timeline, responsibilities, and our next steps."

Desmond introduced himself and provided an overview of his background and experience. Then the clients introduced themselves (see Table 19.4).

"I'm Lisa Conlin. I've been at Lenker Foods for about five years now. I have a background in instructional design and organization development. I oversee our learning management system for our headquarters training, and I'll be the project manager on the Lenker Foods' side."

"And I'm Sameesh Asoka. I've been at Lenker Foods for eight years and I've been a trainer in the field for the last two years. I've also worked in some of the roles that we'll be looking at for this project, so I'll act as an SME. I can help translate some of our industry terminology, and our Lenker Foods-speak, too," he chuckled.

"I should add," said Lisa, "that Marcus Zacharius, who's my boss and our director of learning at Lenker Foods, will be following our work closely too. The good news is he's the one who fought hard to get the needs assessment project approved before we start doing any learning design or development work."

"Okay, great," said Desmond. "So, what additional information could you share that might help us get started on the right foot?"

Lisa was the first to respond. "Well, let's review some background. Pull up the document that I've sent you with breakdowns of the sales roles (see Figure 19.4). Each sales role at Lenker Foods consists of dozens of leaders who are director or manager-level employees, as well as hundreds of individual performers."

Lisa continued, "Page two of the document shows our goals (see Figure 19.5). Lenker Foods has an internal goal of growing our top-selling item—Right Rice—from $1 billion to $2 billion over the next three years," she continued. "There are also many sub-goals for each of the three sales roles, such as minimizing trade costs, growing new business segments, and increasing specific brand profit margins."

Desmond noted that these KPIs would likely be vital later because the tasks, knowledge, and skills that he'd be exploring for the three sales roles should all ultimately align with these.

Role	Employee Type	Quantity
Managers/directors	Management	~50 (estimate)
Sales managers	Management	150
Customer service representatives	Individual performer	750
Merchandising specialists	Individual performer	1500

FIGURE 19.4 Lenker sales roles and head counts.

Lenker Business Goal	KPI	Role
Grow Right Rice to $2 billion	5% increase in up-sells	CSR
	25% increase in pre-order quantity	Sales manager
	Improved placement (obtain floor display or endcap)	Merchandising Specialist
Minimize Trade Costs	1-item shipments reduced to 0 occurrences	CSR
	Reduce the cost of promotions by 10%	Sales manager
	Reduce damaged returns by 10%	Merchandising Specialist
Grow New Business in Asia	-	CSR
	Grow Asia customer base by 100 customers annually	Asia sales manager
	-	Merchandising Specialist
Increase the Right profit Margin	Reduce the number of return authorizations by 10%	CSR
	Reduce the cost of Right Rice promotions by 10%	Sales manager
	Provide store costing data to sales managers weekly	Merchandising Specialist

FIGURE 19.5 Lenker Foods' goals, key performance indicators (KPIs), and roles.

Sameesh then pointed out, "All training and communications updates, as well as business goals, originate primarily from headquarters in Atlanta. However, day-to-day business is managed on a regional or local basis."

"What role does headquarters play in day-to-day business then?" Desmond asked.

Sameesh responded, "I have that information in a document I'll email to you right now" (see Figure 19.6).

Lenker Foods Headquarters' Role in Supporting Sales:

- Supplies annual selling calendar, national events list, price lists, new/discontinued products sheets, and other materials to the regions regularly
- Helps sales personnel sell Lenker Foods products to their markets
- Relies on local employees to manage the business at the store level because of regional variance, e.g., retail customers range from small mom-and-pop stores that want the national brand recognition of Lenker Foods' products to large 'mega stores' who have dedicated Lenker Foods sales directors and custom pricing and programs
- Regional sales directors and managers are responsible for translating directives from headquarters into actionable activities in the stores within their assigned locales

FIGURE 19.6 Lenker Foods headquarters' role.

As Desmond read the document, he speculated headquarters likely had a challenge in trying to send a consistent message to such a variety of stores. He asked, "How well do you think headquarters does in terms of communicating with the regions?"

Sameesh replied, "Well, sometimes communiqués, including training, coming from headquarters are not necessarily received positively. That's because, with the geographic and demographic differences in the regions, headquarters can seem a bit out of touch. One example that comes to mind is from a few years back when we created a national winter promotion for our hot mini sandwiches. It was tied to a marketing campaign, training, and most importantly to local, regional, and national sales goals. Even though the goals were much smaller for stores in our southern regions, because it was a sales goal based on a cold weather winter promotion, it went over badly with our southern stores, and they let us know it!"

Desmond nodded. With a geographic footprint as large as Lenker Foods, in combination with such varied store types, it made sense that corporate communications and training could have a reduced impact because it wasn't fully relevant to each audience. He made a note to especially focus on potential regional issues when he worked on the learning impact maps, most likely in areas of required knowledge with local or regional implications.

Tim guided the rest of the meeting through a discussion of the project timeline, each person's role and responsibilities, and an agreement on the next step—Desmond coming up with a plan to move forward.

EARLY SEPTEMBER

To determine what the key tasks were for the three sales positions, Desmond decided that he needed to strategize the best approach to collecting data about each position. He knew from experience that he needed to consider multiple data collection methods: interviews, focus groups, surveys, extant data, industry-related articles, and publications were all options on the table. Desmond wanted to use at least three data sources to triangulate his findings. He jotted down some questions he needed to have answered (see Figure 19.7).

As he thought through these questions, Desmond recalled that interviews with managers/directors and individual performers were expected to be part of the data collection. But Desmond also wanted to get input directly from a large portion of the sales force about what they thought were the key tasks to accomplishing their jobs. They would have first-hand experiences with what was critical as well as have the expertise to help explain the differences that exist in terms of regional characteristics, store types, and sizes. However, given the large

Guiding Questions:

- *What are the best sources of data in this situation?*
- *Given the situation, what are the most valid and reliable data collection methods?*
- *How will data collection affect resources and the timeline?*
- *Once a plan is decided upon, how will this be effectively communicated to the team?*

FIGURE 19.7 Desmond's questions to guide his thinking.

Brand	Region	Gross Sales (in Millions)	Margin
Right Rice	Northeast	$245	8.6%
	Southeast	$320	7.6%
	Midwest	$230	7.8%
	Mountain	$155	7.8%
	Southwest	$135	8.3%
	Northwest	$125	8.4%
		$1,210	

FIGURE 19.8 Lenker Foods annual sales summary—Right Rice.

number of individual performers, Desmond was concerned that he wouldn't obtain enough information from the limited number of interviews he could conduct. He considered augmenting the interviews with an email survey to reach the large and dispersed population of sales staff. He knew there was a tradeoff—using a survey would take more time but deliver more nuanced data, even though interviews alone would be quicker.

He could also collect data by reviewing information such as job descriptions, job advertisements, online database searches, sales figures, and so on (see Figure 19.8).

Sameesh had provided him with recent job descriptions for each of the three Lenker Foods' sales roles, as well as recent job ads (see Figure 19.9). These detailed the key tasks as well as the required knowledge and skills for each role. He knew that part of his analysis would be to validate these descriptions during the development of the learning impact maps.

Desmond also recalled from the kickoff meeting that Lisa had described some KPIs that were important to these sales roles: minimizing trade costs, growing new business segments, and increasing specific brand profit margins. Lastly, Lisa had granted him access to the training courses in the Lenker Foods corporate LMS. This would provide him with a snapshot of where the organization was now in terms of meeting the immediate knowledge and skills needs of the three sales roles. As he navigated through the LMS, Desmond took some notes on the courses available (see Figure 19.10).

Desmond thought he had a pretty strong set of extant data that he could use to triangulate interviews with managers/directors and individual performers, and email survey responses.

Lenker Customer Service Representative (CSR) Job Description:

This role is responsible for supporting Lenker customers in daily order taking, issuing of return authorizations, and solutions in shipping or back ordered products. Additionally, this role supports regional sales managers and merchandising specialists.

Tasks:

- Supply regional sales personnel with annual selling materials including annual selling calendar, national events list, price lists, and new/discontinued product sheets
- Support sell-in of Lenker Foods' products to all markets
- Interact with customers daily to provide product information, take daily orders, cancel/adjust orders, and solve customer issues

Skills/Abilities:

- CRM, database query, and MS Office software
- Active listening
- Written and oral communication
- Service orientation
- Critical thinking

Knowledge:

- Customer service
- English language
- Clerical

FIGURE 19.9 Lenker Foods' CSR job description.

CSR courses found on the Lenker LMS:

- Lenker 101
- Our Brands and Products
- CSR Processes
- Customer Interactions
- The Annual Marketing Calendar
- Developing the Business Relationship
- Advanced Excel for CSRs
- Advanced Access for CSRs

FIGURE 19.10 Existing courses for CSRs.

To communicate this, he drafted a data collection strategy document and sent it to Tim for review (see Figure 19.11).

MID-SEPTEMBER

"Desmond, we need to talk." Tim's voice on Desmond's voicemail didn't sound happy. "Call me when you get this message."

Desmond felt somewhat puzzled. He was confident his approach was sound. Was Tim dissatisfied with his work, and so soon on the project? He called Tim.

"Hello, Tim, it's Desmond. I got your message."

Data Collection Strategy

Strategy

The collection of meaningful data is a necessary step to determine job tasks and required skills and knowledge of the three Lenker Foods' sales roles. Triangulation of data, using three data sources, is proposed to ensure the validity and reliability of data:

- Extant documentation
- Manager/director and individual performer interviews
- Individual performer surveys

1. **Extant documentation**
   - Job descriptions and related documents (such as job analysis) for each role
   - Existing training courses
   - Role-specific key performance indicators
2. **Manager/director and individual performer interviews**
   - To obtain their perspectives on key tasks, skills, and knowledge
3. **Individual performer surveys**

   Online surveys will capture the perspectives of the three categories of sales performers. The variation in work experience, time in the position, large population (over 2,500 employees), and work settings make for potentially rich data. A supervisor will send a link to each sales force member with an explanation and request to complete the survey. The survey should take about 10 minutes to complete.
4. **Data collection methods**

   The following table outlines the data collection methods proposed for interview and survey data, with approximate numbers of participants for each sales role.

Participant	Interviews/n	Survey/N
Directors/managers of sales managers	4	-
Directors/managers of customer service representatives (CSR)	4	-
Directors/managers of merchandising specialists	4	-
Sales managers	4	150
Customer service representatives (CSRs)	6	750
Merchandising specialists	10	1,500

5. **Timeline**
   - Extant document review: September 20–27
   - Manager/director and individual performer interviews: September 28–October 10
   - Individual sales performer surveys: October 11–31
   - Development of learning impact map: November 1–14

FIGURE 19.11 Proposed data collection strategy.

"Oh, great," said Tim. "So, I read your strategy document. Overall, I think it's a good approach, but I have concerns about the survey. We hadn't talked about that before. You know, implementing that could put our project timeline back at least a couple of weeks."

Admittedly, Desmond knew that designing, reviewing, and then sending out the surveys—with a follow-up reminder email after some time—would take time to complete. However, he was resolute on the value of the survey data from the individual performers on the job.

"Well, that's true. We hadn't talked about that because I hadn't thought about it yet," said Desmond. "But it makes sense because collecting more detailed data from the sales groups is pretty vital."

"But the proposal specified only using interviews," said Tim. "I get that it's not ideal, but remember that you'll be interviewing the people in all three of the sales roles, as well as supervisors of those roles. And I suspect that many of the supervisors have worked in those three roles prior, so they'll have applied experience too."

"But listen, Tim," Desmond replied, "although supervisors can shine a light on the three sales roles, that's not their perspective now. Also, it might be a problem to assume that what was true in the past is still true now. The best way to support or refute this is to collect survey data from the sales force itself. The survey will allow us to get a much broader, more representative picture of the experiences of individual performers in their widely differing contexts."

Tim paused. "I don't know," he said. He agreed with Desmond from a pure methods standpoint, but he was torn because of his project management responsibilities. He was concerned about the timeline being negatively impacted by a survey and he knew that ultimately, he would be accountable for it, despite Desmond's rationale.

Desmond sensed Tim's hesitation. "If we get on it right away," said Desmond, "which I'm prepared to do, and we have support from the Lenker Foods' team, we should be fine on the deliverable dates."

Tim thought about Desmond's professional experience, recognized his rationale for conducting the survey, and finally acquiesced. "Well, okay, go ahead and send it out to Lisa and Sameesh." Desmond emailed the data collection strategy document (see Figure 19.12).

Subject: **Data Collection Strategy**
To: Lisa Conlin <L.Conlin@lenkerfoods.com>, Sameesh Asoka <S.Asoka@lenkerfoods.com>
CC: Tim Mcrue <t.mcrue@xultantlearning.com>
From: Desmond Brower <desmondbrower@dbrower.com>
Date: September 16 11:15 a.m.

Hi Lisa and Sameesh,

Attached is the data collection strategy document that outlines our approach. Please review it at your earliest convenience and let me know if you have any feedback.

Best,
Desmond

DataCollectionStrategy.docx

FIGURE 19.12 Proposed data collection strategy email.

However, later that day Desmond was stunned to read a reply-all email from Tim to the entire team (see Figure 19.13).

"Desmond, I'm sorry," said Tim on the phone. "But I've had a change of heart about the survey. It just won't work. I get the argument for doing it, but we just don't have the wiggle room in the timeline. If we have even one small misstep, such as someone on the client side not meeting a deadline, which is outside of our control, then we're behind. I just can't risk it. We should be fine on the data collection without the survey."

Desmond strongly believed that omitting the survey would reduce the validity of the data collected and decided he had to take a stand. He thought that Tim was taking actions beyond his role as project manager and was getting too much into micromanaging the work that Desmond was hired to do. He also thought that Tim's email potentially hurt the developing trust between him and his Lenker Foods' client.

"Can I have some time to get my head around this?" Desmond responded. He knew that one thing he didn't want to do was to say something in frustration. Calming down a bit would be a wise first move.

Later that evening Desmond asked himself, "So if I can't survey the individual performers, what are my best options?" Desmond knew that he had a very strong set of extant data that would contribute to his work. And he also knew he would interview managers and individual performers in the three roles and would likely get valid data from that. Was that enough? He wasn't convinced. He also remembered that he had sales figures and job descriptions.

At the same time, he was concerned about his now strained relationship with Tim, and perhaps also with Lisa and Sameesh after that last email from Tim. He did not doubt that he needed to communicate directly with Tim about his concerns. But he wasn't sure yet about the approach to take with Lenker Foods.

As he thought more about his situation systemically, Desmond realized that there were significant implications in terms of ethics, contractual agreements, internal and external relationships, project quality, and potential future work both personally and for Xultant. Ethically, he was challenged to navigate the dynamic tensions between his professional standards, the project's resource constraints, and the expectations of the project manager. Yet, at a minimum, he was required to deliver the three sets of documents as defined in his contract. He

Subject: **RE: Data Collection Strategy**
To: Lisa Conlin <L.Conlin@lenkerfoods.com>, Sameesh Asoka <S.Asoka@lenkerfoods.com>, Desmond Brower <desmondbrower@dbrower.com>
From: Tim Mcrue <t.mcrue@xultantlearning.com>
Date: September 16, 2:35 p.m.

Hello all,

I know that Desmond has already sent out the data collection strategy document for your review. But please disregard it until we have time to further refine it.

Please let me know if you have any questions,
Tim

DataCollectionStrategy.docx

FIGURE 19.13 Follow-up email from Tim Mcrue.

knew that it was one thing to go "above and beyond" on a project, which had the added benefits of building trust with the client as well as creating a higher likelihood of potential future work, but at what cost? His tactical decisions would need to be weighed against the potential for missing deadlines or harming personal relationships.

Desmond considered the old metaphor of a project as a three-legged stool. One leg of the stool represents cost, one leg represents time, and one leg represents quality. The tongue-in-cheek question to the client would therefore be "Since you can't realistically have all three the way you want them, which two do you want to choose?" Desmond struggled because as confident as he was in terms of cost and timing, he did not want to sacrifice what he saw as opportunities to deliver the best quality work.

Desmond also knew that there were multiple clients he needed to consider. His immediate client was Xultant, as he was a direct subcontractor to them, so future work from this project was most likely related to how Xultant viewed him and his work. But also critical was Lenker Foods, as their perspective and final assessment of both his work on the project and his working relationship with them would also influence future work. He knew that his best outcome would be to make both of his clients satisfied while meeting his standards.

Preliminary Analysis Questions

1. Viewing needs assessment as a systemic process can be a helpful tool in understanding its constraints. Create a systems diagram of this needs assessment project, including its inputs, outputs, components, and the relationships among them within the system.
2. Identify potential benefits, limitations, and trade-offs to Desmond's proposed data collection strategy.
3. How can Desmond use the extant data that are available when completing his needs assessment?
4. How might Desmond proceed given the current constraints? Describe potential ethical issues that might arise.

Implications for ID Practice

1. Analyze how time constraints can affect the quality of a needs assessment. Describe strategies that might mitigate these effects.
2. What approaches can an ID consultant take to balance the needs of a subcontracting firm with those of the end client? How might these approaches vary in different situations?
3. Define ethics. Describe how ethical considerations might inform the relationship between an ID consultant and a client.

20

Maggie Lochs

Aligning Process at Global Training Innovations

Jill E. Stefaniak

A REQUEST FOR ASSISTANCE

Maggie Lochs, an independent instructional design (ID) consultant, sat at her desk anxiously waiting for her phone to ring. Maggie had 20 years' experience working as an instructional designer. After working for a training and development company that produced training products for healthcare education, Maggie had decided to go out on her own as an independent contractor. A lot of Maggie's work consisted of conducting needs assessments and designing e-learning modules for clients. Last Friday, she received an email from Ted Evans, director of digital production at Global Training Innovations (GTI), inquiring about her availability to conduct a needs assessment to improve their ID efforts.

GTI is an international training consulting firm with clients throughout the world. The firm offers a variety of off-the-shelf courses for purchase on topics related to organizational communication and health and safety. They also design custom-made training for clients. GTI's headquarters is in Chicago, Illinois, but the company is looking to expand its business operations around the world.

As director of digital production, Ted had ever-changing roles. Having worked in employee development for a large manufacturing company for 20 years, Ted was recruited by GTI to assist with their training and development efforts ten years ago. Ted had a master's in industrial technology and completed a couple of courses on adult learning and instructional design. He was instrumental in establishing GTI's process for developing face-to-face training programs. These days, Ted spent most of his time recruiting new clients and setting up contracts that involved the development of face-to-face and e-learning options. In addition, he sometimes worked as a facilitator for their face-to-face training.

Recently, there had been some changes to GTI's leadership structure. As a result, the CEO, Brenda Baxter, had asked Ted to work with the different teams who were involved in ID projects to improve their processes as the new leaders transitioned into their roles. While Ted had not been involved in the day-to-day operations in quite some time, he felt that he could be of assistance. Further, he hoped that this might open other leadership opportunities within the company for which he could be considered.

DOI: 10.4324/9781003354468-23

Maggie had done some freelance work for GTI the previous year, assisting with organizing content and writing test items for some e-learning design projects. As a contractor, she had experienced some challenges with their ID process and had the impression that there was a lack of communication across the various teams that worked on design projects; however, this was merely speculation. She was interested in the prospect of a new project and an opportunity to help GTI improve their ID process.

While she had not worked directly with Ted, she had met him briefly during a kickoff meeting for one of the projects a year earlier. She had responded to Ted immediately, and they had arranged for him to call her that following Monday morning to discuss the details of the project.

Right on time, Maggie's phone rang at 9:00 A.M. It was Ted calling to discuss the details of the project. "Thank you for taking the time to speak with me today, Maggie. I received final approval from our CEO to bring in a consultant to conduct a needs assessment for us, and I knew just the person to call," Ted exclaimed. "We've been expanding our training offerings, which has created, or perhaps highlighted, some difficulties with our current ID practices. With more work coming our way, we thought now is the right time to have someone help us identify possible solutions to mitigate some challenges our design team keeps experiencing. We think having someone like you conduct a needs assessment could really help us explore the ID process and gain more clarity on the challenges some folks are experiencing."

Maggie wanted to know more about the challenges GTI was experiencing. "Well, thanks for thinking of me, Ted. I'm certainly interested. Can you share some more details regarding these tensions? What are you hoping to accomplish with the needs assessment?" Maggie asked.

"Well, now that business is increasing, we're finding it more important for everyone to be on the same page in terms of our design processes so we can complete projects as quickly as possible. We no longer have the flexibility of taking a few extra days to complete these. We have several projects waiting in the queue. We'd really appreciate it if you visited our headquarters and met with our design team to make recommendations on how we can improve our ID processes. If business continues to increase, we'll need to start planning ahead for any additional resources we may need. We're also experiencing some challenges with members of our team complaining about our ID process. We've actually had some individuals ignore the process altogether. I can't tell if it's a personnel issue or if there's a major flaw in the process. I think the results of your needs assessment could help us get a better handle on what those challenges are and what we can do to improve."

"What's your timeline for completing the needs assessment?" Maggie asked.

"Ideally, we'd like to have it completed within this next month. We will need to submit our proposed budgets for the upcoming fiscal year within the next three months. If the needs assessment were completed before then, it could help us justify any new additions to our training budget. I spoke with our leadership team, and we'd like you to visit our headquarters for a couple of days, meet with the ID team, and submit a report. I realize we're not giving you much time, but we will give you access to whatever you need during your visit. We know you're familiar with some of our processes having worked with us as a freelance designer. You've also experienced some of the challenges I've alluded to. Are you interested?"

Maggie chuckled to herself. She knew what Ted was referring to and had witnessed some of those challenges at GTI. She had worked on ten different projects over the past year and half for GTI. Every project seemed to follow a different ID process, and no one seemed to be on the same page during their team meetings. Maggie had just assumed some of the chaos was due to clients changing their minds on different projects and several independent contractors being brought together to work on projects. She figured there might have been issues with contractors not being properly onboarded or oriented to the projects due to a lack of time.

Maggie paused for a moment. "It's certainly an aggressive timeline for a needs assessment. But I am definitely interested. Would it be possible for me to meet with others in your organization who interact with the ID team on the various projects? While I'm somewhat familiar with the process from the times I've worked with GTI, I'd like to see how others, such as the project managers and technical writers, approach the process."

"Sure thing!" Ted exclaimed. "I know you're aware of some of the different units that interact with the ID team. Why don't you put a list together of the different units you are interested in meeting with, and I'll put together a few names as well. We want to make good use of your time with us in Chicago. I'll set up the meetings with everyone in the organization. I think the more people you talk with, the better understanding you will have of the challenges we've been experiencing."

Maggie was excited. She began making a list of the different units she would want to meet with so she could email Ted later that week. Having worked with GTI the previous year, Maggie knew that in addition to the design team, they had a multimedia production team and a technical writing team. Each project was assigned a project manager to oversee the process. It would be really helpful to see how the different units functioned when working together. She remembered some communication challenges she had experienced previously. Perhaps, this needs assessment would provide more insight into why those issues had occurred.

PLANNING THE VISIT

Four days before her visit to GTI, Maggie received an email from Ted with the itinerary for her visit (see Figure 20.1). In addition to the list of units and functions she had identified, Ted had also made some recommendations for individuals he thought Maggie might be

Subject: Maggie Lochs GTI Visit (Itinerary)
To: Margaret Lochs <Margaret.lochs@lochs.com>
From: Ted Evans <tevans@GTI.com>
Date: October 7, 2:30 P.M.

Hi Maggie,

Global Training Innovations is looking forward to your visit later this week. In preparation for your visit, I want to share a list of individuals we have scheduled you to meet. I took the liberty of adding a couple of names to the list that I thought would be informative for your needs assessment.

I will meet you at the office the morning you arrive, and we can talk briefly before you jump into your interviews. If there is anything else you can think of that you may need, please let me know.

I'm not sure why you want to meet with folks in the sales department, but I have asked Lynn Williams in sales to meet with you and hopefully answer your questions. I'm also working on seeing which project managers are available. We currently have three. I'm most interested to have you meet with Brent Franz. The other two project managers tend to deviate from our processes.

FIGURE 20.1 Needs assessment itinerary email to Maggie Lochs from Ted Evans.

October 11th	
8:00 A.M. to 9:00 A.M.	Meeting with Ted Evans, Director of Digital Production (debrief on needs assessment and itinerary)
9:00 A.M. to 9:30 A.M.	Meeting with Paul Jones (instructional designer)
9:30 A.M. to 10:00 A.M.	Meeting with Gina D'Alia (instructional designer)
10:00 A.M. to 10:30 A.M.	Meeting with Claudia Radford (multimedia production supervisor)
10:30 A.M. to 11:00 A.M.	Meeting with Roberto Lopez and Jennifer Trammel (graphic designers)
11:00 A.M. to 1:00 P.M.	Lunch with Ted Evans
1:00 P.M. to 2:00 P.M.	Demo of communication software for design teams
2:00 P.M. to 3:00 P.M.	Meeting with project managers (to be determined depending on availability)
3:00 P.M. to 4:30 P.M.	Open time for Maggie
October 12th	
8:00 A.M. to 9:00 A.M.	Instructional design team meeting
9:00 A.M. to 9:30 A.M.	Meeting with Lynn Williams (sales and customer relations)
9:30 A.M. to 10:30 A.M.	Coffee with project managers (group)
10:30 A.M. to 11:00 A.M.	Meeting with Tamara Parkson and Leonardo Pontini
11:00 A.M. to 12:00 P.M.	Debrief with Ted Evans

FIGURE 20.1 Continued

interested in speaking with. As Maggie reviewed Ted's email, she smiled. She could already identify one challenge, and she hadn't even started.

DAY 1, OCTOBER 11

When Maggie's cab arrived at GTI's headquarters, Ted was waiting in the lobby. "Hi, Maggie! It's great to see you. How was your flight?"

Maggie smiled. "It was a smooth flight. No delays. I can't get over the nice weather. It's been raining for the past three days back home. It was nice to see some sunshine!"

"I've reserved the conference room for you all day. I figured we could have individuals come in and meet with you throughout the day so that you can stay settled. I know your first two meetings are with our instructional designers, Paul and Gina. I just want to warn you that Gina will probably complain about the design process we have in place. I really need you to tell her that it's good and that you recommend we keep the process. I think the challenge is that no one is following the process or filling out the forms correctly. I think they may be more compliant if they hear from an expert that they should."

Maggie nodded. "Do you mind sharing the form with me and walking me through the ID process? It would be especially helpful if you could walk me through what happens when a new project is presented to the group."

Once they sat down at the conference table, Ted pulled up an image on his laptop to show Maggie. "Here's the process (see Figure 20.2). Either I or one of our training consultants will finalize a contract with our client and then bring it forward to the group. The contract

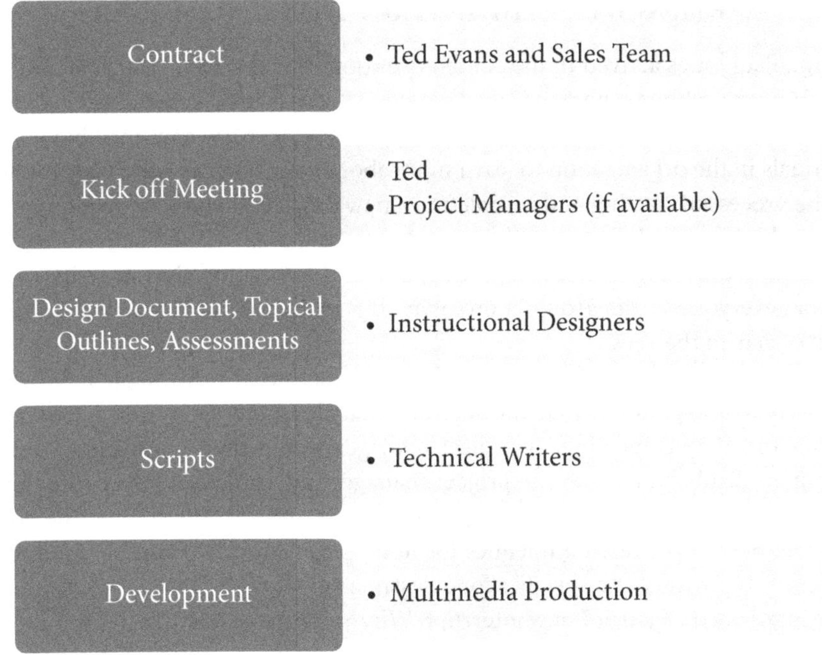

FIGURE 20.2 The project design process.

includes the specifications of the project and the various timelines associated with each task. We typically hold a kickoff meeting with the client and the project manager to discuss the ID process and what information we may need from them along the way."

"Who typically participates in the kickoff meetings?" Maggie asked.

Ted replied, "Either me or one of my training consultants and a project manager if they're available."

Maggie looked perplexed. "What is the difference between an instructional designer and a training consultant?"

"The instructional designers are responsible for facilitating the design and development process of all instructional materials. The training consultants are typically responsible for delivering training if it's a face-to-face course. They also may be hired to stay on contract with the client to help them implement changes in their organization," Ted explained.

Maggie responded, "When do the instructional designers meet with the clients? When do they discuss the specifics of the project?"

"They don't. I'm able to tell the team what they need for the project. They are typically given the information that they need after the project manager completes the design document and gets approval from the client. I helped develop the ID process years ago. Actually, that's how I started with the company. Having the IDs in the meeting would just be a waste of resources. I can get them the information they need, and they can focus on working on their projects. Besides, since I deliver a lot of the training out in the field, I can skip through a lot of stuff in the meetings with the clients."

While Maggie never wanted to wish extra meetings on anyone, she was a little curious how the instructional designers could customize instruction for the clients without ever meeting with them. "Okay, Ted. Can you walk me through the rest of the process in this diagram?"

MEETING WITH THE INSTRUCTIONAL DESIGNERS

At 9:00 a.m., Paul Jones arrived in the conference room. "Come on in," Maggie said. As Paul sat down, Maggie grabbed a notepad to take notes. "Ted has invited me to provide feedback on GTI's instructional design process. I'm spending these next few days meeting with different individuals in the organization to learn more about your ID processes. Can you walk me through the process of starting and completing a new project? If you have recommendations for how you think we could improve the process, please share."

Paul shared, "Sure thing. We have a process, but we don't really follow it. To be honest, I'm not sure that everyone in the group knows what the process is. Ted created it a while back, but it kind of gets in the way."

Maggie replied, "That's okay. Can you walk me through what really happens?"

Paul continued, explaining that the instructional designers were first introduced to a project after the kickoff meeting. A project manager would then reach out to them with the assignment. Paul shared that the project manager was supposed to provide the design team with a design plan that outlined the goals and objectives for the course. The document (see Figure 20.3) also provided guidelines for how long a course should be, whether it was face-to-face or e-learning, and specifics for assessments.

Maggie interjected. "Paul, if I may interrupt. Why are there so many sections for the learning objectives?"

"Ted recommended that we break each objective down so that we know what type of objective and strategies we should use. He said that it's important to incorporate a variety of types of learning objectives in every course."

"Does that ever get confusing for the team?" Maggie asked.

Global Training Innovations

Design Document

Project Name:	**Project Code:**
Start Date:	**End Date:**
Version:	
Summary of Changes and Revisions	

Global Training Innovations Design Team

Project Manager:

Instructional Designer:

Graphic Designer:

Approval Team: **Approval Date:**

FIGURE 20.3 Design document used by GTI.

Overview of Course	
Course Aim:	
Instructional Goal:	*Summary of Objectives*
Learning Audience	
Media Format:	

Course Objectives	
Enabling Learning Objectives	
Affective Learning Objectives	
Behavioral Learning Objectives	
Attitudinal Learning Objectives	

Key Learning Segments	
Sections/Modules	List topics to be included in each section or module. Specify when different multimedia is needed.

Assessment		
Formative Assessment Checkpoints	**Type** Multiple choice Fill-in-the-blank Drag and drop Short answer	**# of Questions**
Summative Assessment	Multiple choice	# of Questions

FIGURE 20.3 Continued

"The project managers usually complain about it when we have team meetings. They don't understand the differences. Clients typically ask a lot of questions when we have meetings to share design drafts with them." Paul continued, "Gina keeps saying that we don't need all the sections, but Ted says she's just being difficult. I don't have a problem with it. If any of the objective sections are missing, I just copy and paste objectives from other courses we've designed, and no one seems to have questioned it."

The official process showed that the instructional designers were responsible for building upon the design document by providing topical outlines and suggested instructional strategies. They were also responsible for writing the test questions. A majority of the assessments that GTI provides are in multiple choice format. Once this information was outlined, the instructional designer would then work with the technical writers who were hired on contract to write scripts that would later be recorded in multimedia production.

"What types of things are typically recorded?" Maggie asked.

"Sometimes it's just the audio that we embed in the e-learning modules. Multimedia production will often use voice actors. Sometimes a client requests that we develop customized videos related to safety in the workplace or how to use a machine properly."

Paul shared that the project managers often had the writers begin writing the script at the same time the instructional designers were mapping out the course. Oftentimes, the writers would ignore the assessment questions that the instructional designers wrote and, instead, write their own.

"It's really frustrating, because we end up writing the design document after a project is in development. By then, it's too late to be useful. The writers don't understand that the assessment questions need to be aligned with the course goals and learning objectives. They think that they are in charge of all writing because they're the technical writing team. Half the time, the questions they write do not make sense."

"Who signs off on the writing? Who do you talk to if problems like this come up during a project?" Maggie asked.

"We usually complain to the project manager. Some of the project managers will send an email to the writers while others just ignore our complaints. They think we're being territorial about design. I don't think they do it intentionally. Oftentimes, we're way past deadlines, and they are trying to get the project done. I think they get to a point where they just need to send something back to the client. They don't care whether it's a good example of instruction."

Maggie followed up with another question. "Why do you think there are so many challenges with meeting project deadlines?"

"Well, I can't say with certainty because I'm not included in the kickoff meetings. I think some of the challenges arise because the project managers are not usually included in the initial discussions with the client. By the time the project manager is assigned a project, Ted and his team have already mapped out a plan, including timelines, and have specified them in a contract. By the time it comes to us, we're told 'just make it work.'"

Maggie looked confused. "I thought the project managers were supposed to be included in the meetings."

"They should be. Most of the time Ted and his team handle it with sales and then let everyone know what's needed."

"Who's on Ted's team?" Maggie asked.

"Sometimes it's just Ted. Other times it's the other training consultants who are hired to deliver training. Every once in a while, a sales representative is included in the call depending upon their relationship with the client."

Maggie wrote a note to herself. She was going to follow up with the project managers when she met with them later that day.

"What about the design document form? Ted shared that you're supposed to add information to the form. Is the form helpful?" Maggie asked.

"Not at all! We actually created our own form that the ID team uses. We never know when we're going to get inundated with project requests. We created our own tracking system on a spreadsheet so that Gina and I know who's working on which projects and the internal deadlines we have before we send things over to multimedia production. We have additional information that we need to know, especially when we're designing the e-learning courses. They've created their own variation based on Ted's form to help them track their projects. The project managers didn't like us expanding their form, so we created our own. We've found it helpful in terms of identifying who should take on the next project as it comes in."

As Maggie wrapped up her meeting with Paul, she was anxiously awaiting her meeting with Gina D'Alia. Ted had warned her that Gina was not a fan of the process, but he had never said anything about Paul. Maggie was curious what Gina might have to say about the process and projects.

Just as Maggie and Paul were wrapping up their conversation, there was a knock on the conference room door. Gina was standing in the doorway.

Maggie smiled. "Perfect timing. Paul and I were just finishing our conversation. Please, grab a seat. Thanks for coming! I appreciate your taking the time to meet with me today. How has your morning been so far?"

"So far so good. We've got four ID projects we're trying to wrap up this week. This is a nice break in between some of those final meetings."

"That's great. GTI has invited me to visit the company and meet with folks in your organization to get a better understanding of the ID process that's used. They've asked me to review the process and offer suggestions if there are opportunities to improve it. I've been asking everyone to walk me through the ID process you follow when a new project comes in."

Gina smirked. "Which process do you want to know about? The one that we don't use or the one that Paul and I created to help with our day-to-day tasks?"

"How about both? I'm trying to get a better understanding of why the process isn't being used or isn't working. And please be honest. If there are certain challenges that you think are interfering with the IDs' abilities to get their work done, I'd like to know. I'm here to help as much as I can. I just started meeting with people this morning, so I haven't talked to everyone yet. Ted has shared the process with me, and Paul walked me through the design document that you use. I'd like to know thoughts from the ID perspective."

Gina smiled. "Sure thing. Everyone seems to have an issue with the design document Ted created. I have a master's degree in instructional design and have worked in the e-learning industry for 12 years and have never seen a design document like this one. It's repetitive and the multiple objectives sections are confusing. It's fine if you're teaching someone how to write objectives for the first time, but for the purposes of what we do here, it's not needed. We really just need one section for the learning objectives.

Whenever we have meetings with the project managers they complain about the form. The clients don't care how the objectives are being labeled. They just want us to design courses. And there's information that the ID team needs that's not included in the design document. We're not allowed to modify the document, so Paul and I use a different one internally."

"What information does the ID team need that is missing?" Maggie asked.

"We have a lot of courses that we work on simultaneously. Right now, there are only two of us in the ID department. We're hoping to hire another ID soon. Paul and I created a document that outlines the status of each project. For instance, when I write the assessment questions for a course, I'll share the document with Paul, and he double checks my questions to see if they align with the course objectives before we send the content back to the project managers for one last review. Half the time, our assessment questions don't address the affective objectives.

"We also have to design mockups for the various screens to be used in the e-learning modules. We share these storyboards with the graphic designers in multimedia production so they can start finding images and work on the branding. We have to wait for them on these items before we can finalize the e-learning modules. Once we finalize the modules on our end, we send them back to the project managers. They'll do a final review of the scripts with the technical writers and send them to multimedia production to add the audio recordings and videos. The last step is for multimedia production to get approval from our creative director, Eugene Phelps, for branding.

"Since there are so many phases of the projects, we created a spreadsheet that we use internally to track where the projects are."

"This is really helpful information, Gina. I haven't had a chance to meet with the project managers or the other departments yet. I saw on my itinerary that I'm supposed to see a demo of the communication software. Is that the spreadsheet you're referring to for tracking the ID projects?"

Gina shook her head. "No. That software only tracks the communication that the project managers have with the clients. It doesn't do a very good job of letting us know the current status of the different projects. Ted has embedded the design document in the software portal and wants us to update the document every time a change is made. That rarely happens. If any changes are made after a client signs off on the objectives and module breakdown, everyone scatters, and each department does their own thing."

"How do you know when you can expect to get a project back from the technical writers or the graphic designers?"

Gina laughed. "We don't. It's always a surprise when someone sends it back to us. It's really frustrating because it would help us with planning and prioritizing our projects if we knew when we could expect things. The other issue we have is that the deadlines aren't realistic.

"When Ted and the sales representatives meet with a client to set up a contract, they promise the moon. They don't care how long it takes us to design a course. They just want the client to sign the contract. Multimedia gets frustrated the most by this. A client will be promised that we can design a course with customized videos and the turnaround time is half what it should be, or the budget isn't what it needs to be."

"Does anyone say anything? What happens when multimedia points this out?" At this point, Maggie was taking copious amounts of notes.

"We're told from the top that we need to make it happen. These are things that the project managers should be handling from the very beginning of the project, but most of the time they aren't brought into the mix until a contract has been signed."

While they talked, Gina described experiencing similar challenges to those expressed by Paul when working with the technical writing team. While talking about the project managers, Gina shared, "It's difficult to work with the project managers because none of them have a background in ID or training. Half the time, they don't attend the meetings and they just rely on what Ted shares with them. It's really telling when they attend the kickoff meetings and report back the information to us. There's so much more information that we need that they do not think to ask. I feel like we're in a constant state of playing the telephone game. Important information seems to be left out every time the information passes through someone. By the time that information gets to the IDs, we're forced to make a lot of assumptions about the project and the clients."

"Can you share some examples of questions you would like the project managers to ask during the kickoff meetings?" Maggie inquired.

Gina responded, "We never know anything about the learners. The design document that the project managers complete usually says 'new employees' or 'employees with some degree of experience.' That doesn't help us at all! I wish they would get us some more details. That would help us with the types of examples we incorporate into our materials. It could inform our choice of the pictures we use for messaging. The project managers are relying on what Ted and his team provide, but it's not enough to do the job correctly. And then it's a completely different problem when we're updating the off-the-shelf courses."

Maggie sat back for a minute, looking confused. "What do you mean it's different? Is there a different process?"

Gina smiled. "We have two types of courses. The first type are the ones that we've been talking about. These are courses that are customized for a client. Oftentimes, our sales team and Ted's team are establishing contracts to create a training program unique to an organization. The second type is our off-the-shelf courses. These are courses that we've developed, which companies may purchase, to add to their training catalogs. The challenge with these courses is that we never know if a company is going to purchase a few modules, or an entire course pack. We don't know who the learning audience is or how the lessons will be used."

"How often are you working on off-the-shelf courses?" Maggie asked.

"It depends on what we have in progress. The contracted projects with clients are prioritized. Sometimes we create new off-the-shelf courses after sales informs Ted that new courses are needed. Sometimes we're asked to upgrade the courses because they're more than five years old."

"What challenges do you encounter with those courses?" Maggie pressed.

Gina continued. "We encounter many of the same challenges with the project managers. They do not always share our updates with the technical writers, the technical writers do their own thing and disregard the instructional designers, and we never really know what we're supposed to be updating. It's easy to figure out that you might have to update the images if some of them look old or update industry standards that may be referenced in a module, but we're never really told why we're updating the courses."

"Does the sales department ever provide that information to you or the project managers?" Maggie asked.

"Nope. They usually just say, 'We need to update these five courses by this time.' It'd be great if they could tell us why. Have sales been steady? Are there certain courses that sell more than others? Why are they selling more than others? Are there certain instructional strategies that buyers seem to be most interested in for their employees? Paul and I are constantly designing in the dark."

Maggie had a few minutes before her next meeting and was making some additional notes based on her conversations with Paul and Gina. She didn't think that their concerns seemed unreasonable. Maggie thought Gina had brought up some really important points.

MULTIMEDIA PRODUCTION SUPERVISOR AND GRAPHIC DESIGNERS

By the time Maggie had her meetings with the graphic designers, Claudia Radford, Roberto Lopez, and Jennifer Trammel, she already knew the response when she asked the question, "Can you walk me through the process of when a new project begins at GTI?"

The multimedia production team had similar concerns as the instructional designers. They expressed that they weren't brought in on a project until it was too late. They felt their team had to go through several design iterations to finalize the message design on a project.

Claudia shared, "We could avoid so many delays with our projects if the project managers asked specific questions regarding messaging and branding when they have a kickoff meeting with the client. Oftentimes, the contracts are set by Ted's team, and they never consult with our department regarding the costs or time associated with different products and services. Doing voice-over for an e-learning course is a lot different than filming a five-minute video. There are different timeframes and resources that are needed. We're in a constant state of running behind our deadlines."

Jennifer added, "The process that Ted created shows multimedia production as the very last step of the project. While we put the final touches on the courses, we really need to be involved much earlier. Even while the ID team is working on their content, we could be setting up the design work on our end. The current process is too linear. It doesn't reflect what really goes on here."

MEETING WITH THE PROJECT MANAGERS

By the time Maggie met with the three project managers, Sarah LeClair, Brent Franz, and Daniel Sterling, she was beginning to see what the problems were. The project managers verified that while there was a process that Ted provided for everyone, no one used it.

When pressed for why they didn't use the process, Brent replied, "Ted added so many things to the form that it's overwhelming. There are so many questions about course goals, course objectives, and the typologies of each learning objective. When we meet with our clients, they don't know the type of objective they want, and I don't think they care. We only fill out the form for what we need so we can estimate how much time each department will need to do their part of the project."

Maggie inquired about the relationship between the instructional designers and the technical writers. "Do you see any challenges with how they work together on your projects?"

Sarah responded, "Let me guess. Paul probably told you that they never use his evaluation questions. The technical writers are just that—writers. They can handle it. It's really just Paul getting territorial about what the ID department gets to do. They like to throw out phrases like "there's no alignment with the course goals," but it's not a big deal.

DAY 2, OCTOBER 12

Maggie was eager to get started with her meetings at GTI. By the time she left for her hotel the night before, her head was spinning with all the information everyone had shared. Maggie spent her evening reviewing her notes and brainstorming how the different processes that were being followed could be merged in such a way as to help everyone out. Everyone seemed to be working in silos, and no one was talking to each other.

She hoped that she could work with everyone to come up with some ways to improve the process and support communication. Maggie was going to have coffee with the project managers later in the morning and had a couple of ideas she wanted to run by the group to get their feedback.

Paul and Gina were waiting for Maggie in the lobby when she arrived. Maggie's first meeting for the day was to join the IDs during their regularly scheduled team meeting. She followed them back to Paul's office.

"We talk everyday but we try to hold a weekly meeting where we focus on status updates on our projects. It helps us know what each of us is working on and if we need an additional set of eyes on any of our projects," Gina shared.

During their meeting, Paul and Gina showed Maggie some of their latest projects. They shared examples of some of the storyboards they mock up for the graphic designers and what the assessment content and narration scripts look like as they evolve throughout the design process.

MEETING WITH SALES REPRESENTATIVE AND CUSTOMER RELATIONS

As Maggie's meeting with Paul and Gina was coming to an end, they walked her back to the conference room for her next meeting. Lynn Williams was one of the sales representatives at GTI and was already waiting in the conference room for Maggie.

"Good morning, Maggie. It's nice to meet you." Lynn stood up to shake Maggie's hand.

Maggie smiled. "Good morning. Thank you so much for taking the time to meet with me today. GTI has asked that I conduct a needs assessment to help them improve their ID process. When I initially spoke with Ted about this project a few weeks ago, I had asked if it'd be possible for me to meet with a member of the sales team."

"I'm happy to help, but I'm not sure how much help I'll be. I'm not an instructional designer, and I'm not involved with that process."

"No worries," said Maggie. "I've been meeting with people who work in different units of GTI. I'm trying to see where different groups come together on projects. Would you mind sharing with me what typically happens when you're lining up a new project with a client? I'm trying to figure out the differences between the projects involving customized instructor-led trainings and the off-the-shelf courses."

"Sure. I'll start with the customized courses. Sometimes those projects are initiated by sales whether a potential client has contacted the company or one of our sales representatives is following up on a lead. If we know it's going to be an instructor-led course, we'll include Ted on a few of the calls or meetings with the prospective client. That's where Ted can talk through our design process and timelines depending upon what they might want to do.

"If the client has worked with GTI in the past, they sometimes bypass sales and contact Ted or one of the other training associates. When that happens, Ted will typically follow up with sales so we're aware and can help with setting up a contract."

"Are the project managers in those meetings?" Maggie asked.

"Not always. Sometimes they are. Most of the time they find out that there is a call right before the meeting, so their schedules don't always allow for them to participate. It's okay. Ted knows what to ask in those meetings and can handle the questions regarding the training materials and forms of delivery. I'm really just there to finalize deadlines for delivering the project and setting up a contract with the client. Once the contract is signed, everything gets turned over to Ted or the project managers and they see the project through completion."

"Thank you, Lynn. This is really helpful in giving me a sense of how these projects are initiated. Can you walk me through what happens with the off-the-shelf courses? I have a few questions about those. How do you determine what courses need to be updated? What drives GTI's decision to revise some courses and not others?"

"There's a few different ways we approach these. If we have developed off-the-shelf courses that are situated around safety in the workplace, the safety standards may have changed which would drive the need for a course revision. If a new technology has been integrated, we might look at trends for the particular industry to see what should be added or removed from existing courses.

"We try to update courses every five years. Sometimes those updates just involve changing the imagery. For instance, we had a few courses that had older pictures and videos of individuals working on computers at their workstations. The computers looked very outdated along with what individuals were wearing and their hairstyles. It was obvious we were using old footage. We'll update the pictures.

"Other times, we might look at sales data to see which courses have sold more than others. If it's a course that has been successful, we prioritize updating it every five years so we can inform those clients that we have an updated course available for purchase."

"Do you collect feedback from your customers on the courses after they've purchased them?" Maggie asked.

"Yes. Some of our clients pay a subscription for access to our modules. We're able to see what their training managers are downloading or using for their employees' training plans. We also send out customer feedback surveys every six months so we can follow up on how they're using the modules or what changes they'd like to see in future courses. That report gets sent to the project managers."

Maggie wrote a note to herself to ask about the sales reports during her coffee meeting with the project managers later that day. She was interested in hearing more about how they used the information from the sales reports. After meeting with Lynn, it was apparent that there was a lot of information that might be useful for the ID team and multimedia production.

Just as Maggie and Lynn were wrapping up their conversation, there was a knock at the door. Ted was standing there.

"Hi, Maggie. Good morning, Lynn. I'm sorry to interrupt, but there's been a slight change to Maggie's schedule."

"No worries, Ted. We just finished. What's up?" Maggie asked.

"I know we had you scheduled to have coffee with the project managers now, but our CEO, Brenda Baxter, is available to talk with you on the phone if you'd like to meet with her. She's traveling on business. I was on a call with her earlier this morning, and she said she had availability to meet with you if you thought that'd be helpful. I've got her waiting on hold."

Maggie didn't really have a chance to respond, but she didn't want to miss out on an opportunity to speak with Brenda. Perhaps Brenda could offer insight into how she envisioned everyone working together on projects. "Thanks, Ted. That sounds like a wonderful opportunity. I'd be happy to speak with Brenda."

Ted helped transfer the phone call to the conference room. Once Brenda was on the phone and introductions were made, he stepped out to give Maggie and Brenda privacy during their phone call.

"Thank you, Maggie, for helping us with this needs assessment. Ted has spoken very highly of you and shared that you have done some contracting work with us in the past. I'm sure you can provide a lot of insight having worked with us before."

"Everyone has been great," Maggie replied. I've been getting a lot of information from everyone and learning more about what each of the different groups do at GTI. It's been very informative.

"In your role, as CEO, how do you envision the process occurring when a new project begins? Do you see any challenges with the current process? Is there anything that you think could be improved?"

"I'm not sure what I can offer in terms of the process. I think our process is very simple. When a new project begins, we need all hands on deck. I think Ted has done an excellent job creating new business for us on a more global scale. I'm not involved in the day-to-day operations with the ID team—that's what the project managers are in place for. Ted typically attends our leadership meetings and provides updates.

"I am interested in the results of your needs assessment. There seems to be issues with some individuals not wanting to comply with the ID process. I know that's caused a lot of challenges for some."

"In what ways?" Maggie pressed.

"Well, Ted seems to be very annoyed by Gina. He's shared with me that she doesn't like following his process and has been outspoken in different meetings. We've lost a few people in the ID and multimedia production teams. If I'm perfectly honest, we've had a hard time keeping people for longer than six months. I guess they get here and find out that GTI is not a good fit for them."

As Maggie continued to talk with Brenda, it became apparent that a lot of the attrition tended to be related to the workload and communication issues others had shared with her the previous day. Maggie had a few more questions for Brenda, but Brenda had to call their meeting short to take an emergency phone call.

"Thank you, Maggie for your help. I'm really looking forward to seeing the results. I hope you enjoy the rest of your visit at GTI."

Due to the adjustments made to the schedule to allow Maggie to meet with Brenda, not all of the project managers were able to adjust their schedules to have coffee at the new time. But two of the project managers, Brent Simmons and Sarah LeClair, were still able to take Maggie to a coffee shop that was located across the street from GTI. Maggie appreciated the change of scenery.

During their meeting, Brent and Sarah talked about the sales reports that Lynn had mentioned earlier that morning. "We typically use the report to see which courses have made more money and which ones we should focus on revising first," Sarah shared.

"Are those reports shared with anyone on the ID or multimedia production teams?" Maggie asked.

"We don't share the specifics of the course. We're more concerned with the number of sales and how quickly we can turn a course around," said Brent. "There are a lot of other data that sales collects that we don't really need. If the course has been successful, then we really don't need to worry about changing what isn't broken."

"Lynn mentioned that the sales team collects customer feedback on the courses. Would it be possible for me to see a copy of one of those reports? I wonder if there might be some information that would be of use to the IDs as they revise courses and change instructional activities."

"I have no problem with that," Sarah said. Let us check with Ted to see if it'd be okay to share that information when we get back to the office."

When they returned to GTI's office, Maggie realized she was nearing the end of her scheduled meetings. Her last meeting was with the technical writers. She was very excited about this meeting. She had heard a lot about the technical writers during her conversations with the others the day before. Several had mentioned that one of the writers, Tamara Parkson, was extremely difficult to work with. They also shared that she was Brenda Baxter's sister-in-law.

Maggie knew she was going to have to be careful with how she worded things in her final report relating to the technical writers.

MEETING WITH THE WRITERS

As Maggie neared the end of her visit at GTI, her last scheduled meeting was with the technical writing team, Tamara Parkson and Leonardo Pontini. They were both contract workers for GTI and were going to meet with Maggie together.

There was a knock on the door. As Maggie looked up, she quickly realized that Leonardo was alone. "Where's Tamara?" Maggie asked.

Leonardo looked sheepish. "Umm. I think it's just going to be me this morning. Tamara didn't really see the value in talking with another instructional designer. I tried calling her to convince her to meet with you, but she's not coming."

Maggie smiled. "That's okay. I appreciate your taking the time to meet with me. I have one question that I've been asking everyone. Do you mind walking me through the process that's used when a new project begins at GTI?"

Maggie enjoyed her conversation with Leonardo. He shared some of the challenges that occur between the instructional designers and the technical writers. He shared that by the time the project managers provide the content for the writers, they're behind and have to make changes to their scripts rather quickly. When they make changes to the scripts, it's easier if they write the evaluation questions for consistency. Leonardo also shared that if they had more time for review, the instructional designers could be brought in to review and assist with the evaluative assessments. He also shared that Tamara wasn't very cooperative and often didn't follow the technical writing process that they adhered to within their team. "She's the CEO's sister-in-law so it makes it difficult when we come across problems. No one feels comfortable discussing her performance."

THE DEBRIEFING MEETING

At the end of the second day, Ted took Maggie to the coffee shop across the street to have a quick debriefing meeting before she headed to the airport to go home.

"It was helpful to see demos of some of your more recent courses. Your staff shared the various forms they use internally to help their respective teams manage their tasks for each project," Maggie began.

"Also, thank you for scheduling time for me to meet with Lynn Williams in sales. Moving forward, I think it would be helpful to facilitate some conversations between sales, your project managers, and instructional designers. Sales has collected a lot of information that could inform the design of future iterations of existing courses and data pertaining to learners. It might be helpful to bring these groups together every once in a while to talk about what information they need and prioritize on a project. It might help improve communication."

Ted replied, "That sounds like a great idea. Maybe we could schedule these meetings quarterly to talk about what work is on the horizon."

He continued, "I hope you were able to talk some sense into these guys these past two days. I just know that if they follow my process, we wouldn't have any issues."

Maggie chose her words carefully. "Ted, I really appreciated that so many people took the time out of their schedules to meet with me. It was interesting for me to hear how the process works or doesn't work depending on their roles with the project. I think it's more than a few folks being insubordinate. I've been taking a lot of notes during this visit, and I've gotten a chance to see some of the forms that are used to launch the projects."

"Oh, of course. I understand," Ted replied. "I think the process would go a lot smoother if Gina wasn't involved. She's constantly complaining about the process. If you could share some specifics about your observations of her in your report, I think that would really help strengthen my arguments with senior leadership when we must make some changes."

"Ted, I've only been here for two days, and I didn't really get an opportunity to observe individuals engaged in their work. I'll go through my notes and share my recommendations with you and the CEO. I should have the report to you both by the end of next week."

Once Maggie boarded the airplane for her trip home, she pulled out her meeting notes. There were more challenges than just fixing a few ID processes—the organization needed a complete overhaul. While Maggie had a good inclination as to why certain things were not working at GTI, she felt uncomfortable making certain recommendations regarding personnel, especially since she had only visited GTI for two days and was given limited information.

Maggie had asked for a copy of a sales report so she could see what types of feedback customers provided related specifically to the content of the courses they purchased. Ted was hesitant to share that information with her. He had called Brenda during their debriefing meeting, but Brenda preferred that he not share. She didn't feel comfortable with Maggie seeing the names of their clients.

During Maggie's visit, the project managers had quickly walked her through the production studio where videos were filmed. It looked like a production studio you'd see on television. Nobody was in the studio during the tour, so Maggie didn't have an opportunity to ask too many questions. She would have liked to meet with the multimedia production director. She wanted to learn more about the timelines involved with developing videos and recording audio for the training materials.

Maggie needed to decide how she should prioritize her recommendations for GTI's ID practices. It seemed that a lot of jobs and tasks were being modified by the various teams based on their individual departmental demands. Clearly, many of the challenges Maggie had identified were intertwined. She was going to need more time to reflect on how to organize her recommendations.

Preliminary Analysis Questions

1. Based on Global Training Innovations' presentation of their problem, what types of data would you want to access if you were hired to conduct a needs assessment?
2. Maggie was not given access to information she needed to complete her needs assessment. What information would have been helpful for her to have during this process? How could Maggie mitigate the challenges caused by the lack of information?
3. How might Maggie communicate some of the challenges others expressed during the needs assessment regarding Ted's communication?
4. Based on the information provided, what strategies might Maggie suggest to help the teams work together throughout the project?

Implications for ID Practice

1. How can instructional designers communicate to their clients the need for access to different reports and materials when conducting a needs assessment?

2. Consider how an instructional designer might present their recommendations when they have not been given access to all the relevant data during a needs assessment.
3. If you were an instructional designer and were not able to meet directly with clients, what questions would you want a project manager to ask on your behalf?
4. Sometimes IDs may be asked to provide feedback or recommendations related to personnel issues. How can an ID remain both professional and apolitical while providing the type of feedback the employer is asking for?

21

Raul Ramirez

Designing Educational Materials for a Neurodiverse Patient Population

Miranda Hawks and Alan Jones

Raul Ramirez sat in the waiting room of Central Valley Medical Center (CVM). He had applied for the position of nurse educator, knowing that the competition was fierce. If hired, Raul would be responsible for designing and implementing comprehensive patient education programs. In addition, his role would involve designing curriculum and delivering training sessions to healthcare professionals and patients. Most critically, Raul's position would involve creating inclusive and accessible educational resources for patients.

As he waited for his interview, Raul reflected on his experiences as a part-time clinical instructor for Central Valley University and his recent completion of a master's in nursing degree, while also working as a registered nurse (RN) in the Emergency Department of CVM during the COVID-19 pandemic. He remembered the moment that he completed the national certified nurse educator (CNE) exam, which was a personal goal for Raul and a requirement to obtain the nurse educator position. After a few minutes, Raul was ushered into a small conference room by Betty Walker, the nursing education coordinator at CVM for the past 27 years. During Raul's interview, he had the opportunity to learn more about the hospital's operations.

Raul felt his excitement grow as he engaged in conversation with Betty. Betty leaned forward, detailing the significance of the nurse educator role at CVM and in the Desert Springs Healthcare System (DSHS). Betty explained, "Here at CVM and across DSHS, nurse educators are highly valued members of our nursing staff. With the recent staffing issues we've experienced for the past two years, mainly due to the COVID-19 pandemic, their role has become even more crucial."

Raul nodded attentively, eager to learn more about the impact he could make. "I understand. How do nurse educators contribute to the team?"

Betty smiled, recognizing Raul's genuine curiosity. "Well, as nurse educators, they serve as the main design team members for newly implemented projects or projects that require revision. They play a vital role in developing patient education materials that align with our mission of providing comprehensive and inclusive care."

DOI: 10.4324/9781003354468-24

Raul's eyes widened with interest. "That sounds like an amazing opportunity to make a difference. How have nurse educators been involved in the pandemic response?"

"Great question, Raul. During the pandemic, the Nevada state government recognized the importance of healthcare-systems-based nurse educators. In fact, they allocated $64.2 million dollars in statewide funding, specifically for the creation and dissemination of updated, inclusive patient education materials." Raul was impressed by the scale of the initiative. "That's incredible! Has CVM already made progress in this area?"

Betty leaned back, reflecting on the achievements of the nurse educators at CVM. "Yes, indeed. Our nurse educators at CVM Unit 34B, a 28-bed medical-surgical unit, have already developed a prototype of the updated patient teaching materials. It has shown promising results and improved patient outcomes."

Raul's excitement grew as he envisioned the potential impact of his work. "It's inspiring to hear about this progress. So, the goal is to expand this initiative to other units throughout the healthcare system?"

Betty nodded enthusiastically. "Yes! That's the long-term goal for DSHS. We aim to scale what was created at Unit 34B and implement it across other units to ensure that our patients receive the same high-quality, inclusive care no matter where they are in our healthcare system."

Raul couldn't help but feel a deep sense of purpose and opportunity in front of him. "It's evident that being a nurse educator here is more than just a job. It's about making a real impact on patients' lives."

Betty smiled warmly, her eyes reflecting a shared passion. "That's exactly right, Raul. We believe that nurse educators, like yourself, are instrumental in finding innovative solutions to improve patient outcomes. Your expertise and dedication are precisely what we're looking for."

Raul stepped out of the CVM building after the interview as his heart raced with excitement. As he walked toward his car, he reached for his phone and dialed his husband, Gregory. "Hey, babe," he said as soon as Gregory picked up. "Guess what? The interview went really well!"

Gregory responded, "That's great news! What made it so exciting?"

"Well," Raul said, grinning from ear to ear, "the position is for a nurse educator at CVM. It's an opportunity to develop patient education materials that could make a real difference in the lives of patients."

Gregory smiled while responding, "That does sound exciting! Tell me more."

Raul explained that CVM is one of fourteen hospitals in the network of DSHS, based in western Nevada. In addition to its fourteen hospitals, DSHS operates two sets of clinics with several branch locations scattered throughout the region. He further explained that the hospital was looking to hire someone like him who was passionate about patient education, had experience working with diverse patient populations, and was committed to staying up-to-date with the latest medical research and best practices.

TUESDAY, MARCH 2: DAY 1 OF THE DESIGN PROJECT

First Project Team Meeting

After being hired and completing his month-long orientation training, Raul was assigned to the mentorship of Rose Langley, a seasoned nurse educator at CVM. Rose had worked at CVM for 24 years and worked closely with Betty. Raul and Betty found themselves waiting in the conference room, eagerly anticipating Rose's arrival for the meeting. Betty took the opportunity to catch Raul up on the details of the project. She began, "Recently, I asked Rose to spearhead a new project focused on designing patient education materials, suitable for all learners including neurodivergent and neurotypical patients. The success of this important initiative could potentially help us secure additional funding for CVM from the statewide allocation since, unfortunately, we will run out of the initial funding this month."

The prospect of making a difference in patient education and securing more resources for the hospital was an exciting challenge for Raul. "That sounds like a significant undertaking. I'm thrilled to be a part of it," said Raul.

Betty nodded, acknowledging the constraints they faced. "Absolutely, Raul. It's a crucial project, but I understand that we all have limited time to dedicate to it due to our responsibilities in providing direct patient care. That's why we need passionate individuals like you and Rose who can balance both responsibilities effectively."

As Betty's words echoed in Raul's mind, he was reminded of the importance of finding innovative solutions despite the time constraints. He felt ready to collaborate with Rose and Betty to merge their skills and knowledge to create patient education materials that would empower and support all learners.

As Rose walked into the conference room, she spotted Betty and Raul already sitting at the conference table. "Rose, I'd like you to meet Raul," Betty said, gesturing toward Raul with a smile. "He's got some incredible ideas, and I think he'll be a great addition to our team."

Rose looked up as she was settling into the meeting and smiled warmly at Raul. "Nice to meet you, Raul," she said, extending her hand. "I've heard a lot about you."

Raul shook her hand with excitement, "It's great to meet you too, Rose. I'm really looking forward to your mentorship and to completing our daily rounds together."

Betty turned to both of them and smiled. "Let's get started then. We've got a lot to cover today."

Rose began, "As you all know, we've been collecting patient feedback surveys over the past few years. The results have been significant." She pulled up a slide on the screen behind her, which showed a graph of patient satisfaction ratings broken down by demographics. "It's become evident that our neurodiverse patients are consistently reporting lower levels of satisfaction than our neurotypical patients. As healthcare professionals, we have a responsibility to ensure that all of our patients feel heard, valued, and included during patient education." Rose continued, indicating that many departing staff members had voiced concerns about the lack of discharge education materials for patients who experience divergence from neurotypical learning processes, such as patients with autism or dyslexia. The hospital had received a number of responses on patient satisfaction surveys indicating that patients were struggling to adhere to discharge instructions, due to the format of the instructions (see Figure 21.1).

Betty nodded in agreement. "That's why I called the meeting today. Let's begin to brainstorm about how we can improve our current approach that still relies on the standard paper pamphlets designed 15 years ago."

Raul leaned forward, ready to contribute. "Yes, I've found that one of the most important strategies for creating a more inclusive environment is to provide a range of accommodations and resources. Also, it's important to educate staff on how to effectively communicate and engage with neurodiverse patients."

Betty smiled. "That's exactly what we're hoping to achieve with this project. Maybe you can elaborate on that idea, Raul."

"Well, I've learned that it is important to use simple direct language to explain procedures and treatment plans to neurodiverse patients," expanded Raul.

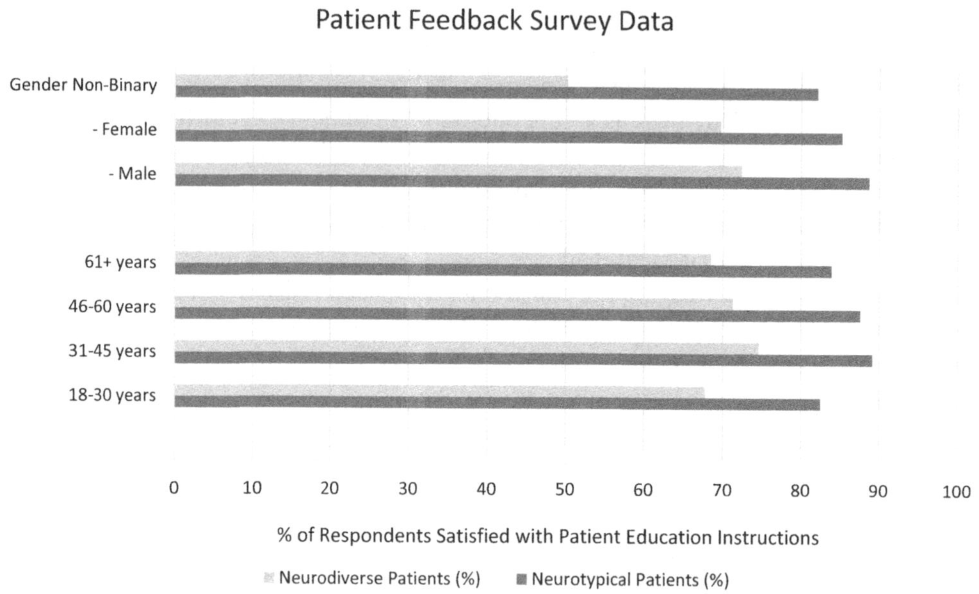

Patient Feedback Survey Data

Gender Non-Binary
- Female
- Male
61+ years
46-60 years
31-45 years
18-30 years
0 10 20 30 40 50 60 70 80 90 100
% of Respondents Satisfied with Patient Education Instructions
Neurodiverse Patients (%)
Neurotypical Patients (%)

FIGURE 21.1 Patient feedback survey data, including demographic information presented by Rose.

"Yes, that makes sense. Can you expand on that a little more?" asked Rose.

"Some of the gold standard organizations, such as the National Inclusivity Alliance and the Agency for Evidence-Based Patient Education, recommend that we design patient education training materials in a manner that avoids complex medical jargon and uses visuals or diagrams," continued Raul.

Raul and Rose began to discuss the notable differences that likely would occur in patient outcomes at home if materials were enhanced to include different learning considerations.

"We could even present our work at the Central Valley University annual conference," exclaimed Rose.

"That sounds like a good plan," Betty said. "Let me go ahead and outline which team member will take on which role in this design process. I have to run to another meeting now, but we're off to a good start. Thanks, team!"

WEDNESDAY, MARCH 17: DAY 16 OF THE DESIGN PROJECT

After initial excitement about the project during the first team meeting, there had been little discussion of the project outcomes or deliverables in the two weeks since. In addition, Betty had recently been assigned to another unit to care for patients due to COVID-19 staffing issues, putting the next planning meeting on hold.

To start their day, Raul and Rose began their daily patient rounds on Unit 34B. During their rounds, they were introduced to Zena Thompkins, a 15-year-old pediatric client admitted to the hospital for acute asthmatic exacerbation associated with her renting situation. Zena's family rented an apartment in the historic area of town, known for poor living conditions associated with a lack of adherence to asbestos and lead housing regulations. In addition, Zena was recently diagnosed as being on the autism spectrum and was being supported by learning accommodations in the school close to their apartment.

As Rose and Raul began to assess the patient and discuss her educational learning materials for inhaler use, the respiratory therapist Michael Lowe and the nurse practitioner Logan Rae walked into the room. Logan informed Zena and her family that Zena had just tested positive for COVID-19. As Zena's mother began to cry, Rose attempted to provide information regarding asthma and COVID-19.

"Watch me demonstrate how to use the inhaler," Rose instructed. Rose continued to quickly verbalize instructions to the family and Zena, as Logan finalized his physical examination and Michael scanned the electronic health record.

As Rose and Raul left Zena's room, Rose turned to Raul and asked, "Should we consider an additional learning tool here? Maybe go back and implement the teach-back method with Zena or bring in a visual aid?"

Raul replied, "Yeah, I was thinking of an additional tool, too—maybe consider repeating the instructions multiple times." Raul recalled learning that repeating instructions and practices can aid in learning and retention for all learners, especially students on the autism spectrum. People with autism spectrum disorder (ASD) can also benefit from visual aids in various forms as they often have strengths in visual processing.

Rose responded, "Yes, I think that's a good idea. Unfortunately, we were pressed for time due to Logan needing to conduct his exam."

As Raul and Rose continued down the hall, Julia Thompkins, one of Zena's sisters, approached Raul. "Do you think Zena could use social media to learn more about the complications occurring if you have asthma and COVID-19? Zena really likes engaging with online videos and seems to like hearing things repeated a lot." Raul began to help Julia identify quality resources on her smartphone.

"I just need to know which resources are most helpful. There's so much information out there," said Julia.

"And in what format would your parents prefer to receive additional information?" asked Raul.

"They would definitely prefer paper or email resources, please," responded Julia.

Rose and Raul quickly moved on to assist during a code blue in Room 1546. After helping the team during the code blue, Raul presented an idea to Rose that included a very detailed scaffolding plan to reduce the quantity of information included in the patient education materials.

Rose seemed to be onboard with the idea but began to ask for clarification by stating, "How much longer would that take?"

"Possibly another three weeks," responded Raul.

As he left his shift, Raul began to ponder the idea of using gaming and virtual reality as a medium to teach asthma care in the home setting. Raul knew from his training that clients experiencing autism often enjoy gaming as a method of learning.

TUESDAY, MARCH 23: DAY 22 OF THE DESIGN PROJECT

Beginning of the Shift

Betty sent several emails to Raul and Rose letting them know that she had been pulled into other departments to cover staffing shortages. There had been no further discussion of a second team meeting about the patient education materials project. Raul emailed Betty a number of times with examples of revisions that could be made to existing materials, based on Zena's case. Eager to continue the project, Raul decided to create a handout listing the different types of media that might support learning for neurodiverse patients.

"Have you received approval from Betty yet to present the handout you created?" Rose asked Raul.

"Not yet. I will try to circle back to her later today. I am working on finalizing the handout [see Figure 21.2] but am still missing critical technology strategies."

As Raul jotted down a note to remind himself to contact Betty, he overheard one of the staff nurses, Lea Thomas, discussing a patient case. "He won't listen to me. I just know he's going to be back here at the hospital because he simply won't pay attention."

As Raul approached, Lea complained, "This patient won't stop interrupting me and does not seem to follow my instructions when I am teaching him how to care for his incision site."

A Summary of Supporting Media for Neurodiverse Learners

Media that will be selected or developed to support patient learning

Visual:

Visual schedules break down complex tasks into smaller, more manageable steps and help individuals with neurodiverse learning styles anticipate what is coming next and stay on track

Visual cues (e.g., posters, flashcards) can be used to help neurodiverse learners understand social cues, emotions, and language

Social stories are short narratives that describe social situations and the appropriate behavior(s) in those situations. They can help neurodiverse learners understand and respond appropriately to social cues

Graphic organizers (e.g., flow charts, mind maps, Venn diagrams) can help neurodiverse learners understand relationships between ideas and organize information

Videos can be an effective way to teach new concepts and skills by providing a clear and concrete way to understand complex ideas

Audio:

Audio mini-lessons can provide an alternative way for neurodiverse learners to access and understand information

Incorporating sound and music into mini-lessons can be used to help neurodiverse learners manage sensory sensitivities during learning

Recording routines and procedures can provide neurodiverse learners with a reference they can listen to and follow, which can help reduce anxiety and promote independence

Kinesthetic:

Incorporating movement breaks into the learning process can help neurodiverse learners stay focused and engaged—this can include simple movements like stretching or more structured movements like exercise

Sensory toys (e.g., stress balls, fidget spinners) can help neurodiverse learners manage sensitivities and improve focus

Manipulatives (e.g., blocks, puzzles) can be used to help neurodiverse learners understand abstract concepts in a concrete and tangible way

Active learning activities (e.g., role playing, hands-on projects) can help neurodiverse learners engage with material in a meaningful and interactive way

Technology Strategies:

TBD

FIGURE 21.2 Raul's handout outlining a summary of different types of supporting media included in patient education for a neurodiverse population.

Raul nodded with understanding. "Would you like me to try to help?"

Lea instantly agreed, "That'd be great if you could."

Raul took a quick look at the patient's record to gather some baseline data (see Figure 21.3). Then, after navigating through a complex series of screens, he noticed a physician's note in the comment section of a past hospitalization.

Upon further review, Raul noted that Anthony was admitted to the hospital for a bowel resection after years of struggling with Crohn's disease. "How are you feeling today, Anthony?" asked Raul after entering his room.

"Not great," exclaimed Anthony. "I was supposed to be discharged over two hours ago. I'm not sure why they are making me wait so long."

As their conversation continued, Raul discovered that Anthony was recently let go from his job as a plumber. He explained that he has had difficulty paying attention at work. The symptoms associated with ADHD and Crohn's disease have made it difficult for Anthony to concentrate, especially during his nutrition education sessions.

"I get so bored and can't remember what the nurses are telling me because they are throwing a lot of information at me at one time," grumbled Anthony.

Raul returned to the nurses' station and continued his review of Anthony's electronic medical record. Anthony had been taking medications for both Crohn's disease and ADHD, which interacted with each other prior to surgery, causing side effects and reducing the effectiveness of both sets of medication. The impulsivity and difficulty with organization and time management associated with ADHD have caused many barriers to Anthony's care. Combined with the chronic nature of Crohn's disease, Anthony's ADHD diagnosis made it difficult for him to consistently follow his self-care regimen, including taking medication and maintaining a diverticulitis-friendly diet, which led to an infection that may have resulted in the bowel resection surgery.

"I've been thinking about the process of patient education with Anthony," Raul said while talking to Lea at the nurses' station. "Patients experiencing neurodiversity like Anthony often require unique adaptations to support their learning and understanding."

Lea looked up from her computer, intrigued. "Okay, but how would we accommodate learning for all our patients, who have a range of different learning needs?"

Raul responded, "While each neurodiversity may require specific approaches, there are overlapping strategies that can benefit patients with an array of needs (see Table 21.1). For example, the use of visual aids has proven effective for many neurodiverse individuals by providing a visual representation that enhances understanding and engagement."

Lea continued to think through the information that Raul suggested. "What about the importance of concise language and clear instructions? Would that be helpful to support learning with neurodivergent patients?"

Raul smiled, acknowledging Lea's contribution. "Absolutely, Lea. Concise language and clear instructions can make a significant difference in communication. Presenting information in a straightforward and concise manner can help patients process and comprehend discharge instructions or patient education more effectively."

After talking with Lea, Raul decided to find Rose to discuss this opportunity to develop specific patient education materials for Anthony since the available materials did not include strategies to support learning for patients like him. "Rose, I think that we have another opportunity to build patient education materials that we can use in our project for Betty," said Raul after passing Rose in the hallway.

"Sounds good. I definitely want to hear more, but right now, I need to help in Room 1583," said Rose hurriedly. Raul recalled seeing animated videos with simple and clear explanations

Patient Record Entry
Patient Name: Anthony L.
Age: 47
Gender: Male
Medical Record Number: WXQRl13863
Chief Complaint:
Patient reports delayed discharge and difficulty paying attention during education sessions.
Presenting Concerns:
Anthony expresses frustration with difficulty in paying attention and retaining information during his hospital stay. He mentions recent job loss due to attention-related challenges.
Medical History:
Anthony has a history of Crohn's Disease, which led to his current admission for a bowel resection. He was diagnosed with Attention Deficit Hyperactivity Disorder (ADHD) at the age of 8, and since then, he has received treatment, including medication and behavioral therapy.
Assessment:
During the conversation, Anthony exhibits signs of ongoing attention difficulties, as reported by both himself and the nursing staff. He expresses boredom during education sessions and struggles to remember the information provided.
Plan:
1. Collaborate with the nursing staff and develop strategies to improve Anthony's engagement during education sessions.
2. Consider adjusting teaching methods to accommodate his ADHD-related challenges, such as breaking down information into smaller, manageable parts.
3. Liaise with the healthcare team to ensure Anthony's timely discharge and address any concerns causing delays.
4. Explore the possibility of involving a behavioral therapist to provide support and guidance in managing his ADHD symptoms.
5. Provide Anthony with educational materials tailored to his learning needs, incorporating visual aids, written instructions, and repeated reinforcement.
Follow-up:
Schedule a follow-up meeting with Anthony to assess the effectiveness of implemented strategies, address any new concerns, and provide ongoing support during his hospital stay.
Note:
Attention deficit symptoms associated with ADHD, combined with the challenges of Crohn's Disease, have impacted Anthony's ability to concentrate and retain information. A multidisciplinary approach involving nursing, medical, and behavioral interventions will be essential to enhance his experience and facilitate effective patient education.

FIGURE 21.3 Anthony's patient record accessed by Raul for baseline data.

TABLE 21.1
Different Manifestations of Neurodiversity and Strategies for Meeting Diverse Learning Needs

Neurodiversity Manifestation	*Strategies for Meeting Diverse Learning Needs*
Autism Spectrum Disorder (ASD)	Visual aids, structured routine, repetition and reinforcement, social stories, sensory integration, assistive technology, clear and concise language, positive reinforcement, individualized instruction
Attention Deficit Hyperactivity Disorder (ADHD)	Breaks and movement breaks, clear and concise instructions, visual aids, chunking tasks into smaller parts, positive reinforcement, individualized instruction
Dyslexia	Multisensory instruction, structured reading programs, assistive technology, detailed and concise instruction, individualized instruction, visual aids
Dyscalculia	Manipulatives, visual aids, repetition and reinforcement, real-world applications, individualized instruction, assistive technology
Dyspraxia	Movement breaks, sensory integration, detailed and concise instruction, visual aids, individualized instruction, assistive technology

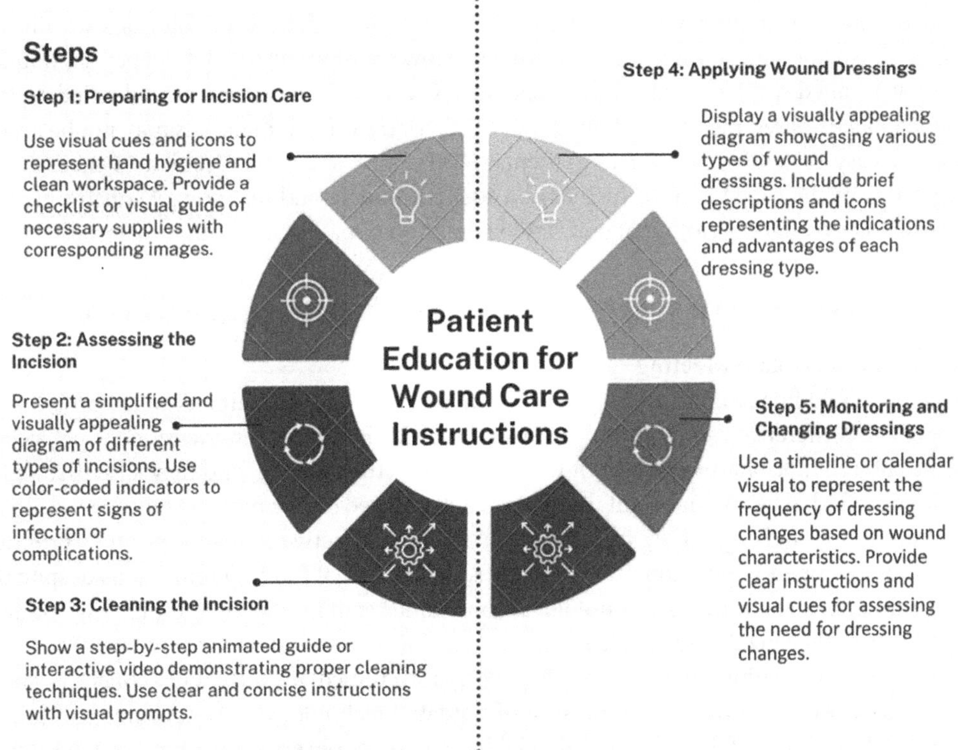

FIGURE 21.4 Interactive patient education diagram for wound care instructions identified by Raul at the local Central Valley Conference.

of the incision care process from his master's curriculum that might help Anthony retain information. Additionally, the use of colorful graphics and animation might help him maintain attention and focus during the nurse's discharge instructions. Raul also remembered a presentation at a local Central Valley Conference that included interactive diagrams highlighting the different steps in incision care including the types of wound dressings and when to change them (see Figure 21.4).

"I bet this diagram could be helpful in breaking down complex information into manageable chunks for not only neurodiverse patients but also the entire patient population," thought Raul.

TUESDAY, MARCH 23: DAY 22 OF THE DESIGN PROJECT

End of the Shift

Raul approached Betty and Rose at the end of the shift at the nurses' station to discuss his ideas for the patient education materials and other ideas for the project. "These seem like big changes that you are suggesting, Raul," Betty stated. "Think about our last budget report. We are already in the red and working overtime to compensate for the impacts of COVID-19. Despite the initial $64 million in state funding, CVM's limited fiscal resources have prevented us from investing in much needed technology upgrades. Our outdated infrastructure is vulnerable to cyber-attacks, and the existing internet connectivity may not support large multimedia files."

Raul nodded. "So, accessing and viewing the materials could be a challenge for both patients and staff?"

Betty nodded in agreement. "Exactly. We need to find alternative solutions within our budget, ensuring accessibility and effectiveness. How about we just stick to paper handouts?"

Rose recalled similar situations, even before COVID-19, where the hospital relied on traditional paper-based materials. Raul knew that these traditional materials may not be accessible or easy to understand for all patients. Raul, Betty, and Rose decided to meet at the beginning of their next shift to further consider the budget and technology constraints and their impact on the development and implementation of patient education materials.

WEDNESDAY, MARCH 31: DAY 30 OF THE DESIGN PROJECT

Second Project Team Meeting

"Glad we could finally meet. It feels like it's been forever," Betty exclaimed, welcoming everyone to the conference room on the first floor of CVM. Benny Rover, the resident physician, and Gabby Nicholson, the director of Unit 34B, joined the meeting, and they all settled in for what promised to be an important discussion. Betty kicked off the meeting by acknowledging the numerous challenges they faced in developing an effective patient education program for neurodivergent populations. She emphasized the internal funding limitations despite the $64 million of state funding, technological constraints, staff hesitancy, and the range of neurodiversities they needed to consider.

As the conversation unfolded, each participant chimed in with their concerns about different barriers. Benny raised the issue of outdated technology infrastructure and how it affected the delivery of digital materials. Gabby shared her observations about staff hesitancy and resistance to change. The team dove into a deep conversation while floating ideas and brainstorming possible solutions.

"This project sounds like a good idea. What can I do to help?" asked Raj Patel, a nurse practitioner on the unit.

Rose continued to discuss the original ideas for the project. "Raul and I could use your expertise to scale this project throughout our hospital system to include all patient education at discharge," said Rose.

Carolyn Gaynai, a respiratory therapist, spoke up, "I appreciate that you are including us, but we are from completely different disciplines with different scopes of practice that require more time and different teaching approaches at discharge."

Raul and Rose started to sense the enormity of the many barriers to the development and implementation of inclusive patient education. The discussion continued to gain momentum, with ideas flowing back and forth. Everyone explored a variety of possibilities such as leveraging existing resources, partnering with external organizations, and finding cost-effective alternatives. Amidst the lively exchange, Raul pondered where they might start to make the biggest impact, given their limited resources. As the meeting concluded, Raul was left with the crucial task of evaluating and prioritizing everyone's ideas while searching for the most efficient approaches that would yield the most productive outcomes without requiring maximum effort or resources.

Preliminary Analysis Questions

1. List barriers to the development of patient education materials in this case and describe their potential impact on possible solutions.
2. What approaches/strategies could Raul and Rose use to overcome the existing barriers identified in Question 1? How can Raul make the best use of available resources to have the biggest impact on patient education?
3. How can Raul and Rose encourage the team to see the value of designing with neurodiversity in mind at the beginning of the instructional design process?
4. Identify the different team members involved in either Anthony's or Zena's care. How can Raul and Rose draw on the team's expertise to enhance their care?

Implications for ID Practice

1. List the pros and cons related to evaluating and addressing existing constraints at the beginning of a design project in a medical context.
2. When beginning a design project, what strategies can designers use to ensure that *all* learners will benefit from their learning designs?
3. How can instructional designers approach, and work with, hesitant or resistant team members? How can designers address the valid concerns expressed by these team members?

22

Fiona Roberts

"Joyne-ing" the Learning Team at a Startup Company

Freddi Rokaw

Fiona received a notification from her job search site that Ed Stoppard, a former colleague and curriculum designer at Gizmo, had a new job at Joyne. "Joyne?" she thought. "What company is that? It must be something really special if Ed left Gizmo after so many years." She was intrigued and wanted to find out more. After a little searching, she learned that Joyne was a new business that Rob Jackson was starting in Silicon Valley. Jackson was a highly respected executive at Gizmo where Fiona once worked as a customer trainer. He had always been a visionary. Fiona couldn't wait to find out more about his next big idea.

Gizmo was a retail store that sold computers and offered customers personalized classes to help them become more proficient with their products. Fiona loved the teaching part of her job and wanted to further her career by formalizing her foundational knowledge in learning and curriculum design, so she left Gizmo to pursue a degree in instructional design through an online program at a prestigious university. She graduated with her MSEd in learning design and technology and was excited to put her new skills to work. Since graduating, she had been looking for the perfect job, but it turned out to be more difficult than she had imagined. It seemed the technology sector wasn't looking to hire women over the age of 35.

Fiona couldn't wait to call her friend, Gwen, to tell her she had seen an open position for an instructional designer at Rob Jackson's new startup company. Gwen had also worked at Gizmo as a customer trainer but left her job to accept a well-paying position as an instructional designer at EverTech, even though she had no formal training in learning design.

"I just found out that Rob Jackson is starting a new company called 'Joyne,'" Fiona said by phone. "Listen to this—not only is Rob Jackson in charge, but Ed is heading up the learning team. You remember Ed, don't you? He was the one who wrote and facilitated the 'train-the-trainer' courses at Gizmo."

"Oh yes," Gwen replied. "I remember what a great training program that was. Ed had so many interesting ways to teach. The customer service skills we gained in that course helped us teach our in-store customers how to use their computers and smartphones. I really believe we were successful because of the amazing training we got at Gizmo. I'm sure it was my experience there that made it easy for me to move right into my instructional design role here at EverTech."

DOI: 10.4324/9781003354468-25

Fiona replied, "I agree. The train-the-trainer courses at Gizmo were very effective. Well, they're looking for an instructional designer, and I think I'm going to apply for the job. If Joyne hires me to be on their learning team, I can create training that's even better than Gizmo's." Continuing, Fiona said, "I'd like to get in on the ground floor of this business and give them everything I know. This is the kind of disruptive tech company I've wanted to work for! It seems like the perfect fit."

Fiona asked Gwen about her interview at EverTech and what she might expect from a company like Joyne. Gwen said, "Well, they already knew they wanted to hire me, so my interview was pretty straightforward. I met with five people in person and had video calls with two global executives. They extended an offer right away, so I guess I made a good impression."

Thinking about Fiona's situation, Gwen said, "I'm sure Joyne will make you a great offer. They'd be foolish not to hire you." She suggested, "Just make sure they offer you a substantial salary and stock options. After all, you've got life experience *and* a graduate degree in learning design and technology. You've learned a lot about organizational learning, motivation theories, methods of instruction, and educational psychology from the program. You should definitely earn more than I do as an instructional designer here at EverTech. Let me know what happens!"

COMPANY DESCRIPTION

Joyne is a Silicon Valley startup company that specializes in selling emerging technologies and dispatching specialized technicians to deliver, set up, and teach customers how to use high-tech products in the comfort of their own homes. It has often been compared to other companies that come to your home to install and repair computer systems.

Joyne's three founders are experienced entrepreneurs who share a common professional background. They were all former executives and colleagues at a successful, well-established technology company. Joyne's major investors are well-known venture capitalists within the Silicon Valley business community.

A startup culture is one in which the focus of the company can change (or "pivot") on any given day. All corporate employees at headquarters (HQ) collaborate to contribute significantly to the direction of the company. "All Hands" meetings are held once a week to update everyone on past, present, and future company initiatives.

To fit into the startup culture, employees need to be agile enough to handle rapid change, have the ability to multitask, take initiative with little direction, work as many hours as needed, and be comfortable with fast-paced growth. If a startup company doesn't do well for its investors, they may choose to stop funding at any time. Founding employees typically have an ownership stake in the company. So theoretically, the harder they work, the more successful the company will be, thereby making their ownership (stock options) more valuable if the company were to go public in the future.

COMPANY GROWTH

Two years ago, Rob Jackson, Joyne's visionary, had the idea to build a company that could provide a personalized, high-touch service to customers, mostly older adults, who wanted help setting up and maintaining technology in their homes. Especially in a world filled with video courses and webinars, Jackson hoped to re-create a sense of community in neighborhoods across the country by sending trained field specialists into local communities to help their neighbors with new technology.

Within a year, Joyne secured enough venture capital funds to move into a new office space and hire key employees. The company also used this investment money to fill middle management positions and hire the first group of field specialists.

FIELD SPECIALISTS

Field specialists are the front line of Joyne, the majority of whom are between the ages of 20 and 25 years old and well educated. They are expected to use excellent customer service skills during every appointment at a customer's home. The company requires field specialists to be proficient with high-tech products so they can install, operate, demonstrate, and troubleshoot any situation. Field specialists are evaluated for their technical expertise before they are allowed to interact with paying customers.

Training for the field specialists is designed and developed by Joyne's learning department. Ed Stoppard, a 30-year-old former employee of Gizmo, was hired to build a learning department to create training for field specialists. Even without a formal education in instructional design, Ed has garnered a reputation for writing and delivering excellent training. His goal at Joyne is to create a training course for field specialists that can address the challenges of learning brand new technology at a fast pace, in a dynamic environment. Also, field specialists must be able to draw on good interpersonal skills to set up and teach new customers how to use specific technologies in their homes.

FIONA'S INTERVIEW

After taking advice from her colleagues, friends, and family, Fiona applied for the "learning experience designer" position at Joyne. Ed Stoppard called her the very next day.

"Fiona, what a nice surprise to hear from you after so many years!" It had been a long time since they had been in touch directly. "I see from your resume that you've recently earned a degree in learning design and technology. I'd love to know more about your recent experiences and how you see yourself fitting into a company like Joyne." He went on, "How about coming to our Silicon Valley headquarters to talk with us in person?"

"That would be wonderful, Ed. Thanks for considering me. I can't wait to learn more about Joyne and what you guys are doing out there. It will also be nice to catch up with you after so long."

"Great!" said Ed. "We'd like to have you come in this Friday for the day. We'll fly you in and out and provide you with transportation to and from the airport. We promise a quick turnaround. You'll receive a call from our recruiter this afternoon to set up a preliminary video screening call with you before you arrive."

"Wow! They really *do* work fast at start-up companies—it's already Tuesday," Fiona thought to herself.

"Oh, just one more thing," Ed added. "Sometimes we have to design workshops on short notice. Can you take a stab at one by 4:00 P.M. today? We will pilot it with a few employees tomorrow before you arrive on Friday. It doesn't have to be fancy, just think of the experience you want the learners to go through to hit the objectives. Remember, these are field specialists entering strangers' homes to help them with their technology."

Ed emailed Fiona a minimal framework for creating a "Safety Workshop."

From: Ed Stoppard <estoppard@joynecorp.com>
Date: Tuesday, January 15 at 11:28 A.M.

To: Fiona Roberts <froberts_msed@pmail.com>
Subject: Safety Workshop

Here are the details for the workshop we'd like to see:
Participants: 10 field specialists
Duration: Up to 1 hour
Materials: Classroom with projector, sticky notes, whiteboard, and a computer
Objective: After this workshop, field specialists will be able to:

- Describe the safety framework (below)
- Demonstrate the safety framework

Safety Framework:

1) Keep your cool!
2) Assess the immediate situation
3) Take the appropriate actions to stay safe

—ed

Just to make sure she was on the right track, Fiona emailed Ed to ask for some clarification about the context:

From: Fiona Roberts <froberts_msed@pmail.com>
Date: Tuesday, January 15 at 12:04 P.M.
To: Ed Stoppard <estoppard@joynecorp.com>
Subject: Re: Safety Workshop

Hi Ed,
Will the workshop be just one component of a day-long training or is it stand alone? If it's part of a full training day, what will the participants be learning before and after this workshop?
—Fiona

Ed replied with a short answer:

From: Ed Stoppard <estoppard@joynecorp.com>
Date: Tuesday, January 15 at 12:28 P.M.
To: Fiona Roberts <froberts_msed@pmail.com>
Subject: Re: Safety Workshop

Stand alone for now
—ed

That was it. Fiona wrote back with another question:

From: Fiona Roberts <froberts_msed@pmail.com>
Date: Tuesday, January 15 at 12:46 P.M.
To: Ed Stoppard <estoppard@joynecorp.com>
Subject: Re: Safety Workshop

Sorry to bother you, but just a couple more questions:

1. Do the 10 participants have previous experience working in the field?
2. Will all participants be in the classroom? Will there be any remote attendees?

~Fiona

Ed answered tersely:

From: Ed Stoppard <estoppard@joynecorp.com>
Date: Tuesday, January 15 at 12:48 P.M.
To: Fiona Roberts <froberts_msed@pmail.com>
Subject: Re: Safety Workshop

1. Yes
2. Maybe

—ed

Fiona was trying to get a bit of information about the needs of the field specialists. She figured she was on her own to do her best with the minimal information she was given. This workshop was going to be facilitated by and presented to people she didn't know. Still, Fiona saw this as an opportunity to showcase her expertise and prove her potential value to the company.

Fiona had time to do just a little bit of research into the topic of situational awareness to justify her content before she started designing the workshop, but she soon realized she only had enough time to stick to the basics. She would explain the parts of the framework and maybe come up with a good acronym for the learners to remember. She could add a quick activity to help the participants recall the parts of the framework.

She finished creating the design document, slides, and facilitator's guide in the allotted time and emailed the whole thing to Ed before the deadline of 4:00 P.M. Although there was so much more she could have added if she had the time, she felt pretty good about it. It was a brief but solid example of what she could do with "soft skills."

Fiona flew to San Francisco three days later. She was immediately greeted by Ed's familiar face as she entered the lobby of Joyne's headquarters.

"Welcome to 'HQ'! I'm so glad you could make it. Thanks for sending your workshop presentation. It looked good," Ed said cheerfully.

Fiona asked how the workshop went. Ed replied, "Oh, we didn't end up facilitating it. No worries, though, we've got a full day of interviews lined up for you. You'll be meeting with seven of my colleagues, including Rob Jackson. We'll make sure you finish on time so you can make your flight home this evening."

All the interviews went well. Fiona always enjoyed meeting new people, and she had many questions about the company and the culture. It seemed everyone felt comfortable with her.

After meeting with Rob Jackson, Ed led her into one of the meeting rooms and handed her a folder with an offer letter in it. "You made a great impression on everyone you met today. We'd like to offer you a position here at Joyne. We all feel you'd be a great asset to the learning team. I hope you'll accept."

The salary seemed very generous. She knew it was more than her friends were making, and stock options were also included in the package. Ed pressured Fiona to sign the offer before she left to go back home. He assured her it was more than fair and that her shares in the company would have the potential to make her a fortune if the company were to go public someday. She signed the offer, and they shook hands on the deal. "Welcome to the Joyne family. We look forward to you moving to Silicon Valley. We have a lot to do."

Fiona certainly did have a lot to do. She needed to pack up her apartment, find someone to sublet it, find movers, find an apartment near Joyne headquarters, move in, unpack, and get settled. All of this was supposed to happen in three weeks while she was also expected to work from home. The move seemed daunting, but she was so excited to join the company she didn't give it a second thought.

GETTING STARTED

Fiona was Ed's first hire on the learning team. Knowing that everything happened quickly at startup companies like Joyne, Fiona still hoped to take some time to settle in and learn the basics from Ed. During her first week on the job, however, it became apparent that Ed was not available to mentor her and that she would be on her own to assess the training needs of the company. She had to step up and take the initiative to start developing Joyne's training on her own.

To begin, Fiona drew from her academic experience. She knew the best place to start was to conduct a comprehensive front-end analysis. The resulting information would be used to begin building solid learning objectives.

When not at the office, Fiona went into the field to observe the veteran field specialists conducting mock appointments with friends and family. She also started looking for learning assets and other resources for a continually growing collection of products the company would sell and support. In addition to these tasks, Ed and Fiona started a search for talented learning professionals to join their team. Ed wasn't kidding when he said that working at a startup company meant being able to multitask and pivot quickly!

A few weeks after Fiona was hired, Ed recruited Chuck White, his old friend and colleague from Gizmo. Ed asked Fiona if she would take a few minutes to interview Chuck by phone. "He's thinking of leaving Gizmo, and I believe he would be a good addition to the team."

Fiona initially thought Chuck would be a natural fit for the team. Chuck was an interesting person. He started out studying music composition and ended up at Gizmo writing curriculum. He had no formal background in instructional design, but he wrote successful 'train-the-trainer' courses at Gizmo. In fact, he was the one who taught Fiona how to facilitate that curriculum for others at the company.

During the phone interview, Chuck managed to turn the conversation around and ask Fiona about *her* experience. Chuck said, "You and I think very differently. If there's a question about learning, you'll probably go look it up in a *book*." He said the word "book" as if it were a bad word. He went on, "I bet your formal education, especially from an *online* university, will hold up our progress. Academia moves much slower than business, and it isn't real. It's all theory."

Fiona was taken aback and even felt insulted. Chuck went on to explain his own agenda and personal goals for creating new training. It sounded as if he had already been given the job. Although she respected Chuck and admired the work he had done at Gizmo, she concluded that Chuck would not be a good collaborator. He obviously had specific ideas of what constituted effective learning. Working with him could be very challenging.

After the phone call, Fiona approached Ed to discuss her conversation with Chuck. She mentioned that she was offended by some of the things Chuck had said. "I don't think we should hire him as a full-time member of our team." Without trying to diminish his abilities, Fiona said, "I think he could be an important contributor, but maybe we should consider hiring him as outside consultant."

Ed replied, "Well then, once Chuck joins the team, your first conversation should be used to clear the air." It was obvious that Ed had already decided, regardless of Fiona's opinion, that Chuck would be hired onto the team.

"Hmmm, it seems as if my opinion has no value," she thought to herself. "I guess I'll need to stand up for what I believe in and be more assertive about it from now on."

Once Chuck arrived, Fiona began to realize that all of the tasks Ed had given her—interviewing candidates, building learning objectives, and conducting research on learning management systems (LMS)—were all just meant to keep her occupied while he and Chuck met with upper management to determine the over-arching goals for the company's learning and development department. She wondered why Chuck had been included in those conversations and not her.

"Could it be that this is one of those 'old boys' clubs' that I've heard about? I wonder if they don't want to include me because I'm a woman. Maybe they think I wouldn't understand the bigger picture. Once again, I'm getting the feeling that my skills and experiences just aren't considered very valuable."

Fiona decided that she would demonstrate, through her actions, that she knew the importance of a thorough front-end analysis, solid learning objectives, and strategic evaluation. "They will recognize my value soon enough," she thought. Fiona compiled an extensive list of learning objectives based on what she had learned from the stakeholders and subject matter experts at Joyne. She even included weighted objectives to use as a solid starting point. When Ed saw the list, he was overwhelmed with the number and complexity of goals she had identified (see Figure 22.1).

"What kind of learning objectives are these?" he asked. "Man! This looks like a school project!" Ed was unable to see the need for identifying knowledge gaps before creating specific learning objectives. "We already know what the field specialists need to learn," he declared. "There's no need to make things more complicated."

OUTCOME	OBJECTIVE (Field Specialists will be able to...)	LEARNING STRATEGY	WEIGHT				
Promote the core principles of Joyne	Recognize the core principles of Joyne in existing press and branding materials	Facilitated discussion/Activity	1	2	3	4	5
	Integrate core principles in all interactions	On-going application	1	2	3	4	5
Create personalized, collaborative customer experiences	Identify individual customer learning styles	Facilitated discussion Role-play	1	2	3	4	5
	Match content delivery to individual customer learning style	Engagement scenarios	1	2	3	4	5
Perform each step of an appointment	Identify the steps of an appointment	Facilitated discussion Share Observe Debrief	1	2	3	4	5
	Use all steps of an appointment	Role-play Mock Engagements Observe/Shadow Engagements On-going application	1	2	3	4	5
	Assess safety concerns	Self-reflection Observe Discuss	1	2	3	4	5
	Apply the Joyne safety framework in potentially unsafe situations	Engagement scenarios	1	2	3	4	5
Communicate clearly	Recognize opportunities to create productive dialogue	Observation Discussion	1	2	3	4	5
	Apply strategies for creating an environment which fosters productive dialogue	Role-play activities Debrief	1	2	3	4	5
	Identify skills needed to organize thoughts that need to be shared	Facilitated discussion Self-reflection	1	2	3	4	5
	Identify skills needed to clarify thoughts that need to be shared	Self-reflection	1	2	3	4	5
	Prioritize thoughts that need to be shared	Self-reflection	1	2	3	4	5
	Apply the skills needed to organize, clarify, and prioritize thoughts that need to be shared	Share	1	2	3	4	5
	Integrate appropriate body language and gestural techniques into conversations in order to put others at ease and instill confidence	Observation Discuss Share	1	2	3	4	5

FIGURE 22.1 Outcome-objective-strategy alignment document.

"We can't use these," Ed said, dismissing her work. He insisted, "Joyne is a fast-paced startup company and we don't have time for all of this." He shut her down saying, "We don't do instructional design here, we do ADDIE!"

She took a deep breath and decided to move on with what she had. She was new on the job and didn't want to cause any friction.

OBSERVATIONS IN THE FIELD

As part of her needs analysis, Fiona interviewed veteran field specialists who had been working with their friends and family, who were acting as paying customers. They hadn't yet had any formal training from Joyne—that was one of the reasons she found their input so valuable.

"Watching the field specialists learn how to use the new products is so much fun," Fiona thought to herself. She could see that most of them were eager to take a new product out of the box and immediately start figuring it out with their peers. This experiential learning environment gave them a safe place to learn by trial and error. They also seemed compelled to reach out and share their new knowledge with each other.

Watching the field specialists learn how to operate the products was one thing, but Fiona wanted to attend an appointment. She asked Jeremy Patterson, one of her favorite field specialists, if she could shadow him during one of his appointments. After just a short time with the customer, Fiona could see that the essential qualities of a successful field specialist included more than knowing how to operate high-tech products; equally important were the skills used for building trusting relationships with customers.

In addition to being technically proficient with products, field specialists needed exemplary customer service skills to make personal connections with, and gain the trust of, their clients during an appointment. They were expected to arrive at appointments on time, be polite, communicate clearly, have respect for the customers and their homes, listen actively to any concerns, share in the excitement of unboxing a new product, set realistic expectations, and create engaging and worthwhile learning experiences.

After the appointment, Fiona asked Jeremy, "How do you feel about walking into a stranger's house and meeting them for the first time?"

"For the most part, it's been great. All of our customers have been really kind. One lady even offered me lunch! But seriously, so far I've felt comfortable teaching all my customers in their homes."

With situational awareness in the back of her mind, Fiona asked Jeremy, "Have you ever encountered a situation that made you feel uncomfortable?"

Jeremy thought about it. "As a matter of fact, I was at a house just last week that had two guard dogs. I could hear them growling the minute I got to the door. I wasn't sure what to do because I'm terrified of big dogs." He continued, "Luckily, the customer was nice enough to put the dogs in the backyard before she answered the door to let me in. I was so relieved!"

Fiona was relieved that Jeremy's experience worked out well, but she had to ask herself, "What if it hadn't been that easy? How would Jeremy have handled a more threatening situation delicately without running away or disrespecting the customer?" And even if they felt uncomfortable, field specialists needed to learn how to recognize and deal with these types of uncomfortable or even dangerous situations. Entering strangers' homes was part of their jobs, and field specialists deserved careful training to help them understand potential risks.

CREATING A SAFETY WORKSHOP

Fiona felt so strongly about the safety of the field specialists that she decided to revisit the workshop she created for her interview and expand it to include some of the concerns from the field. The safety framework workshop that Ed had asked her to design was an excellent start, but there was so much more to know regarding situational awareness. She looked around for some scientific evidence and found academic papers written about the subject from a psychological point of view. Most of the research referred to military decisions, though. She would have to interpret the information and apply it to the job of field specialist.

Fiona decided to design an activity that provided a set of parameters that could guide the actions of the field specialists in threatening situations. She would begin by giving them real or virtual sticky notes and asking them to describe situations they may be concerned about. They could use real or imaginary examples that might make them feel threatened or uncomfortable in the field. The anonymous notes would be compiled for field specialists to read. They would then discuss how each situation might relate to Joyne's safety framework: recognize, assess, and take action.

Using Jeremy's example, she came up with a plausible problem situation for the class to solve together. She created an example with a picture of a growling dog and a possible scenario (see Figure 22.2).

Before the group discussed possible solutions, the facilitator would provide a set of parameters to guide their responses. For example, responses should incorporate the following four components: stating the problem in neutral terms (e.g., "I see you have a very spirited dog"), taking responsibility for the issue (e.g., "I'm nervous around big dogs"), asking directly for a solution (e.g., "Could you please put him in a different room or outside until we're done with

You arrive early at a customer's home. As soon as you ring the doorbell, you hear the deep bark of a large dog. When the customer opens the door, the dog starts for you, but the owner holds the dog back by its pinch collar. The dog is obviously agitated and is baring its teeth. To make matters worse, you've always been afraid of dogs because a dog bit you when you were a little kid. **What would you do?**

FIGURE 22.2 Safety workshop scenario.

our appointment?"), and reinforcing the purpose and intended outcome of the appointment (e.g., "I want to make sure you get my full attention").

Following this, the group would devise other solutions that met this same set of parameters.

Fiona realized it might be challenging to evaluate general common sense, but this workshop would be the first step toward making sure the field specialists were prepared to deal with any threatening situations in the field. She thought it would be possible to assess the reaction to a fictional situation in the workshop and evaluate the ability of the learners to apply the framework, using the parameters she had outlined.

Fiona felt confident about the workshop and was ready to share her ideas with Ed and Chuck. She would make sure to bring up the importance of including it in the curriculum at the planning meeting Ed had scheduled for that afternoon.

BRAINSTORMING PRODUCT TRAINING

Ed, Chuck, and Fiona met at a whiteboard and began sketching out a plan for product training. Ed and Chuck decided it would be an online e-learning module, provided through an LMS. The LMS would also serve as a repository for resources from the product manufacturers like user manuals, installation guides, and compliance statements, as well as links to amateur how-to videos from the Internet.

As the diagram on the whiteboard started to take the form of a sprawling flowchart (see Figure 22.3), Fiona questioned the overall plan by remarking, "This complicated workflow looks like it will be difficult to navigate. I'm concerned it will be more work than necessary for the field specialists."

Chuck disagreed by countering, "It's like a game—everybody their age grew up with gaming, and I think the learning experiences we create should simulate that kind of play." Ed added that badges could be used as an incentive to make the learning more engaging for this group of digital natives.

Chuck jumped in, "Oh yeah, good idea! I could design some really cool badges." Ed agreed. He thought the badges would be a great way to motivate learners to advance along their online learning paths.

The system that Ed and Chuck sketched out, without any contribution from Fiona, was structured to guide learners through three levels of product knowledge. Each level had a "gate" that could be unlocked only by passing a product knowledge quiz. The learner would earn a digital badge if they passed the quiz. The badges would then allow the learner to proceed to the next level. The learner would need to earn all three knowledge badges to achieve "expert status" on any one product. Once recognized as an "expert" on a product, the field specialist would need a manager's approval before they would be permitted to help real customers with that product (see Figure 22.4).

"We'll probably need to create a workshop to teach the field specialists how to follow the process of product expertise," Ed added. "It's a little involved." They agreed that they should include a separate module in the overall curriculum related to the complex LMS navigation of product knowledge training. Ed and Chuck were ready to move on.

Fiona tried again to participate in the conversation. She added, "I'm concerned that this system will not prepare the field specialists for their appointments with customers, and I wonder if the pace is too slow." Her words fell on deaf ears as they looked at her with disdain. She found it difficult to contribute her ideas to the conversation and was rarely acknowledged for trying to collaborate. Fiona knew from her field observations that Joyne's veteran field

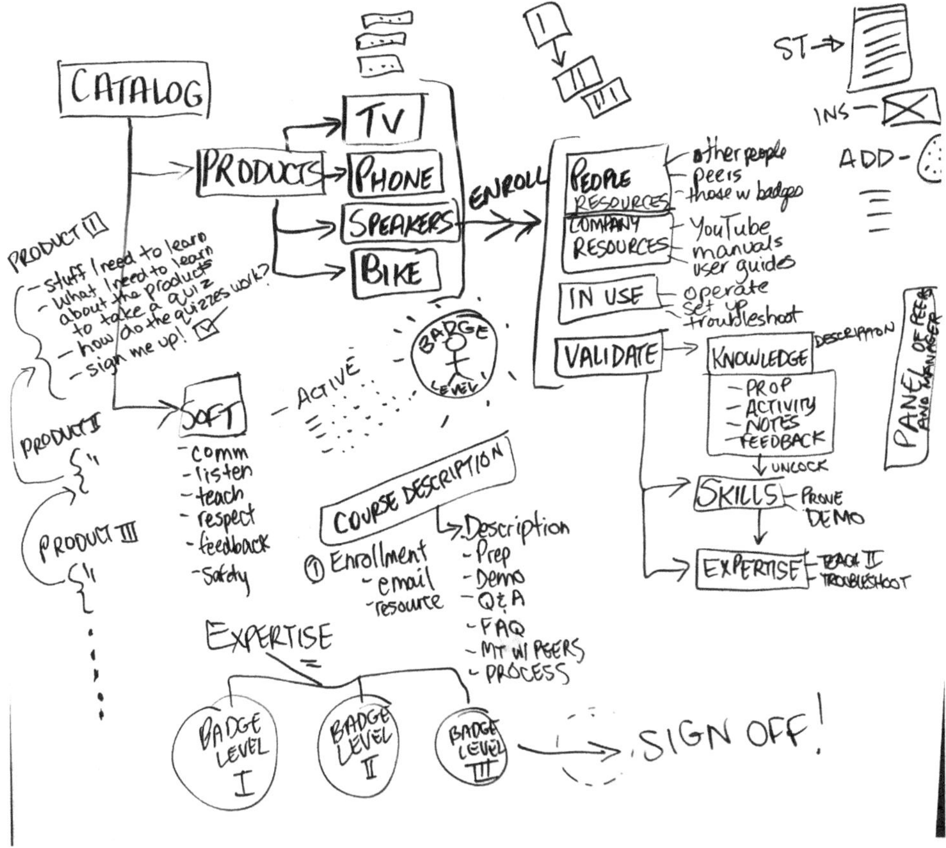

FIGURE 22.3 Whiteboard planning.

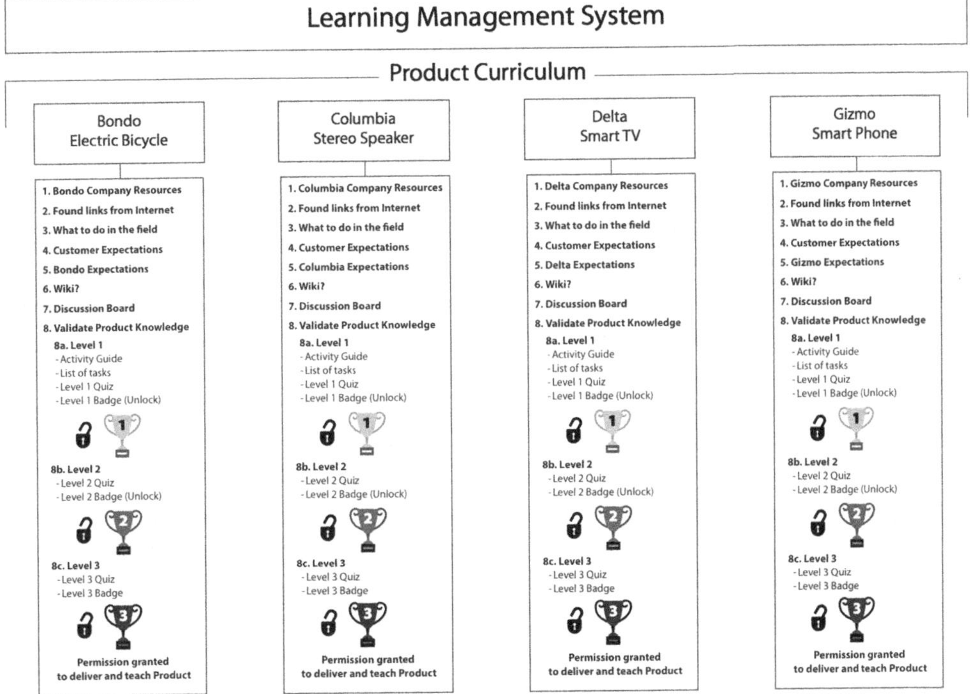

FIGURE 22.4 LMS product curriculum chart.

specialists seemed more interested in learning informally. Her foundational knowledge of instructional design and her past experiences suggested there were more effective ways for these young people to become proficient with the products—far beyond what she saw taking form on the whiteboard—but she deferred to Ed and Chuck's experiences. She figured they must know best.

WHAT ABOUT SAFETY?

Fiona asserted herself by saying, "Hey, let's not forget to talk about customer service and safety training. I would like to add a safety workshop to the overall plan. I've expanded the workshop I created for my interview. It covers Joyne's 'Safety Framework' and how it applies to the field specialist job. They need to know how to recognize potentially dangerous scenarios and what to do if they feel uncomfortable or threatened in any situation. I've added a lot of discussions and activities that should really keep them engaged. I've hit all of Ed's learning objectives and included a few others. I'm in the middle of developing the assessment instruments to measure success." She assured them, "Along with the customer service skills training, both components should fit within the overall time constraints of a two-week course."

"That seems like a lot of work and training time for something they'll never use," Chuck said.

"I agree," Ed added. "We would never put our field specialists in harm's way, so why scare them unnecessarily?"

Remembering what Ed said about ADDIE the other day, she tried to reframe her ideas so she could get their buy-in. She felt strongly that safety training was important and should be a priority. She wasn't going to give in this time. Using a different tactic, Fiona told Ed and Chuck, "I've already done the analysis by talking to the field specialists on-the-job, designed the content, and developed the materials—the only thing left to do is to implement it. I've got half the evaluation figured out, and we'll get more information after the course is over." She added, "Then, we can work together to create the customer service skills portion of training. It shouldn't take too long. We can start with the soft skills modules you wrote at Gizmo and make them relevant to the job of field specialist."

"I don't know," Ed wondered. "We've already got so much to cover." It was apparent Ed didn't like the idea of adding safety training to an already packed curriculum.

Chuck suggested a solution: "Why don't we redo the workshop Fiona created and rework it as an optional self-led activity? We could map out the ideas and activities on a laminated card and have small groups work together to figure it out on their own. Field specialists could choose to do the activity if they had some downtime."

Fiona came back, "I think the course needs more attention than that. Learning these skills shouldn't be optional. It's a delicate subject, and as Ed said, we don't want to scare them."

"Let's figure it out when we get all the pieces together," Ed said, delaying the issue. The meeting ended with a plan to come together later in the afternoon to sketch out the entire training arc. Chuck volunteered to create an interactive storyboard to make it easy for them to map out the two-week plan. He retreated to his desk to work on it alone.

PUTTING IT ALL TOGETHER

Three o'clock rolled around. "It's amazing how fast the time flies when you're busy!" Fiona thought. She collected her computer and notebook and headed off to the conference room.

The "bullpen" office style was great for collaboration, but the constant noise and activity sometimes made it difficult to concentrate.

Ed and Chuck already had the projector set up and were working on the course outline. Fiona showed up at the expected time and was surprised they had started without her.

Chuck was annoyed at Fiona's entrance and said, "Well, I guess we'll have to start over." He went on to explain how his interactive storyboard worked. "We drag the modules from the side and place them into the timeline until we've put them in a logical order and filled all the time slots."

Chuck had boxes for every module: "History of the Company," "Human Resources," "Benefits," "Product Knowledge," "Badging Ceremonies," "Navigating Your Product Training," and "Unnamed Activities." Fiona was happy to see that her safety workshop had a box, as well as other customer service skills, like active listening, communication skills, and time management. However, after an hour of pushing boxes around, Fiona noticed that each day was filled with everything but the soft skills (see Figure 22.5).

Fiona was disappointed and frustrated at the lack of time dedicated to the inclusion of soft skills. It was clear this type of training was going to take a back seat to learning how to use the fun products. The imbalance was apparent. Could it be that Ed and Chuck assumed

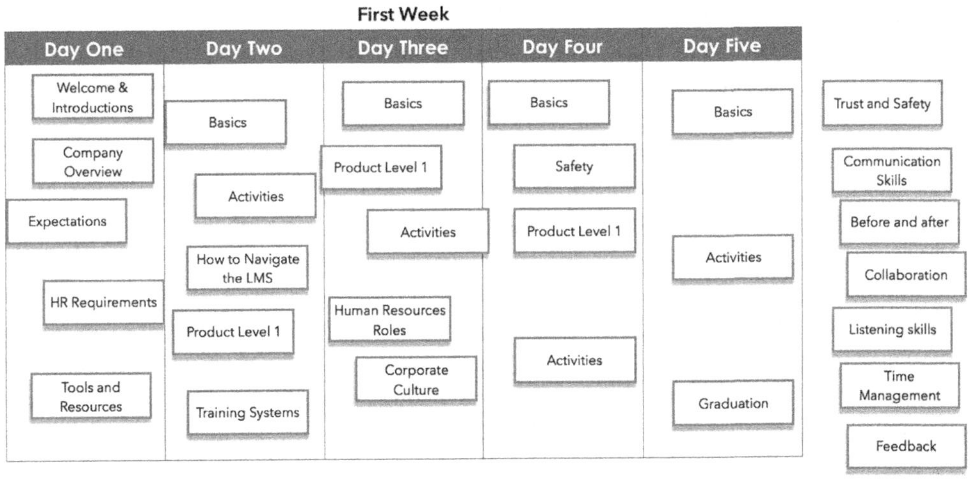

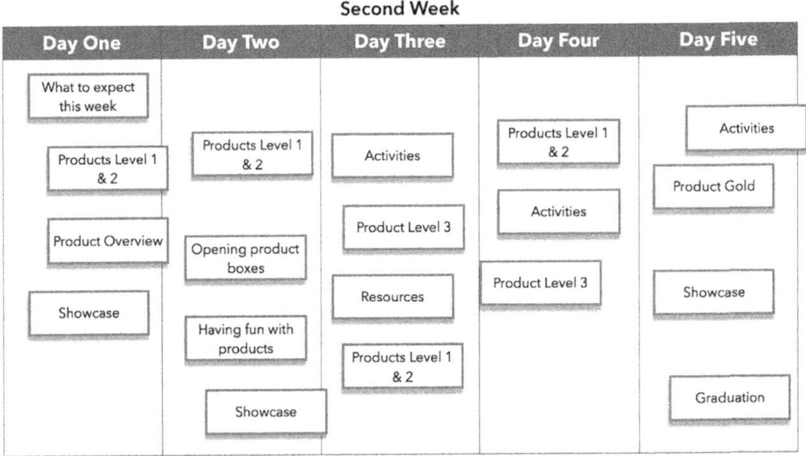

FIGURE 22.5 Course outline storyboard.

that the field specialists already had this kind of training at Gizmo? Perhaps Ed and Chuck thought teaching and assessing behaviors and attitudes would require more effort to develop than technical training.

Most of the field specialists were former employees at Gizmo, so it was assumed they had already learned good customer service skills. Still, they were hired at Joyne because they had friendly dispositions, mature attitudes, and a love for learning new technology. They weren't necessarily hired for their common sense and customer service skills.

When Fiona spoke up about the importance of safety training, Chuck argued, "You can't teach common sense. People either have it or they don't. Learning things like empathy, active listening, and the art of conversation are difficult to assess. How can you tell if someone has more common sense at the end of training than they did before they started? We just don't have that much time. Besides, what could possibly go wrong?"

CHECKING IN WITH THE FIELD SPECIALISTS

The first iteration of product training was built in the LMS and ready for online testing. The veteran field specialists progressed through the badging process to validate their knowledge of a few products and subsequently began conducting appointments. Fiona left the office and joined them in the field. All of the field specialists connected with Fiona. They trusted and respected her and were quick to share their honest feedback. She decided to meet with Jeremy, first, to find out how he was doing. She specifically wanted to assess the impact the LMS training had on his ability to do his job.

"Hi, Jeremy, how are you doing?" she greeted him at the coffee shop.

"Not so good, Fiona. I've spent the last few hours here trying to pass the quizzes and get my badge for the electric bike I'm supposed to deliver this afternoon."

"I'm sorry you're feeling so much pressure, Jeremy. What can I do to help?"

"I'm not sure if you can help, Fiona. This online product training is awkward and confusing. It's the most stressful part of my job." He continued, "It takes too much time away from actually using the product, and I am stuck on my laptop learning it on my own. If I need a user manual or videos to watch, I can just find them for myself. Besides, how is someone supposed to learn how to ride an electric bike by playing an online game and doing quizzes?" Jeremy continued, "I know I'm not the only one who's having trouble with this. I met up with Manuel, Nadja, and Amelia yesterday, and they're all saying the same thing."

Fiona empathized, "I understand your frustrations. Let me see what I can do when I get back to HQ this afternoon. This is great feedback, and I'll be sure to share it with Ed and Chuck. Thanks for testing out the method. I hope we'll be able to make some adjustments to the training that will make it easier and more fun for you and the other field specialists."

Back at HQ, Fiona discussed the feedback with Ed and Chuck, hoping they would at least reconsider using locked gates in the design flow. She knew this wasn't the way the field specialists learned best. Despite the feedback from Jeremy, Ed said there was no time to go back and change anything. A group of new field specialists was set to arrive tomorrow, and the facilitator's guide was done.

Early in the morning the next day, Ed and Chuck approached Fiona. Chuck said, "We want you to facilitate the course today because you know the material and connect easily with your learners." Fiona knew in her heart that they were sending her away from the team because they didn't want her involvement in building or changing content. There wasn't enough time to challenge them. The new group was about to arrive.

Preliminary Analysis Questions

1. How can Fiona assure that the field specialists are adequately prepared to meet all of their customers' needs (e.g., technical, communication, interpersonal)?
2. What strategies can Fiona use to increase the safety and situational awareness of field specialists when it doesn't appear to be a company priority?
3. Jeremy expresses frustration with the online training. Describe differences between the assumptions that Ed and Chuck made about this audience and what Jeremy reported as being the specialists' training experiences. Suggest strategies to better align the learners' needs and the instructional goals.
4. In this case, Fiona wonders why her work is not being valued and considers the possibility that her age and gender are factors. What evidence is provided in the case that either supports or refutes this interpretation of the situation?

Implications for ID Practice

1. In a startup culture, how can training be scaled, maintained, and facilitated in such a dynamically changing environment: frequent software and hardware updates, changes to employee roles, hybrid versus in-person training, and evolving company direction?
2. What issues should an instructional designer consider when developing training for a skill or topic that may rarely, or never, be applied in practice?
3. How can designers promote values around safety, diversity, or other soft skills when the company doesn't prioritize these goals?
4. What strategies can instructional designers use if their skills, methods, or learning approaches are not taken seriously by their peers or superiors?

23

Cassie Standage

Developing a Workplace Violence Prevention Training

Amy Rogers and Jason K. McDonald

CASSIE'S FIRST PROJECT

Wednesday, January 4

Cassie was surprised to see a call coming in from Melissa Jennings, project manager at Arizona ID Experts (AIDE). She wasn't due to start her remote instructional designer position with the company for another few days, so she answered the phone hesitantly.

"Hello?" Cassie said.

"Hi, Cassie. Sorry to bother you before your official start date," replied Melissa.

"Oh, that's no problem. How can I help you?"

"Well," said Melissa, "we just got a time-sensitive request from our primary client, the Emergency Services Association of Arizona, or ESA. As I mentioned in one of your interviews, we are contracted with the ESA to create 10 blended training experiences each year that are available to all 230 fire departments in the state. So, that's training for approximately 9,000 firefighters."

"Right, I remember," Cassie said.

"Well," Melissa went on, "due to a recent tragedy in the firefighter community, the ESA associate director, Chief Kyle Adams, has made an additional request for a workplace violence prevention training to be available to all Arizona firefighters by the end of April."

Melissa went on to tell Cassie that three weeks prior, a firefighter had brought a gun to the fire station where he worked and had shot and killed his co-worker and injured the station captain.

Cassie was too shocked to respond. She had just recently received her master's degree in instructional design (ID), and this was her first full-time position. She hoped she wasn't in over her head.

Melissa continued, "Under normal circumstances, I would assign one of our senior instructional designers to lead the project. But all the IDs are neck deep in their regularly scheduled ESA projects, so I'm going to head this one up myself. I was hoping you'd be willing to work with me so we can get the job done in three months, per Chief Adams' request."

Now Cassie *did* know what to say, and she quickly responded, "That sounds like an amazing opportunity."

DOI: 10.4324/9781003354468-26

From: Jennings, Melissa <m.jennings@aide.com>

Sent: January 4 at 10:27 A.M.

To: Standage, Cassie <cassiestandage@gmail.com>

Subject: Project kickoff

Hi Cassie,

Here's the kickoff event invite. Once you have your work email set up on Monday, you can accept the invite from there, but I wanted you to have the details down now. I'm glad you're willing to work on this project. A quick heads up on who will be at the meeting:

- Chief Kyle Adams: Emergency Services Association Executive Director, 30+ years in the fire service.
- Chief Andy Bingham: retired firefighter chief, lead SME on learner population and how the topic of workplace violence uniquely impacts firefighters.
- Greg Jones: workplace violence prevention SME, chief threat assessment officer. Corporate trainer and management consultant specializing in workplace violence prevention, 20+ years of experience conducting threat assessments and designing risk mitigation plans.
- Michael Kempton: retired firefighter chief, internal SME, working for AIDE.

Workplace Violence Prevention Kickoff

Wednesday, January 11, 9 A.M.–10:30 A.M.

Join with Google Meet

Organizer
Melissa Jennings

Guests
Kyle Adams
Andy Bingham
Greg Jones
Michael Kempton
Cassie Standage

Talk soon!

Melissa

Melissa Jennings
Project Manager
Arizona Instructional Design Experts

FIGURE 23.1 Kickoff meeting email invitation.

Cassie had been very impressed by Melissa throughout the entire hiring process and was excited about the possibility of working closely (well, "virtually" close) with her. Since this was Cassie's first non-higher-education ID role, she knew there was a lot she could learn from Melissa—even with the team being fully remote.

"I want to be fully transparent about the circumstances before I make any official assignments. You'd be working with some great but intense SMEs. The topic is heavy, and the stakes are high. Not to mention, a course like this would typically be developed in five months, not three. What do you think?" Melissa asked.

Again, Cassie didn't hesitate. "I would love to be a part of the project. It seems like a great opportunity to really make a difference. Thanks for trusting me with this."

Melissa thanked Cassie for her willingness to jump on board and said she'd pass on more details once Cassie officially started on Monday. When Cassie checked her email later that day, she saw a calendar invite to the project kickoff meeting, scheduled for three days after her start date (see Figure 23.1).

DAYS 1 AND 2

Monday, January 9

Over the weekend, Cassie googled all the names of the participants attending the kickoff meeting and tried to find news articles about the fire station shooting, but she hadn't found much. She was hoping she'd show up Monday morning and jump right into project work. Unfortunately for Cassie, her first day was like most other first days. There were onboarding courses to watch and HR paperwork to fill out. All the while, Cassie's list of questions about the project grew.

Tuesday, January 10

Day 2 was more onboarding. Cassie familiarized herself with AIDE's style guide and then reviewed previous courses the team had developed. Seeing the style guide "in action" was helpful as she reviewed the courses and saw how the style guide kept the team consistent in their content presentation.

Finally, at 3:30 P.M., an email from Melissa came through (see Figure 23.2).

From: Melissa Jennings <m.jennings@aide.com>

Sent: January 10 at 3:30 P.M.

To: Cassie Standage <c.standage@aide.com>

Subject: Items to review

Hey there,

Hope onboarding is going well! Here are a few things to review before the kickoff meeting tomorrow. I'll facilitate the meeting. We'll meet after so I can answer your questions. See you at 9!

Melissa

Melissa Jennings
Project Manager
Arizona Instructional Design Experts

2 Attachments
ESA demographics.docx
AFTER ACTION REPORT.docx

Note: The email included two attachments for review (see Figures 23.3 and 23.4).

FIGURE 23.2 Email from Melissa to Cassie.

Emergency Services of Arizona Demographics

230 fire stations

Stations serve metropolitan, suburban, and rural communities.

8,050 firefighters

Firefighter demographics range widely from station to station. Overall, demographic information for firefighters in Arizona:

- 7.4% of all firefighters are women, while 92.6% are men.
- Firefighters must be 18 years of age with a high school diploma or GED certificate.
- The average age of an employed firefighter is 38 years old.
- Firefighters are primarily White (69.0%), followed by Hispanic or Latino/a (15.3%), Black or African American (8.1%), and Other (4.8%).

FIGURE 23.3 Email attachment: ESA demographics.

AFTER ACTION REPORT

Incident

At 0700 Firefighter Raven arrived at the station. He made his way to the kitchen where the rest of the crew was gathered. He confronted Firefighter Mack, said a few words, and then pulled out a handgun and shot him. Captain Diaz and others charged Firefighter Raven and were successful in disarming him. Several crew members were able to keep Firefighter Raven restrained until police arrived at the scene. Firefighter Raven was arrested and remains in police custody.

The EMTs on duty transported Firefighter Mack to the hospital. He succumbed to his injuries later that day.

Captain Diaz received minor injuries in the confrontation and was eventually taken to the hospital for evaluation of his injuries. He was discharged later that day.

FIGURE 23.4 Email attachment: After action report.

KICKOFF MEETING

Wednesday, January 11

Cassie was eager to make a good first impression, so she signed onto the call a few minutes early. There was some banter back and forth between the meeting participants before the kickoff officially started.

"You look older than I remember," Michael said to Chief Bingham.

"Oh yeah, retirement will age ya. It's nothing like the carefree days of 24-hour shifts, living with my co-workers," Chief Bingham joked. "Greg, long time no see. How's Kathy doing?"

"Hey, Chief. Kathy is doing great. Are you loving your retirement home in Tennessee? We're looking at properties out there."

Casual conversation continued for a few minutes until Melissa got the meeting started. "First things first, we have a new AIDE team member joining us for this project. Cassie has been brought up to speed on the background of this case."

Cassie chimed in, "Yeah, Kyle, I think it's great that you're prioritizing a training like this. I can't wait to get started and work with all of you."

"Yes, *Chief Adams*, we really can't wait to get started," Melissa expressed.

Cassie flushed and made herself a note: *Chief* Adams, not Kyle!

Then, it was down to business. Melissa opened it up for a team discussion about what everyone thought the training needed to cover. Greg Jones, the workplace violence prevention SME, got the ball rolling.

"From a prevention perspective, there are certain things that must be included. For starters, we've got to talk about behaviors of concern. These are basically the warning signs we see before an act of violence occurs. And there are always warning signs. I've got data on what these behaviors are, who's likely to observe them, and some stats on reporting."

"Thanks, Greg," Chief Adams said. "We definitely want our firefighters aware of these behaviors and passing them up the chain, but I know there is a lot of hesitancy to report because they don't want to get someone in trouble or rat someone out."

"Right. And that's not unique to firefighters. We see this in every workplace environment. One thing that is very important to emphasize in any training on this is that the goal of reporting is not to get someone in trouble. It's to get someone help. And you have to show your people that that's what the response will be. Not probation, not getting fired. Help."

The conversation continued with lots of dialogue among the group members. Cassie tried to take notes, but her head was spinning. *How on earth were they going to fit all of this into one training?*

After giving everyone a chance to speak, Melissa stopped the discussion and shared her screen. She had color-coded sticky notes for each idea that was mentioned (see Figure 23.5).

As she gave everyone a moment to review her notes, Melissa asked, "I've written down all your ideas here. I'm curious as you look at all the ideas together, do you think there is anything that we can or should cut?"

For the first time since the meeting started, it was quiet.

Melissa let the silence sink in and then continued, "Most of you have been in kickoff meetings with me before, where I've cut huge chunks of content. But this training is different. I'm assuming the silence means you all agree with me when I say, there's nothing here that jumps out as needing to be cut. But this is *a lot* of content. So, here's what I propose, Chief Adams: two training courses.

"The first will include the content on the left here. This is content *every single firefighter* needs to know. We could have a training like this done on the expedited timeline requested. The second training would be specifically for chiefs and captains. I heard a lot of comments about providing leadership with more support as they encounter the behaviors Greg has mentioned. If I'm understanding right, crucial conversations aren't really happening with firefighters who are displaying these behaviors, and that seems to stem from chiefs and captains not really knowing how to help these individuals."

To that, Chief Bingham said, "Yeah, in the past when you had a guy causing problems or displaying certain behaviors of concern, captains would get annoyed and get the guy moved to a different station—make him a different captain's problem. But the issues he was causing were never documented, so when he starts doing the same thing at the next station, that captain doesn't realize it's a pattern. He also gets annoyed and sends the guy somewhere else. This can happen over and over. Now you have a guy that's been shuffled from station to station. He hasn't gotten any help or support. There has been no documentation of what's been going on. Everyone thinks he's annoying. And after years of this, the guy snaps—goes absolutely crazy. That's when we have problems like what happened in Cave Creek."

Cassie noticed the other firefighters nodding in agreement.

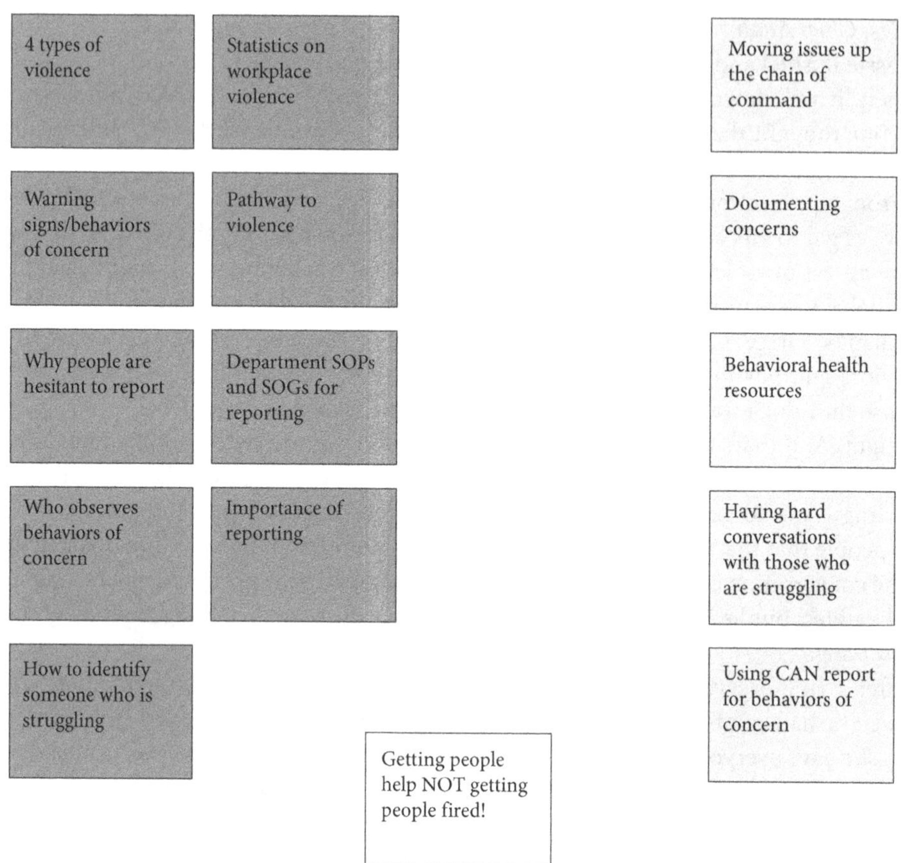

FIGURE 23.5 Melissa's main ideas for training.

"Exactly," Chief Adams said. "We need these issues passed up the chain of command. We need to know when someone is struggling so we can provide them with resources and help."

"But you have to admit, most of the resources we have for firefighters are terrible. No firefighter wants to listen to someone who has no idea what this job is like. And even if they are good, firefighters don't want to admit they need help. They have this mindset of 'I'm the helper,' " said Chief Bingham.

"You're not wrong. We do need better resources, and the stigma is real. Firefighters don't want to be seen as the crazy person. That's a label that'll stick with you your entire career," said Chief Adams. "But there are some departments that have really shifted the mindset and decreased the stigma on this kind of stuff. The firefighters up in Flagstaff have an amazing Employee Assistance Program (EAP) counselor. They've implemented these behavioral wellness checks where firefighters go visit with the counselor every quarter. They've totally normalized it. And these meetings occur during their shifts, so they don't have to take time during their off-time."

Cassie noticed Melissa adding new sticky notes to her screen:

- Shift the mindset of behavioral health.
- How can this be done—case study: Flagstaff behavioral wellness checks.

- Find other examples of departments that have moved the needle when it comes to the behavioral health stigma.
- Highlight the *good* resources! Acknowledge that it's important to find counselors/support who understand firefighter life.

Then she refocused the group, "So, two trainings. One for everyone. And one for chiefs and captains addressing these cultural issues you guys are talking about. Like I said before, the first one will be done by the end of April. The second one could be done by July. Chief Adams?"

"I love it," said Chief Adams.

"Great," Melissa said. "I've taken some notes on what you just shared about the Flagstaff department and the overall goal of the training for chiefs and captains. But since that training will be developed second, I want to take the rest of the time we have today to focus on course one content and action items for all of you."

"I do have a question about the content you've proposed for course one," Chief Bingham said. "No offense, Greg, but that all seems a little too statistic-y for me. And I think most firefighters will feel the same way. I'm not saying it's not good information. Just that I don't know how engaged people will be with it."

"I was thinking the same thing. We're more hands-on people," said Michael.

Greg chimed in, "You're exactly right, Chiefs. And when I've done in-person trainings on this in the past, it's less the numbers and more the stories I share that resonate with people."

Now Melissa joined the conversation, "I love that you've brought this up because it actually ties into one of my requests for you, Michael and Chief Bingham. The firefighters need to feel like the training applies to them, so I'd love to get some stories from each of you about experiences you've had with firefighters who have exhibited behaviors of concern. Cassie and I will figure out the best way to fictionalize and use these stories in the training to help it come to life. Maybe we'll use them for role plays or something more hands-on like Michael mentioned. Whatever it ends up being, know it will be a priority for us to contextualize what we're teaching so it's not just a course with definitions and numbers."

Melissa then divvied out additional assignments and scheduled a weekly SME meeting to keep the team on track and connected during development. She would keep Chief Adams up to date on their progress.

"I hope you don't mind, Melissa, but I have one more question for the group before we end," Chief Adams said. "We all know that the Cave Creek incident is what fast-tracked this training. When the firefighters see this training coming through the pipeline, they'll probably suspect that incident is the reason for it. So, my question is, do we acknowledge that in the training at all? Or no?"

The group then discussed pros and cons of acknowledging the triggering incident, but no consensus was reached regarding its inclusion.

"I suggest we continue to weigh the pros and cons and keep an open dialogue about this during development. Then, we can make a decision closer to launch," Melissa said.

Because there were valid arguments for both sides, the team agreed that keeping this as an open discussion point was the right call for now. The meeting was adjourned.

Less than five minutes after the meeting ended, Cassie and the other team members had an email in their inboxes from Melissa with action items and deadlines (see Figure 23.6).

From: Jennings, Melissa <m.jennings@aide.com>

Sent: January 11 at 10:35 A.M.

To: Standage, Cassie <c.standage@aide.com>, Jones, Greg <gregjones@gmail.com>, Kempton, Michael <michael.kempton@aide.com >, Bingham, Andy <andy.bingham@esa.org>

Subject: Post-kickoff meeting action items

Hi Everyone,

Thanks for a productive kickoff conversation. Here are the action items we discussed. Looking forward to our work together.

Melissa and Cassie

Start on the design/development of Course 1 deliverables; due by April 30

- 45-minute eLearning course
- Facilitator guide for in-person training session

Greg

- Send Melissa and Cassie resource links and PowerPoint presentation with workplace violence "basics" content by tomorrow.

Michael and Chief Bingham

- Write up experiences with workplace violence/behaviors of concern and send them to Melissa by the end of the week.

Let me know if you have any questions or concerns!

Melissa

Melissa Jennings
Project Manager
Arizona Instructional Design Experts

FIGURE 23.6 Post-kickoff meeting email.

DEBRIEF WITH MELISSA AND NEXT STEPS

Cassie had question marks all over her notes. There were times during the meeting that she felt like the SMEs were speaking a different language. Fortunately, Melissa scheduled a meeting for that afternoon to discuss next steps. Cassie took some time to organize her notes and write down specific questions, so she was prepared to meet with Melissa after lunch.

At 2:00 P.M., Cassie hopped on Zoom. As the call started, Melissa gave Cassie a chance to ask questions.

"I wrote down a lot of questions, but I think the one at the top of my list has to do with a comment that Chief Bingham made. He made it in reference to behavioral health counselors, but I suspect the same applies to us and the training we develop. He said firefighters don't want to listen to someone who doesn't understand the firefighter culture. So, my question is, how can I make sure I understand firefighter life and assure that it comes through in the training?"

"I am so glad you've brought this up," Melissa said. "As instructional designers, we know how important it is to understand our audience. But I think this importance is elevated in our work with firefighters. We need to find ways to show our learners we understand them and to gain their trust in the content we present. We've done this in different ways in the past, and one way I think we can do it in this training is by incorporating examples that they can relate to. That's why I've asked Michael and Chief Bingham to come up with scenarios that we can leverage and weave into our training. I'd challenge you to be thinking of other ways we can do that in this training. Brainstorm and don't be afraid to share the ideas you have.

"As for understanding your audience, the first thing I want you to do is to find out more about your learners. You've already started reflecting on comments that were made in the kickoff meeting—keep doing that. Think about the interactions you observed between our firefighter SMEs and the comments they made, because those can give you a glimpse into life as a firefighter.

"I also want you to take some time to research firefighter life, find answers to the questions you wrote down about firefighter culture in the meeting, and talk to Michael. He is a wonderful resource for us. I encourage you to schedule a meeting with him so you can hear firsthand what his career as a firefighter was like."

"Great!" Cassie said. "So, a learner analysis."

"Right," Melissa said. "Except since the timeline for this project is so tight it won't be a formal learner analysis. It'll just be helping you get a handle on firefighter culture—to the extent that's possible in a day or two of research and conversations. Then we'll have to jump into development."

"Okay, I'll do my best with those constraints in mind," Cassie said.

"Thanks, Cassie. While you work on that, I'll create an outline shell with the topics of everything we want included in course one, and the order in which I think we should present them. Then you can use the content provided by the SMEs to fill in the outline and propose how the content should be presented—keeping in mind the trust-building factor we discussed. We'll meet again Monday to see what you've come up with and finalize decisions before starting development."

"Sounds like a plan!"

Cassie ended the call and went to work on her learner analysis.

LEARNER ANALYSIS

Cassie wasn't exactly sure what this less formal learner analysis should entail. But she figured she would start by finding answers to the questions she had written down during the kickoff meeting (see Figure 23.7). Then, she would meet with Michael, and hopefully, she'd have time for a few more analysis activities after that—though she wasn't exactly sure what those should be yet.

Cassie's first undertaking was finding out more about the firefighter hierarchy. In her research, she learned that firefighters are organized along paramilitary lines. Promotions to higher ranks are determined by years of experience, test scores, and other evaluative criteria (e.g., physical evaluations, supervisor references).

While learning about firefighter hierarchy and acronyms was interesting, Cassie's meeting with Michael is what really opened her eyes to some of the realities of firefighter life. Cassie learned that Michael was a third-generation firefighter. He started his career when he was 18 years old and worked at a few different stations as he worked his way up to Fire Chief before retiring at 52. Like most firefighters, he worked ten 24-hour shifts a month and had seen his fair share of traumatic events.

Ranks

Probationary firefighter: Entry-level. Still undergoing training. Typically, 6 months to 1 year

Firefighter: Responsible for hands-on actions during calls

Driver engineer: Drives the fire truck and maintains/operates fire pump and aerial ladder; Technical position; Promotion required

Captain: Oversees day-to-day operations and training of the company; Highest-ranking officer at an emergency

Battalion Chief: Manages personnel; Highest-ranking officer on duty

Fire Chief: Highest-ranking officer in the fire department; Responsible for fire department operations, personnel, and activities

Acronyms

SOP	Standard operating procedures. List of formal policies that specify a firefighter's course of action for all firefighters during emergency response and non-emergency activities.
SOG	Standard operating guidelines. More general overview of firefighter best practices. *SOPs and SOGs are specific to each department, so while there may be some overlap, each department has their own standards.
AAR	After-action review
CAN	Conditions—Actions—Needs
SCBA	Self-contained breathing apparatus
IMT	Incident management team
HOT	Hands-on training

FIGURE 23.7 Cassie's learner analysis notes.

Cassie jotted down a few quotes that really struck her as they discussed his career experiences and the topic of workplace violence. After her call with Michael, she decided it would be a good idea to keep a living document with firefighter quotes and firefighter culture comments to reference. She combined Michael's comments with some quotes she had written down during the kickoff meeting (see Figure 23.8). Fortunately, there were recordings and transcripts of both meetings so she could make sure she got the quotes just right.

A UNIQUE OPPORTUNITY

Monday, January 16

As Cassie was trying to decide what other learner analysis activities to pursue, Melissa called with some exciting news. Chief Adams had scheduled an all-day meeting with some of Tucson's fire chiefs and captains (from 14 departments) on March 5. He reserved a two-hour block on the agenda for Melissa and Cassie. Chief Adams knew the first training wouldn't be complete by then, but he thought it would be a good opportunity for Melissa and Cassie to

Kickoff Meeting

"No firefighter wants to listen to someone who has no idea what this job is like."

"Firefighters don't want to admit they need help. They have this mindset of, 'I'm the helper.'"

"Firefighters don't want to be seen as the crazy person. That's a label that'll stick with you your entire career."

"We're more hands-on [learners]."

Meeting with Michael

"I'll admit, I don't have much to compare it to. But being a firefighter isn't like any other job. You *live* with your co-workers."

"Whenever a call comes in, you have to be ready to go. No matter what the incident. It might be a fire. Or a car crash. There might be no casualties or there might be ten or more. There's really no telling."

"It's interesting how certain calls hit you differently. I remember one time we got called to a pedestrian/vehicle accident. A 10-year-old boy had been hit and killed while riding his bike. Just the weekend before I was teaching my 5-year-old how to ride his bike. That one sticks with me."

"With this workplace violence training we're trying to get firefighters to realize when to ask for help for themselves or for other people. But we're not used to asking for help. We're used to being the helpers."

"When Greg was talking about early signs of workplace violence, he kept saying, you've got to ask yourself: 'Would a reasonable person consider this behavior problematic?' The problem with that is firefighters are not your average reasonable person. I mean, we run into burning buildings for a living. I think it's safe to say, most reasonable people wouldn't do that."

"There is a tough-guy mentality that comes along with being a firefighter. There's a stigma around mental health issues, and we traditionally have done all we can to avoid anything to do with it. We're trying to change things. But this is generations deep. It's not something that can be changed overnight."

"Yeah, firefighter culture is real. There's so much more I could say, but I'm sure you'll learn as you go."

FIGURE 23.8 Quotes that informed Cassie's learner analysis.

discuss the upcoming training with leadership personnel. He said the time was theirs to use any way they'd like to gather or test out learner content and/or gain learner buy-in. Melissa asked Cassie to start brainstorming ways they could use the time. As the call ended, Cassie wondered whether the meeting was a time to learn more about the audience or dive right in and present their plan. She could see advantages to both, but knew the stakes were high enough that she should consider it a little more before making some recommendations.

Preliminary Analysis Questions

1. Cassie was tasked with completing an informal, just-for-her-benefit learner analysis. What are the implications of this? What other learner analysis activities could she complete to increase her understanding of the learners?
2. Cassie and Melissa want to make sure the firefighters know that these trainings are created by individuals who understand firefighter culture. What can they do to make the training both relevant and realistic so the participating firefighters think it is worth their time?

3. Cassie and Melissa need to take advantage of the facetime they have with fire chiefs and captains on March 5. What are the pros and cons to using the time to gain learner buy-in versus piloting potential training activities?
4. The team discussed whether they should acknowledge the triggering incident in the training. What are the pros and cons to incorporating the incident into the training? What would you recommend to the team?

Implications for ID Practice

1. What steps can instructional designers take to better understand and empathize with their learners, especially a very specialized/unique group of learners? How can an instructional designer's familiarity with the audience impact the design and development process?
2. Gaining the trust and respect of SMEs is also important. What steps can instructional designers take to gain respect and foster good working relationships with their SMEs?
3. Why does learner trust matter? What role does an instructional designer play in gaining the buy-in and trust of learners? Describe some strategies for gaining buy-in and fostering trust.

24

Jack Waterkamp

Managing Scope Change in an Instructional Design Project

Shahron Williams van Rooij

EARLY FEBRUARY

Jack Waterkamp, Director of the Curriculum Development Group at Complex Data Systems, Inc. was feeling upbeat as he prepared to log in for the Human Resources (HR) division's monthly meeting. Elizabeth Henderson, his boss and HR VP, had emailed a last-minute agenda item and Jack was certain that it meant a new project for him and his team. He had recently celebrated his two-year anniversary with Complex Data Systems, a $960 million software development company that provided business software systems, classroom-based training, technical support, and annual maintenance agreements to small and medium-sized companies. He smiled as he glanced at the organizational chart hanging on his home office wall (see Figure 24.1), visualizing his name among the other executives reporting directly to the company president.

Jack had arrived at Complex Data Systems with seven years of experience at an e-learning courseware vendor plus a bachelor's degree in computer science and a master's degree in instructional design. His career had been progressing well. Last year, he successfully introduced a small selection of online self-paced refresher courses for employees and for client technical staff using Complex Data System's homegrown LMS, although classroom-based training with some synchronous sessions remained the standard for new products.

Yesterday, Jack learned that the instructional design document he had written for the training curriculum for the new cloud-based Customer Relationship Management (CRM) software product was approved and ready to move into development. Now, this new project, whatever it was, would give him another opportunity to demonstrate his leadership skills and put him on senior management's radar for future executive team candidacy.

THE HR DIVISION MEETING

Elizabeth Henderson shared her laptop screen with the meeting attendees. "Good morning, everyone. Last night I emailed a new agenda item, so I'd like to start with that. The item is called *New Training Directions*. It's the result of an executive team meeting earlier this week,

DOI: 10.4324/9781003354468-27

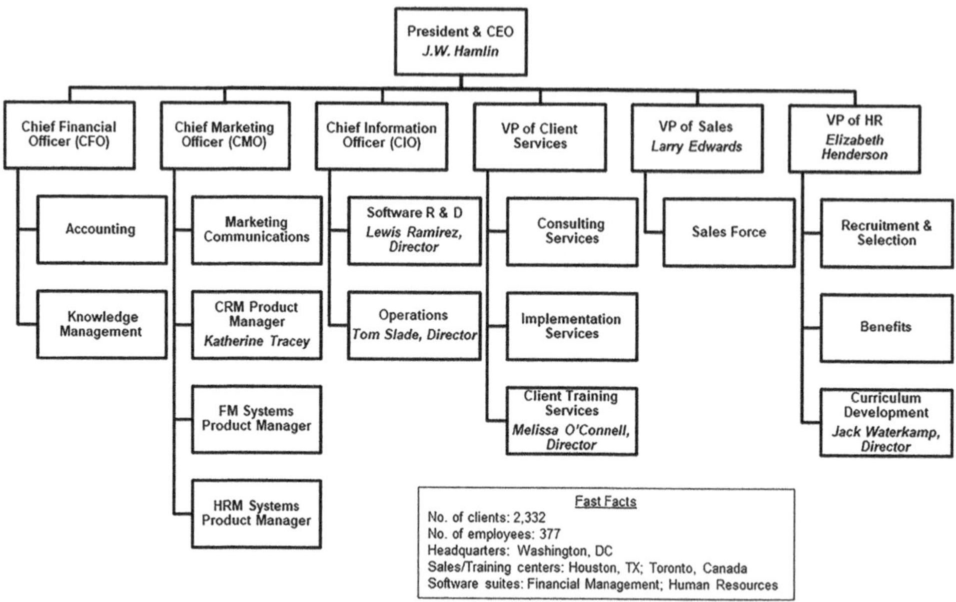

FIGURE 24.1 Complex Data Systems, Inc. organizational chart.

and I thought it would be best if the entire division heard the news at the same time." She reviewed the three-year downward trend in revenues from both classroom-based training offered at Complex Data Systems and classroom-based training offered at individual client sites. "So," she concluded, "JW has decided that the training curriculum for the new CRM product and for our other training offerings should primarily be online. This also aligns with yesterday's announcement about a reduction in the number of trainers."

Jack immediately asked about timelines and resources. Although his current plan called for sales-ready, classroom-based CRM curriculum with some online resources for the November product launch, he had made provisions for neither the scheduling and resourcing of any online CRM training nor for modifications to the curriculum of Complex Data Systems' other software products. Nor was he clear about how the reduction in training staff would impact his plan.

"I have good news and bad news," Elizabeth replied. "The good news is that the executive team did not mandate a timeframe for developing online training for our existing product line. The bad news is that the November delivery date for the CRM software product and training curriculum is not negotiable, nor is your budget and staffing."

Jack logged out of the meeting with two action items: Revise the CRM Curriculum Development Project Charter to reflect the scope change resulting from the executive mandate and send it to Elizabeth for executive sign-off and have a revised instructional design document with a project plan for completing the work ready for Elizabeth's approval at the end of the month. Using previous instructor-led training development projects as a guideline, Jack had originally budgeted this project at $280,000, using his own staff that consisted of one graphic artist, one audio-visual specialist, and one programmer. If what he had learned at industry conferences and from industry networking sites was accurate, he would need three to four times his current resource levels to shift the new CRM curriculum online.

THE FOLLOWING WEEK

Jack requested a Zoom meeting with Katherine Tracey, the CRM product manager; Lewis Ramirez, the software development R&D director; and Melissa O'Connell, the client training services director, to get their feedback on his idea of confining the online CRM training to system administrators (SAs) responsible for deploying and maintaining the new software system at each client site. He began the meeting by explaining that the SAs were the group that is most critical to CRM product success.

"So, what do you think?" Jack asked.

"I've got some serious concerns," Melissa began. "First of all, I'm down to a dozen trainers, and none of them have experience with online training. I'm certainly not going to have them give up billable days to learn how to train online and perhaps ruin a great record of high client satisfaction ratings. Besides," she declared, "I'm not convinced that the self-paced approach you used for the online refresher courses would work for new product training, even with SAs."

"SAs are tech-savvy," Lewis countered, "and aren't as scared of online training as some of the functional users who are subject matter experts as far as what product features do, but know little about what's under the technology hood, so to speak. Besides, we've seen how well this works with SAs from the high satisfaction ratings for those online refresher courses."

"I don't see a problem, either," said Katherine. "Your trainers need to keep up with the times, and anyway, this is what our CEO wants."

Jack reminded the group that the executive mandate had two components—one short-term related to the new CRM product launch, the other long-term related to online training for the total inventory of training offerings, and that the immediate concern was the CRM launch. He also noted that Complex Data Systems' semi-annual Train-the-Trainer Week would take place in May, providing an excellent opportunity for Melissa's trainers to learn about online facilitation. Jack concluded the meeting by proposing next steps.

"Let's have a two-week virtual work session on our company intranet," Jack said. "I'll post a revised instructional design document based on the SA target audience, then the three of us can work collaboratively to finalize it and flesh out a plan for completing the work. Lewis, would it be possible to host the new training modules on the password-protected Clients Only section of the company website? Our LMS hasn't been a hit with our clients."

"Work with Tom Slade in Operations on that," Lewis replied. "He's been hoping we'd replace that clunker of a system with something that's easy to maintain and doesn't add to his budget."

The next day, Jack emailed a summary of the previous day's meeting to Katherine, Melissa, and Lewis and included a link to the intranet workspace where he had posted a revised CRM Curriculum Development Project Charter. He also requested their electronic signatures on the Charter if they agreed with his revisions.

"Before I sign," Melissa responded, "please highlight or bold the concerns that I expressed at the meeting."

Jack revised the Project Charter to include a bulleted list of all of Melissa's concerns (see Appendix 24-A) and uploaded the document to the intranet. Katherine and Lewis submitted their electronic signatures as requested. Two days later, Jack phoned Melissa and left her a voice mail asking for her electronic signature. In her email reply, Melissa acknowledged receipt of his voice mail and of the link to the intranet workspace. Although Melissa had not "signed," Jack felt that her last email was sufficient evidence that she was aware of what was discussed and agreed.

LATE FEBRUARY

The revised instructional design document and project plan were taking shape with a great deal of input from Katherine and a few tweaks from Lewis regarding the software's new technical specifications. Jack had just emailed Elizabeth his weekly project status report (see Figure 24.2) when the phone rang.

"Okay, Jack," Elizabeth began, "I can't wait to hear your explanation as to why Melissa thinks you're trying to eliminate classroom-based training and do everything self-paced online."

"Perhaps she hasn't had a chance to review the minutes of our last meeting," Jack offered, "and is misremembering our goal of developing online training only for the system administrators to learn the product basics. All of our application end-users will initially take our normal classroom-based training, although we'll have more online synchronous sessions."

"Well, I suggest you get moving with the communications plan. The last thing we need is a misunderstanding that leads to panic among clients and employees."

Project Status Report

Project name: CRM Curriculum Training

Team: Curriculum Development Group

Date: February 27

Design/Development Summary

The CRM curriculum consists of two tracks:

1. System administrator/SA Track
   a. Installation foundations (online)
      i. Pre-instructional video with audio
      ii. Seven (7) self-paced instructional modules based on slides created for classroom-based training
      iii. Practice tests after each module
      iv. Post-test using data on client's CRM testing servers
      v. Memory aids in the Tech Doc section of the Clients Only section of Complex Data Systems website
   b. Advanced topics (classroom-based)
      i. Implementation
      ii. Maintenance
2. Application end-user/APPs track (classroom-based w/synchronous sessions)
   a. System overview (2 days, synchronous)
   b. Data entry and retrieval (4 days, classroom)
   c. Reporting (1 day classroom, 1 day synchronous)

Posted to Our Intranet Workspace

1. Revised Project Charter
2. Communications matrix describing the purpose/description of each communication needed for the project, the document or medium used, the audience and frequency

Overall Project Status: On schedule

FIGURE 24.2 CRM curriculum project status report.

"Already started," Jack assured her. "Katherine Tracey has been working with our Marketing Communications folks on a series of information briefings to our clients over the next couple of months. That should nip any potential misinformation in the bud."

Jack also noted that he would include the schedule of client briefings in his project status reports and in the project plan. With this assurance, Elizabeth signed off on the revised CRM curriculum project plan.

EARLY MARCH TO MID-APRIL

Jack's team was on time and on budget for both the online and the classroom-based components of the CRM curriculum. The marketing team had launched a series of webinars announcing Complex Data Systems' plan to include online training opportunities for system administrators. Anecdotal information indicated a strong interest in the online training, and Jack was certain that he had neutralized the misinformation threat successfully. The next step was to figure out a way to incorporate online facilitation training into May's Train-the-Trainer Week schedule. He was about to send Melissa an email about this, when his mobile pinged to indicate a new text message.

"Where's the pricing, Waterkamp?" The text was from was Larry Edwards, the VP of Sales. "I'm in the office. Call me."

Jack had barely gotten past "hello," when Larry began, "Look, I'm on board with this online training thing, but my folks don't have any pricing information or whether the clients still have contact with their favorite trainers."

"As always, it is the product manager who submits a pricing proposal for executive approval six months before product launch," Jack replied. "My understanding is that Katherine won't have the CRM pricing ready until next month."

"I need it now," Larry pressed. "We've fired up the clients with those webinars, and you know that our competitors have been offering training online for as little as $200 a pop."

"I'll email Katherine and see if we can get some preliminary pricing by the end of April," Jack replied. "And I'll cc you so you can follow up with her yourself."

"Okay, but I hope the new pricing won't be a show stopper for new CRM sales," he added. "If nobody buys, you've got nobody to train, online or otherwise."

"I'm on it, Larry," Jack replied.

After sending the pricing request to Katherine, Jack turned his attention back to online facilitation for the field trainers. He and Melissa had not yet agreed on how to include online facilitation into the May Train-the-Trainer Week program, particularly since she was not ready to delete anything from the standard program sessions. Jack picked up the phone and called Melissa.

"What if," he began, "we deliver the online facilitation training as an online workshop for a small group of trainers? Let's start with five trainers that you select to participate, and I'll develop and conduct the workshop myself, just like I did at my previous company. I'll even post the materials on the intranet in advance, making it easier for your trainers," he concluded.

"You're the expert," Melissa replied. "Send me your workshop program, and I'll look it over."

"Great. Feel free to add comments or modifications, since you know your trainers better than I do."

The next day, Jack sent Melissa his workshop program. No sooner had he hit the "send" key, when he received a brief reply agreeing to the program if it would contribute to the overall success of the project. She promised to send out a call for volunteers to her trainers asking them to email Jack if they would like to sign up for his online facilitation workshop.

TWO WEEKS LATER

Three days before the start of Train-the-Trainer Week, Jack still did not have a list of trainers for the online facilitation workshop. He sent out a broadcast email to the Client Services division announcing the online facilitation workshop, its purpose, and its benefit to Client Services employees as well as to clients. Participation would be limited to the first five trainers who responded. Other trainers would be placed on a follow-up list for training at a later date. As a hook, he added that the workshop would be offered totally online, enabling participants to "practice what they are going to preach," and that all participants would receive a $100 pre-paid Visa gift card as a token of thanks for participating. Jack suspected that the remaining trainers might expect the same incentive. Nevertheless, the gift cards would cost less than 1% of his budget, and he was determined to keep his project on track.

At the conclusion of Train-the-Trainer Week, Melissa sent Jack a brief email.

"I hear you not only reached your five-person maximum, but got requests from the remaining seven trainers and 11 client services consultants interested in your next online workshop," she wrote. "Congrats. You're a hero."

Jack smiled. Although he had to figure out a way to schedule more online workshops for the remaining 18 people on the follow-up list, as well as absorb the $2,300 hit to his project budget for the gift cards for all 23 participants, the enthusiastic reviews were certainly worth it.

MID-JUNE TO MID-SEPTEMBER

Pilot testing of the SA track modules was going well, and Melissa's field trainers were reporting that they were becoming more comfortable with online facilitation. There had been several issues with the classroom-based offerings in the end-user Applications tracks, but Jack was confident that his team would be able to make their usual last-minute adjustments as needed.

As he monitored the software R&D area on the company's project management software platform, Jack clicked on the link to the CRM GANTT chart, a bar chart generated by the company's project management software that shows the project schedule, listing target start and finish dates for all project tasks (see Appendix 24-B). His heart sank as he compared the beta testing target completion dates with the graphic showing the percentage of work completed. Software testing of Module 1a should have been completed on June 22, but as of today, only 39% of the work had been completed. There was no indication on the graphic as to if and when that remaining work would be done. Upcoming test dates also appeared to be in question, with software testing of Module 1b scheduled to be completed next week, yet only 43% of the testing had been completed. Jack was sure that these delays would cascade into the software testing of the remaining modules.

Lewis had not posted any status changes to their collaborative work area, so Jack was puzzled by the apparent delays in the software beta testing. Jack phoned Lewis and left a detailed voice mail requesting project status clarification.

"I'm a bit unclear," Jack said when Lewis phoned the following afternoon. "Perhaps I'm not reading your GANTT chart correctly, but it looks like we've got some delays."

"I've got to put out a fire, Jack. Just wanted to let you know I got your message. I'll get back to you shortly."

As soon as Jack ended the call, he saw the instant message alert at the bottom of his laptop screen with a request from Katherine to call him ASAP.

"Tiny glitch," she said. "It looks like a few critical pieces of functionality failed to be programmed into the software. We've got no automated direct mail, no database merge-purge of duplicate entries, and only one entry field for email addresses. Your end-user APPs classroom sessions covering that functionality will have to be skipped during field testing."

"What about—" Jack began.

"There's more," she went on. "Several of the technical procedures required for system implementation have been altered, making three of the seven online modules in the SA track inaccurate. I'm working on getting the missing functionality restored and field tested in time for general delivery, but the technical procedures are another matter. Sorry, Jack," she said and hung up.

The next morning, Melissa phoned Jack.

"What's this about errors in the online modules?" she snapped. "This is going to blow my client satisfaction and trainer satisfaction ratings out of the water."

"Take it easy, Melissa," Jack said. "Katherine has already contacted our beta test clients about the software changes and—"

"This debacle is proof that online training doesn't work for new products," she declared and hung up.

As the beta testing process continued, Jack learned that Katherine had been successful in restoring some, but not all, of the missing functionality. However, the three online modules would still have to be reworked to accommodate changes to the software. In their weekly team meeting that Friday, Jack's staff balked at the idea of having to redo three of the online modules. Jerry, the programmer, was the most vocal.

"We've already scheduled the updates to other workshops in our training inventory," Jerry said. "Do you want us to cancel those?"

When Jack confirmed this, Jerry added, "I've been here 11 years and can't remember when software beta testing has gone off without a hitch. I'll bet there will be a few more unpleasant surprises that are going to land in our laps."

Jack acknowledged that it was still unclear as to what the final software product would contain, as Katherine was still working on restoring the remaining pieces of functionality. He also reminded them that the CRM software would be delivered in November, with or without that functionality, and that it was his team's responsibility to deliver a sales-ready curriculum at the same time as the general delivery of the software. The ball was in his court, but how was he going to drive this curriculum project to successful completion?

Preliminary Analysis Questions

1. To address the change in scope of the CRM curriculum project, announced in the February HR division meeting, Jack decided to focus on a subset of Complex Data's target audience—namely, the system administrators. What other alternatives could Jack have considered to address the change in project scope? Discuss the pros and cons of each alternative.
2. One of the challenges of instructional design project management is knowing what the project manager should and should not be doing, particularly if a task or activity

is deemed to be the responsibility of other project stakeholders. Review Jack's handling of the pricing issue with Lewis and the online facilitation workshop issue with Melissa. Explain whether or not Jack's actions were consistent with his role as CRM curriculum project manager.

3. Given the status of the software beta testing at the end of the case, how might Jack proceed to successfully complete the CRM curriculum by November? Keep in mind the budget and staffing constraints presented in the case as you explain and justify your recommendations.

Implications for ID Practice

1. Develop a set of guidelines for formulating a communications plan to help manage the impact of changes to the scope of an instructional design project.
2. What role does a project charter play in managing changes to the scope of an instructional design project?
3. How can instructional designers develop instruction in the use of a product while the product is still being developed? Identify some potential "red flags" that indicate that product *training* development and product development are moving out of sync.

Appendix 24.A

Revised Project Charter

REVISED PROJECT CHARTER
Customer Relationship Management (CRM) Software System
Product Training Curriculum
Curriculum Development Group, Complex Data Systems, Inc.

Version: 1.5 Revision Date: February 12, 2023

Approval of the Project Charter indicates an understanding of the purpose and content described in this document. By signing this document, each individual agrees work should be initiated on this project and necessary resources should be committed as described herein.

Approver Name	*Title*	*E-signature Received On*
Katherine Tracey	Product Manager, CRM	02/13/2023
Lewis Ramirez	Directors, Software R&D	02/15/2023
Melissa O'Connell	Director, Client Training Services	Email acknowledgement of intranet workspace received on 02/18/2023
E. Henderson	VP, HR	02/21/2023

1. Problem Statement
   Revenues from classroom-based training as well as from on-site training at client offices have been declining. Anecdotal information from field consultants suggests that in addition to the problem of tight budgets, clients are dealing with smaller staff unable to take time out from busy schedules to attend training. At the same time, new, more complex software products, as well as updates to older products, demand a well-trained user for successful implementation.
2. Project Description
   This project will enhance Complex Data Systems' training revenue potential by providing online learning opportunities alongside classroom-based training events to CRM clients.

3. Project Approach
   This project will be undertaken as an add-on to the current CRM Curriculum Training development Project Charter (version 1.0). The current classroom-based CRM Curriculum targets technical system administrators (SAs) and functional users. The add-on online training will target SAs only.
4. Project Scope
   The project includes the following:
   - Review of current CRM training topics to determine which can be parsed to include online as well as classroom-based components
   - Small group evaluation and field testing of online and classroom-based components concurrent with the 90-day software beta testing cycle
   - Standard pre-launch orientation and training of Complex Data Systems field trainers/consultants
   - Standard pre-launch orientation of Complex Data Systems sales force

   The project excludes the creation by the Curriculum Development Group of online training for Complex Data Systems products other than the new CRM software system.
5. Critical Success Factors
   - A written communications plan that indicates . . .
     - Who needs what information
     - When information is needed
     - How information will be given
     - Who will provide the information
6. Assumptions/Constraints
   - There is strong corporate commitment to offering online training to both clients and employees.
   - Any online training offerings must not replicate and thus not cannibalize the classroom-based offerings
   - Client Services field trainers need to be trained in online facilitation without sacrificing either billable days or client satisfaction.
   - Pilot testing of the online training components will include an assessment of client satisfaction with/attitudes toward online versus classroom training.
   - The expansion of project scope to include online training components must be accomplished within the current budget of $280,000 and with the current four-person Curriculum Development group staff
7. Major Milestones

Milestones/Deliverables	*Target Completion Date*
Development of online components for SAs	March 2023
Announcement of online opportunities to clients	April 2023
Online facilitation training for Client Services field trainers	May 2023
Curriculum pilot testing	September 2023
Sales-ready curriculum launch	November 2023

8. Project Stakeholders

Role	*Name/Title/Organization*	*Email*
Executive Sponsor	Elizabeth Henderson, HR VP	ehenderson@complexdata.com
Subject Matter Expert (SME)	Katherine Tracey, CRM Product Manager	ktracey@complexdata.com
Implementation	Melissa O'Connell, Client Training Services Director	moconnell@complexdata.com
Software Product Development	Lewis Ramirez, Director, R&D	lramirez@complexdata.com
Training Module Hosting	Tom Slade, Operations Director	tslade1@complexdata.com
Product and Training Sales	Larry Edwards, VP Sales	ledwards@complexdata.com

Revision History

Version	*Date*	*Name*	*Description*
1.0	02/04/2011	J. Waterkamp	Version approved by E. Henderson
1.5	02/18/2010	J. Waterkamp	Scope changed to include online offerings as add-on

25

Scott Hunter

Developing Online Assessment in an International Setting

David L. Solomon

Scott Hunter. Vice President, Creative Director. Automotive Performance Improvement Consultants (APIC). There I was—staring at my business card minutes before a tough meeting—and the only insight I could seem to muster was that my title didn't really reflect what I did. I had no idea where I would begin when I approached my supervisor, Ken Young, with the most recent challenge facing the international training team. I remembered being thrilled about my international job assignment—a real opportunity to apply so much of my education in instructional design and technology—but frustration soon replaced enthusiasm.

We had confronted so many problems over the past year and we were now so close to launching the sales consultant certification program that everyone could taste it. One last hurdle remained and it was gnawing at me. I had to stop myself from saying what I truly felt when Ken asked, "Can you refresh my memory and help me understand what's going on?"

In the first few minutes of my meeting with Ken, I explained the turmoil that seemed to plague this project. First there was Katarina (Kat) Wilder, the abusive training manager at the client organization, Trans-Continental Motors (TCM), who once held the position currently occupied by Antoine Devereux (see Figure 25.1).

I couldn't believe it had taken so long for Bob Kelly, the senior manager, to do something about her constant diatribes, but there was an ocean between them and so much red tape. Kat was skilled at generating lengthy email messages and creating a lot of "busy work," but she had no vision of the desired outcomes. We flew overseas for several meetings with TCM and found that "next steps" were always unclear and several disparate projects seemed to appear as each conversation with her unfolded. I remembered wondering if she even knew we were the training supplier or merely considered us to be another department in the advertising agency where we resided. Either way, it was clear to me that we were underused. Unknown to APIC, Kat had been working with Antoine, the training manager from France at that time, to create a certification test for sales consultants. She and Antoine were clandestinely working with a close relative of Antoine's to coordinate a pilot.

"So, Kat was working on a pilot program with Antoine, who hired one of his relatives to develop the certification test and no one from APIC knew about it?"

"That's right," I said to Ken, half-surprised that he was following this soap opera. "The certification test was the most critical piece of the certification program and we had a clearly

DOI: 10.4324/9781003354468-28

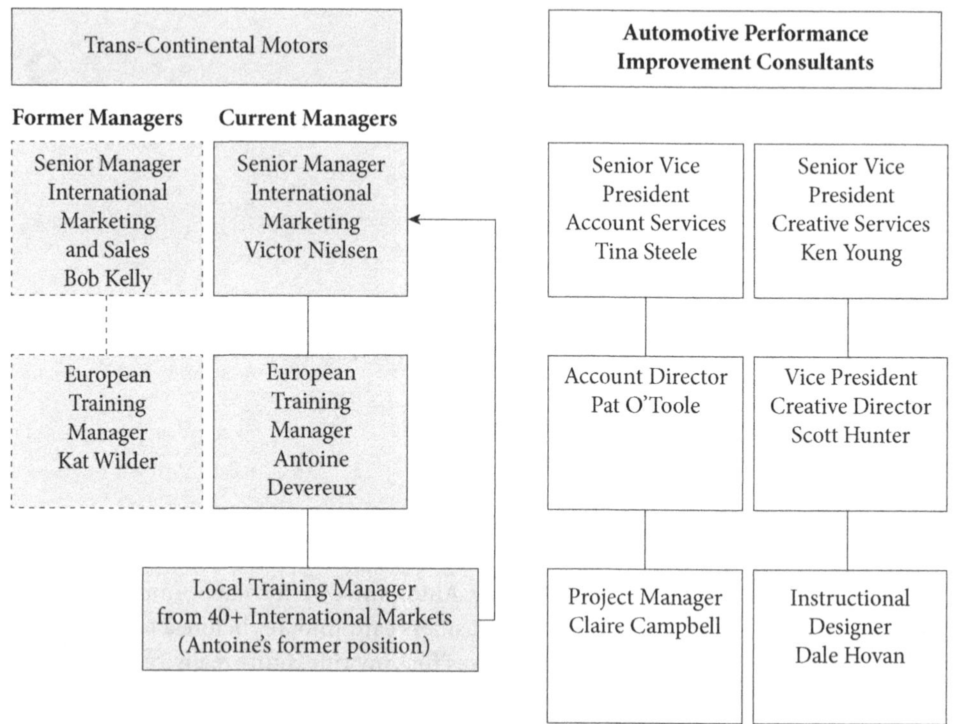

FIGURE 25.1 Client and consultant organizational flowcharts for an international training team.

defined strategy. But there's more to the story and a few twists and turns along the way," I said as I continued with the saga.

"We've had our share of headaches, too. We lost about three or four months due to turnover on the account team. Pat O'Toole, the account director, had to move back to the United States from Europe in the middle of all this, and Claire Campbell, the project manager, didn't start working full-time on this project until about six months ago, so we basically put this entire certification program together in less than nine months."

Once the personnel issues were addressed, I explained other concerns that we had confronted. Many of the training managers at TCM had dual responsibilities for the same manufacturer, which included a large European luxury division and our American brand. The European luxury division had already launched a certification program, and there was pressure to adapt this program for the American brand.

"Makes sense," responded Ken.

"Well, it's true that there is this belief that whatever works for the luxury brand will automatically work for us, but in my experience, this is rarely the case," I explained. "We've got two very different types of cultures operating in this situation, with very different retail environments, product offerings, and customers. Plus, TCM wants everything to be administered online, and the existing program for the luxury brand is mostly paper-based."

"But politically, it looks very good for *everyone* when we can borrow from the luxury brand. Management appreciates when costs can be shared across divisions. Why couldn't we do this?" asked Ken.

At this point, I handed over a copy of my notes from an early meeting of the Block Exemption Regulation (BER) Task Force and offered the following explanation (see Figure 25.2).

Automotive Performance
Improvement Consultants

Block Exemption Regulation (BER) Task Force
Launch Meeting Summary

- Global training already has a certification process in place for a luxury brand.
- It has been difficult to adapt this existing program in international markets where the American brand is sold for several reasons
  - The certification process is complex.
  - The competencies are robust and include more than 250 elements.
  - Behavioral styles and personality characteristics are integrated with the competencies and appear to be culturally specific.
  - The competencies have only been validated locally and may not generalize internationally.
  - The assessment process required a third-party evaluator which can cost up to 2,000 per individual.
  - The curriculum requires a minimum of 18 training days per individual (and does not recognize prior knowledge or experience).
  - The existing program does not indude personal development plans, which is a BER requirement.
  - Product knowledge tests are complicated and costly. Multiple correct answer formats increase the cost of translating the number of answers from multiple-choice questions and the computer programming requirements are more complex traditional multiple-choice formats. This will also increase costs.

FIGURE 25.2 Scott's meeting notes.

"Well, the existing program was highly complex and required a third-party evaluator to assess each sales consultant, which cost about 3,000 euros per day. In addition, in some countries the evaluator had to be an industrial or organizational psychologist. This simply wasn't an option for the smaller markets, as the costs were prohibitive and the ability to pay varied from one country to the next. In addition, the product knowledge tests were multiple-choice with multiple correct answers that required a sophisticated scoring algorithm. Translation costs, alone, for the product knowledge test would be expensive because of the increased number of answer options needed for the multiple correct answer format. In addition, complex programming would be needed, which would require more time and money compared to traditional multiple-choice questions where only one correct answer is needed."

Ken's patience seemed to be wearing thin as he interrupted and asked, "So, what did you do?"

At this point, I pulled out the certification model for the sales consultant certification program and began to summarize some key points (see Figure 25.3).

"We developed this model to explain the certification program to the local training managers. It begins with job descriptions and competencies," I explained. "For this, we *did* use the

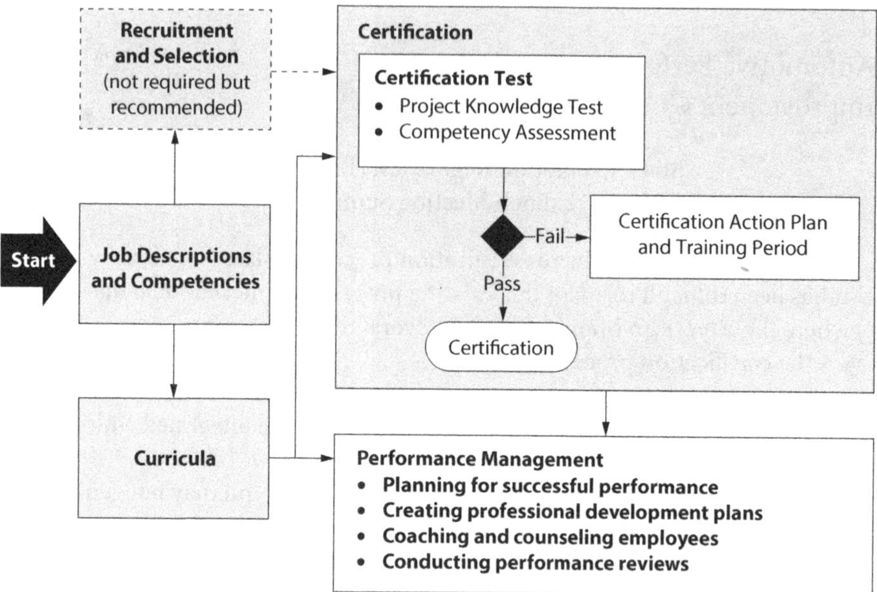

FIGURE 25.3 Certification model.

existing materials from the luxury division's certification program, but we basically edited and simplified the content and their competencies based upon our knowledge and expertise in the automotive industry. We later validated these materials, which I can explain in a minute.

"The next component is recruitment and selection, which is a collection of processes and procedures to ensure that qualified sales consultants are representing the brand, which is a mandatory requirement for the European luxury program. The American brand cannot legally impose recruitment and selection processes for international dealerships because the ability to pay for these activities varies among the different-sized international markets, so it's not required, but recommended, in our program.

"The certification component consists of a product knowledge test and a competency assessment. For the product knowledge test, we're writing basic, multiple-choice items that test a sales consultant's factual knowledge of our client's products. Depending upon the vehicles sold in a given market, and the guidelines we've established, individual tests are generated using randomly selected items from the question pool."

"So how do you handle cheating in the local dealerships?" Ken asked.

"Well, we recommend that the tests are proctored by local training managers or by independent testing facilities, but we've also had to accept that we couldn't prevent cheating from occurring. We'd like to think that people would take the certification process seriously, but those who really want to cheat—or work collaboratively as a group—will figure out a way to do so. Now, that doesn't mean we make it easy for them! The test items and the response options are generated randomly, and every sales consultant is given a unique ID number and receives a unique test. If people work in groups, they'll have to complete a lot of individual tests, but they'll also learn a lot along the way."

Ken looked skeptical. "So, what's to prevent individuals from answering the test questions with the product reference guides right there in their laps or leaving their computer stations to look up an answer?"

"Well, we can't really prevent that from happening, but if sales consultants leave their tests for too long, they are automatically timed-out of their product knowledge tests. The website will bookmark where they left off, saving everything that had already been answered but the sales consultants will be required to log in again, and a different test item will then be randomly assigned where they left off. Sales consultants will have to repeat this process over and over again until the test is completed."

"Okay, so what's up with the competency assessment then?" Ken continued.

"Well, this was our greatest challenge because we needed an alternative to the on-site evaluator, and we had limited resources, both financial and human. We decided to conduct a job analysis with sales consultants in our top five markets using the simplified competencies as a foundation. We removed the parts of the test that assessed behavioral styles and personality characteristics from the luxury program and created operational definitions for eight competencies that would generalize across all of our international markets. For example, we found minimum standards for written and spoken communication and wrote an operational definition for the communication competency. It simply wasn't feasible for us to conduct in-depth evaluations of every sales consultant working in an international market. We decided to conduct the job analysis using the critical incident technique with a small sample of top performers. This approach allowed us to identify a collection of behaviors that were critical to successful job performance. We constructed an online competency assessment using authentic scenarios from the job analysis and, along the way, we were able to validate the competency framework and job descriptions."

Looking impressed, Ken asked, "Great, so how does the competency assessment work?"

"We've aligned a series of questions with each of the competencies, and each item has three response options. The best answer is assigned three points, and it reflects what exemplary performers do in certain situations. There is also an acceptable response, which is assigned two points and a least-acceptable response, which is given one point. This type of scoring procedure was used to discriminate between acceptable performers and those individuals who needed to improve. Once the competency assessment was completed, a score was given for each of the competencies and the candidate either passed or failed. For those sales consultants who failed, a certification action plan had to be developed by the responsible sales manager to improve upon the weaknesses that were identified in the competency assessment. Then, the sales consultants were re-tested after a probationary period of time."

"So what's to prevent someone from cheating on the competency assessment?" Ken wondered.

"The competency assessment is set up online in the same way as the product knowledge test, and there is a bank of questions that are scrambled for each candidate. Again, we won't be able to prevent cheating but we're confident that most sales consultants will recognize the benefit of receiving constructive feedback on their individual performances because it can directly impact their ability to generate sales.

"If they don't pass the required competency assessment, the certification action plan should help them prepare for the re-test. Remember, the competency assessment is only designed to discriminate between acceptable and unacceptable performance, and the program is not intended to be punitive. Continuous improvement is the ultimate goal, and once sales consultants become certified, they receive personal development plans when they enter the performance management phase of the program. From here, the only requirement for recertification is successful completion of product knowledge tests. The program can potentially help sales consultants earn more money if they are truly committed to improving their performance."

"Well, everything sounds great to me. So, what's the problem?"

As I took a deep breath, I mentioned that TCM recently reorganized, and several positions were eliminated or consolidated. Then, I explained that Antoine was now reporting directly to Victor Nielsen in Europe because Bob's position was eliminated.

"And the problem is . . . ?"

"The problem is . . . Bob never felt a need to develop a certification test for vehicle delivery specialists. These are customer-facing employees who are only responsible for handing over the vehicles to customers after the actual sales transactions take place. They answer questions and demonstrate how to use certain features like the in-car entertainment system

Call Report

Client: Antoine Devereux
Author: Pat O'Toole
Participants: Claire Campbell
Antoine Devereux (via telephone)
Dale Hovan
Scott Hunter
Pat O'Toole
Purpose: Certification Program
Date: October 3rd

Purpose

The purpose of this meeting was to discuss the status of the Sales Consultant Certification Program.

Background

- All elements of the Sales Consultant Certification Program were reviewed and approved prior to launch, including:
    - Revised job descriptions and competencies
    - Interface design and functionality
    - Product knowledge test items
    - Competency assessment
    - Certification action plan and personal development plan
- TCM inquired about the status of the vehicle delivery specialist (VDS) certification. APIC informed TCM that Bob did not request VDS certification materials because there were less than 70 job incumbents throughout all international markets.

Discussion

- TCM informed APIC that VDS certification materials must be prepared by the first of the year so that the manufacturer will be compliant with block exemption regulation (BER) standards.

FIGURE 25.4 Call report.

- APIC facilitated a brainstorming session to explore various options, which included:
  - Request quotation from competency assessment supplier to conduct critical incident interviews with top-performing VDS job incumbents
  - Check with domestic training team to see if they have any relevant materials to assist with VDS certification
  - Send e-mail message to all relevant training managers to request information on any existing VDS certification materials
- TCM explained that in most markets, sales consultants (SC) handle vehicle delivery and the VDS position is only implemented in very large markets, often in dealerships that sell both the luxury and American brands. The VDS position is often perceived as an entry-level job for the SC position and a VDS should be able to fulfill the basic functions of the SC position.
- TCM informed APIC that certification materials exist in the United Kingdom for the luxury division. A brief training program is delivered in the dealership, followed by a role-playing scenario where the training manager determines if the VDS should be certified.
- TCM also informed APIC that training support must be available for VDS candidates who fail the certification test.

Next Steps

- APIC to collect existing assets, which are currently known to include:
  - VDS certification materials from the United Kingdom
  - VDS and SC job descriptions and SC competencies
  - SC competency assessment (including approved items that were not used)
  - Domestic training materials for vehicle delivery including five-point vehicle walkaround positions
  - APIC to prepare request for quotation from competency assessment supplier

FIGURE 25.4 Continued

or air-conditioning systems. Bob just didn't think we needed to include them because there are only about 60 or 70 throughout the entire European Union. But Victor insists that the program must include vehicle delivery specialists, and Antoine is demanding it, but we've run out of time and money."

Ken probed further. "So, what was discussed at your last meeting with the client?"

"Here's a copy of the Call Report . . . I'm just not sure what to do" (see Figure 25.4).

"What are your instincts telling you about this one?" Ken asked as he skimmed through the call report.

"One thing I know for sure, TCM does not have enough money to hire an outside supplier to conduct the critical incident interviews for vehicle delivery specialists in order to identify key behaviors critical to their successful performance."

"And how complicated do you think this task would be?"

"Generally, my instincts are telling me that vehicle delivery specialists need to be familiar with basic product features, just in case questions arise at delivery. They need to know which product features to present or demonstrate at various interior and exterior positions around the vehicle, and finally, there are some typical situations that might occur during vehicle delivery that require basic common sense and any customer-facing employee should be able to act accordingly."

"Like what's a typical situation that occurs at delivery?"

"Sometimes the customer is in a hurry and doesn't allow enough time for delivery or the vehicle may not be prepped when the customer arrives."

"Do you think Dale Hovan will have any time to work on this?"

"It's a possibility, and he was very involved in the sales consultant certification program, but I guess it depends upon whether or not we can find any existing training programs that can be repurposed for vehicle delivery specialists."

"I see. Makes sense. Well, it looks like we've got about a week to come up with some recommendations."

At this moment, Ken glanced at his watch and then pointed to a framed quotation on his wall by M. Scott Peck, which stated, "The truth is that our finest moments are most likely to occur when we are feeling deeply uncomfortable, unhappy, or unfulfilled. For it is only in such moments, propelled by our discomfort, that we are likely to step out of our ruts and start searching for different ways or truer answers."

"I know you're very frustrated with all this, but maybe the certification test for vehicle delivery specialists will be one of *your* finest moments on this project. By the way, whatever happened to Kat?" asked Ken.

"Well, Kat was dismissed, and Antoine was promoted to European training manager," I answered matter-of-factly.

Confused, Ken muttered, "But I thought Antoine was—"

I continued, "Yes, Antoine established an inappropriate working relationship with his relative, but he also seemed to get things done, and TCM gave him the promotion with the understanding that his relative could complete the pilot but could not work on any other international business."

"So typical," Ken said as he shook his head and started gathering some papers for his next meeting.

"Thanks for your time," I replied as I found myself thinking that truth is sometimes stranger than fiction. Then I realized that I was the one who would have to fix this mess. One more deliverable, little time, and no budget. "So typical," I echoed as I headed back to my office.

Preliminary Analysis Questions

1. Given the complexity of the existing certification program, critique APIC's approach to the sales consultant certification program it developed.
2. What are the advantages and disadvantages of using a third-party evaluator compared to an online competency assessment?
3. Scott Hunter states, "If people work in groups . . . they'll also learn a lot along the way." What do you think about this statement, given the strategies used to handle cheating in this case?
4. Evaluate the options that resulted from APIC's brainstorming session (see Figure 22.4). Suggest one approach to the certification of the vehicle delivery specialists. Provide your rationale for your suggestion.

Implications for ID Practice

1. Discuss the design challenges associated with working in volatile client environments where turnover, restructuring, and/or job rotation strategies can impact ID projects.
2. What type of communication strategies would you suggest for global project teams that operate in different countries communicating in English, when English is a second language for many members of the team and/or audiences?
3. Propose a range of strategies for addressing performance improvement needs when the intended audience is very small.

9781032379302

TARK!

THE SPORTS CAREER OF FRANCIS TARKENTON

BY:

JAMES & LYNN HAHN

EDITED BY:

DR. HOWARD SCHROEDER

Professor in Reading and Language Arts
Dept. of Elementary Education
Mankato State University

CRESTWOOD HOUSE

Mankato, Minnesota

CIP

LIBRARY OF CONGRESS CATALOGING IN PUBLICATION DATA

Hahn, James.
Tark! The sports career of Francis Tarkenton

(Sports legends)
SUMMARY: A brief biography of the famous quarterback for the Minnesota Vikings who retired in 1979 after 18 years in professional football.
1. Tarkenton, Francis A. — Juvenile literature. 2. Football players — United States — Biography — Juvenile literature. 3. Minnesota Vikings (Football team) — Juvenile literature. [1. Tarkenton, Francis A. 2. Football players] I. Hahn, Lynn, joint author. II. Schroeder, Howard. III. Title. IV. Series.
GV939.T3H33 796.332'092'4 [B] [92] 80-28881
ISBN 0-89686-121-X (lib. bdg.)
ISBN 0-89686—136-8 (pbk.)

INTERNATIONAL STANDARD BOOK NUMBERS:
0-89686-121-X Library Bound
0-89686-136-8 Paperback

LIBRARY OF CONGRESS CATALOG CARD NUMBER:
80-28881

PHOTO CREDITS:

Cover: Focus on Sports, Inc.

Wide World Photos: 3, 7, 15, 23, 30, 36, 40, 42-43
UPI: 5, 18, 20, 24-25, 27, 28-29, 34-35, 38, 45
The Trojan/Louise Anderson & Ruby Anderson: 11
University of Georgia: 12
Minneapolis Star: 16
National Football League/John E. Martin: 32
National Football League: 46

Crestwood House, Inc., Box 3427, Hwy. 66 So., Mankato, MN 56001

TARK!

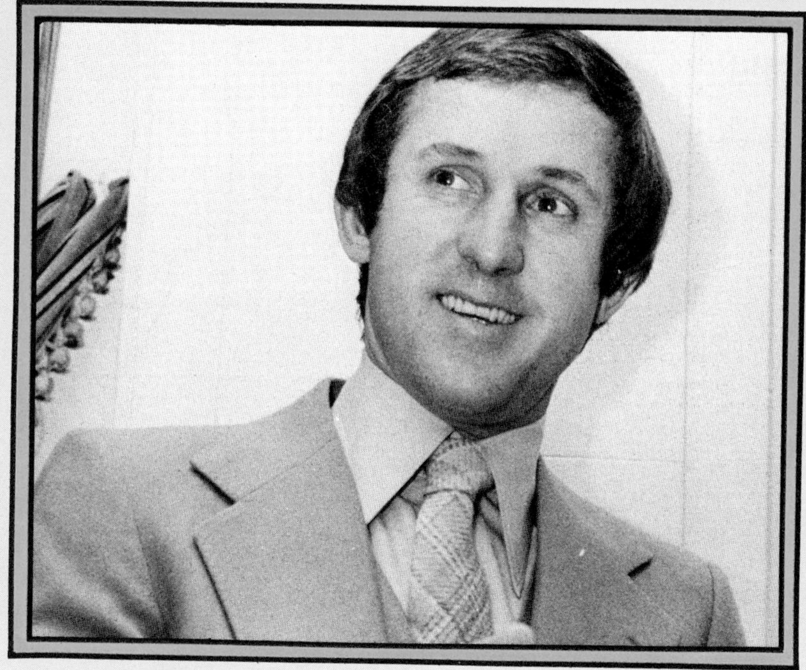

CHAPTER 1

On May 8, 1979, one of the most famous quarterbacks retired from pro football. Football fans would never again see him in action.

After eighteen years as a pro, Fran Tarkenton decided to retire. "I told the Vikings three years ago I was going to quit," Fran said. "There was no one thing that led me to that decision. It was well planned."

Fran went out on top. At the time, he held many all-time pro football records. He had the most passing touchdowns in a career (342). No player ever attempted more passes in one year. In 1978 he passed 572 times, and completed a record 345 passes.

"He's the best quarterback ever to play the game," said Bud Grant, coach of the Minnesota Vikings.

Fran didn't become the best quarterback in one season. It took him almost thirty-nine years.

Francis Asbury Tarkenton was born on February 3, 1940 in Richmond, Virginia. His parents named him after Francis Asbury, a pioneer and Methodist missionary.

Fran's mother's name was Frances and his

father's was Dallas. His father was a preacher in a Pentecostal church.

As a young boy, Fran wanted to be a football player when he grew up. "I dreamed about being a football star from the time I can remember," he said. "When I was five years old, I played touch football in an alley. I made believe I was playing other pro teams."

At age six, Fran started playing tackle football. "We'd go to a park or an empty lot and play," Fran said. "I had a lot of fun playing with my friends and my brother, Dallas."

Fran doing one of the things he was most famous for — "scrambling" away from would-be tacklers.

Temper tantrums caused young Fran many problems. "I used to have a bad temper," he said. "It would go off quick and last. I had fights at school all the time."

As Fran grew up he learned to control his temper. "I realized that losing my temper wouldn't get me anywhere," he said. "I worked on keeping my cool."

A wise man helped Fran learn how to behave. "I was very lucky as a kid," Fran said. "The person who helped me the most was my dad. He wasn't an athlete and didn't push me into sports. But, he was interested in me and watched me play football. He had a good outlook on sports."

Fran's father used strict discipline. Fran didn't see his first movie until he was a freshman in college. Motion pictures were forbidden. His father didn't even allow shoes to be shined in his home.

The Tarkenton family didn't have much money when Fran was young. Fran's father supported his family on fifty dollars a week. "We didn't have many things," Fran said, "but, we never felt poor. The parishioners didn't put much money in the collection basket. Instead, they brought us hams and turkeys. We survived on love."

As a young boy Fran collected football player cards that came with bubble gum. "I made up my own teams," he said. "Then, I staged football games in my room. I'd go through the Philadelphia Eagle

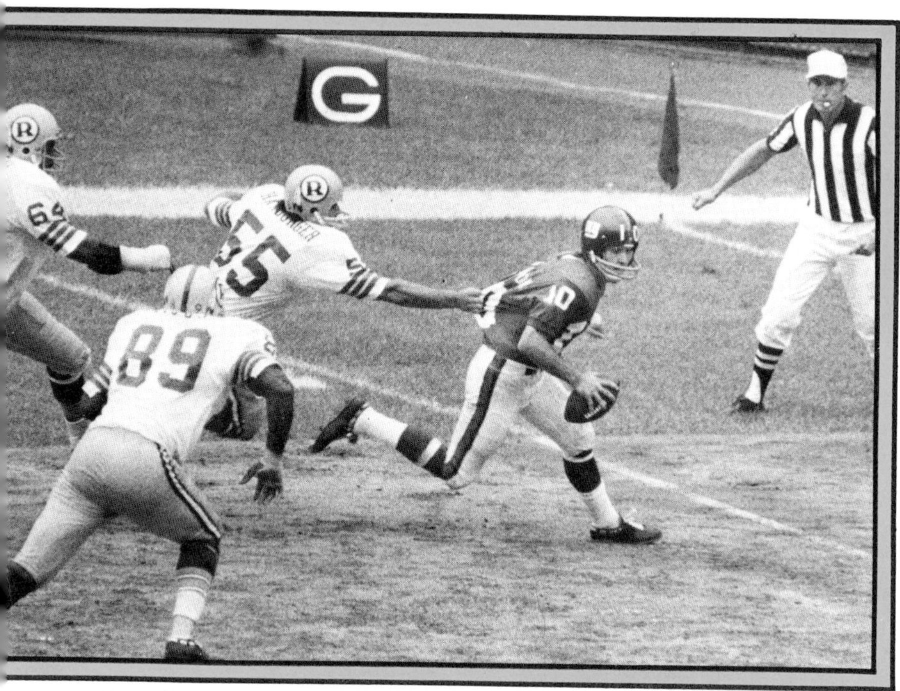

Fran played against the Redskins in real life too! This is a 1971 game when he was quarterback for the New York Giants.

cards and study my players. There'd be Frank Kilroy, Vic Sears, Tommy Thompson, Bosh Pritchard, Steve Van Buren, Pete Pihos, and all the rest."

Fran thought out a game plan based on what the players did best. He remembered hearing how well they had played on Sundays. He also thought about how they played in the exhibition season.

Next, Fran listed the skills of the opposing players. "They would usually be the Washington Redskins," he said, "led by 'Bullet' Bill Dudley."

Then, Fran made up very complex games. "Steve," Fran would say to the Steve Van Buren card, "we're going to be running you a lot today."

"Great, coach," the card would "say" to Fran.

Fran made a mental note for his game plan. The Van Buren card would carry the main load of the offense. "When I needed ten yards," Fran said, "I could always send him on an end run."

Fran's bubble gum card fullback had a charley horse during one game. "But nobody on the other team knew about it," Fran said. "So I thought that for short yardage we could always use him on a center plunge."

All Fran's game plans worked well. "My bubble gum card Philadelphia Eagles were undefeated," he said.

Fran played those make-believe games between the ages of nine and twelve. "I'd come home from school and run off games till suppertime," he said. "After supper, I'd do it for the rest of the evening. While the other kids were doing homework, I was thinking how to use Pete Pihos. Sure, my studies suffered. But, this was my interest, this was my life! I enjoyed every one of those games. I really did learn a lot from those bubble gum cards."

Fran didn't spend all his time playing with bubble gum cards. On Saturdays he played real football with Boys' Club teams. "But," he said, "that wasn't nearly as much fun as playing our own games in the park. You couldn't be yourself in those Boys' Club games. We could only play when told to, and had to follow plays drawn up by the coach. It was much too organized."

When Fran wasn't playing football, he had part-time jobs. He had two paper routes and worked on a chicken farm.

CHAPTER 2

At age twelve, Fran and his family moved to Athens, Georgia. He felt both sad and happy after the move. "I was sad because I couldn't be captain on the Peabody School safety patrol anymore," he said. "But, I was happy because my sixth grade teacher couldn't yell at me anymore for passing out the milk and graham crackers wrong."

One thing bothered Fran after he moved. He related, "I couldn't draw any more freaky football plays in the dirt in Stanton Park with a Popsicle stick."

Fran soon adjusted to his new home in Georgia. Football helped him make new friends. "I played for the YMCA team in Athens," he said. "It was like playground football. I got to play different positions. It wasn't over-organized. I never felt I had to win, win, win. One day I'd play with one group of boys, the next with another group. Those games were a lot of fun."

In high school, Fran met another man who helped shape his life. The man was Weyman Sellers, coach of the Athens High School football team. Coach Sellers taught Fran the basics of playing quarterback.

Like Fran's father, Coach Sellers was very strict. "If we lost a game on Friday night," Fran said, "Coach would bring us back on the field Saturday morning. Then, we'd scrimmage for several hours! At practice after school, we'd run a mile. Next, we had to do exercises. Then, we had to run ten fifty-yard wind sprints. After all that, we'd start playing football. He was tough and I'm glad he was. I learned that nothing in life comes easily."

Later, when Fran was a star quarterback for the Minnesota Vikings, he talked about high school football. "Most of the moves I use today," he said, "I learned from Weyman Sellers and the Athens High School Trojans."

Everything was going fine for Fran until his junior year. "I got a shoulder separation," he said. "It really hurt. I couldn't throw the ball more than fifteen to twenty yards."

Fran didn't sit on the bench feeling sorry for himself. He exercised to make his shoulder muscles stronger. In one game that year, he ran a kick-off

Fran (second from right in back row,) and part of the Athens football team. Coach Sellers is on the far right.

back ninety-five yards!

As a senior, Fran played so well that fifty colleges offered him scholarships. When he graduated from Athens High School in 1957, he had decided to attend the University of Georgia.

Fran led the Georgia freshman football team to an undefeated record. That was the first time in twenty years the Georgia freshman team had been undefeated.

Fran looked forward to joining the varsity team

as a sophomore. However, Wally Butts, his college coach, surprised him by putting him on the third string.

Playing third-string quarterback didn't bother Fran. "I still thought I could be the starting quarterback in a couple of weeks," he said. "I really

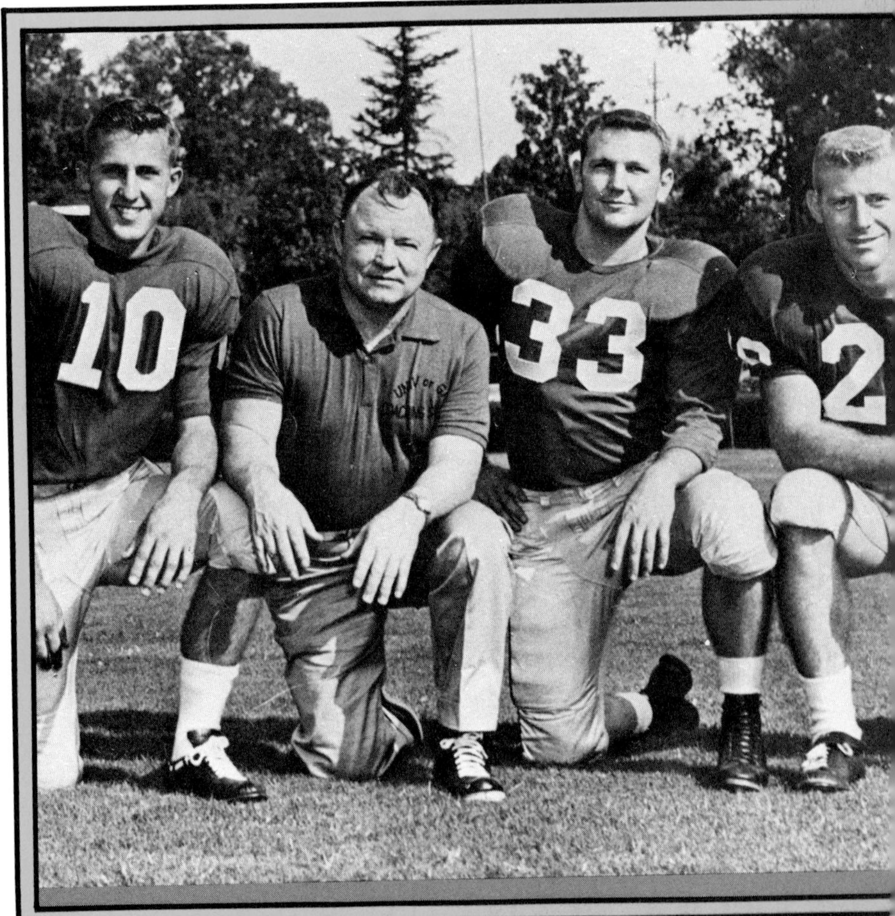

Fran and two other boys from Athens, Billy Slaughter (33) and George Guisler (28), pose with Coach Butts.

thought I had enough to give to the team."

Georgia opened its football season in Texas. Fran watched most of the game from the bench.

"I can do it," Fran told Coach Butts after Georgia hadn't made a first down for three quarters. "I can get you a touchdown in this game! I can get this thing going!"

In the fourth quarter, Coach Butts put Fran in the game. A few minutes later Fran led his teammates ninety-five yards down the field. He passed for a touchdown and the two-point conversion!

Although Fran had played well, he still had not become a star. In another game, he played poorly. During practice the next Monday, Coach Butts yelled at Fran. Fran lost his temper and yelled back at the coach. Then he said he was quitting, and walked off the field.

After a while, Fran and the coach apologized to each other. Fran said he'd play again because he wanted to be part of the team.

When Fran was a junior, he played a great game against Auburn. During one play, Georgia had the ball on Auburn's thirteen yard line, and was losing 13-7. There were only thirty seconds left in the game and it was the fourth down.

Fran called time out and drew up a play in the huddle. He told one of his ends to stay back and block for four seconds.

"After four seconds," Fran said, "I wanted him

to run into the left corner of the end zone."

"We got the play going and I rolled right. After I counted to four, I threw the ball crossfield."

The end caught the ball for a touchdown and Georgia won the game!

As a senior, Fran guided the Georgia Bulldogs to a 9-1 record. In the Orange Bowl, he helped his teammates beat the University of Missouri 14-0. Fran played so well that season he was voted an All-American.

The Minnesota Vikings liked the way Fran played college football. The team drafted Fran in the third round. He signed with the Vikings for $12,500 a year and a $3,500 bonus.

Norm Van Brocklin, the Vikings' coach at the time, had a surprise for Fran. He made Fran his third-string quarterback. "If you could throw, you'd be a real menace," Coach Van Brocklin laughed at Fran.

Fran exercised to strengthen his throwing arm. Before practice, he threw a six pound shot-put. His arm grew stronger and Coach Van Brocklin played Fran in an exhibition game.

That game was rough for the rookie. A player hit Fran's nose and it bled for half an hour. "Welcome to the NFL, kid," Coach Van Brocklin said to Fran. After Fran's nose stopped bleeding, he went back into the game and passed well.

In Fran's first professional game in the 1961 season, the Vikings played the Chicago Bears. Fran

The rookie posed for his official Viking photograph in 1961.

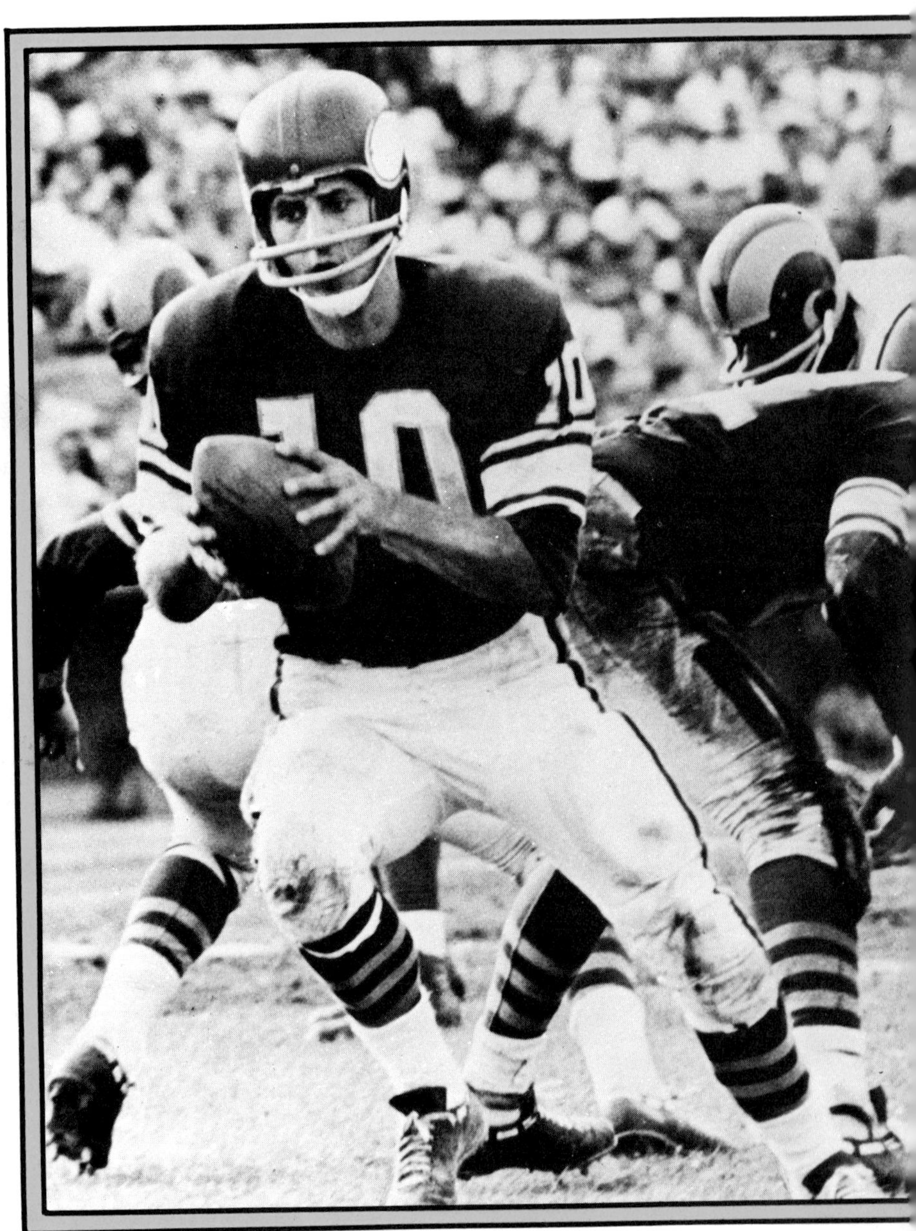

Fran starts back to set up a pass against the Rams.

didn't start the game. However, when the other quarterbacks couldn't get the Vikes moving, Fran got his chance.

At the time, the Bears were one of the best teams in football, but Fran showed the Bears how to play. He completed seventeen of twenty-three passes for 250 yards! The rookie threw four touchdown passes and ran for a fifth! Fran guided the Vikings to a 37-13 win!

That season Fran surprised many fans and players. He didn't play quarterback like other quarterbacks. Sportswriters called his style "scrambling."

"Why do you scramble?" the writers asked Fran.

"I'm not going to stand in the pocket and wait to get tackled," Fran said. "I don't see much sense in giving up. I'm not going to eat the ball if there's a chance of saving the play. The object of football is to win. I do all I can to win. When the blocking breaks down, scrambling is a way out. I refuse to accept defeat."

"What do you think about when you're scrambling?" writers asked.

"When I scramble, I'm trying to figure out a way to make the play work," Fran said. "I don't plot scrambles. I don't lie awake nights dreaming up fakes. I don't look at myself as a hero. When I'm running around out there, winning is everything. I want to win by any way that occurs to me."

Sportswriters asked football players about Fran's scrambling.

"You can expect anything from Tarkenton," one player said. "He might pass the ball to a fan!"

Although Fran had learned to control his temper, occasionally he would get angry. In one

Norm Van Brocklin with his new quarterback.

game, a lineman threw him to the ground and stood there laughing.

"I stood up," Fran said, "and hit him with the ball between the eyes." Since the player was wearing a helmet and face mask, he wasn't hurt. Still, Fran was fined.

Although the Vikings finished with a poor 3-11 record that year, Fran played pretty well. He completed 157 of 280 passes, and passed for 1,997 yards and eighteen touchdowns. He threw seventeen interceptions.

After the football season, Fran opened a business office in Atlanta. On a wall, he hung a poster with his favorite slogan. "I believe the people who make it aren't the most talented. They aren't the smartest, luckiest, or bravest. The ones who make it are the dogged ones. Successful people never give up. They are the ones who take the jolts. Then, they get up and look at the sky. No matter what's there, they'll say, "I've got to do it. So, let's go."

CHAPTER 3

Before the 1962 football season, sportswriters asked Fran how he felt.

"I got discouraged at times last year," he said.

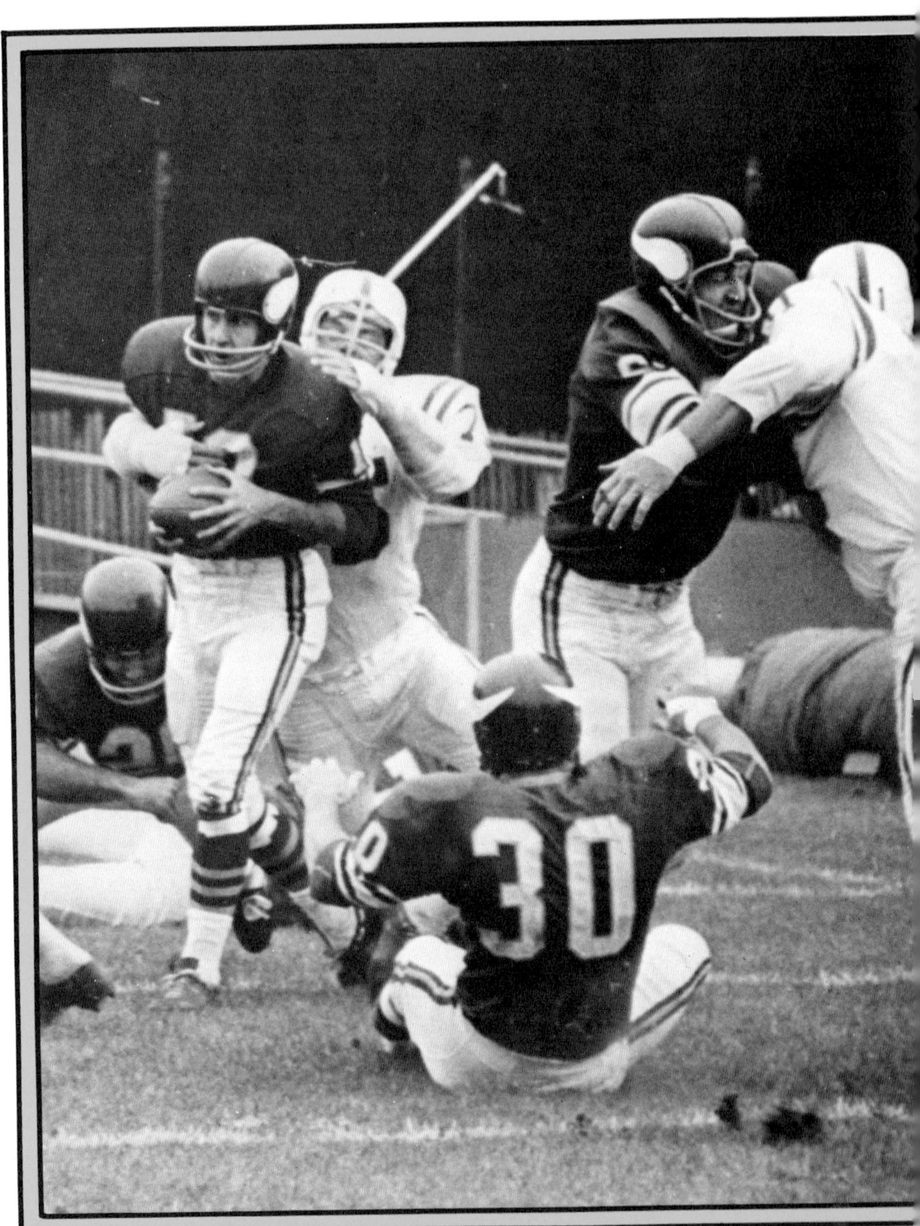

Fran was surrounded in a 1963 game against Baltimore.

"Not because I was getting hit. But, because I was making mistakes. There is so much to learn in this league. The toughest thing to figure out is the defenses. I plan to study the defenses all I can."

During the year he tried 329 passes and completed 163. He gained 2,595 yards and scored twenty-two touchdowns. Tough defenses picked off twenty-five of Fran's passes.

Defenses held the Vikes to two wins and a tie, and handed them eleven losses.

Although Fran had a rough season, he kept a good outlook. Paul Flatley, a teammate, talked with reporters about Fran. "He's a good guy to locker next to. He always enjoys joking with you. If a teammate has a problem, Fran helps him. Sure, he grumbles a little when he feels abused at a team meeting, but, most players do that. Fran has drive, discipline, and a sense of purpose."

Throughout his career, Fran never forgot the discipline he learned from his father. Before games, he didn't eat breakfast. He just drank black coffee. He did give in a little, though. On the nights before games, Fran might enjoy a bowl of chili.

The defenses didn't get any easier for Fran in his third season. In one game he was tackled so hard, he couldn't play for several minutes. Doctors thought he had a concussion.

Fran ended the 1963 season with 170 completed passes. His passes were good for 2,311 yards and fifteen touchdowns. Fifteen passes were intercepted. That year the Vikes won five, lost eight, and tied one.

In 1964, Fran led the Vikings to their best record. The Vikes were 8-5 that year. He passed 306 times and completed 171. Fran's passes gained 2,506 yards and twenty-two touchdowns. He threw just eleven interceptions.

Before the 1965 season, Fran's scrambling still confused some reporters.

"I only scramble in a jam," Fran told them. "Even then, I don't try to run over people. I just head toward daylight. All I'm trying to do is win ball games. I don't want to get killed out there."

At one press conference, Fran talked about fear and football, "I asked John Glenn, the astronaut, about his fears before liftoff. 'I'm scared,' John told me, 'But I don't let my fears hurt what I have to do.' I try to behave the same way during football games."

"Aren't you afraid of getting hurt?" a sportswriter asked.

"I'm never afraid of getting hurt," Fran said. "But, I don't think I have any more courage than the average fan. It's just that I've been playing ball a long time. I'm used to it."

During the 1965 season, Fran completed 171 of 329 passes. He gained 2,609 yards and scored nineteen touchdowns. Still, the Vikings only had a 7-7 record.

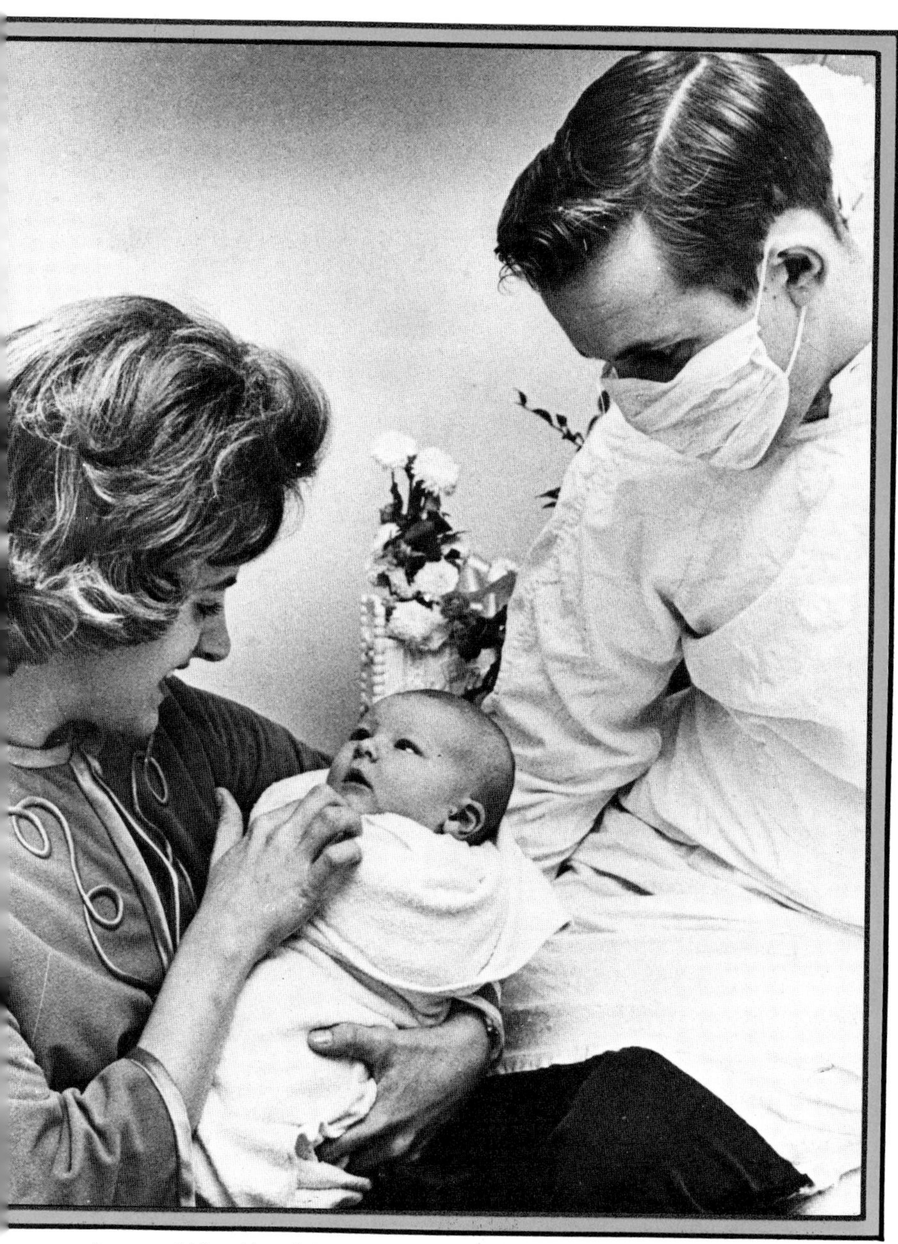

Fran and his wife, Elaine, get to know their daughter, Angela, who was born in 1964.

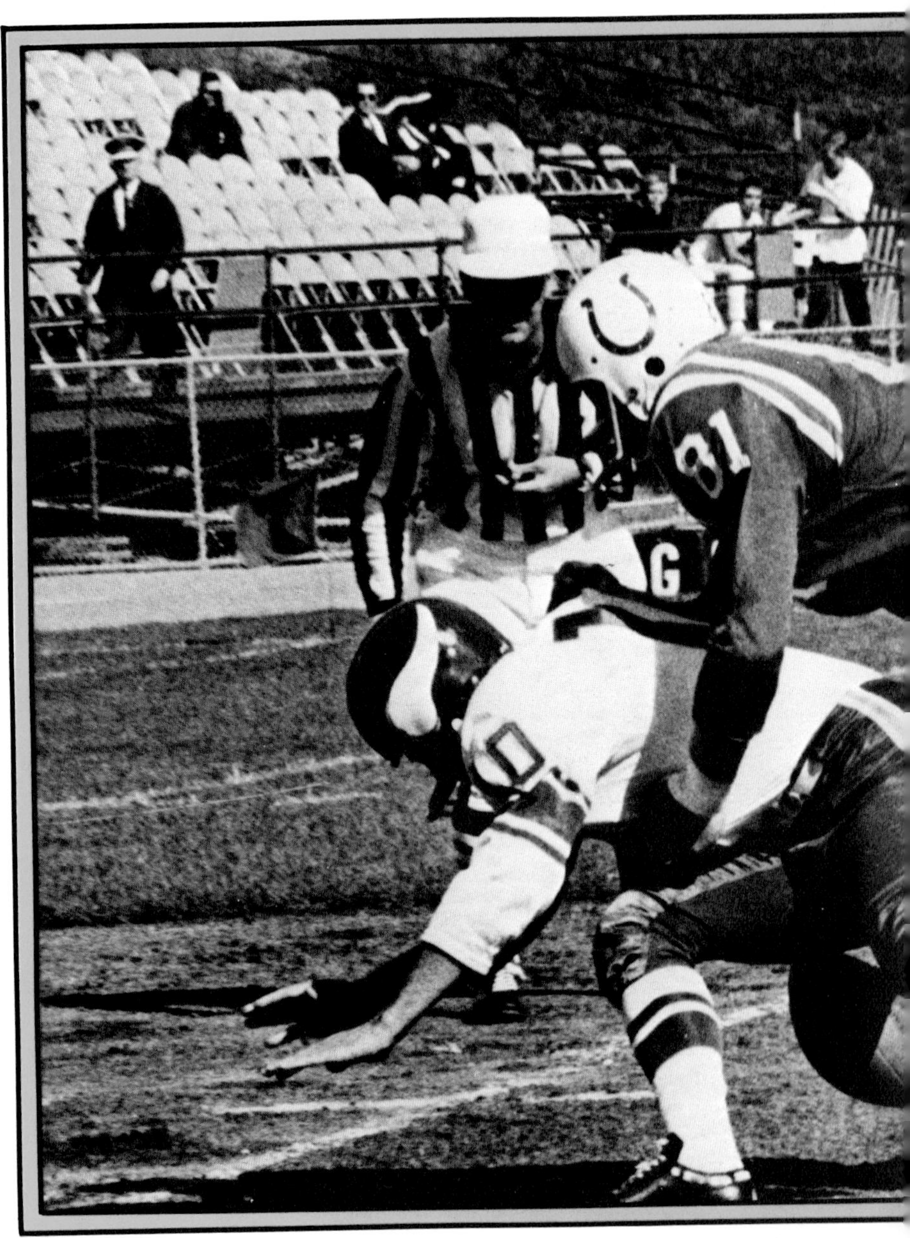

Ordell Braase (81) knocked the ball away from Fran in a game with the Baltimore Colts.

CHAPTER 4

After the season, Fran traveled through the Southern part of the United States. He asked assembly line workers about their jobs, and how they thought their jobs could be made easier.

After his travels, Fran started a new company. He taught businesses how to make their workers feel better about their jobs. "The unhappiest worker is one who is bored." Fran said. "Reward workers when they do good work. Then, they will make better products."

The 1966 season was not a good one for Fran or the Vikings. When the Vikes lost, Coach Van Brocklin blamed Fran and his scrambling passes. "Tarkenton, you're not strong enough to throw passes like that," Coach Van Brocklin told him. "But, you sure are dumb enough!"

After the Vikings lost more games, Coach Van Brocklin said Fran was a selfish player. Finally, he benched Fran.

Fran thought a lot while on the bench. "The hard part of quarterbacking is the mental pressure," he said. "It's hard to make split-second decisions. It came to the point where it was driving me crazy. I would feel unhappy and wouldn't be worth any-

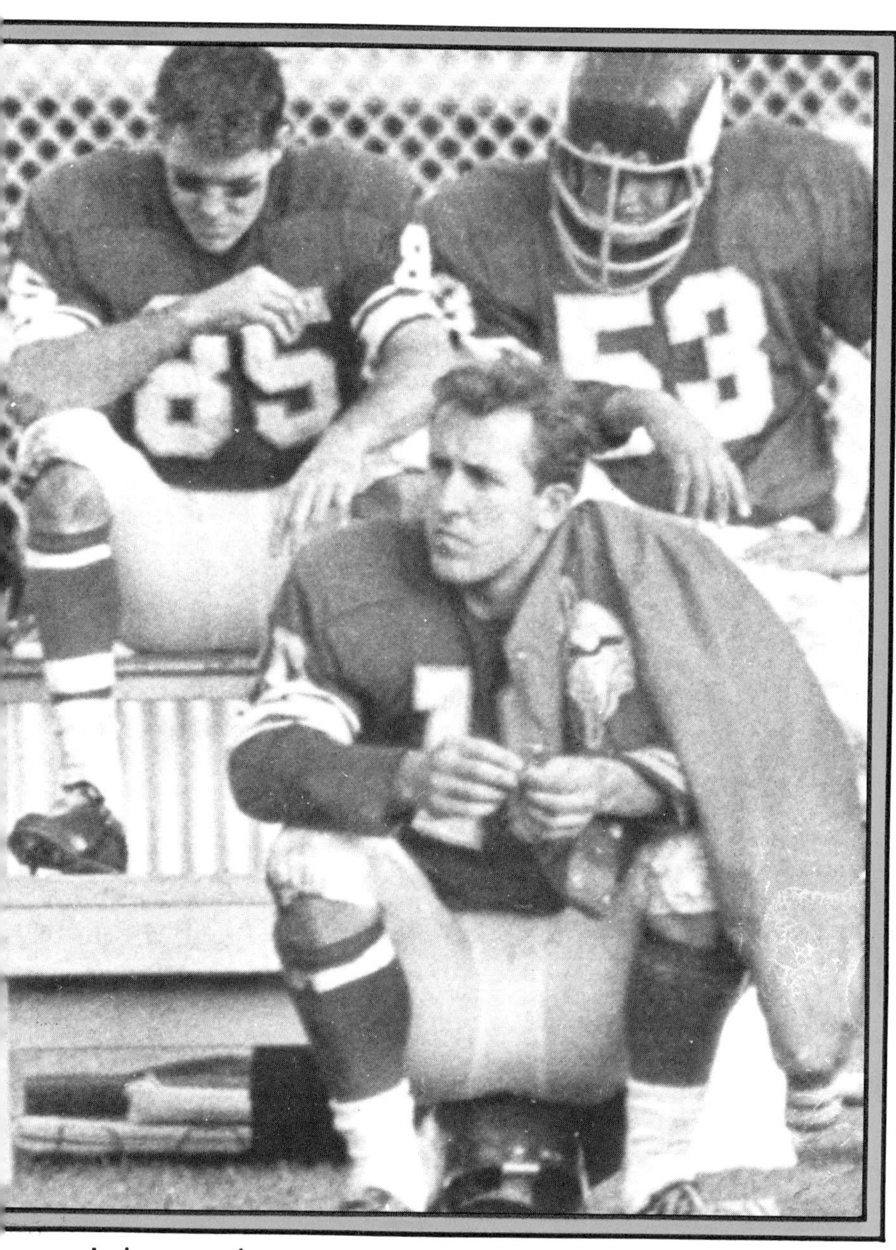

Losing was no fun.

thing to myself or the team. Football wasn't fun for me anymore. So, I had to overcome pressure by conquering myself."

Fran finished the season with 192 completed passes out of 358 attempts. His passes gained 2,561 yards and seventeen touchdowns. Defenders picked

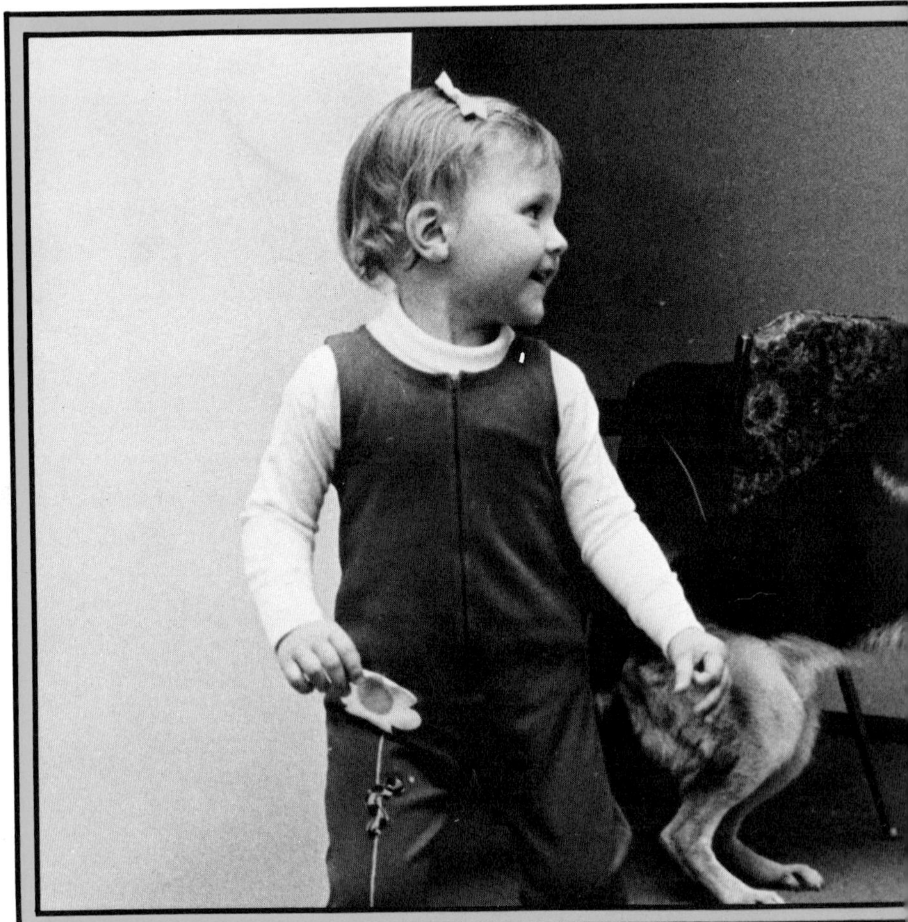

During the off-season Fran played with the family dog, Duke, and two-year-old daughter, Angela.

off sixteen of his passes. The Vikings had a poor 4-9-1 record.

After the season, Fran wrote a letter to Coach Van Brocklin. "I have decided I can't return to play for the Minnesota Vikings next season. It's impossible for me to return to the Vikings with a clear and

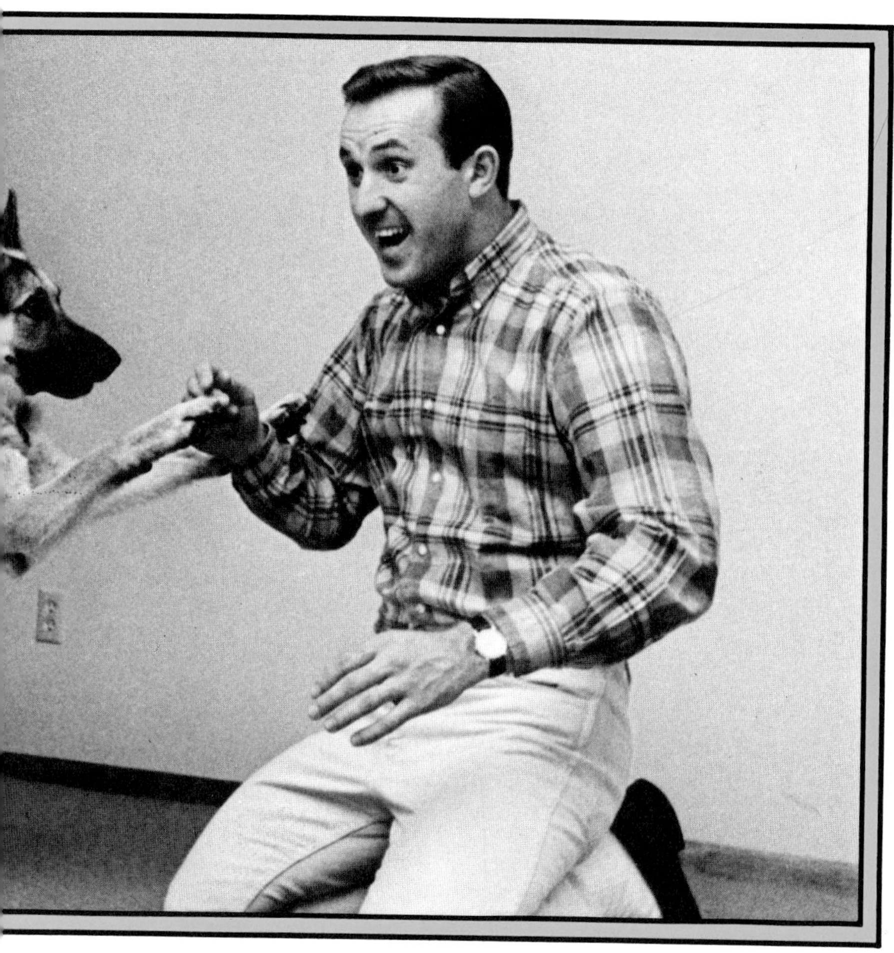

open mind. I'm sure this decision is best for the Vikings, you, and myself. Thank you for your help and guidance during the early years of my career. I wish for you and the Vikings every success."

Since Fran didn't want to play for the Vikings, he was traded to the New York Giants. Fran worked hard during the winter to get in shape for the 1967 football season. "I threw a football at a mattress in my attic between twenty and thirty times every day," he said.

The New York Giants paid Fran $50,000 to play

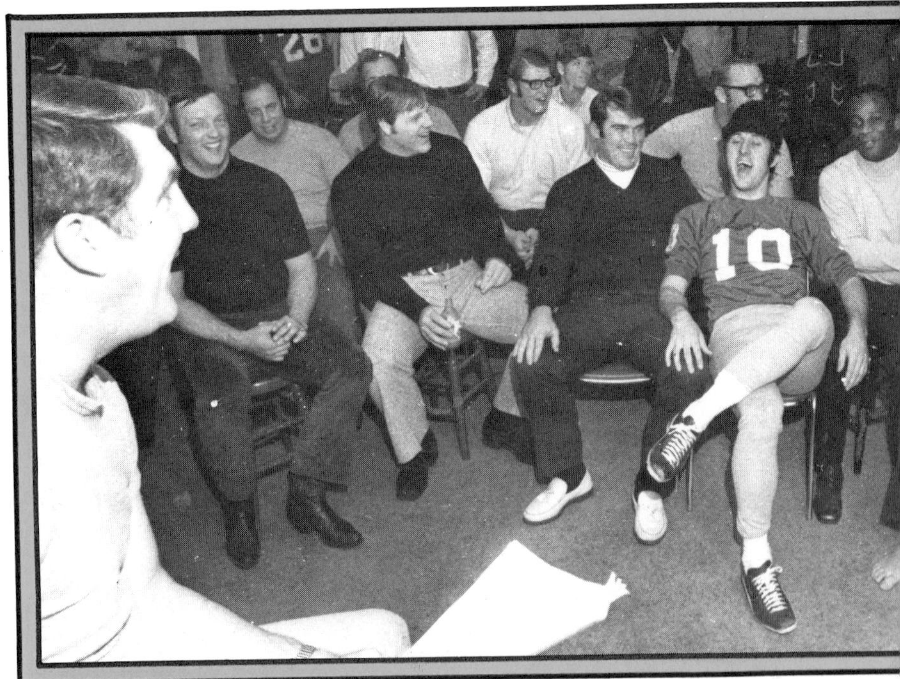

Fran and his teammates share a laugh in the Giants' locker room. Coach Alex Webster is on the left.

football for them in 1967. Fran earned his pay when he completed 204 passes out of 377 attempts. His passes gained the Giants 3,088 yards and twenty-nine touchdowns. However, the Giants only had a 7-7 record.

Fran enjoyed playing football with the New York Giants. "The locker room was relaxed," he said. "There was no yelling, screaming, or name calling. For the first time in my pro career, I really felt joy going to the ballpark. Playing football was fun for me again."

CHAPTER 5

Religion has been important to Fran throughout his life. During the season, he went to chapel meetings with the other members of the Fellowship of Christian Athletes. In the off-season, he attended the Glen Memorial Methodist Church in Atlanta. "I spent many hours talking with people about a proper Christian way of life," Fran said.

Young people meant a lot to him, too. Whenever Fran had time, he spoke with them at sports banquets.

"What are you thinking about when you're scrambling away from linemen?" young people asked Fran.

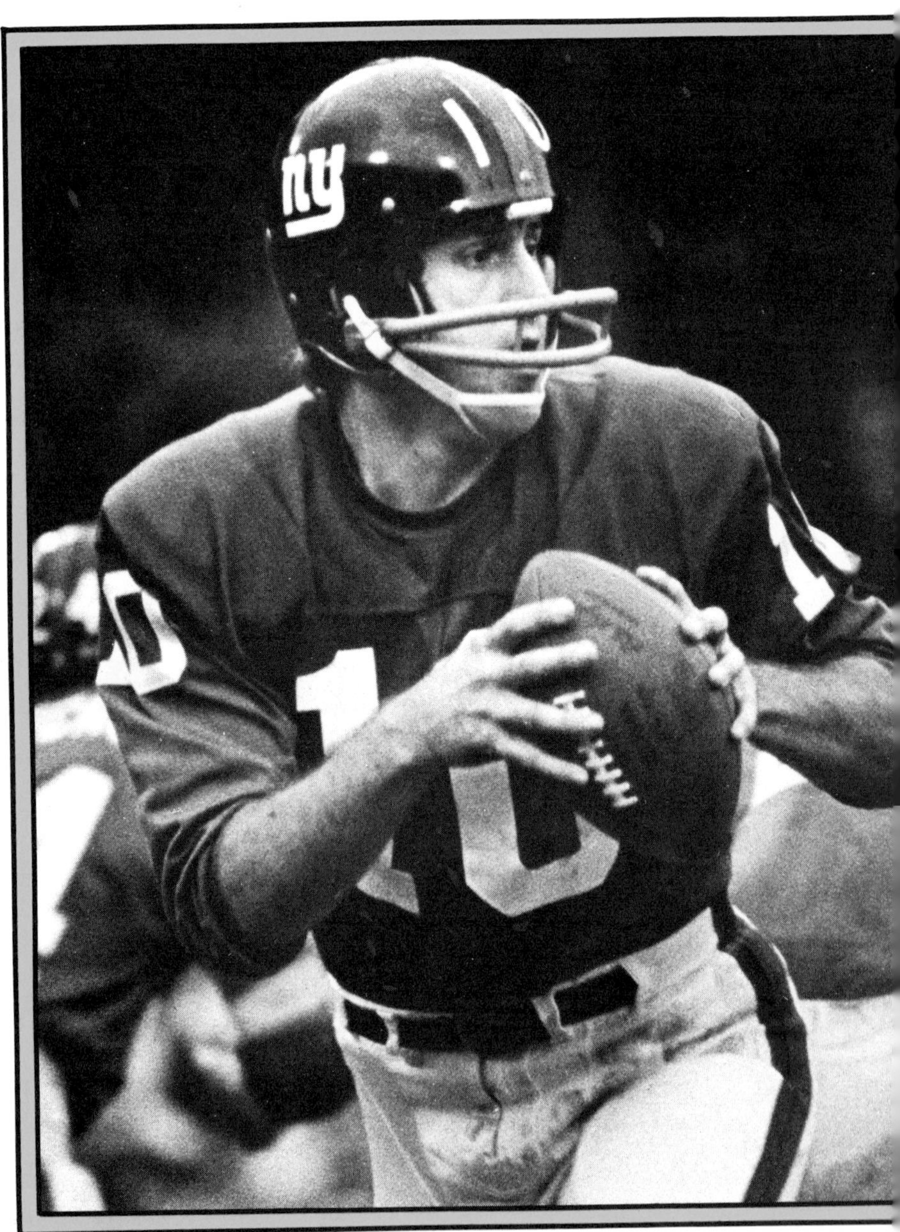

Fran looks for a receiver to get into the open.

"I'm thinking how bad it'll be for me if they catch me!" Fran said.

"What advice do you have for us?" others asked.

"Listen to your coach," Fran said. "Don't beat yourself or your team."

In 1968, Fran suffered an injury. During the fifth game of the season, he separated his right shoulder. Playing with pain, he finished the season with 182 completed passes out of 337 attempts. Fran's passes gained the Giants 2,555 yards and twenty-one touchdowns. Only twelve of his passes were intercepted. Once again, the Giants won seven games and lost seven games.

Before the 1969 season, sportswriters asked Fran how he prepared for games. "First, I tape my ankles," he said. "Then I put on my hip pads. Next, I put my colored team socks and white athletic socks on. Then, I slide into my game pants and a T-shirt. Usually, I read the game program and talk with the other players. I just try to relax and not worry."

The 1969 season was a tough one for Fran. The Giants didn't have many skillful linemen. So, he ran most of the plays off quick counts to surprise the defensive tacklers. Many times he had to throw off-balance, on tip toes, and on a dead run.

In a game against his old team, the Vikings, Carl Eller chased Fran. "I honestly don't think he wanted to tackle me," Fran said later. "I think he

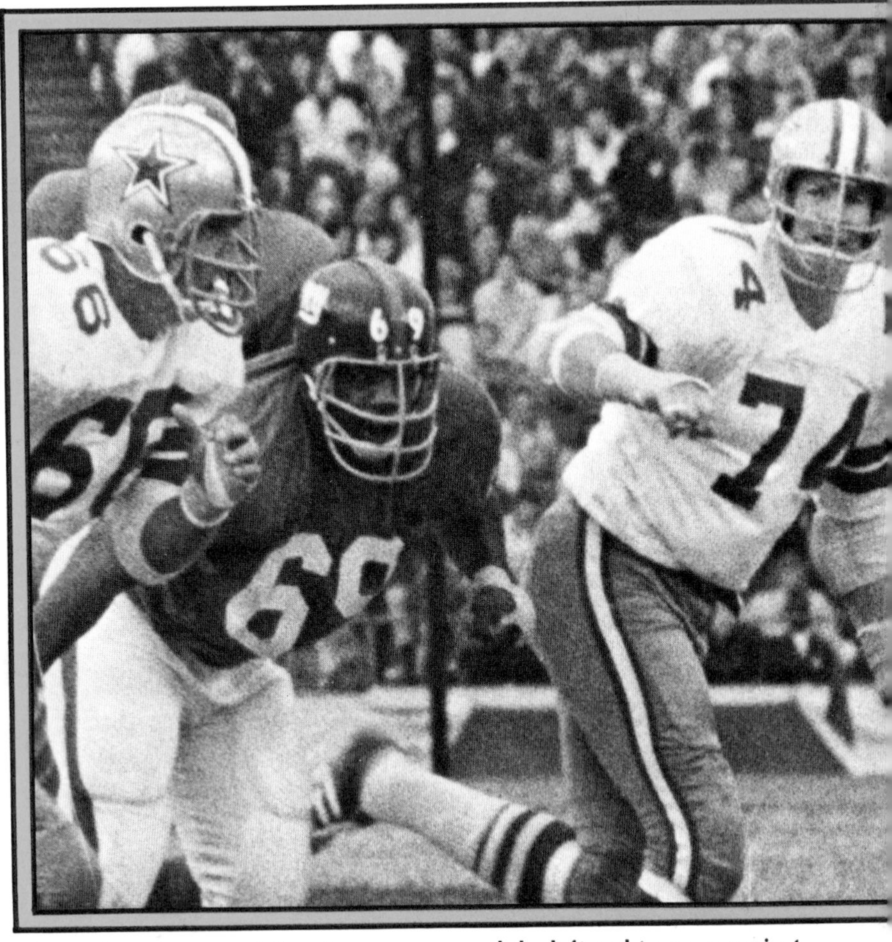

After doing some scrambling, Fran runs around the left end to score against Dallas.

planned to eat me!"

By the end of the season, Fran had 220 pass completions out of 409 attempts. His passes gained the Giants 2,918 yards and twenty-three touchdowns. Only eight of his passes were picked off. But, the Giants finished with a 6-8 record.

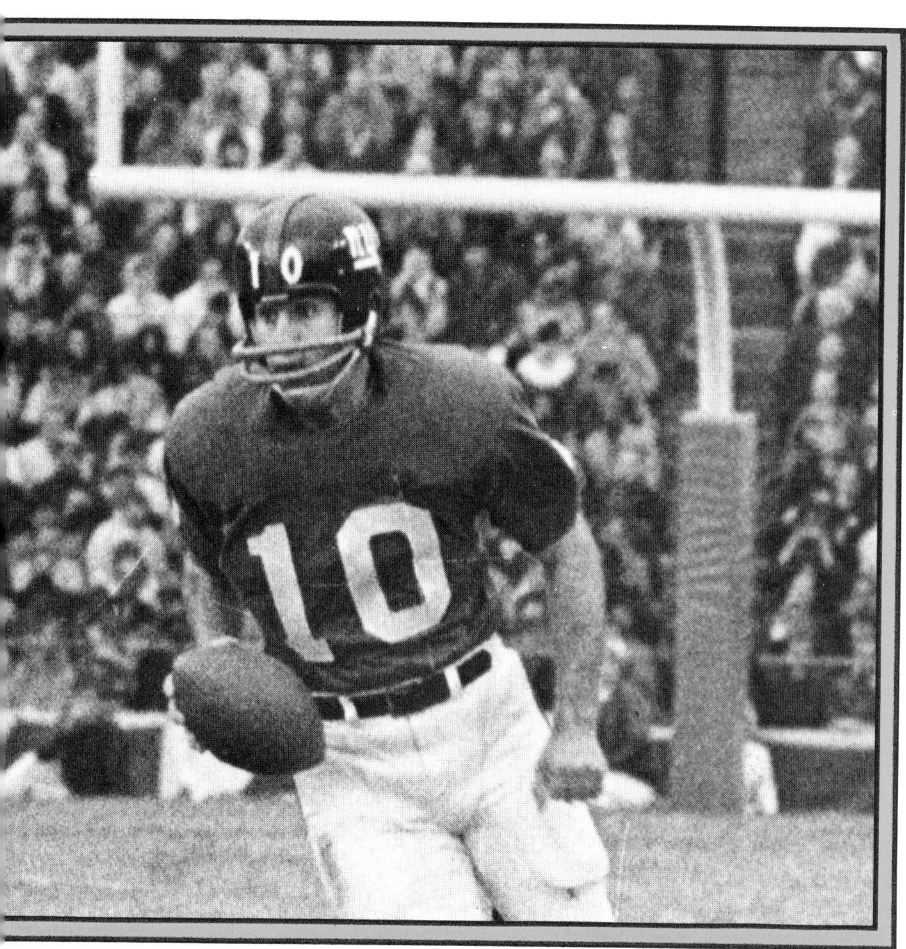

During that season, sportswriters found out that some players used drugs. They asked Fran if he took drugs. "I do not use drugs on or off the field," he said. "I never have." They asked him about smoking and drinking. "I never started," Fran said. Chewing tobacco was his only bad habit.

Before the 1970 season, Fran exercised to stay in shape. "I ran hard each day," he said, "and played a great deal of golf."

In training camp, Fran spent many hours working on handing off, dropping back to pass, and passing.

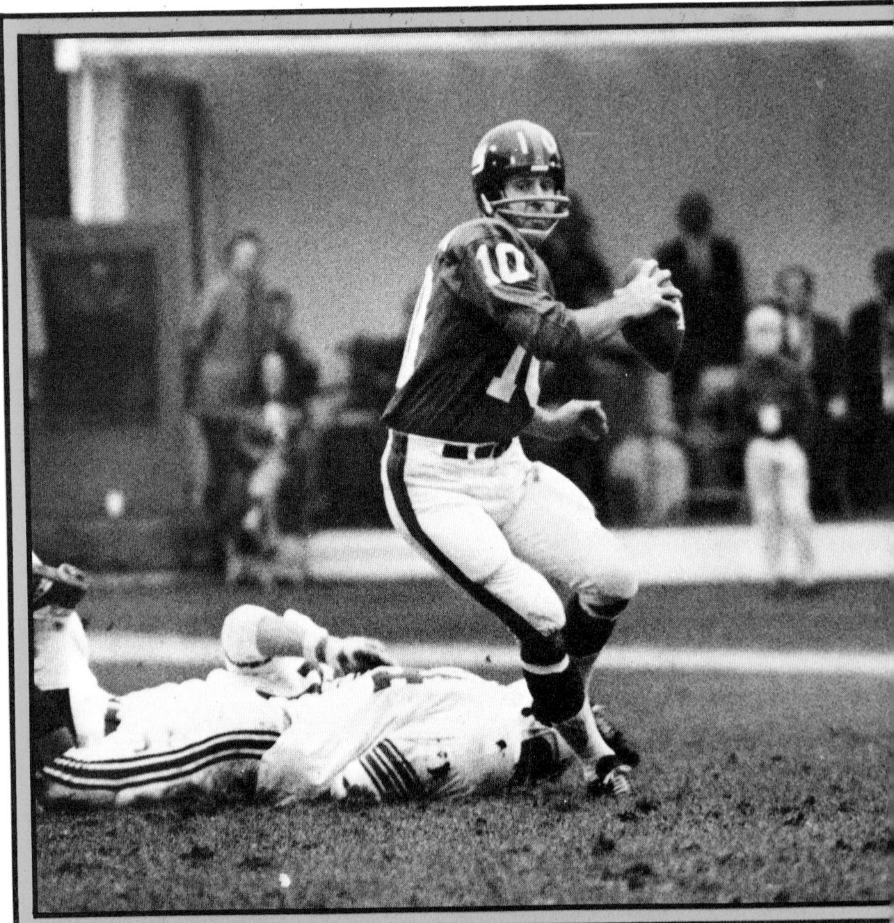

In a 1970 game against the Cardinals, Fran had the best day of his career. He threw five touchdown passes.

All Fran's work paid off when he completed 219 passes out of 389 in 1970. His passes gained 2,777 yards and nineteen touchdowns. The Giants finished 9-5, their best record in years.

Neither the Giants nor Fran had a good year in 1971. Fran threw only eleven touchdown passes. Twenty-one of his passes were intercepted! The Giants had a 4-10 record.

Since the Giants were unorganized and lacked skillful players, Fran said he couldn't play his best with them. "In the last week of the season," Fran said, "I decided I had to get away from the New York Giants. I wanted to play where I could start out with an even chance of winning."

CHAPTER 6

Before the 1972 season began, Fran was traded back to the Minnesota Vikings. He played well for the Vikes, completing 215 passes out of 378 attempts. His passes gained the Vikings 2,651 yards and eighteen touchdowns.

However, the Vikings finished with a 7-7 record. "This has to be my biggest disappointment," Fran said. "I really wanted to have a winning season my first year back with the Vikings."

Viking coach, Bud Grant, and Fran hold a press conference.

To get his mind off football, Fran read books. EXODUS, HAWAII, and TO KILL A MOCKINGBIRD were some of the novels he enjoyed.

The Vikings and Fran improved greatly in 1973. Fran completed 169 passes out of 274, his best passing percentage yet. His passes gained the Vikings 2,113 yards and fifteen touchdowns. The Vikes had a 12-2 record! However, they lost the Super Bowl to the Miami Dolphins 24-7.

Fran gave his entire Super Bowl check to needy people. "The practice of Christian beliefs," he said, "doesn't make you a square. I can be a Christian and play football, too."

During the 1974 season, Fran had some problems with his arm. "I had to start taking heat treatments. I couldn't throw the ball more than fifteen yards. I've had pain in my throwing arm many times, but have been able to put the ball where I wanted. Suddenly my arm didn't have the strength to do what any ten-year-old could do. I was really worried."

Fran worked to strengthen his arm. After many hours of exercise, his arm grew stronger. He completed 199 passes out of 351 attempts, for 2,598 yards and seventeen touchdowns.

With Fran's leadership, the Vikings went all the way to the Super Bowl. However, the Pittsburgh Steelers played better and won the game 16-6.

The Vikings and Fran played well in 1975 until

Fran waits to see if a pass is going to be completed during the 1977 Super Bowl.

the Dallas Cowboys beat them in a play-off game.

At a press conference after the game, reporters asked Fran how he felt.

"I don't play football for the cheers of the fans," Fran said, "or to survive their boos. I don't play it to achieve greatness. I play the game because I enjoy it. When I stop enjoying football, I'll quit the game."

For the season, Fran completed 273 passes out of 425 attempts. He gained 2,994 yards and twenty-five touchdowns. Having played so well, he earned the Jim Thorpe Trophy for the Most Valuable Player in the NFL. The football players in the NFL vote for the winner of the Jim Thorpe Trophy. It is the oldest and highest professional football award.

"I love football," Fran said, after accepting the trophy. "But, football just can't be an end in itself. It's only one thrill in my life. There have to be more."

During the 1976 season, Fran played quite well. He completed 255 passes out of 412 tries. He also gained 2,961 yards and scored seventeen touchdowns. He threw just eight interceptions.

Fran again led his teammates to the Super Bowl. However, the Oakland Raiders won the title 32-14.

Some Viking fans were not happy with Fran in the 1977 season. "I've been booed," Fran said, "and I've fumbled and thrown interceptions. I've done

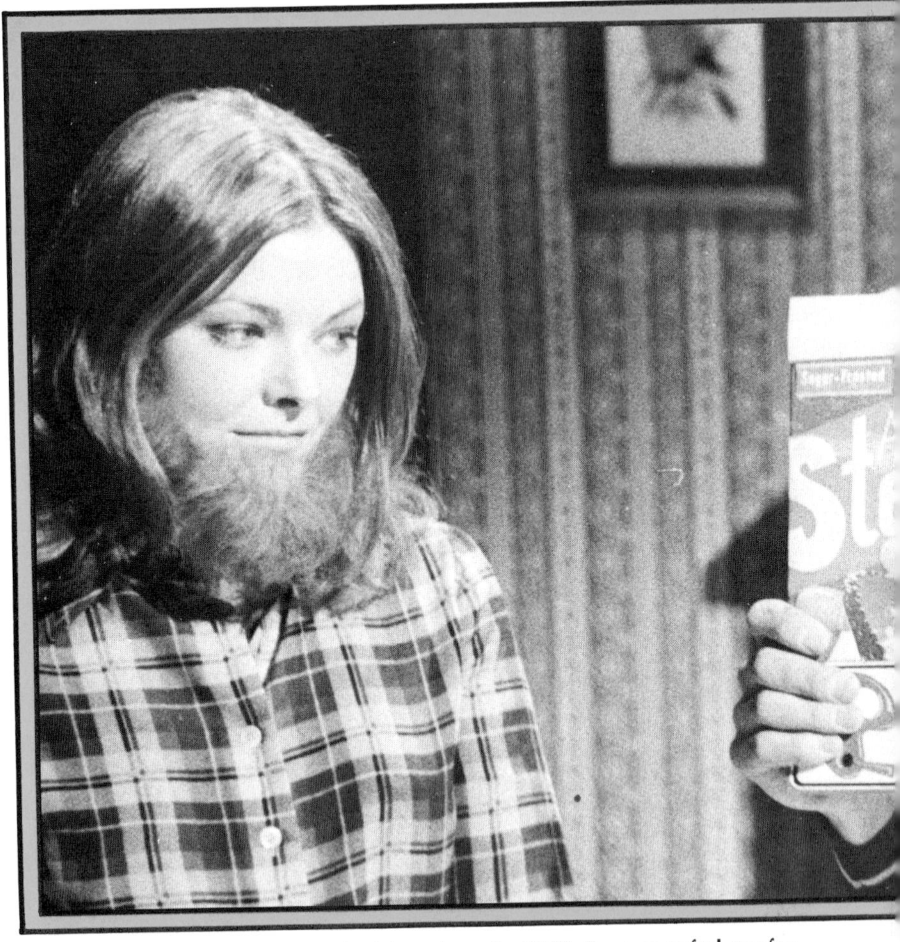

On a "Saturday Night Live" television show in 1977, Fran spoofed professional athletics. Jane Curtin is on the left.

every dumb thing a quarterback can. But, I still try hard to play well. I do what I can to win."

Fran spent many hours practicing to play better. On November 13, 1977, in a game against the Cincinnati Bengals, Fran was playing great. He had

completed 17 of 18 passes for 195 yards.

However, in the third quarter, a Bengal defensive player tackled Fran roughly. Fran had to be carried off the field. A bone was broken in his right leg. Doctors put a cast around the injury.

Fran's season was over. He had passed 258 times and completed 155. He gained just 1,734 yards and scored nine touchdowns. The Vikings finished with a 9-5 record.

CHAPTER 7

Fran's leg healed and he played very well in 1978. However, during one game he was tackled very hard. Three of his top front teeth snapped off. It took sixty stitches to close the wound in his mouth. Fran had to have three hours of plastic surgery.

He didn't let that stop him. Fran had his best season ever! He passed 572 times and completed 345! Both were NFL season records. He gained 3,468 yards (a Vikings season record) and threw twenty-five touchdown passes!

Sadly that was Fran's last season.

At the time he retired, Fran held many NFL records. No one completed more than Fran's 3,686 passes. Fran held the record for the most yards gained passing in a career (47,003), and for the most touchdowns (342). He also held records for most passes attempted (6,467), and for passing for over 2,000 yards for fifteen straight seasons.

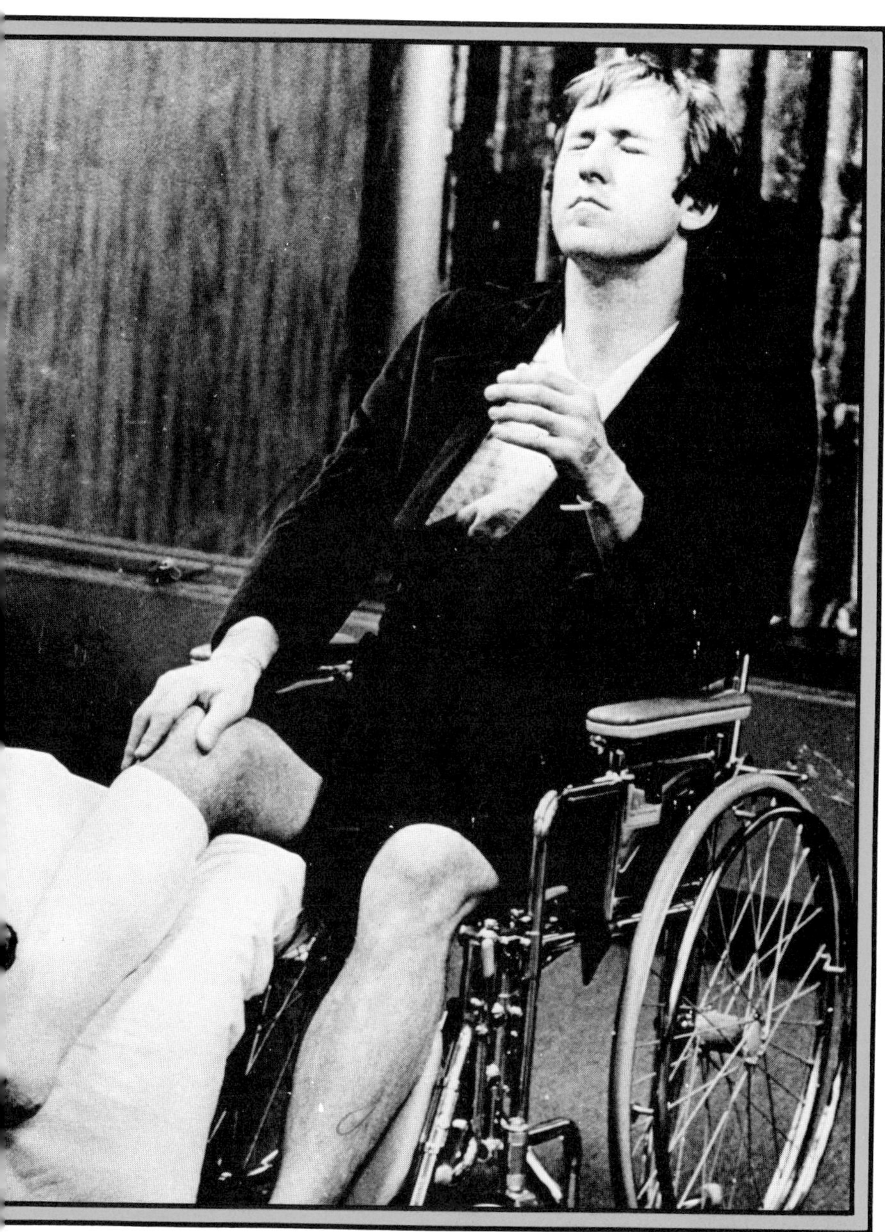

Fran shows pain from his broken leg after finishing a short press conference at the hospital.

Number Ten in action!

"The records are nice," Fran said. "They are a measurement of how you stand with the great quarterbacks. But, they aren't something I've spent hours dreaming about. I never planned to break records. I just wanted to win games for my team."

Although Fran was the best quarterback ever, he was humble. "I am a human being," he said, "nothing more, nothing less. All I did was play a game better than some people. That doesn't make me a better person."

Football meant a lot to Fran. "But," he said, "it isn't everything. It was only part of my life. Now, I want to work where I can do the most to help people." After he quit playing football, Fran helped workers who had problems on the job. He advised bosses to reward workers for doing their jobs well.

Fran enjoyed his new work, and said, "I feel I was put here for a more important purpose than to throw a football."

AFTERWORD:

Fran Tarkenton is currently living in Atlanta, Georgia. He works as a sportscaster for a local TV station, and also announces several football games on nationwide TV.

After the football season, Fran works with his consulting business in Atlanta. Fran's company helps businesses that are having problems with workers.